MIND IS
THE MASTER

ALSO AVAILABLE FROM TARCHER SUCCESS CLASSICS

MIND IS THE MASTER

The Complete James Allen Treasury

JAMES ALLEN

JEREMY P. TARCHER/PENGUIN

a member of Penguin Group (USA) Inc.

New York

JEREMY P. TARCHER/PENGUIN
Published by the Penguin Group
Penguin Group (USA) Inc., 375 Hudson Street, New York, New York 10014, USA • Penguin Group (Canada), 90 Eglinton Avenue East, Suite 700, Toronto, Ontario M4P 2Y3, Canada (a division of Pearson Penguin Canada Inc.) • Penguin Books Ltd, 80 Strand, London WC2R 0RL, England • Penguin Ireland, 25 St Stephen's Green, Dublin 2, Ireland (a division of Penguin Books Ltd) • Penguin Group (Australia), 250 Camberwell Road, Camberwell, Victoria 3124, Australia (a division of Pearson Australia Group Pty Ltd) • Penguin Books India Pvt Ltd, 11 Community Centre, Panchsheel Park, New Delhi–110 017, India • Penguin Group (NZ), 67 Apollo Drive, Rosedale, North Shore 0632, New Zealand (a division of Pearson New Zealand Ltd) • Penguin Books (South Africa) (Pty) Ltd, 24 Sturdee Avenue, Rosebank, Johannesburg 2196, South Africa

Penguin Books Ltd, Registered Offices: 80 Strand, London WC2R 0RL, England

Most Tarcher/Penguin books are available at special quantity discounts for bulk purchase for sales promotions, premiums, fund-raising, and educational needs. Special books or book excerpts also can be created to fit specific needs. For details, write Penguin Group (USA) Inc. Special Markets, 375 Hudson Street, New York, NY 10014.

Library of Congress Cataloging-in-Publication Data

Allen, James, 1864–1912.
Mind is the master: the complete James Allen treasury/James Allen.
p.   cm.
ISBN 978-1-58542-769-7
1. New Thought.   I. Title.
BF639.A636   2010   2009037014
289.9'8—dc22

Printed in the United States of America
1   3   5   7   9   10   8   6   4   2

BOOK DESIGN BY MEIGHAN CAVANAUGH

Neither the publisher nor the author is engaged in rendering professional advice or services to the individual reader. The ideas, procedures, and suggestions contained in this book are not intended as a substitute for consulting with a physician. All matters regarding your health require medical supervision. Neither the author nor the publisher shall be liable or responsible for any loss or damage allegedly arising from any information or suggestion in this book.

While the author has made every effort to provide accurate telephone numbers and Internet addresses at the time of publication, neither the publisher nor the author assumes any responsibility for errors, or for changes that occur after publication. Further, the publisher does not have any control over and does not assume any responsibility for author or third-party websites or their content.

CONTENTS

Posthumously published works are noted by an asterisk (*).

PUBLISHER'S NOTE

The nineteen books that compose *Mind Is the Master* and the remembrance of James Allen by his wife, Lily, appear largely as they did at the time of their original publication. Each has been reproduced from the earliest editions generally available. Other than minor adjustments made to bring the works in line with contemporary typography standards, the publisher has retained the original spellings, usage, and style of the author. As these works were written in the early twentieth century, they occasionally contain an antiquated reference or word choice. For purposes of historical accuracy, the publisher has left these intact.

FROM POVERTY
TO POWER

(1901)

FOREWORD

I looked around upon the world, and saw that it was shadowed by sorrow and scorched by the fierce fires of suffering. And I looked for the cause. I looked around, but could not find it; I looked in books, but could not find it; I looked within, and found there both the cause and the self-made nature of that cause. I looked again, and deeper, and found the remedy. I found one Law, the Law of Love; one Life, the Life of adjustment to that Law; one Truth, the truth of a conquered mind and a quiet and obedient heart. And I dreamed of writing a book which should help men and women, whether rich or poor, learned or unlearned, worldly or unworldly, to find within themselves the source of all success, all happiness, all accomplishment, all truth. And the dream remained with me, and at last became substantial; and now I send it forth into the world on its mission of healing and blessedness, knowing that it cannot fail to reach the homes and hearts of those who are waiting and ready to receive it.

—James Allen

CONTENTS

PART I

THE PATH OF PROSPERITY

THE LESSON OF EVIL

Unrest and pain and sorrow are the shadows of life. There is no heart in all the world that has not felt the sting of pain, no mind that has not been tossed upon the dark waters of trouble, no eye that has not wept the hot, blinding tears of unspeakable anguish. There is no household where the Great Destroyers, disease and death, have not entered, severing heart from heart, and casting over all the dark pall of sorrow. In the strong, and apparently indestructible meshes of evil all are more or less fast caught, and pain, unhappiness, and misfortune wait upon mankind.

With the object of escaping, or in some way mitigating this overshadowing gloom, men and women rush blindly into innumerable devices, pathways by which they fondly hope to enter into a happiness which will not pass away. Such are the drunkard and the harlot, who revel in sensual excitements; such is the exclusive aesthete, who shuts himself out from the sorrows of the world, and surrounds himself with enervating luxuries; such is he who thirsts for wealth or fame, and subordinates all things to the achievement of that object; and such are they who seek consolation in the performance of religious rites.

And to all the happiness sought seems to come, and the soul, for a time, is lulled into a sweet security, and an intoxicating forgetfulness of the existence of evil; but the day of disease comes at last, or some great sorrow, temptation, or misfortune breaks suddenly in on the unfortified soul, and the fabric of its fancied happiness is torn to shreds.

So over the head of every personal joy hangs the Damocletian sword of pain, ready, at any moment, to fall and crush the soul of him who is unprotected by knowledge.

The child cries to be a man or woman; the man and woman sigh for the lost felicity of childhood. The poor man chafes under the chains of poverty by which he is bound, and the rich man often lives in fear of poverty, or scours the world in search of an elusive shadow he calls happiness. Sometimes the soul feels that it has found a secure peace and happiness in adopting a certain religion, in embracing an intellectual philosophy, or in building up an intellectual or artistic ideal; but some overpowering temptation proves the religion to be inadequate or insufficient; the theoretical philosophy is found to be a useless prop; or in a moment, the idealistic statue upon which the devotee has for years been laboring is shattered into fragments at his feet.

Is there, then, no way of escape from pain and sorrow? Are there no means by which the bonds of evil may be broken? Is permanent happiness, secure prosperity, and abiding peace a foolish dream? No, there is a way, and I speak it with gladness, by which evil can be slain forever; there is a process by which disease, poverty, or any adverse condition or circumstance can be put on one side never to return; there is a method by which a permanent prosperity can be secured, free from all fear of the return of adversity, and there is a practice by which unbroken and unending peace and bliss can be partaken of and realized. And the beginning of the way which leads to this glorious realization is *the acquirement of a right understanding of the nature of evil.*

It is not sufficient to deny or ignore evil; it must be understood. It is not enough to pray to God to remove the evil; you must find out why it is there, and what lesson it has for you. It is of no avail to fret and fume and chafe at the chains which bind you; you must know why and how you are bound. Therefore, reader, you must get outside yourself, and must begin to examine and understand yourself. You must cease to be a disobedient child in the school of experience, and must begin to learn, with humility and patience, the lessons that are set for your edification and ultimate perfection; for evil, when rightly understood, is found to be, not an unlimited power or principle in the universe, but a passing phase of human experience, and it therefore becomes a teacher to those who are willing to learn. Evil is not an abstract something outside yourself; it is an experience in your own heart, and by patiently examining and rectifying your heart you will be gradually led into the discovery of the origin and nature of evil, which will necessarily be followed by its complete eradication.

All evil is corrective and remedial, and is therefore not permanent. It is rooted in ignorance, ignorance of the true nature and relation of things, and so long as we remain in that state of ignorance, we remain subject to evil. There is no evil in the universe which is not the result of ignorance, and which would not, if we were ready and willing to learn its lesson, lead us to higher wisdom, and then vanish away. But men remain in evil, and it does not pass away because men are not willing or prepared to learn the lesson which it came to teach them. I knew a child who, every night when its mother took it to bed, cried to be allowed to play with the candle; and one night, when the mother was off guard for a moment, the child took hold of the candle; the inevitable result followed, and the child never wished to play with the candle again. By its one foolish act it learned, and learned perfectly the lesson of obedience, and entered into the knowledge that fire burns. And this incident is a complete illustration of the nature, meaning, and ultimate result of all sin and evil. As the child suffered through its own ignorance of the real nature of fire, so older children suffer through their ignorance of the real nature of the things which they weep for and strive after, and which harm them when they are secured; the only difference being that in the latter case the ignorance and evil are more deeply rooted and obscure.

Evil has always been symbolized by darkness, and Good by light, and hidden within the symbol is contained the perfect interpretation, the reality; for, just as light always floods the universe, and darkness is only a mere speck or shadow cast by a small body intercepting a few rays of the illimitable light, so the Light of the Supreme Good is the positive and life-giving power which floods the universe, and evil the insignificant shadow cast by the self that intercepts and shuts off the illuminating rays which strive for entrance. When night folds the world in its black impenetrable mantle, no matter how dense the darkness, it covers but the small space of half our little planet, while the whole universe is ablaze with living light, and every soul knows that it will awake in the light in the morning. Know, then, that when the dark night of sorrow, pain, or misfortune settles down upon your soul, and you stumble along with weary and uncertain steps, that you are merely intercepting your own personal desires between yourself and the boundless light of joy and bliss, and the dark shadow that covers you is cast by none and nothing but yourself. And just as the darkness without is but a negative shadow, an unreality which comes from nowhere, goes to nowhere, and has no abiding dwelling-place, so the darkness within is equally a negative shadow passing over the evolving and Light-born soul.

"But," I fancy I hear someone say, "why pass through the darkness of evil at all?" Because, by ignorance, you have chosen to do so, and because, by doing so, you may understand both good and evil, and may the more appreciate the light by having passed through the darkness. As evil is the direct outcome of ignorance, so, when the lessons of evil are fully learned, ignorance passes away, and wisdom takes its place. But as a disobedient child refuses to learn its lessons at school, so it is possible to refuse to learn the lessons of experience, and thus to remain in continual darkness, and to suffer continually recurring punishments in the form of disease, disappointment, and sorrow. He, therefore, who would shake himself free of the evil which encompasses him, must be willing and ready to learn, and must be prepared to undergo that disciplinary process without which no grain of wisdom or abiding happiness and peace can be secured.

A man may shut himself up in a dark room, and deny that the light exists, but it is everywhere without, and darkness exists only in his own little room. So you may shut out the light of Truth, or you may begin to pull down the walls of prejudice, self-seeking, and error which you have built around yourself, and so let in the glorious and omnipresent Light.

By earnest self-examination strive to realize, and not merely hold as a theory, that evil is a passing phase, a self-created shadow; that all your pains, sorrows, and misfortunes have come to you by a process of undeviating and absolutely perfect law; have come to you because you deserve and require them, and that by first enduring, and then understanding them, you may be made stronger, wiser, nobler. When you have fully entered into this realization, you will be in a position to mould your own circumstances, to transmute all evil into good and to weave, with a master hand, the fabric of your destiny.

What of the night, O Watchman! see'st thou yet
    The glimmering dawn upon the mountain heights,
    The golden Herald of the Light of lights,
Are his fair feet upon the hilltops set?

Cometh he yet to chase away the gloom,
    And with it all the demons of the Night?
    Strike yet his darting rays upon thy sight?
Hear'st thou his voice, the sound of error's doom?

The Morning cometh, lover of the Light;
    E'en now He gilds with gold the mountain's brow,
    Dimly I see the path whereon e'en now
His shining feet are set toward the Night.

Darkness shall pass away, and all the things
    That love the darkness, and that hate the Light
    Shall disappear for ever with the Night:
Rejoice! for thus the speeding Herald sings.

THE WORLD A REFLEX
OF MENTAL STATES

What you are, so is your world. Everything in the universe is resolved into your own inward experience. It matters little what is without, for it is all a reflection of your own state of consciousness. It matters everything what you are within, for everything without will be mirrored and colored accordingly.

All that you positively know is contained in your own experience; all that you ever will know must pass through the gateway of experience, and so become part of yourself.

Your own thoughts, desires, and aspirations comprise your world, and, to you, all that there is in the universe of beauty and joy and bliss, or of ugliness and sorrow and pain, is contained within yourself. By your own thoughts you make or mar your life, your world, your universe. As you build within by the power of thought, so will your outward life and circumstances shape themselves accordingly. Whatsoever you harbor in the inmost chambers of your heart will, sooner or later by the inevitable law of reaction, shape itself in your outward life. The soul that is impure, sordid, and selfish is gravitating with unerring precision toward misfortune and catastrophe; the soul that is pure, unselfish, and noble is gravitating with equal precision toward happiness and prosperity. Every soul attracts its own, and nothing can possibly come to it that does not belong to it. To realize this is to recognize the universality of Divine Law. The incidents of every human life, which both make and mar, are drawn to it by the quality and power of its own inner thought-life. Every soul is a complex combination of gathered experiences and thoughts, and the body is but an improvised vehicle for its manifestation. What, therefore, your thoughts are, that is your real self; and the world around, both animate and inanimate, wears the aspect with which your thoughts clothe it. "All that we are is the result of what we have thought; it is founded on our thoughts; it is made up of our thoughts." Thus said Buddha, and it therefore follows that if a man is happy, it is because he dwells in happy thoughts; if miserable, because he dwells in despondent and debilitating thoughts. Whether one be fearful or fearless, foolish or wise, troubled or serene, within that soul lies the cause of its own state or states, and never without. And now I seem to hear a chorus of voices exclaim, "But do you really mean to say that outward circumstances do not affect our minds?" I do not say that, but I say this, and know it to be an infallible truth, *that circumstances can only affect you in so far as you allow them to do so.* You are swayed by circumstances because you have not a right understanding of the nature, use, and power of thought. You believe (and upon this little word *belief* hang all our sorrows and joys) that outward things have the power to make or mar your life; by so doing you submit to those outward things, confess that you are their slave, and they your unconditional master; by so doing, you invest them with a power which they do not, of themselves, possess, and you succumb, in reality, not to the mere circumstances, but to the gloom or gladness, the fear or hope, the strength or weakness, which your thought-sphere has thrown around them.

I knew two men who, at an early age, lost the hard-earned savings of years. One was very deeply troubled, and gave way to chagrin, worry, and despondency. The other, on reading in his morning paper that the bank in which his money was deposited had hopelessly failed, and that he had lost all, quietly and firmly remarked, "Well, it's gone, and trouble and worry won't bring it back, but hard work will." He went to work with renewed vigor, and rapidly became prosperous, while the former man, continuing to mourn the loss of his money, and to grumble at his "bad luck," remained the sport and tool of adverse circumstances, in reality of his own weak and slavish thoughts. The loss of money was a curse to the one because he clothed the event with dark and dreary thoughts; it was a blessing to the other, because he threw around it thoughts of strength, of hope, and renewed endeavor.

If circumstances had the power to bless or harm, they would bless and harm all men alike, but the fact that the same circumstances will be alike good and bad to different souls proves that the good or bad is not in the circumstance, but only in the mind of him that encounters it. When you begin to realize this you will begin to control your thoughts, to regulate and discipline your mind, and to rebuild the inward temple of your soul, eliminating all useless and superfluous material, and incorporating into your being thoughts alone of joy and serenity, of strength and life, of compassion and love, of beauty and immortality; and as you do this you will become joyful and serene, strong and healthy, compassionate and loving, and beautiful with the beauty of immortality.

And as we clothe events with the drapery of our own thoughts, so likewise do we clothe the objects of the visible world around us, and where one sees harmony and beauty, another sees revolting ugliness. An enthusiastic naturalist was one day roaming the country lanes in pursuit of his hobby, and during his rambles came upon a pool of brackish water near a farmyard. As he proceeded to fill a small bottle with the water for the purpose of examination under the microscope, he dilated, with more enthusiasm than discretion, to an uncultivated son of the plough who stood close by, upon the hidden and innumerable wonders contained in the pool, and concluded by saying, "Yes, my friend, within this pool is contained a hundred, nay, a million universes, had we but the sense or the instrument by which we could apprehend them." And the unsophisticated one ponderously remarked, "I know the water be full o' tadpoles, but they be easy to catch."

Where the naturalist, his mind stored with the knowledge of natural facts, saw beauty, harmony, and hidden glory, the mind unenlightened upon those things saw only an offensive mud-puddle.

The wild flower which the casual wayfarer thoughtlessly tramples upon is, to the spiritual eye of the poet, an angelic messenger from the invisible. To the many, the ocean is but a dreary expanse of water on which ships sail and are sometimes wrecked; to the soul of the musician it is a living thing, and he hears, in all its changing moods, divine harmonies. Where the ordinary mind sees disaster and confusion, the mind of the philospher sees the most perfect sequence of cause and effect, and where the materialist sees nothing but endless death, the mystic sees pulsating and eternal life.

And as we clothe both events and objects with our own thoughts, so likewise do we clothe the souls of others in the garments of our thoughts. The suspicious believe everybody to be suspicious; the liar feels secure in the thought that he is not so foolish as to believe that there is such a phenomenon as a strictly truthful person; the envious see envy in every soul; the miser thinks everybody is eager to get his money; he who has subordinated conscience in the making of his wealth sleeps with a revolver under his pillow, wrapt in the delusion that the world is full of conscienceless people who are eager to rob him, and the abandoned sensualist looks upon the saint as a hypocrite. On the other hand, those who dwell in loving thoughts see that in all which calls forth their love and sympathy; the trusting and honest are not troubled by suspicions; the good-natured and charitable who rejoice at the good fortune of others, scarcely know what envy means; and he who has realized the Divine within himself recognizes it in all beings, even in the beasts.

And men and women are confirmed in their mental outlook because of the fact that, by the law of cause and effect, they attract to themselves that which they send forth, and so come in contact with people similar to themselves. The old adage "Birds of a feather flock together" has a deeper significance than is generally attached to it, for in the thought-world as in the world of matter, each clings to its kind.

Do you wish for kindness? Be kind.
  Do you ask for truth? Be true.
What you give of yourself you find;
  Your world is a reflex of you.

If you are one of those who are praying for, and looking forward to, a happier world beyond the grave, here is a message of gladness for you: you may enter into and realize that happy world now; it fills the whole universe, and it is within you, waiting for you to find, acknowledge, and possess. Said one who knew the inner laws of Being, "When men shall say lo here, or lo there, go not after them; the kingdom of God is within you." What you have to do is to believe this, simply believe it with a mind unshadowed by doubt, and then meditate upon it till you understand it. You will then begin to purify and to build your inner world, and as you proceed, passing from revelation to revelation, from realization to realization, you will discover the utter powerlessness of outward things beside the magic potency of a self-governed soul.

> If thou would'st right the world,
> And banish all its evils and its woes,
> Make its wild places bloom,
> And its drear deserts blossom as the rose,—
> Then right thyself.

> If thou would'st turn the world
> From its long, lone captivity in sin.
> Restore all broken hearts,
> Slay grief, and let sweet consolation in,—
> Turn thou thyself.

> If thou would'st cure the world
> Of its long sickness, end its grief and pain;
> Bring in all-healing Joy,
> And give to the afflicted rest again,—
> Then cure thyself.

> If thou would'st wake the world
> Out of its dream of death and dark'ning strife,
> Bring it to Love and Peace,
> And Light and brightness of immortal Life,—
> Wake thou thyself.

THE WAY OUT OF UNDESIRABLE CONDITIONS

Having seen and realized that evil is but a passing shadow thrown, by the intercepting self, across the transcedent Form of the Eternal Good, and that the world is a mirror in which each sees a reflection of himself, we now ascend, by firm and easy steps, to that plane of perception whereon is seen and realized the *Vision of the Law*. With this realization comes the knowledge that everything is included in a ceaseless interaction of cause and effect, and that nothing can possibly be divorced from law. From the most trivial thought, word, or act of man, up to the groupings of the celestial bodies, law reigns supreme. No arbitrary condition can, even for one moment, exist, for such a condition would be a denial and an annihilation of law. Every condition of life is, therefore, bound up in an orderly and harmonious sequence, and the secret and cause of every condition is contained within itself. The law "Whatsoever a man sows that shall he also reap" is inscribed in flaming letters upon the portal of Eternity, and none can deny it, none can cheat it, none can escape it. He who puts his hand in the fire must suffer the burning until such time as it has worked itself out, and neither curses nor prayers can avail to alter it. And precisely the same law governs the realm of mind. Hatred, anger, jealousy, envy, lust, covetousness, all these are fires which burn, and whoever even so much as touches them must suffer the torments of burning. All these conditions of mind are rightly called "evil," for they are the efforts of the soul to subvert, in its ignorance, the law, and they, therefore, lead to chaos and confusion within, and are sooner or later actualized in the outward circumstances as disease, failure, and misfortune, coupled with grief, pain, and despair. Whereas love, gentleness, good-will, purity are cooling airs which breathe peace upon the soul that woos them, and, being in harmony with the Eternal Law, they become actualized in the form of health, peaceful surroundings, and undeviating success and good fortune.

A thorough understanding of this Great Law which permeates the universe leads to the acquirement of that state of mind known as *obedience*. To know that justice, harmony, and love are supreme in the universe is likewise to know that all adverse and painful conditions are the result of our own disobedience to that Law. Such knowledge leads to strength and power, and it is upon such knowledge alone that a true life and an enduring success and happiness can be built. To be patient under all circumstances, and to accept all conditions as necessary factors in your training, is to rise superior to all painful conditions, and to overcome them with an overcoming which is sure, and which leaves no fear of their return, for by the power of obedience to law they are utterly slain. Such an obedient one is working in harmony with the law, has in fact, identified himself with the law, and whatsoever he conquers he conquers forever; whatsoever he builds can never be destroyed.

The cause of all power, as of all weakness, is within: the secret of all happiness as of all misery is likewise within. There is no progress apart from unfoldment within, and no sure foothold of prosperity or peace except by orderly advancement in knowledge.

You say you are chained by circumstances; you cry out for better opportunities, for a wider scope, for improved physical conditions, and perhaps you inwardly curse the fate that binds you hand and foot. It is for you that I write; it is to you that I speak. Listen, and let my words burn themselves into your heart, for that which I say to you is truth:—*You may bring about that improved condition in your outward life which you desire, if you will unswervingly resolve to improve your inner life.* I know this pathway looks barren at its commencement (truth always does, it is only error and delusion which are at first inviting and fascinating) but if you undertake to walk it; if you perseveringly discipline your mind, eradicating your weaknesses, and allowing your soul-forces and spiritual powers to unfold themselves, you will be astonished at the magical changes which will be brought about in your outward life. As you proceed, golden opportunities will be strewn across your path, and the power and judgment to properly utilize them will spring up within you. Genial friends will come unbidden to you; sympathetic souls will be drawn to you as the needle is to the magnet; and books and all outward aids that you require will come to you unsought.

Perhaps the chains of poverty hang heavily upon you, and you are friendless and alone, and you long with an intense longing that your load may be lightened; but the load continues, and you seem to be enveloped in an ever-increasing darkness. Perhaps you complain, you bewail your lot; you blame your birth, your parents, your employer, or the unjust Powers who have bestowed upon you so undeservedly poverty and hardship, and upon another affluence and ease. Cease your complaining and fretting; none of these things which you blame are the cause of your poverty; the cause is within yourself, and where the cause is, there is the remedy. The very fact that you are a complainer shows that you deserve your lot; shows that you lack that faith which is the ground of all effort and progress. There is no room for a complainer in a universe of law, and worry is soul-suicide. By your very attitude of mind you are strengthening the chains which bind you, and are drawing about you the darkness by which you are enveloped. Alter your outlook upon life, and your outward life will alter. Build yourself up in the faith and knowledge, and make yourself worthy of better surroundings and wider opportunities. Be sure, first of all, that you are making the best of what you have. Do not delude yourself into supposing that you can step into greater advantages whilst overlooking smaller ones, for if you could, the advantage would be impermanent and you would quickly fall back again in order to learn the lesson which you had neglected. As the child at school must master one standard before passing on to the next, so before you can have that greater good which you so desire must you faithfully employ that which you already possess. The parable of the talents is a beautiful story illustrative of this truth, for does it not plainly show that if we misuse, neglect, or degrade that which we possess, be it ever so mean and insignificant, even that little will be taken from us, for by our conduct we show that we are unworthy of it?

Perhaps you are living in a small cottage, and are surrounded by unhealthy and vicious influences. You desire a larger and more sanitary residence. Then you must fit yourself for such a residence by first of all making your cottage as far as possible a little paradise. Keep it spotlessly clean. Make it look as pretty and sweet as your limited means will allow. Cook your plain food with all care, and arrange your humble table as tastefully as you possibly can. If you cannot afford a carpet, let your rooms be carpeted with smiles and welcomes, fastened down with the nails of kind words driven in with the hammer of patience. Such a carpet will not fade in the sun, and constant use will never wear it away.

By so ennobling your present surroundings you will rise above them, and above the need of them, and at the right time you will pass on into the better house and surroundings which have all along been waiting for you, and which you have fitted yourself to occupy.

Perhaps you desire more time for thought and effort, and feel that your hours of labor are too hard and long. Then see to it that you are utilizing to the fullest possible extent what little spare time you have. It is useless to desire more time, if you are already wasting what little you have; for you would only grow more indolent and indifferent.

Even poverty and lack of time and leisure are not the evils that you imagine they are, and if they hinder you in your progress, it is because you have clothed them in your own weaknesses, and the evil that you see in them is really in yourself. Endeavor to fully and completely realize that in so far as you shape and mould your mind, you are the maker of your destiny, and as, by the transmuting power of self-discipline you realize this more and more, you will come to see that these so-called evils may be converted into blessings. You will then utilize your poverty for the cultivation of patience, hope, and courage; and your lack of time in the gaining of promptness of action and decision of mind, by seizing the precious moments as they present themselves for your acceptance. As in the rankest soil the most beautiful flowers are grown, so in the dark soil of poverty the choicest flowers of humanity have developed and bloomed. Where there are difficulties to cope with, and unsatisfactory conditions to overcome, there virtue most flourishes and manifests its glory.

It may be that you are in the employ of a tyrannous master or mistress, and you feel that you are harshly treated. Look upon this also as necessary to your training. Return your employer's unkindness with gentleness and forgiveness. Practice unceasingly patience and self-control. Turn the disadvantage to account by utilizing it for the gaining of mental and spiritual strength, and by your silent example and influence you will thus be teaching your employer, will be helping him to grow ashamed of his conduct, and will, at the same time, be lifting yourself up to that height of spiritual attainment by which you will be enabled to step into new and more congenial surroundings at the time when they are presented to you. Do not complain that you are a slave, but lift yourself up, by noble conduct, above the plane of slavery. Before complaining that you are a slave to another, be sure that you are not a slave to self. Look within; look searchingly, and have no mercy upon yourself. You will find there, perchance, slavish thoughts, slavish desires, and in your daily life and conduct slavish habits. Conquer these; cease to be a slave to self, and no man will have the power to enslave you. As you overcome self, you will overcome all adverse conditions, and every difficulty will fall before you.

Do not complain that you are oppressed by the rich. Are you sure that if you gained riches you would not be an oppressor yourself? Remember that there is the Eternal Law which is absolutely just, and that he who oppresses to-day must himself be oppressed to-morrow; and from this there is no way of escape. And perhaps you, yesterday (in some former existence) were rich and an oppressor, and you are now merely paying off the debt which you owe to the Great Law. Practice, therefore, fortitude and faith. Dwell constantly in mind upon the Eternal Justice, the Eternal Good. Endeavor to lift yourself above the personal and the transitory into the impersonal and permanent. Shake off the delusion that you are being injured or oppressed by another, and try to realize, by a profounder comprehension of your inner life, and the laws which govern that life, that you are only really injured by what is within you. There is no practice more degrading, debasing, and soul-destroying than that of *self-pity*. Cast it out from you. While such a canker is feeding upon your heart you can never expect to grow into a fuller life. Cease from the condemnation of others, and begin to condemn yourself. Condone none of your acts, desires, or thoughts that will not bear comparison with spotless purity, or endure the light of sinless good. By so doing you will be building your house upon the rock of the Eternal, and all that is required for your happiness and well-being will come to you in its own time.

There is positively no way of permanently rising above poverty, or any undesirable condition, except by eradicating those selfish and negative conditions within, of which these are the reflection, and by virtue of which they continue. The way to true riches is to enrich the soul by the acquisition of virtue. Outside of real heart-virtue there is neither prosperity nor power, but only the appearances of these. I am aware that men make money who have acquired no measure of virtue, and have little desire to do so; but such money does not constitute true riches, and its possession is transitory and feverish. Here is David's testimony:—"For I was envious at the foolish when I saw the prosperity of the wicked. . . . . . Their eyes stand out with fatness; they have more than heart could wish. . . . Verily I have cleansed my heart in vain, and washed my hands in innocency. . . . When I thought to know this it was too painful for me; until I went into the sanctuary of God, then understood I their end." The prosperity of the wicked was a great trial to David until he went into the sanctuary of God, and then he *knew their end*. You likewise may go into that sanctuary. It is within you. It is that state of consciousness which remains when all that is sordid, and personal, and impermanent is risen above, and universal and eternal principles are realized. That is the God state of consciousness; it is the sanctuary of the Most High. When by long strife and self-discipline you have succeeded in entering the door of that holy Temple, you will perceive, with unobstructed vision, the end and fruit of all human though and endeavor, both good and evil. You will then no longer relax your faith when you see the immoral man accumulating outward riches, for you will *know* that he must come again to poverty and degradation. The rich roan who is barren of virtue is, in reality, poor, and as surely as the waters of the river are drifting to the ocean, so surely is he, in the midst of all his riches, drifting towards poverty and misfortune; and though he die rich, yet must he return to reap the bitter fruit of all of his immorality. And though he become rich many times, yet as many times must he be thrown back into poverty, until, by long experience and suffering, he conquers the poverty within. But the man who is outwardly poor, yet rich in virtue, is truly rich, and, in the midst of all his poverty he is surely traveling toward prosperity; and abounding joy and bliss await his coming.

If you would become truly and permanently prosperous, you must first become virtuous. It is therefore unwise to aim directly at prosperity, to make it the one object of life, to reach out greedily for it. To do this is to ultimately defeat yourself. But rather aim at self-perfection, make useful and unselfish service the object of your life, and ever reach out hands of faith toward the supreme and unalterable Good.

You say you desire wealth, not for your own sake, but in order to do good with it, and to bless others. If this is your *real* motive in desiring wealth, then wealth will come to you; for you are strong and unselfish indeed if, in the midst of riches, you are willing to look upon yourself as steward and not as owner. But examine well your motive, for in the majority of instances where money is desired for the admitted object of blessing others, the real underlying motive is a love of popularity, and a desire to pose as a philanthropist or reformer. If you are not doing good with what little you have, depend upon it, the more money you got the more selfish you would become, and all the good you appeared to do with your money, if you attempted to do any, would be so much insinuating self-laudation. If your real desire is to do good, there is no need to wait for money before you do it; you can do it now, this very moment, and just where you are. If you are really so unselfish as you believe yourself to be, you will show it by sacrificing yourself for others now. No matter how poor you are, there is room for self-sacrifice, for did not the widow put her all into the treasury? The heart that truly desires to do good does not wait for money before doing it, but comes to the altar of sacrifice, and, leaving there the unworthy elements of self, goes out and breathes upon neighbor and stranger, friend and enemy alike, the breath of blessedness.

As the effect is related to the cause, so is prosperity and power related to the inward good, and poverty and weakness to the inward evil.

Money does not constitute true wealth, nor position, nor power, and to rely upon it alone is to stand upon a slippery place.

Your true wealth is your stock of virtue, and your true power the uses to which you put it. Rectify your heart, and you will rectify your life. Lust, hatred, anger, vanity, pride, covetousness, self-indulgence, self-seeking, obstinacy—all these are poverty and weakness; whereas, love, purity, gentleness, meekness, patience, compassion, generosity, self-forgetfulness, and self-renunciation—all these are wealth and power.

As the elements of poverty and weakness are overcome, an irresistible and all-conquering power is evolved from within, and he who succeeds in establishing himself in the highest virtue brings the whole world to his feet.

But the rich, as well as the poor, have their undesirable conditions, and are frequently farther removed from happiness than the poor. And here we see how happiness depends, not upon outward aids or possessions, but upon the inward life. Perhaps you are an employer, and you have endless trouble with those whom you employ, and when you do get good and faithful servants they quickly leave you. As a result you are beginning to lose, or have completely lost, your faith in human nature. You try to remedy matters by giving better wages, and by allowing certain liberties, yet matters remain unaltered. Let me advise you. The secret of all your trouble is not in your servants, *it is in yourself;* and if you look within, with a humble and sincere desire to discover and eradicate your error, you will, sooner or later, find the origin of all your unhappiness. It may be some selfish desire, or lurking suspicion, or unkind attitude of mind which sends out its poison upon those about you, and reacts upon yourself, even though you may not show it in your manner or speech. Think of your servants with kindness, consider their happiness and comfort, and never demand of them that extremity of service which you yourself would not care to perform were you in their place. Rare and beautiful is that humility of soul by which a servant entirely forgets himself in his master's good; but far rarer, and beautiful with a divine beauty, is that nobility of soul by which a man, forgetting his own happiness, seeks the happiness of those who are under his authority, and who depend upon him for their bodily sustenance. And such a man's happiness is increased tenfold, nor does he need to complain of those whom he employs. Said a well-known and extensive employer of labor, who never needs to dismiss an employe: "I have always had the happiest relations with my workpeople. If you ask me how it is to be accounted for. I can only say that it has been my aim from the first to do to them as I would wish to be done by." Herein lies the secret by which all desirable conditions are secured, and all that are undesirable are overcome. Do you say that you are lonely and unloved, and have "not a friend in the world"? Then, I pray you, for the sake of your own happiness, blame nobody but yourself. Be friendly towards others, and friends will soon flock round you. Make yourself pure and lovable, and you will be loved by all.

Whatever conditions are rendering your life burdensome, you may pass out of and beyond them by developing and utilizing within you the transforming power of self-purification and self-conquest. Be it the poverty which galls (and remember that the poverty upon which I have been dilating is that poverty which is a source of misery, and not that voluntary poverty which is the glory of emancipated souls), or the riches which burden, or the many misfortunes, griefs, and annoyances which form the dark background in the web of life, you may overcome them by overcoming the selfish elements within which give them life.

It matters not that by the unfailing Law there are past thoughts and acts to work out and to atone for, as, by the same law, we are setting in motion, during every moment of our life, fresh thoughts and acts, and we have the power to make them good or ill. Nor does it follow that if a man (reaping what he has sown) must lose money or forfeit position, that he must also lose his fortitude or forfeit his uprightness, and it is in these that his wealth and power and happiness are to be found.

He who clings to self is his own enemy, and is surrounded by enemies. He who relinquishes self is his own savior, and is surrounded by friends like a protecting belt. Before the divine radiance of a pure heart all darkness vanishes and all clouds melt away, and he who has conquered self has conquered the universe. Come, then, out of your poverty; come out of your pain; come out of your troubles, and sighings, and complainings, and heartaches, and loneliness *by coming out of yourself*. Let the old tattered garment of your petty selfishness fall from you, and put on the new garment of universal Love. You will then realize the inward heaven, and it will be reflected in all your outward life.

He who sets his foot firmly upon the path of self-conquest, who walks, aided by the staff of Faith, the highway of self-sacrifice, will assuredly achieve the highest prosperity, and will reap abounding and enduring joy and bliss.

To them that seek the highest good
   All things subserve the wisest ends;
   Nought comes as ill, and wisdom lends
Wings to all shapes of evil brood.

The dark'ning sorrow veils a Star
   That waits to shine with gladsome light;
   Hell waits on heaven; and after night
Comes golden glory from afar.

Defeats are steps by which we climb
   With purer aim to nobler ends;
   Loss leads to gain, and joy attends
True footsteps up the hills of time.

Pain leads to paths of holy bliss,
    To thoughts and words and deeds divine;
    And clouds that gloom and rays that shine,
Along life's upward highway kiss

    Misfortune does but cloud the way
    Whose end and summit in the sky
    Of bright success, sunkiss'd and high,
Awaits our seeking and our stay.

The heavy pall of doubts and fears
    That clouds the Valley of our hopes,
    The shades with which the spirit copes,
The bitter harvesting of tears.

The heartaches, miseries, and griefs,
    The bruisings born of broken ties,
    All these are steps by which we rise
To living ways of sound beliefs.

Love, pitying, watchful, runs to meet
    The Pilgrim from the Land of Fate;
    All glory and all good await
The coming of obedient feet.

THE SILENT POWER OF THOUGHT: CONTROLLING AND DIRECTING ONE'S FORCES

The most powerful forces in the universe are the silent forces; and in accordance with the intensity of its power does a force become beneficent when rightly directed, and destructive when wrongly employed. This is a common knowledge in regard to the mechanical forces, such as steam, electricity, etc., but few have yet learned to apply this knowledge to the realm of mind, where the thought-forces (most powerful of all) are continually being generated and sent forth as currents of salvation or destruction.

At this stage of his evolution, man has entered into the possession of these forces, and the whole trend of his present advancement is their complete subjugation. All the wisdom possible to man on this material earth is to be found only in complete self-mastery, and the command "Love your enemies" resolves itself into an exhortation to enter here and now, into the possession of that sublime wisdom by taking hold of, mastering, and transmuting those mind forces to which man is now slavishly subject, and by which he is helplessly borne, like a straw on the stream, upon the currents of selfishness.

The Hebrew prophets, with their perfect knowledge of the Supreme Law, always related outward events to inward thought, and associated national disaster or success with the thoughts and desires that dominated the nation at the time. The knowledge of the causal power of thought is the basis of all their prophecies, as it is the basis of all real wisdom and power. National events are simply the working out of the psychic forces of the nation. Wars, plagues, and famines are the meeting and clashing of wrongly-directed thought-forces, the culminating points at which destruction steps in as the agent of the Law. It is foolish to ascribe war to the influence of one man, or to one body of men. It is the crowning horror of national selfishness.

It is the silent and conquering thought-forces which bring all things into manifestation. The universe grew out of thought. Matter in its last analysis is found to be merely objectivized thought. All men's accomplishments were first wrought out in thought, and then objectivized. The author, the inventor, the architect first builds up his work in thought, and having perfected it in all its parts as a complete and harmonious whole upon the thought-plane, he then commences to materialize it, to bring it down to the material or sense-plane.

When the thought-forces are directed in harmony with the over-ruling Law, they are up-building and preservative, but when subverted they become disintegrating and self-destructive.

To adjust all your thoughts to a perfect and unswerving faith in the omnipotence and supremacy of Good is to co-operate with that Good, and to realize within yourself the solution and destruction of all evil. *Believe and ye shall live.* And here we have the true meaning of salvation; salvation from the darkness and negation of evil, by entering into and realizing the living light of the Eternal Good.

Where there is fear, worry, anxiety, doubt, trouble, chagrin, or disappointment, there is igno-rance and lack of faith. All these conditions of mind are the direct outcome of selfishness, and are based upon an inherent belief in the power and supremacy of evil; they therefore constitute practi-cal atheism; and to live in, and become subject to, these negative and soul-destroying conditions of mind is the only real atheism.

It is salvation from such conditions that the race needs, and let no man boast of salvation whilst he is their helpless and obedient slave. To fear or to worry is as sinful as to curse, for how can one fear or worry if he intrinsically believes in the Eternal Justice, the Omnipotent Good, the Boundless Love? To fear, to worry, to doubt is to deny, to disbelieve.

It is from such states of mind that all weakness and failure proceed, for they represent the annul-ling and disintegrating of the positive thought-forces which would otherwise speed to their object with power, and bring about their own beneficent results.

To overcome these negative conditions is to enter into a life of power, is to cease to be a slave, and to become a master, and there is only one way by which they can be overcome, and that is by *steady and persistent growth in inward knowledge.* To mentally deny evil is not sufficient; it must, by daily practice, be risen above and understood. To mentally affirm the good is inadequate; it must, by unswerving endeavor, be entered into and comprehended.

The intelligent practice of self-control quickly leads to a knowledge of one's interior thought-forces, and, later on, to the acquisition of that power by which they are rightly employed and directed. In the measure that you master self, that you control your mental forces instead of being controlled by them, in just such measure will you master affairs and outward circumstances.

Show me a man under whose touch everything crumbles away, and who cannot retain success even when it is placed in his hands, and I will show you a man who dwells continually in those conditions of mind which are the very negation of power. To be forever wallowing in the bogs of doubt, to be drawn continually into the quicksands of fear, or blown ceaselessly about by the winds of anxiety is to be a slave, and to live the life of a slave, even though success and influence be for-ever knocking at your door seeking for admittance. Such a man, being without faith and without self-government, is incapable of the right government of his affairs, and is a slave to circumstances; in reality a slave to himself. Such are taught by affliction, and ultimately pass from weakness to strength by the stress of bitter experience.

Faith and purpose constitute the motive-power of life. There is nothing that a strong faith and an unflinching purpose may not accomplish. By the daily exercise of silent faith, the thought-forces are gathered together, and by the daily strengthening of silent purpose, those forces are directed toward the object of accomplishment.

Whatever your position in life may be, before you can hope to enter into any measure of success, usefulness, and power, you must learn how to focus your thought-forces by cultivating calmness and repose. It may be that you are a business man, and you are suddenly confronted with some overwhelming difficulty or probable disaster. You grow fearful and anxious, and are at your wit's end. To persist in such a state of mind would be fatal, for when anxiety steps in, correct judgment passes out. Now if you will take advantage of a quiet hour or two in the early morning or at night, and go away to some solitary spot, or to some room in your house where you know you will be absolutely free from intrusion, and, having seated yourself in an easy attitude, you forcibly direct your mind right away from the object of anxiety by dwelling upon something in your life that is pleasing and bliss-giving, a calm, reposeful strength will gradually steal into your mind, and your anxiety will pass away. Upon the instant that you find your mind reverting to the lower plane of worry bring it back again, and re-establish it on the plane of peace and strength. When this is fully accomplished, you may then concentrate your whole mind upon the solution of your difficulty, and what was intricate and insurmountable to you in your hour of anxiety will be made plain and easy, and you will see, with that clear vision and perfect judgment which belong only to a calm and untroubled mind, the right course to pursue and the proper end to be brought about. It may be that you will have to try day after day before you will be able to perfectly calm your mind, but if you persevere you will certainly accomplish it. And the course which is presented to you in that hour of calmness *must be carried out.* Doubtless when you are again involved in the business of the day, and worries again creep in and begin to dominate you, you will begin to think that the course is a wrong or foolish one, but do not heed such suggestions. Be guided absolutely and entirely by the vision of calmness, and not by the shadows of anxiety. The hour of calmness is the hour of illumination and correct judgment. By such a course of mental discipline the scattered thought-forces are re-united, and directed, like the rays of the search-light, upon the problem at issue, with the result that it gives way before them.

There is no difficulty, however great, but will yield before a calm and powerful concentration of thought, and no legitimate object but may be speedily actualized by the intelligent use and direction of one's soul-forces.

Not until you have gone deeply and searchingly into your inner nature, and have overcome many enemies that lurk there, can you have any approximate conception of the subtle power of thought, of its inseparable relation to outward and material things, or of its magical potency, when rightly poised and directed, in readjusting and transforming the life-conditions.

Every thought you think is a force sent out, and in accordance with its nature and intensity will it go out to seek a lodgment in minds receptive to it, and will react upon yourself for good or evil. There is ceaseless reciprocity between mind and mind, and a continual interchange of thought-forces. Selfish and disturbing thoughts are so many malignant and destructive forces, messengers of evil, sent out to stimulate and augment the evil in other minds, which in turn send them back upon you with added power. While thoughts that are calm, pure, and unselfish are so many angelic messengers sent out into the world with health, healing, and blessedness upon their wings, counteracting the evil forces; pouring the oil of joy upon the troubled waters of anxiety and sorrow, and restoring to broken hearts their heritage of immortality.

Think good thoughts, and they will quickly become actualized in your outward life in the form of good conditions. Control your soul-forces, and you will be able to shape your outward life as you will. The difference between a savior and a sinner is this, that the one has a perfect control of all the forces within him; the other is dominated and controlled by them.

There is absolutely no other way to true power and abiding peace but by self-control, self-government, self-purification. To be at the mercy of your disposition is to be impotent, unhappy, and of little real use in the world. The conquest of your petty likes and dislikes, your capricious loves and hates, your fits of anger, suspicion, jealousy, and all the changing moods to which you are more or less helplessly subject, this is the task you have before you if you would weave into the web of life the golden threads of happiness and prosperity. In so far as you are enslaved by the changing moods within you, will you need to depend upon others and upon outward aids as you walk through life. If you would walk firmly and securely, and would accomplish any achievement, you must learn to rise above and control all such disturbing and retarding vibrations. You must daily practice the habit of putting your mind at rest, "going into the silence," as it is commonly called. This is a method of replacing a troubled thought with one of peace, a thought of weakness with one of strength. Until you succeed in doing this you cannot hope to direct your mental forces upon the problems and pursuits of life with any appreciable measure of success. It is a process of diverting one's scattered forces into one powerful channel. Just as a useless marsh may be converted into a field of golden corn or a fruitful garden by draining and directing the scattered and harmful streams into one well-cut channel, so he who acquires calmness, and subdues and directs the thought-currents within himself, saves his soul, and fructifies his heart and life.

As you succeed in gaining mastery over your impulses and thoughts you will begin to feel, growing up within you, a new and silent power, and a settled feeling of composure and strength will remain with you. Your latent powers will begin to unfold themselves, and whereas formerly your efforts were weak and ineffectual, you will now be able to work with that calm confidence which commands success. And along with this new power and strength, there will be awakened within you that interior illumination known as "intuition," and you will walk no longer in darkness and speculation, but in light and certainty. With the development of this soul-vision, judgment and mental penetration will be incalculably increased, and there will evolve within you that prophetic vision by the aid of which you will be able to sense coming events, and to forecast, with remarkable accuracy, the result of your efforts. And in just the measure that you alter from within will your outlook upon life alter; and as you alter your mental attitude toward others they will alter in their attitude and conduct toward you. As you rise above the lower, debilitating, and destructive thought-forces, you will come in contact with the positive, strengthening, and up-building currents generated by strong, pure, and noble minds, your happiness will be immeasurably intensified, and you will begin to realize the joy, strength, and power which are born only of self-mastery. And this joy, strength, and power will be continually radiating from you, and without any effort on your part, nay, though you are utterly unconscious of it, strong people will be drawn toward you, influence will be put into your hands, and in accordance with your altered thought-world will outward events shape themselves.

"A man's foes are they of his own household," and he who would be useful, strong, and happy must cease to be a passive receptacle for the negative, beggarly, and impure streams of thought; and as a wise householder commands his servants and invites his guests, so must he learn to command his desires, and to say, with authority, what thoughts he shall admit into the mansion of his soul. Even a very partial success in self-mastery adds greatly to one's power, and he who succeeds in perfecting this divine accomplishment enters into possession of undreamed-of wisdom and inward strength and peace, and realizes that all the forces of the universe aid and protect his footsteps who is master of his soul.

Would you scale the highest heaven,
    Would you pierce the lowest hell,—
Live in dreams of constant beauty,
    Or in basest thinkings dwell.

For your thoughts are heaven above you.
    And your thoughts are hell below;
Bliss is not, except in thinking,
    Torment nought but thought can know.

Worlds would vanish but for thinking;
    Glory is not but in dreams;
And the Drama of the ages
    From the Thought Eternal streams.

Dignity and shame and sorrow,
    Pain and anguish, love and hate
Are but maskings of the mighty
    Pulsing Thought that governs Fate.

As the colors of the rainbow
    Makes the one uncolored beam.
So the universal changes
    Make the One Eternal Dream.

And the Dream is all within you.
    And the Dreamer waiteth long
For the Morning to awake him
    To the living thought and strong.

That shall make the ideal real,
    Make to vanish dreams of hell
In the highest, holiest heaven
    Where the pure and perfect dwell.

Evil is the thought that thinks it;
    Good, the thought that makes it so;
Light and darkness, sin and pureness
    Likewise out of thinking grow.

Dwell in thought upon the Grandest,
    And the Grandest you shall see;
Fix your mind upon the Highest,
    And the Highest you shall be.

THE SECRET OF HEALTH, SUCCESS, AND POWER

We all remember with what intense delight, as children, we listened to the never-tiring fairy-tale. How eagerly we followed the fluctuating fortunes of the good boy or girl, ever protected, in the hour of crisis, from the evil machinations of the scheming witch, the cruel giant, or the wicked king. And our little hearts never faltered for the fate of the hero or heroine, nor did we doubt their ultimate triumph over all their enemies, for we knew that the fairies were infallible, and that they would never desert those who had consecrated themselves to the good and the true. And what unspeakable joy pulsated within us when the Fairy-Queen, bringing all her magic to bear at the critical moment, scattered all the darkness and trouble, and granted them the complete satisfaction of all their hopes, and they were "happy ever after."

With the accumulating years, and an ever-increasing intimacy with the so-called "realities" of life, our beautiful fairy-world became obliterated, and its wonderful inhabitants were relegated, in the archives of memory, to the shadowy and unreal. And we thought we were wise and strong in thus leaving forever the land of childish dreams, but as we re-become little children in the wondrous world of wisdom, we shall return again to the inspiring dreams of childhood and find that they are, after all, realities.

The fairy-folk, so small and nearly always invisible, yet possessed of an all-conquering and magical power, who bestow upon the good health, wealth, and happiness, along with all the gifts of nature in lavish profusion, start again into reality and become immortalized in the soul-realm of he who, by growth in wisdom, has entered into a knowledge of the power of thought, and the laws which govern the inner world of being. To him the fairies live again as thought-people, thought-messengers, thought-powers working in harmony with the over-ruling Good. And they who, day by day, endeavor to harmonize their hearts with the heart of the Supreme Good do in reality acquire true health, wealth, and happiness. There is no protection to compare with goodness, and by "goodness" I do not mean a mere outward conformity to the rules of morality; I mean pure thought, noble aspiration, unselfish love, and freedom from vainglory. To dwell continually in good thoughts is to throw around oneself a psychic atmosphere of sweetness and power which leaves its impress upon all who come in contact with it.

As the rising sun puts to rout the helpless shadows, so are all the impotent forces of evil put to flight by the searching rays of positive thought which shine forth from a heart made strong in purity and faith.

Where there is sterling faith and uncompromising purity there is health, there is success, there is power. In such a one, disease, failure, and disaster can find no lodgment, for there is nothing on which they can feed.

Even physical conditions are largely determined by mental states, and to this truth the scientific world is rapidly being drawn. The old, materialistic belief that a man is what his body makes him is rapidly passing away, and is being replaced by the inspiring belief that man is superior to his body, and that his body is what he makes it by the power of thought. Men everywhere are ceasing to believe that a man is despairing because he is dyspeptic, and are coming to understand that he is dyspeptic because he is despairing, and in the near future, the fact that all disease has its origin in the mind will become common knowledge.

There is no evil in the universe but has its root and origin in the mind, and sin, sickness, sorrow, and affliction do not, in reality, belong to the universal order, are not inherent in the nature of things, but are the direct outcome of our ignorance of the right relations of things.

According to tradition, there once lived, in India, a school of philosophers who led a life of such absolute purity and simplicity that they commonly reached the age of one hundred and fifty years, and to fall sick was looked upon by them as an unpardonable disgrace, for it was considered to indicate a violation of law.

The sooner we realize and acknowledge that sickness, far from being the arbitrary visitation of an offended God, or the test of an unwise Providence, is the result of our own error or sin, the sooner shall we enter upon the highway of health. Disease comes to those who attract it, to those whose minds and bodies are receptive to it, and flees from those whose strong, pure, and positive thought-sphere generates healing and life-giving currents.

If you are given to anger, worry, jealousy, greed, or any other inharmonious state of mind, and expect perfect physical health, you are expecting the impossible, for you are continually sowing the seeds of disease in your mind. Such conditions of mind are carefully shunned by the wise man, for he knows them to be far more dangerous than a bad drain or an infected house.

If you would be free from all physical aches and pains, and would enjoy perfect physical harmony, then put your mind in order, and harmonize your thoughts. Think joyful thoughts; think loving thoughts; let the elixir of goodwill course through your veins, and you will need no other medicine. Put away your jealousies, your suspicions, your worries, your hatreds, your selfish indulgences, and you will put away your dyspepsia, your biliousness, your nervousness and aching joints. If you will persist in clinging to these debilitating and demoralizing habits of mind, then do not complain when your body is laid low with sickness.

The following story illustrates the close relation that exists between habits of mind and bodily conditions: A certain man was afflicted with a painful disease, and he tried one physician after another, but all to no purpose. He then visited towns which were famous for their curative waters, and after having bathed in them all, his disease was more painful than ever. One night he dreamed that a Presence came to him and said, "Brother, hast thou tried all the means of cure?" and he replied, "I have tried all." "Nay," said the Presence, "Come with me, and I will show thee a healing bath which has escaped thy notice." The afflicted man followed, and the Presence led him to a clear pool of water, and said, "Plunge thyself in this water and thou shalt surely recover," and thereupon vanished. The man plunged into the water, and on coming out, lo! his disease had left him, and at the same moment he saw written above the pool the word "Renounce." Upon waking, the full meaning of his dream flashed across his mind, and looking within he discovered that he had, all along, been a victim to a sinful indulgence, and he vowed that he would renounce it forever. He carried out his vow, and from that day his affliction began to leave him, and in a short time he was completely restored to health.

Many people complain that they have broken down through over-work. In the majority of such cases the breakdown is more frequently the result of foolishly wasted energy. If you would secure health you must learn to work without friction. To become anxious or excited, or to worry over needless details is to invite a breakdown. Work, whether of brain or body, is beneficial and health-giving, and the man who can work with a steady and calm persistency, freed from all anxiety and worry, and with his mind utterly oblivious to all but the work he has in hand, will not only accomplish far more than the man who is always hurried and anxious, but he will retain his health, a boon which the other quickly forfeits.

True health and true success go together, for they are inseparably intertwined in the thought-realm. As mental harmony produces bodily health, so it also leads to a harmonious sequence in the actual working out of one's plans. Order your thoughts and you will order your life. Pour the oil of tranquillity upon the turbulent waters of the passions and prejudices, and the tempests of misfortune, howsoever they may threaten, will be powerless to wreck the bark of your soul, as it threads its way across the ocean of life. And if that bark be piloted by a cheerful and never-failing faith its course will be doubly sure, and many perils will pass it by which would otherwise attack it. By the power of faith every enduring work is accomplished. Faith in the Supreme; faith in the over-ruling Law; faith in your work, and in your power to accomplish that work—here is the rock upon which you must build if you would achieve, if you would stand and not fall. To follow, under all circumstances, the highest promptings within you; to be always true to the divine self; to rely upon the inward Light, the inward Voice, and to pursue your purpose with a fearless and restful heart, believing that the future will yield unto you the meed of every thought and effort; knowing that the laws of the universe can never fail, and that your own will come back to you with mathematical exactitude, this is faith and the living of faith. By the power of such a faith the dark waters of uncertainty are divided, every mountain of difficulty crumbles away, and the believing soul passes on unharmed.

Strive. O reader! to acquire, above everything, the priceless possession of this dauntless faith, for it is the talisman of happiness, of success, of peace, of power, of all that makes life great and superior to suffering. Build upon such a faith, and you build upon the Rock of the Eternal, and with the materials of the Eternal, and the structure that you erect will never be dissolved, for it will transcend all the accumulations of material luxuries and riches, the end of which is dust. Whether you are hurled into the depths of sorrow or lifted upon the heights of joy, ever retain your hold upon this faith, ever return to it as your rock of refuge, and keep your feet firmly planted upon its immortal and immovable base. Centered in such a faith, you will become possessed of such a spiritual strength as will shatter, like so many toys of glass, all the forces of evil that are hurled against you, and you will achieve a success such as the mere striver after worldly gain can never know or even dream of. "If ye have faith, and doubt not, ye shall not only do this, . . . but if ye shall say unto this mountain, be thou removed and be thou cast into the sea, it shall be done."

There are those to-day, men and women tabernacled in flesh and blood, who have realized this faith, who live in it and by it day by day, and who, having put it to the uttermost test, have entered into the possession of its glory and peace. Such have sent out the word of command, and the mountains of sorrow and disappointment, of mental weariness and physical pain have passed from them, and have been cast into the sea of oblivion.

If you will become possessed of this faith you will not need to trouble about your success or failure, and success will come. You will not need to become anxious about results, but will work joyfully and peacefully, knowing that right thoughts and right efforts will inevitably bring about right results.

I know a lady who has entered into many blissful satisfactions, and recently a friend remarked to her, "Oh, how fortunate you are! You only have to wish for a thing, and it comes to you." And it did, indeed, appear so on the surface; but in reality all the blessedness that has entered into this woman's life is the direct outcome of the inward state of blessedness which she has, throughout life, been cultivating and training toward perfection. Mere wishing brings nothing but disappointment; it is living that tells. The foolish wish and grumble; the wise work and wait. And this woman had worked; worked without and within, but especially within upon heart and soul; and with the invisible hands of the spirit she had built up, with the precious stones of faith, hope, joy, devotion, and love, a fair temple of light, whose glorifying radiance was ever round about her. It beamed in her eye; it shone through her countenance; it vibrated in her voice; and all who came into her presence felt its captivating spell.

And as with her, so with you. Your success, your failure, your influence, your whole life you carry about with you, for your dominant trends of thought are the determining factors in your destiny. Send forth loving, stainless, and happy thoughts, and blessings will fall into your hands, and your table will be spread with the cloth of peace. Send forth hateful, impure, and unhappy thoughts, and curses will rain down upon you, and fear and unrest will wait upon your pillow. You are the uncon-ditional maker of your fate, be that fate what it may. Every moment you are sending forth from you the influences which will make or mar your life. Let your heart grow large and loving and unself-ish, and great and lasting will be your influence and success, even though you make little money. Confine it within the narrow limits of self-interest, and even though you become a millionaire your influence and success, at the final reckoning, will be found to be utterly insignificant.

Cultivate, then, this pure and unselfish spirit, and combine it with purity and faith, singleness of purpose, and you are evolving from within the elements, not only of abounding health and endur-ing success, but of greatness and power.

If your present position is distasteful to you, and your heart is not in your work, nevertheless perform your duties with scrupulous diligence, and whilst resting your mind in the idea that the better position and greater opportunities are waiting for you, ever keep an active mental outlook for budding possibilities, so that when the critical moment arrives, and the new channel presents itself, you will step into it with your mind fully prepared for the undertaking, and with that intelligence and foresight which is born of mental discipline.

Whatever your task may be, concentrate your whole mind upon it, throw into it all the energy of which you are capable. The faultless completion of small tasks leads inevitably to larger tasks. See to it that you rise by steady climbing, and you will never fall. And herein lies the secret of true power. Learn, by constant practice, how to husband your resources, and to concentrate them, at any moment, upon a given point. The foolish waste all their mental and spiritual energy in frivolity, foolish chatter, or selfish argument, not to mention wasteful physical excesses.

If you would acquire overcoming power you must cultivate poise and passivity. You must be able to stand alone. All power is associated with immovability. The mountain, the massive rock, the storm-tried oak all speak to us of power, because of their combined solitary grandeur and defi-ant fixity; while the shifting sand, the yielding twig, and the waving reed speak to us of weakness, because they are movable and non-resistant, and are utterly useless when detached from their fel-lows. He is the man of power who, when all his fellows are swayed by some emotion or passion, remains calm and unmoved.

He only is fitted to command and control who has succeeded in commanding and controlling himself. The hysterical, the fearful, the thoughtless and frivolous, let such seek company, or they will fall for lack of support; but the calm, the fearless, the thoughtful, and grave, let such seek the solitude of the forest, the desert, and the mountain-top, and to their power more power will be added, and they will more and more successfully stem the psychic currents and whirlpools which engulf mankind.

Passion is not power; it is the abuse of power, the dispersion of power. Passion is like a furious storm which beats fiercely and wildly upon the embattled rock, whilst power is like the rock itself, which remains silent and unmoved through it all. That was a manifestation of true power when Martin Luther, wearied with the persuasions of his fearful friends, who were doubtful as to his safety should he go to Worms, replied, "If there were as many devils in Worms as there are tiles on the housetops I would go." And when Benjamin Disraeli broke down in his first Parliamentary speech, and brought upon himself the derision of the House, that was an exhibition of germinal power when he exclaimed, "The day will come when you will consider it an honor to listen to me."

When a young man whom I knew, passing through continual reverses and misfortunes, was mocked by his friends and told to desist from further effort, and he replied, "The time is not far distant when you will marvel at my good fortune and success," he showed that he was possessed of that silent and irresistible power which has taken him over innumerable difficulties, and crowned his life with success.

If you have not this power, you may acquire it by practice, and the beginning of power is like-wise the beginning of wisdom. You must commence by overcoming those purposeless trivialities to which you have hitherto been a willing victim. Boisterous and uncontrolled laughter, slander and idle talk, and joking merely to raise a laugh, all these things must be put on one side as so much waste of valuable energy. St. Paul never showed his wonderful insight into the hidden laws of human progress to greater advantage than when he warned the Ephesians against "Foolish talking and jesting which is not convenient," for, to dwell habitually in such practices is to destroy all spiritual power and life. As you succeed in rendering yourself impervious to such mental dissipations you will begin to understand what true power is, and you will then commence to grapple with the more powerful desires and appetites which hold your soul in bondage, and bar the way to power, and your further progress will then be made clear.

Above all be of single aim; have a legitimate and useful purpose, and devote yourself unreserv-edly to it. Let nothing draw you aside; remember that "The double-minded man is unstable in all his ways." Be eager to learn, but slow to beg. Have a thorough understanding of your work, and let it be your own; and as you proceed, ever following the inward Guide, the infallible Voice, you will pass on from victory to victory, and will rise step by step to higher resting-places, and your ever-broadening outlook will gradually reveal to you the essential beauty and purpose of life. Self-purified, health will be yours; faith-protected, success will be yours; self-governed, power will be yours, and all that you do will prosper, for, ceasing to be a disjointed unit, self-enslaved, you will be in harmony with the Great Law, working no longer against, but with, the Universal Life, the Eternal Good. And what health you gain will remain with you; what success you achieve will be beyond all human computation, and will never pass away; and what influence and power you wield will continue to increase throughout the ages, for it will be a part of that unchangeable Principle which supports the universe.

This, then, is the secret of health—a pure heart and a well-ordered mind; this is the secret of success—an unfaltering faith, and a wisely-directed purpose; and to rein in, with unfaltering will, the dark steed of desire, this is the secret of power.

All ways are waiting for my feet to tread,
The light and dark, the living and the dead,
The broad and narrow way, the high and low,
The good and bad, and with quick step or slow,
I now may enter any way I will,
And find, by walking, which is good, which ill.

And all good things my wandering feet await,
If I but come, with vow inviolate,
Unto the narrow, high and holy way
Of heart-born purity, and therein stay;
Walking, secure from him who taunts and scorns,
To flowery meads, across the path of thorns.

And I may stand where health, success, and power
Await my coming, if, each fleeting hour,
I cling to love and patience; and abide
With stainlessness; and never step aside
From high integrity; so shall I see
At last the land of immortality.

And I may seek and find; I may achieve;
I may not claim, but, losing, may retrieve.
The law bends not for me, but I must bead
Unto the law, if I would reach the end
Of my afflictions, if I would restore
My soul to Light and Life, and weep no more.

Not mine the arrogant and selfish claim
To all good things: be mine the lowly aim

To seek and find, to know and comprehend,
And wisdom-ward all holy footsteps wend.
Nothing is mine to claim or to command
But all is mine to know and understand.

THE SECRET OF
ABOUNDING HAPPINESS

Great is the thirst for happiness, and equally great is the lack of happiness. The majority of the poor long for riches, believing that their possession would bring them supreme and lasting happiness. Many who are rich, having gratified every desire and whim, suffer from ennui and repletion, and are farther from the possession of happiness even than the very poor. If we reflect upon this state of things it will ultimately lead us to a knowledge of the all-important truth that happiness is not derived from mere outward possessions, nor misery from the lack of them; for if this were so, we should find the poor always miserable, and the rich always happy, whereas the reverse is frequently the case. Some of the most wretched people whom I have known were those who were surrounded with riches and luxury, whilst some of the brightest and happiest people I have met were possessed of only the barest necessities of life. Many men who have accumulated riches have confessed that the selfish gratification which followed the acquisition of riches has robbed life of its sweetness, and that they were never so happy as when they were poor.

What, then, is happiness, and how is it to be secured? Is it a figment, a delusion, and is suffering alone perennial?

We shall find, after earnest observation and reflection, that all, except those who have entered the way of wisdom, believe that happiness is only to be obtained *by the gratification of desire.* It is this belief, rooted in the soil of ignorance, and continually watered by selfish cravings, that is the cause of all the misery in the world. And I do not limit the word *desire* to the grosser animal cravings; it extends to the higher psychic realm, where far more powerful, subtle, and insidious cravings hold in bondage the intellectual and refined, depriving them of all that beauty, harmony, and purity of soul whose expression is happiness.

Most people will admit that selfishness is the cause of all the unhappiness in the world but they fall under the soul-destroying delusion that it is somebody else's selfishness, and not their own. When you are willing to admit that all your unhappiness is the result of your own selfishness you will not be far from the gates of Paradise; but so long as you are convinced that it is the selfishness of others that is robbing you of joy, so long will you remain a prisoner in your self-created purgatory.

Happiness is that inward state of perfect satisfaction which is joy and peace, and from which all desire is eliminated. The satisfaction which results from gratified desire is brief and illusionary, and is always followed by an increased demand for gratification. Desire is as insatiable as the ocean, and clamors louder and louder as its demands are attended to. It claims ever-increasing service from its deluded devotees, until at last they are struck down with physical or mental anguish, and are hurled into the purifying fires of suffering. Desire is the region of hell, and all torments are centered there. The giving up of desire is the realization of heaven, and all delights await the pilgrim there.

> *I sent my soul through the invisible,*
> *Some letter of that after life to spell.*
> *And by-and-by my soul returned to me,*
> *And whispered, "I myself am heaven and hell."*

Heaven and hell are inward states. Sink into self and all its gratifications, and you sink into hell; rise above self into that state of consciousness which is the utter denial and forgetfulness of self, and you enter heaven. Self is blind, without judgment, not possessed of true knowledge, and always leads to suffering. Correct perception, unbiased judgment, and true knowledge belong only to the divine state, and only in so far as you realize this divine consciousness can you know what real happiness is. So long as you persist in selfishly seeking for your own personal happiness, so long will happiness elude you, and you will be sowing the seeds of wretchedness. In so far as you succeed in losing yourself in the service of others, in that measure will happiness come to you, and you will reap a harvest of bliss.

> *It is in loving, not in being loved,*
> *The heart is blessed;*
> *It is in giving, not in seeking gifts,*
> *We find our quest.*

> *Whatever be thy longing or thy need,*
> *That do thou give;*

So shall thy soul be fed, and thou indeed
  Shalt truly live.

Cling to self, and you cling to sorrow; relinquish self, and you enter into peace. To seek selfishly is not only to lose happiness, but even that which we believe to be the source of happiness. See how the glutton is continually looking about for a new delicacy wherewith to stimulate his deadened appetite; and how, bloated, burdened, and diseased, scarcely any food at last is eaten with pleasure. Whereas, he who has mastered his appetite, and not only does not seek, but never thinks of gustatory pleasure, finds delight in the most frugal meal. The angel-form of happiness, which men, looking through the eyes of self, imagine they see in gratified desire, when clasped is always found to be the skeleton of misery. Truly, "He that seeketh his life shall lose it, and he that loseth his life shall find it."

Abiding happiness will come to you when, ceasing to selfishly cling, you are willing to give up. When you are willing to lose, unreservedly, that impermanent thing which is so dear to you, and which, whether you cling to it or not, will one day be snatched from you, then you will find that that which seemed to you like a painful loss, turns out to be a supreme gain. To give up in order to gain, than this there is no greater delusion, nor no more prolific source of misery; but to be willing to yield up and to suffer loss, this is indeed the Way of Life.

How is it possible to find real happiness by centering ourselves in those things which, by their very nature, must pass away? Abiding and real happiness can only be found by centering ourselves in that which is permanent. Rise, therefore, above the clinging to and the craving for impermanent things, and you will then enter into a consciousness of the Eternal, and as, rising above self, and by growing more and more into the spirit of purity, self-sacrifice, and universal Love, you become centered in that consciousness, you will realize that happiness which has no reaction, and which can never be taken from you.

The heart that has reached utter self-forgetfulness in its love for others has not only become possessed of the highest happiness but has entered into immortality, for it has realized the Divine. Look back upon your life, and you will find that the moments of supremest happiness were those in which you uttered some word, or performed some act, of compassion or self-denying love.

Spiritually, happiness and harmony are synonymous. Harmony is one phase of the Great Law whose spiritual expression is love. All selfishness is discord, and to be selfish is to be out of harmony with the Divine order. As we realize that all-embracing love which is the negation of self, we put ourselves in harmony with the divine music, the universal song, and that ineffable melody which is true happiness becomes our own.

Men and women are rushing hither and thither in the blind search for happiness, and cannot find it; nor ever will until they recognize that happiness is already within them and round about them, filling the universe, and that they, in their selfish searching are shutting themselves out from it.

I followed happiness to make her mine,
Past towering oak and swinging ivy vine.
She fled. I chased, o'er slanting hill and dale,
O'er fields and meadows, in the purpling vale;
Pursuing rapidly o'er dashing stream.
I scaled the dizzy cliffs where eagles scream;
I traversed swiftly every land and sea,
But always happiness eluded me.

Exhausted, fainting, I pursued no more,
But sank to rest upon a barren shore.
One came and asked for food, and one for alms;
I placed the bread and gold in bony palms.
One came for sympathy, and one for rest;
I shared with every needy one my best;
When, lo! sweet Happiness, with form divine,
Stood by me, whispering softly, "I am thine."

These beautiful lines of Burleigh's express the secret of all abounding happiness. Sacrifice the personal and transient, and you rise at once into the impersonal and permanent. Give up that narrow cramped self that seeks to render all things subservient to its own petty interests, and you will enter into the company of the angels, into the very heart and essence of universal Love. Forget yourself entirely in the sorrows of others and in ministering to others, and divine happiness will emancipate you from all sorrow and suffering. "Taking the first step with a good thought, the second with a good word, and the third with a good deed, I entered Paradise." And you also may enter into Paradise by pursuing the same course. It is not beyond, it is here. It is realized only by the unselfish. It is known in its fullness only to the pure in heart.

If you have not realized this unbounded happiness you may begin to actualize it by ever holding before you the lofty ideal of unselfish love, and aspiring toward it. Aspiration or prayer is desire turned upward. It is the soul turning toward its Divine source, where alone permanent satisfaction can be found. By aspiration the destructive forces of desire are transmuted into divine and all-preserving energy. To aspire is to make an effort to shake off the trammels of desire; it is the prodigal made wise by loneliness and suffering, returning to his Father's Mansion.

As you rise above the sordid self; as you break, one after another, the chains that bind you, will you realize the joy of giving, as distinguished from the misery of grasping—giving of your substance; giving of your intellect; giving of the love and light that is growing within you. You will then understand that it is indeed "more blessed to give than to receive." But the giving must be *of the heart* without any taint of self, without desire for reward. The gift of pure love is always attended with bliss. If, after you have given, you are wounded because you are not thanked or flattered, or your name put in the paper, know then that your gift was prompted by vanity and not by love, and you were merely giving in order to get; were not really giving, but grasping.

Lose yourself in the welfare of others; forget yourself in all that you do; this is the secret of abounding happiness. Ever be on the watch to guard against selfishness, and learn faithfully the divine lessons of inward sacrifice; so shall you climb the highest heights of happiness, and shall remain in the never-clouded sunshine of universal joy, clothed in the shining garment of immortality.

Are you searching for the happiness that does not fade away?
Are you looking for the joy that lives, and leaves no grievous day?
Are you panting for the waterbrooks of Love, and Life, and Peace?
Then let all dark desires depart, and selfish seeking cease.

Are you ling'ring in the paths of pain, grief-haunted, stricken sore?
Are you wand'ring in the ways that wound your weary feet the more?
Are you sighing for the Resting-Place where tears and sorrows cease?
Then sacrifice your selfish heart and find the Heart of Peace.

THE REALIZATION OF PROSPERITY

It is granted only to the heart that abounds with integrity, trust, generosity, and love to realize true prosperity. The heart that is not possessed of these qualities cannot know prosperity, for prosperity, like happiness, is not an outward possession, but an inward realization. The greedy man may become a millionaire, but he will always be wretched, and mean, and poor, and will even consider himself outwardly poor so long as there is a man in the world who is richer than himself, whilst the upright, the open-handed and loving will realize a full and rich prosperity, even though their outward possessions may be small. "He is poor who is dissatisfied; he is rich who is contented with what he has," and he is richer who is generous with what he has.

When we contemplate the fact that the universe is abounding in all good things, material as well as spiritual, and compare it with man's blind eagerness to secure a few gold coins, or a few acres of dirt, it is then that we realize how dark and ignorant selfishness is; it is then that we know that self-seeking is self-destruction.

Nature gives all, without reservation, and loses nothing; man, grasping all, loses everything.

If you would realize true prosperity do not settle down, as many have done, into the belief that if you do right everything will go wrong. Do not allow the word "competition" to shake your faith in the supremacy of righteousness. I care not what men may say about the "laws of competition," for do I not know the unchangeable Law, which shall one day put them all to rout, and which puts them to rout even now in the heart and life of the righteous man? And knowing this Law I can contemplate all dishonesty with undisturbed repose, for I know where certain destruction awaits it.

Under all circumstances *do that which you believe to be right,* and trust the Law; trust the Divine Power that is imminent in the universe, and it will never desert you, and you will always be protected. By such a trust all your losses will be converted into gains, and all curses which threaten will be transmuted into blessings. Never let go of integrity, generosity, and love, for these, coupled with energy, will lift you into the truly prosperous state. Do not believe the world when it tells you that you must always attend to "number one" first, and to others afterwards. To do this is not to think of others at all, but only of one's own comforts. To those who practice this the day will come when they will be deserted by all, and when they cry out in their loneliness and anguish there will be no one to hear and help them. To consider one's self before all others is to cramp and warp and hinder every noble and divine impulse. Let your soul expand, let your heart reach out to others in loving and generous warmth, and great and lasting will be your joy, and all prosperity will come to you.

Those who have wandered from the highway of righteousness guard themselves against competition; those who always pursue the right need not to trouble about such defense. This is no empty statement. There are men to-day who, by the power of integrity and faith, have defied all competition, and who, without swerving in the least from their methods, when competed with, have risen steadily into prosperity, whilst those who tried to undermine them have fallen back defeated.

To possess those inward qualities which constitute *goodness* is to be armored against all the powers of evil, and to be doubly protected in every time of trial; and to build oneself up in those qualities is to build up a success which cannot be shaken, and to enter into a prosperity which will endure forever.

The White Robe of the Heart Invisible
    Is stained with sin and sorrow, grief and pain,
And all repentant pools and springs of prayer
    Shall not avail to wash it white again.

While in the path of ignorance I walk,
    The stains of error will not cease to cling;
Defilements mark the crooked path of self.
    Where anguish lurks and disappointments sting.

Knowledge and wisdom only can avail
    To purify and make my garment clean.
For therein lie love's waters; therein rests
    Peace undisturbed, eternal, and serene.

Sin and repentance is the path of pain,
    Knowledge and wisdom is the path of Peace;
By the near way of practice I will find
    Where bliss begins, how pains and sorrows cease.

Self shall depart, and Truth shall take its place;
    The Changeless One, the Indivisible
Shall take up His abode in me, and cleanse
    The White Robe of the Heart Invisible.

PART II

THE WAY OF PEACE

THE POWER OF MEDITATION

Spiritual meditation is the pathway to Divinity. It is the mystic ladder which reaches from earth to heaven, from error to Truth, from pain to peace. Every saint has climbed it; every sinner must sooner or later come to it, and every weary pilgrim that turns his back upon self and the world, and sets his face resolutely toward the Father's Home, must plant his feet upon its golden rounds. Without its aid you cannot grow into the divine state, the divine likeness, the divine peace, and the fadeless glories and unpolluting joys of Truth will remain hidden from you.

Meditation is the intense dwelling, in thought, upon an idea or theme, with the object of thoroughly comprehending it, and whatsoever you constantly meditate upon you will not only come to understand, but will grow more and more into its likeness, for it will become incorporated into your very being, will become, in fact, your very self. If, therefore, you constantly dwell upon that which is selfish and debasing, you will ultimately become selfish and debased; if you ceaselessly think upon that which is pure and unselfish you will surely become pure and unselfish.

Tell me what that is upon which you most frequently and intensely think, that to which, in your silent hours, your soul most naturally turns, and I will tell you to what place of pain or peace you are traveling, and whether you are growing into the likeness of the divine or the bestial.

There is an unavoidable tendency to become literally the embodiment of that quality upon which one most constantly thinks. Let, therefore, the object of your meditation be above and not below, so that every time you revert to it in thought you will be lifted up; let it be pure and unmixed with any selfish element; so shall your heart become purified and drawn nearer to Truth, and not defiled and dragged more hopelessly into error.

Meditation, in the spiritual sense in which I am now using it, is the secret of all growth in spiritual life and knowledge. Every prophet, sage, and savior became such by the power of meditation. Buddha meditated upon the truth until he could say, "I am the Truth." Jesus brooded upon the Divine imminence until at last he could declare, "I and my Father are One."

Meditation centered upon divine realities is the very essence and soul of prayer. It is the silent reaching of the soul toward the Eternal. Mere petitionary prayer without meditation is a body without a soul, and is powerless to lift the mind and heart above sin and affliction. If you are daily praying for wisdom, for peace, for loftier purity and a fuller realization of Truth, and that for which you pray is still far from you, it means that you are praying for one thing whilst living out in thought and act another. If you will cease from such waywardness, taking your mind off those things the selfish clinging to which debars you from the possession of the stainless realities for which you pray; if you will no longer ask God to grant you that which you do not deserve, or to bestow upon you that love and compassion which you refuse to bestow upon others, but will commence to think and act in the spirit of Truth, you will day by day be growing into those realities, so that ultimately you will become one with them

He who would secure any worldly advantage must be willing to work vigorously for it, and he would be foolish indeed who, waiting with folded hands, expected it to come to him for the mere asking. Do not then vainly imagine that you can obtain the heavenly possessions without making an effort. Only when you commence to work earnestly in the kingdom of Truth will you be allowed to partake of the Bread of Life, and when you have, by patient and uncomplaining effort, earned the spiritual wages for which you ask, they will not be withheld from you.

If you really seek Truth, and not merely your own gratification; if you love it above all worldly pleasures and gains; more, even than happiness itself, you will be willing to make the effort necessary for its achievement.

If you would be freed from sin and sorrow; if you would taste of that spotless purity for which you sigh and pray; if you would realize wisdom and knowledge, and would enter into the possession of profound and abiding peace, come now and enter the path of meditation, and let the supreme object of your meditation be Truth.

At the outset, meditation must be distinguished from *idle reverie.* There is nothing dreamy and unpractical about it. It is *a process of searching and uncompromising thought which allows nothing to remain but the simple and naked truth.* Thus meditating you will no longer strive to build yourself up in your prejudices, but, forgetting self, you will remember only that you are seeking the Truth. And so you will remove, one by one, the errors which you have built around yourself in the past, and will patiently wait for the revelation of Truth which will come when your errors have been sufficiently removed. In the silent humility of your heart you will realize that

There is an inmost center in us all
Where Truth abides in fullness; and around,
Wall upon wall, the gross flesh hems it in;
This perfect, clear perception, which is Truth,

A baffling and perverting carnal mesh
Blinds it, and makes all error; and to know,
Rather consists in opening out a way
Whence the imprisoned splendor may escape,
Than in effecting entry for a light
Supposed to be without.

Select some portion of the day in which to meditate, and keep that period sacred to your purpose. The best time is the very early morning when the spirit of repose is upon everything. All natural conditions will then be in your favor; the passions, after the long bodily fast of the night, will be subdued, the excitements and worries of the previous day will have died away, and the mind, strong and yet restful, will be receptive to spiritual instruction. Indeed, one of the first efforts you will be called upon to make will be to shake off lethargy and indulgence, and if you refuse you will be unable to advance, for the demands of the spirit are imperative.

To be spiritually awakened is also to be mentally and physically awakened. The sluggard and the self-indulgent can have no knowledge of Truth. He who, possessed of health and strength, wastes the calm, precious hours of the silent morning in drowsy indulgence is totally unfit to climb the heavenly heights.

He whose awakening consciousness has become alive to its lofty possibilities, who is beginning to shake off the darkness of ignorance in which the world is enveloped, rises before the stars have ceased their vigil, and, grappling with the darkness within his soul, strives, by holy aspiration, to perceive the light of Truth while the unawakened world dreams on.

The heights by great men reached and kept,
  Were not attained by sudden flight,
But they, while their companions slept.
  Were toiling upward in the night.

No saint, no holy man, no teacher of Truth ever lived who did not rise early in the morning. Jesus habitually rose early, and climbed the solitary mountains to engage in holy communion. Buddha always rose an hour before sunrise and engaged in meditation, and all his disciples were enjoined to do the same.

If you have to commence your daily duties at a very early hour, and are thus debarred from giving the early morning to systematic meditation, try to give an hour at night, and should this, by the length and laboriousness of your daily task be denied you, you need not despair, for you may turn your thoughts upward in holy meditation in the intervals of your work, or in those few idle minutes which you now waste in aimlessness; and should your work be of that kind which becomes by practice automatic, you may meditate while engaged upon it. That eminent Christian saint and philosopher Jacob Boehme realized his vast knowledge of divine things whilst working long hours as a shoemaker. In every life there is time to think, and the busiest, the most laborious is not shut out from aspiration and meditation.

Spiritual meditation and self-discipline are inseparable; you will therefore commence to meditate upon yourself so as to try and understand yourself, for, remember, the great object you will have in view will be the complete removal of all your errors in order that you may realize Truth. You will begin to question your motives, thoughts, and acts, comparing them with your ideal, and endeavoring to look upon them with a calm and impartial eye. In this manner you will be continually gaining more of that mental and spiritual equilibrium without which men are but helpless straws upon the ocean of life. If you are given to hatred or anger you will meditate upon gentleness and forgiveness, so as to become actually alive to a sense of your harsh and foolish conduct. You will then begin to dwell in thoughts of love, of gentleness, of abounding forgiveness; and as you overcome the lower by the higher, there will gradually, silently steal into your heart a knowledge of the Divine Law of Love with an understanding of its bearing upon all the intricacies of life and conduct. And in applying this knowledge to your every thought, word, and act, you will grow more and more gentle, more and more loving, more and more divine. And thus with every error, every selfish desire, every human weakness; by the power of meditation is it overcome, and as each sin, each error is thrust out, a fuller and clearer measure of the Light of Truth illumines the pilgrim soul.

Thus meditating, you will be ceaselessly fortifying yourself against your only *real* enemy, your selfish, perishable self, and will be establishing yourself more and more firmly in the divine and imperishable self that is inseparable from Truth. The direct outcome of your meditations will be a calm, spiritual strength which will be your stay and resting-place in the struggle of life. Great is the overcoming power of holy thought, and the strength and knowledge gained in the hour of silent meditation will enrich the soul with saving remembrance in the hour of strife, of sorrow, or of temptation.

As, by the power of meditation, you grow in wisdom, you will relinquish, more and more, your selfish desires which are fickle, impermanent, and productive of sorrow and pain; and will take your stand, with increasing steadfastness and trust, upon unchangeable principles, and will realize heavenly rest.

The use of meditation is the acquirement of a knowledge of eternal principles, and the power which results from meditation is the ability to rest upon and trust those principles, and so become one with the Eternal. The end of meditation is, therefore, direct knowledge of Truth, God, and the realization of divine and profound peace.

Let your meditations take their rise from the ethical ground which you now occupy. Remember that you are to *grow* into Truth by steady perseverance. If you are an orthodox Christian, meditate ceaselessly upon the spotless purity and divine excellence of the character of Jesus, and apply his every precept to your inner life and outward conduct, so as to approximate more and more toward his perfection. Do not be as those religious ones, who, refusing to meditate upon the Law of Truth, and to put into practice the precepts given to them by their Master, are content to formally worship, to cling to their particular creeds, and to continue in the ceaseless round of sin and suffering. Strive to rise, by the power of meditation, above all selfish clinging to partial gods or party creeds; above dead formalities and lifeless ignorance. Thus walking the highway of wisdom, with mind fixed upon the spotless Truth, you shall know no halting place short of the realization of Truth. He who earnestly meditates first perceives a truth, as it were, afar off, and then realizes it by daily practice. It is only the doer of the Word of Truth that can know of the doctrine of Truth, for though by pure thought the Truth is perceived, it is only actualized by practice.

Said the divine Gautama, the Buddha, "He who gives himself up to vanity, and does not give himself up to meditation, forgetting the real aim of life and grasping at pleasure, will in time envy him who has exerted himself in meditation," and he instructed his disciples in the following "Five Great Meditations":

"The first meditation is the meditation of love, in which you so adjust your heart that you long for the weal and welfare of all beings, including the happiness of your enemies.

"The second meditation is the meditation of pity, in which you think of all beings in distress, vividly representing in your imagination their sorrows and anxieties so as to arouse a deep compassion for them in your soul.

"The third meditation is the meditation of joy, in which you think of the prosperity of others, and rejoice with their rejoicings.

"The fourth meditation is the meditation of impurity, in which you consider the evil consequences of corruption, the effects of sin and diseases. How trivial often the pleasure of the moment, and how fatal its consequences.

"The fifth meditation is the meditation on serenity, in which you rise above love and hate, tyranny and oppression, wealth and want, and regard your own fate with impartial calmness and perfect tranquillity."

By engaging in these meditations the disciples of the Buddha arrived at a knowledge of the Truth. But whether you engage in these particular meditations or not matters little so long as your object is Truth, so long as you hunger and thirst for that righteousness which is a holy heart and a blameless life. In your meditations, therefore, let your heart grow and expand with ever-broadening love, until, free from all hatred, and passion, and condemnation, it embraces the whole universe with thoughtful tenderness. As the flower opens its petals to receive the morning light, so open your soul more and more to the glorious light of Truth. Soar upward upon the wings of aspiration; be fearless, and believe in the loftiest possibilities. Believe that a life of absolute meekness is possible; believe that a life of stainless purity is possible; believe that a life of perfect holiness is possible; believe that the realization of the highest truth is possible. He who so believes climbs rapidly the heavenly hills, whilst the unbelievers continue to grope darkly and painfully in the fog-bound valleys.

So believing, so aspiring, so meditating, divinely sweet and beautiful will be your spiritual experiences, and glorious the revelations that will enrapture your inward vision. As you realize the divine Love, the divine Justice, the divine Purity, the Perfect Law of Good, or God, great will be your bliss and deep your peace. Old things will pass away, and all things will become new. The veil of the material universe, so dense and impenetrable to the eye of error, so thin and gauzy to the eye of Truth, will be lifted and the spiritual universe will be revealed. Time will cease, and you will live only in Eternity. Change and mortality will no more cause you anxiety and sorrow, for you will become established in the unchangeable, and will dwell in the very heart of immortality.

STAR OF WISDOM

Star that of the birth of Vishnu,
Birth of Krishna, Buddha, Jesus,
Told the wise ones, Heavenward looking,
Waiting, watching for thy gleaming
In the darkness of the night-time,
In the starless gloom of midnight;
Shining Herald of the coming
Of the kingdom of the righteous;
Teller of the Mystic story
Of the lowly birth of Godhead
In the stable of the passions,
In the manger of the mind-soul;
Silent singer of the secret
Of compassion deep and holy
To the heart with sorrow burdened,
To the soul with waiting weary:—
Star of all surpassing brightness,
Thou again dost deck the midnight;
Thou again dost cheer the wise ones
Watching in the creedal darkness,

Weary of the endless battle
With the grinding blades of error;
Tired of lifeless, useless idols,
Of the dead forms of religions;
Spent with watching for thy shining;
Thou hast ended their despairing;
Thou hast lighted up their pathway;
Thou hast brought again the old Truths
To the hearts of all thy Watchers;
To the souls of them that love thee
Thou dost speak of Joy and Gladness,
Of the peace that comes of Sorrow.
Blessed are they that can see thee,
Weary wanderers in the Night-time;
Blessed they who feel the throbbing,
In their bosoms feel the pulsing
Of a deep Love stirred within them
By the great power of thy shining.
Let us learn thy lesson truly;
Learn it faithfully and humbly;
Learn it meekly, wisely, gladly,
Ancient Star of holy Vishnu,
Light of Krishna, Buddha, Jesus.

THE TWO MASTERS,
SELF AND TRUTH

Upon the battlefield of the human soul two masters are ever contending for the crown of supremacy, for the kingship and dominion of the heart; the master of self, called also the "Prince of this world," and the master of Truth, called also the Father God. The master self is that rebellious one whose weapons are passion, pride, avarice, vanity, self-will, implements of darkness; the master Truth is that meek and lowly one whose weapons are gentleness, patience, purity, sacrifice, humility, love, instruments of Light.

In every soul the battle is waged, and as a soldier cannot engage at once in two opposing armies, so every heart is enlisted either in the ranks of self or of Truth. There is no half-and-half course; "There is self and there is Truth; where self is, Truth is not, where Truth is, self is not." Thus spake Buddha, the teacher of Truth, and Jesus, the manifested Christ, declared that "No man can serve two masters; for either he will hate the one and love the other; or else he will hold to the one and despise the other. Ye cannot serve God and Mammon."

Truth is so simple, so absolutely undeviating and uncompromising that it admits of no complexity, no turning, no qualification. Self is ingenious, crooked, and, governed by subtle and snaky desire, admits of endless turnings and qualifications, and the deluded worshippers of self vainly imagine that they can gratify every worldly desire, and at the same time possess the Truth. But the lovers of Truth worship Truth with the sacrifice of self, and ceaselessly guard themselves against worldliness and self-seeking.

Do you seek to know and to realize Truth? Then you must be prepared to sacrifice, to renounce to the uttermost, for Truth in all its glory can only be perceived and known when the last vestige of self has disappeared.

The eternal Christ declared that he who would be His disciple must "deny himself daily." Are you willing to deny yourself, to give up your lusts, your prejudices, your opinions? If so, you may enter the narrow way of Truth, and find that peace from which the world is shut out. The absolute denial, the utter extinction, of self is the perfect state of Truth, and all religions and philosophies are but so many aids to this supreme attainment.

Self is the denial of Truth. Truth is the denial of self. As you let self die, you will be reborn in Truth As you cling to self, Truth will be hidden from you.

Whilst you cling to self, your path will be beset with difficulties, and repeated pains, sorrows, and disappointments will be your lot. There are no difficulties in Truth, and coming to Truth, you will be freed from all sorrow and disappointment.

Truth in itself is not hidden and dark. It is always revealed and is perfectly transparent. But the blind and wayward self cannot perceive it. The light of day is not hidden except to the blind, and the Light of Truth is not hidden except to those who are blinded by self.

Truth is the one Reality in the universe, the inward Harmony, the perfect Justice, the eternal Love. Nothing can be added to it, nor taken from it: It does not depend upon any man, but all men depend upon it. You cannot perceive the beauty of Truth while you are looking out through the eyes of self. If you are vain, you will color everything with your own vanities. If lustful, your heart and mind will be so clouded with the smoke and flames of passion that everything will appear distorted through them. If proud and opinionative, you will see nothing in the whole universe except the magnitude and importance of your own opinions.

There is one quality which preeminently distinguishes the man of Truth from the man of self, and that is *humility.* To be not only free from vanity, stubbornness, and egotism, but to regard one's own opinions as of no value, this indeed is true humility.

He who is immersed in self regards his own opinions as Truth, and the opinions of other men as error. But that humble Truth-lover who has learned to distinguish between opinion and Truth regards all men with the eye of charity, and does not seek to defend his opinions against theirs, but sacrifices those opinions that he may love the more, that he may manifest the spirit of Truth, for Truth in its very nature is ineffable and can only be lived. He who has most of charity has most of Truth.

Men engage in heated controversies, and foolishly imagine they are defending the Truth, when in reality they are merely defending their own petty interests and perishable opinions. The follower of self takes up arms against others. The follower of Truth takes up arms against himself. Truth, being unchangeable and eternal, is independent of your opinion and of mine. We may enter into it, or we may stay outside; but both our defense and our attack are superfluous, and are hurled back upon ourselves.

Men enslaved by self, passionate, proud, and condemnatory, believe their particular creed or religion to be the Truth, and all other religions to be error; and they proselytize with passionate ardor. There is but one religion, the religion of Truth. There is but one error, the error of self. Truth is not a formal belief; it is an unselfish, holy, and aspiring heart, and he who has Truth is at peace with all, and cherishes all with thoughts of love.

You may easily know whether you are a child of Truth or a worshipper of self, if you will silently examine your mind, heart, and conduct. Do you harbor thoughts of suspicion, enmity, envy, lust, pride, or do you strenuously fight against these? If the former, you are chained to self, no matter what religion you may profess; if the latter, you are a candidate for Truth, even though outwardly you may profess no religion. Are you passionate, self-willed, ever seeking to gain your own ends, self-indulgent, and self-centered; or are you gentle, mild, unselfish, quit of every form of self-indulgence, and ever ready to give up your own? If the former, self is your master; if the latter, Truth is the object of your affection. Do you strive for riches? Do you fight, with passion, for your party? Do you lust for power and leadership? Are you given to ostentation and self-praise? Or have you given up the love of riches? Have you relinquished all strife? Are you content to take the lowest place, and to be passed by unnoticed? And have you ceased to talk about yourself and to regard yourself with self-complacent pride? If the former, even though you may imagine you worship God, the god of your heart is self. If the latter, even though you may withhold your lips from worship, you are dwelling with the Most High.

The signs by which the Truth-lover is known are unmistakable. Hear the Holy Krishna declare them, in Sir Edwin Arnold's beautiful rendering of the *Bhagavad Gita*.

> *Fearlessness, singleness of soul, the will*
> *Always to strive for wisdom; opened hand*
> *And governed appetites; and piety,*
> *And love of lonely study; humbleness,*
> *Uprightness, heed to injure nought which lives.*
> *Truthfulness, slowness unto wrath, a mind*
> *That lightly letteth go what others prize;*
> *And equanimity, and charity*
> *Which spieth no man's faults; and tenderness*
> *Towards all that suffer; a contented heart,*
> *Fluttered by no desires; a bearing mild,*
> *Modest and grave, with manhood nobly mixed,*
> *With patience, fortitude and purity;*
> *An unrevengeful spirit, never given*
> *To rate itself too high—such be the signs,*
> *O Indian Prince! of him whose feet are set*
> *On that fair path which leads to heavenly birth!*

When men, lost in the devious ways of error and self, have forgotten the "heavenly birth," the state of holiness and Truth, they set up artificial standards by which to judge one another, and make acceptance of, and adherence to, their own particular theology the test of Truth; and so men are divided one against another, and there is ceaseless enmity and strife, and unending sorrow and suffering.

Reader, do you seek to realize the birth into Truth? There is only one way: *Let self die*. All those lusts, appetites, desires, opinions, limited conceptions and prejudices to which you have hitherto so tenaciously clung, let them fall from you. Let them no longer hold you in bondage, and Truth will be yours. Cease to look upon your own religion as superior to all others, and strive humbly to learn the supreme lesson of charity. No longer cling to the idea, so productive of strife and sorrow, that the Savior whom you worship is the only Savior, and that the Savior whom your brother worships with equal sincerity and ardor is an imposter; but seek diligently the path of holiness, and then you will realize that every holy man is a savior of mankind.

The giving up of self is not merely the renunciation of outward things. It consists of the renunciation of the inward sin, the inward error. Not by giving up vain clothing; not by relinquishing riches; not by abstaining from certain foods; not by speaking smooth words; not by merely doing these things is the Truth found; but by giving up the spirit of vanity; by relinquishing the desire for riches; by abstaining from the lust of self-indulgence; by giving up all hatred, strife, condemnation, and self-seeking, and becoming gentle and pure at heart; by doing these things is the Truth found. To do the former, and not to do the latter, is pharisaism and hypocrisy, whereas the latter includes the former. You may renounce the outward world, and isolate yourself in a cave or in the depths of a forest, but you will take all your selfishness with you, and unless you renounce that, great indeed will be your wretchedness and deep your delusion. You may remain just where you are, performing all your duties, and yet renounce the world, the inward enemy. To be in the world and yet not of the world is the highest perfection, the most blessed peace, is to achieve the greatest victory. The renunciation of self is the way of Truth, therefore.

> *Enter the Path; there is no grief like hate,*
> *No pain like passion, no deceit like sense;*
> *Enter the Path; far hath he gone whose foot*
> *Treads down one fond offence.*

As you succeed in overcoming self you will begin to see things in their right relations. He who is swayed by any passions, prejudice, like, or dislike adjusts everything to that particular bias, and sees only his own delusions. He who is absolutely free from all passion, prejudice, preference, and partiality sees himself as he is; sees others as they are; sees all things in their proper proportions and right relations. Having nothing to attack, nothing to defend, nothing to conceal, and no interests to guard, he is at peace. He has realized the profound simplicity of Truth, for this unbiased, tranquil, blessed state of mind and heart is the state of Truth. He who attains to it dwells with the angels, and sits at the footstool of the Supreme. Knowing the Great Law; knowing the origin of sorrow; knowing the secret of suffering; knowing the way of emancipation in Truth, how can such a one engage in strife or condemnation; for though he knows that the blind, self-seeking world, surrounded with the clouds of its own illusions, and enveloped in the darkness of error and self, cannot perceive the steadfast Light of Truth, and is utterly incapable of comprehending the profound simplicity of the heart that has died, or is dying, to self, yet he also knows that when the suffering ages have piled up mountains of sorrow, the crushed and burdened soul of the world will fly to its final refuge, and that when the ages are completed, every prodigal will come back to the fold of Truth. And so he dwells in good will toward all, and regards all with that tender compassion which a father bestows upon his wayward children.

Men cannot understand Truth because they cling to self, because they believe in and love self, because they believe self to be the only reality, whereas it is the one delusion.

When you cease to believe in and love self you will desert it, and will fly to Truth, and will find the Eternal Reality.

When men are intoxicated with the wines of luxury, and pleasure, and vanity, the thirst of life grows and deepens within them, and they delude themselves with dreams of fleshly immortality, but when they come to reap the harvest of their own sowing, and pain and sorrow supervene, then, crushed and humiliated, relinquishing self and all the intoxications of self, they come, with aching hearts, to the one immortality, the immortality that destroys all delusions, the spiritual immortality in Truth.

Men pass from evil to good, from self to Truth, through the dark gate of sorrow, for sorrow and self are inseparable. Only in the peace and bliss of Truth is all sorrow vanquished. If you suffer disappointment because your cherished plans have been thwarted, or because some one has not come up to your anticipations, it is because you are clinging to self. If you suffer remorse for your conduct, it is because you have given way to self. If you are overwhelmed with chagrin and regret because of the attitude of some one else toward you, it is because you have been cherishing self. If you are wounded on account of what has been done to you or said of you, it is because you are walking in the painful way of self. All suffering is of self. All suffering ends in Truth. When you have entered into and realized Truth, you will no longer suffer disappointment, remorse, and regret, and sorrow will flee from you.

Self is the only prison that can ever bind the soul;
Truth is the only angel that can bid the gates unroll;
And when he comes to call thee, arise and follow fast;
His way may lie through darkness, but it leads to light at last.

The woe of the world is of its own making. Sorrow purifies and deepens the soul, and the extremity of sorrow is the prelude to Truth.

Have you suffered much? Have you sorrowed deeply? Have you pondered seriously upon the problem of life? If so, you are prepared to wage war against self, and to become a disciple of Truth.

The intellectuals, who do not see the necessity for giving up self, frame endless theories about the universe and call them Truth; but do thou pursue that direct line of conduct which is the practice of righteousness, and thou wilt realize the Truth which has no place in theory, and which never changes. Cultivate your heart. Water it continually with unselfish love and deep-felt pity, and strive to shut out from it all thoughts and feelings which are not in accordance with Love. Return good for evil, love for hatred, gentleness for ill-treatment, and remain silent when attacked. So shall you transmute all your selfish desires into the pure gold of Love, and self will disappear in Truth. So will you walk blamelessly amongst men, yoked with the easy yoke of lowliness, and clothed with the divine garment of humility.

O come, weary brother! thy struggling and striving
 End thou in the heart of the Master of Truth;
Across self's drear desert why wilt thou be driving,
 Athirst for the quickening waters of Truth.

When here, by the path of thy searching and sinning,
 Flows Life's gladsome stream, lies Love's oasis green?
Come, turn thou and rest; know the end and beginning,
 The sought and the searcher, the seer and seen.

Thy Master sits not in the unapproached mountains,
 Nor dwells in the mirage which floats on the air,
Nor shalt thou discover His magical fountains
 In pathways of sand that encircle despair.

In selfhood's dark desert cease wearily seeking
 The odorous tracks of the feet of thy King;
And if thou wouldst hear the sweet sound of His speaking,
 Be deaf to all voices that emptily sing.

Flee the vanishing places; renounce all thou hast;
 Leave all that thou lovest, and, naked and bare,

Thyself at the shrine of the *Innermost* cast;
    The Highest, the Holiest, the Changeless is there.

Within, in the heart of the Silence He dwelleth;
    Leave sorrow and sin, leave thy wanderings sore;
Come bathe in His Joy, whilst He, whispering, telleth
    Thy soul what it seeketh, and wander no more.

Then cease, weary brother, thy struggling and striving;
    Find peace in the heart of the Master of Truth;
Across self's dark desert cease wearily driving;
    Come; drink at the beautiful waters of Truth.

THE ACQUIREMENT OF SPIRITUAL POWER

The world is filled with men and women seeking pleasure, excitement, novelty; seeking ever to be moved to laughter or tears; not seeking strength, stability, and power; but courting weakness, and eagerly engaged in dispersing what power they have.

Men and women of real power and influence are few, because few are prepared to make the sacrifice necessary to the acquirement of power, and fewer still are ready to patiently build up character.

To be swayed by your fluctuating thoughts and impulses is to be weak and powerless; to rightly control and direct those forces is to be strong and powerful. Men of strong animal passions have much of the ferocity of the beast, but this is not power. The elements of power are there; but it is only when this ferocity is tamed and subdued by the higher intelligence that real power begins; and men can only grow in power by awakening themselves to higher and ever higher states of intelligence and consciousness.

The difference between a man of weakness and one of power lies not in the strength of the personal will (for the stubborn man is usually weak and foolish), but in that focus of consciousness which represents their states of knowledge.

The pleasure-seekers, the lovers of excitement, the hunters after novelty, and the victims of impulse and hysterical emotion lack that knowledge of principles which gives balance, stability, and influence.

A man commences to develop power when, checking his impulses and selfish inclinations, he falls back upon the higher and calmer consciousness within him, and begins to steady himself upon a principle.

The realization of unchanging principles in consciousness is at once the source and secret of the highest power.

When, after much searching, and suffering, and sacrificing, the light of an eternal principle dawns upon the soul, a divine calm ensues and joy unspeakable gladdens the heart.

He who has realized such a principle ceases to wander, and remains poised and self-possessed. He ceases to be "passion's slave," and becomes a master-builder in the Temple of Destiny.

The man that is governed by self, and not by a principle, changes his front when his selfish comforts are threatened. Deeply intent upon defending and guarding his own interests, he regards all means as lawful that will subserve that end. He is continually scheming as to how he may protect himself against his enemies, being too self-centered to perceive that he is his own enemy. Such a man's work crumbles away, for it is divorced from Truth and power. All effort that is grounded upon self perishes; only that work endures that is built upon an indestructible principle.

The man that stands upon a principle is the same calm, dauntless, self-possessed man under all circumstances. When the hour of trial comes, and he has to decide between his personal comforts and Truth, he gives up his comforts and remains firm. Even the prospect of torture and death cannot alter or deter him. The man of self regards the loss of his wealth, his comforts, or his life as the greatest calamities which can befall him. The man of principle looks upon these incidents as comparatively insignificant, and not to be weighed with loss of character, loss of Truth. To desert Truth is, to him, the only happening which can really be called a calamity.

It is the hour of crisis which decides who are the minions of darkness, and who the children of light. It is the epoch of threatening disaster, ruin, and persecution which divides the sheep from the goats, and reveals to the reverential gaze of succeeding ages the men and women of power.

It is easy for a man, so long as he is left in the enjoyment of his possessions, to persuade himself that he believes in and adheres to the principles of Peace, Brotherhood, and Universal Love; but if, when his enjoyments are threatened, or he imagines they are threatened, he begins to clamor loudly for war, he shows that he believes in and stands upon not Peace, Brotherhood, and Love, but strife, selfishness, and hatred.

He who does not desert his principles when threatened with the loss of every earthly thing, even to the loss of reputation and life, is the man of power; is the man whose every word and work endures; is the man whom the after-world honors, reveres, and worships. Rather than desert that principle of Divine Love on which he rested, and in which all his trust was placed, Jesus endured the utmost extremity of agony and deprivation; and to-day the world prostrates itself at his pierced feet in rapt adoration.

There is no way to the acquirement of spiritual power except by that inward illumination and enlightenment which is the realization of spiritual principles; and those principles can only be realized by constant practice and application.

Take the principle of divine Love, and quietly and diligently meditate upon it with the object of arriving at a thorough understanding of it. Bring its searching light to bear upon all your habits, your actions, your speech and intercourse with others, your every secret thought and desire. As you persevere in this course, the divine Love will become more and more perfectly revealed to you, and your own shortcomings will stand out in more and more vivid contrast, spurring you on to renewed endeavor; and having once caught a glimpse of the incomparable majesty of that imperishable principle, you will never again rest in your weakness, your selfishness, your imperfection, but will pursue that Love until you have relinquished every discordant element, and have brought yourself into perfect harmony with it. And that state of inward harmony is spiritual power. Take also other spiritual principles, such as Purity and Compassion, and apply them in the same way, and, so exacting is Truth, you will be able to make no stay, no resting-place until the inmost garment of your soul is bereft of every stain, and your heart has become incapable of any hard, condemnatory, and pitiless impulse.

Only in so far as you understand, realize, and rely upon these principles will you acquire spiritual power, and that power will be manifested in and through you in the form of increasing dispassion, patience, and equanimity.

Dispassion argues superior self-control; sublime patience is the very hall-mark of divine knowledge; and to retain an unbroken calm amid all the duties and distractions of life marks off the man of power. "It is easy in the world to live after the world's opinion; it is easy in solitude to live after our own; but the great man is he who in the midst of the crowd keeps with perfect sweetness the independence of solitude."

Some mystics hold that perfection in dispassion is the source of that power by which miracles (so-called) are performed, and truly he who has gained such perfect control of all his interior forces that no shock, however great, can for one moment unbalance him must be capable of guiding and directing those forces with a master-hand.

To grow in self-control, in patience, in equanimity is to grow in strength and power; and you can only thus grow by focusing your consciousness upon a principle. As a child, after making many and vigorous attempts to walk unaided, at last succeeds, after numerous falls, in accomplishing this, so you must enter the way of power by first attempting to stand alone. Break away from the tyranny of custom, tradition, conventionality, and the opinions of others, until you succeed in walking lonely and erect amongst men. Rely upon your own judgment; be true to your own conscience; follow the Light that is within you; all outward lights are so many will-o'-the-wisps. There will be those who will tell you that you are foolish; that your judgment is faulty; that your conscience is all awry; and that the Light within you is darkness; but heed them not. If what they say is true the sooner you, as a searcher for wisdom, find it out the better, and you can only make the discovery by bringing your powers to the test. Therefore, pursue your course bravely. Your conscience is at least your own, and to follow it is to be a man; to follow the conscience of another is to be a slave. You will have many falls, will suffer many wounds, will endure many buffetings for a time, but press on in faith, believing that sure and certain victory lies ahead. Search for a rock, a principle, and having found it cling to it; get it under your feet and stand erect upon it, until at last, immovably fixed upon it, you succeed in defying the fury of the waves and storms of selfishness.

For selfishness in any and every form is dissipation, weakness, death; unselfishness in its spiritual aspect is conservation, power, life. As you grow in spiritual life, and become established upon principles, you will become as beautiful and as unchangeable as those principles, will taste of the sweetness of their immortal essence, and will realize the eternal and indestructible nature of the God within.

No harmful shaft can reach the righteous man,
    Standing erect amid the storms of hate,
Defying hurt and injury and ban,
    Surrounded by the trembling slaves of Fate.

Majestic in the strength of silent power,
    Serene he stands, nor changes not nor turns;
Patient and firm in suffering's darkest hour,
    Time bends to him, and death and doom he spurns.

Wrath's lurid lightnings round about him play,
    And hell's deep thunders roll about his head;
Yet heeds he not, for him they cannot slay
    Who stands whence earth and time and space are fled.

Sheltered by deathless love, what fear hath he?
    Armored in changeless Truth, what can he know

Of loss and gain? Knowing eternity,
    He moves not whilst the shadows come and go.

Call him immortal, call him Truth and Light
    And splendor of prophetic majesty
Who bideth thus amid the powers of night.
    Clothed with the glory of divinity.

THE REALIZATION OF SELFLESS LOVE

It is said that Michael Angelo saw in every rough block of stone a thing of beauty awaiting the master-hand to bring it into reality. Even so, within each there reposes the Divine Image awaiting the master-hand of Faith and the chisel of Patience to bring it into manifestation. And that divine Image is revealed and realized as stainless, selfless Love.

Hidden deep in every human heart, though frequently covered up with a mass of hard and almost impenetrable accretions, is the spirit of Divine Love, whose holy and spotless essence is undying and eternal. It is the Truth in man; it is that which belongs to the Supreme: that which is real and immortal. All else changes and passes away; this alone is permanent and imperishable; and to realize this Love by ceaseless diligence in the practice of the highest righteousness, to live in it and to become fully conscious in it, is to enter into immortality here and now, is to become one with Truth, one with God, one with the central Heart of all things, and to know our own divine and eternal nature.

To reach this Love, to understand and experience it, one must work with great persistency and diligence upon his heart and mind, must ever renew his patience and keep strong his faith, for there will be much to remove, much to accomplish before the divine image is revealed in all its glorious beauty.

He who strives to reach and to accomplish the divine will be tried to the very uttermost; and this is absolutely necessary, for how else could one acquire that sublime patience without which there is no real wisdom, no divinity? Ever and anon, as he proceeds, all his work will seem to be futile, and his efforts appear to be thrown away. Now and then a hasty touch will mar his image, and perhaps when he imagines his work is almost completed he will find what he imagined to be the beautiful form of Divine Love utterly destroyed, and he must begin again with his past bitter experience to guide and help him. But he who has resolutely set himself to realize the Highest recognizes no such thing as defeat. All failures are apparent, not real. Every slip, every fall, every return to selfishness is a lesson learned, an experience gained, from which a golden grain of wisdom is extracted, helping the striver toward the accomplishment of his lofty object. To recognize

> *That of our vices we can frame*
> *A ladder if we will but tread*
> *Beneath our feet each deed of shame.*

is to enter the way that leads unmistakably toward the Divine, and the failings of one who thus recognizes are so many dead selves, upon which he rises, as upon stepping-stones, to higher things.

Once come to regard your failings, your sorrows and sufferings as so many voices telling you plainly where you are weak and faulty, where you fall below the true and the divine, you will then begin to ceaselessly watch yourself, and every slip, every pang of pain will show you where you are to set to work, and what you have to remove out of your heart in order to bring it nearer to the likeness of the Divine, nearer to the Perfect Love. And as you proceed, day by day detaching yourself more and more from the inward selfishness, the Love that is selfless will gradually become revealed to you. And when you are growing patient and calm, when your petulances, tempers, and irritabilities are passing away from you, and the more powerful lusts and prejudices cease to dominate and enslave you, then you will know that the divine is awakening within you, that you are drawing near to the eternal Heart, that you are not far from that selfless Love, the possession of which is peace and immortality.

Divine Love is distinguished from human loves in this supremely important particular, *it is free from partiality.* Human loves cling to a particular object to the exclusion of all else, and when that object is removed, great and deep is the resultant suffering to the one who loves. Divine Love embraces the whole universe, and, without clinging to any part, yet contains within itself the whole, and he who comes to it by gradually purifying and broadening his human loves until all the selfish and impure elements are burnt out of them ceases from suffering. It is because human loves are narrow and confined and mingled with selfishness that they cause suffering. No suffering can result from that Love which is so absolutely pure that it seeks nothing for itself. Nevertheless, human loves are absolutely necessary as steps toward the Divine, and no soul is prepared to partake of Divine Love until it has become capable of the deepest and most intense human love. It is only by passing through human loves and human sufferings that Divine Love is reached and realized.

All human loves are perishable like the forms to which they cling; but there is a Love that is imperishable, and that does not cling to appearances.

All human loves are counterbalanced by human hates; but there is a Love that admits of no opposite or reaction; divine and free from all taint of self, that sheds its fragrance on all alike.

Human loves are reflections of the Divine Love, and draw the soul nearer to the reality, the Love that knows neither sorrow nor change.

It is well that the mother, clinging with passionate tenderness to the little helpless form of flesh that lies on her bosom, should be overwhelmed with the dark waters of sorrow when she sees it laid in the cold earth. It is well that her tears should flow and her heart ache, for only thus can she be reminded of the evanescent nature of the joys and objects of sense, and be drawn nearer to the eternal and imperishable Reality.

It is well that lover, brother, sister, husband, wife should suffer deep anguish, and be enveloped in gloom when the visible object of their affections is torn from them, so that they may learn to turn their affections toward the invisible Source of all, where alone abiding satisfaction is to be found.

It is well that the proud, the ambitious, the self-seeking should suffer defeat, humiliation, and misfortune; that they should pass through the scorching fires of affliction; for only thus can the wayward soul be brought to reflect upon the enigma of life; only thus can the heart be softened and purified, and prepared to receive the Truth.

When the sting of anguish penetrates the heart of human love; when gloom and loneliness and desertion cloud the soul of friendship and trust, then it is that the heart turns toward the sheltering love of the Eternal, and finds rest in its silent peace. And whosoever comes to this Love is not turned away comfortless, is not pierced with anguish nor surrounded with gloom; and is never deserted in the dark hour of trial.

The glory of Divine Love can only be revealed in the heart that is chastened by sorrow, and the image of the heavenly state can only be perceived and realized when the lifeless, formless accretions of ignorance and self are hewn away.

Only that Love that seeks no personal gratification or reward, that does not make distinctions, and that leaves behind no heartaches, can be called divine.

Men, clinging to self and to the comfortless shadows of evil, are in the habit of thinking of divine Love as something belonging to a God who is out of reach; as something outside themselves, and that must forever remain outside. Truly, the Love of God is ever beyond the reach of self, but when the heart and mind are emptied of self then the selfless Love, the supreme Love, the Love that is of God or Good becomes an inward and abiding reality.

And this inward realization of holy Love is none other than the Love of Christ that is so much talked about and so little comprehended. The Love that not only saves the soul from sin, but lifts it also above the power of temptation.

But how may one attain to this sublime realization? The answer which Truth has always given, and will ever give to this question is—"Empty thyself, and I will fill thee." Divine Love cannot be known until self is dead, for self is the denial of Love, and how can that which is known be also denied? Not until the stone of self is rolled away from the sepulchre of the soul does the immortal Christ, the pure Spirit of Love, hitherto crucified, dead, and buried, cast off the bands of ignorance, and come forth in all the majesty of His resurrection.

You believe that the Christ of Nazareth was put to death and rose again. I do not say you err in that belief; but if you refuse to believe that the gentle spirit of Love is crucified daily upon the dark cross of your selfish desires, then, I say, you err in this unbelief and have not yet perceived, even afar off, the Love of Christ.

You say that you have tasted of salvation in the Love of Christ. Are you saved from your temper, your irritability, your vanity, your personal dislikes, your judgment and condemnation of others? If not, from what are you saved, and wherein have you realized the transforming Love of Christ?

He who has realized the Love that is divine has become a new man, and has ceased to be swayed and dominated by the old elements of self. He is known for his patience, his purity, his self-control, his deep charity of heart, and his unalterable sweetness.

Divine or selfless Love is not a mere sentiment or emotion; it is a state of knowledge which destroys the dominion of evil and the belief in evil, and lifts the soul into the joyful realization of the supreme Good. To the divinely wise, knowledge and Love are one and inseparable.

It is toward the complete realization of this divine Love that the whole world is moving; it was for this purpose that the universe came into existence, and every grasping at happiness, every reaching out of the soul toward objects, ideas, and ideals, is an effort to realize it. But the world does not realize this Love at present because it is grasping at the fleeting shadow and ignoring, in its blindness, the substance. And so suffering and sorrow continue, and must continue until the world, taught by its self-inflicted pains, discovers the Love that is selfless, the wisdom that is calm and full of peace.

And this Love, this Wisdom, this Peace, this tranquil state of mind and heart may be attained to, may be realized by all who are willing and ready to yield up self, and who are prepared to humbly enter into a comprehension of all that the giving up of self involves. There is no arbitrary power in the universe, and the strongest chains of fate by which men are bound are self-forged. Men are chained to that which causes suffering because they desire to be so, because they love their chains, because they think their little dark prison of self is sweet and beautiful, and they are afraid that if they desert that prison they will lose all that is real and worth having.

Ye suffer from yourselves, none else compels,
  None other holds ye that ye live and die.

And the indwelling power which forged the chains and built around itself the dark and narrow prison can break away when it desires and wills to do so, and the soul does will to do so when it has discovered the worthlessness of its prison, when long suffering has prepared it for the reception of the boundless Light and Love.

As the shadow follows the form, and as smoke comes after fire, so effect follows cause, and suffering and bliss follow the thoughts and deeds of men. There is no effect in the world around us but has its hidden or revealed cause, and that cause is in accordance with absolute justice. Men reap a harvest of suffering because in the near or distant past they have sown the seeds of evil; they reap a harvest of bliss also as a result of their own sowing of the seeds of good. Let a man meditate upon this, let him strive to understand it, and he will then begin to sow only seeds of good, and will burn up the tares and weeds which he has formerly grown in the garden of his heart.

The world does not understand the Love that is selfless because it is engrossed in the pursuit of its own pleasures, and cramped within the narrow limits of perishable interests, mistaking, in its ignorance, those pleasures and interests for real and abiding things. Caught in the flames of fleshly lusts, and burning with anguish, it sees not the pure and peaceful beauty of Truth. Feeding upon the swinish husks of error and self-delusion, it is shut out from the mansion of all-seeing Love.

Not having this Love, not understanding it, men institute innumerable reforms which involve no inward sacrifice, and each imagines that his reform is going to right the world forever, whilst he himself continues to propagate evil by engaging in it in his own heart. That only can be called reform which tends to reform the human heart, for all evil has its rise there, and not until the world, ceasing from selfishness and party strife, has learned the lesson of divine Love, will it realize the Golden Age of universal blessedness.

Let the rich cease to despise the poor, and the poor to condemn the rich; let the greedy learn how to give, and the lustful how to grow pure; let the partisan cease from strife, and the uncharitable begin to forgive; let the envious endeavor to rejoice with others and the slanderers grow ashamed of their conduct. Let men and women take this course, and, lo! the Golden Age is at hand. He, therefore, who purifies his own heart is the world's greatest benefactor.

Yet, though the world is, and will be for many ages to come, shut out from that Age of Gold, which is the realization of selfless Love, you, if you are willing, may enter it now, by rising above your selfish self; if you will pass from prejudice, hatred, and condemnation to gentle and forgiving love.

Where hatred, dislike, and condemnation are, selfless Love does not abide. It resides only in the heart that has ceased from all condemnation.

You say, "How can I love the drunkard, the hypocrite, the sneak, the murderer? I am compelled to dislike and condemn such men." It is true you cannot love such men *emotionally*, but when you say that you must perforce dislike and condemn them you show that you are not acquainted with the Great over-ruling Love; for it is possible to attain to such a state of interior enlightenment as will enable you to perceive the train of causes by which these men have become as they are, to enter into their intense sufferings, and to know the certainty of their ultimate purification. Possessed of such knowledge it will be utterly impossible for you any longer to dislike or condemn them, and you will always think of them with perfect calmness and deep compassion.

If you love people and speak of them with praise until they in some way thwart you, or do something of which you disapprove, and then you dislike them and speak of them with dispraise, you are not governed by the Love which is of God. If, in your heart, you are continually arraigning and condemning others, selfless Love is hidden from you.

He who knows that Love is at the heart of all things, and has realized the all-sufficing power of that Love, has no room in his heart for condemnation.

Men, not knowing this Love, constitute themselves judge and executioner of their fellows, forgetting that there is the Eternal Judge and Executioner, and in so far as men deviate from them in their own views, their particular reforms and methods, they brand them as fanatical, unbalanced, lacking judgment, sincerity, and honesty; in so far as others approximate to their own standard do they look upon them as being everything that is admirable. Such are the men who are centered in self. But he whose heart is centered in the supreme Love does not so brand and classify men; does not seek to convert men to his own views, not to convince them of the superiority of his methods. Knowing the Law of Love, he lives it, and maintains the same calm attitude of mind and sweetness of heart toward all. The debased and the virtuous, the foolish and the wise, the learned and the unlearned, the selfish and the unselfish receive alike the benediction of his tranquil thought.

You can only attain to this supreme knowledge, this divine Love by unremitting endeavor in self-discipline, and by gaining victory after victory over yourself. Only the pure in heart see God, and when your heart is sufficiently purified you will enter into the New Birth, and the Love that does not die, nor change, nor end in pain and sorrow will be awakened within you, and you will be at peace.

He who strives for the attainment of divine Love is ever seeking to overcome the spirit of condemnation, for where there is pure spiritual knowledge, condemnation cannot exist, and only in the heart that has become incapable of condemnation is Love perfected and fully realized.

The Christian condemns the Atheist; the Atheist satirizes the Christian; the Catholic and Protestant are ceaselessly engaged in wordy warfare, and the spirit of strife and hatred rules where peace and love should be.

"He that hateth his brother is a murderer," a crucifier of the divine Spirit of Love; and until you can regard men of all religions and of no religion with the same impartial spirit, with all freedom from dislike, and with perfect equanimity, you have yet to strive for that Love which bestows upon its possessor freedom and salvation.

The realization of divine knowledge, selfless Love, utterly destroys the spirit of condemnation, disperses all evil, and lifts the consciousness to that height of pure vision where Love, Goodness, Justice are seen to be universal, supreme, all-conquering, indestructible.

Train your mind in strong, impartial, and gentle thought; train your heart in purity and compassion; train your tongue to silence and to true and stainless speech; so shall you enter the way of holiness and peace, and shall ultimately realize the immortal Love. So living, without seeking to convert, you will convince; without arguing, you will teach; not cherishing ambition, the wise will find you out; and without striving to gain men's opinions, you will subdue their hearts. For Love is all-conquering, all-powerful; and the thoughts, and deeds, and words of Love can never perish.

To know that Love is universal, supreme, all-sufficing; to be freed from the trammels of evil; to be quit of the inward unrest; to know that all men are striving to realize the Truth each in his own way; to be satisfied, sorrowless, serene; this is peace; this is gladness; this is immortality; this is Divinity; this is the realization of selfless Love.

I stood upon the shore, and saw the rocks
　　Resist the onslaught of the mighty sea,
And when I thought how all the countless shocks
　　They had withstood through an eternity,
I said, "To wear away this solid main
The ceaseless efforts of the waves are vain."

But when I thought how they the rocks had rent,
　　And saw the sand and shingles at my feet
(Poor passive remnants of resistance spent)
　　Tumbled and tossed where they the waters meet,
Then saw I ancient landmarks 'neath the waves,
And knew the waters held the stones their slaves.

I saw the mighty work the waters wrought
　　By patient softness and unceasing flow;
How they the proudest promontory brought
　　Unto their feet, and mossy hills laid low;
How the soft drops the adamantine wall
Conquered at last, and brought it to its fall.

And then I knew that hard, resisting sin

    Should yield at last to Love's soft ceaseless roll

Coming and going, ever flowing in

    Upon the proud rocks of the human soul;

That all resistance should be spent and past,

And every heart yield unto it at last.

ENTERING INTO THE INFINITE

From the beginning of time, man, in spite of his bodily appetites and desires, in the midst of all his clinging to earthly and impermanent things, has ever been intuitively conscious of the limited, transient, and illusionary nature of his material existence, and in his sane and silent moments has tried to reach out into a comprehension of the Infinite, and has turned with tearful aspiration toward the restful Reality of the Eternal Heart.

Whilst vainly imagining that the pleasures of earth are real and satisfying, pain and sorrow continually remind him of their unreal and unsatisfying nature. Ever striving to believe that complete satisfaction is to be found in material things, he is conscious of an inward and persistent revolt against this belief, which revolt is at once a refutation of his essential mortality, and an inherent and imperishable proof that only in the immortal, the eternal, the infinite can he find abiding satisfaction and unbroken peace.

And here is the common ground of faith; here the root and spring of all religion; here the soul of Brotherhood and the heart of Love—that man is essentially and spiritually divine and eternal, and that, immersed in mortality and troubled with unrest, he is ever striving to enter into a consciousness of his real nature.

The spirit of man is inseparable from the Infinite, and can be satisfied with nothing short of the Infinite, and the burden of pain will continue to weigh upon man's heart, and the shadows of sorrow to darken his pathway until, ceasing from his wanderings in the dream-world of matter, he comes back to his home in the reality of the Eternal.

As the smallest drop of water detached from the ocean contains all the qualities of the ocean, so man, detached in consciousness from the Infinite, contains within him its likeness; and as the drop of water must, by the law of its nature, ultimately find its way back to the ocean and lose itself in its silent depths, so must man, by the unfailing law of his nature, at last return to his source, and lose himself in the great ocean of the Infinite.

To re-become one with the Infinite is the goal of man. To enter into perfect harmony with the Eternal Law is Wisdom, Love, and Peace. But this divine state is, and must ever be, incomprehensible to the merely personal. Personality, separateness, selfishness are one and the same, and are the antithesis of wisdom and divinity. By the unqualified surrender of the personality, separateness and selfishness cease, and man enters into the possession of his divine heritage of immortality and infinity.

Such surrender of the personality is regarded by the worldly and selfish mind as the most grievous of all calamities, the most irreparable loss, yet it is the one supreme and incomparable blessing, the only real and lasting gain. The mind unenlightened upon the inner laws of being, and upon the nature and destiny of its own life, clings to transient appearances, things which have in them no enduring substantiality, and so clinging, perishes, for the time being, amid the shattered wreckage of its own illusions.

Men cling to and gratify the flesh as though it were going to last forever, and though they try to forget the nearness and inevitability of its dissolution, the dread of death and of the loss of all that they cling to clouds their happiest hours, and the chilling shadow of their own selfishness follows them like a remorseless spectre.

And with the accumulation of temporal comforts and luxuries, the divinity within men is drugged, and they sink deeper and deeper into materiality, into the perishable life of the senses, and where there is sufficient intellect, theories concerning the immortality of the flesh come to be regarded as infallible truths. When a man's soul is clouded with selfishness in any or every form, he loses the power of spiritual discrimination, and confuses the temporal with the eternal, the perishable with the permanent, mortality with immortality, and error with Truth. It is thus that the world has come to be filled with theories and speculations having no foundation in human experience. Every body of flesh contains within itself, from the hour of birth, the elements of its own destruction, and by the unalterable law of its own nature must it pass away.

The perishable in the universe can never become permanent; the permanent can never pass away; the mortal can never become immortal; the immortal can never die; the temporal cannot become eternal nor the eternal become temporal; appearance can never become reality, nor reality fade into appearance; error can never become Truth, nor can Truth become error. Man cannot immortalize the flesh, but, by overcoming the flesh, by relinquishing all its inclinations, he can enter the region of immortality. "God alone hath immortality," and only by realizing the God state of consciousness does man enter into immortality.

All nature in its myriad forms of life is changeable, impermanent, unenduring. Only the inform-ing Principle of nature endures. Nature is many, and is marked by separation. The informing Prin-ciple is One, and is marked by unity. By overcoming the senses and the selfishness within, which is the overcoming of nature, man emerges from the chrysalis of the personal and illusionary, and wings himself into the glorious light of the impersonal, the region of universal Truth, out of which all perishable forms come.

Let men, therefore, practice self-denial; let them conquer their animal inclinations; let them refuse to be enslaved by luxury and pleasure; let them practice virtue, and grow daily into higher and ever higher virtue, until at last they grow into the Divine, and enter into both the practice and the comprehension of humility, meekness, forgiveness, compassion, and love, which practice and comprehension constitute Divinity.

"Goodwill gives insight," and only he who has so conquered his personality that he has but one attitude of mind, that of goodwill toward all creatures, is possessed of divine insight, and is capable of distinguishing the true from the false. The supremely good man is therefore the wise man, the divine man, the enlightened seer, the knower of the Eternal. Where you find unbroken gentleness, enduring patience, sublime lowliness, graciousness of speech, self-control, self-forgetfulness, and deep and abounding sympathy, look there for the highest wisdom, seek the company of such a one, for he has realized the Divine, he lives with the Eternal, he has become one with the Infinite. Believe not him that is impatient, given to anger, boastful, who clings to pleasure and refuses to renounce his selfish gratifications, and who practices not goodwill and far-reaching compassion, for such a one hath not wisdom, vain is all his knowledge, and his works and words will perish, for they are grounded on that which passes away.

Let a man abandon self, let him overcome the world, let him deny the personal; by this pathway only can he enter into the heart of the Infinite.

The world, the body, the personality are mirages upon the desert of time; transitory dreams in the dark night of spiritual slumber, and those who have crossed the desert, those who are spiritually awakened, have alone comprehended the Universal Reality where all appearances are dispersed and dreaming and delusion are destroyed.

There is one Great Law which exacts unconditional obedience, one unifying principle which is the basis of all diversity, one eternal Truth wherein all the problems of earth pass away like shad-ows. To realize this Law, this Unity, this Truth is to enter into the Infinite, is to become one with the Eternal.

To center one's life in the Great Law of Love is to enter into rest, harmony, peace. To refrain from all participation in evil and discord; to cease from all resistance to evil, and from the omission of that which is good, and to fall back upon unswerving obedience to the holy calm within, is to enter into the inmost heart of things, is to attain to a living, conscious experience of that eternal and infinite principle which must ever remain a hidden mystery to the merely perceptive intellect. Until this principle is realized, the soul is not established in peace, and he who so realizes is truly wise; not wise with the wisdom of the learned, but with the simplicity of a blameless heart and of a divine manhood.

To enter into a realization of the Infinite and Eternal is to rise superior to time, and the world, and the body, which comprise the kingdom of darkness; and is to become established in immortality, Heaven, and the Spirit, which make up the Empire of Light.

Entering into the Infinite is not a mere theory or sentiment. It is a vital experience which is the result of assiduous practice in inward purification. When the body is no longer believed to be, even remotely, the real man; when all appetites and desires are thoroughly subdued and purified; when the emotions are rested and calm, and when the oscillation of the intellect ceases and perfect poise is secured, then, and not till then, does consciousness become one with the Infinite; not until then is childlike wisdom and profound peace secured.

Men grow weary and grey over the dark problems of life, and finally pass away and leave them unsolved because they cannot see their way out of the darkness of the personality, being too much engrossed in its limitations. Seeking to save his personal life, man forfeits the greater impersonal Life in Truth; clinging to the perishable, he is shut out from a knowledge of the Eternal.

By the surrender of self all difficulties are overcome, and there is no error in the universe but the fire of inward sacrifice will burn it up like chaff; no problem, however great, but will disappear like a shadow under the searching light of self-abnegation. Problems exist only in our own self-created illusions, and they vanish away when self is yielded up. Self and error are synonymous. Error is involved in the darkness of unfathomable complexity, but eternal simplicity is the glory of Truth.

Love of self shuts men out from Truth, and seeking their own personal happiness they lose the deeper, purer, and more abiding bliss. Says Carlyle—"There is in man a higher than love of happiness. He can do without happiness, and instead thereof find blessedness.

". . . Love not pleasure, love God. This is the Everlasting Yea, wherein all contradiction is solved; wherein whoso walks and works, it is well with him."

He who has yielded up that self, that personality that men most love, and to which they cling with such fierce tenacity, has left behind him all perplexity, and has entered into a simplicity so profoundly simple as to be looked upon by the world, involved as it is in a network of error, as foolishness. Yet such a one has realized the highest wisdom, and is at rest in the Infinite. He "accomplishes without striving," and all problems melt before him, for he has entered the region of reality, and deals not with changing effects, but with the unchanging principles of things. He is enlightened with a wisdom which is as superior to ratiocination as reason is to animality. Having yielded up his lusts, his errors, his opinions and prejudices, he has entered into possession of the knowledge of God, having slain the selfish desire for heaven, and along with it the ignorant fear of hell; having relinquished even the love of life itself, he has gained supreme bliss and Life Eternal, the Life which bridges life and death, and knows its own immortality. Having yielded up all without reservation, he has gained all, and rests in peace on the bosom of the Infinite.

Only he who has become so free from self as to be equally content to be annihilated as to live, or to live as to be annihilated, is fit to enter into the Infinite. Only he who, ceasing to trust his perishable self, has learned to trust in boundless measure the Great Law, the Supreme Good, is prepared to partake of undying bliss.

For such a one there is no more regret, nor disappointment, nor remorse, for where all selfishness has ceased these sufferings cannot be; and whatever happens to him he knows that it is for his own good, and he is content, being no longer the servant of self, but the servant of the Supreme. He is no longer affected by the changes of earth, and when he hears of wars and rumors of wars his peace is not disturbed, and where men grow angry and cynical and quarrelsome, he bestows compassion and love. Though appearances may contradict it, he knows that the world is progressing, and that

> *Through its laughing and its weeping,*
> *Through its living and its keeping,*
> *Through its follies and its labors, weaving in and out of sight,*
> *To the end from the beginning,*
> *Through all virtue and all sinning,*
> *Reeled from God's great spool of Progress, runs the golden thread of light.*

When a fierce storm is raging none are angered about it, because they know it will quickly pass away, and when the storms of contention are devastating the world, the wise man, looking with the eye of Truth and pity, knows that it will pass away, and that out of the wreckage of broken hearts which it leaves behind the immortal Temple of Wisdom will be built.

Sublimely patient; infinitely compassionate: deep, silent, and pure, his very presence is a benediction; and when he speaks men ponder his words in their hearts, and by them rise to higher levels of attainment. Such is he who has entered into the Infinite, who by the power of utmost sacrifice has solved the sacred mystery of life.

Questioning Life and Destiny and Truth,
I sought the dark and labyrinthine Sphinx,
Who spake to me this strange and wondrous thing:—
"Concealment only lies in blinded eyes,
And God alone can see the Form of God."

I sought to solve this hidden mystery
Vainly by paths of blindness and of pain,
But when I found the Way of Love and Peace,
Concealment ceased, and I was blind no more:
Then saw I God e'en with the eyes of God.

SAINTS, SAGES, AND SAVIORS:
THE LAW OF SERVICE

The spirit of Love which is manifested as a perfect and rounded life is the crown of being and the supreme end of knowledge upon this earth.

The measure of a man's truth is the measure of his love, and Truth is far removed from him whose life is not governed by Love. The intolerant and condemnatory, even though they profess the highest religion, have the smallest measure of Truth; while those who exercise patience, and who listen calmly and dispassionately to all sides, and both arrive themselves at, and incline others to, thoughtful and unbiased conclusions upon all problems and issues have Truth in fullest measure. The final test of wisdom is this—how does a man live? What spirit does he manifest? How does he act under trial and temptation? Many men boast of being in possession of Truth who are continually swayed by grief, disappointment, and passion, and who sink under the first little trial that comes along. Truth is nothing if not unchangeable, and in so far as a man takes his stand upon Truth does he become steadfast in virtue, does he rise superior to his passions and emotions and changeable personality.

Men formulate perishable dogmas, and call them Truth. Truth cannot be formulated; it is ineffable, and ever beyond the reach of intellect. It can only be experienced by practice; it can only be manifested as a stainless heart and a perfect life.

Who, then, in the midst of the ceaseless pandemonium of schools and creeds and parties, has the truth? He who lives it. He who practices it. He who, having risen above that pandemonium by overcoming himself, no longer engages in it, but sits apart, quiet, subdued, calm, and self-possessed, freed from all strife, all bias, all condemnation, and bestows upon all the glad and unselfish love of the divinity within him.

He who is patient, calm, gentle, and forgiving under all circumstances manifests the Truth. Truth will never be proved by wordy arguments and learned treatises, for if men do not perceive the Truth in infinite patience, undying forgiveness, and all-embracing compassion, no words can ever prove it to them.

It is an easy matter for the passionate to be calm and patient when they are alone, or are in the midst of calmness. It is equally easy for the uncharitable to be gentle and kind when they are dealt kindly with, but he who retains his patience and calmness under all trial, who remains sublimely meek and gentle under the most trying circumstances, he, and he alone, is possessed of the spotless Truth. And this is so because such lofty virtues belong to the Divine, and can only be manifested by one who has attained to the highest wisdom, who has relinquished his passionate and self-seeking nature, who has realized the supreme and unchangeable Law, and has brought himself into harmony with it.

Let men, therefore, cease from vain and passionate arguments about Truth, and let them think and say and do those things which make for harmony, peace, love, and goodwill. Let them practice heart-virtue, and search humbly and diligently for the Truth which frees the soul from all error and sin, from all that blights the human heart, and that darkens, as with unending night, the pathway of the wandering souls of earth.

There is one great all-embracing Law which is the foundation and cause of the universe, the Law of Love. It has been called by many names in various countries and at various times, but behind all its names the same unalterable Law may be discovered by the eye of Truth. Names, religions, personalities pass away, but the Law of Love remains. To become possessed of a knowledge of this Law, to enter into conscious harmony with it, is to become immortal, invincible, indestructible.

It is because of the effort of the soul to realize this Law that men come again and again to live, to suffer, and to die; and when realized, suffering ceases, personality is dispersed, and the fleshly life and death are destroyed, for consciousness becomes one with the Eternal.

The Law is absolutely impersonal, and its highest manifested expression is that of Service. When the purified heart has realized Truth it is then called upon to make the last, the greatest and holiest sacrifice, the sacrifice of the well-earned enjoyment of Truth. It is by virtue of this sacrifice that the divinely-emancipated soul comes to dwell amongst men, clothed with a body of flesh, content to dwell amongst the lowliest and least, and to be esteemed the servant of all mankind. That sublime humility which is manifested by the world's saviors is the seal of Godhead, and he who has annihilated the personality, and has become a living, visible manifestation of the impersonal, eternal, boundless Spirit of Love, is alone singled out as worthy to receive the unstinted worship of posterity.

He only who succeeds in humbling himself with that divine humility which is not only the extinction of self, but is also the pouring out upon all the spirit of unselfish love, is exalted above measure, and given spiritual dominion in the hearts of mankind.

All the great spiritual teachers have denied themselves personal luxuries, comforts, and rewards, have abjured temporal power, and have lived and taught the limitless and impersonal Truth. Compare their lives and teachings, and you will find the same simplicity, the same self-sacrifice, the same humility, love, and peace both lived and preached by them. They taught the same eternal Principles, the realization of which destroys all evil. Those who have been hailed and worshipped as the saviors of mankind are manifestations of the Great impersonal Law, and being such, were free from passion and prejudice, and having no opinions, and no special letter of doctrine to preach and defend, they never sought to convert and to proselytize. Living in the highest Goodness, the supreme Perfection, their sole object was to uplift mankind by manifesting that Goodness in thought, word, and deed. They stand between man the personal and God the impersonal, and serve as exemplary types for the salvation of self-enslaved mankind.

Men who are immersed in self, and who cannot comprehend the Goodness that is absolutely impersonal, deny divinity to all saviors except their own, and thus introduce personal hatred and doctrinal controversy, and, whilst defending their own particular views with passion, look upon each other as being heathens or infidels, and so render null and void, as far as their lives are concerned, the unselfish beauty and holy grandeur of the lives and teachings of their own Masters. Truth cannot be limited; it can never be the special prerogative of any man, school, or nation, and when personality steps in, Truth is lost.

The glory alike of the saint, the sage, and the savior is this—that he has realized the most profound lowliness, the most sublime unselfishness; having given up all, even his own personality, all his works are holy and enduring, for they are freed from every taint of self. He gives, yet never thinks of receiving; he works without regretting the past or anticipating the future, and never looks for reward.

When the farmer has tilled and dressed his land and put in the seed, he knows that he has done all that he can possibly do, and that now he must trust to the elements, and wait patiently for the course of time to bring about the harvest, and that no amount of expectancy on his part will affect the result. Even so, he who has realized Truth goes forth as a sower of the seeds of goodness, purity, love, and peace, without expectancy, and never looking for results, knowing that there is the Great Over-ruling Law which brings about its own harvest in due time, and which is alike the source of preservation and destruction.

Men, not understanding the divine simplicity of a profound unselfish heart, look upon their particular savior as the manifestation of a special miracle, as being something entirely apart and distinct from the nature of things, and as being, in his ethical excellence, eternally unapproachable by the whole of mankind. This attitude of unbelief (for such it is) in the divine perfectibility of man paralyzes effort, and binds the souls of men as with strong ropes to sin and suffering. Jesus "grew in wisdom" and was "perfected by suffering." What Jesus was, he became such; what Buddha was, he became such; and every holy man became such by unremitting perseverance in self-sacrifice. Once you recognize this, once you realize that, by watchful effort and hopeful perseverance you can rise above your lower nature, and great and glorious will be the vistas of attainment that will open out before you. Buddha vowed that he would not relax his efforts until he arrived at the state of perfection, and he accomplished his purpose.

What the saints, sages, and saviors have accomplished, you likewise may accomplish if you will only tread the way which they trod and pointed out, the way of self-sacrifice, of self-denying service.

Truth is very simple. It says, "Give up self," "Come unto Me" (away from all that defiles) "and I will give you rest." All the mountains of commentary that have been piled upon it cannot hide it from the heart that is earnestly seeking for righteousness. It does not require learning; it can be known in spite of learning. Disguised under many forms by erring, self-seeking man, the beautiful simplicity and clear transparency of Truth remains unaltered and undimmed, and the unselfish heart enters into and partakes of its shining radiance. Not by weaving complex theories, not by building up speculative philosophies is Truth realized; but by weaving the web of inward purity, by building up the Temple of a stainless life is Truth realized.

He who enters upon this holy way begins by restraining his passions. This is virtue, and is the beginning of saintship, and saintship is the beginning of holiness. The entirely worldly man gratifies all his desires, and practices no more restraint than the law of the land in which he lives demands; the virtuous man restrains his passions; the saint attacks the enemy of Truth in its stronghold within his own heart, and restrains all selfish and impure thoughts; whilst the holy man is he who is free from passion and all impure thought, and to whom goodness and purity have become as natural as scent and color are to the flower. The holy man is divinely wise; he alone knows Truth in its fullness, and has entered into abiding rest and peace. For him evil has ceased; it has disappeared in the universal light of the All-Good. Holiness is the badge of wisdom. Said Krishna to the Prince Arjuna—

Humbleness, truthfulness, and harmlessness,
Patience and honor, reverence for the wise,
Purity, constancy, control of self,
Contempt of sense-delights, self-sacrifice,
Perception of the certitude of ill
In birth, death, age, disease, suffering and sin;

An ever tranquil heart in fortunes good
And fortunes evil . . . .
. . . . Endeavors resolute
To reach perception of the utmost soul,
And grace to understand what gain it were
So to attain—this is true wisdom, Prince!
And what is otherwise is ignorance!

Whoever fights ceaselessly against his own selfishness and strives to supplant it with all-embracing love is a saint, whether he live in a cottage or in the midst of riches and influence; or whether he preaches or remains obscure.

To the worldling, who is beginning to aspire toward higher things, the saint, such as a sweet St. Francis of Assisi, or a conquering St. Anthony, is a glorious and inspiring spectacle; to the saint, an equally enrapturing sight is that of the sage, sitting serene and holy, the conqueror of sin and sorrow, no more tormented by regret and remorse, and whom even temptation can never reach; and yet even the sage is drawn on by a still more glorious vision, that of the savior actively manifesting his knowledge in selfless works, and rendering his divinity more potent for good by sinking himself in the throbbing, sorrowing, aspiring heart of mankind.

And this only is true service—to forget oneself in love toward all, to lose oneself in working for the whole. O thou vain and foolish man, who thinkest that thy many works can save thee; who, chained to all error, talkest loudly of thyself, thy work, and thy many sacrifices, and magnifiest thine own importance; know this, that though thy fame fill the whole earth, all thy work shall come to dust, and thou thyself be reckoned lower than the least in the Kingdom of Truth!

Only the work that is impersonal can live; the works of self are both powerless and perishable. Where duties, howsoever humble, are done without self-interest, and with joyful sacrifice, there is true service and enduring work. Where deeds, however brilliant and apparently successful, are done from love of self, there is ignorance of the Law of Service, and the work perishes.

It is given to the world to learn one great and divine lesson, the lesson of absolute unselfishness. The saints, sages, and saviors of all time are they who have submitted themselves to this task, and have learned and lived it. All the Scriptures of the world are framed to teach this one lesson; all the great teachers reiterate it. It is too simple for the world which, scorning it, stumbles along in the complex ways of selfishness.

A pure heart is the end of all religion and the beginning of divinity. To search for this Righteousness is to walk the Way of Truth and Peace, and he who enters this Way will soon perceive that Immortality which is independent of birth and death, and will realize that in the Divine economy of the universe the humblest effort is not lost.

The divinity of a Krishna, a Gautama, or a Jesus is the crowning glory of self-abnegation, the end of the soul's pilgrimage in matter and mortality, and the world will not have finished its long journey until every soul has become as these, and has entered into the blissful realization of its own divinity.

Great glory crowns the heights of hope by arduous struggle won;
Bright honor rounds the hoary head that mighty works hath done;
Fair riches come to him who strives in ways of golden gain,
And fame enshrines his name who works with genius-glowing brain:
But greater glory waits for him who, in the bloodless strife
'Gainst self and wrong, adopts, in love, the sacrificial life;
And brighter honor rounds the brow of him who, 'mid the scorns
Of blind idolaters of self, accepts the crown of thorns;
And fairer, purer riches come to him who greatly strives
To walk in ways of love and truth to sweeten human lives;
And he who serveth well mankind exchanges fleeting fame
For Light eternal, Joy and Peace, and robes of heavenly flame.

THE REALIZATION OF PERFECT PEACE

In the external universe there is ceaseless turmoil, change, and unrest; at the heart of all things there is undisturbed repose; in this deep silence dwelleth the Eternal.

Man partakes of this duality, and both the surface change and disquietude, and the deep-seated eternal abode of Peace are contained within him.

As there are silent depths in the ocean which the fiercest storm cannot reach, so there are silent, holy depths in the heart of man which the storms of sin and sorrow can never disturb.

To reach this silence and to live consciously in it is peace.

Discord is rife in the outward world, but unbroken harmony holds sway at the heart of the universe. The human soul, torn by discordant passion and grief, reaches blindly toward the harmony of the sinless state, and to reach this state and to live consciously in it is peace.

Hatred severs human lives, fosters persecution, and hurls nations into ruthless war, yet men, though they do not understand why, retain some measure of faith in the overshadowing of a Perfect Love; and to reach this love and to live consciously in it is peace.

And this inward peace, this silence, this harmony, this Love is the Kingdom of Heaven, which is so difficult to reach because few are willing to give up themselves and to become as little children.

Heaven's gate is very narrow and minute,
It cannot be perceived by foolish men
Blinded by vain illusions of the world;
E'en the clear-sighted who discern the way,
And seek to enter, find the portal barred,
And hard to be unlocked. Its massive bolts
Are pride and passion, avarice and lust.

Men cry peace! peace! where there is no peace, but on the contrary, discord, disquietude, and strife. Apart from that Wisdom which is inseparable from self-renunciation, there can be no real and abiding peace.

The peace which results from social comfort, passing gratification, or worldly victory is transitory in its nature, and is burnt up in the heat of fiery trial. Only the Peace of Heaven endures through all trial and only the selfless heart can know the Peace of Heaven.

Holiness alone is undying peace. Self-control leads to it, and the ever-increasing Light of Wisdom guides the pilgrim on his way. It is partaken of in a measure as soon as the path of virtue is entered upon, but it is only realized in its fullness when self disappears in the consummation of a stainless life.

This is peace,
To conquer love of self and lust of life,
To tear deep-rooted passion from the heart
To still the inward strife.

If, O reader! you would realize the Light that never fades, the joy that never ends, and the tranquility that cannot be disturbed; if you would leave behind forever your sins, your sorrows, your anxieties and perplexities; if, I say, you would partake of this salvation, this supremely glorious Life, then conquer yourself. Bring every thought, every impulse, every desire into perfect obedience to the divine power resident within you. There is no other way to peace but this, and if you refuse to walk it, your much praying and your strict adherence to ritual will be fruitless and unavailing, and neither gods nor angels can help you. Only to him that overcometh is given the white stone of the regenerate life, on which is written the New and Ineffable Name.

Come away, for a while, from external things, from the pleasures of the senses, from the arguments of the intellect, from the noise and the excitements of the world, and withdraw yourself into the inmost chamber of your heart, and there, free from the sacrilegious intrusion of all selfish desires, you will find a deep silence, a holy calm, a blissful repose, and if you will rest awhile in that holy place, and will meditate there, the faultless eye of Truth will open within you, and you will see things as they really are. This holy place within you is your real and eternal self; it is the divine within you; and only when you identify yourself with it can you be said to be "clothed and in your right mind." It is the abode of peace, the temple of wisdom, the dwelling-place of immortality. Apart from this inward resting-place, this Mount of Vision, there can be no true peace, no knowledge of the Divine, and if you can remain there for one minute, one hour, or one day, it is possible for you to remain there always.

All your sins and sorrows, your fears and anxieties are your own, and you can cling to them or you can give them up. Of your own accord you cling to your unrest; of your own accord you can come to abiding peace. No one else can give up sin for you; you must give it up yourself. The greatest teacher can do no more than walk the way of Truth for himself, and point it out to you; you yourself must walk it for yourself. You can obtain freedom and peace alone by your own efforts, by yielding up that which binds the soul, and which is destructive of peace.

The angels of divine peace and joy are always at hand, and if you do not see them, and hear them, and dwell with them, it is because you shut yourself out from them, and prefer the company of the spirits of evil within you. You are what you will to be, what you wish to be, what you prefer to be. You can commence to purify yourself, and by so doing can arrive at peace, or you can refuse to purify yourself, and so remain with suffering.

Step aside, then; come out of the fret and the fever of life; away from the scorching heat of self, and enter the inward resting-place where the cooling airs of peace will calm, renew, and restore you.

Come out of the storms of sin and anguish. Why be troubled and tempest-tossed when the haven of peace is so near?

Give up all self-seeking; give up self, and lo! the Peace of God is yours!

Subdue the animal within you; conquer every selfish uprising, every discordant voice; transmute the base metals of your selfish nature into the unalloyed gold of Love, and you shall realize the Life of Perfect Peace. Thus subduing, thus conquering, thus transmuting, you will, O reader! whilst living in the flesh, cross the dark waters of mortality, and will reach that Shore upon which the storms of sorrow never beat, and where sin and suffering and dark uncertainty cannot come. Standing upon that Shore, holy, compassionate, awakened, and self-possessed and glad with unending gladness, you will realize that,

Never the Spirit was born, the Spirit will cease to be never;
Never was time it was not, end and beginning are dreams;
Birthless and deathless and changeless remaineth the Spirit forever:
Death hath not touched it at all, dead though the house of it seems.

You will then know the meaning of Sin, of Sorrow, of Suffering, and that the end thereof is Wisdom; will know the cause and the issue of existence.

And with this realization you will enter into rest, for this is the bliss of immortality, this the unchangeable gladness, this the untrammeled knowledge, undefiled Wisdom, and undying Love; this, and this only, is the realization of Perfect Peace.

O thou who wouldst teach men of Truth!
　　Hast thou passed through the desert of doubt?
Art thou purged by the fires of sorrow? hath Truth
　　　　　The fiends of opinion cast out
Of thy human heart? Is thy soul so fair
That no false thought can ever harbor there?

O thou who wouldst teach men of Love!
　　Hast thou passed through the place of despair?
Hast thou wept through the dark night of grief? does it move
　　　　(Now freed from its sorrow and care)
Thy human heart to pitying gentleness,
Looking on wrong, and hate, and ceaseless stress?

O thou who wouldst teach men of Peace!
　　Hast thou crossed the wide ocean of strife?
Hast thou found on the Shores of the Silence, release
　　　　From all the wild unrest of life?
From thy human heart hath all striving gone,
Leaving but Truth, and Love, and Peace alone?

ALL THESE
THINGS ADDED

(1903)

FOREWORD

In seeking for pleasures here and rewards hereafter men have destroyed (in their hearts) the Temple of Righteousness, and have wandered from the Kingdom of Heaven. By ceasing to seek for earthly pleasures and heavenly rewards, the Temple of Righteousness is restored and the Kingdom of Heaven is found. This truth is for those who are ready to receive it; and this book also is for those whose souls have been prepared for the acceptance of its teaching.

—James Allen

CONTENTS

PART I

ENTERING THE KINGDOM

THE SOUL'S GREAT NEED

I sought the world, but Peace was not there;
I courted learning, but Truth was not revealed;
I sojourned with philosophy, but my heart was sore with vanity.
And I cried, Where is Peace to be found!
And where is the hiding-place of Truth!

—FILIUS LUCIS

Every human soul is in need. The expression of that need varies with individuals, but there is not one soul that does not feel it in some degree. It is a spiritual and casual need which takes the form, in souls of a particular development, of a deep and inexpressible hunger which the outward things of life, however abundantly they may be possessed, can never satisfy. Yet the majority, imperfect in knowledge, and misled by appearances, seek to satisfy this hunger by striving for material possessions, believing that these will satisfy their need, and bring them peace.

Every soul, consciously or unconsciously, hungers for righteousness, and every soul seeks to gratify that hunger in its own particular way, and in accordance with its own particular state of knowledge. The hunger is one, and the righteousness is one, but the pathways by which righteousness is sought are many. They who seek consciously are blessed, and shall shortly find that final and permanent satisfaction of soul which righteousness alone can give, for they have come into a knowledge of the true path. They who seek unconsciously, although for a time they may bathe in a sea of pleasure, are not blessed, for they are carving out for themselves pathways of suffering over which they must walk with torn and wounded feet, and their hunger will increase, and the soul will cry out for its lost heritage—the eternal heritage of righteousness.

Not in any of the three worlds can the soul find lasting satisfaction, apart from the realization of righteousness. Bodied or disembodied, it is ceaselessly driven on by the discipline of suffering, until at last, in its extremity, it flies to its only refuge—the refuge of righteousness—and finds that joy, satisfaction, and peace which it had so long and so vainly sought.

The great need of the soul, then, is the need of this permanent principle, called righteousness, on which it may stand securely and restfully amid the tempest of earthly existence, no more bewildered, and whereon it may build the mansion of a beautiful, peaceful, and perfect life.

It is in the realization of this principle where the Kingdom of Heaven, the abiding home of the soul, resides, and which is the source and storehouse of every permanent blessing. Finding it, all is found; not finding it, all is lost. It is an attitude of mind, a state of consciousness, an ineffable knowledge, in which the struggle for existence ceases, and the soul finds itself at rest in the midst of plenty, where its great need, yea, its every need, is satisfied, without strife and without fear. Blessed are they who earnestly and intelligently seek, for it is impossible that such should seek in vain.

THE COMPETITIVE LAWS AND
THE LAW OF LOVE

When I am pure
I shall have solved the mystery of life,
I shall be sure
(When I am free from hatred, lust and strife)
I am in Truth, and Truth abides in me.
I shall be safe and sane and wholly free
When I am pure.

It has been said that the laws of Nature are cruel; it has likewise been said that they are kind. The one statement is the result of dwelling exclusively upon the fiercely competitive aspect of Nature; the other results from viewing only the protective and kindly aspect. In reality, natural laws are neither cruel nor kind; they are absolutely just—are, in fact, the outworking of the indestructible principle of justice itself.

The cruelty, and consequent suffering, which is so prevalent in Nature, is not inherent in the heart and substance of life; it is a passing phase of evolution, a painful experience, which will ultimately ripen into the fruit of a more perfect knowledge; a dark night of ignorance and unrest, leading to a glorious morning of joy and peace.

When a helpless child is burnt to death, we do not ascribe cruelty to the working of the natural law by virtue of which the child was consumed; we infer ignorance in the child, or carelessness on the part of its guardians. Even so, men and creatures are daily being consumed in the invisible flames of passion, succumbing to the ceaseless interplay of those fiery psychic forces which, in their ignorance, they do not understand, but which they shall at last learn how to control and use to their own protection, and not, as at present, foolishly employ them to their own destruction.

To understand, control, and harmoniously adjust the invisible forces of its own soul is the ultimate destiny of every being and creature. Some men, in the past, have accomplished this supreme and exalted purpose; some, in the present, have likewise succeeded, and, until this is done, that place of rest wherein one receives all that is necessary for one's well-being and happiness, without striving, and with freedom from pain, cannot be entered.

In an age like the present, when, in all civilized countries, the string of life is strained to its highest pitch, when men, striving each with each in every department of life for the vanities and material possessions of this perishable existence, have developed competition to the utmost limit of endurance—in such an age the sublimest heights of knowledge are scaled, the supremest spiritual conquests are achieved; for when the soul is most tired, its need is greatest, and where the need is great, great will be the effort. Where, also, the temptations are powerful, the greater and more enduring will be the victory. Men love the competitive strife with their fellows, while it promises, and seems to bring them gain and happiness; but when the inevitable reaction comes, and the cold steel of selfish strife which their own hands have forged enters their own hearts, then, and not till then, do they seek a better way. "Blessed are they that mourn"—that have come to the end of strife, and have found the pain and sorrow to which it leads; for unto them, and unto them only, can open the door which leads to the Kingdom of Peace.

In searching for this Kingdom, it is necessary to fully understand the nature and origin of that which prevents its realization—namely, the strife of nature, the competitive laws operative in human affairs, and the universal unrest, insecurity, and fear which accompany these factors; for without such an understanding there can be no sound comprehension as to what constitutes the true and the false in life, and therefore no real spiritual advancement. Before the true can be apprehended and enjoyed, the false must be unveiled; before the real can be perceived as the real, the illusions which distort it must be dispersed; and before the limitless expanse of Truth can open out before us, the limited experience which is confined to the world of visible and superficial effects must be transcended.

Let, therefore, those of my readers who are thoughtful and earnest, and who are diligently seeking, or are willing to seek, for that basis of thought and conduct which shall simplify and harmonize the bewildering complexities and inequalities of life, walk with me step by step as I open up the way to the Kingdom; first descending into Hell (the world of strife and self-seeking) in order that, having comprehended its intricate ways, we may afterwards ascend into Heaven (the world of Peace and Love).

It is the custom in my household, during the hard frosts of winter, to put out food for the birds, and it is a noticeable fact that these creatures, when they are really starving, live together most amicably, huddling together to keep each other warm, and refraining from all strife; and if a small quantity of food be given them they will eat it with comparative freedom from contention; but let a quantity of food which is more than sufficient for all be thrown to them, and fighting over the coveted provender at once ensues. Occasionally we would put out a whole loaf of bread, and then the contention of the birds became fierce and prolonged, although there was more than they all could possibly eat during several days. Some, having gorged themselves until they could eat no more, would stand upon the loaf and hover round it, pecking fiercely at all newcomers, and endeavoring to prevent them from obtaining any of the food. And along with this fierce contention there was noticeable a great fear. With each mouthful of food taken, the birds would look round in nervous terror, apprehensive of losing their food or their lives.

In this simple incident we have an illustration—crude, perhaps, but true—of the basis and outworking of the competitive laws in Nature and in human affairs. It is not scarcity that produces competition, *it is abundance;* so that the richer and more luxurious a nation becomes, the keener and fiercer becomes the competition for securing the necessaries and luxuries of life. Let famine overtake a nation, and at once compassion and sympathy take the place of competitive strife; and, in the blessedness of giving and receiving, men enjoy a foretaste of that heavenly bliss which the spiritually wise have found, and which all shall ultimately reach.

The fact that abundance, and not scarcity, creates competition, should be held constantly in mind by the reader during the perusal of this book, as it throws a searching light not only on the statements herein contained, but upon every problem relating to social life and human conduct. Moreover, if it be deeply and earnestly meditated upon, and its lessons applied to individual conduct, it will make plain the Way which leads to the Kingdom.

Let us now search out the *cause* of this fact, in order that the evils connected with it may be transcended.

Every phenomenon in social and national life (as in Nature) is an effect, and all these effects are embodied by a cause which is not remote and detached, but which is the immediate soul and life of the effect itself. As the seed is contained in the flower, and the flower in the seed, so the relation of cause and effect is intimate and inseparable. An effect, also, is vivified and propagated, not by any life inherent in itself, but by the life and impulse existing in the cause.

Looking out upon the world, we behold it as an arena of strife in which individuals, communities, and nations are constantly engaged in struggle, striving with each other for superiority, and for the largest share of worldly possessions. We see, also, that the weaker fall out defeated, and that the strong—those who are equipped to pursue the combat with undiminished ardor—obtain the victory, and enter into possession. And along with this struggle we see the suffering which is inevitably connected with it—men and women, broken down with the weight of their responsibilities, failing in their efforts and losing all; families and communities broken up, and nations subdued and subordinated. We see seas of tears, telling of unspeakable anguish and grief; we see painful partings and early and unnatural deaths; and we know that this life of strife, when stripped of its surface appearances, is largely a life of sorrow.

Such, briefly sketched, are the phenomena connected with that aspect of human life with which we are now dealing; such are the effects as we see them; and they have one common cause which is found in the human heart itself. As all the multiform varieties of plant life have one common soil from which to draw their sustenance, and by virtue of which they live and thrive, so all the varied activities of human life are rooted in, and draw their vitality from, one common source—*the human heart.* The cause of all suffering and of all happiness resides, not in the outer activities of human life, but in the inner activities of the heart and mind; and every external agency is sustained by the life which it derives from human conduct.

The organized life-principle in man carves for itself outward channels along which it can pour its pent-up energies, makes for itself vehicles through which it can manifest its potency and reap its experience, and, as a result, we have our religious, social, and political organizations.

All the visible manifestations of human life, then, are effects; and as such, although they may possess a reflex action, they can never be causes, but must remain forever what they are—*dead effects,* galvanized into life by an enduring and profound cause.

It is the custom of men to wander about in this world of effects, and to mistake its illusions for realities, eternally transposing and readjusting these effects in order to arrive at a solution of human problems, instead of reaching down to the underlying cause which is at once the center of unification and the basis upon which to build a peace-giving solution of human life.

The strife of the world in all its forms, whether it be war, social or political quarreling, sectarian hatred, private disputes, or commercial competition, has its origin in one common cause, namely, *individual selfishness.* And I employ this term selfishness in a far-reaching sense; in it I include all forms of self-love and egotism—I mean by it the desire to pander to, and preserve at all costs, the personality.

This element of selfishness is the life and soul of competition, and of the competitive laws. Apart from it they have no existence. But in the life of every individual in whose heart selfishness in any form is harbored, these laws are brought into play, and the individual is subject to them.

Innumerable economic systems have failed, and must fail, to extirpate the strife of the world. They are the outcome of the delusion that outward systems of government are the causes of that strife, whereas they are but the visible and transient effect of the *inward strife,* the channels through which it must necessarily manifest itself. To destroy the channel is, and must ever be, ineffectual, as the inward energy will immediately make for itself another, and still another and another. Strife cannot cease; and the competitive laws *must prevail so long as selfishness is fostered in the heart.* All reforms will fail where this element is ignored or unaccounted for; all reforms will succeed where it is recognized, and steps are taken for its removal.

Selfishness, then, is the root cause of competition, the foundation on which all competitive systems rest, and the sustaining source of the competitive laws. It will thus be seen that all competitive systems, all the visible activities of the struggle of man with man, are as the leaves and branches of a tree which overspreads the whole earth, the root of that tree being *individual selfishness,* and the ripened fruits of which are pain and sorrow. This tree cannot be destroyed by merely lopping off its branches; to do this effectually, *the root must be destroyed.* To introduce measures in the form of changed external conditions is merely lopping off the branches; and as the cutting away of certain branches of a tree gives added vigor to those which remain, even so the very means which are taken to curtail the competitive strife, when those means deal entirely with its outward effects, will but add strength and vigor to the tree whose roots are all the time being fostered and encouraged in the human heart. The most that even legislation can do is to prune the branches, and so prevent the tree from altogether running wild.

Great efforts are now being put forward to found a "Garden City," which shall be a veritable Eden planted in the midst of orchards, and whose inhabitants shall live in comfort and comparative repose. And beautiful and laudable are all such efforts when they are prompted by unselfish love. But such a city cannot exist, or cannot long remain the Eden which it aims to be in its outward form, unless the majority of its inhabitants have subdued and conquered the inward selfishness. Even one form of selfishness, namely, *self-indulgence,* if fostered by its inhabitants, will completely undermine that city, leveling its orchards to the ground, converting many of its beautiful dwellings into competitive marts, and obnoxious centers for the personal gratification of appetite, and some of its public buildings into institutions for the maintenance of order; and upon its public spaces will rise jails, asylums, and orphanages, for where the spirit of self-indulgence is, the means for its gratification will be immediately adopted, without considering the good of others or of the community (for selfishness is always blind), and the fruits of that gratification will be rapidly reaped.

The building of pleasant houses and the planting of beautiful orchards and gardens can never, of itself, constitute a Garden City unless its inhabitants have learned that self-sacrifice is better than self-protection, and have first established in their own hearts the Garden City of unselfish love. And when a sufficient number of men and women have done this, the Garden City will appear, and it will flourish and prosper, and great will be its peace, for "out of the heart are the issues of life."

Having found that selfishness is the root cause of all competition and strife, the question naturally arises as to how this cause shall be dealt with, for it naturally follows that a cause being destroyed, all its effects cease; a cause being propagated, all its effects, however they may be modified from without, *must* continue. Every man who has thought at all deeply upon the problem of life, and has brooded sympathetically upon the sufferings of mankind, has seen that selfishness is at the root of all sorrow—in fact, this is one of the truths that is first apprehended by the thoughtful mind. And along with that perception there has been born within him a longing to formulate some methods by which that selfishness might be overcome. The first impulse of such a man is to endeavor to frame some outward law, or introduce some new social arrangements or regulations, which shall put a check on *the selfishness of others.* The second tendency of his mind will be to feel his utter helplessness before the great iron wall of selfishness by which he is confronted. Both these attitudes of mind are the result of an incomplete knowledge of what constitutes selfishness. And this partial knowledge dominates him because, although he has overcome the grosser forms of selfishness in himself, and is so far noble, he is yet selfish in other and more remote and subtle directions. This feeling of "helplessness" is the prelude to one of two conditions—the man will either give up in despair, and again sink himself in the selfishness of the world, or he will search and meditate until he finds another way out of the difficulty. And that way he will find. Looking deeper and ever deeper into the things of life; reflecting, brooding, examining, and analyzing; grappling with every difficulty and problem with intensity of thought, and developing day by day a profounder love of Truth—by these means his heart will grow and his comprehension expand, and at last he will realize that the way to destroy selfishness is not to try to destroy *one form* of it in other people, but to destroy it utterly, root and branch, *in himself.*

The perception of this truth constitutes spiritual illumination, and when once it is awakened in the mind, the "straight and narrow way" is revealed, and the shining Gates of the Kingdom already loom in the distance. Then does a man apply to himself (not to others) these words—"And why beholdest thou the mote that is in thy brother's eye, but considerest not the beam that is in thine own eye? Or how wilt thou say to thy brother, let me pull out the mote out of thine eye; and, behold, a beam is in thine own eye? Thou hypocrite, first cast out the beam out of thine own eye; and then shalt thou see clearly to cast out the mote out of thy brother's eye." When a man can apply these words to himself and act upon them, judging himself mercilessly, but judging none other, then will he find his way out of the hell of competitive strife, then will he rise above and render of non-effect the laws of competition, and will find the higher Law of Love, subjecting himself to which every evil thing will flee from him, and the joys and blessings which the selfish vainly seek will constantly wait upon him. And not only this, he will, having lifted himself, lift the world. By his example many will see the Way, and will walk it; and the powers of darkness will be the weaker for his having lived.

It will here be asked, "But will not a man who has risen above his selfishness, and therefore above the competitive strife, suffer through the selfishness and competition of those around him? Will he not, after all the trouble he has taken to purify himself, suffer at the hands of the impure?" No, he will not. The equity of the Divine Order is perfect, and cannot be subverted, so that it is impossible for one who has overcome selfishness to be subject to those laws which are brought into operation by the action of selfishness; in other words, each individual suffers by virtue of his own selfishness. It is true that the selfish all come under the operation of the competitive laws, and suffer collectively, each acting, more or less, as the instrument by which the suffering of others is brought about, which makes it appear, on the surface, as though men suffered for the sins of others rather than their own. But the truth is that in a universe the very basis of which is harmony, and which can only be sustained by the perfect adjustment of all its parts, each unit receives *its own* measure of adjustment, and suffers by and of itself. Each man comes under the laws of his own being, never under those of another. True, he will suffer like another, and even through the instrumentality of another, if he elects to live under the same conditions as that other. But if he chooses to desert those conditions and to live under another and higher set of conditions of which that other is ignorant, he will cease to come under, or be affected by, the lower laws.

Let us now go back to the symbol of the tree, and carry the analogy a little further. Just as the leaves and branches are sustained by the roots, so the roots derive their nourishment from the soil, groping blindly in the darkness for the sustenance which the tree demands. In like manner, selfishness, the root of the tree of evil and of suffering, derives its nourishment from the dark soil of *ignorance*. In this it thrives; upon this it stands and flourishes. By ignorance I mean something vastly different from lack of learning; and the sense in which I use it will be made plain as I proceed.

Selfishness always gropes in the dark. It has no knowledge; by its very nature it is cut off from the source of enlightenment; it is a blind impulse, knowing nothing, obeying no law, for it knows none, and is thereby forcibly bound to those competitive laws by virtue of which suffering is inflicted in order that harmony may be maintained. We live in a world, a universe, abounding with all good things. So great is the abundance of spiritual, mental, and material blessings that every man and woman on this globe could not only be provided with every necessary good, but could live in the midst of abounding plenty, and yet leave much to spare. Yet, in spite of this, what a spectacle of ignorance do we behold! We see on the one hand millions of men and women chained to a ceaseless slavery, interminably toiling in order to obtain a poor and scanty meal and a garment to cover their nakedness; and on the other hand we see thousands, who already have more than they require and can well manage, depriving themselves of all the blessings of a true life and of the vast opportunities which their possessions place within their reach, in order to accumulate more of those material things for which they have no legitimate use. Surely men and women have no more wisdom than the beasts which fight over the possession of that which is more than they can all well dispose of, and which they could all enjoy in peace!

Such a condition of things can only obtain in a state of ignorance deep and dark; so dark and dense as to be utterly impenetrable save to the unselfish eye of wisdom and truth. And in the midst of all this striving after place and food and raiment, there works unseen, yet potent and unerring, the Over-ruling Law of Justice, meting out to every individual his own quota of merit and demerit. It is impartial; it bestows no favors; it inflicts no unearned punishments:

> It knows not wrath nor pardon; utter-true
>> It measures mete, its faultless balance weighs;
> Times are as nought, to-morrow it will judge,
>> Or after many days.

The rich and the poor alike suffer for *their own selfishness;* and none escapes. The rich have their particular sufferings as well as the poor. Moreover, the rich are continually losing their riches; the poor are continually acquiring them. The poor man of to-day is the rich man of tomorrow, and *vice versa.* There is no stability, no security in hell, and only brief and occasional periods of respite from suffering in some form or other. Fear, also, follows men like a great shadow, for the man who obtains and holds by selfish force will always be haunted by a feeling of insecurity, and will continually fear its loss; while the poor man, who is selfishly seeking or coveting material riches, will be harassed by the fear of destitution. And one and all who live in this underworld of strife are overshadowed by one great fear—the fear of death.

Surrounded by the darkness of ignorance, and having no knowledge of those eternal and life-sustaining Principles out of which all things proceed, men labor under the delusion that the most important and essential things in life are food and clothing, and that their first duty is to strive to obtain these, believing that these outward things are the source and cause of all comfort and happiness. It is the blind animal instinct of self-preservation (the preservation of the body and personality), by virtue of which each man opposes himself to other men in order to "get a living" or "secure a competency," believing that if he does not keep an incessant watch on other men, and constantly renew the struggle, they will ultimately "take the bread out of his mouth."

It is out of this initial delusion that comes all the train of delusions, with their attendant sufferings, which obtain in the world around us. Food and clothing are not the *essential* things of life; not the causes of happiness. They are non-essentials, effects, and, as such, proceed by a process of natural law from the essentials, the underlying cause. The essential things in life are the enduring elements in character—integrity, faith, righteousness, self-sacrifice, compassion, love; and out of these all good things proceed. Food, clothing, and money are dead effects; there is in them no life, no power except that with which we invest them. They are without vice and virtue, and can neither bless nor harm. Even the body which men believe to be themselves, to which they pander, and which they long to keep, must very shortly be yielded up to the dust. But the higher elements of character are life itself; and to practice these, to trust them, and to live entirely in them, constitutes the Kingdom of Heaven.

The man who says, "I will first of all earn a competence and secure a good position in life, and will then give my mind to these higher things," does not understand these higher things, does not believe them to be higher, for if he did, it would not be possible for him to neglect them. He believes the material excrescences of life to be the higher, and therefore he seeks them first. He believes money, clothing, and position to be of vast and essential importance, righteousness and truth to be at best secondary; for a man always sacrifices that which he believes to be lesser to that which he believes to be greater. Immediately a man *realizes* that righteousness is of more importance than the getting of food and clothing, he ceases to strive after the latter, and begins to live for the former. It is here where we come to the dividing line between the two Kingdoms—Hell and Heaven.

Once a man perceives the beauty and enduring reality of righteousness, his whole attitude of mind toward himself and others and the things within and around him changes. The love of personal existence gradually loses its hold on him; the instinct of self-preservation begins to die, and the practice of self-renunciation takes its place. For the sacrifice of others, or of the happiness of others, for his own good, he substitutes the sacrifice of self and of his own happiness for the good of others. And thus, rising above self, he rises above the competitive strife which is the outcome of self, and above the competitive laws which operate only in the region of self, and for the regulation of its blind impulses. He is like a man who has climbed a mountain, and thereby risen above all the disturbing currents in the valleys below him. The clouds pour down their rain, the thunders roll and the lightnings flash, the fogs obscure, and the hurricanes uproot and destroy, but they cannot reach him on the calm heights where he stands, and where he dwells in continual sunshine and peace.

In the life of such a man the lower laws cease to operate, and he now comes under the protection of a higher Law—namely, the Law of Love; and, in accordance with his faithfulness and obedience to this Law, will all that is necessary for his well-being come to him at the time when he requires it. The idea of gaining a position in the world cannot enter his mind, and the external necessities of life, such as money, food, and clothing, he scarcely ever thinks about. But, subjecting himself for the good of others, performing all his duties scrupulously and without thinking of reward, and living day by day in the discipline of righteousness, all other things follow at the right time and in the right order. Just as suffering and strife inhere in, and spring from, their root cause, selfishness, so blessedness and peace inhere in, and spring from, their root cause, righteousness. And it is a full and all-embracing blessedness, complete and perfect in every department of life, for that which is morally and spiritually right is physically and materially right.

Such a man is free, for he is freed from all anxiety, worry, fear, despondency, all those mental disturbances which derive their vitality from the elements of self, and he lives in constant joy and peace, and this while living in the very midst of the competitive strife of the world. Yet, though walking in the midst of Hell, its flames fall back before and around him, so that not one hair of his head can be singed. Though he walks in the midst of the lions of selfish force, for him their jaws are closed and their ferocity is subdued. Though on every hand men are falling around him in the fierce battle of life, he falls not, neither is he dismayed, for no deadly bullet can reach him, no poisoned shaft can pierce the impenetrable armor of his righteousness. Having lost the little, personal, self-seeking life of suffering, anxiety, fear, and want, he has found the illimitable, glorious, self-perfecting life of joy and peace and plenty. "Therefore take no thought, saying, What shall we eat? or, What shall we drink? or, Wherewithal shall we be clothed? . . . For your heavenly Father knoweth ye have need of all these things. But seek ye first the Kingdom of God, and His Righteousness; and all these things shall be added unto you."

THE FINDING OF A PRINCIPLE

Be still, my soul, and know that peace is thine.
    Be steadfast, heart, and know that strength divine
Belongs to thee; cease from thy turmoil, mind,
    And thou the everlasting rest shalt find.

How then shall a man reach the Kingdom? By what process shall he find the light which alone can disperse his darkness? And in what way can he overcome the inward selfishness which is strong, and deeply rooted?

A man will reach the Kingdom by purifying himself, and he can only do this by pursuing a process of self-examination and self-analysis. The selfishness must be discovered and understood before it can be removed. It is powerless to remove itself, neither will it pass away of itself. Darkness ceases only when light is introduced; so ignorance can only be dispersed by Knowledge; selfishness by Love. Seeing that in selfishness there is no security, no stability, no peace, the whole process of seeking the Kingdom resolves itself into a search for a Principle; a divine and permanent Principle on which a man can stand secure, freed from himself—that is, from the personal element, and from the tyranny and slavery which that personal self exacts and demands. A man must first of all be willing to lose himself (his self-seeking self) before he can find himself (his divine self). He must realize that selfishness is not worth clinging to, that it is a master altogether unworthy of his service, and that divine Goodness alone is worthy to be enthroned in his heart as the supreme master of his life. This means that he must have faith, for without this equipment there can be neither progress nor achievement. He must believe in the desirability of purity, in the supremacy of righteousness, in the sustaining power of integrity; he must ever hold before him the Ideal and Perfect Goodness, and strive for its achievement with ever-renewed effort and unflagging zeal. This faith must be nurtured and its development encouraged. As a lamp, it must be carefully trimmed and fed and kept burning in the heart, for without its radiating flame no way will be seen in the darkness; he will find no pathway out of self. And as this flame increases and burns with a steadier light, energy, resolution, and self-reliance will come to his aid, and with each step, his progress will be accelerated until at last the Light of Knowledge will begin to take the place of the lamp of faith, and the darkness will commence to disappear before its searching splendor. Into his spiritual ken will come the Principles of the divine Life, and as he approaches them, their incomparable beauty and majestic symmetry will astonish his vision, and gladden his heart with a gladness hitherto unknown.

Along this pathway of self-control and self-purification (for such it is) every soul must travel on its way to the Kingdom. So narrow is this way, and so overgrown with the weeds of selfishness is its entrance, that it is difficult to find, and, being found, cannot be retained except by *daily meditation.* Without this the spiritual energies grow weaker, and the man loses the strength necessary to continue. As the body is sustained and invigorated by material food, so the spirit is strengthened and renewed by its own food—namely, meditation upon spiritual things.

He, then, who earnestly resolves to find the Kingdom will commence to meditate, and to rigidly examine his heart and mind and life in the light of that Supreme Perfection which is the goal of his attainment. On his way to that goal, he must pass through *three Gateways of Surrender.* The first is *the Surrender of Desire;* the second is *the Surrender of Opinion;* the third is *the Surrender of Self.* Entering into meditation, he will commence to examine his desires, tracing them out in his mind, and following up their effects in his life and upon his character; and he will quickly perceive that, without the renunciation of desire, a man remains a slave both to himself and to his surroundings and circumstances. Having discovered this, the first Gate, that of *the Surrender of Desire,* is entered. Passing through this Gate, he adopts a process of self-discipline which is the first step in the purification of the soul. Hitherto he has lived as a slavish beast; eating, drinking, sleeping, and pursuing enjoyment at the beck and call of his lower impulses; blindly following and gratifying his inclinations without method, not questioning his conduct, and having no fixed center from which to regulate his character and life. Now, however, he begins to live as a man; he curbs his inclinations, controls his passions, and steadies his mind in the practice of virtue. He ceases to pursue enjoyment, but follows the dictates of his reason, and regulates his conduct in accordance with the demands of an ideal. With the introduction of this regulating factor in his life, he at once perceives that certain habits must be abandoned. He begins to select his food, and to have his meals at stated periods, no longer eating at any time when the sight of food tempts his inclination. He reduces the number of meals per day and also the quantity of food eaten. He no longer goes to bed, by day or night, to indulge in pleasurable indolence, but to give his body the rest it needs, and he therefore regulates his hours of sleep, rising early, and never encouraging the animal desire to indulge in dreamy indolence after waking. All those foods and drinks which are particularly associated with gluttony, cruelty, and drunkenness he will dispense with altogether, selecting the mild and refreshing sustenance which Nature provides in such rich profusion.

These preliminary steps will be at once adopted; and as the path of self-government and self-examination is pursued, a clearer and ever clearer perception of the nature, meaning, and effects of desire will be developed, until it will be seen that the mere regulation of one's desires is altogether inadequate and insufficient, and that *the desires themselves must be abandoned,* must be allowed to fall out of the mind and to have no part in the character and life. It is at this point where the soul of the seeker will enter the dark Valley of Temptation, for these desires will not die without a struggle, and without many a fierce effort to reassert the power and authority with which they have hitherto been invested. And here the lamp of faith must be constantly fed and assiduously trimmed, for all the light that it can throw out will be required to guide and encourage the traveler in the dense gloom of this dark Valley. At first his desires, like so many wild beasts, will clamor loudly for gratification. Failing in that, they will then tempt him to struggle with them that they may overthrow him. And this last temptation is greater and more difficult to overcome than the first, for *the desires will not be stilled until they are utterly ignored;* until they are left unheeded, unconditionally abandoned, and allowed to perish for want of food. In passing through this Valley, the searcher will develop certain powers which are necessary to his further advancement, and these powers are—*self-control, self-reliance, fearlessness,* and *independence of thought.* Here also he will have to pass through ridicule and mockery and false accusation; so much so that some of his best friends, yea, even those whom he most unselfishly loves, will accuse him of folly and inconsistency, and will do all they can to argue him back to the life of animal indulgence, self-seeking, and petty personal strife. Nearly everybody around him will suddenly discover that they know his duty better than he knows it himself, and, knowing no other and higher life than their own of mingled excitement and suffering, they will take great pains to win him back to it, imagining, in their ignorance, that he is losing so much pleasure and happiness, and is gaining nothing in return. At first this attitude of others toward him will arouse in him acute suffering, but he will rapidly discover that this suffering is caused by his own vanity and selfishness, and is the result of his own subtle desire to be appreciated, admired, and thought well of; and immediately this knowledge is arrived at, he will rise into a higher state of consciousness, where these things can no longer reach him and inflict pain. It is here where he will begin to stand firm, and to wield with effect the powers of mind already mentioned. Let him therefore press on courageously, heeding neither the revilings of his friends without nor the clamorings of his enemies within; aspiring, searching, striving; looking ever toward his Ideal with eyes of holy love; day by day ridding his mind of selfish motive, his heart of impure desire; stumbling sometimes, sometimes falling, but ever traveling onward and rising higher; and, recording each night in the silence of his own heart the journey of the day, let him not despair if but each day, in spite of all its failures and falls, record some holy battle fought, though lost, some silent victory attempted, though unachieved. The loss of to-day will add to the gain of to-morrow for him whose mind is set on the conquest of self.

Passing along the Valley, he will at last come to the Fields of Sorrow and Loneliness. His desires, having received at his hands neither encouragement nor sustenance, have grown weak, and are now falling away and perishing. He is now climbing out of the Valley, and the darkness is less dense; but now he realizes, for the first time, that he is alone. He is like a man standing upon the lowest level of a great mountain, and it is night. Above him towers the lofty peak, beyond which shine the everlasting stars; a short distance below him are the glaring lights of the city which he has left, and from it there come up to him the noises of its inhabitants—a confused mingling of shouts, screams, laughter, rumblings of traffic, and the strains of music. He thinks of his friends, all of whom are in the city, pursuing their own particular pleasures, and he is alone upon the mountain. That city is the City of Desire and Pleasure, the mountain is the Mountain of Renunciation, and the climber now knows that he has left the world, that henceforth for him its excitements and strifes are lifeless things, and can tempt him no more. Resting awhile in this lonely place, he will taste of sorrow and learn its secret; harshness and hatred will pass from him; his heart will grow soft, and the first faint broodings of that divine compassion, which shall afterwards absorb his whole being, will over-shadow and inspire him. He will begin to feel with every living thing in its strivings and sufferings, and gradually, as this lesson is learned, his own sorrow and loneliness will be forgotten in his great calm love for others, and will pass away.

Here, also, he will begin to perceive and understand the working of those hidden laws which govern the destinies of individuals and nations. Having risen above the lower region of strife and selfishness within himself, he can now look calmly down upon it in others and in the world, and analyze and comprehend it, and he will see how selfish striving is at the root of all the world's suffering. His whole attitude toward others and the world now undergoes a complete change, and compassion and love begin to take the place of self-seeking and self-protection in his mind; and as a result of this, the world alters in its attitude toward him. At this juncture he perceives the folly of competition, and, ceasing from striving to overtop and get the better of others, he begins to encourage them, both with unselfish thoughts, and, when necessary, with loving acts; and this he does even to those who selfishly compete with him, no longer defending himself against them. As a direct result of this, his worldly affairs begin to prosper as never before; many of the friends who at first mocked him commence to respect, and even to love him, and he suddenly wakes up to the fact that he is coming in contact with people of a distinctly unworldly and noble type, of whose existence he had no knowledge while living in his lower selfish nature. From many parts and from long distances these people will come to him to minister to him and that he may minister to them, spiritual fellowship and loving brotherhood will become potent factors in his life, and so he will pass beyond the Fields of Sorrow and Loneliness.

The lower competitive laws have now ceased to operate in his life, and their results, which are *failure, disaster, exposure, and destitution,* can no longer enter into and form part of his experience; and this not merely because he has risen above the lower forms of selfishness in himself, but because also, in so rising, he has developed certain power of mind by which he is enabled to direct and govern his affairs with a more powerful and masterly hand.

He, however, has not yet traveled far, and unless he exercise constant watchfulness, may at any time fall back into the lower world of darkness and strife, revivifying its empty pleasures, and galvanizing back to life its dead desires. And especially is there this danger when he reaches the greatest temptation through which man is called to pass—*the temptation of doubt.* Before reaching, or even perceiving, the second Gate, that of *Surrender of Opinion,* the pilgrim will come upon a great soul-desert, the Desert of Doubt. And here for a time he will wander around, and despondency, indecision, and uncertainty, a melancholy brood, will surround him like a cloud, hiding from his view the way immediately in front of him. A new and strange fear, too, will possibly overtake him, and he will begin to question the wisdom of the course he is pursuing. Again the allurements of the world will be presented to him, dressed in their most attractive garb, and the drowning din and stimulating excitement of worldly battle will once more assume a desirable aspect. "After all, am I right?" "What gain is there in this?" "Does not life itself consist of pleasure and excitement and battle, and in giving these up am I not giving up all?" "Am I not sacrificing the very substance of life for a meaningless shadow?" "May it not be that, after all, I am a poor deluded fool, and that all these around me who live the life of the senses and stand upon its solid, sure, and easily procured enjoyments are wiser than I?" By such dark doubtings and questionings will he here be tempted and troubled, and these very doubts will drive him to a deeper searching into the intricacies of life, and arouse within him the feeling of necessity for some permanent Principle upon which to stand and take refuge. He will therefore, while wandering about in this dark Desert, come into contact with the higher and more subtle delusions of his own mind, the delusions of the intellect; and, by contrasting these with his Ideal, will learn to distinguish between the real and the unreal, the shadow and the substance, between effect and cause, between fleeting appearances and permanent Principles.

In the Desert of Doubt a man is confronted with all forms of illusion, not only the illusions of the senses, but also those of abstract thought and religious emotion. It is in the testing of, grappling with, and ultimately destroying these illusions that he develops still higher powers, those of *discrimination, spiritual perception, steadfastness of purpose,* and *calmness of mind,* by the exercise of which he is enabled to unerringly distinguish the true from the false, both in the world of thought and that of material appearances. Having acquired these powers, and learned how to use them in his holy warfare as weapons against himself, he now emerges from the Desert of Doubt, the mists and mirages of delusion vanish from his pathway, and there looms before him the second Gate, the *Gateway of the Surrender of Opinion.*

As he approaches this Gate, he sees before him the whole pathway along which he is traveling, and, for a space, obtains a glimpse of the glorious heights of attainment toward which he is moving; he sees the Temple of the Higher Life in all its majesty, and already he feels within him the strength and joy and peace of conquest. With Sir Galahad he can now exclaim:

> *I . . . saw the Grail,*
> *The Holy Grail . . .*
> *. . . And one will crown me king*
> *Far in the spiritual city,*

for he knows that his ultimate victory is assured.

He now enters upon a process of self-conquest, which is altogether distinct from that which he has hitherto pursued. Up to the present he has been overcoming, transmuting, and simplifying his animal desires; now he commences to transmute and simplify his intellect. He has, so far, been adjusting his *feelings* to his Ideals; he now begins to adjust his *thoughts* to that Ideal, which also assumes at this point larger and more beautiful proportions, and for the first time he perceives what really constitutes *a permanent and imperishable Principle.* He sees that the righteousness for which he has been searching is fixed and unvariable; that it cannot be accommodated to man, but that man must reach up to, and obey it; that it consists of an undeviating line of conduct, apart from all considerations of loss or gain, of reward or punishment; that, in reality, it consists in abandoning self, with all the sins of desire, opinion, and self-interest of which that self is composed, and in living the blameless life of perfect love toward all men and creatures. Such a life is fixed and perfect; it is without turning, change, or qualification, and demands a sinless and perfect conduct. It is, therefore, the direct antithesis of the worldly life of self.

Perceiving this, the seeker sees that, although he has freed himself from the baser passions and desires which enslave mankind, he is still in bondage to the fetters of opinion; that although he has purified himself with a purity to which few aspire, and which the world cannot understand, he is still defiled with a defilement which is difficult to wash away—*he loves his own opinions,* and has all along been confounding them with Truth, with the Principle for which he is seeking. He is not yet free from strife, and is still involved in the competitive laws as they obtain in the higher realm of thought. He still believes that he (in his opinions) is right, and that others are wrong; and, in his egotism, has even fallen so low as to bestow a mock pity on those who hold opinions the reverse of his own. But now, realizing this more subtle form of selfishness with which he is enslaved, and perceiving all the train of sufferings which spring from it, having also acquired the priceless possession of spiritual discernment, he reverently bends his head and passes through the second Gateway toward his final peace.

And now, clothing his soul with the colorless Garment of Humility, he bends all his energies to the uprooting of those opinions which he has hitherto loved and cherished. He now learns to distinguish between Truth, which is one and unchangeable, and his own and others' opinions about Truth, which are many and changeable. He sees that his *opinions* about Goodness, Purity, Compassion, and Love are very distinct from those qualities themselves, and that he must stand upon those divine Principles, and not upon his opinions. Hitherto he has regarded his own opinions as of great value, and the opinions of others as worthless, but now he ceases to so elevate his own opinions and to defend them against those of others, and comes to regard them as utterly worthless. As a direct result of this attitude of mind, he takes refuge in the practice of *pure Goodness,* unalloyed with base desire and subtle self-love, and takes his stand upon the divine Principles of Purity, Wisdom, Compassion, and Love, incorporating them into his mind, and manifesting them in his life. He is now clothed with *the Righteousness of Christ* (which is incomprehensible to the world) and is rapidly becoming divine. He has not only realized the darkness of desire; he has also perceived the vanity of speculative philosophy, and so he rids his mind of all those metaphysical subtleties which have no relation to practical holiness, and which have hitherto encumbered his progress, and prevented him from seeing the enduring realities in life.

And now he casts from him, one after another, his opinions and speculations, and commences to live the life of perfect love toward all beings. With each opinion overcome and abandoned as a burden, there is an increased lightness of spirit, and he now begins to realize the meaning of being "free." The divine flowers of Gladness, Joy, and Peace spring up spontaneously in his heart, and his life becomes a blissful song. And as the melody in his heart expands, and grows more and more perfect, his outward life harmonizes itself with the inward music. All the effort he puts forth being now free from strife, he obtains all that is necessary for his well-being, without pain, anxiety, or fear. He has almost entirely transcended the competitive laws, and the Law of Love is now the governing factor in his life, adjusting all his worldly affairs harmoniously, and without struggle or difficulty on his part. Indeed, the competitive laws, as they obtain in the commercial world, have here been long left behind, and have ceased to touch him at any point in his material affairs. Here, also, he enters into a wider and more comprehensive consciousness, and, viewing the universe and humanity from the higher altitudes of purity and knowledge to which he has ascended, perceives the orderly sequence of law in all human affairs. The pursuit of this Path brings about the development of still higher powers of mind, arid these powers are—*divine patience, spiritual equanimity, non-resistance,* and *prophetic insight.* By prophetic insight I do not mean the foretelling of events, but direct perception of those hidden causes which operate in human life, and, indeed, in all life, and out of which spring the multifarious and universal effects and events.

The man here rises above the competitive laws as they operate in the thought world, so that their results, which are *violence, ignominy, grief, humiliation,* and *distress* and *anxiety* in all their forms, no more obtain in his life. As he proceeds, the imperishable Principles which form the foundation and fabric of the universe loom before him, and assume more and more symmetrical proportions. For him there is no more anguish; no evil can come near his dwelling; and there breaks upon him the dawning of the abiding Peace.

But he is not yet free. He has not yet finished his journey. He may rest here, and that as long as he chooses; but sooner or later he will rouse himself to the last effort, and will reach the final goal of achievement—the selfless state, the divine life. He is not yet free from self, but still clings, though with less tenacity, to the love of personal existence, and to the idea of exclusive interest in his personal possessions. And when he at last realizes that these selfish elements must also be abandoned, there appears before him the third Gate—*the Gateway of Surrender of Self.* It is no dark portal which he now approaches, but one luminous with divine glory, one radiant with a radiance with which no earthly splendor can vie, and he advances toward it with no uncertain step. The clouds of Doubt have long been dispersed; the sounds of the voices of Temptation are lost in the valley below; and with firm gait, erect carriage, and a heart filled with unspeakable joy, he nears the Gate that guards the Kingdom of God. He has now given up all but self-interest in those things which are his by legal right, but he now perceives that he must hold nothing as his own; and as he pauses at the Gate, he hears the command which cannot be evaded or denied: "Yet lackest thou one thing; sell all that thou hast, and distribute unto the poor, and thou shalt have treasure in Heaven." And passing through the last great Gate, he stands glorious, radiant, free, detached from the tyranny of desire, of opinion, of self; a divine man—harmless, patient, tender, pure; he has found that for which he has been searching—the Kingdom of God and His Righteousness.

The journey to the Kingdom may be a long and tedious one, or it may be short and rapid. It may occupy a minute, or it may take a thousand ages. Everything depends on the faith and belief of the searcher. The majority cannot "enter in because of their unbelief"; for how can men realize righteousness when they do not believe in it nor in the possibility of its accomplishment? Neither is it necessary to leave the outer world, and one's duties therein. Nay, it can only be found through the unselfish performance of one's duty. Some there are whose faith is so great that, when this truth is presented to them, they can let all the personal elements drop almost immediately out of their minds, and enter into their divine heritage. But all who believe and aspire to achieve will sooner or later arrive at victory if, amid all their worldly duties, they faint not, nor lose sight of the Ideal Goodness, and continue, with unshaken resolve, to "press on to Perfection."

AT REST IN THE KINGDOM
AND ALL THINGS ADDED

My life is glad—
Nowise forgetting yet those other lives
Painful and poor, wicked and miserable,
Whereon the gods grant pity!

—Sir Edwin Arnold

The whole journey from the Kingdom of Strife to the Kingdom of Love resolves itself into a process which may be summed up in the following words: *The regulation and purification of conduct.* Such a process must, if assiduously pursued, necessarily lead to perfection. It will also be seen that as the man obtains the mastery over certain forces within himself, he arrives at a knowledge of all the laws which operate in the realm of those forces, and by watching the ceaseless working of cause and effect within himself, until he understands it, he then understands it in its universal adjustments in the body of humanity. Moreover, seeing that all the laws which govern human affairs are the direct outcome of the necessities of the human heart, he, having reformed and transmuted those necessities, has brought himself under the guidance of other laws which operate in accordance with his altered condition, and that, having mastered and overcome the selfish forces within himself, he can no longer be subject to the laws which exist for their governance.

The process is also one of *simplification of the mind,* a sifting away of all but the essential gold in character. And as the mind is thus simplified, the apparently unfathomable complexity of the universe assumes simpler and simpler aspects, until the whole is seen to resolve itself into, and to rest upon, a few unalterable Principles; and these Principles are ultimately seen to be contained in *one,* namely LOVE.

The mind thus simplified, the man arrives at peace, and he now really begins to *live.* Looking back on the personal life which he has forever abandoned, he sees it as a horrible nightmare out of which he has awakened; but looking out and down with the eyes of the spirit, he sees that others continue to live it. He sees men and women struggling, fighting, suffering, and perishing for that which is abundantly given to them by the bountiful hand of the Father, if they would only cease from all covetousness, and take it without hurt or hindrance; and compassion fills his heart, and also gladness, for he knows that humanity will wake at last from its long and painful dream. In the early part of his journey he seemed to be leaving humanity far behind, and he sorrowed in his loneliness. But now, having reached the highest, having attained the goal, he finds himself nearer to humanity than ever before—yea, living in its very heart, sympathizing with all its sorrows, rejoic-ing in all its joys; for, having no longer any personal considerations to defend, he lives entirely in the heart of humanity. He lives no longer for himself; he lives for others; and so living, he enjoys the highest bliss, the deepest peace. For a time he searched for Compassion, Love, Bliss, Truth; but now he has verily become Compassion, Love, Bliss, Truth; and it may literally be said of him that he has ceased to be a personality, for all the personal elements have been extinguished, and there remain only those qualities and principles which are entirely impersonal. And those qualities are now manifested in the man's life, and henceforth *the man's character.*

And having ceased from the protection of self, and living constantly in compassion, wisdom, and love, he comes under the protection of the highest Law, the Law of Love; and he understands that Law, and consciously co-operates with it; yea, is himself inseparately identified with the Law.

Forgoing self, the universe grows I

and he whose nature is compassion, wisdom, and love cannot possibly need any protection; for those Principles themselves constitute the highest protection, being the real, the divine, the immor-tal in all men, and constituting the indestructible reality in the cosmic order. Neither does he need to seek enjoyment whose very nature is Bliss, Joy, Peace. As for competing with others, with whom should he compete who has lovingly identified himself with all? With whom should he struggle who has sacrificed himself for all? Whose blind, misguided, and ineffectual competition should he fear who has reached the source of all blessedness, and who receives at the hands of the Father all necessary things? Having lost himself (his selfish personality), he has found himself (his divine nature, Love); and Love and all the effects of Love now compose his life. He can now joyfully exclaim—

I have made the acquaintance of the Master of Compassion;
I have put on the Garment of the Perfect Law;
I have entered the realm of the Great Reality;
Wandering is ended, for Rest is accomplished;
Pain and sorrow have ceased, for Peace is entered into;
Confusion is dissolved, for Unity is made manifest;
Error is vanquished, for Truth is revealed!

The Harmonizing Principle, Righteousness, or Divine Love, being found, all things are seen as they are, and not through the illusory mediums of selfishness and opinion; the universe is *One,* and all its manifold operations are the manifestation of *one Law.* Hitherto in this work *laws* have been referred to, and also spoken of as being *higher* and *lower,* and this distinction was necessary; but now the Kingdom is reached, we see that all the forces operative in human life are the varied manifestations of the One Supreme Law of Love. It is by virtue of this Law that Humanity suffers, that, by the intensity of its sufferings, it shall at last become purified and wise, and so relinquish the source of suffering, which is selfishness.

The Law and foundation of the universe being Love, it follows that all self-seeking is opposed to that Law, is an effort to overcome or ignore the Law, and as a result, every self-seeking act and thought is followed by the exact quota of suffering which is required to annul its effect, and so maintain the universal harmony. All suffering is, therefore, the *restraint* which the Law puts upon ignorance and selfishness, and out of such painful restraint Wisdom at last emerges.

There being no strife and no selfishness in the Kingdom, there is therefore no suffering, no restraint; there is perfect harmony, equipoise, rest. Those who have entered it do not follow any animal inclinations (they have none to follow), but live in accordance with the highest Wisdom. Their nature is Love, and they live in love toward all. They are never troubled about "making a living," as they are Life itself, living in the very Heart of Life; and should any material or other need arise, that need is immediately supplied without any anxiety or struggle on their part. Should they be called to undertake any work, the money and friends needed to carry out that work are immediately forthcoming. Having ceased to violate their principles, all their needs are supplied through legitimate channels. Any money or help required always comes through the instrumentality of good people who are either living in the Kingdom themselves, or are working for its accomplishment. Those who live in the Kingdom of Love have all their needs supplied by the Law of Love, with all freedom from unrest, just as those who live in the kingdom of self only meet their needs by much strife and suffering. Having altered the root cause in their heart they have altered all the effects in their inner and outer life. As self is the root cause of all strife and suffering, so Love is the root cause of all peace and bliss.

Those who are at rest in the Kingdom do not look for happiness to any outward possession. They see that all such possessions are mere transient effects that come when they are required, and after their purpose is served, pass away. They never think of these things (money, clothing, food, etc.) except as mere accessories and *effects* of the true Life. They are therefore freed from all anxiety and trouble, and resting in Love, they are the embodiment of happiness. Standing upon the imperishable Principles of Purity, Compassion, Wisdom, and Love, they are immortal, and know they are immortal; they are one with God (the Supreme Good), and know they are one with God. Seeing the realities of things, they can find no room anywhere for condemnation. All the operations that obtain upon the earth they see as instruments of the Good Law, even those called *evil*. All men are essentially divine, though unaware of their divine nature, and all their acts are efforts, even though many of them are dark and impotent, to realize some higher good. All so-called evil is seen to be rooted in ignorance, even those deeds that are called *deliberately wicked*, so that condemnation ceases, and Love and Compassion become all in all.

But let it not be supposed that the children of the Kingdom live in ease and indolence (these two sins are the first that have to be eradicated when the search for the Kingdom is entered upon); they live in a peaceful activity; in fact, *they only* truly live, for the life of self with its train of worries, griefs, and fears, is not *real* life. They perform all their duties with the most scrupulous diligence, apart from thoughts of self, and employ all their means, as well as powers and faculties, which are greatly intensified, in building up the Kingdom of Righteousness in the hearts of others and in the world around them. This is their work—first by example, then by precept. Having sold all that they have (renounced all self-interest in their possessions), they now give to the poor (give of their rich store of wisdom, love, and peace to the needy in spirit, the weary and broken-hearted), and follow the Christ whose name is Love. And they sorrow no more, but live in perpetual gladness, for though they see the suffering in the world, they also see the final Bliss and the Eternal Refuge of Love, to which whosoever is ready may come *now*, and to which all will come at last.

The children of the Kingdom *are known by their life*. They manifest the fruits of the Spirit—"love, joy, peace, long-suffering, kindness, goodness, faithfulness, meekness, temperance, self-control"— under all circumstances and vicissitudes. They are entirely free from anger, fear, suspicion, jealousy, caprice, anxiety, and grief. Living in the Righteousness of God, they manifest qualities which are the very reverse of those which obtain in the world, and which are regarded by the world as foolishness. They demand no *rights*; they do not defend themselves; do not retaliate; do good to those who attempt to injure them; manifest the same gentle spirit toward those who oppose and attack them

AT REST IN THE KINGDOM AND ALL THINGS ADDED

as toward those who agree with them; do not pass judgment on others; condemn no man and no system, and live at peace with all.

The Kingdom of Heaven is perfect trust, perfect knowledge, perfect peace. All is music, sweetness, and tranquillity. No irritations, no bad tempers, no harsh words, no suspicions, no lust, and no disturbing elements can enter there. Its children live in perfect sweetness, forgiving and forgiven, ministering to others with kindly thoughts, words, and deeds. And that Kingdom is in the heart of every man and woman; it is their rightful heritage, their own Kingdom; theirs to enter *now*. But *no sin can enter therein;* no self-born thought or deed can pass its Golden Gates; no impure desire can defile its radiant robes. All may enter it who will, but all *must pay the price*, and that is—*the unconditional abandonment of self.* "If thou wilt be perfect, sell all that thou hast"; but at these words the world turns away "sorrowful, for it is very rich"; rich in money which it cannot keep; rich in fears which it cannot let go; rich in selfish loves to which it greedily clings; rich in grievous partings which it would fain escape; rich in seeking enjoyment; rich in pain and sorrow; rich in strife and suffering; rich in excitement and woe; rich in all things which are not riches, but poor in riches themselves which are not to be found outside the Kingdom; rich in all things that pertain to darkness and death, but poor in those things which are Light and Life.

He, then, who would realize the Kingdom, let him pay the price and enter. If he have a great and holy faith he can do it *now*, and, letting fall from him like a garment the self to which he has been clinging, stand free. If he have less faith, he must rise above self more slowly, and find the Kingdom by daily effort and patient work.

The Temple of Righteousness is built, and its four walls are the four Principles—Purity, Wisdom, Compassion, Love. Peace is its roof, its floor its Steadfastness, its entrance-door is Selfless Duty, its atmosphere is Inspiration, and its music is the Joy of the perfect. It cannot be shaken, and, being eternal and indestructible, there is no more need to seek protection in taking thought for the things of the morrow. And the Kingdom of Heaven being established in the heart, the obtaining of the material necessities of life is no more considered, for, having found the Highest, all these things are added as effect to cause; the struggle for existence has ceased, and the spiritual, mental, and material needs are daily supplied from the universal abundance:

> *Long I sought thee, Spirit holy,*
> *Master Spirit, meek and lowly;*
> *Sought thee with a silent sorrow, brooding o'er the woes of men;*
> *Vainly sought thy yoke of meekness*
> *'Neath the weight of woe and weakness;*
> *Finding not, yet in my failing, seeking o'er and o'er again.*

In unrest and doubt and sadness
  Dwelt I, yet I knew thy Gladness
Waited somewhere; somewhere greeted torn and sorrowing hearts like mine;
  Knew that somehow I should find thee,
  Leaving sin and woe behind me,
And at last thy Love would bid me enter into Rest divine.

  Hatred, mockery, and reviling
  Scorched my seeking soul, defiling
That which should have been thy Temple, wherein thou should'st move and dwell;
  Praying, striving, hoping, calling;
  Suffering, sorrowing in my falling,
Still I sought thee, groping blindly in the gloomy depths of Hell.

  And I sought thee till I found thee;
  And the dark Powers all around me
Fled, and left me silent, peaceful, brooding o'er thy holy themes;
  From within me and without me
  Fled they when I ceased to doubt thee;
And I found thee in thy Glory, mighty Master of my dreams!

  Yea, I found thee, Spirit holy,
  Beautiful and pure and lowly;
Found thy Joy and Peace and Gladness; found thee in thy House of Rest;
  Found thy strength in Love and Meekness,
  And my pain and woe and weakness
Left me, and I walked the Pathway trodden only by the blest.

PART II

THE HEAVENLY LIFE

THE DIVINE CENTER

The secret of life, of abundant life, with its strength, its felicity, and its unbroken peace is to find the Divine Center within oneself, and to live in and from that, instead of in that outer circumference of disturbances—the clamors, cravings, and argumentations which make up the animal and intellectual man. These selfish elements constitute the mere husks of life, and must be thrown away by him who would penetrate to the Central Heart of things—to Life itself.

Not to know that within you that is changeless, and defiant of time and death, is not to know anything, but is to play vainly with unsubstantial reflections in the Mirror of Time. Not to find within you those passionless Principles which are not moved by the strifes and shows and vanities of the world is to find nothing but illusions which vanish as they are grasped.

He who resolves that he will not rest satisfied with appearances, shadows, illusions shall, by the piercing light of that resolve, disperse every fleeting phantasy, and shall enter into the substance and reality of life. He shall learn how to live, and he shall *live*. He shall be the slave of no passion, the servant of no opinion, the votary of no fond error. Finding the Divine Center within his own heart, he will be pure and calm and strong and wise, and will ceaselessly radiate the Heavenly Life in which he lives—*which is himself*.

Having betaken himself to the Divine Refuge within, and remaining there, a man is free from sin. All his yesterdays are as the tide-washed and untrodden sands; no sin shall rise up against him to torment and accuse him and destroy his sacred peace; the fires of remorse cannot scorch him, nor can the storms of regret devastate his dwelling-place. His tomorrows are as seeds which shall germinate, bursting into beauty and potency of life, and no doubt shall shake his trust, no uncertainty rob him of repose. The *Present* is his, only in the immortal Present does he live, and it is as the eternal vault of blue above which looks down silently and calmly, yet radiant with purity and light, upon the upturned and tear-stained faces of the centuries.

Men love their desires, for gratification seems sweet to them, but its end is pain and vacuity; they love the argumentations of the intellect, for egotism seems most desirable to them, but the fruits thereof are humiliation and sorrow. When the soul has reached the end of gratification and reaped the bitter fruits of egotism, it is ready to receive the Divine Wisdom and to enter into the Divine Life. Only the crucified can be transfigured; only by the death of self can the Lord of the heart rise again into the Immortal Life, and stand radiant upon the Olivet of Wisdom.

Thou hast thy trials? Every outward trial is the replica of an inward imperfection. Thou shalt grow wise by knowing this, and shalt thereby transmute trial into active joy, finding the Kingdom where trial cannot come. When wilt thou learn thy lessons, O child of earth! All thy sorrows cry out against thee; every pain is thy just accuser, and thy griefs are but the shadows of thy unworthy and perishable self. The Kingdom of Heaven is thine; how long wilt thou reject it, preferring the lurid atmosphere of Hell—the hell of thy self-seeking self?

Where self is not, there is the Garden of the Heavenly Life, and

> *There spring the healing streams*
> *Quenching all thirst! there bloom the immortal flowers*
> *Carpeting all the way with joy! there throng*
> *Swiftest and sweetest hours!*

The redeemed sons of God, the glorified in body and spirit, are "bought with a price," and that price is the crucifixion of the personality, the death of self; and having put away that within which is the source of all discord, they have found the universal Music, the abiding Joy.

Life is more than motion, it is Music; more than rest, it is Peace; more than work, it is Duty; more than labor, it is Love; more than enjoyment, it is Blessedness; more than acquiring money and position and reputation, it is Knowledge, Purpose, strong and high Resolve.

Let the impure turn to Purity, and they shall be pure; let the weak resort to Strength, and they shall be strong; let the ignorant fly to Knowledge, and they shall be wise. All things are man's, and he chooses that which he will have. To-day he chooses in ignorance, to-morrow he shall choose in Wisdom. He shall "work out his own salvation" whether he believe it or not, for he cannot escape himself, nor transfer to another the eternal responsibility of his own soul. By no theological subterfuge shall he trick the Law of his being, which shall shatter all his selfish makeshifts and excuses for right thinking and right doing. Nor shall God do for him that which it is destined his soul shall accomplish for itself. What would you say of a man who, wanting to possess a mansion in which to dwell peacefully, purchased the site and then knelt down and asked God to build the house for him? Would you not say that such a man was foolish? And of another man who, having purchased the land, set the architects and builders and carpenters at work to erect the edifice, would you not say that he was wise? And as it is in the building of a material house, even so it is in the building of a spiritual mansion. Brick by brick, pure thought upon pure thought, good deed upon good deed, must the habitation of a blameless life rise from its sure foundation until at last it stands out in all the majesty of its faultless proportions. Not by caprice, nor gift, nor favor does a man obtain the spiritual realities, but by diligence, watchfulness, energy, and effort.

> *Strong is the soul, and wise and beautiful;*
> *The seeds of God-like power are in us still;*
> *Gods are we, bards, saints, heroes, if we will.*

The spiritual Heart of man is the Heart of the universe, and, finding that Heart, man finds the strength to accomplish all things. He finds there also the Wisdom to see things as they are. He finds there the Peace that is divine. At the center of man's being is the Music which orders the stars—the Eternal Harmony. He who would find Blessedness, let him find himself; let him abandon every discordant desire, every inharmonious thought, every unlovely habit and deed, and he will find that Grace and Beauty and Harmony which form the indestructible essence of his own being.

Men fly from creed to creed, and find—unrest; they travel in many lands, and discover—disappointment; they build themselves beautiful mansions, and plant pleasant gardens, and reap—ennui and discomfort. Not until a man falls back upon the Truth within himself does he find rest and satisfaction; not until he builds the inward Mansion of Faultless Conduct does he find the endless and incorruptible Joy, and, having obtained that, he will infuse it into all his outward doings and possessions.

If a man would have peace, let him exercise the spirit of Peace; if he would find love, let him dwell in the spirit of Love; if he would escape suffering, let him cease to inflict it; if he would do noble things for humanity, let him cease to do ignoble things for himself. If he will but quarry the mine of his own soul, he shall find there all the materials for building whatsoever he will, and he shall find there also the central Rock on which to build in safety.

Howsoever a man works to right the world, it will never be righted until he has put himself right. This may be written upon the heart as a mathematical axiom. It is not enough to preach Purity, men must cease from lust; to exhort to love, they must abandon hatred; to extol self-sacrifice, they must yield up self; to adorn with mere words the Perfect Life, they must *be* perfect.

When a man can no longer carry the weight of his many sins, let him fly to the Christ, whose throne is the center of his own heart, and he shall become lighthearted, entering the glad company of the Immortals.

When he can no longer bear the burden of his accumulated learning, let a man leave his books,

his science, his philosophy, and come back to himself, and he shall find within that which he outwardly sought and found not—his own divinity.

He ceases to argue about God who has found God within. Relying upon that calm strength
which is not the strength of self, he *lives* God, manifesting in his daily life the Highest Goodness,
which is Eternal Life.

THE ETERNAL NOW

Now is the reality in which time is contained. It is more and greater than time; it is an
ever-present reality. It knows neither past nor future, and is eternally potent and substantial. Every minute, every day, every year is a dream as soon as it has passed, and exists
only as an imperfect and unsubstantial picture in the memory, if it be not entirely obliterated.

Past and future are dreams; *now* is a reality. All things are now; all power, all possibility, all action
is now. Not to act and accomplish now is not to act and accomplish at all. To live in thoughts of what
you might have done, or in dreams of what you mean to do, this is folly; but to put away regret, to
anchor anticipation, and to do and to work *now*, this is wisdom.

While a man is dwelling upon the past or future he is missing the present; he is forgetting to live
now. All things are possible now, and *only* now. Without wisdom to guide him, and mistaking the
unreal for the real, a man says, "If I had done so and so last week, last month, or last year, it would
have been better with me to-day"; or, "I know what is best to be done, and I will do it to-morrow."
The selfish cannot comprehend the vast importance and value of the present, and fail to see it as the
substantial reality of which past and future are the empty reflections. It may truly be said that past
and future do not exist except as negative shadows, and to live in them—that is, in the regretful and
selfish contemplation of them—is to miss the reality in life.

> The Present, the Present is all thou hast
> 　　For thy sure possessing;
> Like the patriarch's angel, hold it fast,
> 　　Till it gives its blessing.

All which is real now remaineth,
   And fadeth never:
The hand which upholds it now sustaineth
   The soul for ever.

Then of what is to be, and of what is done,
   Why queriest thou?
The past and the time to be are one,
   And both are NOW!

Man has all power now; but not knowing this, he says, "I will be perfect next year, or in so many years, or in so many lives." The dwellers in the Kingdom of God, who live only in the now, say, "I am perfect now," and refraining from all sin now, and ceaselessly guarding the portals of the mind, not looking to the past nor to the future, nor turning to the left or right, they remain eternally holy and blessed. "Now is the accepted time; now is the day of salvation."

Say to yourself, "I will live in my Ideal now; I will manifest my Ideal now; I will be my Ideal now; and all that tempts me away from my Ideal I will not listen to; I will listen only to the voice of my Ideal." Thus resolving and thus doing, you shall not depart from the Highest, and shall eternally manifest the True.

Afoot and light-hearted, I take to the open road.
Henceforth I ask not good fortune: I myself am good fortune.
Henceforth I whimper no more, postpone no more, need nothing;
Done with indoor complaints, libraries, querulous criticisms.
Strong and content, I take to the open road.

Cease to tread every byway of dependence, every winding side-way that tempts thy soul into the shadow-land of the past and the future, and manifest thy native and divine strength now. Come out into "the open road."

That which you would be, and hope to be, you may be now. Non-accomplishment resides in your perpetual postponement, and, having the power to postpone, you also have the power to accomplish—to perpetually accomplish: realize this truth, and you shall be to-day, and every day, the ideal man of whom you dreamed.

Virtue consists in fighting sin day after day, but holiness consists in leaving sin, unnoticed and ignored, to die by the wayside; and this is done, can only be done, in the living now. Say not unto thy soul, "Thou shalt be purer to-morrow"; but rather say, "Thou shalt be pure now." To-morrow is too late for anything, and he who sees his help and salvation in to-morrow shall continually fail and fall to-day.

Thus didst fall yesterday? Didst sin grievously? Having realized this, leave it instantly and forever, and watch that thou sinnest not now. The while thou art bewailing the past every gate of thy soul remains unguarded against the entrance of sin now. Thou shall not rise by grieving over the irre-mediable past, but by remedying the present.

The foolish man, loving the boggy side-path of procrastination rather than the firm Highway of Present Effort, says, "I will rise early to-morrow; I will get out of debt to-morrow; I will carry out my intentions to-morrow." But the wise man, realizing the momentous import of the Eternal Now, rises early to-day; keeps out of debt to-day; carries out his intentions to-day; and so never departs from strength and peace and ripe accomplishment.

That which is done now remains; that which is to be done to-morrow does not appear. It is wisdom to leave that which has not arrived, and to attend to that which is; and to attend to it with such a consecration of soul and concentration of effort as shall leave no possible loophole for regret to creep in.

A man's spiritual comprehension being clouded by the illusions of self, he says, "I was born on such a day, so many years ago, and shall die at my allotted time." But he was not born, neither will he die, for how can that which is immortal, which eternally *is*, be subject to birth and death? Let a man throw off his illusions, and then he will see that the birth and death of the *body* are the mere incidents of a journey, and not its beginning and end.

Looking back to happy beginnings, and forward to mournful endings, a man's eyes are blinded, so that he beholds not his own immortality; his ears are closed, so that he hears not the ever-present harmonies of Joy; and his heart is hardened, so that it pulsates not to the rhythmic sounds of Peace.

The universe, with all that it contains, is now. Put out thy hand, O man, and receive the fruits of Wisdom! Cease from thy greedy striving, thy selfish sorrowing, thy foolish regretting, and be content to *live*. Act now, and, lo! all things are done; live now, and, behold! thou art in the midst of Plenty; *be* now, and *know* that thou art perfect.

THE "ORIGINAL SIMPLICITY"

Life is simple. Being is simple. The universe is simple. Complexity arises in ignorance and self-delusion. The "Original Simplicity" of Lao-tze is a term expressive of the universe as it *is*, and not as it *appears*. Looking through the woven network of his own illusions, man sees interminable complication and unfathomable mystery, and so loses himself in the labyrinths of his own making. Let a man put away egotism, and he will see the universe in all the beauty of its pristine simplicity. Let him annihilate the delusion of the personal "I," and he will destroy all the illusions which spring from that "I." He will thus "rebecome a little child," and will "revert to Original Simplicity."

When a man succeeds in entirely forgetting (annihilating) his personal self, he becomes a mirror in which the universal Reality is faultlessly reflected. He is awakened, and henceforward he lives, not in dreams, but realities.

Pythagoras saw the universe in the ten numbers, but even this simplicity may be further reduced, and the universe ultimately be found to be contained in the number ONE, for all the numerals and all their infinite complications are but additions of the *One*.

Let life cease to be lived as a fragmentary thing, and let it be lived as a perfect Whole; the simplicity of the Perfect will then be revealed. How shall the fragment comprehend the Whole? Yet how simple that the Whole should comprehend the fragment. How shall sin perceive Holiness? Yet how plain that Holiness should understand sin. He who would become the Greater let him abandon the lesser. In no form is the circle contained, but in the circle all forms are contained. In no color is the radiant light imprisoned, but in the radiant light all colors are embodied. Let a man destroy all the forms of self, and he shall apprehend the Circle of Perfection; let him submerge, in the silent depths of his being, the varying colors of his thoughts and desires, and he shall be illuminated with the White Light of Divine Knowledge. In the perfect chord of music the single note, though forgotten, is indispensably contained, and the drop of water becomes of supreme usefulness by losing itself in the ocean. Sink thyself compassionately in the heart of humanity, and thou shalt reproduce the harmonies of Heaven; lose thyself in unlimited love toward all, and thou shalt work enduring works and shalt become one with the eternal Ocean of Bliss.

Man evolves outward to the periphery of complexity, and then involves backward to the Central Simplicity. When a man discovers that it is mathematically impossible for him to know the universe before knowing himself, he then starts upon the Way which leads to the Original Simplicity. He begins to unfold from within, and as he unfolds himself, he enfolds the universe.

Cease to speculate about God, and find the all-embracing Good within thee, then shalt thou see the emptiness and vanity of speculation, knowing thyself one with God.

He who will not give up his secret lust, his covetousness, his anger, his opinion about this or that can see nor know nothing; he will remain a dullard in the school of Wisdom, though he be accounted learned in the colleges.

If a man would find the Key of Knowledge, let him find himself. Thy sins are not thyself; they are not any part of thyself; they are diseases which thou hast come to love. Cease to cling to them, and they will no longer cling to thee. Let them fall away, and thy self shall stand revealed. Thou shalt then know thyself as Comprehensive Vision, Invincible Principle, Immortal Life, and eternal Good.

The impure man believes impurity to be his rightful condition, but the pure man knows himself as pure being; he also, penetrating the Veils, sees all others as pure being. Purity is extremely simple, and needs no argument to support it; impurity is interminably complex, and is ever involved in defensive argument. Truth *lives* itself. A blameless life is the only witness of Truth. Men cannot see, and will not accept the witness until they find it within themselves; and having found it, a man becomes silent before his fellows. Truth is so simple that it cannot be found in the region of argument and advertisement, and so silent that it is only manifested in actions.

So extremely simple is Original Simplicity that a man must let go his hold of everything before he can perceive it. The great arch is strong by virtue of the hollowness underneath, and a wise man becomes strong and invincible by emptying himself.

Meekness, Patience, Love, Compassion, and Wisdom—these are the dominant qualities of Original Simplicity; therefore the imperfect cannot understand it. Wisdom only can apprehend Wisdom; therefore the fool says, "No man is wise." The imperfect man says, "No man can be perfect," and he therefore remains where he is. Though he live with a perfect man all his life, he shall not behold his perfection. Meekness he will call cowardice; Patience, Love, and Compassion he will see as weakness; and Wisdom will appear to him as folly. Faultless discrimination belongs to the Perfect Whole, and resides not in any part; therefore men are exhorted to refrain from judgment until they have themselves manifested the Perfect Life.

Arriving at Original Simplicity, opacity disappears, and the universal transparency becomes apparent. He who has found the indwelling Reality of his own being has found the original and universal Reality. Knowing the Divine Heart within, all hearts are known, and the thoughts of all men become his who has become the master of his own thoughts; therefore the good man does not defend himself, but molds the minds of others to his own likeness.

As the problematical transcends crudity, so Pure Goodness transcends the problematical. All problems vanish when Pure Goodness is reached; therefore the good man is called "The slayer of illusions." What problem can vex where sin is not? O thou who strivest loudly and restest not! Retire into the holy silence of thine own being, and live therefrom. So shalt thou, finding Pure Goodness, rend in twain the Veil of the Temple of Illusion, and shalt enter into the Patience, Peace, and transcendent Glory of the Perfect, for Pure Goodness and Original Simplicity are one.

THE UNFAILING WISDOM

A man should be superior to his possessions, his body, his circumstances and surroundings, and the opinions of others and their attitude toward him. Until he is this, he is not strong and steadfast. He should also rise superior to his own desires and opinions; and until he is this, he is not wise.

The man who identifies himself with his possessions will feel that all is lost when these are lost; he who regards himself as the outcome and the tool of circumstances will weakly fluctuate with every change in his outward condition; and great will be his unrest and pain who seeks to stand upon the approbation of others.

To detach oneself from every outward thing, and to rest securely upon the inward Virtue, this is the Unfailing Wisdom. Having this Wisdom, a man will be the same whether in riches or poverty. The one cannot add to his strength, nor the other rob him of his serenity. Neither can riches defile him who has washed away all the inward defilement, nor the lack of them degrade him who has ceased to degrade the temple of his soul.

To refuse to be enslaved by any outward thing or happening, regarding all such things and happenings as for your use, for your education, this is Wisdom. To the wise all occurrences are *good*, and, having no eye for evil, they grow wiser every day. They utilize all things, and thus put all things under their feet. They see all their mistakes as soon as made, and accept them as lessons of intrinsic value, knowing that there are no mistakes in the Divine Order. They thus rapidly approach the Divine Perfection. They are moved by none, yet learn from all. They crave love from none, yet give love to all. To learn, and not to be shaken; to love where one is not loved; herein lies the strength which shall never fail a man. The man who says in his heart, "I will teach all men, and learn from none" will neither teach nor learn while he is in that frame of mind, but will remain in his folly.

All strength and wisdom and power and knowledge a man will find within himself, but he will not find it in egotism; he will only find it in obedience, submission, and willingness to learn. He must obey the Higher, and not glorify himself in the lower. He who stands upon egotism, rejecting reproof, instruction, and the lessons of experience, will surely fall; yea, he is already fallen. Said a great Teacher to his disciples, "Those who shall be a lamp unto themselves, relying upon themselves only, and not relying upon any external help, but holding fast to the Truth as their lamp, and, seeking their salvation in the Truth alone, shall not look for assistance to any besides themselves, it is they among my disciples who shall reach the very topmost height! *But they must be willing to learn.*" The wise man is always anxious to learn, but never anxious to teach, for he knows that the true Teacher is in the heart of every man, and must ultimately be found there by all. The foolish man, being governed largely by vanity, is very anxious to teach, but unwilling to learn, not having found the Holy Teacher within who speaks wisdom to the humbly listening soul. Be self-reliant, but let thy self-reliance be saintly and not selfish.

Folly and wisdom, weakness and strength are within a man, and not in any external thing, neither do they spring from any external cause. A man cannot be strong for another, he can only be strong for himself; he cannot overcome for another, he can only overcome of himself. You may learn of another, but you must accomplish for yourself. Put away all external props, and rely upon the Truth within you. A creed will not bear a man up in the hour of temptation; he must possess the inward Knowledge which slays temptation. A speculative philosophy will prove a shadowy thing in the time of calamity; a man must have the inward Wisdom which puts an end to grief.

Goodness, which is the aim of all religions, is distinct from religions themselves. Wisdom, which is the aim of every philosophy, is distinct from all philosophies. The Unfailing Wisdom is found only by constant practice in pure thinking and well-doing, by harmonizing one's mind and heart to those things which are beautiful, lovable, and true.

In whatever condition a man finds himself, he can always find the True; and he can find it only by so utilizing his present condition as to become strong and wise. The effeminate hankering after rewards, and the craven fear of punishment, let them be put away forever, and let a man joyfully bend himself to the faithful performance of all his duties, forgetting himself and his worthless pleasures, and living strong and pure and self-contained; so shall he surely find the Unfailing Wisdom, the God-like Patience and strength. "The situation that has not its Duty, its Ideal, was never yet occupied by man. . . . Here or nowhere is thy Ideal. Work it out therefrom, and, working, believe, live, be free. The Ideal is in thyself, the impediment, too, is in thyself; thy condition is but the stuff thou art to shape that same Ideal out of. What matters whether such stuff be of this sort or that, so the form thou give it be heroic, be poetic? Oh, thou that pinest in the imprisonment of the Actual, and criest bitterly to the gods for a kingdom wherein to rule and create, know this of a truth: the thing thou seekest is already within thee, here and now, couldest thou only see!"

All that is beautiful and blessed is in thyself, not in thy neighbor's wealth. Thou art poor? Thou art poor indeed if thou art not stronger than thy poverty! Thou hast suffered calamities? Well, wilt thou cure calamity by adding anxiety to it? Canst thou mend a broken vase by weeping over it, or restore a lost delight by thy lamentations? There is no evil but will vanish if thou wilt wisely meet it. The God-like soul does not grieve over that which has been, is, or will be, but perpetually finds the Divine Good, and gains wisdom by every occurrence.

Fear is the shadow of selfishness, and cannot live where loving Wisdom is. Doubt, anxiety, and worry are unsubstantial shades in the underworld of self, and shall no more trouble him who will climb the serene altitudes of his soul. Grief, also, will be forever dispelled by him who will comprehend the Law of his being. He who so comprehends shall find the Supreme Law of Life, and he shall find that it is Love, that it is imperishable Love. He shall become one with that Love, and loving all, with mind freed from all hatred and folly, he shall receive the invincible protection which Love affords. Claiming nothing, he shall suffer no loss; seeking no pleasure, he shall find no grief; and employing all his powers as instruments of service, he shall evermore live in the highest state of blessedness and bliss.

Know this: Thou makest and unmakest thyself; thou standest and fallest by what thou art. Thou art a slave if thou preferrest to be; thou art a master if thou wilt make thyself one. Build upon thy animal desires and intellectual opinions, and thou buildest upon the sand; build upon Virtue and Holiness, and no wind nor tide shall shake thy strong abode. So shall the Unfailing Wisdom uphold thee in every emergency, and the Everlasting Arms gather thee to thy peace.

Lay up each year
Thy harvest of well-doing, wealth that kings
Nor thieves can take away. When all the things
Thou callest thine, goods, pleasures, honors fall,
Thou in thy virtue shalt survive them all.

THE MIGHT OF MEEKNESS

The mountain bends not to the fiercest storm, but it shields the fledgling and the lamb; and though all men tread upon it, yet it protects them, and bears them up upon its deathless bosom. Even so is it with the meek man who, though shaken and disturbed by none, yet compassionately bends to shield the lowliest creature, and, though he may be despised, lifts all men up, and lovingly protects them.

As glorious as the mountain in its silent might is the divine man in his silent Meekness; like its form, his loving compassion is expansive and sublime. Truly his body, like the mountain's base, is fixed in the valleys and the mists; but the summit of his being is eternally bathed in cloudless glory, and lives with the Silences.

He who has found Meekness has found divinity; he has realized the divine consciousness, and knows himself as divine. He also knows all others as divine, though they know it not themselves, being asleep and dreaming. Meekness is a divine quality, and as such is all-powerful. The meek man overcomes by not resisting, and by allowing himself to be defeated he attains to the Supreme Conquest.

The man who conquers another by force is strong; the man who conquers himself by Meekness is mighty. He who conquers another by force will himself likewise be conquered; he who conquers himself by Meekness will never be overthrown, for the human cannot overcome the divine. The meek man is triumphant in defeat. Socrates lives the more by being put to death; in the crucified Jesus the risen Christ is revealed, and Stephen in receiving his stoning defies the hurting power of stones. That which is real cannot be destroyed, but only that which is unreal. When a man finds that within him which is real, which is constant, abiding, changeless, and eternal, he enters into that Reality, and becomes meek. All the powers of darkness will come against him, but they will do him no hurt, and will at last depart from him.

The meek man is found in the time of trial; when other men fall he stands. His patience is not destroyed by the foolish passions of others, and when they come against him he does not "strive nor cry." He knows the utter powerlessness of all evil, having overcome it in himself, and lives in the changeless strength and power of divine Good.

Meekness is one aspect of the operation of that changeless Love which is at the Heart of all things, and is therefore an imperishable quality. He who lives in it is without fear, knowing the Highest, and having the lowest under his feet.

The meek man shines in darkness, and flourishes in obscurity. Meekness cannot boast, nor advertise itself, nor thrive on popularity. It is *practiced*, and is seen or not seen; being a spiritual quality it is perceived only by the eye of the spirit. Those who are not spiritually awakened see it not, nor do they love it, being enamored of, and blinded by, worldly shows and appearances. Nor does history take note of the meek man. Its glory is that of strife and self-aggrandizement; his is the glory of peace and gentleness. History chronicles the earthly, not the heavenly acts. Yet though he lives in obscurity he cannot be hidden (how can light be hid?); he continues to shine after he has withdrawn himself from the world, and is worshiped by the world which knew him not.

That the meek man should be neglected, abused, or misunderstood is reckoned by him as of no account, and therefore not to be considered, much less resisted. He knows that all such weapons are the flimsiest and most ineffectual of shadows. To them, therefore, who give him evil he gives good. He resists none, and thereby conquers all.

He who imagines he can be injured by others, and who seeks to justify and defend himself against them, does not understand Meekness, does not comprehend the essence and meaning of life. "He abused me, he beat me, he defeated me, he robbed me.—In those who harbor such thoughts hatred will never cease . . . for hatred ceases not by hatred at any time; hatred ceases by love." What sayest thou, thy neighbor has spoken of thee falsely? Well, what of that? Can a falsity hurt thee? That which is false is false, and there is an end of it. It is without life, and without power to hurt any but him who seeks to hurt by it. It is nothing to thee that thy neighbor should speak falsely of thee, but it is much to thee that thou shouldst resist him, and seek to justify thyself, for, by so doing, thou givest life and vitality to thy neighbor's falseness, so that thou art injured and distressed. Take all evil out of thine own heart, then shalt thou see the folly of resisting it in another. Thou wilt be trodden on? Thou art trodden on already if thou thinkest thus. The injury that thou seest as coming from another comes only from thyself. The wrong thought, or word, or act of another has no power to hurt thee unless thou galvanize it into life by thy passionate resistance, and so receivest it into thyself. If any man slander me, that is his concern, not mine. I have to do with my own soul, not with my neighbor's. Though all the world misjudge me, it is no business of mine; but that I should possess my soul in Purity and Love, that is all my business. There shall be no end to strife until men cease to justify themselves. He who would have wars cease let him cease to defend any party—let him cease to defend himself. Not by strife can peace come, but by ceasing from strife. The glory of Cæsar resides in the resistance of his enemies. They resist and fall. Give to Cæsar that which Cæsar demands, and Cæsar's glory and power are gone. Thus, by submission does the meek man conquer the strong man; but it is not that outward show of submission which is slavery, it is that inward and spiritual submission which is *freedom*.

Claiming no *rights*, the meek man is not troubled with self-defense and self-justification; he lives in love, and therefore comes under the immediate and vital protection of the Great Love which is the Eternal Law of the universe. He neither claims nor seeks his own; thus do all things come to him, and all the universe shields and protects him.

He who says, "I have tried Meekness, and it has failed" has not tried Meekness. It cannot be tried as an experiment. It is only arrived at by unreserved self-sacrifice. Meekness does not consist merely in non-resistance in action; it consists preëminently in non-resistance in *thought*, in ceasing to hold or to have any selfish, condemnatory, or retaliatory thoughts. The meek man, therefore, cannot "take offense" or have his "feelings hurt," living above hatred, folly, and vanity. Meekness can never fail.

O thou who searchest for the Heavenly Life! Strive after Meekness; increase thy patience and forbearance day by day; bid thy tongue cease from all harsh words; withdraw thy mind from selfish arguments, and refuse to brood upon thy wrongs; so living, thou shalt carefully tend and cultivate the pure and delicate flower of Meekness in thy heart, until at last, its divine sweetness and purity and beauteous perfection shall be revealed to thee, and thou shalt become gentle, joyful, and strong. Repine not that thou art surrounded by irritable and selfish people; but rather rejoice that thou art so favored as to have thine own imperfections revealed to thee, and that thou art so placed as to necessitate within thee a constant struggle for self-mastery and the attainment of perfection. The more there is of harshness and selfishness around thee, the greater is the need of thy Meekness and love. If others seek to wrong thee, all the more is it needful that thou shouldst cease from all wrong, and live in love; if others preach Meekness, humility, and love, and do not practice these, trouble not, nor be annoyed; but do thou, in the silence of thy heart, and in thy contact with others, *practice* these things, and they shall preach themselves. And though thou utter no declamatory word, and stand before no gathered audience, thou shalt teach the whole world. As thou becomest meek, thou shalt learn the deepest secrets of the universe. Nothing is hidden from him who overcomes himself. Into the cause of causes shalt thou penetrate, and lifting, one after another, every veil of illusion, shalt reach at last the inmost Heart of Being. Thus becoming one with Life, thou shalt know all life, and, seeing into causes, and knowing realities, thou shalt be no more anxious about thyself, and others, and the world, but shalt see that all things that are are engines of the Great Law. Canopied with gentleness, thou shalt bless where others curse; love where others hate; forgive where others condemn; yield where others strive; give up where others grasp; lose where others gain. And in their strength they shall be weak; and in thy weakness thou shalt be strong; yea, thou shalt mightily prevail. He that hath not unbroken gentleness hath not Truth:

Therefore when Heaven would save a man, it enfolds him with gentleness.

THE RIGHTEOUS MAN

The righteous man is invincible. No enemy can possibly overcome or confound him; and he needs no other protection than that of his own integrity and holiness.

As it is impossible for evil to overcome Good, so the righteous man can never be brought low by the unrighteous. Slander, envy, hatred, malice can never reach him, nor cause him any suffering, and those who try to injure him only succeed ultimately in bringing ignominy upon themselves.

The righteous man, having nothing to hide, committing no acts which require stealth, and harboring no thoughts and desires which he would not like others to know, is fearless and unashamed. His step is firm, his body upright, and his speech direct and without ambiguity. He looks everybody in the face. How can he fear any who wrongs none? How can he be ashamed before any who deceives none? And ceasing from all wrong he can never be wronged; ceasing from all deceit he can never be deceived.

The righteous man, performing all his duties with scrupulous diligence, and living above sin, is invulnerable at every point. He who has slain the inward enemies of virtue can never be brought low by any outward enemy; neither does he need to seek any protection against them, righteousness being an all-sufficient protection.

The unrighteous man is vulnerable at almost every point; living in his passions, the slave of prejudices, impulses, and ill-formed opinions, he is continually suffering (as he imagines) at the hands of others. The slanders, attacks, and accusations of others cause him great suffering because they have a basis of truth in himself; and not having the protection of righteousness, he endeavors to justify and protect himself by resorting to retaliation and specious argument, and even to subterfuge and deceit.

The partially righteous man is vulnerable at all those points where he falls short of righteousness, and should the righteous man fall from his righteousness, and give way to *one* sin, his invincibility is gone, for he has thereby placed himself where attack and accusation can justly reach and injure him, because he has first injured himself.

If a man suffers or is injured through the instrumentality of others, let him look to himself, and, putting aside self-pity and self-defense, he will find in his own heart the source of all his woe.

No evil can happen to the righteous man who has cut off the source of evil in himself; living in the All-Good, and abstaining from sin in thought, word, and deed, whatever happens to him is good; neither can any person, event, or circumstance cause him suffering, for the tyranny of circumstance is utterly destroyed for him who has broken the bonds of sin.

The suffering, the sorrowing, the weary, and broken-hearted ever seek a sorrowless refuge, a haven of perpetual peace. Let such fly to the refuge of the righteous life; let them come now and enter the haven of the sinless state, for sorrow cannot overtake the righteous; suffering cannot reach him who does not waste in self-seeking his spiritual substance; and he cannot be afflicted by weariness and unrest whose heart is at peace with all.

PERFECT LOVE

The Children of Light, who abide in the Kingdom of Heaven, see the universe, and all that it contains, as the manifestation of one Law—the Law of Love. They see Love as the molding, sustaining, protecting, and perfecting Power immanent in all things animate and inanimate. To them Love is not merely and only a rule of life, it is the Law of Life, it is Life itself. Knowing this, they order their whole life in accordance with Love, not regarding their own personality. By thus practicing obedience to the Highest, to divine Love, they become conscious partakers of the power of Love, and so arrive at perfect Freedom as Masters of Destiny.

The universe is preserved because Love is at the Heart of it. Love is the only preservative power. While there is hatred in the heart of man, he imagines the Law to be cruel, but when his heart is mellowed by Compassion and Love, he perceives that the Law is Infinite Kindness. So kind is the Law that it protects man against his own ignorance. Man, in his puny efforts to subvert the Law by attaching undue importance to his own little personality, brings upon himself such trains of suffering that he is at last compelled, in the depth of his afflictions, to seek for Wisdom; and finding Wisdom, he finds Love, and knows it as the Law of his being, the Law of the universe. Love does not punish; man punishes himself by his own hatred; by striving to preserve evil which has no life by which to preserve itself, and by trying to subvert Love, which can neither be overcome nor destroyed, being of the substance of Life. When a man burns himself, does he accuse the fire? Therefore, when a man suffers, let him look for some ignorance or disobedience within himself.

Love is Perfect Harmony, pure Bliss, and contains, therefore, no element of suffering. Let a man think no thought and do no act which is not in accordance with pure Love, and suffering shall no more trouble him. If a man would know Love, and partake of its undying bliss, he must practice it in his heart; he must become Love.

He who always acts from the spirit of Love is never deserted, is never left in a dilemma or difficulty, for Love (impersonal Love) is both Knowledge and Power. He who has learned how to Love has learned how to master every difficulty, how to transmute every failure into success, how to clothe every event and condition in garments of blessedness and beauty.

The way to Love is by self-mastery, and, traveling that way, a man builds himself up in Knowledge as he proceeds. Arriving at Love, he enters into full possession of body and mind, by right of the divine Power which he has earned.

"Perfect Love casteth out fear." To know Love is to know that there is no harmful power in the whole universe. Even sin itself, which the worldly and unbelieving imagine is so unconquerable, is known as a very weak and perishable thing that shrinks away and disappears before the compelling power of Good. Perfect Love is perfect Harmlessness. And he who has destroyed, in himself, all thoughts of harm, and all desire to harm, receives the universal protection, and knows himself to be invincible.

Perfect Love is perfect Patience. Anger and irritability cannot dwell with it nor come near it. It sweetens every bitter occasion with the perfume of holiness, and transmutes trial into divine strength. Complaint is foreign to it. He who loves bewails nothing, but accepts all things and conditions as heavenly guests; he is therefore constantly blessed, and sorrow does not overtake him.

Perfect Love is perfect Trust. He who has destroyed the desire to grasp can never be troubled with the fear of loss. Loss and gain are alike foreign to him. Steadfastly maintaining a loving attitude of mind toward all, and pursuing, in the performance of his duties, a constant and loving activity, Love protects him and evermore supplies him in fullest measure with all that he needs.

Perfect Love is perfect Power. The wisely loving heart commands without exercising any authority. All things and all men obey him who obeys the Highest. He thinks, and lo! he has already accomplished! He speaks, and behold! a world hangs upon his simple utterances! He has harmonized his thoughts with the Imperishable and Unconquerable Forces, and for him weakness and uncertainty are no more. His every thought is a purpose; his every act an accomplishment; he moves with the Great Law, not setting his puny personal will against it, and he thus becomes a channel through which the divine Power can flow in unimpeded and beneficent expression. He has thus become Power itself.

Perfect Love is perfect Wisdom. The man who loves all is the man who knows all. Having thoroughly learned the lessons of his own heart, he knows the tasks and trials of other hearts, and adapts himself to them gently and without ostentation. Love illuminates the intellect; without it the intellect is blind and cold and lifeless. Love succeeds where the intellect fails; sees where the intellect is blind;

knows where the intellect is ignorant. Reason is only completed in Love, and is ultimately absorbed in it. Love is the Supreme Reality in the universe, and as such it contains all Truth. Infinite Tenderness enfolds and cherishes the universe; therefore is the wise man gentle and childlike and tender-hearted. He sees that the one thing which all creatures need is Love, and he gives unstintingly. He knows that all occasions require the adjusting power of Love, and he ceases from harshness.

To the eye of Love all things are revealed, not as an infinity of complex effects, but in the light of Eternal Principles, out of which spring all causes and effects, and back into which they return. "God is Love"; therefore than Love there is nothing more perfect. He who would find pure knowledge, let him find pure Love.

Perfect Love is perfect Peace. He who dwells with it has completed his pilgrimage in the underworld of sorrow. With mind calm and heart at rest, he has banished the shadows of grief, and knows the deathless Life.

If thou wouldst perfect thyself in Knowledge, perfect thyself in Love. If thou wouldst reach the Highest, ceaselessly cultivate a loving and compassionate heart.

PERFECT FREEDOM

There is no bondage in the Heavenly Life. There is Perfect Freedom. This is its great glory. This Supreme Freedom is gained only by obedience. He who obeys the Highest coöperates with the Highest, and so masters every force within himself and every condition without. A man may choose the lower and neglect the Higher, but the Higher is never overcome by the lower; herein lies the revelation of Freedom. Let a man choose the Higher and abandon the lower; he shall then establish himself as an Overcomer, and shall realize Perfect Freedom.

To give the reins to inclination is the only slavery; to conquer oneself is the only freedom. The slave to self loves his chains, and will not have one of them broken for fear he would be depriving himself of some cherished delight. He clings to his gratifications and vanities, regarding freedom from them as an empty and undesirable condition. He thus defeats and enslaves himself.

By self-enlightenment is Perfect Freedom found. While a man remains ignorant of himself, of his desires, of his emotions and thoughts, and of the inward causes which mold his life and destiny, having neither control nor understanding of himself, he will remain in bondage to passion, sorrow, suffering, and fluctuating fortune. The Land of Perfect Freedom lies through the Gate of Knowledge.

All outward oppression is but the shadow and effect of the real oppression within. For ages the oppressed have cried for liberty, and a thousand man-made statutes have failed to give it to them. They can give it only to themselves; they shall find it only in obedience to the Divine Statutes which are inscribed upon their hearts. Let them resort to the inward Freedom, and the shadow of oppression shall no more darken the earth. Let men cease to oppress themselves, and no man shall oppress his brother.

Men legislate for an *outward* freedom, yet continue to render such freedom impossible of achievement by fostering an inward condition of enslavement. They thus pursue a shadow without, and ignore the substance within. Man will be free when he is freed from self. All outward forms of bondage and oppression will cease to be when man ceases to be the willing bond-slave of passion, error, and ignorance. Freedom is to the free.

While men cling to weakness they cannot have strength; while they love darkness they can receive no light; and so long as they prefer bondage they can enjoy no liberty. Strength, light, and freedom are ready now, and can be had by all who love them, who aspire to them. Freedom does not reside in coöperative aggression, for this will always produce, reactively, coöperative defense—hence warfare, hatred, party strife, and the destruction of liberty. Freedom resides in individual self-conquest. The emancipation of Humanity is frustrated and withheld by the self-enslavement of the unit. Thou who criest to man and God for liberty, liberate thyself!

The Heavenly Freedom is freedom from passion, from cravings, from opinions, from the tyranny of the flesh, and the tyranny of the intellect—this first, and then all outward freedom, as effect to cause. The Freedom that begins within, and extends outwardly until it embraces the whole man, is an emancipation so complete, all-embracing, and perfect as to leave no galling fetter unbroken. Free thy soul from all sin, and thou shalt walk a freed and fearless man in the midst of a world of fearful slaves; and, seeing thee, many slaves shall take heart and shall join thee in thy glorious freedom.

He who says, "My worldly duties are irksome to me; I will leave them and go into solitude, where I shall be as free as the air," and thinks to gain freedom thus, will find only a harder slavery. The tree of Freedom is rooted in Duty, and he who would pluck its sweet fruits must discover joy in Duty.

Glad-hearted, calm and ready for all tasks is he who is freed from self. Irksomeness and weariness cannot enter his heart, and his divine strength lightens every burden so that its weight is not felt. He does not run away from Duty with his chains about him, but breaks them and stands free.

Make thyself pure; make thyself proof against weakness, temptation, and sin; for only in thine own heart and mind shalt thou find that Perfect Freedom for which the whole world sighs and seeks in vain.

GREATNESS AND GOODNESS

Goodness, simplicity, greatness—these three are one, and this trinity of perfection cannot be separated. All greatness springs from goodness, and all goodness is profoundly simple. Without goodness there is no greatness. Some men pass through the world as destructive forces, like the tornado or the avalanche, but they are not great; they are to greatness as the avalanche is to the mountain. The work of greatness is enduring and preservative, and not violent and destructive. The greatest souls are the most gentle.

Greatness is never obtrusive. It works in silence, seeking no recognition. This is why it is not easily perceived and recognized. Like the mountain, it towers up in its vastness, so that those in its immediate vicinity, who receive its shelter and shade, do not see it. Its sublime grandeur is only beheld as they recede from it. The great man is not seen by his contemporaries; the majesty of his form is only outlined by its recession in time. This is the awe and enchantment of distance. Men occupy themselves with the small things; their houses, trees, lands. Few contemplate the mountain at whose base they live, and fewer still essay to explore it. But in the distance these small things disappear, and then the solitary beauty of the mountain is perceived. Popularity, noisy obtrusiveness, and shallow show, these superficialities rapidly disappear, and leave behind no enduring mark; whereas greatness slowly emerges from obscurity, and endures forever.

Jewish Rabbi and rabble alike saw not the divine beauty of Jesus; they saw only an unlettered carpenter. To his acquaintances, Homer was only a blind beggar, but the centuries reveal him as Homer the immortal poet. Two hundred years after the farmer of Stratford (and all that is known of him) has disappeared, the *real* Shakespeare is discerned. All true genius is impersonal. It belongs not to the man through whom it is manifested; it belongs to all. It is a diffusion of pure Truth; the Light of Heaven descending on all mankind.

Every work of genius, in whatsoever department of art, is a symbolic manifestation of impersonal Truth. It is universal, and finds a response in every heart in every age and race. Anything short of this is not genius, is not greatness. That work which defends *a* religion perishes; it is *religion* that lives. Theories about immortality fade away; immortal man endures; commentaries upon Truth come to the dust; Truth alone remains. That only is true in art which represents the True; that only is great in life which is universally and eternally true. And the True is the Good; the Good is the True.

Every immortal work springs from the Eternal Goodness in the human heart, and it is clothed with the sweet and unaffected simplicity of goodness. The greatest art is, like nature, *artless*. It knows no trick, no pose, no studied effort. There are no stage-tricks in Shakespeare; and he is the greatest of dramatists because he is the *simplest.* The critics, not understanding the wise simplicity of greatness, always condemn the loftiest work. They cannot discriminate between the *childish* and the *childlike.* The True, the Beautiful, the Great, is always childlike, and is perennially fresh and young.

The great man is always the good man; he is always simple. He draws from, nay, lives in, the inexhaustible fountain of divine Goodness within; he inhabits the Heavenly Places; communes with the vanished great ones; lives with the Invisible: he is inspired, and breathes the airs of Heaven.

He who would be great let him learn to be good. He will therefore become great by not seeking greatness. Aiming at greatness a man arrives at nothingness; aiming at nothingness he arrives at greatness. The desire to be great is an indication of littleness, of personal vanity and obtrusiveness. The willingness to disappear from gaze, the utter absence of self-aggrandizement is the witness of greatness.

Littleness seeks and loves authority. Greatness is never authoritative, and it thereby becomes the authority to which the after ages appeal. He who seeks, loses; he who is willing to lose wins all men. Be thy simple self, thy better self, thy impersonal self, and lo! thou art great! He who selfishly seeks authority shall succeed only in becoming a trembling apologist courting protection behind the back of acknowledged greatness. He who will become the servant of all men, desiring no personal authority, shall live as a man, and shall be called *great.* "Abide in the simple and noble regions of thy life, obey thy heart, and thou shalt reproduce the foreworld again." Forget thine own little self, and fall back upon the Universal self, and thou shalt reproduce, in living and enduring forms, a thousand beautiful experiences; thou shalt find within thyself that simple goodness which is greatness.

"It is as easy to be great as to be small," says Emerson; and he utters a profound truth. Forgetfulness of self is the whole of greatness, as it is the whole of goodness and happiness. In a fleeting moment of self-forgetfulness the smallest soul becomes great; extend that moment indefinitely, and there is a great soul, a great life. Cast away thy personality (thy petty cravings, vanities, and ambitions) as a worthless garment, and dwell in the loving, compassionate, selfless regions of thy soul, and thou art no longer small—thou art great.

Claiming personal authority, a man descends into littleness; practicing goodness, a man ascends into greatness. The presumptuousness of the small may, for a time, obscure the humility of the great, but it is at last swallowed up by it, as the noisy river is lost in the calm ocean.

The vulgarity of ignorance and the pride of learning must disappear. Their worthlessness is equal. They have no part in the Soul of Goodness. If thou wouldst do, thou must *be.* Thou shalt not mistake information for Knowledge; thou must know thyself as pure Knowledge. Thou shalt not confuse learning with Wisdom; thou must apprehend thyself as undefiled Wisdom.

Wouldst thou write a living book? Thou must first *live;* thou shalt draw around thee the mystic garment of a manifold experience, and shalt learn, in enjoyment and suffering, gladness and sorrow, conquest and defeat, that which no book and no teacher can teach thee. Thou shalt learn of life, of thy soul; thou shalt tread the Lonely Road, and shalt *become;* thou shalt *be.* Thou shalt then write thy book, and it shall live; it shall be more than a book. Let thy book first live in thee, then shalt thou live in thy book.

Wouldst thou carve a statue that shall captivate the ages, or paint a picture that shall endure? Thou shalt acquaint thyself with the divine Beauty within thee. Thou shalt comprehend and adore the Invisible Beauty; thou shalt know the Principles which are the soul of Form; thou shalt perceive the matchless symmetry and faultless proportions of Life, of Being, of the Universe; thus knowing the eternally True thou shalt carve or paint the indescribably Beautiful.

Wouldst thou produce an imperishable poem? Thou shalt first live thy poem; thou shalt think and act rhythmically; thou shalt find the never-failing source of inspiration in the loving places of thy heart. Then shall immortal lines flow from thee without effort, and, as the flowers of wood and field spontaneously spring, so shall beautiful thoughts grow up in thine heart and, enshrined in words as molds to their beauty, shall subdue the hearts of men.

Wouldst thou compose such music as shall gladden and uplift the world? Thou shalt adjust thy soul to the Heavenly Harmonies. Thou shalt know that thyself, that life and the universe is Music. Thou shalt touch the chords of Life. Thou shalt know that Music is everywhere; that it is the Heart of Being; then shalt thou hear with thy spiritual ear the Deathless Symphonies.

Wouldst thou preach the living Word? Thou shalt forgo thyself, and become that Word. Thou shalt know one thing—*that the human heart is good, is divine;* thou shalt live one thing—*Love.* Thou shalt love all, seeing no evil, thinking no evil, believing no evil; then, though thou speak but little, thy every act shall be a power, thy every word a precept. By thy pure thought, thy selfless deed, though it appear hidden, thou shalt preach, down the ages, to untold multitudes of aspiring souls.

To him who chooses Goodness, sacrificing all, is given that which is more than and includes all. He becomes the possessor of the Best, communes with the Highest, and enters the company of the Great.

The greatness that is flawless, rounded, and complete is above and beyond all art. It is Perfect Goodness in manifestation; therefore the greatest souls are always Teachers.

HEAVEN IN THE HEART

The toil of life ceases when the heart is pure. When the mind is harmonized with the Divine Law the wheel of drudgery ceases to turn, and all work is transmuted into joyful activity. The pure-hearted are as the lilies of the field, which toil not, yet are fed and clothed from the abundant storehouse of the All-Good. But the lily is not lethargic; it is ceaselessly active, drawing nourishment from earth and air and sun. By the Divine Power immanent within it, it builds itself up, cell by cell, opening itself to the light, growing and expanding toward the perfect flower. So is it with those who, having yielded up self-will, have learned to coöperate with the Divine Will. They grow in grace, goodness, and beauty, freed from anxiety and without friction and toil. And they never work in vain; there is no waste action. Every thought, act, and thing done subserves the Divine Purpose, and adds to the sum-total of the world's happiness.

Heaven is in the heart. They will look for it in vain who look elsewhere. In no outward place will the soul find Heaven until it finds it within itself; for, wherever the soul goes, its thoughts and desires will go with it; and, howsoever beautiful may be its outward dwelling-place, if there is sin within, there will be darkness and gloom without, for sin always casts a dark shadow over the pathway of the soul—the shadow of sorrow.

This world is beautiful, transcendently and wonderfully beautiful. Its beauties and inspiring wonders cannot be numbered; yet, to the sin-sodden mind, it appears as a dark and joyless place. Where passion and self are, there is hell, and there are all the pains of hell; where Holiness and Love are, there is Heaven, and there are all the joys of Heaven.

Heaven is here. It is also everywhere. It is wherever there is a pure heart. The whole universe is abounding with joy, but the sin-bound heart can neither see, hear, nor partake of it. No one is, or can be, arbitrarily shut out from Heaven; each shuts himself out. Its Golden Gates are eternally ajar, but the selfish cannot find them; they mourn, yet see not; they cry, but hear not. Only to those who turn their eyes to heavenly things, their ears to heavenly sounds, are the happy Portals of the Kingdom revealed, and they enter and are glad.

All life is gladness when the heart is right, when it is attuned to the sweet chords of holy Love. Life is Religion, Religion is life, and all is Joy and Gladness. The jarring notes of creeds and parties, the black shadows of sin, let them pass away forever; they cannot enter the Door of Life; they form no part of Religion. Joy, Music, Beauty—these belong to the True Order of things; they are of the texture of the universe; of these is the divine Garment of Life woven. Pure Religion is glad, not gloomy. It is Light without darkness or shadow.

Despondency, disappointment, grief—these are the reflex aspects of pleasurable excitement, self-seeking, and desire. Give up the latter, and the former will forever disappear; then there remains the perfect Bliss of Heaven.

Abounding and unalloyed Happiness is man's true life; perfect Blessedness is his rightful portion; and when he loses his false life and finds the true he enters into the full possession of his Kingdom. The Kingdom of Heaven is man's Home: and it is here and now, it is in his own heart, and he is not left without Guides, if he wills to find it. All man's sorrows and sufferings are the result of his own self-elected estrangement from the Divine Source, the All-Good, the Father, the Heart of Love. Let him return to his Home; his peace awaits him.

The Heavenly-hearted are without sorrow and suffering, because they are without sin. What the worldly-minded call *troubles* they regard as pleasant tasks of Love and Wisdom. Troubles belong to hell; they do not enter Heaven, This is so simple it should not appear strange. If you have a trouble it is in your own mind, and nowhere else; you make it, it is not made for you; it is not in your task; it is not in that outward thing. You are its creator, and it derives its life from you only. Look upon all your difficulties as lessons to be learned, as aids to spiritual growth, and lo! they are difficulties no longer! This is one of the Pathways up to Heaven.

To transmute everything into Happiness and Joy, this is supremely the work and duty of the Heavenly-minded man. To reduce everything to wretchedness and deprivation is the process which the worldly-minded unconsciously pursue. To live in Love is to work in Joy. Love is the magic that transforms all things into power and beauty. It brings plenty out of poverty, power out of weakness, loveliness out of deformity, sweetness out of bitterness, light out of darkness, and produces all blissful conditions out of its own substantial but indefinable essence.

He who loves can never want. The universe belongs to Goodness, and it therefore belongs to the good man. It can be possessed by all without stint or shrinking, for Goodness, and the abundance of Goodness (material, mental, and spiritual abundance), is inexhaustible. Think lovingly, speak lovingly, act lovingly, and your every need shall be supplied; you shall not walk in desert places, and no danger shall overtake you.

Love sees with faultless vision, judges true judgment, acts in wisdom. Look through the eyes of Love, and you shall see everywhere the Beautiful and True; judge with the mind of Love, and you shall err not, shall awake no wail of sorrow; act in the spirit of Love, and you shall strike undying harmonies upon the Harp of Life.

Make no compromise with self. Cease not to strive until your whole being is swallowed up in Love. To love all and always—this is the Heaven of heavens. "Let there be nothing within thee that is not very beautiful and very gentle, and then will there be nothing without thee that is not beautified and softened by the spell of thy presence." All that you do, let it be done in calm wisdom, and not from desire, impulse, or opinion; this is the Heavenly way of action.

Purify your thought-world until no stain is left, and you will ascend into Heaven while living in the body. You will then see the things of the outward world clothed in all beautiful forms. Having found the Divine Beauty within ourselves, it springs to life in every outward thing. To the beautified soul the world is beautiful.

Undeveloped souls are merely unopened flowers. The perfect Beauty lies concealed within, and will one day reveal itself to the full-orbed light of Heaven. Seeing men thus, we stand where evil is not, and where the eye beholds only good. Herein lies the peace and patience and beauty of Love—*it sees no evil.* He who loves thus becomes the protector of all men. Though in their ignorance they should hate him, he shields and loves them.

What gardener is so foolish as to condemn his flowers because they do not develop in a day? Learn to love, and you shall see in all souls, even those called "degraded," the Divine Beauty, and shall know that it will not fail to come forth in its own season. This is one of the Heavenly Visions; it is out of this that Gladness comes.

Sin, sorrow, suffering—these are the dark gropings of the unopened soul for Light. Open the petals of your soul and let the glorious Light stream in.

Every sinful soul is an unresolved harmony. It shall at last strike the Perfect Chord, and swell the joyful melodies of Heaven.

Hell is the preparation for Heaven; and out of the débris of its ruined hovels are built pleasant mansions wherein the perfected soul may dwell.

Night is only a fleeting shadow which the world casts, and sorrow is but a transient shade cast by the self. "Come out into the Sunlight." Know this, O reader! that you are divine. You are not cut off from the Divine except in your own unbelief. Rise up, O Son of God! and shake off the nightmare of sin which binds you; accept your heritage—the Kingdom of Heaven! Drug your soul no longer with the poisons of false beliefs. You are not "a worm of the dust" unless you choose to make your-self one. You are a divine, immortal, God-born being, and this you may know if you will to seek and find. Cling no longer to your impure and groveling thoughts, and you shall know that you are a radiant and celestial spirit, filled with all pure and lovable thoughts. Wretchedness and sin and sorrow are not your portion here unless you accept them as such; and if you do this, they will be your portion hereafter, for these things are not apart from your soul-condition; they will go wherever you go; they are only within you.

Heaven, not hell, is your portion here and always. It only requires you to take that which belongs to you. You are the master, and you choose whom you will serve. You are the maker of your state, and your choice determines your condition. What you pray and ask for (with your mind and heart, not with your lips merely), this you receive. You are served as you serve. You are conditioned as you condition. You garner in your own.

Heaven is yours; you have but to enter in and take possession; and Heaven means Supreme Happiness, Perfect Blessedness; it leaves nothing to be desired; nothing to be grieved over. It is complete satisfaction *now and in this world.* It is within you; and if you do not know this, it is because you persist in turning the back of your soul upon it. *Turn round* and you shall behold it.

Come and live in the sunshine of your being. Come out of the shadows and the dark places. You are framed for Happiness. You are a child of Heaven. Purity, Wisdom, Love, Plenty, Joy, and Peace—these are the eternal Realities of the Kingdom, and they are yours, but you cannot possess them in sin; they have no part in the Realm of Darkness. They belong to "the Light which lighteth every man that cometh into the world," the Light of spotless Love. They are the heritage of the holy Christ-Child who shall come to birth in your soul when you are ready to divest yourself of all your impurities. They are your real self.

But he whose soul has been safely delivered of the Wonderful Joy-Child does not forget the travail of the world.

AS A MAN THINKETH

(1903)

Mind is the Master power that moulds and makes,
And Man is Mind, and evermore he takes
The tool of Thought, and, shaping what he wills,
Brings forth a thousand joys, a thousand ills:—
He thinks in secret and it comes to pass:
Environment is but his looking-glass.

FOREWORD

This little volume (the result of meditation and experience) is not intended as an exhaustive treatise on the much-written-upon subject of the power of thought. It is suggestive rather than explanatory, its object being to stimulate men and women to the discovery and perception of the truth that—

They themselves are makers of themselves

by virtue of the thoughts which they choose and encourage; that mind is the master weaver, both of the inner garment of character and the outer garment of circumstance, and that, as they may have hitherto woven in ignorance and pain they may now weave in enlightenment and happiness.

—JAMES ALLEN
Broad Park Avenue
Ilfracombe, England

CONTENTS

THOUGHT AND CHARACTER

The aphorism "As a man thinketh in his heart so is he" not only embraces the whole of a man's being, but is so comprehensive as to reach out to every condition and circumstance of his life. A man is literally *what he thinks*, his character being the complete sum of all his thoughts.

As the plant springs from, and could not be without, the seed, so every act of a man springs from the hidden seeds of thought, and could not have appeared without them. This applies equally to those acts called "spontaneous" and "unpremeditated" as to those which are deliberately executed.

Act is the blossom of thought, and joy and suffering are its fruits; thus does a man garner in the sweet and bitter fruitage of his own husbandry.

> Thought in the mind hath made us. What we are
> By thought was wrought and built. If a man's mind
> Hath evil thoughts, pain comes on him as comes
> The wheel the ox behind. . . .
>   . . . If one endure
> In purity of thought, joy follows him
> As his own shadow—sure.

Man is a growth by law, and not a creation by artifice, and cause and effect is as absolute and undeviating in the hidden realm of thought as in the world of visible and material things. A noble and Godlike character is not a thing of favor or chance, but is the natural result of continued effort in right thinking, the effect of long-cherished association with Godlike thoughts. An ignoble and bestial character, by the same process, is the result of the continued harboring of groveling thoughts.

Man is made or unmade by himself; in the armory of thought he forges the weapons by which he destroys himself; he also fashions the tools with which he builds for himself heavenly mansions of joy and strength and peace. By the right choice and true application of thought, man ascends to the Divine Perfection; by the abuse and wrong application of thought, he descends below the level of the beast. Between these two extremes are all the grades of character, and man is their maker and master.

Of all the beautiful truths pertaining to the soul which have been restored and brought to light in this age, none is more gladdening or fruitful of divine promise and confidence than this—that man is the master of thought, the molder of character, and the maker and shaper of condition, environment, and destiny.

As a being of Power, Intelligence, and Love, and the lord of his own thoughts, man holds the key to every situation, and contains within himself that transforming and regenerative agency by which he may make himself what he wills.

Man is always the master, even in his weakest and most abandoned state; but in his weakness and degradation he is the foolish master who misgoverns his "household." When he begins to reflect upon his condition, and to search diligently for the Law upon which his being is established, he then becomes the wise master, directing his energies with intelligence, and fashioning his thoughts to fruitful issues. Such is the *conscious* master, and man can only thus become by discovering *within himself the* laws of thought; which discovery is totally a matter of application, self-analysis, and experience.

Only by much searching and mining are gold and diamonds obtained, and man can find every truth connected with his being if he will dig deep into the mine of his soul; and that he is the maker of his character, the molder of his life, and the builder of his destiny, he may unerringly prove, if he will watch, control, and alter his thoughts, tracing their effects upon himself, upon others, and upon his life and circumstances, linking cause and effect by patient practice and investigation, and utilizing his every experience, even to the most trivial, everyday occurrence, as a means of obtaining that knowledge of himself which is Understanding, Wisdom, Power. In this direction, as in no other, is the law absolute that "He that seeketh findeth; and to him that knocketh it shall be opened"; for only by patience, practice, and ceaseless importunity can a man enter the Door of the Temple of Knowledge.

EFFECT OF THOUGHT
ON CIRCUMSTANCES

A man's mind may be likened to a garden, which may be intelligently cultivated or allowed to run wild; but whether cultivated or neglected, it must, and will, *bring forth*. If no useful seeds are *put* into it, then an abundance of useless weed seeds will *fall* therein, and will continue to produce their kind.

Just as a gardener cultivates his plot, keeping it free from weeds, and growing the flowers and fruits which he requires, so may a man tend the garden of his mind, weeding out all the wrong, useless, and impure thoughts, and cultivating toward perfection the flowers and fruits of right, useful, and pure thoughts. By pursuing this process, a man sooner or later discovers that he is the master gardener of his soul, the director of his life. He also reveals, within himself, the laws of thought, and understands, with ever-increasing accuracy, how the thought forces and mind elements operate in the shaping of his character, circumstances, and destiny.

Thought and character are one, and as character can only manifest and discover itself through environment and circumstance, the outer conditions of a person's life will always be found to be harmoniously related to his inner state. This does not mean that a man's circumstances at any given time are an indication of his *entire* character, but that those circumstances are so intimately connected with some vital thought element within himself that, for the time being, they are indispensable to his development.

Every man is where he is by the law of his being; the thoughts which he has built into his character have brought him there, and in the arrangement of his life there is no element of chance, but all is the result of a law which cannot err. This is just as true of those who feel "out of harmony" with their surroundings as of those who are contented with them.

As a progressive and evolving being, man is where he is that he may learn that he may grow; and as he learns the spiritual lesson which any circumstance contains for him, it passes away and gives place to other circumstances.

Man is buffeted by circumstances so long as he believes himself to be the creature of outside conditions, but when he realizes that he is a creative power, and that he may command the hidden soil and seeds of his being out of which circumstances grow, he then becomes the rightful master of himself.

That circumstances *grow* out of thought every man knows who has for any length of time practiced self-control and self-purification, for he will have noticed that the alteration in his circumstances has been in exact ratio with his altered mental condition. So true is this that when a man earnestly applies himself to remedy the defects in his character, and makes swift and marked progress, he passes rapidly through a succession of vicissitudes.

The soul attracts that which it secretly harbors; that which it loves, and also that which it fears; it reaches the height of its cherished aspirations; it falls to the level of its unchastened desires—and circumstances are the means by which the soul receives its own.

Every thought seed sown or allowed to fall into the mind, and to take root there, produces its own, blossoming sooner or later into act, and bearing its own fruitage of opportunity and circumstance. Good thoughts bear good fruit, bad thoughts bad fruit.

The outer world of circumstance shapes itself to the inner world of thought, and both pleasant and unpleasant external conditions are factors which make for the ultimate good of the individual. As the reaper of his own harvest, man learns both by suffering and bliss.

Following the inmost desires, aspirations, thoughts, by which he allows himself to be dominated (pursuing the will-o'-the-wisps of impure imaginings or steadfastly walking the highway of strong and high endeavor), a man at last arrives at their fruition and fulfillment in the outer conditions of his life. The laws of growth and adjustment everywhere obtain.

A man does not come to the almshouse or the jail by the tyranny of fate or circumstance, but by the pathway of groveling thoughts and base desires. Nor does a pure-minded man fall suddenly into crime by stress of any mere external force; the criminal thought had long been secretly fostered in the heart, and the hour of opportunity revealed its gathered power. Circumstance does not make the man; it reveals him to himself. No such conditions can exist as descending into vice and its attendant sufferings apart from vicious inclinations, or ascending into virtue and its pure happiness without the continued cultivation of virtuous aspirations; and man, therefore, as the lord and master of thought, is the maker of himself, the shaper and author of environment. Even at birth the soul comes to its own, and through every step of its earthly pilgrimage it attracts those combinations of conditions which reveal itself, which are the reflections of its own purity and impurity, its strength and weakness.

Men do not attract that which they *want*, but that which they *are*. Their whims, fancies, and ambitions are thwarted at every step, but their inmost thoughts and desires are fed with their own food, be it foul or clean. The "divinity that shapes our ends" is in ourselves; it is our very self. Man is manacled only by himself: thought and action are the jailers of Fate—they imprison, being base; they are also the angels of Freedom—they liberate, being noble. Not what he wishes and prays for does a man get, but what he justly earns. His wishes and prayers are only gratified and answered when they harmonize with his thoughts and actions.

In the light of this truth, what, then, is the meaning of "fighting against circumstances"? It means that a man is continually revolting against an *effect* without, while all the time he is nourishing and preserving its *cause* in his heart. That cause may take the form of a conscious vice or an unconscious weakness; but whatever it is, it stubbornly retards the efforts of its possessor, and thus calls aloud for remedy.

Men are anxious to improve their circumstances, but are unwilling to improve themselves; they therefore remain bound. The man who does not shrink from self-crucifixion can never fail to accomplish the object upon which his heart is set. This is as true of earthly as of heavenly things. Even the man whose sole object is to acquire wealth must be prepared to make great personal sacrifices before he can accomplish his object; and how much more so he who would realize a strong and well-poised life?

Here is a man who is wretchedly poor. He is extremely anxious that his surroundings and home comforts should be improved, yet all the time he shirks his work, and considers he is justified in trying to deceive his employer on the ground of the insufficiency of his wages. Such a man does not understand the simplest rudiments of those principles which are the basis of true prosperity, and is not only totally unfitted to rise out of his wretchedness, but is actually attracting to himself a still deeper wretchedness by dwelling in, and acting out, indolent, deceptive, and unmanly thoughts.

Here is a rich man who is the victim of a painful and persistent disease as the result of gluttony. He is willing to give large sums of money to get rid of it, but he will not sacrifice his gluttonous desires. He wants to gratify his taste for rich and unnatural viands and have his health as well. Such a man is totally unfit to have health, because he has not yet learned the first principles of a healthy life.

Here is an employer of labor who adopts crooked measures to avoid paying the regulation wage, and, in the hope of making larger profits, reduces the wages of his workpeople. Such a man is altogether unfitted for prosperity, and when he finds himself bankrupt, both as regards reputation and riches, he blames circumstances, not knowing that he is the sole author of his condition.

I have introduced these three cases merely as illustrative of the truth that man is the causer (though nearly always unconsciously) of his circumstances, and that, while aiming at a good end, he is continually frustrating its accomplishment by encouraging thoughts and desires which cannot possibly harmonize with that end. Such cases could be multiplied and varied almost indefinitely, but this is not necessary, as the reader can, if he so resolves, trace the action of the laws of thought in his own mind and life, and until this is done, mere external facts cannot serve as a ground of reasoning.

Circumstances, however, are so complicated, thought is so deeply rooted, and the conditions of happiness vary so vastly with individuals that a man's *entire* soul condition (although it may be known to himself) cannot be judged by another from the external aspect of his life alone. A man may be honest in certain directions, yet suffer privations; a man may be dishonest in certain directions, yet acquire wealth; but the conclusion usually formed that the one man fails *because of his particular honesty,* and that the other prospers *because of his particular dishonesty,* is the result of a superficial judgment, which assumes that the dishonest man is almost totally corrupt, and the honest man almost entirely virtuous. In the light of a deeper knowledge and wider experience, such judgment is found to be erroneous. The dishonest man may have some admirable virtues which the other does not possess; and the honest man obnoxious vices which are absent in the other. The honest man reaps the good results of his honest thoughts and acts; he also brings upon himself the sufferings which his vices produce. The dishonest man likewise garners his own suffering and happiness.

It is pleasing to human vanity to believe that one suffers because of one's virtue; but not until a man has extirpated every sickly, bitter, and impure thought from his mind, and washed every sinful stain from his soul, can he be in a position to know and declare that his sufferings are the result of his good, and not of his bad qualities; and on the way to, yet long before he has reached, that supreme perfection, he will have found, working in his mind and life, the Great Law which is absolutely just, and which cannot, therefore, give good for evil, evil for good. Possessed of such knowledge, he will then know, looking back upon his past ignorance and blindness, that his life is, and always was, justly ordered, and that all his past experiences, good and bad, were the equitable outworking of his evolving, yet unevolved self.

Good thoughts and actions can never produce bad results; bad thoughts and actions can never produce good results. This is but saying that nothing can come from corn but corn, nothing from nettles but nettles. Men understand this law in the natural world, and work with it; but few understand it in the mental and moral world (though its operation there is just as simple and undeviating), and they, therefore, do not coöperate with it.

Suffering is *always* the effect of wrong thought in some direction. It is an indication that the individual is out of harmony with himself, with the Law of his being. The sole and supreme use of suffering is to purify, to burn out all that is useless and impure. Suffering ceases for him who is pure. There could be no object in burning gold after the dross had been removed, and a perfectly pure and enlightened being could not suffer.

The circumstances which a man encounters with suffering are the result of his own mental inharmony. The circumstances which a man encounters with blessedness are the result of his own mental harmony. Blessedness, not material possessions, is the measure of right thought; wretchedness, not lack of material possessions, is the measure of wrong thought. A man may be cursed and rich; he may be blessed and poor. Blessedness and riches are only joined together when the riches are rightly and wisely used; and the poor man only descends into wretchedness when he regards his lot as a burden unjustly imposed.

Indigence and indulgence are the two extremes of wretchedness. They are both equally unnatural and the result of mental disorder. A man is not rightly conditioned until he is a happy, healthy, and prosperous being; and happiness, health, and prosperity are the result of a harmonious adjustment of the inner with the outer, of the man with his surroundings.

A man only begins to be a man when he ceases to whine and revile, and commences to search for the hidden justice which regulates his life. And as he adapts his mind to that regulating factor, he ceases to accuse others as the cause of his condition, and builds himself up in strong and noble thoughts; ceases to kick against circumstances, but begins to *use* them as aids to his more rapid progress, and as a means of discovering the hidden powers and possibilities within himself.

Law, not confusion, is the dominating principle in the universe; justice, not injustice, is the soul and substance of life; and righteousness, not corruption, is the molding and moving force in the spiritual government of the world. This being so, man has but to right himself to find that the universe is right; and during the process of putting himself right, he will find that as he alters his thoughts toward things, and other people, things and other people will alter toward him.

The proof of this truth is in every person, and it therefore admits of easy investigation by systematic introspection and self-analysis. Let a man radically alter his thoughts, and he will be astonished at the rapid transformation it will effect in the material conditions of his life. Men imagine that thought can be kept secret, but it cannot; it rapidly crystallizes into habit, and habit solidifies into circumstance. Bestial thoughts crystallize into habits of drunkenness and sensuality, which solidify into circumstances of destitution and disease; impure thoughts of every kind crystallize into enervating and confusing habits, which solidify into distracting and adverse circumstances; thoughts of fear, doubt, and indecision crystallize into weak, unmanly, and irresolute habits, which solidify into circumstances of failure, indigence, and slavish dependence; lazy thoughts crystallize into habits of uncleanliness and dishonesty, which solidify into circumstances of foulness and beggary; hateful and condemnatory thoughts crystallize into habits of accusation and violence, which solidify into circumstances of injury and persecution; selfish thoughts of all kinds crystallize into habits of self-seeking, which solidify into circumstances more or less distressing. On the other hand, beautiful thoughts of all kinds crystallize into habits of grace and kindliness, which solidify into genial and sunny circumstances; pure thoughts crystallize into habits of temperance and self-control, which solidify into circumstances of repose and peace; thoughts of courage, self-reliance, and decision crystallize into manly habits, which solidify into circumstances of success, plenty, and freedom; energetic thoughts crystallize into habits of cleanliness and industry, which solidify into circumstances of pleasantness; gentle and forgiving thoughts crystallize into habits of gentleness, which solidify into protective and preservative circumstances; loving and unselfish thoughts crystallize into habits of self-forgetfulness for others, which solidify into circumstances of sure and abiding prosperity and true riches.

A particular train of thought persisted in, be it good or bad, cannot fail to produce its results on the character and circumstances. A man cannot *directly* choose his circumstances, but he can choose his thoughts, and so indirectly, yet surely, shape his circumstances.

Nature helps every man to the gratification of the thoughts which he most encourages, and opportunities are presented which will most speedily bring to the surface both the good and evil thoughts.

Let a man cease from his sinful thoughts, and all the world will soften toward him, and be ready to help him; let him put away his weakly and sickly thoughts, and lo! opportunities will spring up on every hand to aid his strong resolves; let him encourage good thoughts, and no hard fate shall bind him down to wretchedness and shame. The world is your kaleidoscope, and the varying combinations of colors which at every succeeding moment it presents to you are the exquisitely adjusted pictures of your ever-moving thoughts.

> You will be what you will to be;
> Let failure find its false content
> In that poor word, "environment,"
> But spirit scorns it, and is free.
>
> It masters time, it conquers space;
> It cows that boastful trickster, Chance,
> And bids the tyrant Circumstance
> Uncrown, and fill a servant's place.
>
> The human Will, that force unseen,
> The offspring of a deathless Soul,
> Can hew a way to any goal,
> Though walls of granite intervene.
>
> Be not impatient in delay,
> But wait as one who understands;
> When spirit rises and commands,
> The gods are ready to obey.

EFFECT OF THOUGHT ON
HEALTH AND THE BODY

The body is the servant of the mind. It obeys the operations of the mind, whether they be deliberately chosen or automatically expressed. At the bidding of unlawful thoughts the body sinks rapidly into disease and decay; at the command of glad and beautiful thoughts it becomes clothed with youthfulness and beauty.

Disease and health, like circumstances, are rooted in thought. Sickly thoughts will express themselves through a sickly body. Thoughts of fear have been known to kill a man as speedily as a bullet, and they are continually killing thousands of people just as surely though less rapidly. The people who live in fear of disease are the people who get it. Anxiety quickly demoralizes the whole body, and lays it open to the entrance of disease; while impure thoughts, even if not physically indulged, will soon shatter the nervous system.

Strong, pure, and happy thoughts build up the body in vigor and grace. The body is a delicate and plastic instrument, which responds readily to the thoughts by which it is impressed, and habits of thought will produce their own effects, good or bad, upon it.

Men will continue to have impure and poisoned blood so long as they propagate unclean thoughts. Out of a clean heart comes a clean life and a clean body. Out of a defiled mind proceeds a defiled life and a corrupt body. Thought is the font of action, life, and manifestation; make the fountain pure, and all will be pure.

Change of diet will not help a man who will not change his thoughts. When a man makes his thoughts pure, he no longer desires impure food.

Clean thoughts make clean habits. The so-called saint who does not wash his body is not a saint. He who has strengthened and purified his thoughts does not need to consider the malevolent microbe.

If you would perfect your body, guard your mind. If you would renew your body, beautify your mind. Thoughts of malice, envy, disappointment, despondency rob the body of its health and grace.

A sour face does not come by chance; it is made by sour thoughts. Wrinkles that mar are drawn by folly, passion, pride.

I know a woman of ninety-six who has the bright, innocent face of a girl. I know a man well under middle age whose face is drawn into inharmonious contours. The one is the result of a sweet and sunny disposition; the other is the outcome of passion and discontent.

As you cannot have a sweet and wholesome abode unless you admit the air and sunshine freely into your rooms, so a strong body and a bright, happy, or serene countenance can only result from the free admittance into the mind of thoughts of joy and good will and serenity.

On the faces of the aged there are wrinkles made by sympathy; others by strong and pure thought; and others are carved by passion: who cannot distinguish them? With those who have lived righteously, age is calm, peaceful, and softly mellowed, like the setting sun. I have recently seen a philosopher on his deathbed. He was not old except in years. He died as sweetly and peacefully as he had lived.

There is no physician like cheerful thought for dissipating the ills of the body; there is no comforter to compare with good will for dispersing the shadows of grief and sorrow. To live continually in thoughts of ill will, cynicism, suspicion, and envy is to be confined in a self-made prison hole. But to think well of all, to be cheerful with all, to patiently learn to find the good in all—such unselfish thoughts are the very portals of heaven; and to dwell day by day in thoughts of peace toward every creature will bring abounding peace to their possessor.

THOUGHT AND PURPOSE

Until thought is linked with purpose there is no intelligent accomplishment. With the majority the bark of thought is allowed to "drift" upon the ocean of life. Aimlessness is a vice, and such drifting must not continue for him who would steer clear of catastrophe and destruction.

They who have no central purpose in their life fall an easy prey to petty worries, fears, troubles, and self-pityings, all of which are indications of weakness, which lead, just as surely as deliberately planned sins (though by a different route), to failure, unhappiness, and loss, for weakness cannot persist in a power-evolving universe.

A man should conceive of a legitimate purpose in his heart, and set out to accomplish it. He should make this purpose the centralizing point of his thoughts. It may take the form of a spiritual ideal, or it may be a worldly object, according to his nature at the time being; but whichever it is, he should steadily focus his thought forces upon the object which he has set before him. He should make this purpose his supreme duty, and should devote himself to its attainment, not allowing his thoughts to wander away into ephemeral fancies, longings, and imaginings. This is the royal road to self-control and true concentration of thought. Even if he fails again and again to accomplish his purpose (as he necessarily must until weakness is overcome), the *strength of character gained* will be the measure of his *true* success, and this will form a new starting point for future power and triumph.

Those who are not prepared for the apprehension of a *great* purpose should fix their thoughts upon the faultless performance of their duty, no matter how insignificant their task may appear. Only in this way can the thoughts be gathered and focused, and resolution and energy be developed, which being done, there is nothing which may not be accomplished.

The weakest soul, knowing its own weakness, and believing this truth—*that strength can only be developed by effort and practice*—will, thus believing, at once begin to exert itself, and, adding effort to effort, patience to patience, and strength to strength, will never cease to develop, and will at last grow divinely strong.

As the physically weak man can make himself strong by careful and patient training, so the man of weak thoughts can make them strong by exercising himself in right thinking.

To put away aimlessness and weakness, and to begin to think with purpose, is to enter the ranks of those strong ones who only recognize failure as one of the pathways to attainment; who make all conditions serve them, and who think strongly, attempt fearlessly, and accomplish masterfully.

Having conceived of his purpose, a man should mentally mark out a *straight* pathway to its achievement, looking neither to the right nor the left. Doubts and fears should be rigorously excluded; they are disintegrating elements which break up the straight line of effort, rendering it crooked, ineffectual, useless. Thoughts of doubt and fear never accomplish anything, and never can. They always lead to failure. Purpose, energy, power to do, and all strong thoughts cease when doubt and fear creep in.

The will to do springs from the knowledge that we *can* do. Doubt and fear are the great enemies of knowledge, and he who encourages them, who does not slay them, thwarts himself at every step.

He who has conquered doubt and fear has conquered failure. His every thought is allied with power, and all difficulties are bravely met and wisely overcome. His purposes are seasonably planted, and they bloom and bring forth fruit which does not fall prematurely to the ground.

Thought allied fearlessly to purpose becomes creative force: he who *knows* this is ready to become something higher and stronger than a mere bundle of wavering thoughts and fluctuating sensations; he who *does* this has become the conscious and intelligent wielder of his mental powers.

THE THOUGHT-FACTOR
IN ACHIEVEMENT

All that a man achieves and all that he fails to achieve is the direct result of his own thoughts. In a justly ordered universe, where loss of equipoise would mean total destruction, individual responsibility must be absolute. A man's weakness and strength, purity and impurity, are his own, and not another man's; they are brought about by himself, and not by another; and they can only be altered by himself, never by another. His condition is also his own, and not another man's. His suffering and his happiness are evolved from within. As he thinks, so he is; as he continues to think, so he remains.

A strong man cannot help a weaker unless that weaker is *willing* to be helped, and even then the weak man must become strong of himself; he must, by his own efforts, develop the strength which he admires in another. None but himself can alter his condition.

It has been usual for men to think and to say, "Many men are slaves because one is an oppressor; let us hate the oppressor." Now, however, there is among an increasing few a tendency to reverse this judgment, and to say, "One man is an oppressor because many are slaves; let us despise the slaves." The truth is that oppressor and slave are coöperators in ignorance, and, while seeming to afflict each other, are in reality afflicting themselves. A perfect Knowledge perceives the action of law in the weakness of the oppressed and the misapplied power of the oppressor; a perfect Love, seeing the suffering which both states entail, condemns neither; a perfect Compassion embraces both oppressor and oppressed.

He who has conquered weakness, and has put away all selfish thoughts, belongs neither to oppressor nor oppressed. He is free.

A man can only rise, conquer, and achieve by lifting up his thoughts. He can only remain weak, abject, and miserable by refusing to lift up his thoughts.

Before a man can achieve anything, even in worldly things, he must lift his thoughts above slavish animal indulgence. He may not, in order to succeed, give up *all* animality and selfishness, by any means; but a portion of it must, at least, be sacrificed. A man whose first thought is bestial indulgence could neither think clearly nor plan methodically; he could not find and develop his latent resources, and would fail in any undertaking. Not having commenced manfully to control his thoughts, he is not in a position to control affairs and to adopt serious responsibilities. He is not fit to act independently and stand alone. But he is limited only by the thoughts which he chooses.

There can be no progress, no achievement without sacrifice, and a man's worldly success will be in the measure that he sacrifices his confused animal thoughts, and fixes his mind on the development of his plans, and the strengthening of his resolution and self-reliance. And the higher he lifts his thoughts, the more manly, upright, and righteous he becomes, the greater will be his success, the more blessed and enduring will be his achievements.

The universe does not favor the greedy, the dishonest, the vicious, although on the mere surface it may sometimes appear to do so; it helps the honest, the magnanimous, the virtuous. All the great Teachers of the ages have declared this in varying forms, and to prove and know it a man has but to persist in making himself more and more virtuous by lifting up his thoughts.

Intellectual achievements are the result of thought consecrated to the search for knowledge, or for the beautiful and true in life and nature. Such achievements may be sometimes connected with vanity and ambition, but they are not the outcome of those characteristics; they are the natural outgrowth of long and arduous effort, and of pure and unselfish thoughts.

Spiritual achievements are the consummation of holy aspirations. He who lives constantly in the conception of noble and lofty thoughts, who dwells upon all that is pure and unselfish, will, as surely as the sun reaches its zenith and the moon its full, become wise and noble in character, and rise into a position of influence and blessedness.

Achievement, of whatever kind, is the crown of effort, the diadem of thought. By the aid of self-control, resolution, purity, righteousness, and well-directed thought a man ascends; by the aid of animality, indolence, impurity, corruption, and confusion of thought a man descends.

A man may rise to high success in the world, and even to lofty altitudes in the spiritual realm, and again descend into weakness and wretchedness by allowing arrogant, selfish, and corrupt thoughts to take possession of him.

Victories attained by right thought can only be maintained by watchfulness. Many give way when success is assured, and rapidly fall back into failure.

All achievements, whether in the business, intellectual, or spiritual world, are the result of definitely directed thought, are governed by the same law and are of the same method; the only difference lies in *the object of attainment.*

He who would accomplish little must sacrifice little; he who would achieve much must sacrifice much; he who would attain highly must sacrifice greatly.

VISIONS AND IDEALS

The dreamers are the saviors of the world. As the visible world is sustained by the invisible, so men, through all their trials and sins and sordid vocations, are nourished by the beautiful visions of their solitary dreamers. Humanity cannot forget its dreamers; it cannot let their ideals fade and die; it lives in them; it knows them as the *realities* which it shall one day see and know.

Composer, sculptor, painter, poet, prophet, sage, these are the makers of the afterworld, the architects of heaven. The world is beautiful because they have lived; without them, laboring humanity would perish.

He who cherishes a beautiful vision, a lofty ideal in his heart, will one day realize it. Columbus cherished a vision of another world, and he discovered it; Copernicus fostered the vision of a multiplicity of worlds and a wider universe, and he revealed it; Buddha beheld the vision of a spiritual world of stainless beauty and perfect peace, and he entered into it.

Cherish your visions; cherish your ideals; cherish the music that stirs in your heart, the beauty that forms in your mind, the loveliness that drapes your purest thoughts, for out of them will grow all delightful conditions, all heavenly environment; of these, if you but remain true to them, your world will at last be built.

To desire is to obtain; to aspire is to achieve. Shall man's basest desires receive the fullest measure of gratification, and his purest aspirations starve for lack of sustenance? Such is not the Law: such a condition of things can never obtain: "Ask and receive."

Dream lofty dreams, and as you dream, so shall you become. Your Vision is the promise of what you shall one day be; your Ideal is the prophecy of what you shall at last unveil.

The greatest achievement was at first and for a time a dream. The oak sleeps in the acorn; the bird waits in the egg; and in the highest vision of the soul a waking angel stirs. Dreams are the seedlings of realities.

Your circumstances may be uncongenial, but they shall not long remain so if you but perceive an Ideal and strive to reach it. You cannot travel *within* and stand still *without*. Here is a youth hard pressed by poverty and labor; confined long hours in an unhealthy workshop; unschooled, and lacking all the arts of refinement. But he dreams of better things: he thinks of intelligence, of refinement, of grace and beauty. He conceives of, mentally builds up, an ideal condition of life; the vision of a wider liberty and a larger scope takes possession of him; unrest urges him to action, and he utilizes all his spare time and means, small though they are, to the development of his latent powers and resources. Very soon so altered has his mind become that the workshop can no longer hold him. It has become so out of harmony with his mentality that it falls out of his life as a garment is cast aside, and, with the growth of opportunities which fit the scope of his expanding powers, he passes out of it forever. Years later we see this youth as a full-grown man. We find him a master of certain forces of the mind which he wields with worldwide influence and almost unequaled power. In his hands he holds the cords of gigantic responsibilities; he speaks, and lo! lives are changed; men and women hang upon his words and remold their characters, and, sunlike, he becomes the fixed and luminous center around which innumerable destinies revolve. He has realized the Vision of his youth. He has become one with his Ideal.

And you, too, youthful reader, will realize the Vision (not the idle wish) of your heart, be it base or beautiful, or a mixture of both, for you will always gravitate toward that which you, secretly, most love. Into your hands will be placed the exact results of your own thoughts; you will receive that which you earn; no more, no less. Whatever your present environment may be, you will fall, remain, or rise with your thoughts, your Vision, your Ideal. You will become as small as your controlling desire; as great as your dominant aspiration: in the beautiful words of Stanton Kirkham Davis, "You may be keeping accounts, and presently you shall walk out of the door that for so long has seemed to you the barrier of your ideals, and shall find yourself before an audience—the pen still behind your ear, the ink stains on your fingers—and then and there shall pour out the torrent of your inspiration. You may be driving sheep, and you shall wander to the city—bucolic and open mouthed; shall wander under the intrepid guidance of the spirit into the studio of the master, and after a time he shall say, 'I have nothing more to teach you.' And now you have become the master, who did so recently dream of great things while driving sheep. You shall lay down the saw and the plane to take upon yourself the regeneration of the world."

The thoughtless, the ignorant, and the indolent, seeing only the apparent effects of things and not the things themselves, talk of luck, of fortune, and chance. Seeing a man grow rich, they say, "How lucky he is!" Observing another become intellectual, they exclaim, "How highly favored he is!" And noting the saintly character and wide influence of another, they remark, "How chance aids him at every turn!" They do not see the trials and failures and struggles which these men have voluntarily encountered in order to gain their experience; have no knowledge of the sacrifices they have made, of the undaunted efforts they have put forth, of the faith they have exercised, that they might overcome the apparently insurmountable, and realize the Vision of their heart. They do not know the darkness and the heartaches; they only see the light and joy, and call it "luck"; do not see the long and arduous journey, but only behold the pleasant goal, and call it "good fortune"; do not understand the process, but only perceive the result, and call it "chance."

In all human affairs there are *efforts,* and there are *results,* and the strength of the effort is the measure of the result. Chance is not. "Gifts," powers, material, intellectual, and spiritual possessions are the fruits of effort; they are thoughts completed, objects accomplished, visions realized.

The Vision that you glorify in your mind, the Ideal that you enthrone in your heart—this you will build your life by, this you will become.

SERENITY

Calmness of mind is one of the beautiful jewels of wisdom. It is the result of long and patient effort in self-control. Its presence is an indication of ripened experience, and of a more than ordinary knowledge of the laws and operations of thought.

A man becomes calm in the measure that he understands himself as a thought-evolved being, for such knowedge necessitates the understanding of others as the result of thought, and as he develops a right understanding, and sees more and more clearly the internal relations of things by the action of cause and effect, he ceases to fuss and fume and worry and grieve, and remains poised, steadfast, serene.

The calm man, having learned how to govern himself, knows how to adapt himself to others; and they, in turn, reverence his spiritual strength, and feel that they can learn of him and rely upon him. The more tranquil a man becomes, the greater is his success, his influence, his power for good. Even the ordinary trader will find his business prosperity increase as he develops a greater self-control and equanimity, for people will always prefer to deal with a man whose demeanor is strongly equable.

The strong, calm man is always loved and revered. He is like a shade-giving tree in a thirsty land, or a sheltering rock in a storm. "Who does not love a tranquil heart, a sweet-tempered, balanced life? It does not matter whether it rains or shines, or what changes come to those possessing these blessings, for they are always sweet, serene, and calm. That exquisite poise of character which we call serenity is the last lesson of culture; it is the flowering of life, the fruitage of the soul. It is precious as wisdom, more to be desired than gold—yea, than even fine gold. How insignificant mere money-seeking looks in comparison with a serene life—a life that dwells in the ocean of Truth, beneath the waves, beyond the reach of tempests, in the Eternal Calm!

"How many people we know who sour their lives, who ruin all that is sweet and beautiful by explosive tempers, who destroy their poise of character, and make bad blood! It is a question whether the great majority of people do not ruin their lives and mar their happiness by lack of self-control. How few people we meet in life who are well-balanced, who have that exquisite poise which is characteristic of the finished character!"

Yes, humanity surges with uncontrolled passion, is tumultuous with ungoverned grief, is blown about by anxiety and doubt. Only the wise man, only he whose thoughts are controlled and purified, makes the winds and the storms of the soul obey him.

Tempest-tossed souls, wherever ye may be, under whatsoever conditions ye may live, know this—in the ocean of life the isles of Blessedness are smiling, and the sunny shore of your ideal awaits your coming. Keep your hand firmly upon the helm of thought. In the bark of your soul reclines the commanding Master; He does but sleep; wake Him. Self-control is strength; Right Thought is mastery; Calmness is power. Say unto your heart, "Peace, be still!"

BYWAYS OF

BLESSEDNESS

(1904)

FOREWORD

Along the highways of Burma there are placed, at regular distances away from the dust of the road and under the cool shade of groups of trees, small wooden buildings called "rest-houses," where the weary traveller may rest a while, and allay his thirst and assuage his hunger and fatigue by partaking of the food and the water that the kindly inhabitants place there as a religious duty.

Along the great highways of life there are such resting-places; away from the heat of passion and the dust of disappointment, under the cool and refreshing shade of lowly Wisdom, are the humble, unimposing "rest-houses" of peace, and the little, almost unnoticed, byways of blessedness, where alone the weary and footsore can find strength and healing.

Nor can these byways be ignored without suffering. Along the great road of life, hurrying, and eager to reach some illusive goal, presses the multitude, despising the apparently insignificant "rest-houses" of true thought, not heeding the narrow little byways of blessed action, regarded by them as unimportant; and hour by hour men are fainting and falling, and numbers that cannot be counted perish of heart-hunger, heart-thirst, and heart-fatigue.

But he who will step aside from the passionate press, and deign to enter the byways here presented, his happy feet shall press the incomparable flowers of blessedness, his eyes be gladdened with their beauty, and his mind refreshed with their sweet perfume. Rested and sustained, he shall escape the fever and delirium of life, and, strong and happy, he will not fall fainting in the dust nor perish by the way, but will successfully accomplish his journey.

—James Allen

CONTENTS

RIGHT BEGINNINGS

All common things, each day's events,
That with the hour begin and end;
Our pleasures and our discontents
Are rounds by which we may ascend.
We have not wings, we cannot soar;
But we have feet to scale and climb.

—Longfellow

For common life its wants
And ways, would I set forth in beauteous hues.

—Browning

Life is full of beginnings. They are presented every day and every hour to every person. Most beginnings are small and appear trivial and insignificant, but in reality they are the most important things in life.

See how in the material world everything proceeds from small beginnings. The mightiest river is at first a rivulet over which the grasshopper could leap; the great flood commences with a few drops of rain; the sturdy oak, that has endured the storms of a thousand winters, was once an acorn.

Consider how in the spiritual world the greatest things proceed from smallest beginnings. A light fancy may be the inception of a wonderful invention or an immortal work of art; a spoken sentence may turn the tide of history; a pure thought entertained may lead to the exercise of a world-wide regenerative power.

Have you yet discovered the vast importance of beginnings? Do you really know what is involved in a beginning? Do you know the number of beginnings you are continuously making, and do you realize their full import? If not, come with me for a short time, thoughtfully to explore this much ignored byway of blessedness; for blessed it is when wisely resorted to, and much strength and comfort it holds for the understanding mind.

A beginning is a cause, and as such it must be followed by an effect or a train of effects, and the effect will be of the same nature as the cause. The nature of an initial impulse determines the body of its results. A beginning also presupposes an ending, a consummation, achievement, or goal. A gate leads to a path, and the path to some particular destination; so a beginning leads to results, and results lead to a completion.

There are right beginnings and wrong beginnings, followed by effects of a like nature. You can, by careful thought, avoid wrong beginnings and make right beginnings, and so escape evil results and enjoy good results.

There are beginnings over which you have no control and authority—these are without, in the universe, in the world of nature around you, and in other people possessing the same liberty as yourself.

Do not concern yourself with these beginnings, but direct your energies and attention to those beginnings over which you have complete control and authority, which bring about the complicated web of results which compose your life. These beginnings are to be found in the realm of your own thoughts and actions; in your mental attitude toward the variety of circumstances through which you pass; in your conduct day by day—in short, in your life as you make it, which is your world of good or ill.

In aiming at the life of Blessedness one of the simplest beginnings to be considered and rightly made is that which we all make every day—the beginning of each day's life.

How do you begin each day? At what hour do you rise? How do you begin your work? In what frame of mind do you enter upon the sacred life of a new day? What answer can you give your heart to these important questions? You will find that much happiness or unhappiness follows upon the right or wrong beginning of the day, and that, when every day is wisely begun, happy and harmonious sequences will mark its course, and life in its totality will not fall far short of the ideal blessedness.

It is a right and strong beginning of the day to rise at an early hour. Even if your worldly work does not demand it, it is wise to make of it a habit, and begin the day strongly by shaking off indolence and by putting on vigor and energy. How are you to develop strength of will and mind and body if you begin every day by yielding to weakness? Self-indulgence is followed by unhappiness. Those who lie a-bed till late are not necessarily bright and cheerful and fresh, but often the prey of irritabilities, depressions, debilities, nervous disorders, abnormal fancies, and all unhappy moods. This is the heavy price they have to pay for their daily indulgence. Yet, so blinding is the pandering to self that, like the man taking his daily dram in the belief that it is bracing the nerves which it is all the time shattering, so the lie-a-bed is convinced that long hours of ease are necessary for him as a possible remedy for those very moods and weaknesses and disorders of which his indulgence is the cause. Men and women are unaware of the losses that they entail upon themselves by this common indulgence: loss of strength both of mind and body, loss of prosperity, loss of knowledge, and loss of happiness.

Begin the day by rising early. If you have no object in doing so, never mind; arise, go for a gentle walk among the beauties of nature, and you will experience a buoyancy, a freshness, and a delight, not to say a peace of mind, that will reward you for your effort. One good effort is followed by another; and when a man begins the day by rising early, even though with no other purpose in view, he will find the silent early hour so conducive to clearness of mind and calmness of thought, his early morning walk so profitable in enabling him to become a consecutive thinker and so to see life and its problems, as well as himself and his affairs, in a clearer light; that in time he will rise early for the express purpose of preparing and harmonizing his mind to meet any and every difficulty with wisdom and calm strength.

There is, indeed, so spiritual an influence in the early morning hour, so divine a silence and inexpressible repose, that he who, purposeful and strong, throws off the mantle of ease and climbs the hills to greet the morning sun will thereby climb no inconsiderable distance up the hills of blessedness and truth.

The right beginning of the day will be followed by cheerfulness at the first meal, permeating the household with a sunny influence; and the work of the day will be undertaken in a strong and confident spirit, and the whole day will be well lived.

There is also a sense in which every day is to be regarded as the beginning of a new life, in which one can think, act, and live newly, and in a wiser and better spirit.

> *Every day is a fresh beginning;*
> *Every morn is the world made new.*
> *Ye who are weary of sorrow and sinning,*
> *Here is a beautiful hope for you,*
> *A hope for me and a hope for you.*

Do not dwell upon the sins and mistakes of yesterday so exclusively as to have no energy and mind left for living rightly to-day, and do not think that the sins of yesterday can prevent you from living aright to-day. Begin to-day right with the world, and aided by the accumulated experiences of all your past days, live it better than any of your previous days; but you cannot possibly live it better unless you *begin* it better. The character of the whole day depends upon the way it is begun.

Another beginning of great importance is the beginning of any particular and responsible undertaking. How does a man begin the building of a house? He secures a plan of the proposed edifice, and proceeds to build according to the plan, scrupulously following it in every detail, from the foundation up. Should he neglect the beginning—the obtaining of an architectural plan—his labor would be wasted, and his building, should it reach completion without tumbling to pieces, would be insecure and worthless. The same law holds good in any important work: the right beginning and first essential is *a definite mental plan on which to build*. Nature will have no slip-shod work, no slovenliness, and she annihilates confusion, or rather, confusion is in itself annihilation. Order, definiteness, purpose, eternally and universally prevail; and he who in his operations ignores these elements of precision at once deprives himself of substantiality, completeness, success.

> *Life without a plan,*
> *As useless as the moment it began,*
> *Serves merely as a soil for discontent*
> *To thrive in, an encumbrance ere half spent.*

Let a man start in business without having in his mind a well formed plan to pursue systematically, and he will be incoherent in his efforts and must fail in his business operations. The laws to be observed in the building of a house also operate in the building up of a business. A definite plan is followed by coherent effort; and coherent effort is followed by well-knit and orderly results—completeness, perfection, success, happiness.

But not only mechanical and commercial enterprise—all undertakings, of whatsoever nature, come under this law. The author's book, the artist's picture, the orator's speech, the reformer's work, the inventor's machine, the general's campaign, are all carefully organized and planned in the mind before the attempt to actualize them is commenced; and in accordance with the unity, solidarity, and perfection of the original mental plan will be the actual and ultimate success of the undertaking.

Successful men, influential men, good men are those who, among other things, have learned the value and utilized the power hidden in the obscure beginnings that the foolish man passes by as insignificant.

But the most important beginning of all—that upon which affliction or blessedness inevitably depends, yet the one most neglected and least understood—is the inception of thought in the hidden, but causal, region of the mind. Your whole life is a series of effects, having their cause in thought—in your own thought. All conduct is made and moulded by thought; all deeds, good or bad, are thoughts made visible. A seed put into the ground is the beginning of a plant or tree; the seed germinates, the plant or tree comes forth into the light and evolves. A thought put into the mind is the beginning of a line of conduct: the thought first sends down its roots into the mind, thence to push forth into the light in the form of actions or conduct, which evolve into character and destiny.

Loving, gentle, kind, unselfish, and pure thoughts are right beginnings, leading to blissful results. This is so simple, so plain, so absolutely true; and yet how neglected, how evaded, and how little understood!

The gardener who most carefully studies how, when, and where to put in his seeds gains the greater horticultural knowledge and obtains the best results. The best crops gladden the soul of him who makes the best beginning. The man who most patiently studies how to put into his mind the seeds of strong, wholesome, and charitable thoughts, will obtain the best results in life, and gain the greater knowledge of truth. The greatest blessedness comes to him who infuses into his mind the purest and noblest thoughts.

None but right acts can follow right thoughts; none but a right life can follow right acts—and by living a right life all blessedness is achieved.

He who considers the nature and import of his thoughts, who strives daily to eliminate bad thoughts and supplant them with good, comes at last to see that thoughts are the beginnings of results which affect every fibre of his being, which potently influence every event and circumstance of his life. And when he thus sees, he thinks only right thoughts, chooses to make only those mental beginnings which lead to peace and blessedness.

Wrong thoughts are painful in their inception, painful in their growth, and painful in their fruitage. Right thoughts are blissful in their inception, blissful in their growth, and blissful in their fruitage.

Many are the right beginnings which a man must discover and adopt on his way to wisdom; but that which is first and last, most important and all-embracing, which is the source and fountain of all abiding happiness, is the right beginning of the mental operations—this implies the steady development of self-control, willpower, steadfastness, strength, purity, gentleness, insight, and comprehension. It leads to the perfecting of life, for he who thinks perfectly has abolished all unhappiness, his every moment is peaceful, his years are rounded with bliss—he has attained to the complete and perfect blessedness.

SMALL TASKS AND DUTIES

Wrapped in our nearest duty is the key
Which shall unlock for us the Heavenly Gate:
Unveiled, the Heavenly Vision he shall see.
Who cometh not too early or too late.

Like the star
That shines afar,

Without haste
And without rest,
Let each man wheel with steady sway
Round the task that rules the day,
And do his best.

—GOETHE

As pain and bliss inevitably follow on wrong and right beginnings, so unhappiness and blessedness are inseparably bound up with small tasks and duties. Not that a duty has any power of itself to bestow happiness or the reverse—this is contained in the attitude of mind which is assumed toward the duty—and everything depends upon the way in which it is approached and done.

Not only great happiness but great power arises from doing little things unselfishly, wisely, and perfectly, for life in its totality is made up of little things. Wisdom inheres in the common details of everyday existence, and when the *parts* are made perfect the *Whole* will be without blemish.

Everything in the universe is made up of little things, and the perfection of the great is based upon the perfection of the small. If any detail of the universe were imperfect the Whole would be imperfect. If any particle were omitted the aggregate would cease to be. Without a grain of dust there could be no world, and the world is perfect because the grain of dust is perfect. Neglect of the small is confusion of the great. The snowflake is as perfect as the star; the dewdrop is as symmetrical as the planet; the microbe is not less mathematically proportioned than the man. By laying stone upon stone, plumbing and fitting each with perfect adjustment, the temple at last stands forth in all its architectural beauty. The small precedes the great. The small is not merely the apologetic attendant of the great, it is its master and informing genius.

Vain men are ambitious to be great, and look about to do some great thing, ignoring and despising the little tasks which call for immediate attention, and in the doing of which there is no vainglory, regarding such "trivialities" as beneath the notice of great men. The fool lacks knowledge because he lacks humility, and, inflated with the thought of self-importance, he aims at impossible things.

The great man has become such by the scrupulous and unselfish attention which he has given to small duties. He has become wise and powerful by sacrificing ambition and pride in the doing of those necessary things which evoke no applause and promise no reward. He never sought greatness; he sought faithfulness, unselfishness, integrity, truth; and in finding these in the common round of small tasks and duties he unconsciously ascended to the level of greatness.

The great man knows the vast value that inheres in moments, words, greetings, meals, apparel, correspondence, rest, work, detached efforts, fleeting obligations, in the thousand-and-one little things which press upon him for attention—briefly, in the common details of life. He sees everything as divinely apportioned, needing only the application of dispassionate thought and action on his part to render life blessed and perfect. He neglects nothing, does not hurry; seeks to escape nothing but error and folly; attends to every duty as it is presented to him, and does not postpone and regret. By giving himself unreservedly to his nearest duty, forgetting alike pleasure and pain, he attains to that combined childlike simplicity and unconscious power which is greatness.

The advice of Confucius to his disciples: "Eat at your own table as you would at the table of a king," emphasises the immeasurable importance of little things, as also does that aphorism of another great teacher, Buddha: "If anything is to be done, let a man do it, let him attack it vigorously." To neglect small tasks, or to execute them in a perfunctory or slovenly manner, is a mark of weakness and folly.

The giving of one's entire and unselfish attention to every duty in its proper place evolves, by a natural growth, higher and ever higher combinations of duties, because it evolves power and develops talent, genius, goodness, character. A man ascends into greatness as naturally and unconsciously as the plant evolves a flower, and in the same manner, by fitting with unabated energy and diligence, every effort and detail in its proper place, thus harmonising his life and character without friction or waste of power.

Of the almost innumerable recipes for the development of "will-power" and "concentration" which are now scattered abroad, one looks almost in vain for any wholesome hint applicable to vital experience. "Breathings," "postures," "visualisings," "occult methods" are practices as delusive as they are artificial and remote from all that is real and essential in life; while the true path of—path of duty, of earnest and undivided application to one's daily task—along which alone will-power and concentration of thought can be wholesomely and normally developed, remains unknown, untrodden, unexplored even by the elect.

All unnatural forcing and straining in order to gain "power" should be abandoned. There is no way from childhood to manhood but by growth; nor is there any other way from folly to wisdom, from ignorance to knowledge, from weakness to strength. A man must learn how to grow little by little and day after day, by adding thought to thought, effort to effort, deed to deed.

It is true the fakir gains some sort of power by his long persistence in "postures," and "mortifications," but it is a power which is bought at a heavy price, and that price is an equal loss of strength in another direction. He is never a strong, useful character, but a mere fantastic specialist in some psychological trick. He is not a developed man, he is a maimed man.

True will-power consists in overcoming the irritabilities, follies, rash impulses, and moral lapses which accompany the daily life of the individual, and which are apt to manifest themselves on every slight provocation; and in developing calmness, self-possession, and dispassionate action in the press and heat of worldly duties, and in the midst of the passionate and unbalanced throng. Anything short of this is not true power, and this can only be developed along the normal pathway of steady growth in executing ever more and more masterfully, unselfishly, and perfectly the daily round of legitimate tasks and pressing obligations.

The master is not he whose "psychological accomplishments," rounded by mystery and wonder, leave him in unguarded moments the prey of irritability, of regret, of peevishness, or other petty folly or vice, but he whose "mastery" is manifested in fortitude, non-resentment, steadfastness, calmness, and infinite patience. The true Master is master of himself; anything other than this is not mastery but delusion.

The man who sets his whole mind on the doing of each task as it is presented, who puts into it energy and intelligence, shutting all else out from his mind, and striving to do that one thing, no matter how small, completely and perfectly, detaching himself from all reward in his task— that man will every day be acquiring greater command over his mind, and will, by ever-ascending degrees, become at last a man of power—a Master.

Put yourself unreservedly into your present task, and so work, so act, so live that you shall leave each task a finished piece of labor—this is the true way to the acquisition of will-power, concentration of thought, and conservation of energy. Look not about for magical formulas, for strained and artificial methods. Every resource is already with you and within you. You have but to learn how wisely to apply yourself in that place which you now occupy. Until this is done those other and higher places which are waiting for you cannot be taken possession of, cannot be reached.

There is no way to strength and wisdom but by acting strongly and wisely in the present moment, and each present moment reveals its own task. The great man, the wise man, does small things greatly, regarding nothing as "trivial" that is necessary. The weak man, the foolish man, does small things carelessly and meanly, hankering the while after some greater work for which, in his neglect and inability in small matters, he is ceaselessly advertising his incapacity. The man who least governs himself is always more ambitious to govern others and assume important responsibilities. "Whoso neglects a thing which he suspects he ought to do because it seems too small a thing is deceiving himself; it is not too little but too great for him that he doeth it not."

And just as the strong doing of small tasks leads to greater strength, so the doing of those tasks weakly leads to greater weakness. What a man is in his fractional duties that he is in the aggregate of his character. Weakness is as great a source of suffering as sin, and there can be no true blessedness until some measure of strength of character is evolved. The weak man becomes strong by attaching value to little things and doing them accordingly. The strong man becomes weak by falling into looseness and neglect concerning small things, thereby forfeiting his simple wisdom and squandering his energy. Herein we see the beneficent operation of that law of growth which is expressed in the little-understood words: "To him that hath shall be given, and from him that hath not shall be taken away even that which he hath." Man instantly gains or loses by every thought he thinks, every word he says, every act he does, and every work to which he puts hand and heart.

His character from moment to moment is a graduating quantity, to or from which some measure of good is added or subtracted during every moment, and the gain or loss is involved, even to absoluteness, in each thought, word, and deed as these follow each other in rapid sequence.

He who masters the small becomes the rightful possessor of the great. He who is mastered by the small can achieve no superlative victory.

Life is a kind of co-operative trust in which the whole is of the nature of, and dependent upon, the unit.

A successful business, a perfect machine, a glorious temple, or a beautiful character is evolved from the perfect adjustment of a multiplicity of parts.

The foolish man thinks that little faults, little indulgences, little sins, are of no consequence; he persuades himself that so long as he does not commit flagrant immoralities he is virtuous, and even holy; but he is thereby deprived of virtue and holiness, and the world knows him accordingly; it does not reverence, adore, and love him; it passes him by; he is reckoned of no account; his influence is destroyed. The efforts of such a man to make the world virtuous, his exhortations to his fellow-men to abandon great vices, are empty of substance and barren of fruitage. The insignificance which he attaches to his small vices permeates his whole character and is the measure of his manhood: he is regarded as an insignificant man. The levity with which he commits his errors and publishes his weakness comes back to him in the form of neglect and loss of influence and respect: he is not sought after, for who will seek to be taught of folly? His work does not prosper, for who will lean upon a reed? His words fall upon deaf ears, for they are void of practice, wisdom, and experience, and who will go after an echo?

The wise man, or he who is becoming wise, sees the danger which lurks in those common personal faults which men mostly commit thoughtlessly and with impunity; he also sees the salvation which inheres in the abandonment of those faults, as well as in the practice of virtuous thoughts and acts which the majority disregard as unimportant, and in those quiet but momentous daily conquests over self which are hidden from other's eyes.

He who regards his smallest delinquencies as of the gravest nature becomes a saint. He sees the far-reaching influence, good or bad, which extends from his every thought and act, and how he himself is made or unmade by the soundness or unsoundness of those innumerable details of conduct which combine to form his character and life, and so he watches, guards, purifies, and perfects himself little by little and step by step.

As the ocean is composed of drops, the earth of grains, and the stars of points of light, so is life composed of thoughts and acts; without these life would not be. Every man's life, therefore, is what his apparently detached thoughts and acts make it. Their combination is himself. As the year consists of a given number of sequential moments, so a man's character and life consists of a given number of sequential thoughts and deeds, and the finished whole will bear the impress of the parts.

All sorts of things and weather
Must be taken in together,
To make up a year
And a sphere.

Little kindnesses, generosities, and sacrifices make up a kind and generous character. Little renunciations, endurances and victories over self make up a strong and noble character. The truly honest man is honest in the minutest details of his life. The noble man is noble in every little thing he says and does.

It is a fatal delusion with men to think that life is detached from the momentary thought and act, and not to understand that the passing thought and deed is the foundation and substance of life. When this is fully understood all things are seen as sacred, and every act becomes religious. Truth is wrapped up in infinitesimal details. Thoroughness is genius.

Possessions vanish, and opinions change,
And passions hold a fluctuating seat:
But, by the storms or circumstance unshaken,
And subject neither to eclipse nor wane,
Duty exists.

You do not live your life in the mass; you live it in the fragments, and from these the mass emerges. You can will to live each fragment nobly if you choose, and, this being done, there can be no particle of baseness in the finished whole. The saying "Take care of the pence and the pounds will take care of themselves" is seen to be more than worldly-wise when applied spiritually, for, to take care of the present, passing act, knowing that by so doing the total sum and amount of life and character will be safely preserved, is to be divinely wise. Do not long to do great and laudable things; these will do themselves if you do your present task nobly. Do not chafe at the restrictions and limitations of your present duty, but be nobly unselfish in the doing of it, putting aside discontent, listlessness, and the foolish contemplation of great deeds which lie beyond you—and lo! already the greatness for which you sighed begins to appear. There is no weakness like peevishness. Aspire to the attainment of inward nobility, not outward glory, and begin to attain it where you now are.

The irksomeness and sting which you feel to be in your task are in your mind only. Alter your attitude of mind toward it, and at once the crooked path is made straight, the unhappiness is turned into joy.

See that your every fleeting moment is strong, pure, and purposeful; put earnestness and unselfishness into every passing task and duty; make your every thought, word, and deed sweet and true; thus learning, by practice and experience, the inestimable value of the small things of life, you will gather, little by little, abundant and enduring blessedness.

TRANSCENDING DIFFICULTIES AND PERPLEXITIES

Man who would be
Must rule the empire of himself; in it
Must be supreme, establishing his throne
On vanquished will, quelling the anarchy
Of hopes and fears, being himself alone.

—SHELLEY

Have you missed in your aim? Well, the mark is still shining.
Did you faint in the race? Well, take breath for the next.

—ELLA WHEELER WILCOX

To suggest that any degree of blessedness may be extracted from difficulties and perplexities will doubtless appear absurd to many; but truth is ever paradoxical, and the curses of the foolish are the blessings of the wise. Difficulties arise in ignorance and weakness, and they call for the attainment of knowledge and the acquisition of strength.

As understanding is acquired by right living, difficulties become fewer, and perplexities gradually fade away, like the perishable mists which they are.

Your difficulty is not contained, primarily, in the situation which gave rise to it, but in the mental state with which you regard that situation and which you bring to bear upon it. That which is difficult to a child presents no difficulty to the matured mind of the man; and that which to the mind of an unintelligent man is surrounded with perplexity would afford no ground for perplexity to an intelligent man.

To the untutored and undeveloped mind of the child how great, and apparently insurmountable, appear the difficulties which are involved in the learning of some simple lesson. How many anxious and laborious hours and days, or even months, its solution costs; and, frequently, how many tears are shed in hopeless contemplation of the unmastered, and apparently insurmountable, wall of difficulty! Yet the difficulty is in the ignorance of the child only, and its conquest and solution is absolutely necessary for the development of intelligence and for the ultimate welfare, happiness, and usefulness of the child.

Even so is it with the difficulties of life with which older children are confronted, and which it is imperative, for their own growth and development, that they should solve and surmount; and each difficulty solved means so much more experience gained, so much more insight and wisdom acquired; it means a valuable lesson learned, with the added gladness and freedom of a task successfully accomplished.

What is the real nature of a difficulty? Is it not a situation which is not fully grasped and understood in all its bearings? As such, it calls for the development and exercise of a deeper insight and broader intelligence than has hitherto been exercised. It is an urgent necessity calling forth unused energy, and demanding the expression and employment of latent power and hidden resources. It is, therefore, a good angel, albeit disguised; a friend, a teacher; and, when calmly listened to and rightly understood, leads to larger blessedness and higher wisdom.

Without difficulties there could be no progress, no unfoldment, no evolution; universal stagnation would prevail, and humanity would perish of ennui.

Let a man rejoice when he is confronted with obstacles, for it means that he has reached the end of some particular line of indifference or folly, and is now called upon to summon up all his energy and intelligence in order to extricate himself, and to find a better way; that the powers within him are crying out for greater freedom, for enlarged exercise and scope.

No situation can be difficult of itself; it is the lack of insight into its intricacies and the want of wisdom in dealing with it, which give rise to the difficulty. Immeasurable, therefore, is the gain of a difficulty transcended.

Difficulties do not spring into existence arbitrarily and accidentally; they have their causes, and are called forth by the law of evolution itself, by the growing necessities of the man's being. Herein resides their blessedness.

There are ways of conduct which end inevitably in complications and perplexities, and there are ways of conduct which lead, just as inevitably, out of troublesome complexities. Howsoever tightly a man may have bound himself round he can always unbind himself. Into whatsoever morasses of trouble and trackless wastes of perplexity he may have ignorantly wandered he can always find his way out of them, can always recover the lost highway of uninvolved simplicity which leads, straight and clear, to the sunny city of wise and blessed action. But he will never do this by sitting down and weeping in despair, nor by complaining and worrying and aimlessly wishing he were differently situated. His dilemma calls for alertness, logical thought, and calm calculation. His position requires that he shall strongly command himself; that he shall think and search, and rouse himself to strenuous and unremitting exertion in order to regain himself. Worry and anxiety only serve to heighten the gloom and exaggerate the magnitude of the difficulty. If he will but quietly take himself to task, and retrace, in thought, the more or less intricate way by which he has come to his present position, he will soon perceive where he made mistakes; will discover those places where he took a false turn, and where a little more thoughtfulness, judgment, economy, or self-denial would have saved him. He will see how, step by step, he has involved himself, and how a riper judgment and clearer wisdom would have enabled him to take an altogether different and truer course. Having proceeded thus far, and extracted from his past conduct this priceless grain of golden wisdom, his difficulty will already have assumed less impregnable proportions, and he will then be able to bring to bear upon it the searchlight of dispassionate thought, thoroughly to anatomize it, to comprehend it in all its details, and to perceive the relation which those details bear to the motive source of action and conduct within himself. This being done, the difficulty will have ceased, for the straight way out of it will plainly appear, and the man will thus have learned, for all time, his lesson; will have gained an item of wisdom and a measure of blessedness of which he can never again be deprived.

Just as there are ways of ignorance, selfishness, folly, and blindness which end in confusion and perplexity, so there are ways of knowledge, self-denial, wisdom, and insight which lead to pleaseant and peaceful consummations. He who knows this will meet difficulties in a courageous spirit, and, in overcoming them, will evolve truth out of error, bliss out of pain, and peace out of perturbation.

No man can be confronted with a difficulty which he has not the strength to meet and subdue. Worry is not merely useless, it is folly, for it defeats that power and intelligence which is otherwise equal to the task. Every difficulty can be overcome if rightly dealt with; anxiety is, therefore, unnecessary. The task which cannot be overcome ceases to be a difficulty, and becomes an *impossibility;* and anxiety is still unnecessary, for there is only one way of dealing with an impossibility—namely, to submit to it. The inevitable is the best.

Heartily know,
When half-gods go,
The gods arrive.

And just as domestic, social, and economic difficulties are born of ignorance and lead to riper knowledge, so every religious doubt, every mental perplexity, every heart-beclouding shadow, presages greater spiritual gain, is prophetic of a brighter dawn of intelligence for him on whom it falls.

It is a great day in the life of a man (though at the time he knows it not) when bewildering perplexities concerning the mystery of life take possession of his mind, for it signifies that his era of dead indifference, of animal sloth, of mere vegetative happiness, has come to an end, and that henceforth he is to live as an aspiring, self-evolving being. No longer a mere human animal, he will now begin to live as a man, exerting all his mental energies to the solution of life's problems, to the answering of those haunting perplexities which are the sentinels of truth, and which stand at the gate and threshold of the Temple of Wisdom.

He it is who, when great trials come,
Nor seeks nor shuns them, but doth calmly stay.

Nor will he ever rest again in selfish ease and listless ignorance; nor sleekly sate himself upon the swine's husks of fleshly pleasures; nor find a hiding-place from the ceaseless whisperings of his heart's dark and indefinable interrogatories. The divine within him has awakened; a sleeping god is shaking off the incoherent visions of the night, never again to slumber, never again to rest until his eyes rest upon the full, broad day of Truth.

It is impossible for such a man to hush, for any length of time, the call to higher purposes and achievements which is aroused within him, for the awakened faculties of his being will ceaselessly urge him on to the unravelling of his perplexities; for him there is no more peace in sin, no more rest in error, no final refuge but in Wisdom.

Great will be the blessedness of such a man when, conscious of the ignorance of which his doubts and perplexities are born, and acknowledging and understanding that ignorance, not striving to hide himself from it, he earnestly applies himself to its removal, seeks unremittingly, day after day, for that pathway of light which shall enable him to dispel all the dark shadows, dissolve his doubts, and find the solution to all his pressing problems. And as a child is glad when it has mastered a lesson long toiled over, just so a man's heart becomes light and free when he has satisfactorily met some worldly difficulty; even so, but to a far greater degree, is the heart of a man rendered joyous and peaceful when some vital and eternal question which has been long brooded over and grappled with is at last completely answered, and its darkness is forever dispelled.

Do not regard your difficulties and perplexities as portentous of ill; by so doing you will make them ill; but regard them as prophetic of good, which, indeed, they are. Do not persuade yourself that you can evade them; you cannot. Do not try to run away from them; this is impossible, for wherever you go they will still be there with you—but meet them calmly and bravely; confront them with all the dispassion and dignity which you can command; weigh up their proportions; analyse them; grasp their details; measure their strength; understand them; attack them, and finally vanquish them. Thus will you develop strength and intelligence; thus will you enter one of those byways of blessedness which are hidden from the superficial gaze.

BURDEN-DROPPING

This to me is life;
That it life be a burden, I will join
To make it but the burden of a song.

—BAILEY

Have you heard that it was good to gain the day?
I also say it is good to fall, battles are lost in the same spirit in which they are won.

—WALT WHITMAN

We hear and read much about burden-bearing, but of the better way of burden-dropping very little is heard or known. Yet why should you go about with an oppressive weight at your heart when you might relieve yourself of it and move amongst your fellows heart-free and cheerful? No man carries a load upon his back except necessarily to transfer something from one place to another; he does not saddle his shoulders with a perpetual burden, and then regard himself as a martyr for his pains; and why should you impose upon your mind a useless burden, and then add to its weight the miseries of self-condolence and self-pity? Why not abandon both your load and your misery, and thus add to the gladness of the world by first making yourself glad? No reason can justify, and no logic support, the ceaseless carrying of a grievous load. As in things material a load is only undertaken as a necessary means of transference, and is never a source of sorrow; so in things spiritual a burden should only be taken up as a means toward some good and necessary end, which, when attained, the burden is put aside; and the carrying of such a burden, far from being a source of grief, would be a cause for rejoicing.

We say that bodily mortifications which some religious ascetics inflict upon themselves are unnecessary and vain; and are the mental mortifications which so many people inflict upon themselves less unnecessary and vain?

Where is the burden which should cause unhappiness or sorrow? It does not exist. If a thing is to be done let it be done cheerfully, and not with inward groanings and lamentations. It is of the highest wisdom to embrace necessity as a friend and guide. It is of the greatest folly to scowl upon necessity as an enemy, and to wish or try to overcome or avoid her. We meet our own at every turn, and duties only become oppressive loads when we refuse to recognise and embrace them. He who does any necessary thing in a niggardly and complaining spirit, hunting the while after unnecessary pleasures, lashes himself with the scorpions of misery and disappointment, and imposes upon himself a doubly-weighted burden of weariness and unrest under which he incessantly groans.

> Wake thou, O self, to better things;
> To yonder heights uplift thy wings;
> Take up the psalm of life anew;
> Sing of the good, sing of the true;
> Sing of full victory o'er wrong;
> Make thou a richer, sweeter song;
> Out of thy doubting, care, and pain
> Weave thou a joyous, glad refrain;
> Out of thy thorns a crown weave thou
> Of rare rejoicing. Sing thou, now.

I will give my cheerful, unselfish and undivided attention to the doing of all those things which enter into my compact with life, and, though I walk under colossal responsibilities, I shall be unconscious of any troublesome weight or grievous burden.

You say a certain thing (a duty, a companionship, or a social obligation) troubles you, is burdensome, and you resign yourself to oppression with the thought: "I have entered into this, and will go through with it, but it is a heavy and grievous work." But is the thing really burdensome, or is it your selfishness that is oppressing you? I tell you that that very thing which you regard as so imprisoning a restriction is the first gateway to your emancipation; that work which you regard as a perpetual curse contains for you the actual blessedness which you vainly persuade yourself lies in another and unapproachable direction. All things are mirrors in which you see yourself reflected, and the gloom which you perceive in your work is but a reflection of that mental state which you bring to it. Bring a right, unselfish, state of heart to the thing, and lo! it is at once transformed, and becomes a means of strength and blessedness, reflecting back that which you have brought to it. If you bring a scowling face to your looking-glass will you complain of the glass that it glowers upon you with a deformed visage, or will you put your face right, and so get back from the reflector a more pleasing countenance?

If it is right and necessary that a thing should be done then the doing of it is good, and it can only become burdensome in wishing not to do it. The selfish wish makes the thing appear evil. If it is neither right nor necessary that a thing should be done then the doing of it in order to gain some coveted pleasure is folly, which can only lead to burdensome issues.

The duty which you shirk is your reproving angel; the pleasure which you race after is your flattering enemy. Foolish man! when will you turn round and be wise?

It is the beneficence of the universe that it is everywhere, and at all times, urging its creatures to wisdom as it demands coherence of its atoms. That folly and selfishness entail suffering in ever-increasing degrees of intensity is preservative and good, for agony is the enemy of apathy and the herald of wisdom.

What is painful? What is grievous? What is burdensome? Passion is painful; folly is grievous; selfishness is burdensome.

> It is the dark idolatry of self
> Which, when our thoughts and actions once are done,
> Demands that man should weep, and bleed, and groan.

Eliminate passion, folly, and selfishness from your mind and conduct and you will eliminate suffering from your life. Burden-dropping consists in abandoning the inward selfishness and putting pure love in its place. Go to your task with love in your heart and you will go to it light-hearted and cheerful.

The mind, through ignorance, creates its own burdens and inflicts its own punishments. No one is doomed to carry any load. Sorrow is not arbitrarily imposed. These things are self-made. Reason is the rightful monarch of the mind, and anarchy reigns in his spiritual kingdom when his throne is usurped by passion. When love of pleasure is to the fore heaviness and anguish compose the rear. You are free to choose. Even if you are bound by passion, and feel helpless, you have bound

yourself, and are not helpless. Where you have bound you can unbind. You have come to your present state by degrees, and you can recover yourself by degrees, can reinstate reason and dethrone
passion. The time to avoid evil is before pleasure is embraced, but, once embraced, its train of consequences should teach you wisdom. The time to decide is before responsibilities are adopted, but,
once adopted, all selfish considerations, with their attendant grumblings, whinings, and complainings, should be religiously excluded from the heart. Responsibilities lose their weight when carried
lovingly and wisely.

What heavy burden is a man weighted with which is not made heavier and more unendurable
by weak thoughts or selfish desires? If your circumstances are "trying" it is because you need them,
and can evolve the strength to meet them. They are trying because there is some weak spot within
you, and they will continue to be trying until that spot is eradicated. Be glad that you have the
opportunity of becoming stronger and wiser. No circumstances can be trying to wisdom; nothing
can weary love. Stop brooding over your own trying circumstances and contemplate the lives of
some of those about you.

Here is a woman with a large family who has to make ends meet on a pound a week. She performs
all her domestic duties, down to the washing, finds time to attend on sick neighbors, and manages
to keep entirely out of the two common quagmires—debt and despondency. She is cheerful from
morning to night, and never complains of her "trying circumstances." She is perennially cheerful
because she is unselfish. She is happy in the thought that she is the means of happiness to others.
Were she to brood upon the holidays, the pretty baubles, the lazy hours of which she is deprived;
of the plays she cannot see, the music she cannot hear, the books she cannot read, the parties she
cannot attend, the good she might do, the friendships she is debarred from forming; of the many
pleasures which might only be hers if her circumstances were more favorable—if she brooded thus
what a miserable creature she would be! How unbearably laborious her work would become! How
every little domestic duty would hang like a millstone about her neck, dragging her down to the
grave which, unless she altered her state of mind, she would quickly reach, killed by—selfishness!
But, not living in vain desires for herself, she is relieved of all burdens, and is happy. Cheerfulness
and unselfishness are sworn friends. Love knows no heavy toil.

Here is another woman, with a private income which is more than sufficient, combined with leisure and luxury, yet, because she is called upon to forfeit a portion of her time, pleasure, and money
to discharge some obligation which she wishes to be rid of, and which should be to her a work of
loving service, or fostering in her heart some ungratified desire, she is perpetually discontented
and unhappy, and complains of "trying circumstances." Discontent and selfishness are inseparable
companions. Self-love knows no joyful labor.

Of the two sets of circumstances above depicted (and life is crowded with such contrasted
instances) which are the "trying" conditions? Is it not true that neither of them are trying, and

that both are blest or unblest in accordance with the measure of love or selfishness which is infused into them? Is not the root of the whole matter in the mind of the individual and not in the circumstance?

When a man, who has recently taken up the study of some branch of theology, religion, or "occultism," says; "If I had not burdened myself with a wife and family I could have done a great work; and had I known years ago what I know now I would never have married," I know that that man has not yet found the commonest and broadest way of wisdom (for there is no greater folly than regret,) and that he is incapable of the great work which he is so ambitious to perform. If a man has such deep love for his fellow-men that he is anxious to do a great work for humanity he will manifest that surpassing love always and in the place where he now is. His home will be filled with it, and the beauty and sweetness and peace of his unselfish love will follow wherever he goes, making happy those about him and transmuting all things into good. The love that goes abroad to air itself, and is undiscoverable at home, is not love—it is vanity.

Have I not seen (Oh, pitiful sight!) the cheerless home and neglected children of the misguided missioner and religionist? It is on such self-delusion as this that self-pity and self-martyrdom ever wait, and its self-inflicted misery is regarded by the deluded one as a holy and religious burden which he or she is called upon to bear.

Only a great man can do a great work; and he will be great wherever he is, and will do his noble work under whatsoever conditions he may find himself when he has unfolded and revealed that work.

Thou who art so anxious to work for humanity, to help thy fellow-men, begin that work at home; help thyself, thy neighbor, thy wife, thy child. Do not be deluded; until thou doest, with utmost faithfulness, the nearer and the lesser thou canst not do the farther and greater.

If a man has lived many years of his life in lust and selfish pleasure it is in the order of things that his accumulated errors should at last weigh heavily upon him, as, until they are thus brought home to him, he will not abandon them, will not exert himself to find a better life; but whilst he regards his self-made, self-imposed burdens as "holy crosses" imposed upon him by the Supreme, or as marks of superior virtue, or as loads which Fate, circumstances, or other people have heaped undeservedly and unjustly upon him, he is but lengthening out his folly, increasing the weight of his burdens, and multiplying his pains and sorrows. Only when such a man wakes up to the truth that his burdens are of his own making, that they are the accumulated effects of his own acts, will he cease from unmanly self-pity and find the better way of burden-dropping; only when he opens his eyes to see that his every thought and act is another brick, another stone, built into the temple of his life will he develop the insight which will enable him to recognise his own unstable handiwork, the unflinching manliness to acknowledge it, and the courage to build more nobly and enduringly.

Painful burdens are necessary, but only so long as we lack love and wisdom.

The Temple of Blessedness lies beyond the outer courts of suffering and humiliation and to reach it the pilgrim must pass through the outer courts. For a time he will linger in the outer, but only so long as, through his own imperfect understanding, he mistakes it for the inner. While he pities himself and confounds suffering with holiness he will remain in suffering; but when, casting off the last unholy rag of self-pity, he perceives that suffering is a means and not an end, that it is a state self-originated and self-propagated, then converted and right-minded, he will rapidly pass through the outer courts, and reach the inner abode of peace.

Suffering does not originate in the perfect but in the imperfect; it does not mark the complete but the incomplete; it can, therefore, be transcended. Its self-born cause can be found, investigated, comprehended, and for ever removed.

It is true, therefore, that we must pass through agony to rest, through loneliness to peace; but let the sufferer not forget that it *is* a "passing through;" that the agony is a gateway and not a habitation; that the loneliness is a pathway and not a destination; and that a little farther on he will come to the painless and blissful repose.

Little by little is a burden accumulated; imperceptibly and by degrees is its weight increased. A thoughtless impulse, a gross self-indulgence, a blind passon yielded to and gratified again and again; an impure thought fostered, a cruel word uttered, a foolish thing done time after time, and at last the gathered weight of many follies becomes oppressive. At first, and for a time, the weight is not felt; but it is being added to day after day, and the time comes when the accumulated burden is felt in all its galling weight, when the bitter fruits of selfishness are gathered, and the heart is troubled with the weariness of life. When this period arrives let the sufferer look to himself; let him search for the blessed way of burden-dropping, finding which he will find wisdom to live better, purity to live sweeter, love to live nobler: will find, in the reversal of that conduct by which his burdens were accumulated, light-hearted nights and days, cheerful action, and unclouded joy.

> *Come out of the world—come above it—*
>   *Up over its crosses and graves;*
> *Though the green earth is fair and I love it,*
>   *We must love it as masters, not slaves.*
> *Come up where the dust never rises—*
>   *But only the perfume of flowers—*
> *And your life shall be glad with surprises*
>   *Of beautiful hours.*

HIDDEN SACRIFICES

What need hath man
Of Eden passed, or Paradise to come,
When heaven is round us and within ourselves?

Lowliness is the base of every virtue:
Who goes the lowest, builds, doubt not, the safest.

—BAILEY

Truth is within ourselves; it takes norise
From outward things, whate'er you may believe.

—BROWNING

It is one of the paradoxes of Truth that we gain by giving up; we lose by greedily grasping. Every gain in virtue necessitates some loss in vice; every accession of holiness means some selfish pleasure yielded up; and every forward step on the path of Truth demands the forfeit of some self-assertive error.

He who would be clothed in new garments must first cast away the old, and he who would find the True must sacrifice the false. The gardener digs in the weeds in order that they may feed, with their decay, the plants which are good for food; and the Tree of Wisdom can only flourish on the compost of uprooted follies. Growth—gain—necessitates sacrifice—loss.

The true life, the blessed life, the life that is not tormented with passions and pains, is reached only through sacrifice, not necessarily the sacrifice of outward things, but the sacrifice of the inward errors and defilements, for it is these, and these only, which bring misery into life. It is not the good and true that needs to be sacrificed but the evil and false; therefore all sacrifice is ultimately gain, and there is no essential loss. Yet at first the loss seems great, and the sacrifice is painful, but this is because of the self-delusion and spiritual blindness which always accompany selfishness, and pain must always accompany the cutting away of some selfish portion of one's nature. When the drunkard resolves to sacrifice his lust for strong drink he passes through a period of great suffering, and he feels that he is forfeiting a great pleasure; but when his victory is complete, when the lust is dead, and his mind is calm and sober, then he knows that he has gained incalculably by the giving up of his selfish animal pleasure. What he has lost was evil and false, and not worth keeping—nay, its keeping entailed continual misery—but what he has gained, in character, in self-control, in soberness and greater peace of mind, is good and true, and it was necessary that he should acquire it.

So it is with all true sacrifice; it is at first, and until it is completed, painful, and this is why men shrink from it. They cannot see any purpose in abstaining from and overcoming selfish gratification; it seems to them like losing so much that is sweet, seems to them like courting misery, and giving up all happiness and pleasure. And this must be so; for if a man could know that by giving up his particular forms of selfishness his gain in happiness would be immeasurably greater, unselfishness (which is now so difficult of attainment) would then be rendered infinitely more difficult of achievement, for his desire for the greater gain his selfishness—would thereby be greatly intensified.

No man can become unselfish, and thereby arrive at the highest bliss, until he is willing to lose, looking for neither gain nor reward: it is this state of mind which constitutes unselfishness. A man must be willing humbly to sacrifice his selfish habits and practices because they are untrue and unworthy, and for the happiness of those about him, without expecting any reward or looking for any good to accrue to himself; nay, he must be prepared to lose for himself, to forfeit pleasure and happiness, even life itself, if by so doing he can make the world more beautiful and happy. But does he lose? Does the miser lose when he gives up his lust for gold? Does the thief lose when he abandons stealing? Does the libertine lose when he sacrifices his unworthy pleasures? No man loses by the sacrifice of self, or some portion of self; nevertheless he thinks he will lose by so doing, and because he so thinks he suffers, and this is where the sacrifice comes in—this is where he gains by losing.

All true sacrifice is within; it is spiritual and hidden, and is prompted by deep humility of heart. Nothing but the sacrifice of self can avail, and to this must all men come sooner or later during their spiritual evolution. But in what does this self-abnegation consist? How is it practised? Where is it sought and found? It consists in overcoming the daily proneness to selfish thoughts and acts; it is practised in our common intercourse with others; and it is found in the hour of tumult and temptation.

There are hidden sacrifices of the heart which are infinitely blessed both to him that makes them and those for whom they are made, albeit their making costs much effort and some pain. Men are anxious to do some great thing, to perform some great sacrifice which lies beyond the necessities of their experience, while all the time, perhaps, they are neglecting the one thing needful, are blind to that sacrifice which by its very nearness is rendered imperative. Where lurks your besetting sin? Where lies your weakness? Where does temptation assail you most strongly? There shall you make your first sacrifice, and shall find thereby the way unto your peace. Perhaps it is anger or unkindness. Are you prepared to sacrifice the angry impulse and word, the unkind thought and deed? Are you prepared silently to endure abuse, attack, accusation, and unkindness, refusing to pay back these in their own coin? Nay, more, are you prepared to give in return for these dark follies kindness and loving protection? If so, then you are ready to make those hidden sacrifices which lead to beatific bliss.

If you are given to anger or unkindness offer it up. These hard, cruel, and wrong conditions of mind never brought you any good; they can never bring you anything but unrest, misery, and spiritual blindness. Nor can they ever bring to others anything but unhappiness. Perhaps you will say: "But he was unkind to me first; he treated me unjustly." Perhaps so, but what a poor excuse is this! What an unmanly and ineffectual refuge! For if his unkindness toward you is so wrong and hurtful yours to him must be equally so. Because another is unkind to you is no justification of your own unkindness, but is rather a call for the exercise of greater kindness on your part. Can the pouring in of more water prevent a flood? Neither can unkindness lessen unkindness. Can fire quench fire? Neither can anger overcome anger.

Offer up all unkindness, all anger. "It takes two to make a quarrel;" don't be the "other one." If one is angry or unkind to you try to find out where you have acted wrongly; and, whether you have acted wrongly or not, do not throw back the angry word or unkind act. Remain silent, self-contained, and kindly disposed; and learn, by continual effort in right-doing, to have compassion upon the wrong-doer.

Perhaps you are habitually impatient and irritable. Know, then, the hidden sacrifice which is needful that you should make. *Give up your impatience.* Overcome it there where it is wont to assert itself. Resolve that you will yield no longer to its tyrannical sway but will conquer it and cast it out. It is not worth keeping a single hour, nor would it dominate you for another moment if you were not laboring under the delusion that the follies and perversities of others render impatience on your part necessary. Whatever others may do or say, even though they may mock and taunt you, impatience is not only unnecessary, it can never do any other than aggravate the evil which it seeks to remove. Calm, strong, and deliberate action can accomplish much, but impatience and its accompanying irritability are always indications of weakness and inefficiency. And what do they bestow upon you? Do they bestow rest, peace, happiness, or bring these to those about you? Do they not, rather, make you and those about you wretched? But though your impatience may hurt others it certainly hurts and wounds and impoverishes yourself most of all.

Nor can the impatient man know aught of true blessedness, for he is a continual source of trouble and unrest to himself. The calm beauty and perpetual sweetness of patience are unknown to him, and peace cannot draw near to soothe and comfort him.

There is no blessedness anywhere until impatience is sacrificed; and the sacrifice means the development of endurance, the practice of forbearance, and the creation of a new and gentler habit of mind. When impatience and irritability are entirely put away, are finally offered up on the altar of unselfishness, then is realised and enjoyed the blessedness of a strong, quiet, and peaceful mind.

Each hour we think
Of others more than self, that hour we live again,
And every lowly sacrifice we make
For others' good shall make life more than self,
And ope the windows of thy soul to light
From higher spheres. So hail thy lot with joy.

Then there are little selfish indulgences, some of which appear harmless, and are commonly fostered; but no selfish indulgence can be harmless, and men and women do not know what they lose by repeatedly and habitually succumbing to effeminate and selfish gratifications. If the God in man is to rise strong and triumphant, the beast in man must perish. The pandering to the animal nature, even when it appears innocent and seems sweet, leads away from truth and blessedness. Each time you give way to the animal within you, and feed and gratify him, he waxes stronger and more rebellious, and takes firmer possession of your mind, which should be in the keeping of Truth. Not until a man has sacrificed some apparently trivial indulgence does he discover what strength, what joy, what poise of character and holy influence he has all along been losing by that gratification; not until a man sacrifices his hankering for pleasure does he enter into the fulness of abiding joy.

By his personal indulgences a man degrades himself, forfeits self-respect to the extent and frequency of his indulgence, and deprives himself of exemplary influence and the power to accomplish lasting good in his work in the world. He also, by allowing himself to be led by blind desire, increases his mental blindness, and fails of that ultimate clearness of vision, that clarified percipience which pierces to the heart of things and comprehends the real and the true. Animal indulgence is alien to the perception of Truth. By the sacrifice of his indulgences man rises above confusion and doubt, and arrives at the possession of insight and surety.

Sacrifice your cherished and coveted indulgence; fix your mind on something higher, nobler, and more enduring than ephemeral pleasure; live superior to the craving for sense-excitement, and you will live neither vainly nor uncertainly.

Very far-reaching in its effect upon others, and rich with the revelations of Truth for him who makes it, is the sacrifice of self-assertion—the giving up of all interference with the lives, views, or religion of other people, substituting for it an understanding love and sympathy. Self-assertion or opinionativeness is a form of egotism or selfishness most generally found in connection with intellectualism and dialectical skill. It is blindly presumptive and uncharitable, and, more often than not, is regarded as a virtue; but when once the mind has opened to perceive the way of gentleness and self-sacrificing love then the ignorance, deformity, and painful nature of self-assertion become apparent.

The victim of self-assertion, setting up his own opinions as the standard of right and the measure of judgment, regards all those as wrong whose lives and opinions run counter to his own, and, being eager to put others right, is thereby prevented from putting himself right. His attitude of mind brings about him opposition and contradiction from people who are anxious to put *him* right, and this wounds his vanity and makes him miserable, so that he lives in an almost continual fever of unhappy, resentful, and uncharitable thoughts. There can be no peace for such a man, no true knowledge, and no advancement until he sacrifices his desire to bend others to his own way of thinking and acting. Nor can he understand the hearts of others, and enter lovingly into their strivings and aspirations. His mind is cramped and embittered, and he is shut out from all sweet sympathy and spiritual communion.

He who sacrifices the spirit of self-assertion, who in his daily contact with others puts aside his prejudices and opinions, and strives both to learn from others and to understand them as they are, who allows to others perfect liberty (such as he exercises himself) to choose their own opinions, their own way in life—such a man will acquire a deeper insight, a broader charity, and a richer bliss than he has hitherto experienced, and will strike a byway of blessedness from which he was formerly shut out.

Then there is the sacrifice of greed and all greedy thoughts. The willingness that others should possess rather than we; the not-coveting of things for ourselves but rejoicing that they are possessed and enjoyed by others, that they bring happiness to others; the ceasing to claim one's "own," and the giving up to others, unselfishly and without malice, that which they exact. This attitude of mind is a source of deep peace and great spiritual strength. It is the sacrifice of *self-interest*.

Material possessions are temporary, and in this sense we cannot truly call them our own—they are merely in our keeping for a short time—but spiritual possessions are eternal and must ever remain with us. Unselfishness is a spiritual possession which is only secured by ceasing to covet material possessions and enjoyments, by ceasing to regard things as for our own special and exclusive pleasure, and by our readiness to yield them up for the good of others.

The unselfish man, even though he finds himself involved in riches, stands aloof, in his mind, from the idea of "exclusive possession," and so escapes the bitterness and fear and anxiety which ever accompany the covetous spirit. He does not regard any of his outward accretions as being too valuable to lose, but he regards the virtue of unselfishness as being too valuable to the world—to suffering humanity—to lose or to cast away.

And who is the blessed man? He who is ever hankering after more possessions, thinking only of the personal pleasure he can get out of them? or he who is ever ready to give up what he has for the good and happiness of others? By greed happiness is destroyed; by not-greed happiness is restored.

Another hidden sacrifice, one of great spiritual beauty and of powerful efficacy in the healing of human sorrows, is the sacrifice of *hatred*—the giving up of all bitter thoughts against others, of all malice, dislike, and resentment. Bitter thoughts and blessedness cannot dwell together. Hatred is a fierce fire that scorches up, in the heart of him who harbors it, all the sweet flowers of peace and happiness, and makes a hell of every place where it comes.

Hatred has many names and many forms but only one essence—namely, burning thoughts of resentment against others. It is sometimes, by its blind votaries, called by the name of religion, causing them to attack, slander, and persecute each other because they will not accept each other's views of life and death, thus filling the earth with miseries and tears.

All resentment, dislike, ill-thinking, and ill-speaking of others is hatred, and where there is hatred there is always unhappiness. No one has conquered hatred while thoughts of resentment toward others spring up in his mind. This sacrifice is not complete until a man can think kindly of those who try to do him wrong. Yet it must be made before true blessedness can be realised and known. Beyond the hard, cruel, steely gates of hatred waits the divine angel of love, ready to reveal herself to him who will subdue and sacrifice his hateful thoughts, and conduct him to his peace.

Whatever others may say of you, whatever they may do to you, *never take offence.* Do not return hatred with hatred. If another hates you perhaps you have, consciously or unconsciously, failed somewhere in your conduct, or there may be some misunderstanding which the exercise of a little gentleness and reason may remove; but, under all circumstances, "Father, forgive them" is infinitely better, sweeter, and nobler than "I will have nothing more to do with them." Hatred is so small and poor, so blind and wretched. Love is so great and rich, so far-seeing and blissful.

The highest culture is to speak no ill:
The best reformer is the man whose eyes
Are quick to see all beauty and all worth;
And by his own discreet, well-ordered life
Alone reproves the erring.

Sacrifice all hatred, slay it upon the holy altar of devotion—devotion to others. Think no more of any injury to your own petty self, but see to it that henceforth you injure and wound no other. Open the floodgates of your heart for the inpouring of that sweet, great, beautiful love which embraces all with strong yet tender thoughts of protection and peace, leaving not one, nay, not even he who hates or despises or slanders you, out in the cold.

Then there is the hidden sacrifice of impure desires, of weak self-pity and degrading self-praise, of vanity and pride, for these are unblest attitudes of mind, deformities of heart. He who makes them, one by one, gradually subduing and overcoming them, will, according to the measure of his success, rise above weakness and suffering and sorrow, and will comprehend and enjoy the perfect and imperishable blessedness.

Now, all these hidden sacrifices which are here mentioned are pure, humble heart-offerings. They are made within; are offered up on the sacred, lonely, unseen altar of one's own heart. Not one of them can be made until the fault is first silently acknowledged and confessed. No man can sacrifice an error until he first of all confess (to himself) "I am in error;" when, yielding it up, he will perceive and receive the truth which his error formerly obscured.

"The kingdom of heaven cometh not by observation," and the silent sacrifice of self for the good of others, the daily giving up of one's egotistic tendencies, is not seen and rewarded of men, and brings no loud blazon of popularity and praise. It is hidden away from the eyes of all the world, nay, even from the gaze of those who are nearest to you, for no eyes of flesh can perceive its spiritual beauty. But think not that because it is unperceived it is therefore futile. Its blissful radiance is enjoyed by you, and its power for good over others is great and far-reaching, for though they cannot see it, nor, perhaps, understand it, yet they are unconsciously influenced by it. They will not know what silent battles you are fighting, what eternal victories over self you are achieving, but they will *feel* your altered attitude, your new mind wrought of the fabric of love and loving thoughts, and will share somewhat in its happiness and bliss. They will know nothing of the frequent fierceness of the fight you are waging, of the wounds you receive and the healing balm you apply, of the anguish and the after-peace; but they will know that you have grown sweeter and gentler, stronger and more silently self-reliant, more patient and pure, and that they are rested and helped by your presence. What rewards can compare with this? Beside the fragrant offices of love the praises of men are gross and fulsome, and in the pure flame of a selfless heart the flatteries of the world are turned to ashes. Love is its own reward, its own joy, its own satisfaction; it is the final refuge and resting-place of passion-tortured souls.

The sacrifice of self, and the acquisition of the supreme knowledge and bliss which it confers, is not accomplished by one great and glorious act but by a series of lesser and successive sacrifices in the ordinary life of the world, by a succession of steps in the daily conquest of Truth over selfishness. He who each day accomplishes some victory over himself, who subdues and puts behind him some unkind thought, some impure desire, some tendency to sin, is every day growing stronger, purer, and wiser, and every dawn finds him nearer to that final glory of Truth which each self-sacrificing act reveals in part.

Look not outside thee nor beyond thee for the light and blessedness of Truth, but look within; thou wilt find it within the narrow sphere of thy duty, even in the humble and hidden sacrifices of thine own heart.

SYMPATHY

When thy gaze
Turns it on thine own soul, be most severe:
But when it falls upon a fellow-man
Let kindliness control it; and refrain
From that belittling censure that springs forth
From common lips like weeds from marshy soil.

—Ella Wheeler Wilcox

I do ask the wounded person how he feels,
I myself become the wounded person.

—Walt Whitman

We can only sympathise with others in so far as we have conquered ourselves. We cannot think and feel for others while we are engaged in condoling with and pitying ourselves; cannot deal tenderly and lovingly with others while we are anxious for our own pre-eminence or for the exclusive preservation of ourselves, our opinions, and our own generally. What is sympathy but thoughtfulness for others in the forgetfulness of self?

To sympathise with others we must first understand them, and to understand them we must put away all personal preconceptions concerning them, and must see them as they are. We must enter into their inner state and become one with them, looking through their mental eyes and comprehending the range of their experience. You cannot, of course, do this with a being whose wisdom and experiences are greater than your own; nor can you do it with any if you regard yourself as being on a higher plane than others (for egotism and sympathy cannot dwell together), but you can practice it with all those who are involved in sins and sufferings from which you have successfully extricated yourself, and, though your sympathy cannot embrace and overshadow the man whose greatness is beyond you, yet you can place yourself in such an attitude toward him as to receive the protection of his larger sympathy, and so make for yourself an easier way out of the sins and sufferings by which you are still enchained.

Prejudice and ill-will are complete barriers to the giving of sympathy, while pride and vanity are total barriers to its reception. You cannot sympathise with a person for whom you have conceived a hatred; you cannot enjoy the sympathy of one whom you envy. You cannot understand the person whom you dislike, or him for whom, through animal impulse, you have framed an ill-formed affection. You do not, cannot, see him as he is, but see only your own imperfect notions of him; see only a distorted image of him through the exaggerating medium of your ill-grounded opinions.

To see others as they are you must not allow impulsive likes or dislikes, powerful prejudices, or egotistic considerations to come between you and them. You must not resent their actions or condemn their beliefs and opinions. You must leave yourself entirely out, and must, for the time being, assume their position. Only in this way can you become *en rapport* with them, and so fathom their life, their experience, and understand it, and when a man is understood it becomes impossible to condemn him. Men misjudge, condemn, and avoid each other because they do not understand each other, and they do not understand each other because they have not overcome and purified themselves.

Life is growth, development, evolution, and there is no essential distinction between the sinner and the saint—there is only a difference in degree. The saint was once a sinner; the sinner will one day be a saint. The sinner is the child; the saint is the grown man. He who separates himself from sinners, regarding them as wicked men to be avoided, is like a man avoiding contact with little children because they are unwise, disobedient, and play with toys.

All life is one, but it has a variety of manifestations. The grown flower is not something distinct from the tree: it is a part of it; is only another form of leaf. Steam is not something apart from water: it is but another form of water. And in like manner good is transmuted evil: the saint is the sinner developed and transformed.

The sinner is one whose understanding is undeveloped, and he ignorantly chooses wrong modes of action. The saint is one whose understanding is ripened, and he wisely chooses right modes of action. The sinner condemns the sinner, condemnation being a wrong mode of action. The saint never condemns the sinner, remembering that he himself formerly occupied the same place, but thinks of him with deep sympathy, regarding him in the light of a younger brother or a friend, for sympathy is a right and enlightened mode of action.

The perfected saint, who gives sympathy to all, needs it of none, for he has transcended sin and suffering, and lives in the enjoyment of lasting bliss; but all who suffer need sympathy, and all who sin *must* suffer. When a man comes to understand that every sin, whether of thought or deed, receives its just quota of suffering he ceases to condemn and begins to sympathise, seeing the sufferings which sin entails; and he comes to such understanding by purifying himself.

As a man purges himself of passions, as he transmutes his selfish desires and puts under foot his egotistic tendencies, he sounds the depths of all human experiences—all sins and sufferings and sorrows, all motives and thoughts and deeds—and comprehends the moral law in its perfection. Complete self-conquest is perfect knowledge, perfect sympathy, and he who views men with the stainless vision of a pure heart views them with a pitying heart, sees them as part of himself, not as something defiled and separate and distinct, but as his very self, sinning as he has sinned, suffering as he has suffered, sorrowing as he has sorrowed, yet, withal, glad in the knowledge that they will come, as he has come, to perfect peace at last.

The truly good and wise man cannot be a passionate partisan, but extends his sympathy to all, seeing no evil in others to be condemned and resisted, but seeing the sin which is pleasant to the sinner, and the after-sorrow and pain which the sinner does not see, and, when it overtakes him, does not understand.

A man's sympathy extends just so far as his wisdom reaches, and no further; and a man only grows wiser as he grows tenderer and more compassionate. To narrow one's sympathy is to narrow one's heart, and so to darken and embitter one's life. To extend and broaden one's sympathy is to enlighten and gladden one's life, and to make plainer to others the way of light and gladness.

To sympathise with another is to receive his being into our own, to become one with him, for unselfish love indissolubly unites, and he whose sympathy reaches out to and embraces all human-kind and all living creatures has realised his identity and oneness with all, and comprehends the universal Love and Law and Wisdom.

Man is shut out from Heaven and Peace and Truth only in so far as he shuts out others from his sympathy. Where his sympathy ends his darkness and torment and turmoil begin, for to shut others out from our love is to shut ourselves out from the blessedness of love, and to become cramped in the dark prison of self.

Whoever walks a furlong without sympathy walks to his own funeral dressed in a shroud.

Only when one's sympathy is unlimited is the Eternal Light of Truth revealed; only in the Love that knows no restrictions is the boundless bliss enjoyed.

Sympathy is bliss; in it is revealed the highest, purest blessedness. It is divine, for in its reciprocal light all thought of self is lost, and there remains only the pure joy of oneness with others, the ineffable communion of spiritual identity. Where a man ceases to sympathise he ceases to live, ceases to see and realise and know.

One cannot truly sympathise with others until all selfish considerations concerning them are put away, and he who does this, and strives to see others as they are, strives to realise their particular sins, temptations, and sorrows, their beliefs, opinions, and prejudices, comes at last to see exactly where they stand in their spiritual evolution, comprehends the arc of their experience, and knows that they cannot for the present act otherwise than they do. He sees that their thoughts and acts are prompted by the extent of their knowledge, or their lack of knowledge, and that if they act blindly and foolishly it is because their knowledge and experience are immature, and they can only come to act more wisely by gradual growth into more enlightened states of mind. He also sees that though this growth can be encouraged, helped, and stimulated by the influence of a riper example, by seasonable words and well-timed instruction, it cannot be unnaturally forced; the flowers of love and wisdom must have time to grow, and the barren branches of hatred and folly cannot be all cut away at once.

Such a man finds the doorway into the inner world of those with whom he comes in contact, and he opens it and enters in and dwells with them in the hidden and sacred sanctuary of their being. And he finds nothing to hate, nothing to revile, nothing to condemn in that sacred place, but something to love and tend, and, in his own heart, room only for greater pity, greater patience, greater love.

He sees that he is one with them, that they are but another aspect of himself, that their natures are not different from his own, except in modification and degree, but are identical with it. If they are acting out certain sinful tendencies he has but to look within to find the same tendencies in himself, albeit, perhaps, restrained or purified; if they are manifesting certain holy and divine qualities he finds the same pure spirit within himself, though, perhaps, in a lesser degree of power and development.

One touch of nature makes the whole world kin.

The sin of one is the sin of all; the virtue of one is the virtue of all. No man can be separate from another. There is no difference of nature but only difference of condition. If a man thinks he is separated from another by virtue of his superior holiness he is not so separated, and his darkness and delusion are very great. Humanity is one, and in the holy sanctuary of sympathy saint and sinner meet and unite.

It is said of Jesus that He took upon Himself the sins of the whole world—that is, He identified Himself with those sins, and did not regard Himself as essentially separate from sinners but as being of a like nature with them—and this realisation of His oneness with all men was manifested in His life as profound sympathy with those who, for their deep sins, were avoided and cast off by others.

And who is it that is in the greatest need of sympathy? Not the saint, not the enlightened seer, not the perfect man. It is the sinner, the unenlightened man, the imperfect one; and the greater the sin the greater is the need. "I came not to call the righteous but sinners to repentance" is the statement of One who comprehended all human needs. The righteous man does not need your sympathy, but the unrighteous; he who, by his wrong-doing, is laying up for himself long periods of suffering and woe is in need of it.

The flagrantly unrighteous man is condemned, despised, and avoided by those who are living in a similar condition to him, though, for the time being, they may not be subject to his particular form of sin, for that withholding of sympathy and that mutual condemnation which are so rife is the commonest manifestation of that lack of understanding in which all sin takes its rise.

While a man is involved in sin he will condemn others who are likewise involved, and the deeper and greater his sin the more severe will be his condemnation of others. It is only when a man begins to sorrow for his sin, and so to rise above it into the clearer light of purity and understanding, that he ceases from condemning others and learns to sympathise with them. But this ceaseless condemnation of each other by those who are involved in the fierce play of the passions must needs be, for it is one of the modes of operation of the Great Law which universally and eternally obtains, and the unrighteous one who falls under the condemnation of his fellows will the more rapidly reach a higher and nobler condition of heart and life if he humbly accepts the censure of others as the effect of his own sin, and resolves henceforward to refrain from all condemnation of others.

The truly good and wise man condemns none; having put away all blind passion and selfishness he lives in the calm regions of love and peace, and understands all modes of sin, with their consequent sufferings and sorrows. Enlightened and awakened, freed from all selfish bias, and seeing men as they are, his heart responds in holy sympathy with all. Should any condemn, abuse, or slander him he throws around them the kindly protection of his sympathy, seeing the ignorance which prompts them so to act, and knowing that they alone will suffer for their wrong acts.

Learn, by self-conquest and the acquisition of wisdom, to love him whom you now condemn, to sympathise with those who condemn you. Turn your eyes away from their condemnation and search your own heart, to find, perchance, some hard, unkind, or wrong thoughts which, when discovered and understood, you will condemn yourself.

Much that is commonly called sympathy is personal affection. To love them who love us is human bias and inclination; but to love them who do not love us is divine sympathy.

Sympathy is needed because of the prevalence of suffering, for there is no being or creature who has not suffered. Through suffering sympathy is evolved. Not in a year or a life or an age is the human heart purified and softened by suffering, but after many lives of intermittent pain, after many ages of ever-recurring sorrow, man reaps the golden harvest of his experiences, and garners in the rich, ripe sheaves of love and wisdom. And then he understands, and, understanding, he sympathises.

All suffering is the result of ignorantly violated law, and after many repetitions of the same wrong act, and the same kind of suffering resulting from that act, knowledge of the law is acquired, and the higher state of obedience and wisdom is reached. Then there blossoms the pure and perfect flower of sympathy.

One aspect of sympathy is that of pity—pity for the distressed or pain-stricken, with a desire to alleviate or help them bear their sufferings. The world needs more of this divine quality.

For pity makes the world
Soft to the weak, and noble for the strong.

But it can only be developed by eradicating all hardness and unkindness, all accusation and resentment. He who, when he sees another suffering for his sin, hardens his heart and thinks or says: "It serves him right"—such a one cannot exercise pity nor apply its healing balm. Every time a man acts cruelly toward another (be it only a dumb creature,) or refuses to bestow needed sympathy, he dwarfs himself, deprives himself of ineffable blessedness, and prepares himself for suffering.

Another form of sympathy is that of rejoicing with those who are more successful than ourselves, as though their success were our own. Blessed indeed is he who is free from all envy and malice, and can rejoice and be glad when he hears of the good fortune of those who regard him as an enemy.

The protecting of creatures weaker and more indefensible than oneself is another form in which this divine sympathy is manifested. The helpless frailty of the dumb creation calls for the exercise of the deepest sympathy. The glory of superior strength resides in its power to shield, not to destroy. Not by the callous destruction of weaker things is life truly lived, but by their preservation:

All life
Is linked and kin.

and the lowest creature is not separated from the highest but by greater weakness, by lesser intelligence. When we pity and protect we reveal and enlarge the divine life and joy within ourselves. When we thoughtlessly or callously inflict suffering or destroy, then our divine life becomes obscured, and its joy fades and dies. Bodies may feed bodies, and passions passions, but man's divine nature is only nurtured, sustained, and developed by kindness, love, sympathy, and all pure and unselfish acts.

By bestowing sympathy on others we increase our own. Sympathy given can never be wasted. Even the meanest creature will respond to its heavenly touch, for it is the universal language which all creatures understand. I have recently heard a true story of a Dartmoor convict whose terms of incarceration in various convict stations extended to over forty years. As a criminal he was considered one of the most callous and hopelessly abandoned, and the warders found him almost intractable. But one day he caught a mouse—a weak, terrified, hunted thing like himself—and its helpless frailty, and the similarity of its condition with his own, appealed to him, and started into flame the divine spark of sympathy which smouldered in his crime-hardened heart, and which no human touch had ever wakened into life.

He kept the mouse in an old boot in his cell, fed, tended, and loved it, and in his love for the weak and helpless he forgot and lost his hatred for the strong. His heart and his hand were no longer against his fellows. He became tractable and obedient to the uttermost. The warders could not understand his change; it seemed to them little short of miraculous that this most hardened of all criminals should suddenly become transformed into the likeness of a gentle, obedient child. Even the expression of his features altered remarkably: a pleasing smile began to play around the mouth which had formerly been moved to nothing better than a cruel grin, and the implacable hardness of his eyes disappeared and gave place to a soft, deep mellow light. The criminal was a criminal no longer; he was saved, converted; clothed, and in his right mind; restored to humaneness and to humanity, and set firmly on the pathway to divinity by pitying and caring for a defenceless creature. All this was made known to the warders shortly afterwards, when, on his discharge, he took the mouse away with him.

Thus sympathy bestowed increases its store in our own hearts, and enriches and fructifies our own life. *Sympathy given is blessedness received;* sympathy withheld is blessedness forfeited. In the measure that a man increases and enlarges his sympathy so much nearer does he approach the ideal life, the perfect blessedness; and when his heart has become so mellowed that no hard, bitter, or cruel thought can enter and detract from its permanent sweetness, then indeed is he richly and divinely blessed.

FORGIVENESS

If men only understood
All the emptiness and aching
Of the sleeping and the waking
Of the souls they judge so blindly,
Of the hearts they pierce unkindly,
They, with gentler words and feeling,
Would apply the balm of healing—
If they only understood.

Kindness, nobler ever than revenge.

—Shakespeare

The remembering of injuries is spiritual darkness; the fostering of resentment is spiritual suicide. To resort to the spirit and practice of forgiveness is the beginning of enlightenment; it is also the beginning of peace and happiness. There is no rest for him who broods over slights and injuries and wrongs; no quiet repose of mind for him who feels that he has been unjustly treated, and who schemes how best to act for the discomfiture of his enemy.

How can happiness dwell in a heart that is so disturbed by ill-will? Do birds resort to a burning bush wherein to build and sing? Neither can happiness inhabit in that breast that is aflame with burning thoughts of resentment. Nor can wisdom come and dwell where such folly resides.

Revenge seems sweet only to the mind that is unacquainted with the spirit of forgiveness; but when the sweetness of forgiveness is tasted then the extreme bitterness of revenge is known. Revenge seems to lead to happiness to those who are involved in the darkness of passion; but when the violence of passion is abandoned, and the mildness of forgiveness is resorted to, then it is seen that revenge leads to suffering.

Revenge is a virus which eats into the very vitals of the mind, and poisons the entire spiritual being. Resentment is a mental fever which burns up the wholesome energies of the mind, and "taking offence" is a form of moral sickness which saps the healthy flow of kindliness and good-will, and from which men and women should seek to be delivered. The unforgiving and resentful spirit is a source of great suffering and sorrow, and he who harbors and encourages it, who does not overcome and abandon it, forfeits much blessedness, and does not obtain any measure of true enlightenment. To be hard-hearted is to suffer, is to be deprived of light and comfort; to be tender-hearted is to be serenely glad, is to receive light and be well comforted. It will seem strange to many to be told that the hard-hearted and unforgiving suffer most; yet it is profoundly true, for not only do they, by the law of attraction, draw to themselves the revengeful passions in other people, but their hardness of heart itself is a continual source of suffering. Every time a man hardens his heart against a fellow-being he inflicts upon himself five kinds of suffering—namely, the suffering of loss of love; the suffering of lost communion and fellowship; the suffering of a troubled and confused mind; the suffering of wounded passion or pride; and the suffering of punishment inflicted by others. Every act of unforgiveness entails upon the doer of that act these five sufferings; whereas every act of forgiveness brings to the doer five kinds of blessedness—the blessedness of love; the blessedness of increased communion and fellowship; the blessedness of a calm and peaceful mind; the blessedness of passion stilled and pride overcome; and the blessedness of kindness and good-will bestowed by others.

Numbers of people are to-day suffering the fiery torments of an unforgiving spirit, and only when they make an effort to overcome that spirit can they know what a cruel and exacting taskmaster they are serving. Only those who have abandoned the service of such a master for that of the nobler master of forgiveness can realise and know how grievous a service is the one, how sweet the other.

Let a man contemplate the strife of the world: how individuals and communities, neighbors and nations, live in continual retaliations toward each other; let him realise the heartaches, the bitter tears, the grievous partings and misunderstandings—yea, even the bloodshed and woe which spring from that strife—and, thus realising, he will never again yield to ignoble thoughts or resentment, never again take offence at the actions of others, never again live in unforgiveness toward any being.

Have good-will
To all that lives, letting unkindness die,
And greed and wrath; so that your lives be made
Like soft airs passing by.

When a man abandons retaliation for forgiveness he passes from darkness to light. So dark and ignorant is unforgiveness that no being who is at all wise or enlightened could descend to it; but its darkness is not understood and known until it is left behind, and the better and nobler course of conduct is sought and practised. Man is blinded and deluded only by his own dark and sinful tendencies; and the giving up of all unforgiveness means the giving up of pride and certain forms of passion, the abandonment of the deeply-rooted idea of the importance of oneself and of the necessity for protecting and defending that self; and when that is done the higher life, greater wisdom, and pure enlightenment, which pride and passion completely obscured, are revealed in all their light and beauty.

Then there are petty offences, little spites and passing slights, which, while of a less serious nature than deep-seated hatreds and revenges, dwarf the character and cramp the soul. They are due to the sin of self and self-importance, and thrive on vanity. Whosoever is blinded and deluded by vanity will continually see something in the actions and attitudes of others toward him at which to take offence, and the more there is of vanity the more greatly will the imaginary slight or wrong be exaggerated. Moreover, to live in the frequent indulgence of petty resentments increases the spirit of hatred, and leads gradually downward to greater darkness, suffering, and self-delusion.

Don't take offence or allow your feelings to be hurt, which means—get rid of pride and vanity. Don't give occasion for offence or hurt the feelings of others, which means—be gently considerate, forgiving, and charitable toward all.

The giving up—the total uprooting—of vanity and pride is a great task; but it is a blessed task, and it can be accomplished by constant practice in non-resentment and by meditating upon one's thoughts and actions so as to understand and purify them; and the spirit of forgiveness is perfected in one in the measure that pride and vanity are overcome and abandoned.

The not-taking-offence and the not-giving-offence go together. When a man ceases to resent the actions of others he is already acting kindly toward them, considering them before himself or his own defence. Such a man will be gentle in what he says and does, will arouse love and kindness in others, and not stir them up to ill-will and strife. He will also be free from all fear concerning the actions of others toward him, for he who hurts none fears none. But the unforgiving man, he who is eager to "pay back" some real or imaginary slight or injury, will not be considerate toward others, for he considers himself first, and is continually making enemies; he also lives in the fear of others, thinking that they are trying to do toward him as he is doing toward them. He who contrives the hurt of others fears others.

That is a beautiful story of Prince Dîrghayu which was told by an ancient Indian teacher to his disciples in order to impress them with the truth of the sublime precept that "hatred ceases not by hatred at any time; hatred ceases by not-hatred." The story is as follows:—Brahmadatta, a powerful king of Benares, made war upon Dirgheti, the king of Kosala, in order to annex his kingdom, which was much smaller than his own. Dirgheti, seeing that it was impossible for him to resist the greater power of Brahmadatta, fled, and left his kingdom in his enemy's hand. For some time he wandered from place to place in disguise, and at last settled down with his queen in an artisan's cottage; and the queen gave birth to a son, whom they called Dîrghayu.

Now, King Brahmadatta was anxious to discover the hiding-place of Dirgheti, in order to put to death the conquered king, for he thought, "Seeing that I have deprived him of his kingdom he may some day treacherously kill me if I do not kill him."

But many years passed away, and Dirgheti devoted himself to the education of his son, who, by diligent application became learned and skilful and wise.

And after a time Dîrgheti's secret became known, and he, fearing that Brahmadatta would discover him and slay all three, and thinking more of the life of his son than his own, sent away the prince. Soon after the exile king fell into the hands of Brahmadatta, and was, along with his queen, executed.

Now Brahmadatta thought: "I have got rid of Dirgheti and his queen, but their son, Prince Dîrghayu, lives, and he will be sure to contrive some means of effecting my assassination; yet he is unknown to any, and I have no means of discovering him." So the king lived in great fear and continual distress of mind.

Soon after the execution of his parents, Dîrghayu, under an assumed name, sought employment in the king's stables, and was engaged by the master of the elephants.

Dîrghayu quickly endeared himself to all, and his superior abilities came at last under the notice of the king, who had the young man brought before him, and was so charmed with him that he employed him in his own castle, and he proved to be so able and diligent that the king shortly placed him in a position of great trust under himself.

One day the king went on a long hunting expedition, and became separated from his retinue,

Dîrghayu alone remaining with him. And the king, being fatigued with his exertions, lay down, and slept with his head in Dîrghayu's lap.

Then Dîrghayu thought: "This king has greatly wronged me. He robbed my father of his kingdom, and slew my parents, and he is now entirely in my power." And he drew his sword, thinking to slay Brahmadatta. But, remembering how his father had taught him never to seek revenge but to forgive to the uttermost, he sheathed his sword.

At last the king awoke out of a disturbed sleep, and the youth inquired of him why he looked so frightened. "My sleep," said the king, "is always restless, for I frequently dream that I am in the power of young Dîrghayu, and that he is about to slay me. While lying here I again dreamed that dream with greater vividness than ever before, and it has filled me with dread and terror."

Then the youth, drawing his sword, said: "I am Prince Dîrghayu, and you are in my power; the time of vengeance has arrived."

Then the king fell upon his knees and begged Dîrghayu to spare his life. And Dîrghayu said: "It is you, O king! who must spare my life. For many years you have wished to find me in order that you might kill me; and, now that you have found me, let me beg of you to grant to me my life."

And there and then did Brahmadatta and Dîrghayu grant each other life, took hands, solemnly vowed never to harm each other. And so overcome was the king by the noble and forgiving spirit of Dîrghayu that he gave him his daughter in marriage, and restored to him his father's kingdom.

Thus hatred ceases by not-hatred—by forgiveness, which is very beautiful, and is sweeter and more effective than revenge. It is the beginning of love, of that divine love that does not seek its own; and he who practises it, who perfects himself in it, comes at last to realize that blessed state wherein the torments of pride and vanity and hatred and retaliation are for ever dispelled, and good-will and peace are unchanging and unlimited. In that state of calm, silent bliss, even forgiveness passes away, and is no longer needed, for he who has reached it sees no evil to resent but only ignorance and delusion on which to have compassion, and forgiveness is only needed so long as there is any tendency to resent, retaliate, and take offence. Equal love toward all is the perfect law, the perfect life, the perfect state in which all lesser states find their completion. Forgiveness is one of the doorways in the faultless Temple of Divine Love.

SEEING NO EVIL

The solid, solid universe
Is pervious to Love;
With bandaged eyes he never errs,
Around, below, above,
His blinding light
He flingeth white
On God's and Satan's brood,
And reconciles
By mystic wiles
The evil and the good.

—Emerson

If thou thinkest evil, be thou sure
Thine acts will bear the shadow of the stain;
And if thy thought be perfect, then thy deed
Will be as of the perfect, true and pure.

—After Confucius

After much practice in forgiveness, and having cultivated the spirit of forgiveness up to a certain point, knowledge of the actual nature of good and evil dawns upon the mind, and a man begins to understand how thoughts and motives are formed in the human heart, how they develop, and how take birth in the form of actions. This marks the opening of a new vision in the mind, the commencement of a nobler, higher, diviner life; for the man now begins to perceive that there is no necessity to resist or resent the actions of others toward him, whatever those actions may be, and that all along his resentment has been caused by his own ignorance, and that his own bitterness of spirit is wrong. Having arrived thus far he will tax himself with some such questionings as these: "Why this continual retaliation and forgiveness? Why this tormenting anger against another and then this repentance and forgiveness? Is not forgiveness the taking back of one's anger, the giving up of one's resentment; and if anger and resentment are good and necessary why repent of them and give them up? If it is so beautiful, so sweet, so peaceful to get rid of all feelings of bitterness and utterly and wholly to forgive, would it not be still more beautiful and sweet and peaceful never to grow bitter at all, never to know anger, never to resent as evil the actions of another, but always to live in the experience of that pure, calm, blissful love which is known when an act of forgiveness is done, and all unruly passion toward another is put away? If another has done me wrong is not my hatred toward him wrong, and can one wrong right another? Moreover, has he by his wrong *really* injured me, or has he injured himself? Am I not injured by my own wrong rather than by his? Why, then, do I grow angry? Why do I resent, retaliate, and engage in bitter thoughts? Is it not because my pride is piqued or my vanity wounded or my selfishness thwarted? Is it not because my blind animal passions are aroused and allowed to subdue my better nature? Seeing that I am hurt by another person's attitude toward me because of my own pride or vanity or ungoverned and unpurified passions, would it not be better to look to the wrong in myself rather than the wrong in another, to get rid of pride and vanity and passion, and so avoid being hurt at all?"

By such self-questionings and their elucidation in the light of mild thoughts and dispassionate conduct a man, gradually overcoming passion and rising out of the ignorance which gave rise to passion, will at last reach that blessed state in which he will cease to see evil in others, and will dwell in universal good-will and love and peace. Not that he will cease to see ignorance and folly; not that he will cease to see suffering and sorrow and misery; not that he will cease to distinguish between acts that are pure and impure, right and wrong, for, having put away passion and prejudice, he will see these things in the full, clear light of knowledge, and exactly as they are; but he will cease to see anything—any evil power—in another which can do him injury, which he must violently oppose and strive to crush, and against which he must guard himself. Having arrived at a right understanding of evil by purging it away from his own heart he sees that it is a thing that does not call for hatred and fear and resentment but for consideration, compassion, and love.

Shakespeare through one of his characters says: "There is no darkness but ignorance." All evil is ignorance, is dense darkness of mind, and the removal of sin from one's mind is a coming out of darkness into spiritual light. Evil is the negation of good, just as darkness is the negation, or absence, of light, and what is there in a negation to arouse anger or resentment? When night settles down upon the world who is so foolish as to rail at the darkness? The enlightened man, likewise, does not accuse or condemn the spiritual darkness in men's hearts which is manifested in the form of sin, though by gentle reproof he may sometimes point out where the light lies.

Now the ignorance to which I refer as evil, or as the source of evil, is two-fold. There is wrong-doing which is committed without any knowledge of good and evil, and where there is no choice—this is unconscious wrong-doing. Then there is wrong-doing which is done in the knowledge that it ought not to be done—this is conscious wrong-doing; but both unconscious and conscious wrong-doing arise in ignorance—that is, *ignorance of the real nature and painful consequences of the wrong-doing.*

Why does a man continue to do certain things which he feels he ought not to do? If he knows that what he is doing is wrong where lies the ignorance?

He continues to do those things because his knowledge of them is incomplete. He only knows he ought not to do them by certain precepts without and qualms of conscience within, but he does not fully and completely understand what he is doing. He knows that certain acts bring him immediate pleasure, and so, in spite of the troubled conscience which follows that pleasure, he continues to commit them. He is convinced that the pleasure is good and desirable, and therefore to be enjoyed. He does not know that pleasure and pain are one, but thinks he can have the one without the other. He has no knowledge of the law which governs human actions, and never thinks of associating his sufferings with his own wrong-doing, but believes that they are caused by the wrong-doing of others or are the mysterious dispensations of Providence, and therefore not to be inquired into or understood. He is seeking happiness, and does those things which he believes will bring him most enjoyment, but he acts in entire ignorance of the hidden and inevitable consequences which attach to his actions.

Said a man to me once who was the victim of a bad habit: "I know the habit is a bad one, and that it does me more harm than good." I said: "If you *know* that what you are doing is bad and harmful why do you continue to do it?" And he replied: "Because it is pleasant, and I like it."

This man, of course, did not really *know* that his habit was bad. He had been told that it was, and he thought he knew or believed it was, but in reality he thought it was good, that it was conducive to his happiness and well-being, and therefore he continued to practice it. When a man knows by experience that a thing is bad, and that every time he does it he injures body or mind, or both; when his knowledge of that thing is so complete that he is acquainted with its whole train of baneful effects, then he cannot only not do it any longer, he cannot even desire to do it, and even the pleasure that was formerly in that thing becomes painful. No man would put a venomous snake in his pocket because it was prettily coloured. Man knows that a deadly sting lurks in those beautiful markings. Nor, when a man knows the unavoidable pain and hurt which lie hidden in wrong thoughts and acts, does he continue to think and commit them. Even the immediate pleasure which formerly he greedily sought is gone from them; their surface attractiveness has vanished; he is no longer ignorant concerning their true nature; he sees them as they are.

I knew a young man who was in business, and, although a member of a church, and occupying the position of a voluntary religious instructor, he told me that it was absolutely necessary to practice lying and deception in business, otherwise sure and certain ruin would follow. He said he *knew* lying was wrong, but while he remained in business he must continue to do it. Upon questioning him I found, of course, that he had never tried truth and honesty in his business, had not even thought of trying the better way, so firmly convinced was he that it was not a "better way," so that it was not possible for him to know whether or not it would be productive of ruin. Now did this young man *know* that lying was wrong? There was a preceptial sense only in which he knew, but there was a deeper and more real sense in which he did not know. He had been taught to regard lying as wrong, and his conscience bore out that teaching, but he believed that it brought to him profit, prosperity, and happiness, and that honesty would bring him loss, poverty, and misery—in a word, he regarded lying, deep in his heart, as the right thing to do, and honesty as the wrong prac- tice. He had no knowledge whatever of the real nature of the act of lying: how it *is*, on the instant of its committal, loss of character, loss of self-respect, loss of power, usefulness, and influence, and loss of blessedness; and how it unerringly leads to loss of reputation and loss of material profit and pros- perity. Only when such a man begins to consider the happiness of others, and prefers to embrace the loss which he fears rather than clutch at the gain which he desires, will he obtain that real knowledge which lofty moral conduct alone can reveal; and then, experiencing the greater blessedness, he will see how, all along, he has been deceiving and defrauding himself rather than others, has been living in darkest ignorance and self-delusion.

These two common instances of wrong-doing will serve to illustrate and make plainer, to those of my readers who, while searching for Truth, are as yet doubtful, uncertain, and confused, the deep Truth that all sin, or evil, is a condition of ignorance, and therefore to be dealt with in a loving and not a hateful spirit.

And as with bad habits and lying so with all sin—with lust, hatred, malice, envy, pride, vanity, self-indulgence, and selfishness in all its forms: it is a state of spiritual darkness, the absence of the Light of Truth in the heart, the negation of knowledge.

Thus when, by overcoming the wrong condition in one's own heart, the nature of evil is fully realised, and mere belief gives place to living knowledge, evil can no longer be hatefully condemned and violently resisted, and the wrong-doer is thought of with tender compassion.

And this brings us to another aspect of evil—namely, that of individual freedom; the right of every person to choose his own actions. Along with the seeing of evil in others is the desire to con- vert or coerce others into one's own ways of thinking and acting. Probably the commonest delusion in which men are involved is that of thinking that what they themselves believe and think and do is good, and all that is otherwise is evil, and therefore to be powerfully condemned and resisted. It is out of this delusion that all persecution springs. There are Christians who regard all Atheists as men wholly evil, as given up to the service of an evil power; and there are Atheists who firmly believe that all Christians are doing the greatest harm to the whole human race by their "superstitious and false doctrines." The truth is that neither the Christian nor the Atheist is evil, nor in the service of evil, but each is choosing his own way, and is pursuing that course which he is convinced is right.

Let a man quietly contemplate the fact that numbers of followers of various religions the world over are, as they ever were, engaged in condemning each other as evil and wrong, and regarding themselves as good and right, and it will help him to realise how all evil is merely ignorance, spiritual darkness; and earnest meditation on that fact will be found to be one of the greatest aids in developing greater kindness, charity, insight, and breadth of mind.

The truly wise and good man sees good in all, evil in none. He has abandoned the folly of wanting others to think and act as he thinks and acts, for he sees that men are variously constituted, are at different points in their spiritual evolution, and must, of necessity, think and act differently. Having put away hatred, condemnation, egotism, and prejudice he has become enlightened, and sees that purity, love, compassion, gentleness, patience, humility, and unselfishness are manifestations of light and knowledge; while impurity, hatred, cruelty, passion, anger, pride, and selfishness are manifestations of darkness and ignorance; and that whether men are living in light or darkness they are one and all doing that which they think is necessary, are acting in accordance with their own measure of light or darkness. The wise man understands, and, understanding, he ceases from all bitterness and accusation.

Every man acts in accordance with his nature, with his own sense of right and wrong, and is surely gathering in the results of his own experience. There is one supreme right which every being possesses—the right to think and act as he chooses. If he chooses to think and act selfishly, thinking of his own immediate happiness only and not of that of others, then he will rapidly bring upon himself, by the action of the moral law of cause and effect, such afflictions as will cause him to pause and consider, and so find a better way. There is no teacher to compare with experience, no chastisement so corrective and purifying as that which men ignorantly inflict upon themselves. The selfish man is the ignorant man; he chooses his own way, but it is a way which leads to suffering, and through suffering to knowledge and bliss. The good man is the wise man: he likewise chooses his own way, but he chooses it in the full light of knowledge, having passed through the stages of ignorance and suffering, and arrived at knowledge and bliss.

A man begins to understand what "seeing no evil" is when, putting away all personal desires in his judgments of others, he considers them from their own standpoint, and judges their actions not from his own standard *but from theirs.* It is because men set up arbitrary standards of right and wrong, and are anxious that all should conform to their particular standard, that they see evil in each other. A man is only rightly judged when he is judged not from my standard or yours but from his own, and to deal with him thus is not judgment—it is Love. It is only when we look through the eyes of Impersonal Love that we become enlightened, and see others as they really are; and a man is approaching that Love when he can say in his heart: "Who am I that I should judge another? Am I so pure and sinless that I arraign men and pass the judgment of evil upon them? Rather let me humble myself, and correct mine own errors, before assuming the position of supreme judge of those of other men."

It was said by one of old to those who were about to stone, as evil, a woman taken in the act of committing one of the darkest of sins: "He that is without sin let him cast the first stone;" and though he who said it was without sin yet he took up no stone, nor passed any bitter judgment, but said, with infinite gentleness and compassion: "Neither do I condemn thee; go, and sin no more."

In the pure heart there is no room left where personal judgments and hatreds can find lodgment, for it is filled to overflowing with tenderness and love: it sees no evil; and only as men succeed in seeing no evil in others will they become free from sin and sorrow and suffering.

No man sees evil in himself or his own acts except the man who is becoming enlightened, and then he abandons those acts which he has come to see are wrong. Every man justifies himself in what he does, and, however evil others may regard his conduct, he himself thinks it to be good and necessary; if he did not he would not, could not, do it. The angry man always justifies his anger; the covetous man his greed; the impure man his unchastity; the liar considers that his lying is altogether necessary; the slanderer believes that, in vilifying the characters of those whom he dislikes, and warning other people against their "evil" natures, he is doing well; the thief is convinced that stealing is the shortest and best way to plenty, prosperity, and happiness; and even the murderer thinks that there is a ground of justification for his deed.

Every man's deeds are in accordance with the measure of his own light or darkness, and no man can live higher than he is or act beyond the limits of his knowledge. Nevertheless, he can improve himself, and thereby gradually increase his light and extend the range of his knowledge. The angry man indulges in raillery and abuse because his knowledge does not extend to forbearance and patience. Not having practised gentleness he does not understand it, and cannot choose it; nor can he know, by its comparison with the light of gentleness, the darkness of anger. It is the same with the liar, the slanderer, and the thief: he lives in this dark condition of mind and action because he is limited to it by his immature knowledge and experience, because, never having lived in the higher conditions, he has no knowledge of them, and it is, to him, as if they were non-existent: "The light shineth in the darkness, and the darkness comprehendeth it not." Nor can he understand even the conditions in which he is living, because, being dark, they are necessarily devoid of all knowledge.

When a man, driven by repeated sufferings at last to reflect upon his conduct, comes to see that his anger or lying, or whatever ignorant condition he may have been living in, is productive only of trouble and sorrow, then he abandons it, and begins to search for, and practice, the opposite and enlightened condition; and when he is firmly established in the better way, so that his knowledge of both conditions is complete, then he realises in what great darkness he had formerly lived. This knowledge of good and evil by experience constitutes enlightenment.

When a man begins to look, as it were, through the eyes of others, and to measure them by their own standard and not by his, then he ceases from the seeing of evil in others, for he knows that every man's perception and standard of good and evil is different; that there is no vice so low but some men regard it as good; no virtue so high but some men regard it as evil; and what a man regards as good that to him is good; what he regards as evil that to him is evil.

Nor will the purified man, who has ceased to see evil in others, have any desire to win men to his own ways or opinions, but will rather help them in their own particular groove, knowing that an enlarged experience only, and not merely change of opinion, can lead to higher knowledge and greater blessedness.

It will be found that men see evil in those who differ from them, good in those who agree with them. The man who greatly loves himself and is enamored of his opinions will love all those who agree with him and will dislike all those who disagree with him. "If ye love them that love ye, what reward have ye? . . . Love your enemies, do good to them that hate you." Egotism and vanity make men blind. Men of opposing religious views hate and persecute each other; men of opposing political views fight and condemn each other. The partisan measures all men by his own standard, and sets up his judgments accordingly. So convinced is he that he is right and others wrong that he at last persuades himself that to inflict cruelty on others is both good and necessary in order to coerce them into his way of thinking and acting, and so bring them to the right—his right—against their own reason and will.

Men hate, condemn, resist, and inflict suffering upon each other, not because they are intrinsically evil, not because they are deliberately "wicked," and are doing, in the full light of truth, what they know to be wrong, but because they regard such conduct as necessary and right. All men are intrinsically good, but some are wiser than others, are older in experience than others.

I recently heard, in substance, the following conversation between two men whom I will call D—— and E——. The third person referred to as X—— is a prominent politician:

E. Every man reaps the result of his own thoughts and deeds, and suffers for his own wrong.

D. If that is so, and if no man can escape from the penalty of his evil deeds, what an inferno some of our men in power must be preparing for themselves.

E. Whether a man is in power or not, so long as he lives in ignorance and sin, he will reap sorrow and suffering.

D. Look, for instance, at X——, a man totally evil, given up entirely to selfishness and ambition; surely great torments are reserved for so unprincipled a man.

E. But how do you know he is so evil?

D. By his works, his fruits. When I see a man doing evil I know that he is evil; and I cannot even think of X—— but I burn with righteous indignation. I am sometimes inclined to doubt that there is an overruling power for good when I see such a man in a position where he can do so much harm to others.

E. What evil is he committing?

D. His whole policy is evil. He will ruin the country if he remains in power.

E. But, while there are large numbers of people who think of X—— as you do, there are also large numbers, equally intelligent, who look upon him as good and able, who admire him for his excellent qualities, and regard his policy as beneficent and making for national progress. He owes his position to these people, are they also evil?

D. They are deceived and misled. And this only makes X——'s evil all the greater, in that he can so successfully employ his talents in deceiving others in order to gain his own selfish ends. I hate the man.

E. May it not be possible that you are deceived?

D. In what way?

E. Hatred is self-deception; love is self-enlightenment. No man can see either himself or others clearly until he ceases from hatred and practises love.

D. That sounds very beautiful, but it is impracticable. When I see a man doing evil to others, and deceiving and misleading them, I *must* hate him. It is right that I should do so. X—— is without a spark of conscience.

E. X—— may or may not be all you believe him to be, but, even if he is, according to your own words, he should be pitied and not condemned.

D. How so?

E. You say he is without a conscience.

D. Entirely so.

E. Then he is a mental cripple. Do you hate the blind because they cannot see, the dumb because they cannot speak, or the deaf because they cannot hear? When a captain has lost his rudder or broken his compass do you condemn him because he did not keep his ship off the rocks? Do you hold him responsible for the loss of life?

  If a man is totally devoid of conscience he is without the means of moral guidance, and all his selfishness must, perforce, appear to him good and right and proper. X—— may appear evil to you, but is he evil to himself? Does he regard his own conduct as evil?

D. Whether he regards himself as evil or not he is evil.

E. If I were to regard you as evil because of your hatred for X——, should I be right?

D. No.

E. Why not?

D. Because in such a case hatred is necessary, justifiable, and righteous. There is such a thing as righteous anger, righteous hatred.

E. Is there such a thing as righteous selfishness, righteous ambition, righteous evil? I should be quite wrong in regarding you as evil, because you are doing what you are convinced is right, because you regard your hatred for X—— as part of your duty as a man and a citizen; nevertheless, there is a better way than that of hatred, and it is the knowledge of this better way that prevents me from hating X—— as you do, because, however wrong his conduct might appear to me, it is not wrong to him, nor to his supporters; moreover, all men reap as they sow.

D. What, then, is that better way?

E. It is the way of Love; the ceasing to regard others as evil. It is a blessed and peaceful state of heart.

D. Do you mean that there is a state which a man can reach wherein he will not grow angry when he sees people doing evil?

E. No, I do not mean that, for while a man regards others as evil he will continue to grow angry with them; but I mean that a man can reach a state of calm insight and spotless love wherein he sees no evil to grow angry with, wherein he understands the various natures of men— how they are prompted to act, and how they reap, as the harvest of their own thoughts and deeds, the tares of suffering and the corn of bliss. To reach that state is to regard all men with compassion and love.

D. The state that you picture is a very high one—it is, no doubt, a very holy and beautiful one— but it is a state that I should be sorry to reach; and I should pray to be preserved from a state of mind wherein I could not hate a man like X—— with an intense hatred.

Thus by this conversation it will be seen that D—— regarded his hatred as good. Even so all men regard that which they do as necessary to be done. The things which men habitually practice those things they believe in. When faith in a thing wholly ceases it ceases to be practised. D——'s individual liberty is equal to that of other men, and he has a right to hate another if he so wishes; nor will he abandon his hatred until he discovers, by the sorrow and unrest which it entails, how wrong and foolish and blind it is, and how, by its practice, he is injuring himself.

A great Teacher was once asked by one of His disciples to explain the distinction between good and evil, and, holding His hand with the fingers pointing downward, He said: "Where is my hand pointing?"

And the disciple replied: "It is pointing downward."

Then, turning His hand upward, the Teacher asked: "Where now is my hand pointing?"

And the disciple answered: "It is pointing upward."

"That," said the Teacher, "is the distinction between evil and good."

By this simple illustration He indicated that evil is merely wrongly-directed energy, and good rightly-directed energy, and that the so-called evil man becomes good by reversing his conduct.

To understand the true nature of evil by living in the good is to cease to see other men as evil. Blessed is he who, turning from the evil in others, exerts himself in the purification of his own heart. He shall one day become of "too pure eyes to behold evil."

Knowing the nature of evil, what does it behoove a man to do? It behooves him to live only in that which is good; therefore, if a man condemn me, I will not condemn him in return; if he revile me I will give him kindness; if he slander me I will speak of his good qualities; if he hate me then he greatly needs, and shall receive, my love. With the impatient I will be patient; with the greedy I will be generous; and with the violent and quarrelsome I will be mild and peaceable. Seeing no evil, whom should I hate, or who regard as mine enemy?

Were mankind murderous or jealous upon you, my brother, my sister?
I'm so sorry for you. They are not murderous or jealous upon me;
All has been gentle with me, I keep no account with lamentation;
What have I to do with lamentation?

He who sees men as evil imagines that behind those acts which are called "wicked" there is a corporate and substantial evil prompting those particular sins, but he of stainless vision sees the deeds themselves as the evil, and knows that there is no evil power, no evil soul or man behind those deeds. The substance of the universe is good; there is no substance of evil. Good alone is permanent; there is no fixed or permanent evil.

As brothers and sisters, born of the same parents and being of one household, love each other through all vicissitudes, see no evil in each other, but overlook all errors, and cling together in the strong bonds of affection—even so the good man sees humanity as one spiritual family, born of the same Father-Mother, being of the same essence and making for the same goal, and he regards all men and women as his brothers and sisters, makes no divisions and distinctions, sees none as evil, but is at peace with all. Happy is he who attains to this blessed state.

ABIDING JOY

Who carry music in their heart
Through dusky lane and wrangling mart,
Plying their daily toil with busier feet,
Because their secret souls a holier strain repeat.

—KEBLE

Serene will be our days and bright,
And happy will our nature be,
When love is an unerring light,
And joy its own security.

—WORDSWORTH

Abiding joy! Is there such a thing? Where is it? Who possesses it? Yea; there is such a thing. It is where there is no sin. It is possessed by the pure-hearted.

As darkness is a passing shadow, and light is substance that remains, so sorrow is fleeting, but joy abides forever. No true thing can pass away and become lost; no false thing can remain and be preserved. Sorrow is false, and it cannot live; joy is true, and it cannot die. Joy may become hidden for a time, but it can always be recovered; sorrow may remain for a period, but it can be transcended and dispersed.

Do not think your sorrow will remain; it will pass away like a cloud. Do not believe that the torments of sin are ever your portion; they will vanish like a hideous nightmare. Awake! arise! Be holy and joyful!

You are the creator of your own shadows; you desire and then you grieve; renounce, and then you shall rejoice.

You are not the impotent slave of sorrow; the Never-Ending Gladness awaits your Home-coming. You are not the helpless prisoner of the darkness and dreams of sin; even now the beautiful light of holiness shines upon your sleeping lids, ready to greet your awakening vision.

In the heavy, troubled sleep of sin and self the abiding joy is lost and forgotten; its undying music is no more heard and the fragrance of its fadeless flowers no longer cheers the heart of the wayfarer.

But when sin and self are abandoned, when the clinging to things for personal pleasure is put away, then the shadows of grief disappear, and the heart is restored to its Imperishable Joy.

Joy comes and fills the self-emptied heart; it abides with the peaceful; its reign is with the pure. Joy flees from the selfish; it deserts the quarrelsome; it is hidden from the impure.

Joy is as an angel so beautiful and delicate and chaste that she can only dwell with holiness. She cannot remain with selfishness; she is wedded to Love.

Joy is revealed just in the measure that selfish desire is put away, and although the full, living consciousness of its abidingness, the unbroken continuance of its presence from moment to moment, is reserved only for the altogether pure, its sweetness is tasted by all in their moments or hours of unselfish exaltation. In every truly unselfish thought and act the joy which is not excitement, not that feverish thing called pleasure, and which is followed by no tearful reaction, is revealed.

Every man is truly happy in so far as he is unselfish; he is miserable in so far as he is selfish. All truly good men, and by good men I mean those who have fought victoriously the battle against self, are men of joy. How great is the jubilation of the saint! No true teacher promises sorrow as the ultimate of life; he promises joy. He points to sorrow, but only as a *process* which sin has rendered necessary. Where self ends grief passes away. Joy is the companion of righteousness. In the divine life tender compassion fills the place where weeping sorrow sat. During the process of *becoming* unselfish there are periods of deep sorrow. Purification is necessarily severe. All becoming is painful. Abiding joy in its completion is realised only in the perfection of being, and this is

> *A state*
> *Where all is loveliness, and power and love,*
> *With all sublimest qualities of mind,*
> > *. . . Where all*
> *Enjoy entire dominion o'er themselves,*
> *Acts, feelings, thoughts conditions qualities.*

Consider how a flower evolves and becomes: at first there is a little germ groping its way in the dark soil toward the upper light; then the plant appears, and leaf is added unto leaf; and finally the perfected flower appears, in the sweet perfume and chaste beauty of which all effort ceases.

So with human life: at first the blind groping for the light in the dark soil of selfishness and ignorance; then the coming into the light, and the gradual overcoming of selfishness with its accompanying pain and sorrow; and finally the perfect flower of a pure, unselfish life, giving forth, without effort, the perfume of holiness and the beauty of joy.

The good, the pure, are the superlatively happy. However men may argumentatively deny or qualify this, humanity instinctively knows it to be true. Do not men everywhere picture their angels as the most joyful of beings? There are joyful angels in bodies of flesh; we meet them and pass on;

and how many of those who come in contact with them are sufficiently pure to see the vision within the form—to see the incorruptible angel in its common instrument of clay?

> They needs must grope who cannot see,
> The blade before the ear must be;
> The outward symbols disappear
> From him whose inward sight is clear.

Yes; the pure are the joyful. We look almost in vain for any expressions of sorrow in the words of Jesus. The "Man of Sorrows" is only completed in the Man of Joy.

> I Buddh, who wept with all my brothers' tears,
>   Whose heart was broken by a whole world's woe,
> Laugh and am glad, for there is Liberty!

In sin, and in the struggle against sin, there is unrest and affliction, but in the perfection of Truth, in the Path of Righteousness, there is abiding joy.

> Enter the Path! There spring the healing streams
>   Quenching all thirst! There bloom th' immortal flowers
> Carpeting all the way with joy! There throng
>   Swiftest and sweetest hours!

Tribulation lasts only so long as there remains some chaff of self which needs to be removed. The *tribulum,* or threshing-machine, ceases to work when all the grain is separated from the chaff; and when the last impurities are blown away from the soul tribulation has completed its work, and there is no more need for it; then abiding joy is realised.

All the saints and prophets and saviours of the race have proclaimed with rejoicing the "Gospel," or the "Good News." All men know what good news is—an impending calamity avoided, a disease cured, friends arrived or returned in safety, difficulties overcome, success in some enterprise assured—but what is the "Good News" of the saintly ones? This: that there is peace for the troubled, healing for the afflicted, gladness for the grief-stricken, victory for the sinful, a home-coming for the wanderer, and joy for the sorrowing and broken-hearted. Not that these beautiful realities *shall be* in some future world, but that they are here and now, that they are known and realised and enjoyed; and are, therefore, proclaimed that all may accept them who will break the galling bonds of self and rise into the glorious liberty of unselfish love.

Seek the highest Good, and as you find it, as you practice it and realise it, you will taste the deepest, sweetest joy. As you succeed in forgetting your own selfish desires in your thoughtfulness for others, in your care and love for others, in your service for others, just so far and no further will you find and realise the abiding joy in life.

Inside the gateway of unselfishness lies the elysium of Abiding Joy, and whosoever will may enter in, whosoever doubts let him come and see.

And knowing this—that selfishness leads to misery, and unselfishness to joy, not merely for one's self alone—for if this were all how unworthy would be our endeavors!—but for the whole world, and because all with whom we live and come in contact will be the happier and the truer for our unselfishness; because Humanity is one, and the joy of one is the joy of all—knowing this, let us scatter flowers and not thorns in the common ways of life—yea, even in the highway of our enemies let us scatter the blossoms of unselfish love—so shall the pressure in their footprints fill the air with the perfume of holiness and gladden the world with the aroma of joy.

SILENTNESS

Be still! The crown of life is silentness.
    Give thou a quiet hour to each long day,
Too much of time we spend in profitless
    And foolish talk. Too little do we say.

If thou wouldst gather words that shall avail,
    Learning a wisdom worthy to express,
Leave for a while thy chat and empty tale—
    Study the golden speech of silentness.

—A. L. Salmon

Be still, my soul.
Rest awhile from the feverish activities in which you lose yourself.
Be not afraid to be left alone with yourself for one short hour.

—Ernest Crosby

In the words of a wise man there is great power, but his silence is more powerful still. The greatest men teach us most effectively when they are purposely silent. The silent attitude of the great man, noted, perhaps, by one or two of his disciples only, is recorded and preserved through the ages; while the obtrusive words of the merely clever talker, heard, perhaps, by thousands, and at once popularised, are neglected and forgotten in, at most, a few generations. The silence of Jesus, when asked by Pilate "What is Truth?" is the impressive, the awful silence of profound wisdom; it is pregnant with humility and reproof, and perpetually rebukes that shallowness that, illustrating the truth that "fools step in where angels fear to tread," would in terms of triteness parcel out the universe, or think to utter the be-all and the end-all of the mystery of things in some textual formula or theological platitude. When, plied with questions about Brahma (God) by the argumentative Brahmans, Buddha remained silent, he taught them better than they knew, and if by his silence he failed to satisfy the foolish he thereby profoundly instructed the wise. Why all this ceaseless talk about God, with its accompaniment of intolerance? Let men practice some measure of kindliness and good-will, and thereby acquaint themselves with the simple rudiments of wisdom. Why all these speculative arguments about the nature of God? Let us first understand somewhat of ourselves. There are no greater marks of folly and moral immaturity than irreverence and presumption; no greater manifestations of wisdom and moral maturity than reverence and humility. Lao-Tze, in his own life, exemplified his teaching that the wise man "teaches without words." Disciples were attracted to him by the power which ever accompanies a wise reserve. Living in comparative obscurity and silence, not courting the ear of men, and never going out to teach, men sought him out and learned of him wisdom.

The silent acts of the Great Ones are beacons to the wise, illuminating their pathway with no uncertain radiance, for he who would attain to virtue and wisdom must learn, not only when to speak and what to say, but also when to remain silent and what not to say. The right control of the tongue is the beginning of wisdom; the right control of the mind is the consummation of wisdom. By curbing his tongue a man gains possession of his mind, and to have complete possession of one's mind is to be a Master of Silence.

The fool babbles, gossips, argues, and bandies words. He glories in the fact that he has had the last word and has silenced his opponent. He exults in his own folly, is ever on the defensive, and wastes his energies in unprofitable channels. He is like a gardener who continues to dig and plant in unproductive soil.

The wise man avoids idle words, gossip, vain argument, and self-defence. He is content to appear defeated; rejoices when he *is* defeated, knowing that, having found and removed another error in himself, he has thereby become wiser. Blessed is he who does not strive for the last word!

Backward I see in my own days where I sweated through fog with linguists and contenders;
I have no mockings or arguments, I witness and wait.

Silence under provocation is the mark of a cultured and sympathetic soul. The thoughtless and unkind are stirred by every slight provocation, and will lose their mental balance by even the appearance of a personal encroachment. The self-possession of Jesus is not a miracle; it is the flower of culture, the diadem of wisdom. When we read of Jesus that "He answered never a word," and of Buddha that "He remained silent," we get a glimpse of the vast power of silence, of the silent majesty of true greatness.

The silent man is the powerful man. The victim of garrulity is devoid of influence; his spiritual energies are dissipated. Every mechanic knows that before a force can be utilised and definitely directed it must be conserved and stored; and the wise man is a spiritual mechanic who conserves the energies of his mind, holds them in masterful abeyance, ready at any moment to direct them, with effective purpose, to the accomplishment of some necessary work.

The true strength is in silentness. It is well said that "The dog that barks does not bite." The grim and rarely broken silence of the bull-dog is the necessary adjunct to that powerfully concentrated and effectual action for which the animal is known and feared. This, of course, is a lower form of silentness, but the principle is the same. The boaster fails; his mind is diverted from the main purpose; and his energies are frittered away upon self-glorification. His forces are divided between his task and the reward to himself, the greater portion going to feed the lust of reward. He is like an unskilful general who loses the battle through dividing his forces instead of concentrating them upon a point. Or he is like a careless engineer who leaves open the waste-valve of his engine and allows the steam to run down. The modest, silent, earnest man succeeds: freed from vanity, and avoiding the dissipation of self-glorification, all his powers are concentrated upon the successful performance of his task. Even while the other man is talking about his powers he is already about his work, and is so much nearer than the other to its completion. It is a law everywhere and always that energy distributed is subject unto energy conserved. The noisy and boasting Charles will ever be thrown by the quiet and modest Orlando.

It is a law universally applicable that quietness is strength. The business man who succeeds never talks about his plans, methods and affairs, and should he, turned giddy by success, begin to do this he will then commence to fail. The man of great moral influence never talks about himself and his spiritual victories, for, should he do so, in that moment his moral power and influence would be gone, and, like Samson, he would be shorn of his strength. Success, worldly or spiritual, is the willing servant of strong, steady, silent, unflinching purpose. The most powerful disintegrating forces make no noise. The greatly-overcoming mind works silently.

If you would be strong, useful, and self-reliant learn the value and power of silentness. Do not talk about yourself. The world instinctively knows that the vain talker is weak and empty, and so it leaves him to his own vanity. Do not talk about what you are going to do but do it, and let your finished work speak for itself. Do not waste your forces in criticising and disparaging the work of others but set about to do your own work thoroughly and well. The worst work with earnestness and sweetness behind it is altogether better than barking at others. While you are disparaging the work of others you are neglecting your own. If others are doing badly help and instruct them by doing better yourself. Neither abuse others nor account their abuse of any weight. When attacked remain silent; in this way you will conquer yourself, and will, without the use of words, teach others.

But the true silence is not merely a silent tongue; it is a *silent mind*. To merely hold one's tongue, and yet to carry about a disturbed and rankling mind, is no remedy for weakness and no source of power. Silentness, to be powerful, must envelop the whole mind, must permeate every chamber of the heart; it must be the silence of peace. To this broad, deep, abiding silentness a man attains only in the measure that he conquers himself. While passions, temptations, and sorrows disturb, the holier, profounder depths of silence are yet to be sounded. To smart under the words and actions of others means that you are yet weak, uncontrolled, unpurified. So rid your heart of the disturbing influences of vanity and pride and selfishness that no petty spite can reach you, no slander or abuse disturb your serene repose. As the storm rages ineffectually against a well-built house, while its occupant sits composed and happy by his fireside within, so no evil without can disturb or harm him who is well fortified with wisdom; self-governed and silent, he remains at peace within. To this great silence the self-conquered man attains.

> *Envy and calumny, and hate and pain,*
> *And that unrest which men miscall delight,*
> *Can touch him not, nor torture him again.*

There is no commoner error amongst men than that of supposing that nothing can be accomplished without much talking and much noise The busy, shallow talker regards the quiet thinker or silent doer as a man wasted; he thinks silentness means "doing nothing," and that hurrying, bustling, and ceaseless talking means "doing much." He also confounds popularity with power. But the thinker and doer is the real and effectual worker. His work is at the root and core and substance of things, and as Nature silently, yet with hidden and wondrous alchemy, transmutes the rude elements of earth and air into tender leaves, beautiful flowers, delectable fruits,—yea, into a myriad forms of beauty—even so does the silent, purposeful worker transform the ways of men and the face of the world by the might and magic of his silently-directed energy. He wastes no time and force in tinkering with the everchanging and artificial surface of things, but goes to the living vital centre, and works therefrom and thereon; and in due season, perhaps when his perishable form is withdrawn from the world, the fruits of his obscure but imperishable labors come forth to gladden the world. But the words of the talker perish. The world reaps no harvest from the sowing of sound.

He who conserves his mental forces also conserves his physical forces. The strongly quiet, calm man lives to a greater age, and in the possession of better health, than the hurrying, noisy man. Quiet, subdued mental harmony is conducive to physical harmony—health. The followers of George Fox are to-day the healthiest, longest-lived, and most successful portion of the British community, and they live quiet, unostentatious, purposeful lives, avoiding all worldly excitements and unnecessary words. They are a silent people, all their meetings being conducted on the principle that "silence is power."

Silentness is powerful because it is the outcome of self-conquest, and the more successfully a man governs himself the more silent be becomes. As he succeeds in living to a purpose and not to the pleasures of self he withdraws himself from the outer discords of the world and reaches to the inward music of peace. Then when he speaks there is purpose and power behind his words, and when he maintains silence there is equal or even greater power therein. He does not utter that which is followed by pain and tears; does not do that which is productive of sorrow and remorse. But, saying and doing those things only which are ripe with thoughtfulness, his conscience is quiet, and all his days are blessed.

> *Why idly seek from outward things*
> *The answer inward silence brings?*
> *Why climb the far-off hills with pain,*
> *A nearer view of heaven to gain?*
> *In lowliest depths of bosky dells*
> *The hermit Contemplation dwells,*
> *Whence, piercing heaven, with screened sight,*
> *He sees at noon the stars, whose light*
> *Shall glorify the coming night.*
>
> —WHITTIER

> *In the still hour when passion is at rest,*
> *Gather up stores of wisdom in thy breast.*
>
> —WORDSWORTH

SOLITUDE

Man's essential being is inward, invisible, spiritual, and as such it derives its life, its strength, from within, not from without. Outward things are channels through which its energies are expended, but for renewal it must fall back on the inward silence.

In so far as man strives to drown this silence in the noisy pleasures of the senses, and endeavors to live in the conflicts of outward things, just so much does he reap the experiences of pain and sorrow, which, becoming at last intolerable, drive him back to the feet of the inward Comforter, to the shrine of the peaceful solitude within.

As the body cannot thrive on empty husks, neither can the spirit be sustained on empty pleasures. If not regularly fed the body loses its vitality, and, pained with hunger and thirst, cries out for food and drink. It is the same with the spirit: it must be regularly nourished in solitude on pure and holy thoughts or it will lose its freshness and strength, and will at last cry out in its painful and utter starvation. The yearning of an anguish-stricken soul for light and consolation is the cry of a spirit that is perishing of hunger and thirst. All pain and sorrow is spiritual starvation, and aspiration is the cry for food. It is the Prodigal Son who, perishing of hunger, turns his face longingly toward his Father's home.

The pure life of the spirit cannot be found, but is lost, in the life of the senses. The lower desires are ever clamorous for more, and they afford no rest. The outward world of pleasure, personal contact, and noisy activities is a sphere of wear and tear which necessitates the counterbalancing effect of solitude. Just as the body requires rest for the recuperation of its forces, so the spirit requires solitude for the renewal of its energies. Solitude is as indispensable to man's spiritual welfare as sleep is to his bodily well-being; and pure thought, or meditation, which is evoked in solitude, is to the spirit what activity is to the body. As the body breaks down when deprived of the needful rest and sleep, so do the spirits of men break down, being deprived of the necessary silence and solitude. Man, as a spiritual being, cannot be maintained in strength, uprightness, and peace except he periodically withdraw himself from the outer world of perishable things and reach inwardly toward the abiding and imperishable realities. The consolations of the creeds are derived from the solitude which those creeds enforce. The regular observance of the ceremonies of formal religion, attended, as they are, with concentrated silence and freedom from worldly distractions, compels men to do unconsciously that which they have not yet learned to do consciously—namely, to concentrate the mind periodically on the inward silence, and meditate, though very briefly, on high and holy things. The man who has not learned to control and purify his mind in seasons of chosen solitude, yet whose awakening aspirations grope for something higher and nobler than he yet possesses, feels the necessity for the aid of ceremonial religion; but he who has taken himself in hand with a view to self-conquest, who withdraws into solitude in order to grapple with his lower nature, and masterfully bend his mind in holy directions, requires no further aid from book or priest or Church. The Church does not exist for the pleasure of the saint but for the elevation of the sinner.

In solitude a man gathers strength to meet the difficulties and temptations of life, knowledge to understand and conquer them, and wisdom to transcend them. As a building is preserved and sustained by virtue of the foundation which is hidden and unobserved, so a man is maintained perpetually in strength and peace by virtue of his lonely hour of intense thought which no eye beholds.

It is in solitude only that a man can be truly revealed to himself, that he can come to understand his real nature, with all its powers and possibilities. The voice of the spirit is not heard in the hubbub of the world and amid the clamors of conflicting desires. There can be no spiritual growth without solitude.

There are those who shrink from too close a scrutiny of themselves, who dread too complete a self-revelation, and who fear that solitude which would leave them alone with their own thoughts and call up before their mental vision the wraith of their desires. And so they go where the din of pleasure is loudest and where the reproving voice of Truth is drowned. But he who loves Truth, who desires and seeks wisdom, will be much alone. He will seek the fullest, clearest revelation of himself, will avoid the haunts of frivolity and noise, and will go where the sweet, tender voice of the spirit of Truth can speak within him and be heard.

Men go after much company, and seek out new excitements, but they are not acquainted with peace; in divers paths of pleasure they search for happiness, but they do not come to rest; through diverse ways of laughter and feverish delirium they wander after gladness and life, but their tears are many and grievous, and they do not escape death.

Drifting upon the ocean of life in search of selfish indulgences men are caught in its storms, and only after many tempests and much privation do they fly to the Rock of Refuge which rests in the deep silence of their own being.

While a man is absorbed in outward activities he is giving out his energies, and is becoming spiritually weaker, and in order to retain his moral vigor he must resort to solitary meditation. So needful is this that he who neglects it loses or does not attain the right knowledge of life; nor does he comprehend and overcome those most deeply-rooted and subtlest of sins which appear like virtues, deceiving the elect, and to which all but the truly wise succumb.

True dignity abides with him alone,
Who, in the silent hour of inward thought,
Can still suspect and still revere himself
In lowliness of heart.

He who lives, without ceasing, in outward excitement lives most in disappointments and griefs. Where the sounds of pleasure are greatest heart-emptiness is the keenest and deepest. He, also, whose whole life, even if not one of lust for pleasure, is centered in outward works, who deals only with the changing panorama of visible things, never falling back, in solitude, upon the inner and invisible world of permanent being, such a man does not attain knowledge and wisdom, but remains empty; he cannot aid the world, cannot feed its aspirations, for he has no food to offer it, his spiritual store being empty. But he who courts solitude in order to search for the truth of things, who subdues his senses and makes quiet his desires, such a man is daily attaining knowledge and wisdom; he becomes filled with the spirit of truth; he can aid the world, for his spiritual store is full, and is kept well replenished.

While a man is absorbed in the contemplation of inward realities he is receiving knowledge and power; he opens himself, like a flower, to the universal light of Truth, and receives and drinks in its life-imparting rays; he also goes to the eternal fountain of knowledge and quenches his thirst in its inspiring waters. Such a man gains, in one hour of concentrated thought, more essential knowledge than a whole year's reading could impart. Being is infinite, and knowledge is illimitable and its source inexhaustible, and he who draws upon the innermost depths of his being drinks from the spring of divine wisdom which can never run dry, and quaffs the waters of immortality.

It is this habitual association with the deep realities of Being, this continual drinking in of the Water of Life at its perennial source, that constitutes *genius*. The resources of genius are inexhaustible because they are drawn from the original and universal source, and for the same reason the works of genius are ever new and fresh. The more a genius gives out the fuller he becomes. With the accomplishment of every work his mind extends and expands, reaches out more vastly, and sees wider and ever wider ranges of power. The genius is inspired. He has bridged the gulf between the finite and the infinite. He needs no secondary aids, but draws from that universal spring which is the source of every noble work. The difference between a genius and an ordinary man is this— the one lives in inward realities, the other in outward appearances; the one goes after pleasure, the other after wisdom; the one relies on books, the other relies upon his own being. Book-learning is good when its true place is understood, but it is not the source of wisdom. The source of wisdom is in life itself, and is comprehended by effort, practice, and experience. Books give information but they cannot bestow knowledge; they can stimulate but cannot accomplish—you must put forth effort, and achieve for yourself. The man who relies entirely upon books, and does not go to the silent resources within himself, is superficial, and becomes rapidly exhausted. He is uninspired (though he may be extremely clever), for he soon reaches the end of his stock of information, and so becomes void and repetitious. His work lacks the sweet spontaneity of life and the ever-renewed freshness of inspiration. Such a man has cut himself off from the infinite supply, and deals, not with life itself, but with dead or decaying appearances. Information is limited; knowledge is boundless.

The inspiration of genius and greatness is fostered, evolved, and finally completed in solitude. The most ordinary man who conceives a noble purpose, and, summoning all his energies and will, broods upon and ripens his purpose in solitude will accomplish his object and become a genius. The man who renounces the pleasures of the world, who avoids popularity and fame, and who works in obscurity and thinks in solitude for the accomplishment of a lofty ideal for the human race, becomes a seer and a prophet. He who silently sweetens his heart, who attunes his mind to that which is pure and beautiful and good, who in long hours of lonely contemplation strives to reach to the central and eternal heart of things, brings himself in touch with the inaudible harmonies of being, opens himself for the reception of the cosmic song, and becomes at last a singer and a poet.

And so with all genius: it is the child of solitude—a very simple-hearted child—wide-eyed and listening and beautiful, yet withal to the noise-enamored world an incomprehensible mystery, of which it is only now and then vouchsafed a glimpse from beyond the well-guarded Portals of Silence.

> *In man's self arise*
> *August anticipations, symbols, types*
> *Of a dim splendor ever on before*
> *In that eternal circle life pursues.*

St. Paul, the cruel persecutor and blind bigot, after spending three years alone in the desert, comes forth a loving apostle and an inspired seer. Gautama Siddartha, the man of the world, after six years (in the forest) of lonely struggle with his passions and intense meditation upon the deep mysteries of his nature, becomes Buddha, the enlightened one, the embodiment of calm, serene wisdom, to whom a heart-thirsty world turns to receive the refreshing waters of immortality. Lao-Tze, an ordinary citizen filling a worldly office, in his search for knowledge courts solitude, and discovers Tao, the Supreme Reason, by virtue of which he becomes a world-teacher. Jesus, the unlettered carpenter, after many years of solitary communion upon the mountains with the Unfailing Love and Wisdom, comes forth a blessed savior of mankind.

Even after they had attained, and had scaled the lofty heights of divine knowledge these Great Souls were much alone, and retired frequently for brief seasons of solitude. The greatest man will fall from his moral height and lose his influence if he neglects that renewal of power which can only be obtained in solitude. These Masters attained their power by consciously harmonising their thoughts and lives with the creative energies within themselves, and by transcending individuality and sinking their petty personal will in the Universal Will they became Masters of Creative Thought, and stand as the loftiest instruments for the outworking of cosmic evolution.

And this is not miraculous, it is a matter of law; it is not mysterious except in so far as law is mysterious. Every man becomes a creative master in so far as he subordinates himself to the universally good and true. Every poet, painter, saint, and sage is the mouthpiece of the Eternal. The perfection of the message varies with the measure of individual selfishness. In so far as self intervenes the distinctness of the work and message becomes blurred. Perfect selfishness is the acme of genius, the consummation of power.

Such self-abnegation can only be begun, pursued, and completed in solitude. A man cannot gather together and concentrate his spiritual forces while he is engaged in spending those forces in worldly activities, and although after power is attained the balance of forces can be maintained under all circumstances, even in the midst of the antagonistic throng, such power is only secured after many years of frequent and habitual solitude.

Man's true Home is in the Great Silence—this is the source of all that is real and abiding within him; his present nature, however, is dual, and outer activities are necessary. Neither entire solitude nor entire action is the true life in the world, but that is the true life which gathers, in solitude, strength and wisdom to rightly perform the activities of life; and as a man returns to his home in the evening, weary with labor, for that sweet rest and refreshment which will prepare him for another day's toil, so must he who would not break down in the labor of life come away from the noise and toil of the world's great workshop and rest for brief periods in his abiding Home in the Silence. He who does this, spending some portion of each day in sacred and purposeful solitude, will become strong and useful and blessed.

Solitude is for the strong, or for those who are ready to become strong. When a man is becoming great he becomes solitary. He goes in solitude to seek, and that which he seeks he finds, for there is a Way to all knowledge, all wisdom, all truth, all power. And the Way is forever open, but it lies through soundless solitudes and the unexplored silences of man's being.

STANDING ALONE

By all means use to be alone.
Salute thyself; see what thy soul doth wear.

—George Herbert

He that has light within his own clear breast
May sit in the centre and enjoy bright day.

—Milton

In the life of blessedness self-reliance is of the utmost importance. If there is to be peace there must be strength; if there is to be security there must be stability; if there is to be lasting joy there must be no leaning upon things which at any moment may be snatched away forever.

A man does not begin truly to live until he finds an immovable centre within himself on which to stand, by which to regulate his life, and from which to draw his peace. If he trusts to that which fluctuates he also will fluctuate; if he leans upon that which may be withdrawn he will fall and be bruised; if he looks for satisfaction in perishable accumulations he will starve for happiness in the midst of plenty.

Let a man learn to stand alone, looking to no one for support; expecting no favors, craving no personal advantages; not begging nor complaining, not craving nor regretting, but relying upon the truth within himself, deriving his satisfaction and comfort from the integrity of his own heart.

If a man can find no peace within himself where shall he find it? If he dreads to be alone with himself what steadfastness shall he find in company? If he can find no joy in communion with his own thoughts, how shall he escape misery in his contact with others? The man who has yet found nothing within himself upon which to stand will nowhere find a place of constant rest.

Men everywhere are deluded by the superstition that their happiness rests with other people and with outward things, and, as a result, they live in continual disappointments, regrets, and lamentations. The man who does not look for happiness to any others or to external things, but finds within himself its inexhaustible source, will be self-contained and serene under all circumstances, and will never become the helpless victim of misery and grief. The man who looks to others for support, who measures his happiness by the conduct of others and not by his own, who depends upon their co-operation for his peace of mind—such a man has no spiritual foothold, his mind is tossed hither and thither with the continual changes going on around him, and he lives in that ceaseless ebb and flow of the spirits which is wretchedness and unrest. He is a spiritual cripple, and has yet to learn how to maintain his mental centre of gravity, and so go without the aid of crutches.

As a child learns to walk in order to go about from place to place of itself strong and unaided, so should a man learn to stand alone, to judge and think and act for himself, and to choose, in the strength of his own mind, the pathway which he shall walk.

Without is change and decay and insecurity, within is all surety and blessedness. The soul is sufficient of itself. Where the need is there is the abundant supply. Your eternal dwelling-place is within; go there and take possession of your mansion; there you are a king, elsewhere you are a vassal. Be contented that others shall manage or mismanage their own little kingdom, and see to it that you reign strongly over your own. Your entire well-being and the well-being of the whole world lies there. You have a conscience, follow it; you have a mind, clarify it; you have judgment, use and improve it; you have a will, employ and strengthen it; you have knowledge, increase it; there is a light within your own soul, watch it, tend it, encourage it, shield it from the winds of passion, and help it to burn with a steadier and ever steadier radiance. Leave the world and come back to yourself. Think as a man, act as a man, live as a man. Be rich in yourself, be complete in yourself. Find the abiding centre within you and obey it. The earth is maintained in its orbit by its obedience to its centre the sun. Obey the centre of light that is within you; let others call it darkness if they will. You are responsible for yourself, are accountable to yourself, therefore rely upon yourself. If you fear yourself who will place confidence in you? If you are untrue to yourself where shall you find the sweet satisfaction of Truth?

The great man stands alone in the simple dignity of independent manhood; he pursues his own path fearlessly, and does not apologise or "beg leave." Criticism and applause are no more to him than the dust upon his coat, of which he shakes himself free. He is not guided by the changing opinions of men but guides himself by the light of his own mind. Other men barter away their manhood for messes of flattery or fashion.

Until you can stand alone, looking for guidance neither to spirits nor mortals, gods nor men, but guiding yourself by the light of the truth within you, you are not unfettered and free, not altogether blessed. But do not mistake pride for self-reliance. To attempt to stand upon the crumbling foundation of pride is to be already fallen. No man depends upon others more than the proud man. He drinks in their approbation and resents their censure. He mistakes flattery for sound judgment, and is most easily hurt or pleased by the opinions of others. His happiness is entirely in the hands of others. But the self-reliant man stands, not upon personal pride, but on an abiding law, principle, ideal, reality, within himself. Upon this he poises himself, refusing to be swept from his strong foothold either by the waves of passion within or the storms of opinion without, but should he at any time lose his balance he quickly regains himself, and is fully restored. His happiness is entirely in his own hands.

Find your centre of balance and succeed in standing alone, and, whatever your work in life may be, you will succeed; you will accomplish what you set your mind upon, for the truly self-reliant man is the invincible man. But though you do not rely upon others, learn of them. Never cease to increase in knowledge, and be ever ready to receive that which is good and useful. You cannot have too much humility; the most self-reliant men are the most humble. "No aristocrat, no prince born to the purple, can begin to compare with the self-respect of the saint. Why is he lowly, but that he knows that he can well afford it, resting on the largeness of God in him." Learn of all men, and especially of the masters of Truth, but do not lose your hold upon the truth that the ultimate guidance is in yourself. A master can say: "Here is the path," but he can neither compel you to walk it nor walk it for you. You must put forth your own efforts, must achieve by your own strength, must make his truth your truth by your own unaided exertions; you must implicitly trust yourself.

> *This thing is God—to be man with thy might,*
> *To grow great in the strength of thy spirit,*
> *And live out thy life as the light.*

You are to be master of yourself, lord over yourself, not fawning and imitating, but doing your work as a living, vital portion of the universe; giving love but not expecting it; giving sympathy but not craving for it; giving aid but not depending upon it. If men should censure your work, heed them not. It sufficeth that your work be true: rest you in this sufficiency. Do not ask: "Will my work please?" but: "Is it real?" If your work be true the criticism of men cannot touch it; if it be false their disapproval will not slay it quicker than it will die of itself. The words and acts of Truth cannot pass away until their work is fully accomplished; the words and acts of error cannot remain, for they have no work to do. Criticism and resentment are alike superfluous.

Free yourself from the self-imposed tyranny of slavish dependence, and stand alone, not as an isolated unit, but as a sympathetic portion of the whole. Find the joy that results from well-earned freedom, the peace that flows from wise self-possession, the blessedness that inheres in native strength.

> *Honor to him who, self-complete, if lone,*
> *Carves to the grave one pathway all his own,*
> *And heeding naught that men may think or say,*
> *Asks but his soul if doubtful of the way.*

UNDERSTANDING THE SIMPLE
LAWS OF LIFE

Watch narrowly
The demonstration of a truth, its birth,
And you trace back the effluence to its spring
And source within us.

—BROWNING

More is the treasure of the Law than gems;
Sweeter than comb its sweetness. Its delights,
Delightful past compare.

—THE LIGHT OF ASIA

Walking those byways which I have so far pointed out, resting in their beauty and drinking in their blessedness, the pilgrim along life's broad highway will in due time come to one wherein his last burden will fall from him, where all his weariness will pass away, where he will drink of light-hearted liberty, and rest in perpetual peace. And this most blessed of spiritual byways, the richest source of strength and comfort, I call *The Right Understanding of the Simple Laws of Life.* He who comes to it leaves behind him all lack and longing, all doubt and perplexity, all sorrow and uncertainty. He lives in the fulness of satisfaction, in light and knowledge, in gladness and surety. He who comprehends the utter simplicity of life, who obeys its laws and does not step aside into the dark paths and complex mazes of selfish desire, stands where no harm can reach him, where no enemy can lay him low—and he doubts, desires, and sorrows no more. Doubt ends where reality begins; painful desire ceases where the fulness of joy is perpetual and complete; and when the Unfailing and Eternal Good is realised what room is there for sorrow?

Human life when rightly lived is simple with a beautiful simplicity, but it is not rightly lived while it is bound to a complexity of lusts, desires, and wants—these are not the real life but the burning fever and painful disease which originate in an unenlightened condition of mind. The curtailing of one's desires is the beginning of wisdom; their entire mastery its consummation. This is so because life is bounded by law, and, being inseparable from law, life has no need that is not already supplied. Now lust, or desire, is not need, but a rebellious superfluity, and as such it leads to deprivation and misery. The prodigal son, while in his father's house, not only had all that he required, but was surrounded with a superabundance. Desire was not necessary, because all things were at hand; but when desire entered his heart he "went into a far country," and "began to be in want," and it was only when he became reduced to the utmost extremity of starvation that he turned with longing toward his father's home. This parable is symbolical of the evolution of the individual and the race. Man has come into such a complexity of cravings that he lives in continual discontent, dissatisfaction, want, and pain; and his only cure lies in a return to the Father's Home—that is, to actual *living* or *being* as distinguished from *desiring*. But a man does not do this until he is reduced to the last extremity of spiritual starvation; he has then reaped the experience of pain and sorrow as the result of desire, and looks back with longing toward the true life of peace and plenty; and so he turns round, and begins his toilsome journey back toward his Home, toward that rich life of simple being wherein is emancipation from the thraldom and fever and hunger of desire, and this longing for the true life, for Truth, Reality, should not be confounded with desire: it is *aspiration*. Desire is *the craving for possession; aspiration is the hunger of the heart for peace.* The craving for things leads ever farther and farther from peace, and not only ends in deprivation but is, in itself, a state of perpetual want. Until it comes to an end rest, satisfaction, is an impossibility. The hunger for things can never be satisfied, but the hunger for peace can, and the satisfaction of peace is found, is fully possessed, when all selfish desire is abandoned. Then there is fulness of joy, abounding plenty, and rich and complete blessedness. In this supremely blessed state life is comprehended in its perfect symmetry and simplicity, and the acme of power and usefulness is attained. Then even the hunger for peace ceases, for peace becomes the normal condition, is fully possessed, constant, and never-varying. Men, immersed in desire, ignorantly imagine that the conquest of desire leads to inactivity, loss of power, and lifelessness. Instead, it leads to highly concentrated activity, to the full employment of power, and to a life so rich, so glorious, and so abundantly blessed as to be incomprehensible to those who hunger for pleasures and possessions. Of this life only can it be said:

> *Here are no sounds of discord—no profane*
> *Or senseless gossip of unworthy things—*
> *Only the songs of chisels and of pens,*
> *Of busy brushes, and ecstatic strains*
> *Of souls surcharged with music most divine.*
> *Here is no idle sorrow, no poor grief*
> *For any day or object left behind—*

For time is counted precious, and herein
Is such complete abandonment of Self
That tears turn into rainbows, and enhance
The beauty of the land where all is fair.

When a man is rescued from selfish desire his mind is unencumbered, and he is free to work for humanity. No longer racing after those gratifications which leave him hungry still, all his powers are at his immediate command. Seeking no rewards he can concentrate all his energies upon the faultless completion of his duties, and so accomplish all things and fulfil all righteousness.

The fully enlightened and fully blessed man is not prompted to action by desire but works from *knowledge*. The man of desire needs the promise of a reward to urge him to action. He is as a child working for the possession of a toy. But the man of knowledge, living in the fulness of life and power, can at any moment bring his energies into requisition for the accomplishment of that which is necessary. He is, spiritually, a full-grown man; for him all rewards have ceased; to him all occurrences are good; he lives always in complete satisfaction. Such a man has attained to life, and his delight (and it is a sweet, perpetual, and never-failing delight) is in obedience to the simple demands of exact and never-failing law.

But this life of supreme blessedness is an end, and the pilgrim who is striving towards it, the prodigal returning to it, must travel thither, and employ means to get there. He must pass through the country of his animal desires, disentangling himself from their intricacies, simplifying them, overcoming them; this is the way, and he has no enemies but what spring within himself.

At first the way seems hard because, blinded by desire, he does not perceive the simple structure of life, and its laws are hidden from him; but as he becomes more simple in his mind the direct laws of life become unfolded to his spiritual perception, and at once the point is reached where these laws begin to be understood and obeyed; then the way becomes plain and easy; there is no more uncertainty and darkness, but all is seen in the clear light of knowledge.

It will help to accelerate the progress of the searcher for the true and blessed life if we now turn to a consideration of some of these simple laws which are rigidly mathematical in their operations.

The elementary laws never apologise.

All life is one, though it has a diversity of manifestations; all law is one, but it is applicable and operative in a variety of ways. There is not one law for matter and another for mind, not one for the material and visible and another for the spiritual and invisible; there is the same law throughout. There is not one kind of logic for the world and another for the spirit, but the same logic is applicable to both. Men faithfully, and with unerring worldly wisdom, observe certain laws or rules of action in material things, knowing that to ignore or disobey them would be great folly on their part, ending in disaster for themselves and confusion for society and the state, but they err in supposing and believing that the same rules do not apply in spiritual things, and thereby suffer for their ignorance and disobedience.

It is a law in worldly things that a man shall support himself, that he shall earn his living, and that "He that will not work, neither shall he eat." Men observe this law, recognising its justice and goodness, and so earn the necessary material sustenance. But in spiritual things men, broadly speaking, deny and ignore the operation of this law. They think that, while it is absolutely just that a man should earn his material bread, and that the man who shirks this law should wander in rags and want, it is right that they should beg for their spiritual bread, think it to be just that they should receive all spiritual blessings without either deserving or attempting to earn them. The result is that most men wander in spiritual beggary and want—that is, in suffering and sorrow—deprived of spiritual sustenance, of joy and knowledge and peace.

If you are in need of any worldly thing—food, clothing, furniture, or other necessary—you do not beg of the store-keeper to give it to you; you ask the price of it, pay for it with your money, and then it becomes your own. You recognise the perfect justice in giving an equivalent for what you receive, and would not wish it to be otherwise. The same just law prevails in spiritual things. If you are in need of any spiritual thing—joy, assurance, peace, or what else soever—you can only come into full possession of it by giving an equivalent; you must pay the price for it. As you must give a portion of your material substance for a worldly thing so you must give a portion of your immaterial substance for a spiritual thing. You must yield up some passion or lust or vanity or indulgence before the spiritual possession can be yours. The miser who clings to his money and will not give up any of it because of the pleasure which its possession affords him cannot have any of the material comforts of life. He lives in continual want and discomfort in spite of all his wealth. The man who will not give up his passions, who clings to anger, unkindness, sensuality, pride, vanity, self-indulgence, for the momentary pleasure which their gratification affords him is a spiritual miser; he cannot have any spiritual comforts, and suffers continual spiritual want and uneasiness in spite of the wealth of worldly pleasures which he fondly hugs and refuses to give up.

The man who is wise in worldly things neither begs nor steals, but labors and purchases, and the world honors him for his uprightness. The man who is wise in spiritual things neither begs nor steals, but labours in his own inner world, and purchases his spiritual possessions. Him the whole universe honours for his righteousness.

It is another law in worldly things that a man who engages himself to another in any form of employment shall be content with the wages upon which he agreed. If at the end of his week's work, and on receiving his wages, he were to ask his employer for a larger sum, pleading that, though he could not justly claim it and did not really deserve it, yet he expected it, he would not only not receive the larger sum but would, doubtless, be discharged from his post. Yet in spiritual things men do not think it to be either foolish or selfish to ask for those blessings—spiritual wages—upon which they never agreed, for which they never labored, and which they do not deserve. Every man gets from the law of the universe that upon which he agrees and for which he works—no more, no less; and he is continually entering into agreements with the Supreme Law—the Master of the universe. For every thought and act which he gives he receives its just equivalent; for all work done in the form of deeds he receives the wages due to him. Knowing this, the enlightened man is always content, always satisfied, and in perfect peace, knowing that whatever he receives (be it what men call misfortune or good fortune) he has earned. The Great Law never cheats any man of his just due, but it says to the railer and the complainer: "Friend, didst thou not agree with me for a penny a day?"

Again, if a man would grow rich in worldly goods he must economise, and husband his financial resources until he has accumulated sufficient capital to invest in some branch of industry; then he must judiciously invest his little store of capital, neither holding it too tightly nor letting it go carelessly. He thus increases both in worldly wisdom and worldly riches. The idle spendthrift cannot grow rich; he is wasteful and riotous. He who would grow rich in spiritual things must also economise, and husband his mental resources. He must curb his tongue and his impulses, not wasting his energy in idle gossip, vain argument, or excesses of temper. In this way he will accumulate a little store of wisdom which is his spiritual capital, and this he must send out into the world for the good of others, and the more he uses it the richer will he become. Thus does a man increase in both heavenly wisdom and heavenly riches. The man who follows his blind impulses and desires and does not control and govern his mind is a spiritual spendthrift: he can never become rich in divine things.

It is a physical law that if we would reach the summit of a mountain we must climb thither. The path must be sought and then carefully followed, and the climber must not give up and go back because of the labour involved and the difficulties to be overcome, nor on account of aching limbs, otherwise his object cannot be accomplished. And this law is also spiritual. He who would reach the high altitudes of moral or intellectual grandeur must climb thither by his own efforts. He must seek out the pathway and then assiduously follow it, not giving up and turning back, but surmounting all difficulties, and enduring for a time trials, temptations, and heartaches, and at last he will stand upon the glorious summit of moral perfection, the would of passion, temptation, and sorrow beneath his feet, and the boundless heavens of divinity stretching vast and silent above his head.

If a man would reach a distant city, or any place of destination, he must travel thither. There is no law by which he can be instantly transported there. He can only get there by putting forth the necessary exertion. If he walks he will put forth great exertion, but it will cost him nothing in money; if he drives or takes train, there will be less actual labor, but he must pay in money for which he has laboured. To reach any place requires labour; this cannot be avoided: it is law. Equally so spiritually. He who would reach any spiritual destination, such as purity, compassion, wisdom, or peace, must travel thither, and must labour to get there. There is no law by which he can suddenly be transported to any of these beautiful spiritual cities. He must find the most direct route and then put forth the necessary labour, and at last he will come to the end of his journey.

These are but a few of the many laws, or manifestations of the One Great Law, which are to be understood, applied, and obeyed before the full manhood and maturity of spiritual life and blessedness can be attained. There is no worldly or physical law which is not operative, with equal exactness, in the spiritual realm—that is, the inner and invisible world of man's being. Just as physical things are the shadows and types of spiritual realities, so worldly wisdom is the reflected image of Divine Wisdom. All those simple operations of human life in worldly things which men never question, but follow and obey implicitly because of their obvious plainness and exactness, obtain in spiritual things with the same unerring accuracy; and when this is understood, and these laws are as implicitly obeyed in spiritual as in worldly matters, then has a man reached the firm standing-ground of exact knowledge; his sorrows are at an end, and he can doubt no more.

Life is uninvolved, uncompromising justice; its operations are simple, invincible logic. Law reigns forever, and the heart of law is love. Favoritism and caprice are the reverse of both law and love. The universe has no favorites; it is supremely just, and gives to every man his rightful earnings. All is good because all is according to law, and because all is according to law, man can find the right way in life, and, having found it, can rejoice and be glad. The Father of Jesus is the Unfailing Good which is embodied in the law of things. "No evil can happen to a good man either in life or death." Jesus recognised the good in his own fate, and exonerated all his persecutors from blame. "No man," he declared, "taketh my life from me, but I lay it down of myself." That is, he himself had brought about his own end.

He who has, by simplifying his life and purifying his mind, arrived at an understanding of the beautiful simplicity of being, perceives the unvarying operation of law in all things, and knows the result of all his thoughts and deeds upon himself and the world—knows what effects are bound up with the mental causes which he sets in motion. He then thinks and does only those thoughts and deeds that are blessed in their inception, blessed in their growth, and blessed in their completion. Humbly accepting the lawful results of all the deeds done when in a state of ignorance, he neither complains nor fears nor questions, but is at rest in obedience, is perfectly blessed in his knowledge of the Good Law.

The tissue of our life to be
    We weave with colors all our own,
And in the field of Destiny
    We reap as we have sown.

And if we reap as we have sown,
    And take the dole we deal,
The law of pain is love alone,
    The wounding is to heal.

HAPPY ENDINGS

Such is the Law which moves to righteousness,
    Which none at last can turn aside or stay;
The heart of it is Love, the end of it
    Is peace and consummation sweet. Obey.

—The Light of Asia

So, haply, when thy task shall end,
    The wrong shall lose itself in right,
And all thy week-day Sabbaths blend
    With the long Sabbath of the Light!

—Whittier

Life has many happy endings, because it has much that is noble and pure and beautiful. Although there is much sin and ignorance in the world, many tears, and much pain and sorrow, there is also much purity and knowledge, many smiles, and much healing and gladness. No pure thought, no unselfish deed can fall short of its felicitous result, and every such result is a happy consummation.

A pleasant home is a happy ending; a successful life is a happy ending; a task well and faithfully done is a happy ending; to be surrounded by kind friends is a happy ending. A quarrel put away, grudges wiped out, unkind words confessed and forgiven, friend restored to friend—all these are happy endings. To find that which one has long and tediously sought; to be restored from tears to gladness; to awaken in the bright sunlight out of the painful nightmare of sin; to strike, after much searching, the Heavenly Way in life—these are, indeed, blessed consummations.

He who looks for, finds, and enters the byways which I have indicated will come to this one without seeking it, for his whole life will be filled with happy endings. He who begins right and continues right does not need to desire and search for felicitous results; they are already at hand; they follow as consequences: they are the certainties, the realities of life.

There are happy endings which belong solely to the material world; these are transient, and they pass away. There are happy endings which belong to the spiritual world; these are eternal, and they do not pass away. Sweet are companionships, pleasures, and material comforts, but they change and fade away. Sweeter still are Purity, Wisdom, and the knowledge of Truth, and these never change nor fade away. Wherever a man goes in this world he can take his worldly possessions with him; but soon he must part company with them, and if he stands upon these alone, deriving all his happiness from them, he will come to a spiritual ending of great emptiness and want. But he who has attained to the possession of spiritual things can never be deprived of his source of happiness: he will never have to part company with it, and wherever he goes in the whole universe he will carry his possessions with him. His spiritual end will be the fulness of joy.

Happy in the Eternal Happiness is he who has come to that Life from which the thought of self is abolished. Already, even now and in this life, he has entered the Kingdom of Heaven, Nirvana, Paradise, the New Jerusalem, the Olympus of Jupiter, the Valhalla of the Gods. He knows the Final Unity of Life, the Great Reality of which these fleeting and changing names are but feeble utterances. He is at rest on the bosom of the Infinite.

Sweet is the rest and deep the bliss of him who has freed his heart from its lusts and hatreds and dark desires; and he who, without any shadow of bitterness or selfishness resting upon him, and looking out upon the world with boundless compassion and love, can breathe, in his inmost heart, the blessing:

Peace unto all living things, making no exceptions or distinctions—such a man has reached that happy ending which can never be taken away, for this is the perfection of life, the fulness of peace, the consummation of Perfect Blessedness.

OUT FROM

THE HEART

(1904)

FOREWORD

Confucius said, "The perfecting of one's self is the fundamental base of all progress and all moral development;" a maxim as profound and comprehensive as it is simple, practical, and uninvolved, for there is no surer way to knowledge, nor no better way to help the world than by perfecting one's self. Nor is there any nobler work or higher science than that of self-perfection. He who studies how to become faultless, who strives to be pure-hearted, who aims at the possession of a calm, wise, and seeing mind, engages in the most sublime task that man can undertake, and the results of which are perceptible in a well-ordered, blessed, and beautiful life.

—James Allen

CONTENTS

THE HEART AND THE LIFE

As the heart, so is the life. The within is ceaselessly becoming the without. Nothing remains unrevealed. That which is hidden is but for a time; it ripens and comes forth at last. Seed, tree, blossom, and fruit is the fourfold order of the universe. From the state of a man's heart proceed the conditions of his life; his thoughts blossom into deeds, and his deeds bear the fruitage of character and destiny.

Life is ever unfolding from within, and revealing itself to the light, and thoughts engendered in the heart at last reveal themselves in words, actions, and things accomplished.

As the fountain from the hidden spring, so issues man's life from the secret recesses of his heart. All that he is and does is generated there. All that he will be and do will take its rise there.

Sorrow and gladness, suffering and enjoyment, hope and fear, hatred and love, ignorance and enlightenment, are nowhere but in the heart; they are solely mental conditions.

Man is the keeper of his heart; the watcher of his mind; the solitary sentinel of his citadel of life. As such, he can be diligent or negligent. He can keep his heart more and more carefully; he can more strenuously watch and purify his mind; and he can guard himself against the thinking of unrighteous thoughts: this is the way of enlightenment and bliss. On the other hand, he can live loosely and carelessly, neglecting the supreme task of rightly ordering his life: this is the way of self-delusion and suffering.

Let a man realize that life in its totality proceeds from the mind, and lo, the way of blessedness is opened up to him! For he will then discover that he possesses the power to rule his mind, and to fashion it in accordance with his Ideal. So will be elect to strongly and steadfastly walk those pathways of thought and action which are altogether excellent; to him life will become beautiful and sacred; and, sooner or later, he will put to flight all evil, confusion and suffering; for it is impossible for a man to fall short of liberation, enlightenment, and peace, who guards with unwearying diligence the gateway of his heart.

THE NATURE AND POWER
OF MIND

Mind is the arbiter of life; it is the creator and shaper of conditions, and the recipient of its own results. It contains within itself both the power to create illusion and to perceive reality.

Mind is the infallible weaver of destiny; thought is the thread, good and evil deeds are the warp and woof, and the web, woven upon the loom of life, is character. Mind clothes itself in garments of its own making.

Man, as a mental being, possesses all the powers of mind, and is furnished with illimitable choice. He learns by experience, and he can accelerate or retard his experience. He is not arbitrarily bound at any point, but he has bound himself at many points, and having bound himself he can, when he chooses, liberate himself. He can become bestial or pure, ignoble or noble, foolish or wise, just as he chooses. He can, by recurring practice, form habits, and he can, by renewed effort, break them off. He can surround himself with illusions until Truth is completely lost, and he can destroy one and another of those illusions until Truth is entirely recovered. His possibilities are limitless; his freedom is complete.

It is in the nature of mind to create its own conditions, and to choose the states in which it shall dwell. It also has the power to alter any condition and to abandon any state, and this it is continually doing as it gathers knowledge of state after state by repeated choice and exhaustive experience.

Inward processes of thought make up the sum of character and life, and man can modify and alter these processes by bringing will and effort to bear upon them. The bonds of habit, impotence, and sin are self-made, and can only be destroyed by one's self; they exist nowhere but in one's mind, and although they are directly related to outward things, they have no real existence in those things. The outer is moulded and vivified by the inner, and never the inner by the outer. Temptation does not arise in the outer object, but in the lust of the mind for that object; nor do suffering and sorrow inhere in the external things and happenings of life, but in an undisciplined attitude of mind toward those things and happenings. The mind that is disciplined by Purity and fortified by Wisdom, avoids all those lusts and desires which are inseparably bound up with affliction, and so arrives at enlightenment and peace.

To condemn others as evil, and to rail against outside conditions as the source of evil, increases, and does not lessen, the world's suffering and unrest. The outer is but the shadow and effect of the inner, and when the heart is pure all outward things are pure.

All growth and life is from within outward; all decay and death is from without inward; this is a universal law. All evolution proceeds from within. All adjustment must take place within. He who ceases to strive against others, and employs his powers in the transformation, regeneration, and development of his own mind, conserves his energies and preserves himself; and as he succeeds in harmonizing his own mind, he leads others by consideration and charity into a like blessed state, for not by assuming authority and guidance over other minds is the way of enlightenment and peace discovered, but by exercising a lawful authority over one's own, and by guiding one's self in pathways of steadfast and lofty virtue.

A man's life proceeds from his heart, his mind: he has compounded that mind by his own thoughts and deeds: it is in his power to re-fashion that mind by his choice of thought: he can therefore transform his life. Let us see how this is to be done.

FORMATION OF HABIT

Every established mental condition is an acquired habit, and it has become such by continuous repetition of thought. Despondency and cheerfulness, anger and calmness, covetousness and generosity—indeed, all states of mind—are habits built up by choice, until they have become automatic. A thought constantly repeated at last becomes a fixed habit of the mind, and from such habits proceeds the life.

It is in the nature of the mind to acquire knowledge by the repetition of its experiences. A thought which it is very difficult, at first, to hold and to dwell upon, at last becomes, by constantly being held in the mind, a natural and habitual condition. Just as a boy, when commencing to learn a trade, cannot even handle his tools aright, much less use them correctly, but after long repetition and practice plies them with perfect ease and consummate skill, so a state of mind, at first apparently impossible of realization, is, by perseverance and practice, at last acquired and built into the character as a natural and spontaneous condition.

In this power of the mind to form and re-form its habits, its conditions, is contained the basis of man's salvation, and the open door to perfect liberty by the mastery of self, for as a man has the power to form harmful habits, so he has the same power to create habits that are essentially good. And here we come to a point which needs some elucidating, and which calls for deep and earnest thought on the part of my reader.

It is commonly said to be easier to do wrong than right, to sin than to be holy; such condition has come to be regarded, almost universally, as axiomatic, and no less a teacher than the Buddha has said:—"Bad deeds, and deeds hurtful to ourselves, are easy to do; what is beneficial and good, that is very difficult to do,"—and as regards humanity generally, this is true, but it is only true as a passing experience, a fleeting factor in human evolution; it is not a fixed condition of things, is not of the nature of an eternal truth. It is easier for men to do wrong than right, because of the prevalence of ignorance, because the true nature of things, and the essence and meaning of life, are not apprehended. When a child is learning to write, it is extremely easy for it to hold the pen wrongly, and to form its letters incorrectly, but it is painfully difficult to hold the pen and to write properly; and this because of the child's ignorance of the art of writing, which can only be dispelled by persistent effort and practice, until, at last, it becomes natural and easy to hold the pen properly, and to write correctly, and difficult, as well as altogether unnecessary, to do the wrong thing. It is the same in the vital things of mind and life. To think and do rightly requires much practice and renewed effort, but the time at last comes when it becomes habitual and easy to think and do rightly, and difficult, as it is then seen to be altogether unnecessary, to do that which is wrong.

Just as an artisan becomes, by practice, accomplished in his craft, so a man can become, by practice, accomplished in goodness; it is entirely a matter of forming new habits of thought, and he to whom right thoughts have become easy and natural, and wrong thoughts and acts difficult to do, has attained to the highest virtue, to pure, spiritual knowledge.

It is easy and natural for men to sin, because they have formed, by incessant repetition, harmful and unenlightened habits of thought. It is very difficult for the thief to refrain from stealing when opportunity occurs, because he has lived so long in covetous and avaricious thoughts; but such difficulty does not exist for the honest man who has lived so long in upright and honest thoughts, and has thereby become enlightened as to the wrong, folly, and fruitlessness of theft, that even the remotest idea of stealing does not enter his mind. The sin of theft is a very extreme one, and I have introduced it in order to the more clearly illustrate the force and formation of habit; but all sins and virtues are formed in the same way. Anger and impatience are natural and easy to thousands of people, because they are constantly repeating the angry and impatient thought and act, and with each repetition the habit is more firmly established and more deeply rooted. Calmness and patience can become habitual in the same way—by first grasping, through effort, a calm and patient thought, and then continuously thinking it, and living in it, until "use becomes second nature," and anger and impatience pass away for ever. It is thus that every wrong thought may be expelled from the mind; thus that every untrue act may be destroyed; thus that every sin may be overcome.

DOING AND KNOWING

L et a man realize that his life, in its totality, proceeds from his mind, and that that mind is a combination of habits which he can, by patient effort, modify to any extent, and over which he can thus gain complete ascendancy and control, and he has at once obtained possession of the key which shall open the door to his complete emancipation.

But emancipation from the ills of life (which are the ills of one's mind) is a matter of steady growth from within, and not a sudden acquisition from without. Hourly and daily must the mind be trained to think stainless thoughts, and to adopt right and dispassionate attitudes under those circumstances in which it is prone to fall into wrong and passion. Like the patient sculptor upon his marble, the aspirant to the Right Life must gradually work upon the crude material of his mind until he has wrought out of it the Ideal of his holiest dreams.

In working toward such supreme accomplishment, it is necessary to commence at the lowest and easiest steps, and proceed by natural and progressive stages to the higher and more difficult. This law of growth, progress, evolution, unfoldment, by gradual and ever ascending stages, is absolute in every department of life, and in every human accomplishment, and where it is ignored, total failure will result. In acquiring learning, in learning a trade, or in pursuing a business, this law is fully recognized and minutely obeyed by all; but in acquiring Virtue, in learning Truth, and in pursuing the right conduct and knowledge of life, it is unrecognized and disobeyed by nearly all; hence Virtue, Truth, and the Perfect Life remain unpractised, unacquired, and unknown.

It is a common error to suppose that the Higher Life is a matter of reading, and the adoption of theological or metaphysical hypotheses, and that Spiritual Principles can be apprehended by this method. The Higher Life is a higher living in thought, word, and deed, and the knowledge of those Spiritual Principles, which are imminent in man and in the universe can only be acquired after long discipline in the pursuit and practice of Virtue.

The lesser must be thoroughly grasped and understood before the greater can be known, and practice always precedes real knowledge. The schoolmaster never attempts to teach his pupils the abstract principles of mathematics at the commencement; he knows that by such a method teaching would be vain, and learning impossible. He first places before them a simple sum, and, having explained it, leaves them to do it. When, after repeated failures and ever-renewed effort, they have succeeded in doing it correctly, a more difficult task is set them, and then another and another; and not until the pupils have, through many years of diligent application, mastered all the lessons in arithmetic, does he attempt to unfold to them the underlying mathematical principles.

In learning a trade, say that of a mechanic, the boy is not at first taught the principles of mechanics, but a simple tool is put into his hand and he is told how rightly to use it, and is then left to do it by effort and practice. As he succeeds in plying his tools correctly, more and more difficult tasks are set him, until, after several years of successful practice, he is prepared to study and grasp the principles of mechanics.

In a properly governed household, the child is first taught to be obedient, and to conduct itself properly under all circumstances. The child is not even told why it must do this, but is commanded to do it, and only after it has so far succeeded in doing what is right and proper, is it told why it should do it. No father would attempt to teach his child the principles of ethics before exacting from it the practice of filial duty and social virtue.

Thus practice ever precedes knowledge even in the ordinary things of the world, and in spiritual things, in the living of the Higher Life, this law is rigid in its exactions. Virtue can only be known by doing, and the knowledge of Truth can only be arrived at by perfecting oneself in the practice of Virtue and to be complete in the practice and acquisition of Virtue is to complete in the knowledge of Truth.

Truth can only be arrived at by daily and hourly doing the lessons of Virtue, beginning at the simplest, and passing on to the more difficult; and as a child patiently and obediently learns its lessons at school, constantly practising, ever exerting itself until all failures and difficulties are surmounted, even so does the child of Truth apply himself to right-doing in thought and action, undaunted by failure, and made stronger by difficulties; and as he succeeds in acquiring Virtue, his mind unfolds itself in the knowledge of Truth, and it is a knowledge in which he can securely rest.

FIRST STEPS IN THE HIGHER LIFE

Seeing that the Path of Virtue is the Path of Knowledge, and that before the all-embracing Principles of Truth can be comprehended, perfection in the more lowly steps must be acquired, how, then, shall a disciple of Truth commence? How shall one who aspires to the righting of his mind and the purification of his heart—that heart which is the fountain and repository of all the issues of life—learn the lessons of Virtue, and thus build himself up in the strength of knowledge, destroying ignorance and the ills of life? What are the first lessons, the first steps? How are they learned? How are they practised? How are they mastered and understood?

The first lessons consist in overcoming those wrong mental conditions which are most easily eradicated, and which are the common barriers to spiritual progress, as well as in practising the simple domestic and social virtues; and the reader will be the better aided if I group and classify the first ten steps in three lessons as follows:—

VICES TO BE OVERCOME AND ERADICATED.

VICES OF THE BODY.

1. Indolence.
2. Self-Indulgence.

First Lesson.
Discipline of the Body.

VICES OF THE TONGUE.

1. Slander.
2. Gossip and idle conversation.
3. Abusive and unkind speech.
4. Levity, or irreverent speech.
5. Captiousness, or fault-finding speech.

Second Lesson.
Discipline of Speech.

VIRTUES TO BE PRACTICED AND ACQUIRED.

1. Unselfish performance
   of duty.   *Third Lesson.*
2. Unswerving rectitude.   Discipline of Inclination.
3. Unlimited forgiveness.

The two vices of the body, and five of the tongue, are so called because they are manifested in the body and tongue, and also because, by so definitely classifying them, the mind of the reader will be the better helped; but it must be clearly understood that these vices arise primarily in the mind, and are wrong conditions of heart worked out in the body and the tongue.

The existence of such chaotic conditions is an indication that the mind is altogether unenlightened as to the real meaning and purpose of life, and their eradication is the beginning of a virtuous, steadfast, and enlightened life.

But how shall they be overcome and eradicated? By first, and at once, checking and controlling their outward manifestations, by suppressing the wrong act; this will stimulate the mind to watchfulness and reflection until, by repeated practice, it will at last come to perceive and understand the dark and wrong conditions of mind, out of which such acts spring, and will abandon them entirely.

It will be seen that the first step in the discipline of the mind is the overcoming of indolence. This is the easiest step, and until it is perfectly accomplished, the other steps cannot he taken. The clinging to indolence constitues a complete barrier to the Path of Truth. Indolence consists in giving the body more ease and sleep than it requires, in procrastinating, and in shirking and neglecting those things which should receive immediate attention. This condition of laziness must be overcome by rousing up the body at any early hour, giving it just the amount of sleep it requires for complete recuperation, and by doing promptly and vigorously, every task and duty, no matter how small, as it comes along. On no account should food or drink be taken in bed, and to lie in bed after one has wakened, indulging in ease and reverie, is a habit fatal to promptness and resolution of character, and purity of mind. Nor should one attempt to do his thinking at such a time. Strong, pure, and true thinking is impossible under such circumstances. A man should go to bed to sleep, not to think. He should get up to think and work, not to sleep.

The next step is the overcoming of self-indulgence, or gluttony. The glutton is he who eats for animal gratification only, without considering the true end and object in eating, who eats more than his body requires, and is greedy after sweet things and rich dishes. Such undisciplined desire can only be overcome by reducing the quantity of food eaten, and the number of meals per day, and by resorting to a simple and uninvolved dietary. Regular hours should be set apart for meals, and eating at other times should be rigidly avoided. Suppers should be abolished, as they are altogether unnecessary, and conduce to heavy sleep and cloudiness of mind. The pursuit of such a method of discipline will rapidly bring the hitherto ungoverned appetite under control, and as the sensual sin of self-indulgence is taken out of the mind, the right selection of food will be instinctively and infallibly adapted to the purified mental condition.

It should be well borne in mind that change of heart is the needful thing, and that any change of diet which does not subserve this end is futile. Whilst one eats for enjoyment he is gluttonous. The heart must be purified of sensual craving and gustatory lust.

When the body is well controlled and firmly guided; when that which is to be done is done vigorously; when no task or duty is delayed; when early rising has become a delight; when frugality, temperance, and abstinence are firmly established; when one is contented with the food which is put before him, no matter how scanty and plain, and the craving for gustatory pleasure is at an end,—then are the first two steps in the Higher Life accomplished; then is the first great lesson in Truth learned. Thus is established in the heart the foundation of a poised, self-governed, virtuous life.

The next lesson is the lesson of Virtuous Speech, in which are five orderly steps. The first step is the overcoming of slander. Slander consists in inventing or repeating evil reports about others, in exposing and magnifying the faults of others, or of absent friends, and in introducing unworthy insinuations. The elements of thoughtlessness, cruelty, insincerity, and untruthfulness enter into every slanderous act. He who aims at the living of the right life will commence to check the cruel word of slander before it has gone forth from his lips, and will then check and eliminate the insincere thought which gave rise to it. He will watch himself that he does not vilify any, and will refrain from disparaging and condemning the absent friend, whose face he has so recently kissed, or shaken his hand, or smiled into his face. He will not say of another that which he dare not say to him. Thus, coming at last to think sacredly of the character and reputation of others, he will destroy those wrong conditions of mind which give rise to slander.

The next step is the overcoming of gossip and idle conversation. Idle speech consists in talking about the private affairs of others, in talking merely to pass away the time, and in engaging in aimless and irrelevant conversation. Such an ungoverned condition of speech is the outcome of an ill-regulated mind. The man of virtue will bridle his tongue, and thus learn how rightly to govern the mind. He will not let his tongue run idly and foolishly, but will make his speech strong and pure and will either talk with a purpose or remain silent.

Abusive and unkind speech is the next vice to be overcome. The man who abuses and accuses others has himself wandered far from the Right Way. To hurl hard words and names at others is to sink deeply into folly. When a man is inclined to abuse and condemn others, let him restrain his tongue and look in upon himself. The virtuous man refrains from abuse and quarrelling, and employs only words that are useful, necessary, pure, and true.

The next step is the overcoming of levity, or irreverent speech. Light and frivolous talking; the repeating of coarse jokes; the telling of vulgar stories, having no other purpose than to raise an empty laugh; offensive familiarity, and the employment of contemptuous and irreverent terms when speaking to or of others, and particularly of one's elders and those who rank as one's teachers, guardians, or superiors,—all this will be put away by the lover of Virtue and Truth.

Upon the altar of irreverence absent friends and companions are immolated for the passing excitement of a momentary laugh, and all the sanctity of life is sacrificed to the zest for ridicule. When respect toward others and the giving of reverence where reverence is due are abandoned, Virtue is abandoned. When modesty, gravity, and dignity are eliminated from speech and behavior, Truth is lost, yea, even its entrance gate is hidden away and forgotten. Irreverence is degrading even in the young, but when it accompanies grey hairs, and appears in the demeanor of the preacher,— this is indeed a piteous spectacle; and when this can be imitated and followed after, then are the blind leading the blind, then have elders and preacher and people lost their way.

The virtuous man will be of grave and reverent speech; he will think and speak of the absent as he thinks and speaks of the dead—tenderly and sacredly; he will put away thoughtlessness, and watch that he does not sacrifice his dignity to gratify a passing impulse to lightness and frivolity. His mirth will be pure and innocent, and his voice will become subdued and musical, and his soul be filled with grace and sweetness as he succeeds in conducting himself as becomes a man of Truth.

The last step in the second lesson is the overcoming of captiousness, or fault-finding speech. This vice of the tongue consists in magnifying and harping on small or apparent faults, in foolish quibbling and hair-splitting, and in pursuing vain arguments based upon groundless suppositions, beliefs, and opinions. Life is short and real, and sin and sorrow and pain are not remedied by carping and contention. The man who is ever on the watch to catch at the words of others in order to contradict and controvert them, has yet to reach the higher way of holiness, the truer life of self-surrender. The man who is ever on the watch to check his own words in order to soften and purify them will find the higher way and the truer life; he will conserve his energies, maintain his composure of mind, and preserve within himself the spirit of Truth.

When the tongue is well controlled and wisely subdued; when selfish impulses and unworthy thoughts no longer rush to the tongue demanding utterance; when the speech has become harmless, pure, gentle, gracious, and purposeful, and no word is uttered but in sincerity and truth,—then are the five steps in virtuous speech accomplished, then is the second great lesson in Truth learned and mastered.

And now some will ask, "But why all this discipline of the body and restraint of the tongue? Surely the Higher Life can be realized and known without such strenuous labor, such incessant effort and watchfulness?" No, it cannot. In the spiritual as the material, nothing is done without labor, and the higher cannot be known until the lower is fufilled. Can a man make a table before he has learned how to handle a tool and drive a nail? And can a man fashion his mind in accordance with Truth before he has overcome the slavery of his body? As the intricate subtleties of language cannot be apprehended and wielded before the alphabet and the simplest words are mastered, neither can the deep subtleties of the mind be understood and purified before the A B C of right conduct is perfectly acquired. As for the labor involved—does not the youth joyfully and patiently submit himself to a seven-years' apprenticeship in order to master a craft? And does he not day by day carefully and faithfully carry out every detail of his master's instructions, looking forward to the time when, perfected through obedience and practice, he shall be himself a master? Where is the man who sincerely aims at excellence in music, painting, literature, in any trade, business, or profession who is not willing to give his whole life to the acquirement of his particular perfection? Shall labor, then, be considered where the very highest excellence is concerned—the excellence of Truth? He who says, "The Path which you point out is too difficult; I must have Truth without labor, salvation without effort," that man will not find his way out of the confusions and sufferings of self-hood; he will not find the calm and well-fortified mind and the wisely ordered life. His love is for ease and enjoyment, and not for Truth. He who, deep in his heart, adores Truth, and aspires to know it, will consider no labor too great to be undertaken, but will adopt it joyfully and pursue it patiently, and by perseverance in practice he will come to the knowledge of Truth.

The necessity for this preliminary discipline of the body and tongue will be the more clearly perceived when it is fully understood that all these wrong outward conditions are merely the expressions of wrong conditions of heart. An indolent body means an indolent mind; an ill-regulated tongue reveals an ill-regulated mind, and the process of remedying the manifested condition is really a method of rectifying the inward state. Moreover, the overcoming of these conditions is only a small part of what is really involved in the process. The ceasing from evil leads to, and is inseparably connected with, the practice of good. While a man is overcoming indolence and self-indulgence, he is really cultivating and developing the virtues of abstinence, temperance, punctuality, and self-denial, and is acquiring that strength, energy, and resolution which are indispensable to the successful accomplishment of the higher tasks. While he is overcoming the vices of speech, he is developing the virtues of truthfulness, sincerity, reverence, kindliness, and self-control, and is gaining that mental steadiness and fixedness of purpose, without which the remoter subtleties of the mind cannot be regulated, and the higher stages of conduct and enlightenment cannot be reached. Also, as he has to do right, his knowledge deepens, and his insight is intensified, and as the child's heart is glad when his school task is mastered, so with each victory achieved, the man of virtue experiences a bliss which the seeker after pleasure and excitement can never know.

And now we come to the third lesson in the Higher Life, which consists in practising and mastering, in one's daily life, three great fundamental. Virtues—(1) Unselfish Performance of Duty;

(2) Unswerving Rectitude; and (3) Unlimited Forgiveness. Having prepared the mind by overcoming the more surface and chaotic conditions mentioned in the two first lessons, the striver after Virtue and Truth is now ready to enter upon greater and more difficult tasks, and to control and purify the deeper motives of the heart. Without the right performance of duty, the higher virtues cannot be known, and Truth cannot be apprehended. Duty is generally regarded as an irksome labor, a compulsory something which must be toiled through, or be in some way circumvented. This way of regarding Duty proceeds from a selfish condition of mind, and a wrong understanding of life. All duty should be regarded as sacred, and its faithful and unselfish performance one of the leading rules of conduct. All personal and selfish considerations should be extracted and cast away from the doing of one's duty, and when this is done, Duty ceases to be irksome, and becomes joyful. Duty is only irksome to him who craves some selfish enjoyment or benefit for himself. Let the man who is chafing under the irksomeness of his duty look to himself, and he will find that his wearisomeness proceeds, not from the duty itself, but from his selfish desire to escape it. He who neglects duty, be it great or small, or of a public or private nature, neglects Virtue; he who in his heart rebels against Duty, rebels against Virtue. When Duty has become a thing of love, and when every particular duty is done accurately, faithfully, and dispassionately, there is much subtle selfishness removed from the heart, and a great step is taken toward the heights of Truth. The virtuous man concentrates his mind on the perfect doing of his own duty, and does not interfere with the duty of another.

The second step in the third lesson is the practice of Unswerving Rectitude. This Virtue must be firmly established in the mind, and so enter into every detail of man's life. All dishonesty, deception, trickery, and misrepresentation must be for ever put away, and the heart be purged of every vestige of insincerity and subterfuge. The least swerving from the path of rectitude is a deviation from Virtue. There must be no extravagance and exaggeration of speech, but the simple truth should be stated. Engaging in deception, no matter how apparently insignificant, for vain-glory, or with the hope of personal advantage, is a state of delusion which one should make efforts to dispel. It is demanded of the man of Virtue that he shall not only practice the most rigid honesty in thought, word, and deed, but that he shall be exact in his statements, omitting and adding nothing to the actual truth. In thus shaping his mind to the principle of Rectitude, he will gradually come to deal with people and things in a just and impartial spirit, considering equity before himself, and viewing all things with freedom from personal bias, passion, and prejudice. When the Virtue of Rectitude is fully practised, acquired, and comprehended, so that all temptation to untruthfulness and insincerity has ceased, then is the heart made purer and nobler, then is character strengthened, and knowledge enlarged, and life takes on a new meaning and a new power. Thus is the second step accomplished.

The third step is the practice of Unlimited Forgiveness. This consists in overcoming the sense of injury which springs from vanity, selfishness, and pride; and in exercising disinterested charity and large-heartedness toward all. Spite, retaliation, and revenge are so utterly ignoble, and so small and foolish, as to be altogether unworthy of being noticed or harbored. No one who fosters such conditions in his heart can lift himself above folly and suffering, and guide his life aright. Only by casting them away, and ceasing to be moved by them, can a man's eyes be opened to the true way in life; only by developing a forgiving and charitable spirit can he hope to approach and perceive the strength and beauty of a well-ordered life. In the heart of the strongly virtuous man no feeling of personal injury can arise; he has put away all retaliation, and has no enemies; and if men should constitute themselves his enemies, he will regard them kindly, understanding their ignorance, and making full allowance for it. When this state of heart is arrived at, then is the third step in the discipline of one's self-seeking inclinations accomplished; then is the third great lesson in Virtue and Knowledge learned and mastered.

Having thus laid down the first ten steps and three lessons in right-doing and right-knowing, I leave those of my readers who are prepared for them to learn and master them in their everyday life. There is, of course, a still higher discipline of the body, a more far-reaching discipline of the tongue, and greater and more all-embracing virtues to acquire and understand before the highest state of bliss and knowledge can be apprehended, but it is not my purpose to deal with them here. I have expounded only the first and easiest lessons on the Higher Path, and by the time these are thoroughly mastered, the reader will have become so purified, strengthened, and enlightened, that he will not be left in the dark as to his future progress. Those of my readers who have completed these three lessons will already have perceived, beyond and above, the high altitudes of Truth, and the narrow and precipitous track which leads to them, and will choose whether they shall proceed.

The straight Path which I have laid down can be pursued by all with greater profit to themselves and to the world, and even those who do not aspire to the attainment of Truth, will develop greater intellectual and moral strength, finer judgment, and deeper peace of mind by perfecting themselves in this Path. Nor will their material prosperity suffer by this change of heart; nay, it will be rendered truer, purer, and more enduring, for if there is one who is capable of succeeding and fitted to achieve, it is the man who has abandoned the petty dissipations and everyday vices of his kind, who is strong to rule his body and his mind, and who pursues with fixed resolve the path of unswerving integrity and sterling virtue.

MENTAL CONDITIONS AND THEIR EFFECTS

Without going into the details of the greater steps and lessons in the right life (a task outside the scope of this small work) a few hints and statements concerning those mental conditions from which life in its totality springs, will prove helpful to those who are ready and willing to penetrate further into that inner realm of heart and mind where Love and Wisdom and Peace await the strenuous comer.

All sin is ignorance. It is a condition of darkness and undevelopment. The wrong-thinker and wrong-doer is in the same position in the school of life as is the ignorant pupil in the school of learning. He has yet to learn how to think and act correctly, that is, in accordance with Law. The pupil in learning is not happy so long as he does his lessons wrongly, and unhappiness cannot be escaped while sin remains unconquered.

Life is a series of lessons. Some are diligent in learning them, and they become pure, wise, and altogether happy. Others are negligent, and do not apply themselves, and they remain impure, foolish, and unhappy.

Every form of unhappiness springs from a wrong condition of mind. Happiness inheres in right conditions of mind. Happiness is mental harmony; unhappiness is mental inharmony. While a man lives in wrong conditions of mind, he will live a wrong life, and will suffer continually. Suffering is rooted in error. Bliss inheres in enlightenment. There is salvation for man only in the destruction of his own ignorance, error, and self-delusion. Where there are wrong conditions of mind there is bondage and unrest; where there are right conditions of mind there is freedom and peace.

Here are some of the leading wrong mental conditions and their disastrous effects upon the life:—

Wrong Mental Conditions.	*Their Effects.*
Hatred.	Injury, violence, disaster, and suffering.
Lust.	Confusion of intellect, remorse, shame, and wretchedness.
Covetousness.	Fear, unrest, unhappiness, and loss.
Pride.	Disappointment, chagrin, lack of self-knowledge.

Wrong Mental Conditions.	Their Effects.
Vanity.	Distress, and mortification of spirit.
Condemnation.	Persecution, hatred from others.
Ill-will.	Failures and troubles.
Self-indulgence.	Misery, loss of judgment, grossness, disease, and neglect.
Anger.	Loss of power and influence.
Desire, or Self-slavery.	Grief, folly, sorrow, uncertainty, and loneliness.

The above wrong conditions of mind are merely negations; they are states of darkness and deprivation and not of positive power. Evil is not a power; it is ignorance and misuse of good. The hater is he who has failed to do the lesson of Love correctly, and he suffers in consequence. When he succeeds in doing it rightly, the hatred will have disappeared, and he will see and understand the darkness and impotence of hatred. It is so with every wrong condition.

The following are some of the more important right mental conditions and their beneficent effects upon the life:—

Right Mental Conditions.	Their Effects.
Love.	Gentle conditions, bliss, and blessedness.
Purity.	Intellectual clearness, joy, invincible confidence.
Selflessness.	Courage, satisfaction, happiness, and plenty.
Humility.	Calmness, restfulness, knowledge of Truth.
Meekness	Equipoise, contentment under all circumstances.
Compassion.	Protection, love and reverence from others.
Goodwill.	Gladness and success.
Self-control.	Peace of mind, true judgment, refinement, health, and honor.
Patience.	Mental power, far-reaching influence.
Self-conquest.	Enlightenment, wisdom, insight, and profound peace.

The above right conditions of mind are states of positive power, of light, of joyful possession, and of knowledge. The good man knows. He has learned to do his lessons correctly, and thereby understands the exact proportions which make up the sum of life. He is enlightened, and knows good and evil. He is supremely happy, doing only that which is divinely right.

The man who is involved in the wrong conditions of mind, does not know. He is ignorant of good and evil, of himself, of the inward causes which make his life. He is unhappy, and believes other people are entirely the cause of his unhappiness. He works blindly, and lives in darkness, seeing no central purpose in existence, and no orderly and lawful sequence in the course of things.

He who aspires to the attainment of the Higher Life in its completion—who would perceive with unveiled vision the true order of things and the meaning of life—let him abandon all the wrong conditions of heart, and persevere unceasingly in the practice of the good. If he suffers, or doubts, or is unhappy, let him search within until he finds the cause, and having found it, let him cast it away. Let him so guard and purify his heart that every day less of evil and more of good shall issue therefrom; so will he daily become stronger, nobler, wiser; so will his blessedness increase, and the Light of Truth, growing ever brighter and brighter within him, will dispel all gloom, and illuminate his Pathway.

EXHORTATION

Disciples of Truth, lovers of Virtue, seekers of Wisdom; ye, also, who are sorrow stricken, knowing the emptiness of the self-life, and who aspire to the life that is supremely beautiful, and serenely glad,—take now yourselves in hand, enter the Door of Discipline, and know the Better Life.

Put away self-delusion; behold yourself as you are, and see the Path of Virtue as it is. There is no lazy way to Truth. He who would stand upon the mountain's summit must strenuously climb, and must rest only to gather strength. But if the climbing is less glorious than the cloudless summit, it is still glorious. Discipline in itself is beautiful, and the end of discipline is sweet.

Rise early and meditate. Begin each day with a conquered body, and a mind fortified against error and weakness. Temptation will never be overcome by unprepared fighting. The mind must be armed and arrayed in the silent hour. It must be trained to perceive, to know, to understand. Sin and temptation disappear when right understanding is developed.

Right understanding is reached through unabated discipline. Truth cannot be reached but through discipline. Patience will increase by effort and practice, and patience will make discipline beautiful.

Discipline is irksome to the impatient man and the self-lover, so he avoids it, and continues to live loosely and confusedly.

Discipline is not irksome to the Truth-lover, and he will find the infinite patience which can wait and work and overcome. As the joy of the gardener who sees his flowers develop day by day, so is the joy of the man of discipline who sees the divine flowers of Purity, Wisdom, Compassion, and Love, grow up in his heart.

The loose-liver cannot escape sorrow and pain. The undisciplined mind falls, weak and helpless, before the fierce onslaught of passion.

Array well your mind, then, lover of Truth. Be watchful, thoughtful, resolute. Your salvation is at hand; your readiness and effort are all that are needed. If you should fail ten times, do not be disheartened; if you should fail a hundred times, rise up and pursue your way; if you should fail a thousand times, do not despair. When the right Path is entered, success is sure if the Path is not utterly abandoned.

First strife, and then victory. First labor, and then rest. First weakness, and then strength. In the beginning the lower life, and the glare and confusion of battle, and at the end the Life Beautiful, the Silence, and the Peace.

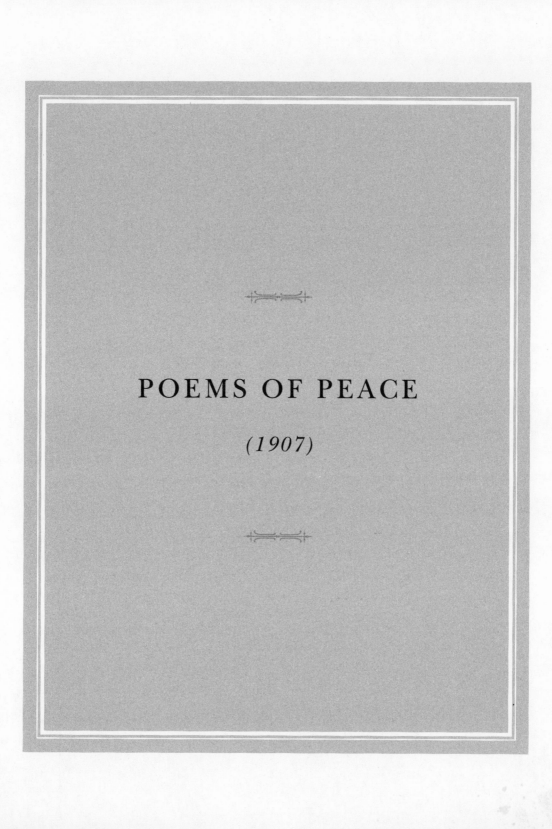

POEMS OF PEACE

(1907)

TO

G. A. D.

WHOSE ESTEEMED FRIENDSHIP ENLARGED MY LABOURS

WHOSE GENEROUS AID STRENGTHENED THE WORK OF TRUTH

AND WHOSE NAME

WILL EVER BE HELD IN AFFECTIONATE REMEMBRANCE

THIS BOOK OF POEMS

IS LOVINGLY

DEDICATED

PREFACE

Wordsworth held that every true poet was a teacher; and he said, "I wish either to be considered as a teacher, or as nothing." The poems in this volume are designed to teach; and as instruction is best administered by methods which please while they elevate, the immediate object of these poems is to comfort, to bless, and to make happy; and, being framed on the principles of Truth, I doubt not that they will inspire men to embrace loftier ideals of life, draw them to a closer acquaintance with virtue, and lead them to a more intimate union with that perfect Wisdom whose ways are "ways of pleasantness," and whose paths are "paths of peace."

—JAMES ALLEN
Bryngoleu,
Ilfracombe, England
November, 1907

CONTENTS

EOLAUS

A Lyrical-Dramatic Poem

Dramatis Personae.

Eolaus.	Cosmos.
The Prophet.	Voices of Nature.
Earth.	Voices of Truth.
Heaven.	Echoes.

Scene.—*A beautiful Island, wooded. EOLAUS sitting on a fallen tree near the sea-shore.*

Eolaus. Unto this lonely Island I repair
To search for peace. After long days and nights
Upon the waters, storm-tossed and fatigued,
My skiff touched they fair harbour, blessed Isle.
Now on thy fragrant bosom I will rest,
And in thy spiritual ecstasy
Sweetly participate: thy loveliness
Entrances me; thy restfulness enweaves
My thoughts with peace imperishable; thou
Art silent, solitary, beautiful,
And I am lonely; yet thy solitude
Perchance will comfort me, and take away
My loneliness and pain. O Solitude!
Thou habitation of aspiring hearts;
Thou light and beacon of the pure; thou guide
Of them that cry in darkness; thou sweet friend
Of sorrow-stricken wanderers; thou staff
And stay of the strong climber up the hills,
Trackless and strange, of Truth; instructor thou,
And teacher of the teachable and true,
Beloved of the lowly, wise, and good,
Be my companion now, and take away

The world's ache from my bosom! I am tired
Of the vain Highways, where the noise and din
Drowns all but sad remembrance; tired of all
The tumult and the terror and the tears
That rule discordant in the House of Life,
Shaking but not destroying, as the storms,
Confederate with the oceans, shake the shores
And rock-bound margins of the continents.
I seek the peace that does not change; the calm
That knows no storm; the Silence that remains.
Pleasure disturbs, and does not satisfy:
When the excitements of the senses fade,
Sorrow and pain return, and leave the heart
Remorseful, desolate. As o'er the waste
And barren moor the lonely curlew cries,
So wails the bird of anguish o'er the mind
Sated with pleasure; Woe and Want repair
To the abode of Selfishness, and take
Legions of miseries with them. I would find
Where Wisdom is, where Peace abides, where
  Truth,
Majestic, changeless, and eternal, stands

Untouched by the illusions of the world:
For surely there is Knowledge, Truth, and Peace
For him who seeks, seeing that ignorance
And error and affliction are; these prove
The unseen truths obversely: darkness makes
Light sure and certain, though we see it not.
We sleep and wake, and, waking, know the
    dream
That troubled us in sleep; how it arose,
Phantasmal and chaotic, in the mind
Left all ungoverned; even so perchance
This life of passion and of wild desire
(Troubled, chaotic, and not understood),
May be, as 'twere, a dream; and if a dream
Of the unmastered mind, we shall awake
Out of the nightmare of our miseries,
And know the gladness of Reality.
But how shall one awake? How, if not by
Bridling his passions, curbing his desires
By masterful dominion of the will?
If passions be the troubled dreams of life,
And not its substance and reality,
Then he who shakes off passion shall awake
And know the Truth: surely this must be so!
Therefore unto this unfrequented place
Have I addressed myself, that I may gain,
By purity and strong self-mastery,
Th' awakened vision that doth set men free
From painful slumber and the night of grief.
Here unobserved and solitary, I
Will purify my heart and train my mind
In the true ways of sweet unselfishness,
Subduing self and passion; so perchance
The changeless Truth will be revealed to me,
And I shall move, wherever Duty calls,
Serene and sorrowless.
                    Moreover, here
An aged Prophet dwells, so I am told,

Who will instruct me in the Silent Way
Which winds through the morasses of the mind
Unto the firm heights of accomplished Truth.
Him will I seek when I have slept awhile,
For weariness now urges me to rest.
                              Lies down.
Thou Zephyrus! thou sweet and cooling breath
That temperest the broiling mid-day rays
Of June's extremest heat, blow o'er me now,
And fan me into sweet forgetfulness!
I am a-wearied, battling with the waves.
Now will I sleep: after my long, long search
Upon the waters, I am spent with toil.
Watch o'er me, Nature, I am safe with thee.
                              Sleeps.

VOICES OF NATURE.
First Voice.
        Listen, O Eolaus!
Woven of passion is the Universe;
Vain is thy puny strength to break its web.
Submit thyself to that which in thee cries:
Gratify nature; do not fly delight.
            Eolaus, come!
        Let me lead thee, Eolaus!
        Let me guide thee, Eolaus!
Come, Eolaus! Eolaus, come!
                Echo.
            Eolaus, come!
            Second Voice.
        There is sweet intoxication
            In the Pleasure-house of Earth;
        Aye-renewed exhilaration,
            Love and happiness and mirth.
            First Voice.
Come, Eolaus! Eolaus, come!
                Echo.
            Eolaus, come!

Third Voice.

What is seen is sure;

What is felt is known

Pleasure is secure;

Joy is life alone.

First Voice.

Come, Eolaus! Eolaus, come!

Echo.

Eolaus, come!

Second Voice.

Come and drink the wine of life;

Pleasure's vintage come and taste;

Leave thy fruitless search and strife;

Holy vigils wear and waste

Youth, for love and revels framed:

Nature thus is blindly blamed.

First Voice.

Come, Eolaus! Eolaus, come!

Echo.

Eolaus, come!

Third Voice.

Think no more of low and high;

Leave thy climbings, and forget

Aim and struggle, doubt and sigh;

Level is the pathway set

Of enjoyment: seek no more;

Rest thou here, thy woe is o'er.

First Voice.

Eolaus, come!

Let me lead thee, Eolaus!

Let me guide thee, Eolaus!

Come, Eolaus! Eolaus, come!

Echo.

Eolaus, come!

EARTH.

Unnumbered ages have I rolled

Through the abysmal spaces;

And eons new from eons old

Th' Eternal Finger traces;

And I must follow where it moves:

No rest! No rest!

With hopes and fears and hates and loves

Unblest! Unblest!

Fourth Voice.

Listen, O Eolaus!

Sorrow doth darken all the universe;

Its creatures are involved in pain and woe;

Helpless they cry, and no one hears or aids;

Dark, dark is life, and none its meaning know.

Eolaus, hear!

None can lead thee, Eolaus!

None can guide thee, Eolaus!

Hear, Eolaus! Eolaus, hear!

Echo.

Eolaus, hear!

Fifth Voice.

There is pain and woe and sorrow

In the hospital of Earth;

Every night and morn and morrow

Bringeth drought and death and dearth.

Fourth Voice.

Hear, Eolaus! Eolaus, hear!

Echo.

Eolaus, hear!

Sixth Voice.

What is seen's unsure;

What is felt is blown;

Self is insecure;

Life is pain alone.

Fourth Voice.

Hear, Eolaus! Eolaus, hear!

Echo.

Eolaus, hear!

Several Voices.

We moan and sigh;

We sob and cry;

We wander, like the wind upon the stream,

Vainly for peace,

Seeking release

From the keen pain of our unending dream.

Fourth Voice.

Eolaus, hear!

None can lead thee, Eolaus!

None can guide thee, Eolaus!

Hear, Eolaus! Eolaus, hear!

Echo.

Eolaus, hear!

VOICES OF TRUTH.

First Voice.

Awake, O Eolaus!

Arise! shake off the dreams of Night,

Open thine eyes, and see the Light;

Passionless Wisdom waits for thee

In sorrowless serenity.

Leave thou the fleeting shapes of Time,

The rugged Way of Truth sublime

Walk thou; nor fear, nor grieve, nor lust,

Scorning the self whose end is dust.

Wake, Eolaus! Eolaus, wake!

Chorus of Voices.

Eolaus, wake!

Second Voice.

Knowledge is for him who seeks;

Wisdom crowneth him who strives;

Peace in sinless silence speaks;

All things perish, Truth survives.

First Voice.

Wake, Eolaus! Eolaus, wake!

Voices.

Eolaus, wake!

Third Voice.

Follow where Virtue leads,

High and still higher;

Listen when Pureness pleads,

Quench not her fire.

Lo! he shall see

Reality,

Who cometh upward, cleansed from all desire.

First Voice.

Wake, Eolaus! Eolaus, wake!

Voices.

Eolaus, wake!

Fourth Voice.

He who attaineth unto Purity

The faultless Parthenon of Truth doth see.

Awake! disperse the dreams of self and sin!

Behold the Shining Gateway! enter in!

First Voice.

Wake, Eolaus! Eolaus, wake!

Voices.

Eolaus, wake!

Fifth Voice.

Conquer thyself,

Then thou shalt know;

Climb to the high,

Leave thou the low.

Deliverance

Shall him entrance

Who strives with sins and sorrows, tears and pains

Till he attains.

First Voice.

Wake, Eolaus! Eolaus, wake!

Voices.

Eolaus, wake!

HEAVEN.

In the visions of the ages

I am evermore reflected;

In the precepts of the Sages

I am spoken and rejected.

I can suffer no distortion,
   Sin and sorrow cannot stain me;
Fixed and faultless in proportion,
   He must bend who would attain me.

EOLAUS, *waking*.
  Who will lead me, who will guide me
  In my deep perplexity?

HEAVEN.
In the middle of the Island
Waits the Sage whom you are seeking!
On the Rock which cannot crumble
Sits the Prophet who will guide you.
                   Eolaus *wakes*.

Eolaus. 'Mid the conflicting visions of the mind
I darkly grope, and nevermore can find
The steadfastness and surety that I seek:
Where clamour reigns the silence cannot speak.
So many voices and so many ways!
So many wand'rings through the nights and days!
One way I seek, one Voice I long to hear,
But Truth eludes me and does not appear.—
Now to this Island's centre I repair
To seek the Prophet who abideth there.

*The scene changes to the centre of the Island.
An aged and venerable man appears, sitting
upon a rock.*

Eolaus. Art thou the Prophet whom I seek?
Prophet.   I am.
  Eolaus. Be thou my guide, for thou art wise, and I
Am ignorant; speak thou, and I will hear;
Teach me, and I will be instructed; make
Me to behold the Path which leads to Truth,
And I will walk it though it be o'entrewn
With flints and burrs; and if it needs must come

Within the round of holy discipline
That one shall walk that way with naked feet,
Or else forego the end and view of Truth,
Then barefoot I will walk it, and account
Bleedings and wounds and lacerations
As aids unto my will and fortitude,
As tasks wisely ordained, and so to be
Gladly encountered in my pilgrimage.
Mine ears are open, open thou mine eyes,
For I am blind, and cannot find my way.
  Prophet. He who would see with the all-seeing eye
Single of Truth, must first his blindness know.
He cannot see who does not wish to see,
Thinking he sees already, while his acts
Proclaim his spiritual blindness.   Truth
Waits on the lowly-hearted.   He who knows
That being passion-bound, he yet is blind,
Has groped his way to Wisdom.   Thou dost see.
  Eolaus. I see naught but the darkness of my mind,
And in that darkness ever-changing shapes
Of things phantasmal that perplex and haunt,
Eluding knowledge; I am ignorant,
Yet strive to know; nor will I cease to strive
Till I attain.
  Prophet.   Seeing thy darkness, thou
So far dost see; knowing thine ignorance,
So far hast thou attained to knowledge: seek,
And thou shalt surely find.
  Eolaus.   How shall I seek?
  Prophet.   Increase thy strength and self-reliance;
  make
The spectres of thy mind obey thy will:
See thou command thyself; nor let no mood,
No subtle passion nor no swift desire
Hurl thee to baseness; but, should'st thou be
  hurled,
Rise, and regain thy manhood, taking gain
Of lowliness and wisdom from thy fall.

Strive ever for the mastery of thy mind,
And glean some good from every circumstance
That shall confront thee; make thy store of strength
Richer for ills encountered and o'ercome.
Submit to naught but nobleness; rejoice
Like a strong athlete straining for the prize,
When thy full strength is tried; be not the slave
Of lusts and cravings and indulgences,
Of disappointments, miseries and griefs,
Fears, doubts, and lamentations, but control
Thyself with calmness: master that in thee
Which masters others, and which heretofore
Has mastered thee: let not thy passions rule,
But rule thy passions; subjugate thyself
Till passion is transmuted into peace,
And wisdom crown thee; so shalt thou attain
And, by attaining, know.

    Eolaus.   Hard is the path
Which thou hast set before me; steep and strange
Its ascent; unfamiliar and unknown
The Place whereto it leads: I see it rise
Precipitous but yet accessible,
Beyond the reach of vision: what awaits
The climber, none but he who climbs may know;
For if one ask, and, with believing ears
Attend the spiritual Mountaineer
In his depicture of the unknown heights,
What knows he more, though more believing? What
Gains he but words, and wonderings, and dreams,
Unless he also climb? I would o'ermount
Faith, and ascend to knowledge; I would not
Rest idly in the valleys of belief,
Content with speculation; I would be
The Mountaineer, and know.

    Prophet.   The Mountaineer
Is he who, dauntless, climbs.

    Eolaus.   But yet the way,—
Where leads it? All beyond the reach of sight

Is dark, unknown, mysterious. What avails
The strenuous ascent, if some precipice
The daring climber claim, or loosened rock
Dash him to death, or cold and hunger make
Ravage upon his strength?   Passion is sweet,
And 'tis enjoyed and known; and round about
The habitations at the mountain's base,
In the familiar valleys of the mind,
Twine the sweet flowers of soft affections,
Filling the air with fragrance and delight,
And mellow fruits of love and labour hang
Ripe for the plucking; shall I these renounce,
The sure and known, for the unsure, unknown?
Are these not safe, substantial and possessed?
While that I seek,—where is it?   Is this Truth,
This idea of Reality which haunts
My mind, and drives me whither I know not,
Itself a speculation?   What abides?
Alas! all that we have and know is caught
In transiency; changes that never end
Roll wave-like o'er the restless universe,
And man is tossed therein; so it befalls
That everything which comes into his grasp—
Bearing the face of an enduring joy—
After a little fever of delight
Is torn away again: nothing endures:
All things are dying even while they live;
And life is passing while it seems to wait.
There is no sweet possession, no rare joy,
No cherished circumstance, no prized delight,
No lovely thing, of which it can be said,—
"There is no time when this will never be."
What comes to pass, passes, and comes no more;
What grows, decays; what rises, falls; what lives
And flourishes, dies and doth fade away:
Where then is surety? Where is knowledge? Where
Is rest and refuge?

    Prophet.   There is rest in Truth.

Eolaus.   Is there no rest in death?

Prophet.   There is no rest
In death.

Eolaus.   No rest in death nor life?

Prophet.   No rest
In death nor life; yet or in death or life,
Where Truth is, there is rest.

   Eolaus.   Prophet of Good,
Lead me to the Abiding; set my feet
Upon the austere Highway which doth lead
To the Eternal City: I would find
The rest and refuge of undying Truth.

   Prophet.   Look thou within. Lo, in the midst
     of change
Abides the Changeless; at the heart of strife
The Perfect Peace reposes. At the root
Of all the restless striving of the world
Is passion, and at passion's heart is stored
Truth; yes, the Law of laws is in thy mind,
And written on the tablet of thy heart
Are its eternal edicts: subjugate
Thy passions, and the truth will be revealed,
For whoso follows passion findeth pain,
But whose conquers passion findeth peace.

   Eolaus.   Not to be subject unto passion, but
To subject passion,—is this then the way?

   Prophet.   Thou hast well said. As the sweet
     nut is held
In the hard shell, and cannot be enjoyed
But by destruction of the husk, so Truth
In passion is preserved, but is not known
Till passion be destroyed and cast away.
He who preserveth passion, dreading loss
Of sweetness and enjoyment, cannot know
The bliss of Truth, nor find where wisdom is:
He is a prodigal, feeding upon
The husks of life, the empty shows of things,
And knowing not its kernel, seeing not

The changeless substance of Reality.
He only knows who conquers evil; he
Who masters self, passes beyond the dim
Uncertain light of faith, and on him breaks
The light of Perfect Knowledge which enfolds
Emancipation, gladness, perfect peace.

   Eolaus.   I know that sorrow follows passion; know
That grief and emptiness and heartaches wait
Upon all earthly joys; so am I sad;
Yet Truth must be, and, being, can be found;
And though I am in sorrow, this I know—
I shall be glad when I have found the Truth.

   Prophet.   There is no gladness like the joy of
     Truth.
The pure in heart swim in a sea of bliss
That evermore nor sorrow knows, nor pain;
For who can see the Cosmos and be sad?
To know is to be happy; they rejoice
Who have attained Perfection; these are they
Who live, and know, and realize the Truth.

Eolaus. I strive for that Perfection; shall I reach
The Heights of Blessed Vision?

   Prophet.   Comfort ye,
The Heights of Blessed Vision ye shall reach.

   Eolaus.   Yet how, and when, and where? I am
     confused.
The Way is near, and yet I see it not!

   Prophet.   He must be friendly with the worm
     and toad
Who would be the companion of the wise,
And know the Cosmic Splendour; he must stoop
Who seeks to stand; must fall who fain would rise;
Must know the low, ascending to the high;
He who would know the Great, must not disdain
To diligently wait upon the small:
He wisdom finds who finds humility.

   Eolaus.   Speak on, O Prophet! I attend thy
     words.

Prophet.   The beasts can neither bend nor
　　stand erect,
Being beasts,—abandon bestial tendencies;
But man can bend, and man can stand erect,
　　Being man,—embrace pure thoughts and
　　　stainless deeds;
Here is deliverance. Man's redemption lies
In man himself, yet is not born of self,
But takes its rise in Truth: man can achieve:
He findeth Truth who findeth self-control.
　　Eolaus.   When I have found the meaning of
　　　thy words,
I know I shall be wise as thou art wise;
But now I hear thee, and yet hear thee not.
　　Prophet.   Thou wilt perceive the substance of
　　　my words,
And understand their meaning, when they stir
That meaning in thyself, and in thy mind
Stand clear and well-reflected; thou canot know
Only by subjugation of thyself,
And practice of the highest: all that's real
Is inward; outward things are fleeting shows,
Vain and illusory, holding nor rest
Nor refuge for the wise: obey the Right,
And wrong shall ne'er again assail thy peace,
Nor error hurt thee more: attune thy heart
To Purity, and thou shalt reach the Place
Where sorrow is not, and all evil ends.
The Holy Ones know not the name of sin;
Goodness and Truth make glad the good and true;
The Perfect Ones behold the Perfect Law;
Struggle and strife are ended in the Truth.
All things are holy to the holy mind,
All uses are legitimate and pure,
All occupations blest and sanctified,
And every day a Sabbath.
　　Eolaus.　　　　　　　　I perceive
Some glimmering of a Light transcending light,

Some outline of a mighty Principle
More beautiful than beauty; see some dim
Appearing of the vision of a Life
Vaster than life: the Cosmos is sublime!
My eyes will open, I shall see the Truth,
And, seeing, shall be glad for evermore!
　　Prophet.   Be mindful, or the thought that soars
　　　will sink:
Be lowly, patient, well-instructed; hold
Thyself in check; by many single steps
All journeys reach completion: as the tree
That rears its stately head toward the sky—
Bestowing shade and shelter—issued from
A tiny seed, and, waiting patiently
Upon the law of growth, it came to be
The thing majestic that it now appears,—
So wisdom from a single act of good
Well-planted, watched, and watered, comes at last
To its sublime proportions.
　　Eolaus.　　　　　　　　I will tend
The plant of wisdom with all diligence,
And watch its growth toward perfection.
Show me the unobserved and lowly Way;
Let praise, reward, and popularity
Be no more sweet to me, and no more sought;
Let self be blotted out, I seek the Truth.
　　Prophet.   Now listen, and attend:—the
　　　pigeons pick
Holes in the buildings, and the storm o'erturns
That they had weakened: little failings eat
Holes in the citadel of Character
Which, weakened thus, cannot withstand the
　　storms
Of circumstance, but weakly falls before
Tempestuous temptations. As the bee
Buildeth the honeycomb, the bird its nest,
The builder his strong house, e'en bit by bit,
Straw unto straw, and stone laid upon stone,

Until the finished thing and perfect whole
Crowns effort with success,—so the wise man,
By adding thought to thought and deed to deed
In ways of good, buildeth his character.
Little by little he accomplishes
His noble ends; in quiet patience works
Diligently, while others sleep, or slake
Their hot desires in riot; nowise moved
From his main purpose by perplexities,
Falls, errors, failures, difficulties, pains,
Daily he builds into his heart and mind
Pure thoughts, high aspirations, selfless deeds,
Until at last the edifice of Truth
Is finished, and behold! There rises and appears
The Temple of Perfection.

  Eolaus.   I have found
The little Gate mean and moss-grown which leads
Into a dark, despised, neglected Way
Which, further, leads to glorious esplanades
And heights of Splendour; foolish men avoid
The lowly, and thereby the lofty lose;
Despise the small, and the majestical
Miss, and see not. Prophet of Good and Truth,
Wisely and well hast thou instructed me;
Thou hast revealed to me the Path of Peace;
My eyes are opened, and at last I see
Thy lowly Way, and I will enter in.

  Prophet. The Perfect Way awaits thy strenuous
   tread;
Behold where rise, precipitous, yet grand,
The Hills of Virtue; higher, and beyond,
The Peaks of Blessedness; and yet again,
Upon the lofty Summits of the Truth,
Where clouds and darkness are not, and where
  rests
Eternal Splendour; there, abiding Joy
Awaits thy coming. Onward, and disperse
The dark delusions of thy self! Evil

Is Good denied, is darkness and no more.
Let self be nothing, and the Truth be all;
Thus conquer pain: acquire serenity;
Wisdom accompanies tranquillity;
The self-subdued the fadeless Glory know:
Be watchful, fearless, faithful, patient, pure:
By earnest meditation sound the depths
Profound of life, and scale the heights sublime
Of Love and Wisdom. He who does not find
The Way of Meditation, cannot reach
Emancipation and enlightenment.
But thou wilt find the Way of Holy Thought;
With mind made calm and steadfast, thou wilt see
The Permanent amid the mutable,
The Truth eternal in the things that change:
Thou wilt behold the Perfect Law: Cosmos
From Chaos rises when the conquered self
Lies underneath man's heel: Love be thy strength;
Look on the passion-tortured multitudes,
And have compassion on them; know their pain
By thy long sorrow ended. Thou wilt come
To perfect peace, and so wilt bless the world,
Leading unto the High and Holy Way
The feet of them that seek.—And now I go
To my Abode; go thou unto thy work.

  Eolaus. Prophet of Peace, I go: and unto Thee,
Spirit of Truth, I come. To all the world,
And all that lives, for evermore be peace.

COSMOS.

I am; Perfection is, and Peace;
 Evil is gone, beholding Me;
And they from sin and sorrow cease
 Who look upon my Symmetry.
When fault and failure find my Form,
 Lo, fault and failure are no more!
I am the sunshine and the storm,
 The whisper, and the ocean's roar!

The creeping action that deceives,
    The lie, the theft, the murderer's ire,
All these my Crucible receives,
    They burn in my Celestial Fire.
All superstitions, errors, wiles,
    The crawling craft, the cruel lust,
All that debases and defiles
    I grind, and scatter in the dust.
The Nations rise, the Empires fall,
    And I eternally rehearse,

To scene and strain majestical,
    The Drama of the Universe.
The Eons pass, the Systems pale,
    Unchanged their changes I behold;
They listen, and I tell my Tale;
    I all their fleeting forms enfold.
Who knoweth Me, becometh Me;
    Who hath my Vision finds release
From Darkness and Captivity.
    I am; Perfection is, and Peace.

MISCELLANEOUS POEMS

BUDDHA

Under Mount Ratnagira's western shade,
Weary and worn with his long search for Truth,
Sorrowing, unsatisfied, disconsolate,
Sat Buddha, knowing not where he should turn
To find the Truth that he had so long sought—
The Truth that maketh steadfast, strong, and pure,
The Truth that bringeth peace and blessed rest.
The Schools had failed him; the philosophies,
Hoary and ancient, had not stilled the cry
Of passion in his heart; and passion's child,
Sorrow, was with him still; the scriptures, creeds,
Proud pillars of the State, had failed to bear
The weight of his great woe, crumbling away
Under temptation, leaving him the prey
Still of desire and pain and clouded mind.
Mortifications he had tried, and they
Had left him strengthless, wan, wanting the Truth;
And now he seemed as one defeated, borne
Upon the stream of Fate, helpless, alone.

But while the Buddha brooded in the shade,
Suddenly on his ear there fell a cry,
A sob of pain, a pitiful strange sigh;
Whereat he rose, and left the shade, and sought
(He scarce knew why, but that there leaped within
His sorrowing heart a mighty unknown love)

Whence came the cry; and presently he saw,
Upon the road, 'mid thirsty clouds of dust,
Under the fierce blaze of the Indian sun,
A shepherd, driving hard a flock of sheep;
And in the rear there lagged a little lamb
With wounded feet, bleating most piteously,
The while the ewe, with anguish deep and sore,
Cried o'er her little one, knowing that she
Was helpless to relieve her.

          When Buddh saw
The piteous spectacle, compassion slew
His own deep sorrow; and he straightway took
The wounded lamb, and bore it in his arms,
Saying, "Vain are the strivings of the soul
After vain knowledge; vain the learnèd lore
That hath not pity in it; vain is life
That hath not love; and whatsoe'er is false,

And what uncertain, though it seemeth true,
This thing is true, that I should pity thee.
The priests who pray and read, and read and pray,
Die in their sins at last, and do not find
The Love I mourn for, the deep Truth I seek;
And better were it that I ease thy pain
Than pray with them, and seek and never find.
Thee will I love; yes, I will pity thee
Whom none will pity; thee will I relieve;
Tired of the soulless theories of men,

I, Buddh, will stoop to thee, thou dumb, weak
   thing,
Whom men despise, knowing that this is true,
Whate'er is doubtful, and whate'er unsure,
Pity and Love are right; whatever fades
And perishes, Compassion will not fade,
And Love will never perish." So he took
Into his arms the weary, wounded thing
Which nestled in his bosom, and became
Quiet and peaceful; and the anxious ewe
Walked by his side, looking into his face,
Glad that her lamb had found those blessed arms:
And so she walked, and dumbly worshipped him,
Knowing him Buddha, the compassionate.

And Buddha in that hour entered the Way
Which he had vainly sought in schools and creeds;
Entered the Path which no philosophy
Leads unto, and which none shall ever find
But by sweet deeds of Love, forgetting self;
And in his heart there grew a holy Love;
And in his mind a knowledge new and strange;
And his whole being felt a painless peace;
Sorrow and pain were not; and then he knew
That he had found the holy Truth at last.

And from thenceforward Buddha lived the Truth,
And taught its practice; and from far and near
Came men and women who had sought the
   Truth,
And at his feet they sat and worshipped him,
Learning of love and pity; finding bliss
And peace that cannot fail; and him they called
Deliverer, Redeemer, Blessed Lord.
And even they who understood not, sensed
Faintly this truth which one day they should
   know:—

Better than learning is a loving heart;
And to give comfort to one wounded lamb
Is higher than the wisdom of the schools,
And greater than the world's philosophy.

IF MEN ONLY UNDERSTOOD

If men only understood
That the wrong act of a Brother
Should not call from them another,
But should be annulled with kindness,
That *their* eyes should did his blindness,
They would find the Heavenly Portal
Leading on to Love immortal—
   If they only understood.

If men only understood
That *their* wrong can never smother
The wrong-doing of another;
That by hatred hate increases,
And by Good all evil ceases,
They would cleanse their hearts and actions,
Banish thence all vile detractions—
   If they only understood.

If men only understood
That the heart that sins *must* sorrow,
That the hateful mind to-morrow
Reaps its barren harvest, weeping,
Starving, resting not, nor sleeping;
Tenderness would fill their being,
They would see with Pity's seeing—
   If they only understood.

If men only understood
All the emptiness and aching
Of the sleeping and the waking
Of the souls they judge so blindly,
Of the hearts they pierce unkindly,
They, with gentler words and feeling,
Would apply the balm of healing—
    If they only understood.

If men only understood
That their hatred and resentment
Slays their peace and sweet contentment,
Hurts themselves, helps not another,
Does not cheer one lonely Brother,
They would seek the better doing
Of good deeds which leaves no rueing—
    If they only understood.

If men only understood
How Love conquers; how prevailing
Is its might, grim hate assailing;
How Compassion endeth sorrow,
Maketh wise, and doth not borrow
Pain of passion; they would ever
Live in Love, in hatred never—
    If they only understood.

PRACTICE AND PERCEPTION

Questioning Life and Destiny and Truth,
I sought the dark and labyrinthine Sphinx,
Who spake to me this strange and wondrous
    thing:—

"Concealment only lies in blinded eyes,
And God alone can see the Form of God."

I sought to solve this hidden mystery
Vainly by paths of blindness and of pain,
But when I found the Way of Love and Peace,
Concealment ceased, and I was blind no more:
Then saw I God e'en with the eyes of God.

LIBERTY

The unwise say, "Our sufferings are unjust,
Our pains and woes rise from the scattered dust
Of sinful ancestors; we are not free;
Our fathers robbed us of our liberty
By what they did; and we are weak and frail
Because they erred; they fell, and we must fail.

"Our drunkenness comes from their love
    of wine;
Our lusts their revels made; and we divine
Our manifold diseases by the ways
In which they walked; and as they trod the maze
Made by their feet, so we must likewise tread,
For we are bound and driven by the dead."

Thy sins are thine, O man! and from thy deeds
Thy life, with all its weal and woe, proceeds;
By self, and not by others, thou art bound;
In thine own will and heart the root is found
Of all thy lack of peace; ope thou thine eyes,
Leave the dead past, and look within; be wise.

Make pure thy heart, and thou wilt make thy life
Rich, sweet, and beautiful, unmarred by strife;

Guard well thy mind, and, noble, strong, and free,
Nothing shall harm, disturb, or conquer thee;
For all thy foes are in thy heart and mind;
There also thy salvation thou wilt find.

Mind is the Master-power that moulds and
    makes,
And Man is Mind, and evermore he takes
The Tool of Thought, and, shaping what
    he wills,
Brings forth a thousand joys, a thousand ills;—
He thinks in secret, and it comes to pass;
Environment is but his looking-glass.

In his own heart he fosters dark desires,
Or strives for good, or loftily aspires;
In his own life he reaps what he has sown,
Or pain or peace, he garners in his own.
Thou man, that bowest to heredity,
Know this—the Law of life is Liberty.

By Thought we rise; by Thought we fall; by
    Thought
We stand or go: all destiny is wrought
By its swift potency; and he who stands
Master of Thought, and his desires commands,
Willing and weaving thoughts of Love and
    Might,
Shapes his high end in Truth's unerring Light.

LONG I SOUGHT THEE

Long I sought thee, Spirit holy,
Master Spirit, meek and lowly;

Sought thee with a silent sorrow, brooding o'er the
    woes of men;
    Vainly sought thy yoke of meekness
    'Neath the weight of woe and weakness;
Finding not, yet in my failing, seeking o'er and
    o'er again.

    In unrest and doubt and sadness
    Dwelt I, yet I knew thy Gladness
Waited somewhere; somewhere greeted torn and
    sorrowing hearts like mine;
    Knew that somehow I should find thee,
    Leaving sin and woe behind me,
And at last thy Love would bid me enter into Rest
    divine.

    Hatred, mockery, and reviling
    Scorched my seeking soul, defiling
That which should have been thy Temple, wherein
    thou should'st move and dwell;
    Praying, striving, hoping, calling;
    Suffering, sorrowing in my falling,
Still I sought thee, groping blindly in the gloomy
    depths of hell.

    And I sought thee till I found thee;
    And the dark Powers all around me
Fled, and left me silent, peaceful, brooding o'er thy
    holy themes;
    From within me and without me
    Fled they when I ceased to doubt thee;
And I found thee in thy Glory, mighty Master of
    my dreams!

    Yea, I found thee, Spirit holy,
    Beautiful and pure and lowly;

Found thy Joy and Peace and Gladness; found thee
    in thy House of Rest;
    Found thy strength in Love and Meekness,
    And my pain and woe and weakness
Left me, and I walked the Pathway trodden only
    by the blest.

REALITY

I see men gaze upon the distant skies
    Of ideals inaccessible and vain;
And miss the Holy Way which near them lies—
    The hourly conquest over sin and pain.

I see uplifted and imploring hands
    Aching with emptiness; I see the cause,
Self-made, of man's long sorrow; see his bands
    Self-wrought, self-bound; I see the
        broken laws.

Wisdom lies hidden in our common life,
    And he will find it who shall rightly ask;
Where springs the fretful fever and the strife
    There Truth abides—e'en in the daily task.

Behold where Love Eternal rests concealed!
    (The deathless Love that seemed so far away!)
E'en in the lowly heart; it stands revealed
    To him who lives the sinless life to-day.

Wrapped in our nearest duty is the Key
    Which shall unlock for us the Heavenly
        Gate;
Unveiled, the Heavenly Vision he shall see,
    Who cometh not too early nor too late.

The glory of the Truth no Future veils
    From tear-stained eyes; no Past obliterates,
For toil-worn feet, the narrow, weed-grown trails
    Which wind through common ways to joyful
        Gates.

Where'er we go immortal splendour goes;
    But eyes, self-blinded, look and cannot see;
Th' Eternal Glory shines upon man's woes,
    Piercing the dark night of his misery.

Lo! where the shadowless Effulgence gleams—
    In tasks well done, in stainless thoughts and
        deeds,
In words of love and pity, not in dreams!
    Of sky-bound glories holding future meeds.

Peace cometh only to the peaceful soul;
    Love, painless, nestles in the Love-born heart;
Joy springs where self is sunken for the whole;
    From conquered sins immortal beauties start.

Our task is with us, and the Path Sublime,
    Rising from swamps of self, through Duty's way,
Cuts its clear course up the steep hills of Time
    Unto the splendour of the Perfect Day.

TO-MORROW AND
TO-DAY

    In the dark land of To-morrow
    I dwelt with pain and sorrow,
And I sighed for joys and blessings that escaped
    me as I ran;

And the darkness gathered round me,
For the morrow ever found me
Living in "what I ought to do," and not in *what I can.*

And I sought for loving-kindness
In the dim, dark haunts of blindness;
In the lightless caves of self I searched for blessed-
ness and rest;
And I reached out hands appealing,
Sadly groped for light and healing,
Striving for "what I want to have," not *what is true
and best.*

Then I found that selfish hoping,
Darkly seeking, blindly groping
In vain wishing and regretting chased life's glory
from my brow;
So I ceased from selfish fretting,
Turned to Love, and, self-forgetting,
Left "what I hope to get and keep," for *what I will
be now.*

So I fled from self and sorrow,
Left the dark land of To-morrow,
And thought of what kind deeds to do, what lov-
ing words to say;
And the light of peace and gladness
Chased away the clouds of sadness,
For I lost the past and future in the bright world
of To-day.

STAR OF WISDOM

Star that of the birth of Vishnu,
Birth of Krishna, Buddha, Jesus,

Told the wise ones, Heavenward looking,
Waiting, watching for thy gleaming
In the darkness of the night-time,
In the starless gloom of midnight;
Shining Herald of the coming
Of the kingdom of the righteous;
Teller of the mystic story
Of the lowly birth of Godhead
In the stable of the passions,
In the manger of the mind-soul;
Silent singer of the secret
Of compassion deep and holy
To the heart with sorrow burdened,
To the soul with waiting weary:—
Star of all-surpassing brightness,
Thou again dost deck the midnight;
Thou again dost cheer the wise ones
Watching in the creedal darkness,
Weary of the endless battle
With the grinding blades of error;
Tired of lifeless, useless idols,
Of the dead forms of religions;
Spent with watching for thy shining;
Thou hast ended their despairing;
Thou hast lighted up their pathway;
Thou hast brought again the old Truths
To the hearts of all thy Watchers;
To the souls of them that love thee
Thou dost speak of Joy and Gladness,
Of the Peace that endeth sorrow.
Blessed are they that can see thee,
Weary wanderers in the Night-time;
Blessed they who feel the throbbing,
In their bosoms feel the pulsing
Of a deep Love stirred within them
By the great power of thy shining.
Let us learn thy lesson truly;
Learn it faithfully and humbly;

Learn it meekly, wisely, gladly,
Ancient Star of holy Vishnu,
Light of Krishna, Buddha, Jesus.

WOULD YOU SCALE THE HIGHEST HEAVEN

Would you scale the highest heaven,
    Would you pierce the lowest hell,—
Live in dreams of constant beauty,
    Or in basest thinkings dwell.

For your thoughts are heaven above you,
    And your thoughts are hell below;
Bliss is not, except in thinking,
    Torment naught but thought can know.

Worlds would vanish but for thinking;
    Glory is not but in dreams;
And the Drams of the ages
    From the Thought Eternal streams.

Dignity and shame and sorrow,
    Pain and anguish, love and hate
Are but maskings of the mighty
    Pulsing Thought that governs Fate.

As the colours of the rainbow
    Make the one uncoloured beam,
So the universal changes
    Make the One Eternal Dream.

And the Dream is all within you,
    And the Dreamer waiteth long
For the Morning to awake him
    To the living thought and strong

That shall make the ideal real,
    Make to vanish dreams of hell
In the highest, holiest heaven
    Where the pure and perfect dwell.

Evil is the thought that thinks it;
    Good, the thought that makes it so;
Light and darkness, sin and pureness
    Likewise out of thinking grow.

Dwell in thought upon the Grandest,
    And the Grandest you shall see;
Fix your mind upon the Highest,
    And the Highest you shall be.

TO THEM THAT SEEK THE HIGHEST GOOD

To them that seek the highest Good
    All things subserve the wisest ends;
    Naught comes as ill, and wisdom lends
Wings to all shapes of evil brood.

The dark'ning sorrow veils a Star
    That waits to shine with gladsome light;
    Hell waits on heaven; and after night
Comes golden glory from afar.

Defeats are steps by which we climb
    With purer aim to nobler ends;
    Loss leads to gain, and joy attends
True footsteps up the hills of time.

Pain lead to paths of holy bliss,
    To thoughts and words and deeds divine;

And clouds that gloom and rays that shine,
Along life's upward highway kiss.

Misfortune does but cloud the way
　　Whose end and summit in the sky
　　Of bright success, sunkiss'd and high,
Awaits our seeking and our stay.

The heavy pall of doubts and fears
　　That clouds the Valley of our hopes,
　　The shades with which the spirit copes,
The bitter harvesting of tears,

The heartaches, miseries, and griefs,
　　The bruisings born of broken ties,
　　All these are steps by which we rise
To living ways of sound beliefs.

Love, pitying, watchful, runs to meet
　　The Pilgrim from the Land of Fate;
　　All glory and all good await
The coming of obedient feet.

ONE THING LACKING

E'en at the Master's holy feet, low kneeling,
　　Came one who knew nor worldly want nor stress,
Yet sad with fruitless search for Truth, and feeling
　　Perchance the Teacher of the world might bless;
Then asked he softly, and with humble pleading,—
　　"Good Master, canst Thou calm my inward
　　　　strife?
Show me the lofty highway of Thy leading;
　　What shall I do to gain Eternal Life?"

Then He, the Lord of Life, looked down in kindness
　　Upon the kneeling form, and, answering, said,—
"Thou knowest the commandments, be not
　　mindless
　　Of these, and thou shalt live, though thou wert
　　　　dead."
Replied the kneeling one,—"All these things
　　keeping
　　From my youth up, I sought Thee out this day,
Yet still I wander unawakened, sleeping;
　　I have not found the high and holy Way."

"Yet lackest thou one thing, yield thy desiring,"
　　(Thus spake the Master), "do not grasp, but give;
Sell that thou holdest, and, with free aspiring,
　　Come, follow Me, and thou shalt surely live;
For whoso follows Me, all selfish clinging
　　Yielding with pure and undivided mind
Shall nothing lack; yes, for his earthly bringing
　　Surely the Heavenly Treasure he shall find."

Now he who knelt was very rich, and cherished
　　His earthly treasure in his inmost heart;
And even there his spirit paused and perished,
　　Losing renunciation's better part:
Noble but not complete, the Master leaving
　　To cleave unto his perishable day,
He chose the path of passing things and grieving,
　　And, sorrow-stricken, went his lonely way.

YASHAS

Lo, in the night, when all the world was sleeping,
　　Yashas, the noble and aspiring youth,

Pondering upon the world's great sorrow,
   weeping,
   Searched for the holy pathway unto Truth.
"I search in vain," said he, "and will betake me
   Unto the Blessed One, and seek release;
Healer of sorrow, he perchance will make me
   Partaker in his deep, Nirvanic peace."

Then came the youth, with footsteps fast and
   faster,
   Unto the Blessed Teacher of mankind,
And, weeping, fell before the Holy Master,
   Saying, "Great Lord, I seek and cannot find.
How great is my distress and tribulation!
   Thou knowest all my sorrow and my pain;
Give me the holy balm of thy salvation,
   Let me depart not from thy side again."

The Blessed One, seeing his perturbation,
   Spake softly thus unto the gentle youth,—
"Lo, here is no distress, no tribulation;
   Come unto Me, and I will show you Truth.
The Truth will bring you joy, dispelling
   sadness,
   And as the night before the light of day
Flees and departs, e'en so your rising gladness
   Sorrow and pain and care will chase away."

Then spake He of things pure and high and
   holy,
   Giving full freely of His wisdom's store,
And Yashas, listening, rapt, all meek and lowly,
   Drank deeply of the Master's wondrous lore;
And lo! the cooling breath of Wisdom o'er him
   Stole softly, fanning all his care to rest;
Sorrow departed, and Compassion bore him
   Unto the Path the Master's feet had prest.

THE LOWLY WAY

All ways are waiting for my feet to tread,
The light and dark, the living and the dead,
The broad and narrow way, the high and low,
The good and bad, and with quick step or slow,
I now may enter any way I will,
And find, by walking, which is good, which ill.

And all good things my wand'ring fest await,
If I but come, with vow inviolate,
Unto the narrow, high and holy way
Of heart-born purity, and therein stay;
Walking, secure from him who taunts and scorns,
To flowery meads, across the path of thorns.

And I may stand where health, success, and power
Await my coming, if, each fleeting hour,
I cling to love and patience; and abide
With stainlessness; and never step aside
From high integrity; so shall I see
At last the land of immortality.

And I may seek and find; I may achieve;
I may not claim, but, losing, may retrieve.
The Law bends not for me, but I must bend
Unto the Law, if I would reach the end
Of my afflictions, if I would restore
My soul of Light and Life, and weep no more.

Not mine the arrogant and selfish claim
To all good things; be mine the lowly aim
To seek and find, to know and comprehend,
And wisdom-ward all holy footsteps wend.

Nothing is mine to claim or to command,
But all is mine to know and understand.

THE MUSIC OF THE SEA

I love to hear the music of the sea,
    As, playing on the everlasting shore,
Its strange, profound, and mystic melody,
    It chants the soul of man for evermore.

It sings of wreckful passion when it beats
    With unrestrained wildness on the rocks;
Then with succeeding sorrow it retreats,
    Sobbing o'er pain of self-inflicted shocks.

Of martyrdom and silent pain it speaks
    When, dumbly moaning, languidly it rolls;
And weirdly wails, as on the rocks it breaks,
    The deadness and despair of human souls.

Its scintillations on the pebbly beach,
    Mingling which sunshine and the playful
        breeze,
Are bubbling merriment and mirth that reach
    No deeper than the sensuous vision sees.

When, scarcely murmuring, placidly it lies,
    It whispers of the silent heart of peace;
Of that unutterable state where dies
    Passion, and all our human sorrows cease.

Playful, perturbed, peaceful, tempestuous,
    Reflected in thy heart, thy peace, thy strife,
Is the strange passion and the peace in us,
    The madness and the wisdom of our life.

Thou symbol of the human soul, O sea!
    I love to heart thee, on the lonely shore
Chanting thy everlasting melody,
    Singing the soul of man for evermore.

LOVE'S CONQUEST

I stood upon the shore, and saw the rocks
    Resist the onslaught of the mighty sea,
And when I thought how all the countless shocks
    They had withstood through an eternity,
I said, "To wear away this solid main
    The ceaseless efforts of the waves are vain."

But when I thought how they the rocks had rent,
    And saw the sand and shingles at my feet
(Poor passive remnants of resistance spent)
    Tumbled and tossed where they the waters
        meet,
Then saw I ancient landmarks 'neath the waves,
    And knew the waters held the stones their slaves.

I saw the mighty work the waters wrought
    By patient softness and unceasing flow;
How they the proudest promontory brought
    Unto their feet, and massy hills laid low;
How the soft drops the adamantine wall
    Conquered at last, and brought it to its fall.

And then I knew that hard, resisting sin
    Should yield at last to Love's soft ceaseless roll
Coming and going, ever flowing in
    Upon the proud rocks of the human soul;
That all resistance should be spent and past,
    And every heart yield unto it at last.

TO MY DAUGHTER NORA ON HER TENTH BIRTHDAY

Since when thou camest, with thy native charms,
A weeping infant to thy mother's arms,
Ten fleeting years have lifted up thy head
Unto my breast; ten years of love are fled,
But all their score of innocence and bliss
Remains with thee; thy mother's and my kiss
Seal it for over thine! Those guileless ways
Which, walking, have filled up thy tender days,
May'st thou for ever keep; may thy pure heart
Keep always pure, that no unholy dart
Pierce it with anguish; may remorse and pain
Shrink from thy hallowed presence, and no stain
Soil thy white robes of peace. O! be thou sure
Bliss follows in the footsteps of the pure.
And whatsoe'er shall tempt of wrong or strife,
Hold fast the rare gem of a blameless life;
Nor lose, nor lightly hold, but bind to thee
The priceless jewel of thy purity.

THE INWARD PURITY

Find ye that life is anguish, and that self-love is a
    chain
That binds thy quivering soul, and cuts with biting
    stings of pain?
Grieve ye where Slander's serpents train beneath
    fair flowers of Trust?
Or weep where Friendship buried lies 'neath
    Hatred's fulsome dust?

Then listen,—Selfish sweets are brief, and fleeting
    self-hood's ties,
But there abides a fadeless Love, a Life that never
    dies;
A path there is which Serpent slime hath never yet
    defiled,
Where weary feet find rest and peace, and are no
    more beguiled:
And that pure Love and Life are his whose inmost
    heart is free
From unforgiveness, judgment false, and self and
    enmity;
And that fair Path of Peace he walks whose mem-
    ory holds no stain
Of injuries past; that blameless heart hath reached
    the end of pain.

SELF-SACRIFICE

Great glory crowns the heights of hope by arduous
    struggle won;
Bright honour rounds the hoary head that mighty
    works hath done;
Fair riches come to him who strives in ways of
    golden gain,
And fame enshrines his name who works with
    genius-glowing brain:
But greater glory waits for him who, in the
    bloodless strife
'Gainst self and wrong, adopts, in love, the
    sacrificial life;
And brighter honour rounds the brow of him
    who, 'mid the scorns
Of blind idolaters of self, accepts the crown of
    thorns;

And fairer, purer riches come to him who greatly
    strives
To walk in ways of love and truth to sweeten
    human lives;
And he who serveth well mankind exchanges
    fleeting fame
For Light eternal, Joy and Peace, and robes of
    heavenly flame.

I TAKE REFUGE
IN TRUTH

I come to thee, O Master! On thy breast
    I lay my weary head; I lave thy feet
With tears and kisses, travail of my quest;
    I bring my aching heart and sore defeat,
And seek thy holy joy an perfect rest.

Place thou thy hand upon my burning brow;
    Soothe thou my soul, and bid my sins depart;
I ask thy sweet salvation even now;
    Thy rest I seek to ease my throbbing heart;
Thou art the Truth, to thee I cling and bow.

Thou changest not amid Earth's changing scenes;
    All worldly joys, strong passions that decay,
The sordid thought, the action that demeans,
    These are not thee, and they will pass away:
On thy abiding strength my spirit leans.

Lead thou my feet unto thy Holy Place;
    I take thy chastening; thy great love I see;
Thy rod I kiss, and in my deep disgrace,
    With longing, humble heart I cling to thee,
Knowing thou wilt not turn away thy face.

I, TRUTH, AM THY
REDEEMER

I, Truth, am thy Redeemer, come to Me;
    Lay down thy sin and pain and wild unrest;
And I will calm thy spirit's stormy sea,
    Pouring the oil of peace upon thy breast:
Friendless and long—lo, I abide with thee.

Defeated and deserted, cast away;
    What refuge hast thou? Whither canst thou fly?
Upon My changeless breast thy burdens lay;
    I am thy certain refuge, even I:
All things are passing; I along can stay.

Lo I, the Great Forsaken, am the Friend
    Of the forsaken; I, whom men despise,
The weak, the helpless, and despised defend;
    I gladden aching hearts and weeping eyes:
Rest thou in Me, I am thy sorrow's end.

Lovers and friends and wealth, pleasures and
    fame—
    These fail and change, and pass into decay;
But my Love does not change; and in thy blame
    I blame thee not, nor turn My face away:
In My calm bosom hide thy sin and shame.

THE WHITE ROBE

The White Robe of the Heart Invisible
    Is stained with sin and sorrow, grief and pain,

And all repentant pools and springs of prayer
    Shall not avail to wash it white again.

While in the path of ignorance I walk,
    The stains of error will not cease to cling;
Defilements mark the crooked path of self,
    Where anguish lurks and disappointments sting.

Knowledge and wisdom only can avail
    To purify and make my garment clean,
For therein lie love's waters; therein rests
    Peace undisturbed, eternal, and serene.

Sin and repentance is the path of pain,
    Knowledge and wisdom is the path of Peace;
By the near way of practice I will find
    Where bliss begins, how pains and sorrows cease.

Self shall depart, and Truth shall take its place;
    The Changeless Once, the Indivisible
Shall take up His abode in me, and cleanse
    The White Robe of the Heart Invisible.

THE RIGHTEOUS MAN

No harmful shaft can reach the righteous man,
    Standing erect amid the storms of hate,
Defying hurt and injury and ban,
    Surrounded by the trembling slaves of Fate.

Majestic in the strength of silent power,
    Serene he stands, nor changes not nor turns;
Patient and firm in suffering's darkest hour,
    Time bends to him, and death and doom he
        spurns.

Wrath's lurid lightnings round about him play,
    And hell's deep thunders roll about his head;
Yet heeds he not, for him they cannot slay
    Who stands whence earth and time and space
        are fled.

Sheltered by deathless love, what fear hath he?
    Armoured in changeless Truth, what can he
        know
Of loss and gain? Knowing eternity,
    He moves not whilst the shadows come and go.

Call him immortal, call him Truth and Light
    And splendour of prophetic majesty
Who bideth thus amid the powers of Night,
    Clothed with the glory of divinity.

CHOICE

The will to evil and the will to Good
    Are both within thee; which wilt thou employ?
Thou knowest what is right and what is wrong;
    Which wilt thou love and foster? Which
        destroy?

Thou art the chooser of thy thoughts and deeds;
    Thou art the maker of thine inward state;
The power is thine to be what thon wilt be;
    Thou buildest Truth and Love, or lies and hate.

If thou dost choose the evil, loving self,
    Thy cries and prayers for Good shall all
        be vain;
Thy thought and act bringeth thee good or ill;
    Deep in thy heart thou makest joy and pain.

As thou pursuest Good, striving to make
  Evil depart, thou shalt rejoice and say,—
"Lo! Light and Love and Peace attend on me;
  Truth fadeth not, and Good abounds always."

Choose as thou wilt thy thoughts and words and
    deeds,
  And as thou choosest so shall be thy life;
The will to Good shall bring thee Joy and Peace,
  The will to evil, wretchedness and strife.

TRUTH TRIUMPHANT

There is no height to which thou canst not
    climb;
  There is no grandeur that thou may'st
      not view,
If thou wilt reach beyond the things of Time,
  Unto the Pure, the Beautiful, the True.

There is no saintly vision, no glad sight
  Of seer, nor no dream of holy sage
But may be thine; nay, is thy heavenly right,
  If thou wilt claim thy regal appanage.

There is no sin but thou may'st overthrow;
  There is no vileness that, octopus-like,
Binds thee its victim, but thou soon canst know
  The way and weapon thy strong foe to strike.

Thou art not framed for sin and grief and shame;
  Thou art not bent to grovel in the mire;
But thou art made erect, and given a name,
  Hast hands to reach, and spirit to aspire.

Glory and strength and triumph—these are thine;
  Rise up, and conquer every inward foe;
Behold the heavens, how radiantly they shine!
  Stand up and strike, O conqueror of woe!

O THOU WHO WOULD'ST TEACH!

O thou who would'st teach men of Truth!
  Hast thou passed through the desert of
      doubt?
Art thou purged by the fires of sorrow?
  Hath ruth
    The fiends of opinion east out
Of thy human heart? Is thy soul so fair
  That no false though can ever harbour there?

O thou who would'st teach men of Love!
  Hast thou passed through the place of
      despair?
Hast thou wept through the dark night of grief?
  Does it move
    (Now freed from its sorrow and care)
Thy human heart to pitying gentleness,
  Looking on wrong, and hate, and ceaseless
      stress?

O thou who would'st teach men of Peace!
  Hast thou crossed the wide ocean of strife?
Hast thou found on the Shores of the Silence,
    release
  From all the wild unrest of life?
From thy human heart hath all striving gone,
  Leaving but Truth, and Love, and Peace alone?

IF THOU WOULD'ST
RIGHT THE WORLD

If thou would'st right the world,
And banish all its evils and its woes,
Make its wild places bloom,
And its drear deserts blossom as the rose,—
Then right thyself.

If thou would'st turn the world
From its long, lone captivity in sin,
Restore all broken hearts,
Slay grief, and let sweet consolation in,—
Turn thou thyself.

If thou would'st cure the world
Of its long sickness, end its grief and pain,
Bring in all-healing Joy,
And give to the afflicted rest again,—
The cure thyself.

If thou would'st wake the world
Out of its dreams of death and dark'ning strife,
Bring it to Love and Peace,
And Light and brightness of immortal Life,—
Wake thou thyself.

WHAT OF THE NIGHT?

What of the night, O Watchman! see'st thou yet
The glimmering dawn upon the mountain heights,
The golden Herald of the Light of lights,
Are his fair feet upon the hilltops set?

Cometh he yet to chase away the gloom,
And with it all the demons of the Night?
Strike yet his darting rays upon thy sight?
Hear'st thou his voice, the sound of error's doom!

The Morning cometh, lover of the Light;
E'en now He gilds with gold the mountain's
brow,
Dimly I see the path whereon e'en now
His shining feet are set toward the Night.

Darkness shall pass away, and all the things
That love the darkness, and that hate the Light
Shall disappear for ever with the Night:
Rejoice! for thus the speeding Herald sings.

KNOWLEDGE

We find the Good by being good, the True
By being true, the Real by dissolving
Our fond illusions, thereby piercing through
Shadow, and knowing substance. By resolving,
We can attain, and by attaining, know;
And, knowing, who shall cause us grief or
harm?
What trembling victim of the world's vain show
Shall pierce the armoured heart, or foil the arm
Of him whose Shield is Wisdom? What event,
What circumstance, what mutability
Can shake the Changeless? And whoso hath blent
His life with Changeless Good, stands steadfastly

In Knowledge, fearing nothing, hating naught;
   His heart and mind Love-fashioned, Wisdom-
      wrought.

THE END OF EVIL

All evil passes from us when we find
The Way of Good; when word and deed
   and mind
Are shaped to Truth and Wisdom; then we see
The end of bondage and captivity.

All good is ever with us; we but want
Wisdom to take it; we are poor and scant
Only in lacking wisdom; that acquired,
The good is ours that we so long desired.

Be still, my soul, and know that peace is thine;
Be steadfast, heart, and know that strength
   divine
Belongs to thee; cease from thy turmoil, mind,
And thou the Everlasting rest shalt find.

MAN DIVINE

Man is superior to sin and shame,
   Evil and error he will yet dethrone,
The beasts within he will o'ercome and tame,
   The brute will pass, the angel will be known;
Yea, even now the Man divine appears,
   Crownèd with conquest, victor o'er all fears.

Hail to thee, Man divine! the conqueror
   Of sin and shame and sorrow; no more weak,
Wormlike and groveling art thou; no, nor
   Wilt thou again bow down to things that
      wreak
Scourgings and death upon thee; thou dost rise
   Triumphant in thy strength; good, pure,
      and wise.

PATIENCE

Why this fierce struggle to achieve thine ends?
This selfish argument? This fire which lends
   Heat to resentment, ashes to remorse?
Canst thou bend Truth and Nature to thy will?
Bend thou, and work and wait; be strong
   and still;
   Soft growth is stronger than vehement force.

Be as a flower, content to be, to grow
In sweetness day by day; content to know
   The hidden blessing in the seeming curse;
A child of Love, unargumentative;
Content to be and know—as thou dost live—
   The simple secret of the Universe.

RESTORED

Eager for strife and struggle, self and gain,
   And heeding not the gentle Voice of Truth,
We strive and wrestle in dark ways of pain,

And, blind and lost in passion, we disdain
    The unobtrusive Way of Love and Truth;
So live we on in sorrow and in woe,
Nor rest can find, nor blessèd gladness know.

Tired of strife and anger, hate and pain,
    And weary of the wranglings of the Schools,
We turn, and look into your face again,
Belovèd brother, sister; nor in vain
    Search we with purer eyes; but as in pools
Soft, deep, and silent, gaze we, finding rest;
So pass we on our way, refreshed and blest.

ON RELEASING A CAPTIVE BIRD

I found a little bird held fast, ensnared
    By ruthless hands; a gentle, captive prey
Thirsting for freedom, piteously scared,
    Struggling in vain to 'scape and soar away.

I marked his terror, and I took him up;
    His fluttering heart spoke out his wild
      despair.
"Look, you and I with the great gods shall sup
    This day," I said; then threw him into air.

Whereat he soared, and wheeled, and flew
    away;
    Great was his joy, and ruth-born bliss was
      mine;
Thus supped we both with the high gods
    that day;
    Thus tasted we their nectar, drank their wine.

ART THOU IN SORROW?

Art thou in sorrow? Art thou in despair,
    Involved in doubt and deep perplexity?
Leave thou thyself, and with thy fellows share
    The good thou hast, and thou wilt blessèd be.

Let Love's bright sunshine play upon your heart;
    Come now unto your gladness, peace, and rest;
Bid the dark shades of selfishness depart,
    And now and evermore be truly blest.

WHEN I AM PURE

    When I am pure
I shall have solved the mystery of life,
    I shall be sure,
When I am free from hatred, lust, and strife,
I am in Truth, and Truth abides in me.
I shall be safe and sane and wholly free
    When I am pure.

IMMORTALITY

He shall not die who seeks the Way of Truth;
He shall not see corruption who doth walk
With stainless feet the Path of Purity;
He shall not wander in dark worlds of woe

Who finds the Gate of Good and enters; there,
For he shall taste of immortality
While feasting at the table of his Lord.

ARE YOU SEARCHING?

Are you searching for the happiness that does not
  fade away?
Are you looking for the joy that lives, and leaves
  no grievous day?

Are you panting for the waterbrooks of Love, and
  Life, and Peace?
Then let all dark desires depart, and selfish seeking
  cease.

Are you ling'ring in the paths of pain,
  grief-haunted, stricken sore?
Are you wand'ring in the ways that wound your
  weary feet the more?
Are you sighing for the Resting-Place where tears
  and sorrows cease?
Then sacrifice the heart of self, and find the Heart
  of Peace.

THE LIFE TRIUMPHANT

(1907)

FOREWORD

Every being lives in his own mental world; his joys and sorrows are the creations of his own mind, and are dependent upon the mind for their existence. In the midst of the world, darkened with many sins and many sorrows, in which the majority live, there abides another world, lighted up with shining virtues and unpolluted joy, in which the perfect ones live. This world can be found and entered, and the way to it is by self-control and moral excellence. It is the world of the perfect life, and rightly belongs to man, who is not complete until crowned with perfection. The perfect life is not the far-away, impossible thing that men who are in darkness imagine it to be; it is supremely possible, and very near and real. Man remains a craving, weeping, sinning, repenting creature just so long as he wills to do so by clinging to these weak conditions; but when he wills to shake off his dark dreams and to rise, he arises and achieves.

—JAMES ALLEN

CONTENTS

FAITH AND COURAGE

For those who will fight bravely, and not yield, there is triumphant victory over all the dark things of life. I state this at the beginning, that the reader may know there is no uncertainty about it; and in the course of this book I shall show what are the elements, in character and conduct, which go to build up the life of calm strength and superlative victory.

To stand face to face with Truth; to arrive, after innumerable wanderings and pains, at wisdom and bliss; not to be finally defeated and cast out, but ultimately to triumph over every inward foe—such is man's divine destiny, such his glorious goal; and this, every saint, sage, and saviour has declared.

In the present stage of the life of humanity, comparatively few reach this place of triumph—though all will reach it at last—yet there is a glorious company of perfect ones who have attained in the past, and their number is being added to with each succeeding age. Men are as yet learners in the school of life, and most men die learners; but some there are who, in this life, through fixity of purpose and strenuous fighting against darkness, pain, and ignorance, acquire a right knowledge of life, and pass joyfully beyond the pupil stage. Man is not to remain *for ever* a schoolboy in the universe, to be whipped for follies and errors; when he wills and wishes, he can set his mind upon his task, and master the lessons of life, becoming a confident and skilled scholar, living in understanding and peace, and not in ignorance and misery.

The sorrows of life are profound and deeply rooted, but they can be fathomed and rooted out; the passions and emotions of human nature are, in their ungoverned state, overwhelming and painfully conflicting, but they can be so softened down, harmonized, and wisely directed and understood, as to become obedient servants for the outworking of enlightened purposes. The difficulties of life are great, its battles fierce, and its wished-for issues are uncertain and elusive; so much so, that every hour men and women are breaking down under the strain; yet these conditions have no objective and arbitrary existence; in their true nature they are subjective and purely mental, and can be transcended. There is no inherent and permanent evil in the universal order; and the mind can be lifted up to that moral altitude where evil can touch it no more.

A steadfast faith in an Eternal and Universal Justice, in an over-ruling Good, is the prelude to the Life Triumphant. The man who aims to become strong, serene, and steadfast at heart, must, at the outset, have no doubt that the Heart of Life is good. He who is to gaze upon the Cosmic Order, and experience the rapture of emancipation, must realize that there is no disorder in his life but that which he creates. This realization is difficult, so prone is the mind, in its imperfect stages, to self-pity and self-justification, but it can be attained, and must be attained by him who is to live the freed life. At first it must be believed, and the belief must be adhered to until it ripens into realization and knowledge.

The sufferings of life are greatly reduced when they are accepted as disciplinary experiences, and the man of faith does so accept them. The sufferings of life are transcended and put away when all experiences are accounted good, and are utilized in the development of character, and the man of knowledge does so regard and utilize them.

Faith is the grey dawn which precedes the full and perfect day of knowledge. Without it there can be no attainment of strength, no permanent security of heart. The man of faith does not succumb when difficulties present themselves; he does not despair when troubles overtake him. However steep and dark his path may seem, he looks forward to a brighter pathway ahead; sees a destination of rest and light beyond.

They who have no faith in the triumph of good ignominiously succumb to the elements of evil. And this must be so; for he who does not elevate good, elevates evil, and, seeing evil as the master of life, he receives the wages of evil.

There are those who, having yielded to defeat in the battle of life, talk thoughtlessly about the wrongs they have suffered at the hands of others. They believe—and try to make others believe—that they would have been successful, or rich, or famous but for the treachery and villainy of those about them. They tell, for the thousandth time, how they have been deceived, defrauded, and degraded by others. They imagine that they themselves are all trust, all innocence, all honesty and good nature, and that nearly everybody else is all that is bad and malicious. They tell how they would have been just as prosperous and honoured as others if they had been as selfish as those others; and that their great drawback, and the chief source, in themselves, of their failures, is that they were born with too great an endowment of unselfishness. Such self-praising complainers cannot distinguish between good and evil, and their faith in human nature and the goodness of the universe is dead. Looking upon others, they have eyes for evil only; looking upon themselves, they see only suffering innocence. Rather than discover any evil in themselves, they would have all humanity bad. In their hearts they have enthroned the wretched Demon of Evil as the Lord of Life, and see in the course of things only a selfish scramble in which the good is always crushed, and evil rises triumphant. Blind to their own folly and ignorance and weakness, they see nothing but injustice in their fate, nothing but misery and wretchedness in their present condition.

He who would have even a useful and successful life—much more so a spiritually noble and victorious one—must at once root out and cast away this wretched condition of mind that negatives all that is good and pure, and gives the pre-eminence to all that is base and impure. Misfortune, misery and defeat most surely await the man who believes that dishonesty, deceit, and selfishness are the best weapons whereby to achieve a successful life. What courage and strength can a man develop, and what quiet and happiness can he enjoy, who believes that in order to keep pace with others he must continually deny and discourage the better qualities of his nature? The man who believes that evil is more powerful than good, and that bad men have the best of life, is still involved in the elements of evil; and, being so involved, he suffers—must necessarily suffer—defeat.

It may appear to you that the world is given over to wickedness; that the bad prosper, and the good fail; that there is nothing but chance, injustice, and disorder; but do not believe this: regard it as an illusive appearance; conclude that you do not see life as it really is; that you have not yet fathomed the causes of things, and that when you can look upon life through a purer heart and a wiser mind, you will see and understand its equity. And truly when you do so look at life, you will see good where you now see evil, order where now appears disorder, justice where now injustice seems to prevail.

The universe is a cosmos, not a chaos, and the bad do not prosper. It is true there is much evil in the world, otherwise there would be no necessity for moral aims, but there is also much misery in the world, and the evil and misery are related as cause and effect. It is equally true that there is much good in the world, and much abiding gladness, and the good and gladness are related as cause and effect.

He who has acquired that faith in the power and supremacy of good which no apparent injustice, no amount of suffering, and no catastrophe can shake, will pass through all emergencies, all trials and difficulties, with a sublime courage that defies the demons of doubt and despair. He may not succeed in all his plans; he may even encounter much failure; but when he fails, it will be that he may frame nobler purposes and ascend to higher achievements. He will only fail in order to reach a success greater than that of which he at first dreamed. His life will not, cannot, be a failure; some of its details may fail, but this will be but the breaking of weak links in the chain of character and events, in order that the whole may be made more strong and complete.

There is an animal courage which can calmly face the fire of an enemy in battle, or the fierce rage of wild beasts, but which fails in the battle of life, and breaks down when confronted with the beasts that rage within one's own heart. It requires a higher, diviner courage to remain calm in the hour of deprivation and calamity than in the heat of battle, to overcome self than to overcome another. And this diviner courage is the companion of faith.

A mere theological belief (commonly confounded with faith) will not avail. Beliefs about God, Jesus, Creation, etc., are mere surface opinions (derived chiefly from custom) which do not reach down to the real life of a man, and have no power to bestow faith. Such beliefs may accompany faith, but they are distinct from it. Frequently those who hold most tenaciously to particular beliefs about God, Jesus, and the Bible, are most lacking in faith—that is, they give way to complaint, despondency, and grief immediately some petty trouble overtakes them. If one is given to irritability, anxiety, hopelessness, and lamentations over the untoward things of life, let him know that, in spite of his religious belief or metaphysical philosophy, he lacks faith; for where faith is there is courage, there is fortitude, there is steadfastness and strength.

The opinions of men are lightly to be considered, for they are changing with every new breeze of thought. They have very little part in the reality of things, being the bubbles of a surface effervescence; but behind all opinions there is the same human heart. The "godless" are they who are godless, even though they be members of churches and make great profession of faith in God. The "godly" are they who are goodly even though they make no profession of religion, the complainers and bewailers are the faithless and unbelieving. Those who deny or belittle the power of good, and in their lives and actions affirm and magnify the power of evil, are the only real atheists. Faith bestows that sublime courage that rises superior to the petty and selfish disappointments and troubles of life, that acknowledges no defeat except as a step to victory; that is strong to endure, patient to wait, and energetic to struggle; that perceives the benign law to Truth in all things, and is assured of the final triumph of the heart, of the kingly power of the mind.

Light up, then, O man! the lamp of faith in your heart, and walk through the darkness guided by its illuminating rays. Its light is dim, and cannot be compared with the sun-like effulgence of knowledge, but it suffices to lead one safely through the mists of doubt and the black darkness of despair; along the narrow, thorny ways of sickness and sorrow, and over the treacherous places of temptation and uncertainty; it enables him to ward off and outstrip the foul beasts that rage in the jungle of his heart, and to reach safely the open plains of a pure life and the mountain levels of conquest where the dim light of faith is no longer needed, for, leaving behind him all the darkness, all the doubt and error and sorrow, he enters into a new consciousness and upon a higher round of life, and works, acts, and lives selfcontained and peaceful, in the full and glorious light of knowledge.

MANLINESS AND SINCERITY

Before a man can be truly godly, he must be manly; before a woman can be truly godly, she must be womanly. There can be no true goodness apart from moral strength. Simperings, affectations, flatteries, insincerities and smiling hypocrisies—let these things be for ever destroyed, and banished from our minds. Evil is inherently weak, ineffectual, cowardly. Good is essentially strong, effective, courageous. In teaching men and women to be good, I teach them to be strong, free, self-reliant. They will greatly misunderstand me and the principles which I enunciate who imagine that because I teach gentleness and purity and patience I teach the cultivation of an effeminate weakness. It is only the manly man and womanly woman that can properly understand those divine qualities, and none are better equipped to achieve the Life Triumphant than they who, along with active moral qualities and a high sense of purity and honour, are also possessed of the strong animal nature of the normal man.

That animal force which, in various forms, surges within you, and which, in the hour of excitement, carries you blindly away, causing you to forget your higher nature and to forfeit your manly dignity and honour—that same force controlled, mastered, and rightly directed, will endow you with a divine strength by which you can achieve the highest, noblest, most blissful victories of true living.

The Caliban within you is to be scourged and disciplined into obedience. You are to be master of your heart, your mind, yourself. Man is only weak and abject when he gives up the reins of government to the lower, instead of directing the lower by the higher. Your passions are to be your servants and slaves, not your masters. See that you keep them in their places, duly controlled and commanded, and they shall render you faithful, strong, and happy service.

You are not "vile." There is no part of your body or mind that is vile. Nature does not make mistakes. The universe is framed on Truth. All your functions, faculties, and powers are good, and to direct them rightly is wisdom, holiness, happiness; to direct them wrongly is folly, sin, and misery.

Men waste themselves in excesses; in bad tempers, hatreds, gluttonies, and unworthy and unlawful pleasures, and then blame life. They should blame themselves.

A man should have more self-respect than to abuse his nature in any way. He should command himself always; should avoid excitement and hurry; should be too noble to give way to anger, to resent the actions and opinions of others, or fruitlessly to argue with an abusive and cantankerous assailant.

A quiet, unobtrusive, and unoffending dignity is the chief mark of a ripe and perfect manhood. Honour others and respect yourself. Choose your own path and walk it with a firm, unflinching step, but avoid a meddlesome interference with others. In the true man opposing qualities are blended and harmonized; a yielding kindness accompanies an unbending strength. He adapts himself gently and wisely to others without sacrificing the steadfast principles upon which his manhood is built. To have that iron strength that can go calmly to death rather than yield one jot of truth, along with that tender sympathy that can shield the weak and mistaken enemy, is to be manly with a divine manhood.

Be true to the dictates of your own conscience, and respect all who do the same, even though their conscience should lead them in a direction the reverse of your own. One of the most unmanly tendencies is to pity another because he chooses opinions or religion contrary to those of one's self. Why pity a man because he is an Agnostic, or an Atheist, or a Buddhist, or a Christian? Because he does not hold this opinion or that belief? Such pity would be rightly named contempt. It is the office of pity to feel for the weak, the afflicted, and the helpless. Pity never says "I pity you;" it does kind deeds. It is superciliousness that professes pity for the strong, the self-reliant, for those who have the courage to mark out their own path and to walk it boldly. Why should he perforce hold my opinion or yours? If what I say and do appeal to his reason and conscience as right, then he will be one with me and will work hand in hand with me. But if my work be not his work, he is none the less a man. He has his duty, though it be not my duty. When I meet one who is self-respecting, and who dares to think for himself, I will salute him as a man, and not harbour in my heart a contemptible pity for him, because, forsooth, he rejects my conclusions.

If we are to be responsible, self-acting beings in a law-begirt universe, let us be masters of our own wills, and respect the free-will of others; if we are to be strong and manly, let us be large-hearted and magnanimous; if we are to triumph over the miseries of life, let us rise superior to the pettiness of our nature.

Men weep in their weakness, and cry out in misery of heart and degradation of mind. How plain, then, is the way of emancipation; how sublime the task of triumph! *be master of yourself.* Eliminate weakness. Exorcise the mocking fiend, selfishness, in whom is all weakness and wretchedness. Do not pander to effeminate and unnatural cravings, to unlawful desires, or to morbid self-love and self-pity; give them no quarter, but promptly stamp them out with disciplinary decision and strength. A man should hold himself, as it were, in the hollow of his hand. He should be able to take up and to lay down. He should know how to use things, and not be used by them. He should neither be the helpless captive of luxury nor the whipped slave of want, but should be self-contained and self-sufficient, master of himself under all conditions. He must train and direct his will in the way of self-mastery which is the way of obedience—obedience to the law of his nature. Disobedience to law is the supreme evil in man, the source of all his sin and sorrow. In his ignorance he imagines he can triumph over law and subdue the wills of others. He thus destroys his power. Man can triumph over his disobedience, over ignorance, sin, egotism, and lawlessness, he can conquer self; and herein lies his manly strength and divine power. He can comprehend the law of his being, and obey it as a child understands and obeys the will of its father. He can sit the crowned king of all his functions and faculties, using them wisely in unselfish service, and not as instruments of selfishness and greed. There is no bad habit that he cannot uproot, no sin that he cannot subdue, no sorrow that he cannot comprehend and conquer. "Let a man then know his worth, and keep things under his feet. Let him not peep or steal, or skulk up and down with the air of a charity-boy, or a bastard, or an interloper, in the world which exists for him."

A manly self-reliance is not only compatible with, but is the accompaniment of, a divine humility. A man is only arrogant and egotistic when he usurps authority over others. He cannot claim nor exercise too great an authority over himself. Strong self-command with gentle consideration for others, combine to make the truly manly man.

To begin with, a man must be honest, upright, sincere. Deceit is the blindest folly. Hypocrisy is the weakest thing on earth. In trying to deceive others, a man most of all deceives himself. A man should be so free from guile, meanness, and deceit as to be able to look everybody in the face with a clear, open, unflinching gaze, free from shame and confusion, and with no inward shrinking or misgivings. Without sincerity a man is but a hollow mask, and whatsoever work he attempts to do, it will be lifeless and ineffectual. Out of a hollow vessel nothing but the sound of hollowness can come; and from insincerity nothing but empty words can proceed.

Many who are not consciously hypocrites, yet fall victims, thoughtlessly, to little insincerities which undermine happiness and destroy the moral fabric of their character. Some of these people go regularly to their place of worship: they pray daily, year after year, for a purer heart and life, yet come from their devotions to vilify an enemy, or, worse still, to ridicule or slander an absent friend for whom, when they meet him, or her, they will have nothing but smiles and smooth words. The pitiful part of it is that they are totally unconscious of their insincerity, and when their friends desert them, they speak complainingly of the faithlessness and hollowness of the world, and of people generally, and tell you sadly that there are no true friends in this world.

Truly, for such there are no abiding friendships, for insincerity, even if not seen, is felt, and those who are incapable of bestowing trust and truth, cannot receive it. Be true to others, and others will be true to you. Think well of an enemy, and defend the absent friend. If you have lost faith in human nature, discover where you have gone wrong yourself.

In the Confucian code of morals sincerity is one of the "Five Great Virtues," and Confucius thus speaks of it: "It is sincerity which places a crown upon our lives; without it, our best actions would be valueless; the seeming virtuous, mere hypocrites; and the shining light, which dazzles us with its splendors, but a poor passing gleam ready to be extinguished by the slightest breath of passion. . . . To be pure in mind, you must be free from self-deception—you must hate vice, as you would a disagreeable odor, and love virtue, as you would some beautiful object. There can be no self-respect without it, and this is why the superior man must be guarded in his hours of solitude.

"The worthless man secretly employs his idle moments in vicious acts, and there is no limit to his wickedness. In the presence of the pure he plays the hypocrite, and puts forward none but his good qualities; yet how does this dissembling avail him when his true character is revealed to the first scrutinizing glance?

"It has been said that there is a strict watch kept over that which is pointed at by many hands, and gazed at by many eyes; it is in solitude, then, that the upright man has the greatest reason to be most guarded."

Thus the sincere man does not do or say that which he would be ashamed of were it brought to light. His uprightness of spirit enables him to walk upright and confident among his fellow-men. His presence is a strong protection, and his words are direct and powerful because they are true. Whatever may be his work, it prospers. Though he may not always please the ears of men, he wins their hearts; they rely on him, trust and honour him.

Courage, self-reliance, sincerity, generosity and kindness—these are the virtues which constitute a robust manhood; without them, a man is but clay in the hands of circumstances; a weak, wavering thing that cannot rise into the freedom and joy of a true life. Every young man should cultivate and foster these virtues, and as he succeeds in living them, will he prepare himself to achieve the Life Triumphant.

I see coming upon the earth a new race of men and women—men who will be men indeed strong, upright, noble; too wise to stoop to anger, uncleanness, strife and hatred—women who will be women indeed, gentle, truthful, pure; too pitying to stoop to gossip, slander and deception; and from their loins will proceed superior beings of the same noble type; and the dark fiends of error and evil will fall back at their approach; they will regenerate the earth; they will dignify man, and vindicate nature, restoring humanity to love, happiness, and peace; and the life of victory over sin and sorrow will be established in the earth.

ENERGY AND POWER

How wonderful is the universal energy! Never-tiring, inexhaustible, and apparently eternal in its operation, it moves in atom and in star, informing the fleeting shapes of time with its restless, glowing, pulsating power.

Man is a portion of this creative energy, and in him it manifests, through a combination of mental faculties, as affection, passion, intelligence, morality, reason, understanding, and wisdom. He is not merely a blind conductor of energy, but he consciously uses, controls, and directs it. Slowly, but with certainty, is he gaining control of the forces without, and is making them do him obedient service; and just as surely will he gain control of the forces within—the subtle energies of thought— and direct them into channels of harmony and happiness.

Man's true place in the Cosmos is that of a king, not a slave, a commander under the Law of Good, and not a helpless tool in the reign of Evil. His own body and mind are the dual dominion over which he is to reign, a Lord of Truth, the master of himself, the wise user and controller of his store of pure, eternal, creative energy. Let him walk the earth unashamed, strong, valiant, tender, and benign; no longer prostrate in self-abasement, but walking erect in the dignity of perfect manhood; not groveling in selfishness and remorse, and crying for pardon and mercy, but standing firm and free in the sublime majesty of a sinless life.

Long has man regarded himself as vile, and weak, and unworthy, and has been content to remain so; but in the new era which has just now burst upon the world, he is to make the glorious discovery that he is pure, and powerful, and noble when he rises up and wills; and the rising up is not against any outward enemy; not against neighbour, nor governments, nor laws, nor spirits, nor principalities, nor powers, but against the ignorance, folly, and misery which beset him in the dominion of his own mind. For it is only by ignorance and folly that man is slavish; by knowledge and wisdom his kingship is restored.

Let them who will, preach man's weakness and helplessness, but I will teach his strength and power. I write for men, not for babes; for those who are eager to learn, and earnest to achieve; for those who will put away (for the world's good) a petty personal indulgence, a selfish desire, a mean thought, and live on as though it were not, sans craving and regret. The Truth is not for the frivolous and the thoughtless; the Life Triumphant is not for triflers and loiterers.

Man is a master. If he were not, he could not act contrary to law. Thus his so-called weakness is an indication of strength; his sin is the inversion of his capacity for holiness. For what is his weakness and sin but misdirected energy, misapplied power? In this sense, the wrong-doer is strong, not weak; but he is ignorant and exerts his strength in wrong directions instead of right, against the law of things instead of with it. Suffering is the recoil of misdirected strength. The bad man becomes good by reversing his conduct. If you are weeping over your sins, cease to commit those sins, and establish yourself in their opposing virtues. It is thus that weakness is converted into strength, helplessness into power, and suffering into bliss. By turning his energies from the old channels of vice, and directing them into the new channels of virtue, the sinner becomes the saint.

While the universal energy may be unlimited, in particular forms its sum is strictly limited. A man is possessed of a given amount of energy, and he can use or misuse it, can conserve and concentrate it, or dissipate and disperse it. Power is concentrated energy; wisdom is that energy adapted to beneficent ends. He is the man of influence and power who directs all his energies toward one great purpose, and patiently works and waits for its fulfillment, sacrificing his desires in other and more pleasant directions. He is the man of folly and weakness who, thinking chiefly of pleasure, gratifies the desire of the hour, or follows the whim and impulse of the moment, and so drifts thoughtlessly into peevishness and poverty of mind.

The energy used in one direction is not available for use in other directions; this is a universal law both in mind and matter. Emerson calls it "the law of compensation." Gain in a given direction necessitates loss in its opposite direction. The force placed in one scale is deducted from the other scale. Nature is always endeavoring to strike a balance. The energy which is dissipated in idleness is not given to work. The pleasure-seeker cannot also be the Truth-seeker. The force wasted in a fit of bad temper is drawn from the man's store of virtue, particularly the virtue of patience. Spiritually, this law of compensation is the law of sacrifice. Selfish pleasure must be sacrificed if purity is to be gained; hatred must be yielded up if love is to be acquired; vice must be renounced if virtue is to be embraced.

Earnest men soon discover that if they are to accomplish anything that is successful, strong, and enduring, either is worldly, intellectual, or spiritual channels, they must curb their desires, and sacrifice much that seems sweet; yea, even much that seems important. Hobbies, bodily and mental indulgences, enticing companionships, alluring pleasures, and all work that does not tend to some central purpose in his life, must be sacrificed by the man of strong resolve. He opens his eyes to the fact that time and energy are strictly limited, and so he economizes the one and concentrates the other.

Foolish men waste their energies in swinish ease and gluttonous indulgence, in frivolous pleasures and empty talk; in hateful thoughts and irritable outbursts of passion; in vain controversy and meddlesome interference; and then complain that many are more "fortunately" equipped than they are for a useful, successful, or great life, and they envy their honoured neighbour who has sacrificed self to duty, and has devoted all his energies to the faithful performance of the business of his life. "He who is just, speaks the truth, and does what is his own business, him the world will hold dear." Let a man attend to his own business, consecrating all his faculties to, and concentrating all his energies upon, the perfect accomplishment of the task of his life, not stepping aside to condemn or interfere with the duties of others, and he will find life simple, strong, and happy.

The universe is girt with goodness and strength, and it protects the good and the strong. Evil and weakness are self-destructive. Dissipation is annihilation. All nature loves strength. I see no inherent cruelty in "the survival of the fittest." It is a spiritual as well as a natural law. The stronger qualities in the beast are the fittest to evolve a higher type. The nobler moral qualities in man are his emancipators, and it is well that they should dominate and ultimately crush out the ignoble tendencies. Most certain it is that he who gives dominion to the lower, courts destruction, and does not survive, either in the struggle of life without or the battle of Truth within. The life given to the lower is lost to the higher; yea, it is finally lost also to the lower, and so all is lost, for evil is ultimately nothingness. But the life given to the higher is preserved, and is not lost to anything, for, while it sacrifices much that the world holds precious, it does not sacrifice anything that is precious in reality. The untrue and worthless must perish, and he who consecrates himself to the good and the true is content that they should perish, and so at last he stands where sacrifice ends, and all is gain—such a one survives in the struggle of life without, and he conquers in the battle of Truth within.

First, then, he strong. Strength is the firm basis on which is built the temple of the Triumphant Life. Without a central motive and fixed resolve, your life will be a poor, weak drifting, unstable thing. Let the act of the moment be governed by the deep abiding purpose of the heart. You will act differently at different times, but the act will not be wrong if the heart is right. You may fall and go astray at times, especially under great stress, but you will quickly regain yourself, and will grow wiser and stronger thereby so long as you guide yourself by the moral compass within, and do not throw it away to gratify effeminate indulgence and give yourself up to uncertain drifting. Follow your conscience. Be true to your convictions. Do at the moment what you regard as right, and put away all procrastination, vacillation, and fear. If you are convinced that in the performance of your duty under certain circumstances the severest measures are necessary, carry out those measures, and let there be no uncertainty about it. Err on the side of strength rather than weakness. The measures you adopt may not be the best, but if they are the best your know, then your plain duty is to carry them out; by so doing you will discover the better way, if you are anxious for progress, and are willing to learn. Deliberate beforehand, but in the time for action do not hesitate. Avoid anger and stubbornness, lust and greed. The angry man is the weak man. The stubborn man, who refuses to learn or mend his ways, is the foolish man. He grows old in folly, and gray hairs do not bring him reverence or honour. The sensualist has energy for pleasure only, and reserves none for manliness and self-respect. The greedy man is blind to the nobility of human nature and the glory of a true life; he spends his energies in perpetuating the miseries of hell, instead of enjoying the happiness of heaven.

Your strength is with you, and you can spend it in burrowing downward or in climbing upward. You can dissipate it in selfishness or conserve it in goodness. The same energy will enable you to become a beast or a god. The course along which you direct it will determine its effect. Do not think the thought, "My mind is weak," but convert weakness into strength, and energy into power by redirecting your mental forces. Turn your thoughts into noble channels. Put away vain longings and foolish regrets; abolish complaint and self-condolence, and have no dalliance with evil. Lift your face upward. Rise up in your divine strength, and spurn from your mind and life all meanness and weakness. Do not live the false life of a pulling slave, but live the true life of a conquering master.

SELF-CONTROL AND HAPPINESS

When mental energy is allowed to follow the line of least resistance, and to fall into easy channels, it is called weakness; when it is gathered, focused, and forced into upward and difficult directions, it becomes power; and this concentration of energy and acquisition of power is brought about by means of self-control.

In speaking of self-control, one is easily misunderstood. It should not be associated with a destructive repression, but with a constructive expression. The process is not one of death, but of life; it is a divine and masterly transmutation in which the weak in converted into the strong, the coarse into the fine, and the base into the noble; in which virtue takes the place of vice, and dark passion is lost in bright intellectuality.

The man who merely smothers up and hides away his real nature without any higher object in view than to create a good impression upon others concerning his character, is practising hypocrisy, and not self-control. As the mechanic transmutes coal into gas, and water into steam, and then concentrates and utilizes the finer forces thus generated for the comfort and convenience of men, so the man who intelligently practises self-control transmutes his lower inclinations into the finer qualities of intelligence and morality to the increase, of his own and the world's happiness.

A man is happy, wise, and great in the measure that he controls himself; he is wretched, foolish, and mean in the measure that he allows his animal nature to dominate his thoughts and actions.

He who controls himself, controls his life, his circumstances, his destiny; and wherever he goes he carries his happiness with him as an abiding possession. He who does not control himself, is controlled by his passions, by his circumstances, and by his fate; and if he cannot gratify the desire of the moment, he is disappointed and miserable. He depends for his fitful happiness on external things.

There is no force in the universe which can be annihilated or lost. Energy is transformed, but not destroyed. To shut the door upon old and bad habits is to open it to new and better ones. Renunciation precedes regeneration. Every self-indulgence, every forbidden pleasure, every hateful thought renounced is transformed into something more purely and permanently beautiful. Where debilitating excitements are cut off, there spring up rejuvenating joys. The seed dies that the flower may appear; the grub perishes, but the dragon-fly comes forth.

Truly, the transformation is not instantaneous; nor is the transition a pleasant and painless process. Nature demands effort and patience as the price of growth. In the march of progress, every victory is contested with struggle and pain; but the victory is achieved, and it abides. The struggle passes; the pain is temporary only. To demolish a firmly fixed habit, to break up a mental tendency that has become automatic with long use, and to force into birth and growth a fine characteristic or lofty virtue—to accomplish this necessitates a painful metamorphosis, a transitional period of darkness, to pass through which, patience and endurance are required: and this is where men fail; this is where they slip back into their old, easy, animal ruts, and abandon self-control as too strenuous and severe. Thus they fall short of permanent happiness, and the life of triumph over evil is hidden from their eyes.

The permanent happiness which men seek in dissipation, excitement, and abandonment to unworthy pleasures is found only in the life which reverses all this—the life of self-control. So far as a man deviates from perfect self-command, just so far does he fall short of perfect happiness, and sink into misery and weakness, the lowest limit of which is madness, entire lack of mental control, the condition of irresponsibility. In so far as a man approximates to perfect self-command, just so near does he approach to perfect happiness, and rise into joy and strength; and so glorious are the possibilities of such divine manhood, that no limit can be set to its grandeur and bliss.

If a man will understand how intimately, yea, how inseparably, self-control and happiness are associated, he has but to look into his own heart, and upon the world around, to find there the joy destroying effects of uncontrolled tendencies. Looking upon the lives of men and women, he will perceive how the hasty word, the bitter retort, the act of deception, the blind prejudice and foolish resentment bring wretchedness and even ruin in their train. Looking into his own life, what days of consuming remorse, of restless anxiety, and of crushing sorrow rise up before his mind—periods of intense suffering through which he has passed through lack of self-control.

But in the right life, the well-governed life, the victorious life, all these things pass away. New conditions obtain, and purer, more espiritual instruments are employed for the achievements of happy ends. There is no more remorse, because there is no more wrong-doing; there is no more anxiety, because there is no more selfishness; there is no more sorrow, because Truth is the source of action.

That much-desired thing which self pursues with breathless and uncontrolled eagerness, yet fails to overtake, comes unbidden, and begs to be admitted, to him who works and waits in perfect self-command. Hatred, impatience, greed, self-indulgence, vain ambitions, and blind desires—the instruments by which self shapes its ill-finished existence, what clumsy tools they are, and how ignorant and unskillful are they who employ them! Love, patience, kindness, self-discipline, trans-muted ambitions and chastened desires—instruments of Truth, by which is shaped a well-finished existence, what perfect tools they are, and how wise and skilful are they who use them!

Whatsoever is gained by feverish haste and selfish desire, is attained in fuller measure by quiet-ness and renunciation. Nature will not be hastened. She brings all to perfection in due season. Truth will not be commanded. He has his conditions, and must be obeyed. Than haste and anger nothing is more superfluous. A man has to learn that he cannot command things, but that he can command himself; that he cannot coerce the wills of others, but that he can mold and master his own will: and things serve him who serves Truth; people seek guidance of him who is master of himself.

It is a little understood, yet simple and profound truth, that the man who cannot command himself under the severest external stress, is unfit to guide others or to control affairs. It is the fundamental principle in the moral and political teaching of Confucius that, before attempting to govern affairs, a man should learn to govern himself. Men who habitually give way, under pressure, to hysterical suspicions, outbursts of resentment, and explosions of anger, are unfit for weighty responsibilities and lofty duties, and usually fail, sooner or later, even in the ordinary duties of life, such as the management of their own family or business. Lack of self-control is foolishness, and folly cannot take precedence of wisdom.

He who is learning how to subdue and control his turbulent, wandering thoughts, is becom-ing wiser every day; and though for a time the Temple of Joy will not be completed, he will gather strength in laying its foundations and building up its walls; and the day will come when, like a wise master-builder, he will rest at peace in the beautiful habitation which he has built. Wisdom inheres in self-control, and in wisdom is "pleasantness and peace."

The life of self-control is no barren deprivation, no wilderness of monotony. Renunciation there is, but it is the renunciation of the ephemeral and false in order that the abiding and true may be realized. Enjoyment is not cut off; it is intensified. Enjoyment is life; it is the slavish desire for it that kills. Is there anywhere a more miserable man than he who is always longing for some new sensation? Is there anywhere a more blessed being than he who, by self-control, is satisfied, calm, and enlightened? Who has most of physical life and joy—the glutton, the drunkard, and the sensualist who lives for pleasure only, or the temperate man who holds his body in subjection, considering its needs and obeying its uses? I was once eating a ripe, juicy apple as it came from the tree, and a man near me said, "I would give anything if I could enjoy an apple like that." I asked, "Why can't you?" His answer was, "I have drunk whisky and smoked tobacco until I have lost all enjoyment in such things." In pursuit of elusive enjoyments, men lose the abiding joys of life.

And as he who controls his senses has most of physical life, and joy, and strength so he who controls his thoughts has most of spiritual life, and bliss, and power; for not only happiness, but knowledge and wisdom also are revealed by self-control. As the avenues of ignorance and selfishness are closed, the open gates of knowledge and enlightenment appear. Virtue attained is knowledge gained. The pure mind is the enlightened mind. He has well-being who controls himself well.

I hear men speak of the "monotony of goodness." If longing for things in the spirit which one has given up in the letter were "goodness," then indeed would it be monotonous. The man of self-control does not merely give up his base pleasures, he abandons all longing for them. He presses forward, and does not look back; and fresh beauties, new glories, sublimer vistas await him at every step.

I am astonished at the revelations which lie hidden in self-control; I am captivated by the infinite variety of Truth; I am filled, with joy at the grandeur of the prospect; I am gladdened by its splendor and its peace.

Along the way of self-control there is the joy of victory; the consciousness of expanding and increasing power; the acquisition of the imperishable riches of divine knowledge; and the abiding bliss of service to humankind. Even he who travels only a portion of the way will develop a strength, achieve a success, and experience a joy which the idle and the thoughtless cannot know; and he who goes all the way will become a spiritual conqueror; he will triumph over all evil, and will blot it out; he will gaze with enrapt vision upon the majesty of the Cosmic Order, and will enjoy the immortality of Truth.

SIMPLICITY AND FREEDOM

You have known what is is to be physically encumbered by some superfluous load; you have experienced the happy relief of dispensing with such load. Your experience illustrates the difference between a life burdened with a complexity of desires, beliefs, and speculations, and one rendered simple and free by the satisfaction of its natural needs, and a calm contemplation of the facts of existence, eliminating all argument and speculation.

There are those who cumber their drawers, cupboards, and rooms with rubbish and lumber. To such an extent is this carried sometimes, that the house cannot be properly cleaned, and vermin swarms. There is no use for the rubbish, but they will not part with it, even though, by so doing, they would also get rid of the vermin; but they like to think that it is there; like to feel that they have *got* it, especially if they are convinced that nobody else has its like; or they reason that it may be of some use some day; or it may become valuable; or it brings up old associations which they occasionally resuscitate, and take a paradoxical pleasure in sorrowing over.

In a sweet, methodical, well-managed house, such superfluities, bringing with them dirt, discomfort, and care, are not allowed to accumulate; or should they have accumulated, they are gathered up and consigned to the fire and the dust-bin, when it is decided to cleanse and restore the house, and give it light, comfort and freedom.

In like manner men hoard up in their minds mental rubbish and lumber, and cling tenaciously to it, and fear its loss. Insatiate desires; thirsty cravings for unlawful and unnatural pleasures; conflicting beliefs about miracles, gods, angels, demons, and interminable theological complexities, hypothesis is piled upon hypothesis, speculation is added to speculation, until the simple, beautiful, all sufficient facts of life are lost to sight and knowledge beneath the metaphysical pile.

Simplicity consists in being rid of this painful confusion of desires and superfluity of opinions, and adhering only to that which is permanent and essential.

And what is permanent in life? What is essential? Virtue alone is permanent; character is essential. So simple is life when it is freed from all superfluities and rightly understood and lived, that it can be reduced to a few unmistakable, easy-to-be-understood, though hard-to-practice principles; and all great minds have so simplified life. Buddha reduced it to eight virtues, in, the practice of which he declared that men would acquire perfect enlightenment; and these eight virtues he reduced to one, which he called *Compassion*. Confucius taught that the perfection of knowledge was contained in five virtues, and these he expressed in one which he called *Reciprocity, or Sympathy*.

Jesus reduced the whole of life to the principle of *Love*. Compassion, Sympathy, Love, these three are identical. How simple they are, too! yet I cannot find a man who fully understands the depths and heights of these virtues, for who so fully understood them would embody them in practice. He would be complete, perfect, divine. There would be nothing lacking in him of knowledge and virtue and wisdom. It is only when a man sets earnestly to work to order his life in accordance with the simple precepts of virtue, that he discovers what piles of mental rubbish he has hoarded up, and which he is now compelled to throw away. The exactions, too, which such a course of conduct makes upon his faith, endurance, patience, kindness, humility, reason, and strength of will, are, until the mind approaches the necessary condition of purity and simplicity, painful in their severity. The clearing-out process, whether of one's mind, home, or place of business, is not a light and easy one, but it ends in comfort and repose.

All complexities of detail, whether in things material or mental, are reducible to a few fundamental laws or principles by virtue of which they exist and are regulated. Wise men govern their lives by a few simple rules. A life governed by the central principle of love will be found to be divinely consistent in all its details. Every thought, word, act, will fall into its proper place, and there will be no conflict and confusion.

"What," asked the learned man of the Buddhist saint who had acquired a wide reputation for sanctity and wisdom—"what is the most fundamental thing in Buddhism?" The saint replied, "The most fundamental thing in Buddhism is to cease from evil and to learn to do good." "I did not ask you," said the learned man, "to tell me what every child of three knows; I want you to tell me what is the most profound, the most subtle, the most important thing in Buddhism." "The most profound, the most subtle, the most important thing in Buddhism," said the saint, "is to cease from evil and to learn to do well. It is true that a child of three may know it, but grey-haired old men fail to put it into practice." The commentator then goes on to say that the learned man did not want facts; he did not want Truth; he wanted to be given some subtle metaphysical speculation which would give rise to another speculation, and then to another and another, and so afford him an opportunity of bringing into play the wonderful intellect of which he was so proud.

A member of a philosophical school once proudly said to me, "Our system of metaphysics is the most perfect and complicated in the world." I discovered how complicated it was by becoming involved in it and then pursuing the process of extrication back to the facts of life, to simplicity and freedom. I have since learned how better to utilize my energy and occupy my time in the pursuit and practice of those virtues that are firm and sure, rather than to waste it in the spinning of the pretty but unsubstantial threads of metaphysical cobwebs.

But while discountenancing assumption and pride, and that vanity which mistakes its own hypothesis for reality, I set no premium on ignorance and stupidity. Learning is a good thing. As an end in itself, as a possession to be proud of, it is a dead thing; but as a means to the high ends of human progress and human good it becomes a living power. Accompanied with a lowly mind, it is a powerful instrument for good. The Buddhist saint was no less learned than his proud questioner, but he was more simple and wise. Even hypotheses will not lead us astray if they are perceived as mere hypotheses and are not confounded with facts. Yet the wisest men dispense with all hypotheses, and fall back on the simple practice of virtue. They thus become divine, and arrive at the acme of simplicity, enlightenment, and emancipation.

To arrive at the freedom and joy of simplicity, one must not think less, he must think more; only the thinking must be set to a high and useful purpose, and must be concentrated upon the facts and duties of life, instead of dissipated in unprofitable theorizing.

A life of simplicity is simple in all its parts because the heart which governs it has become pure and strong; because it is centered and rested in Truth. Harmful luxuries in food, and vain superfluities in dress; exaggerations of speech and insincerities of action; thoughts that tend to intellectual display and empty speculation—all these are set aside in order that virtue may be better understood and more earnestly embraced; the duties of life are undertaken in a spirit from which self is eliminated, and they become transfigured with a new and glorious light, even the light of Truth; the great fundamental facts of life, heretofore hidden from knowledge, and plainly revealed, and the Eternal Verities about which the wordy theorizers can only guess and argue, become substantial possessions.

The simple-hearted, the true-hearted, the virtuous and wise, are no longer troubled with doubts and fears about the future and the unknown and unknowable. They take their stand upon the duty of the hour, and on the known and the knowable. They do not barter away the actual for the hypothetical. They find in virtue an abiding security; they find in Truth an illuminating light which, while it reveals to them the true order of the facts of life, throws a halo of divine promise about the abyss of the unknown; and so they are at rest.

Simplicity works untrammelled, and becomes greatness and power. Suspicions, deceptions, impurities, despondencies, bewailings, doubts, and fears—all these things are cast away, left behind and ignored, and the freed man, strong, self-possessed, calm and pure, works in unclouded assurance, and inhabits heavenly places.

RIGHT-THINKING AND REPOSE

Life is a combination of habits, some baneful, some beneficent, all of which take their rise in the one habit of thinking. The thought makes the man, therefore right-thinking is the most important thing in life. The essential difference between a wise man and a fool is that the wise man controls his thinking, the fool is controlled by it. A wise man, determines how and what he shall think, and does not allow external things to divert his thought from the main purpose; but a fool is carried captive by every tyrant thought as it is aroused within him by external things, and he goes through life the helpless tool of impulse, whim, and passion.

Careless, slovenly thinking, commonly called thoughtlessness, is the companion of failure, wrong-doing, and wretchedness. Nothing, no prayers, no religious ceremonies, not even acts of charity, can make up for wrong thinking. Only right-thinking can rectify a wrong life. Only the right attitude of mind toward men and things can bring repose and peace.

The Triumphant Life is only for him whose heart and intellect are attuned to lofty virtue. He must make his thought logical, sequential, harmonious, symmetrical. He must mould and shape his thinking to fixed principles, and thereby establish his life on the sure foundation of knowledge. He must not merely be kind, he must be intelligently kind; must know why he is kind. His kindness must be an invariable quality, and not an intermittent impulse interspersed with fits of resentment and acts of harshness. He must not merely be virtuous under virtuous circumstances; his virtue must be of that kind that shall continue to shine with unabated light when he is assailed with vicious circumstances. He must not allow himself to be hurled from the throne of divine manhood by the shocks of fate or the praise and blame of those about him. Virtue must be his abiding habitation; his refuge from the whirlwind and the storm.

And virtue is not only of the heart; it is of the intellect also; and without this virtue of the intellect, the virtue of the heart is imperilled. Reason, like passion, has its vices. Metaphysical speculations are the riot of the intellect, as sensuality is the riot of the affections. The highest flights of speculation—pleasing as they are—reveal no place of rest, and the strained mind must return to facts and moral principles to find that truth which it seeks. As the soaring bird returns for refuge and rest to its nest in the rock, so must the speculative thinker return to the rock of virtue for surety and peace.

The intellect must be trained to comprehend the principles of virtue, and to understand all that is involved in their practice. Its energies must be restrained from wasteful indulgence in vain subtleties, and be directed in the path of righteousness and the way of wisdom. The thinker must distinguish, in his own mind, between reality and assumption. He must discover the extent of his actual knowledge. He must know what he knows. He must also know what he does not know. He must learn to discriminate between facts and opinions about facts, between belief and knowledge, error and Truth In his search for the right attitude of mind which perceives truth, and works out a wise and radiant life, he must be more logical than logic, more merciless in exposing the errors of his own mind than the most sarcastic logician is in exposing the errors of the minds of others. After pursuing this course of discrimination for a short time, he will be astonished to find how small is the extent of his actual knowledge; yet he will be gladdened by its possession, for small as it is, it is the pure gold of knowledge; and what is better, to have a few grains of gold hidden away in tons of ore, where it is useless, or to extract the gold and throw away the ore? As the miner sifts away bushels of dull earth to find the sparkling diamond, so the spiritual miner, the true thinker, sifts away from his mind the accumulation of opinions, beliefs, speculations, and assumptions to find the bright jewel of Truth which bestows upon its possessor wisdom and enlightenment.

And the concentrated knowledge which is ultimately brought to light by this sifting process is found to be so closely akin to virtue that it cannot be divided from it, cannot be set apart as something different. In his search for knowledge. Socrates discovered virtue. The divine maxims of the Great Teachers are maxims of virtue. When knowledge is separated from virtue, wisdom is lost. What a man practises, that he knows. What he does not practice, that he does not know. A man may write treatises or preach sermons on Love, but if he treat his family harshly, or think spitefully of his enemy, what knowledge has he concerning Love? In the heart of the man of knowledge there dwells a silent and abiding compassion that shames the fine words of the noisy theorist. He only knows what peace is whose heart is free from hatred; who lives at peace with all. Cunning definitions of virtue only serve to deepen ignorance when they proceed from vice-stained lips. Knowledge has a deeper source than the mere memorizing of information. That knowledge is divine which proceeds from acquaintance with virtue. The humility which purges the intellect of its empty opinions and vain assumptions, also fortifies it with a searching insight and invincible power. There is a divine logic which is in-distinguished from love. The reply, "He that is without sin among you, let him first cast a stone at her," is unanswerable logic; it is also perfect love.

The wrong-thinker is known by his vices; the right-thinker is known by his virtues. Troubles and unrest assail the mind of the wrong-thinker, and he experiences no abiding repose. He imagines that others can injure, snub, cheat, degrade and ruin him. Knowing nothing of the protection of virtue, be seeks the protection of self, and takes refuge in suspicion, spite, resentment, and retaliation, and is burnt in the fire of his own vices. When slandered, he slanders in return; when accused, be recriminates; when assailed, he turns upon his adversary with double fierceness. "I have been treated unjustly!" exclaims the wrong thinker, and then abandons himself to resentment and misery. Having no insight, and unable to distinguish evil from good, he cannot see that it is his own evil, and not his neighbour's, that is the cause of all his trouble.

The right-thinker is not concerned with thoughts about self and self-protection, and the wrong actions of others toward him cannot cause him trouble or unrest. He cannot think—"This man has wronged me." He perceives that no wrong can reach him but by his own evil deeds. He understands that his welfare is in his own hands, and thus none but himself can rob him of repose. Virtue is his protection, and retaliation is foreign to him. He holds himself steadfastly in peace, and resentment cannot enter his heart. Temptation does not find him unprepared, and it assails in vain the strong citadel of his mind. Abiding in virtue, he abides in strength and peace.

The right-thinker has discovered and acquired the right attitude of mind toward men and things—the attitude of a profound and loving repose. And this is not resignation, it is wisdom. It is not indifference, but watchful and penetrating insight. He has comprehended the facts of life; he sees things as they are. He does not overlook the particulars of life, but reads them in the light of cosmic law; sees them in their right relations as portions of the universal scheme. He sees that the universe is upheld by justice. He watches, but does not engage in, the petty quarrels and fleeting strifes of men. He cannot be a partisan. His sympathy is with all. He cannot favor one portion more than another. He knows that good will ultimately conquer in the world, as it has conquered in individuals; that there is a sense in which good already conquers, for evil defeats itself.

Good is not defeated; justice is not set aside. Whatever man may do, justice reigns, and its eternal throne cannot be assailed and threatened, much less conquered and overthrown; and this is the source of the true thinker's abiding repose. Having become righteous, he perceives the righteous law; having acquired Love, he understands the Eternal Love; having conquered evil, he knows that good is supreme.

He only is the true thinker whose heart is free from hatred, lust, and pride; who looks out upon the world through eyes washed free from evil; whose bitterest enemy arouses no enmity, but only tender pity in his heart; who does not talk vainly about things of which he has no knowledge, and whose heart is always at peace.

And by this a man may know that his thoughts are in accordance with Truth—that there is no more bitterness in his heart, that malice has departed from him; that he loves where he formerly condemned.

A man may be learned, but if he is not wise he will not be a true thinker. Not by learning will a man triumph over evil; not by much study will he overcome sin and sorrow. Only by conquering himself will he conquer evil; only by practising righteousness will he put an end to sorrow.

Not for the clever, nor the learned, nor the self-confident is the Life Triumphant, but for the pure, the virtuous, the wise. The former achieve their particular success in life, but the latter alone achieve the Great Success, a success so invincible and complete that even an apparent defeat shines with added victory.

Virtue cannot be shaken; virtue cannot be confounded; virtue cannot be overthrown. He who thinks in accordance with virtue, who acts righteously, whose mind is the servant of Truth, he it is who conquers in life and in death; for virtue must triumph, and Righteousness and Truth are the pillars of the universe.

CALMNESS AND RESOURCE

He who has Truth is always self-possessed. Hurry and excitement, anxiety and fear have no place in the purified mind and the true life. Self-conquest results in a perpetual calm. Calmness is the radiant light which adds a lustre to all the virtues. Like the nimbus round the head of a saint, it surrounds virtue with its shining halo. Without calmness a man's greatest strength is but a kind of exaggerated weakness. Where is a man's spiritual strength—where, indeed, is his ordinary manly strength—who loses his balance with almost every petty disturbance from without? And what enduring influence can a man have who forgets himself in sinful abandonment or unseemly rage in the hour of temptation and crisis?

The virtuous put a check upon themselves, and set a watch upon their passions and emotions; in this way they gain possession of the mind, and gradually acquire calmness; and, as they acquire calmness, they acquire influence, power, greatness, abiding joy, and fulness and completeness of life.

Those who do not put a check upon themselves, whose emotions and passions are their masters, who crave excitements and race after unholy pleasures—these are not yet fit for a life of joyful victory, and can neither appreciate nor receive the beautiful jewel of calmness. Such may pray for peace with their lips, but they do not desire it in their hearts; or the word "peace" may only mean to them another kind of periodic pleasure which they desire to enjoy.

In the life of calm there are no fitful periods of sinful excitement followed by reactionary hours of sorrow and remorse. There are no foolish elations followed by equal foolish depressions; no degrading actions followed by misery and loss of self-respect; but all these things are put away, and what remains is Truth, and Truth is for ever encircled with peace. The calm life is one unbroken bliss. Duties which are irksome to the ungoverned, are things of joy to the calm man; indeed, in the calm life, the word "duty" receives a new meaning; it is no longer opposed to happiness, but it is one with happiness. The calm man, the right-seeing man, cannot separate joy from duty; such separation belongs to the mind and life of the pleasure-hunter and lover of excitement.

Calmness is difficult to attain because men cling blindly to the lower disturbances of the mind for the passing pleasure which those disturbances afford. Even sorrow is sometimes selfishly gloated over as a kind of occasional luxury. But though difficult to attain, the way which leads to its attainment is simple; it consists in abandoning all those excitements and disturbances which are opposed to it, and in fortifying one's self in those steadfast virtues which do not change with changing events and circumstances, which have no violent reactions, and which therefore bestow perpetual satisfaction and abiding peace.

He only finds peace who conquers himself, who strives, day by day, after greater self-possession, greater self-control, greater calmness of mind. One can only be a joy to himself and a blessing to others in the measure that he has command of himself; and such self-command is gained only by persistent practice. A man must conquer his weaknesses by daily effort; he must understand them and study how to eliminate them from his character; and if he continues to strive, not giving way, he will gradually become victorious; and each little victory gained (though there is a sense in which no victory can be called *little*) will be so much more calmness acquired and added to his character as an eternal possession. He will thus make himself strong and capable and blessed, fit to perform his duties faultlessly, and to meet all events with an untroubled spirit. But even if he does not, in this life, reach that supreme calm which no shock can disturb, he will become sufficiently self-possessed and pure to enable him to fight the battle of life fearlessly, and to leave the world a little richer for having known the benignity of his presence.

By constantly overcoming self, a man gains a knowledge of the subtle intricacies of his mind; and it is this divine knowledge which enables him to become established in calmness. Without self-knowledge there can be no abiding peace of mind, and those who are carried away by tempestuous passions, cannot approach the holy place where calmness reigns. The weak man is like one who, having mounted a fiery steed, allows it to run away with him, and carry him withersoever it wills; the strong man is like one who, having mounted the steed, governs it with a masterly hand, and makes it go in whatever direction, and at whatever speed he commands.

Calmness is the crowning beauty of a character that has become, or is becoming, divine, and is restful and peace-giving to all who come in contact with it. Those who are still in their weakness and doubt, find the presence of the calm mind restful to their troubled minds, inspiring to their faltering feet, and rich with healing and comfort in the hour of sorrow; for he who is strong to overcome self, is strong to help others; he who has conquered soul-weariness is strong to help the weary on the way.

That calmness of mind which is not disturbed or overthrown by trials and emergencies, or by the accusations, slanders, and misrepresentations of others, is born of great spiritual strength, is the true indication of an enlightened and wise understanding. The, calm mind is the exalted mind. Divinely gentle and eternally strong, is that man who does not lose his serenity, nor forget his peace when falsehoods and indignities are heaped upon him. Such calmness is the perfect flower of self-control; it has been slowly and laboriously gained, by patiently passing through the fires of suffering, by subjecting the mind to a long process of purification.

The calm man has discovered the spring of both happiness and knowledge within himself, and it is a spring that can never run dry. His powers are at his full command, and there is no limit to his resources. In whatever direction he employs his energies, he will manifest originality and power. And this is so because he deals with things as they are, and not with mere opinions about things. If he has any opinions left, he is no longer enamoured of them, but sees them as they are—mere opinions, and therefore of no intrinsic value. He has abolished egotism, and, by obedience to law, has become one with the power in nature and the universe. His resources are untrammeled by selfishness; his energies are unhindered by pride. There is a sense in which he has ceased to regard anything as his own. Even his virtues belong to Truth, and not exclusively to his person. He has become a conscious instrument of Cosmic Power, and is no longer a mean, dwarfed thing, seeking petty personal ends. And having put away self, he has put away the greed, the misery, the troubles and fears which belong to self. He acts calmly, and accepts all consequences with equal calmness. He is efficient and accurate, and perceives all that is involved in any undertaking. He does not work blindly; he knows there is no chance of favour.

The mind of the calm man is like the surface of a still lake; it reflects life and the things of life truly. Whereas the troubled mind, like the troubled surface of a lake, gives back a distorted image of all things which fall upon it. Gazing into the serene depths within him, the self-conquered man sees a just reflection of the universe. He sees the Cosmic Perfection; sees the equity in his own lot; even those things which are regarded by the world as unjust and grievous (and which formerly appeared so to him) are now known to be the effects of his own past deeds, and are therefore joyfully accepted as portions of the perfect whole. Thus his calmness remains with him with its illimitable fund of resource in joy and enlightenment.

The calm man succeeds where the disturbed man fails. He is fitted to deal with any external difficulty, who has successfully grappled with the most intricate difficulties and problems within his own heart. He who has succeeded in governing the within, is best equipped to govern the without.

The calm mind perceives a difficulty in all its bearings, and understands best how to meet it. The disturbed mind is the lost mind. It has become blind, seeing not whither to go, but *only feeling* its own unhappiness and fear. The resources of the calm man are superior to all incidents which may befall him. Nothing can alarm him, nothing can find him unprepared, nothing can shake his strong and steadfast mind. Wheresoever duty may call him, there will his strength manifest itself; there will his mind, free from the frictions of self, exhibit its silent and patient power. Whether he be engaged in things worldly or things spiritual, he will do his work with concentrated vigor and penetrating insight.

Calmness means that the mind is harmoniously adjusted, perfectly poised; all its extremes, once so antagonistic and painful, are reconciled, merged into one grand central principle with which the mind has identified itself. It means that the runaway passions are tamed and subjected, the intellect is purified, and the will is merged into the Cosmic Will; that is, it is no longer centered upon narrow personal ends, but is concerned with the good of all.

A man is not wholly victorious until he is perpetually calm. While passing things disturb him, his understanding is unripe, his heart is not altogether pure. A man cannot advance in the triumph of life while he flatters and deceives himself. He must awake, and be fully alive to the fact that his sins, sorrows, and troubles are of his own making, and belong to his own imperfect condition. He must understand that his miseries have their root in his own sins, and not in the sins of others. He must strive after calmness as the covetous man strives after riches; and he must not rest satisfied with any partial attainment. He will thus grow in grace and wisdom, in strength and peace, and calmness will descend upon his spirit as the refreshing dew descends upon the flowers.

Where the calm mind is, there is strength and rest, there is love and wisdom; there is one who has fought successfully innumerable battles against self, who, after long toil in secret against his own failings, has triumphed at last.

INSIGHT AND NOBILITY

In the pursuit and practice of virtue, there at last comes a time when a divine insight dawns upon the mind, an insight that searches into the causes and principles of things, and which, once attained, establishes its possessor firmly in virtue, renders him invulnerable to the assaults of temptation, and invincible in his work for the world.

When the understanding is ripened by the culture of virtue, vicious inclinations disappear, and wrong-doing becomes impossible. When individual human conduct is perceived as an unbroken series of causes and effects, the perceiving, mind finally decides for virtue, and the lower selfish elements are cast away for ever.

Until a man perceives the just law which operates in human life, whatever virtue he may manifest at any given time, he is not firmly established in nobility of character, he is not fully armoured with righteousness, is not safely lodged in his final refuge. Not having acquired that perfect insight which knows good and evil and which perceives the effects of all deeds both good and bad, he breaks down when assailed by temptation at those points in his character which are not well fortified, and which have, so far, dimmed his spiritual sight, and barred him from perfect vision. And by thus breaking down, he discovers that within which has hindered him, and by setting to work to remove the hindrance, he ascends still higher in the scale of virtue, and approaches nearer to that perfect insight into the true order of life which makes a man divine.

Under certain circumstances a man, held in restraint by the influence of friends, by custom and environment, and not by his own inherent purity and strength, will appear to have, and may believe himself to possess, a virtue of which he knows nothing in reality; and his lack of such virtue only appears when all outward restraints are withdrawn, and, under temptation, the concealed weakness and vice make themselves manifest.

On the other hand, the man of superior virtue will seem, in a familiar environment, to be much the same as his weaker fellows, and his virtue will not be apparent to those about him; but when he is suddenly brought in contact with great temptations or extraordinary events, his latent virtue appears in all its beauty and strength.

Insight destroys the dominion of evil, and reveals the faultless operation of the Good Law. The man of perfect insight cannot sin, because he fully understands the nature of good and evil, and it is impossible for one who knows good and evil in all their ramifications of cause and effect to choose the evil and reject the good. Just as the sane man would not choose ashes in preference to food, so the spiritually awakened man would not choose evil in preference to good. The presence of sin is an indication of self-delusion, of ignorance; the spiritual vision is warped or undeveloped, and there is confusion of mind concerning the nature of good and evil.

In the early stages of virtue, a man arrays himself against the forces of evil which appear to him to be overpowering in their might, and almost, if not entirely, unconquerable; but with the advent of insight, a new light is thrown upon the nature of things, and evil appears as it actually is—a small, dark, powerless thing, a mere negation, and not a formidable force or combination of forces. The man of insight knows that the root of evil is ignorance—and not an intelligent power—and that all sins and sufferings proceed therefrom. Thus, knowing evil to be merely deprivation of good, he cannot hate it, but manifests compassion for all sinning and suffering beings.

Indeed, be who has so far conquered the evil in his own heart as to know the nature and source of evil, cannot possibly hate, dislike, or despise any being, no matter how far removed from virtue it may be, but, while fully perceiving the degradation of character, he understands the dark spiritual condition from which such degradation springs, and so he pities and helps where, without insight, he would hate and despise. Love ever attends upon insight, and pity waits on knowledge.

That insight which proceeds, from self-purification and long acquaintance with virtue makes itself manifest in the form of *ripeness of character,* there is an unchanging strength and sweetness combined; a clearness of intellect, a virile strength of will, and a gentleness of heart—combination which denotes a cultured, mellowed, perfected being; one who has acquired sympathy, compassion, purity, and—wisdom. Thus while "Goodness gives insight," insight renders goodness permanent, fixes the mind in the love and practice of all that is pure and noble, and stamps upon man's brow the seal of divinity.

The man whose goodness is of that kind that does not alter with altered environment, or change with the changing attitudes of those around him, has reached the Divine Goodness; he understands the Supreme Good. He is no longer concerned with evil as a thing that can harm him, but he is concerned with good only; and so he ignores evil, and recognizes only good. He perceives that men commit evil out of a mistaken idea of good, and, thus perceiving, no hatred against any can enter his peaceful heart.

The life of such a man is powerful, no matter how obscure it may be, for goodness is the most powerful thing in the world, and the fact of his living and moving amongst men confers incalculable benefit upon the race, although during his lifetime, this may not be perceived and understood. So powerful is goodness that the destiny of the world was, is, and will be, in the hands of the good. The good men are the guides and emancipators of humanity. In the present period of its development, they are taking the race rapidly along in its evolutionary journey; and this, not in any mystical or miraculous sense, but in a very practical and normal sense, by their exemplary lives, by the power of their deeds. The good men who help the world are not wonder-workers, though undeveloped minds have ever tried to make them such—but the workers of righteousness, servants of the Good Law.

The world never was, is not, and will not be, under the dominion of evil, for such a condition would mean non-existence, evil being merely the negation of good, as darkness is the negation of light; and it is light, and not darkness, which is the sustaining power. Evil is the weakest thing in the world, and cannot accomplish anything. The universe not only makes for good, the universe *is* good, and evil always falls short and fails.

Insight is *seeing in the Light of Truth*, that Light which is the revealer of all things. As the light of day reveals all objects in the world in their proper forms, so when the Light of Truth enters the mind it reveals all the things of life in their proper proportions. He who searches his own heart by the aid of Truth, searches all hearts. He who, by long searching, has perceived the Perfect Law which is operative in his own mind, has revealed the Divine Law which is the stay and substance of the universe.

Insight disperses error and puts an end to superstition. Sin is the only error. Men attack each other's beliefs and remain in ignorance. When they get rid of their own sins they will become enlightened. Superstition springs from sin. Looking through darkened eyes, men see evil things which are delusions of ignorance; conceiving in their hearts unlawful things, their imagination is troubled with monsters and terrors which have no existence in reality. Where there is pure insight there is no fear; and devils, demons, wrathful and jealous gods, vampires and evil spirits, and all the hideous host of theological monsters, have vanished from the universe along with the feverish nightmare which gave them birth, and before the rapt gaze of the purified one there spreads a universe of orderly beauty and inviolate law.

The man of insight lives in the beatific vision of the saints, not as a fleeting experience in a moment of exceptional purity, but as a constant, normal condition of mind. He has completed his long journey through self and sorrow, and is at peace; he has conquered, and is glad. He sees all the sin and misery and pain that are in the world more plainly and vividly than other men, but he now sees it as it is in its cause, inception, growth and fruitage, and not as it appeared to him when he was blindly involved in it, and his mind was distorted by impurities. He watches the growth of beings, from the immature to the mature, through periods of change and pain, with tender compassion and solicitude, as the mother watches the growth of her child through the helpless period of its infancy.

He sees justice operating in all things. While men are waxing wrathful over the triumph of wrong, he knows that wrong has not triumphed, but is brought to naught. He sees the overruling Right which, though concealed from worldly eyes, remains forever unshaken. He sees the littleness, the puny weakness, the blind folly of evil as compared with the majesty, the invincible power, and the all-seeing wisdom of Good. And thus knowing and seeing, his mind is finally fixed in that which is good. He is devoted to Truth, and his delight is in the doing of righteousness.

When insight is born in the mind, Reality stands revealed; not a metaphysical reality distinct from the universe; not a speculative reality other than the things of life, but the. Reality of the universe itself, the Reality of "things-in-themselves." Insight is triumphant over change and decay, for it perceives the abiding in change, the eternal in the transient, the immortal in the things which pass away.

And herein is the meaning of that fixed nobility of character of the saints and sages, and, superlatively, of the Great Teachers of the Race—that they perceive and abide in Reality; they know life as it is in its completion; they understand and obey the Righteous Law. Having conquered self, they have conquered all delusions; having triumphed over sin, they have triumphed over sorrow, having purified themselves, they see the Perfect Cosmos.

He who chooses the right, the pure, the good, and clings to them through all misunderstanding, contumely, and defeat, reaches, at last, the place of insight, and his eyes open upon the world of Truth; then his painful discipline is ended; the lower conditions no more effect him or cause him sorrow; purity and joy abide with him, and the universe again rejoices in the triumph of good, and hails another conqueror.

MAN THE MASTER

By the mastery of self, a distinct form of consciousness is evolved which would call *divine* as distinguished from that ordinary *human* consciousness which craves personal advantages and gratification on the one hand, and is involved in remorse and sorrow on the other. This divine consciousness concerns itself with humanity and the universe, with eternal verities, with righteousness, wisdom, and truth, and not with pleasures, protection, and preservation of the personality. Not that personal pleasure is destroyed, but it is no longer craved and sought, it no longer takes a foremost place; it is purified, and is received as the effect of right thought and action, and is no longer an end in itself. In divine consciousness there is neither sin nor sorrow. Even the sense of sin has passed away, and the true order and purpose of life being revealed, no cause is found for lamentation. Jesus called this state of consciousness "The Kingdom of Heaven;" Buddha named it "Nirvana;" Lao-Tze's term for it was "Tao;" Emerson refers to it as "The Over-Soul," and Dr. Bucke calls it "Cosmic Consciousness" in his valuable work bearing that title.

The ordinary human consciousness is *self-consciousness*. Self, the personality, is placed before everything else; there are ceaseless anxieties and fears concerning the self; its possible loss is thought to be the most grievous calamity, and its eternal preservation the most important thing in the universe.

In divine consciousness all this has passed away. Self has disappeared, therefore there can be no more fears and anxieties concerning the self, and things are considered and known as they are, and not as they afford pleasure or cause pain to self, not as self wishes them to be for its own temporal or eternal happiness.

The self-conscious man is subject to desire; the divinely conscious man is master of desire. The former considers what is pleasant or unpleasant; the latter acts from the righteous law without reference to pleasure or pain.

The race is passing through self-consciousness to divine consciousness; through the slavery of self, with its sense of sin and shame, to the freedom of Truth, with its sense of purity and power. The Great Teachers and Saviours of the race have already attained. In former existences they have passed through all forms of self-consciousness, and now, having subjugated self have become divinely conscious. They have reached the summit of evolution on this earth, and have no further need to be re-born in the self-conscious form. They are Masters of Life. Having conquered self, they have acquired the Supreme Knowledge. Some of them are worshipped as God because they manifest a wisdom and a consciousness which is quite distinct from the normal self-consciousness of humanity, and which is therefore regarded with, and surrounded by, incomprehenisbie mystery. Yet in this divine consciousness there is no mystery, but, on the contrary, a transparent simplicity which becomes apparent when the confusions of self are dispersed.

The abiding gentleness, the sublime wisdom, the perfect calm of the Great Teachers—qualities which appear supernatural when viewed from the self-conscious state—are seen to be simple and natural when the first glimmering of divine consciousness dawns in the mind; and such divine consciousness does not appear until a high degree of morality is attained by self-conscious man.

Man becomes divinely conscious, divinely wise, divinely gentle and strong in the measure that he subdues and dominates, in himself, those passions by which humanity is subdued and dominated. He only is the divine master who is master of himself. The abiding nobility, beneficent characteristics, and unobtrusive virtue which mark off the spiritually enlightened man from his fellows, are the fruits of self-conquest, the logical outcome of a long struggle to master and comprehend those mental forces which self-conscious man blindly obeys without understanding.

Self-conscious man is man the slave. He obeys his inclinations and is in submission to his passions, and to the sorrows and pains which his allegiance to those passions inflicts upon him. He is conscious of sin and sorrow, but sees no way out of these conditions; and so he invents theologies which he substitutes for effort, and which, while affording him fitful comfort through uncertain hope, leave him the easy victim of sin, and the willing subject of sorrow.

Divinely conscious man is man the master. He obeys Truth, and not self. He curbs and directs his inclinations, is conscious of a growing power over sin and sorrow, and sees that there is a way out of these conditions by the path of self-mastery. He needs no theologies to aid him, but exerts himself in right-doing, and is gladdened by a sense of victory and increasing purity and power. When his mastery is complete, he has no inclinations but those which accord with Truth; he has then become the conqueror of sin, and is no longer subject to sorrow.

Enlightened, wise and evermore peaceful and happy is he who has subjected, overcome, and cast out the turbulent self that reigned within him; the tempests of sorrow do not chill him; the cares and troubles which beset man pass him by, and no evil thing overtakes him. Secure in divine virtue, no enemy can overthrow him; no foe can do him harm. Benign and peaceful, no person, power, nor place can rob him of repose.

Man has no enemy but self, no darkness but ignorance, no suffering but that which springs from the insubordinate elements of his own nature.

No man is truly wise who is involved in likes and dislikes, wishes and regrets, desires and disappointments, sins and sorrows. All these conditions belong to the self-conscious state, and are indications of folly, weakness, and subjection.

He is truly wise who, in the midst of his worldly duties, is always calm, always gentle, always patient; who accepts things as they are, and does no wish and grieve, desire and regret. These things belong to the divinely conscious state, the dominion of Truth, and are indications of enlightenment, strength, and mastery.

He who does not desire riches, or fame, or pleasures; who enjoys what he has, yet does not lament when it is taken from him, he is indeed wise.

He who desires riches and fame, and pleastres; who is discontended with what he has, yet laments when it is taken from him, he is indeed foolish.

Man is fitted for conquest, but the conquest of territory will not avail; he must resort to the conquest of self. The conquest of territory renders man a temporal ruler, but the conquest of self makes him an eternal conqueror.

Man is destined for mastery; not the mastery of his fellow-men by force, but the mastery of his own nature by self-control. The mastery of his fellow-men by force is the crown of egotism, but the mastery of self by self-control is the crown of humility.

He is man the master who has shaken off the service of self for the service of Truth, who has established himself in the Eternal Verities. He is crowned, not only with perfect manhood, but with divine wisdom. He has overcome the disturbances of the mind and the shocks of life. He is superior to all circumstances. He is the calm spectator, but no longer the helpless tool, of events. No more a sinning, weeping, repenting mortal, he is pure, rejoicing, erect, immortal. He perceives the course of things with a glad and peaceful heart; a divine conqueror, master of life and death.

KNOWLEDGE AND VICTORY

Faith is the beginning of the Triumphant Life, but knowledge is its consummation. Faith reveals the way, but knowledge is the goal. Faith suffers many afflictions; knowledge has transcended affliction. Faith endures; knowledge loves. Faith walks in darkness, but *believes;* knowledge acts in light, and *knows.* Faith inspires to effort; knowledge crowns effort with success. "Faith is the substance of things hoped for;" knowledge is the substance of things possessed. Faith is the helpful staff of the pilgrim; knowledge is the City of Refuge at his journey's end. Without faith there will be no knowledge, but when knowledge is acquired, the work of faith is finished.

The Life Triumphant is a life of knowledge; and by knowledge is meant, not book-learning, but life-knowing; not superficial facts committed to memory, but the deep facts and truths of life grasped and comprehended. Apart from this knowledge there is no victory for man, no rest for his weary feet, no refuge for his aching heart. There is no salvation for the foolish except by becoming wise; there is no salvation for the sinful except by becoming pure; there is no liberation for man from the turmoils and troubles of life but through divine knowledge reached by the pathway of a pure and blameless life. Nowhere is there permanent peace except in an enlightened condition of mind; and a pure life and an enlightened mind are identical.

But there *is* salvation for the foolish because wisdom can be acquired; there, is salvation for the sinful because purity can be embraced; there is liberation for all men from the troubles and tur-moils of life because whosoever wills to do so—whether rich or poor, learned or unlearned—can enter the lowly way of blamelessness which leads to perfect knowledge. And because of this—that there is deliverance for the captives and victory for the defeated—there is rejoicing in the High Places, and the universe is glad.

The man of knowledge, being victorious over himself, is victorious over sin, over evil, over all the inharmonies of life. Out of the old mind marred by sin and sorrow, be has framed a new mind glori-fied by purity and peace. He has died out of the old world of evil, and is reborn in a new world where love and faultless law prevail, where evil is not, and he has become deathless in immortal Good.

Anxiety and fear, grief and lamentation, disappointment and regret, wretchedness and remorse—these things have no part in the world of the wise. They are the shadowy inhabitants of the world of self, and cannot live, nay, they are seen to have no substantiality—in the light of wisdom. The dark things of life are the dark conditions of a mind not yet illuminated by the light of wisdom. They follow self as the shadow the substance. Where selfish desires go, there they follow; where sin is, there they are.

There is no rest in self; there is no light in self, and where the flames of turbulent passions and the fires of consuming desires are rife, the cool airs of wisdom and peace are not felt.

Safety and assurance, happiness and repose, satisfaction and contentment, joy and peace—these are the abiding possessions of the wise, earned by right of self-conquest, the results of righteous-ness, the wages of a blameless life.

The substance of a right life is enlightenment (knowledge), and the spirit of knowledge is peace. To be victorious over self in all the issues of life is to know life as it is in reality, and not as it appears in the nightmare of self; it is to be in peace in all passages, and not to be stricken with trouble and grief in the common happenings of life.

As the ripe scholar is no more troubled by incorrect work and lessons imperfectly done, and the painful reproof and punishment formerly inflicted by his teachers are left behind forever, so the perfected scholar in virtue, the wise man, the enlightened doer of righteousness, is no more troubled with wrong-doing and folly (which are merely the imperfectly accomplished lessons of life), and the scourgings of sorrow and remorse have passed away forever.

The skilled scholar has no more doubt or fear concerning his ability. He has overcome and dis-persed the ignorance of his intellect. He has attained to learning, and he *knows* that he has attained; and he so knows because, having undergone innumerable intellectual tests in the form of lessons and examinations, he has at last proved his skill by passing successfully through the severest tests of scholarship. And now he no longer fears, but rejoices when severe tests are applied to prove his ability. He is capable, confident, and glad.

Even so the skilled doer of righteousness is no more troubled with doubt and fear concerning his destiny. He has overcome and dispersed the ignorance of his heart. He has attained to wisdom, and he *knows* that he has attained; and he so knows because where he formerly failed and fell when tested by the wrong conduct of others, he now maintains his patience and calmness under the severest tests of accusation and reproof.

Herein is the glory and victory of divine knowledge, that, understanding the nature of deeds both good and bad, the enlightened doer of good deeds no longer suffers through the bad deeds of others. Their actions towards him can never cause him pain and sorrow, nor rob him of his peace. Having taken refuge in good, evil can no more reach or harm him. He returns good for evil, and overcomes the weakness of evil by the power of good.

The man who is involved in bad deeds imagines that the bad deeds of others are powerful to do him injury, are filled with grievous harm against him, and he is stung with pain and overwhelmed with sorrow, not for his own bad deeds (for these be does not see) but for the wrong deeds of others. Involved in ignorance, he has no spiritual strength, no refuge, and no abiding peace.

The man victorious over self is the true seer; not the seer of spirits or supernatural phenomena, for such seeing is narrow and illusory, but the seer of life as it is, both in its particular aspects and in its divine principles; the seer of the spiritual universe, of cosmic law, cosmic love, and cosmic liberty.

The man of knowledge and victory, who has shaken off the painful dreams of self, has awakened with a new vision which beholds a new and glorified universe. He is the seer of the Eternal, and is blessed with perfect love and endless peace. He is lifted far above all sordid desires, narrow aims, and selfish love and hate; and being so lifted up he perceives the lawful course of things, and does not grieve when overtaken by the inevitable. He is above the world of sorrow, not because he has become cold and cruel, but because he abides, in a love where no thought of self can enter, and where the well-being of others is all-in-all. He is sorrowless because he is selfless. He is serene because he knows that whatever he receives, it is good, and whatever is taken from him, that also is good. He has transmuted sorrow into love, and is filled with infinite tenderness and abounding compassion. His power is not violent, ambitious, worldly, but pure, peaceful, heavenly, and he is possessed of a hidden strength which knows how to stand and when to bend for the good of others and the world. He is a Teacher, though he speak but little; he is a Master, yet he has no desire to rule others; he is a Conqueror, but makes no attempt to subdue his fellowmen. He has become a conscious instrument for the outworking of cosmic law, and is an intelligent, enlightened power directing the evolution of the Race.

At this, the beginning of a new epoch, let the Good News again go forth throughout the world that there is purity for the sinful, comfort for the afflicted, healing for the broken-hearted, and triumph for the defeated. In your heart, O man! stained as it is with sin, and torn with conflicting desires, there is a place of power, a citadel of strength; you are the dwelling-place of the Supreme Good, and the Sceptre of Victory awaits you: deep in your consciousness is the High Seat of Empire. Arise O stricken one! ascend your kingly throne.

MORNING AND EVENING THOUGHTS

(1908)

Conquer thyself,
Then thou shalt know;
Climb to the high,
Leave thou the low.
Deliverance
Shall him entrance
Who strives with sins and sorrows,
tears and paina.
Till he attains.

—JAMES ALLEN

FIRST MORNING

In aiming at the life of blessedness, one of the simplest beginnings to be considered, and rightly made, is that which we all make every day—namely, the beginning of each day's life. There is a sense in which every day may be regarded as the beginning of a new life, in which one can think, act, and live newly, and in a wiser and better spirit. The right beginning of the day will be followed by cheerfulness permeating the household with a sunny influence, and the tasks and duties of the day will be undertaken in a strong and confident spirit, and the whole day will be well lived.

FIRST EVENING

There can be no progress, no achievement, without sacrifice, and a man's worldly success will be in the measure that he sacrifices his confused animal thoughts, and fixes his mind on the development of his plans, and on the strengthening of his resolution and self-reliance. And the higher he lifts his thoughts, the more manly, upright, and righteous he becomes, the greater will be his success, the more blessed and enduring will be his achievements.

SECOND MORNING

None but right acts can follow right thoughts; none but a right life can follow right acts; and by living a right life all blessedness is achieved.

Mind is the Master-power that moulds and makes.
And Man is Mind, and evermore he takes
The Tool of Thought, and, shaping what he wills,
Brings forth a thousand joys, a thousand ills;—
He thinks in secret, and it comes to pass;
Environment is but his looking-glass.

SECOND EVENING

Calmness of mind is one of the beautiful jewels of wisdom. A man becomes calm in the measure that he understands himself as a thought-evolved being . . . and as he develops a right understanding, and sees more and more clearly the internal relations of things by the action of cause and effect, he ceases to fret and fume, and worry and grieve, and remains poised, steadfast, serene.

THIRD MORNING

To follow, under all circumstances, the highest promptings within you; to be always true to the divine self; to rely upon the inward Voice, the inward Light, and to pursue your purpose with a fearless and restful heart, believing that the future will yield unto you the need of every thought and effort; knowing that the laws of the universe can never fail, and that your own will come back to you with mathematical exactitude—this is faith and the living of faith.

THIRD EVENING

Have a thorough understanding of your work, and let it be your own; and as you proceed, ever following the inward Guide, the infallible Voice, you will pass on from victory to victory, and will rise step by step to higher resting-places, and your ever-broadening outlook will gradually reveal to you the essential beauty and purpose of life. Self-purified, health will be yours; self-governed, power will be yours, and all that you do will prosper.

> And I may stand where health, success, and power
> Await my coming, if, each fleeting hour,
> I cling to love and patience; and abide
> With stainlessness; and never step aside
> From high integrity; so shall I see
> At last the land of immortality.

FOURTH MORNING

When the tongue is well controlled and wisely subdued; when selfish impulses and unworthy thoughts no longer rush to the tongue demanding utterance; when the speech has become harmless, pure, gracious, gentle, and purposeful, and no word is uttered but in sincerity and truth—then are the five steps in virtuous speech accomplished, then is the second great lesson in Truth learned and mastered.

Make pure thy heart, and thou wilt make thy life
Rich, sweet and beautiful.

FOURTH EVENING

Having clothed himself with humility, the first questions a man asks himself are:—"How am I acting toward others?" "What am I doing to others?" "How am I thinking of others?" "Are my thoughts of, and acts toward, others prompted by unselfish love?" As a man, in the silence of his soul, asks himself these searching questions, he will unerringly see where he has hitherto failed.

FIFTH MORNING

To dwell in love always and toward all is to live the true life, is to have Life itself. Knowing this, the good man gives up himself unreservedly to the Spirit of Love, and dwells in Love toward all, contending with none, condemning none, but loving all.

The Christ Spirit of Love puts an end, not only to all sin, but to all division and contention.

FIFTH EVENING

When sin and self are abandoned, the heart is restored to its imperishable Joy.

Joy comes and fills the self-emptied heart; it abides with the peaceful; its reign is with the pure.

Joy flees from the selfish, it deserts the quarrelsome; it is hidden from the impure.

Joy cannot remain with the selfish; it is wedded to Love.

SIXTH MORNING

In the pure heart there is no room left where personal judgments and hatreds can find lodgment, for it is filled to overflowing with tenderness and love; it sees no evil, and only as men succeed in seeing no evil in others will they become free from sin, and sorrow, and suffering.

> If men only understood
> That the heart that sins must sorrow,
> That the hateful mind to-morrow
> Reaps its barren harvest, weeping,
> Starving, resting not, nor sleeping;
> Tenderness would fill their being,
> They would see with Pity's seeing
>   If they only understood.

SIXTH EVENING

To stand face to face with truth; to arrive, after innumerable wanderings and pains, at wisdom and bliss; not to be finally defeated and cast out, but to ultimately triumph over every inward foe—such is man's divine destiny, such his glorious goal; and this, every saint, sage, and savior has declared.

A man only begins to be a man when he ceases to whine and revile, and commences to search for the hidden justice which regulates his life. And as he adapts his mind to that regulating factor, he ceases to accuse others as the cause of his condition, and builds himself up in strong and noble thoughts; ceases to kick against circumstances; but begins to use them as aids to his more rapid progress, and as a means of discovering the hidden powers and possibilities within himself.

SEVENTH MORNING

The will to evil and the will to good
Are both within thee, which wilt thou employ?
Thou knowest what is right and what is wrong,
Which wilt thou love and foster? which destroy?
Thou art the chooser of thy thoughts and deeds;
Thou art the maker of thine inward state;
The power is thine to be what thou wilt be;
Thou buildest Truth and Love, or lies and hate.

SEVENTH EVENING

The teaching of Jesus brings men back to the simple truth that righteousness, or *right-doing,* is entirely a matter of individual conduct, and not a mystical something apart from a man's thoughts and deeds.

Calmness and patience can become habitual by first grasping, through effort, a calm and patient thought, and then continuously thinking it, and living in it, until "use becomes second nature," and anger and impatience pass away for ever.

EIGHTH MORNING

Man is made or unmade by himself; in the armoury of thought he forges the weapons by which he destroys himself; he also fashions the tools with which he builds for himself heavenly mansions of joy and strength and peace. By the right choice and true application of thought man ascends to the Divine Perfection; by the abuse and wrong application of thought he descends below the level of the beast. Between these two extremes are all the grades of character, and man is their maker and master.

As a being of Power, Intelligence, and Love, and the lord of his own thoughts, man holds the key to every situation.

EIGHTH EVENING

Whatsoever you harbour in the inmost chambers of your heart will, sooner or later, by the inevitable law of reaction, shape itself in your outward life.

Every soul attracts its own, and nothing can possibly come to it that does not belong to it. To realize this is to recognize the universality of Divine Law.

If thou would'st right the world,
And banish all its evils and its woes.
Make its wild places bloom,
And its drear deserts blossom as the rose—
Then right thyself.

NINTH MORNING

Whatever conditions are rendering your life burdensome, you may pass out of and beyond them by developing and utilizing within you the transforming power of self-purification and self-conquest.

Before the divine radiance of a pure heart all darkness vanishes and all clouds melt away, and he who has conquered self has conquered the universe.

He who sets his foot firmly upon the path of self-conquest, who walks, aided by the staff of faith, the highway of self-sacrifice, will assuredly achieve the highest prosperity, and will reap abounding and enduring joy and bliss.

NINTH EVENING

It is the silent and conquering thought-forces which bring all things into manifestation. The universe grew out of thought.

To adjust all your thoughts to a perfect and unswerving faith in the omnipotence and supremacy of Good, is to co-operate with that Good, and to realize within yourself the solution and destruction of all evil.

To mentally deny evil is not sufficient; it must, by daily practice, be risen above and understood. To affirm the Good mentally is inadequate; it must, by unswerving endeavor, be entered into and comprehended.

TENTH MORNING

Every thought you think is a force sent out.

Whatever your position in life may be, before you can hope to enter into any measure of success, usefulness, and power, you must learn how to focus your thought-forces by cultivating calmness and repose.

There is no difficulty, however great, but will yield before a calm and purposeful concentration of thought, and no legitimate object but may be speedily actualized by the intelligent use and direction of one's soul-forces.

Think good thoughts, and they will quickly become actualized in your outward life in the form of good conditions.

TENTH EVENING

That which you would be and hope to be, you may be now. Non-accomplishment resides in your perpetual postponement, and, having the power to postpone, you also have the power to accomplish—to perpetually accomplish: Realize this truth, and you shall be to-day, and every day, the ideal being of whom you dreamed.

Say to yourself, "I will live in my Ideal now; I will manifest my Ideal now; I will be my Ideal now; and all that tempts me away from my Ideal I will not listen to; I will listen only to the voice of my Ideal."

ELEVENTH MORNING

Be as a flower, content to be, to grow in sweetness day by day.

If thou would'st perfect thyself in knowledge, perfect thyself in Love. If thou would'st reach the Highest, ceaselessly cultivate a loving and compassionate heart.

To him who choose Goodness, sacrificing all, is given that which is more than, and includes, all.

ELEVENTH EVENING

The Great Law never cheats any man of his just due.

Human life, when rightly lived, is simple with a beautiful simplicity.

He who comprehends the utter simplicity of life, who obeys its laws, and does not step aside into the dark paths and complex mazes of selfish desire, stands where no harm can reach him.

Then there is fulness of joy, abounding plenty, and rich and complete blessedness.

TWELFTH MORNING

Every man reaps the results of his own thoughts and deeds, and suffers for his own wrong.

He who begins right, and continues right, does not need to desire and search for felicitous results; they are already at hand; they follow as consequences; they are the certainties, the realities, of life.

Sweet is the rest and deep the bliss of him who has freed his heart from its lusts and hatreds and dark desires.

TWELFTH EVENING

You are the creator of your own shadows; you desire, and then you grieve; renounce, and then you shall rejoice.

Of all the beautiful truths pertaining to the soul, . . . none is more gladdening or fruitful of divine promise and confidence than this—that man is the master of thought, the moulder of character, and the maker and shaper of character, environment, and destiny.

THIRTEENTH MORNING

As darkness is a passing shadow, and light is substance that remains, so sorrow is fleeting, but joy abides for ever. No true thing can pass away and become lost; no false thing can remain and be preserved. Sorrow is false, and it can not live; Joy is true, and it can not die. Joy may become hidden for a time, but it can always be recovered; sorrow may remain for a period, but it can be transcended and dispersed.

Do not think your sorrow will remain; it will pass away like a cloud. Do not believe that the torments of sin are ever your portion; they will vanish like a hideous nightmare. Awake! Arise! Be holy and joyful.

THIRTEENTH EVENING

Tribulation lasts only so long as there remains some chaff of self which needs to be removed. The *tribulum,* or threshing machine, ceases to work when all the grain is separated from the chaff; and when the last impurities are blown away from the soul, tribulation has completed its work, and there is no more need for it; then abiding joy is realized.

The sole and supreme use of suffering is to purify, to burn out all that is useless and impure. Suffering ceases for him who is pure. There can be no object in burning gold after the dross had been removed.

FOURTEENTH MORNING

In speaking of self-control, one is easily misunderstood. It should not be associated with a destructive repression, but with a constructive expression.

A man is happy, wise and great in the measure that he controls himself; he is wretched, foolish, and mean in the measure that he allows his animal nature to dominate his thoughts and actions.

He who controls himself, controls his life, his circumstances, his destiny; and wherever he goes he carries his happiness with him as an abiding possession.

Renunciation precedes regeneration.

The permanent happiness which men seek in dissipation, excitement, and abandonment to unworthy pleasures, is found only in the life which reverses all this—the life of self-control.

FOURTEENTH EVENING

Law, not confusion, is the dominating principle in the universe; justice, not injustice, is the soul and substance of life; and righteousness, not corruption, is the moulding and moving force in the spiritual government of the world. This being so, man has but to right himself to find that the universe is right.

When I am pure,
I shall have solved the mystery of life;
I shall be sure,
When I am free from hatred, lust and strife,
I am in Truth, and Truth abides in me;
I shall be safe, and sane, and wholly free,
When I am pure.

FIFTEENTH MORNING

If men only understood.
That their hatred and resentment.
Slays their peace and sweet contentment
Hurts themselves, helps not another,
Does not cheer one lonely brother,
They would seek the better doing
Of good deeds which leaves no rueing—
If they only understood.

If men only understood
How Love conquers; how prevailing
Is its might, grim hate assailing;
How compassion endeth sorrow,
Maketh wise, and doth not borrow
Pain of passion, they would ever
Live in Love, in hatred never:—
If they only understood.

FIFTEENTH EVENING

The grace and beauty that were in Jesus can be of no value to you—cannot be understood by you—unless they are also *in you,* and they can never be in you, until you practice them, for, apart from *doing,* the qualities which constitute Goodness do not, as far as you are concerned, exist. To adore Jesus for his good qualities is a long step toward Truth, but to practice those qualities is Truth itself; and he who truly adores the perfection of another will not rest content in his own imperfection, but will fashion his soul after the likeness of that other.

Therefore thou who adorest Jesus for his divine qualities, practice those qualities thyself, and thou too shalt be divine.

SIXTEENTH MORNING

Let a man realize that life in its totality proceeds from the mind, and lo, the way of blessedness is opened up to him! For he will then discover that he possesses the power to rule his mind, and to fashion it in accordance with his Ideal. So will he elect to strongly and steadfastly walk those pathways of thought and action which are altogether excellent; to him life will become beautiful and sacred; and, sooner or later, he will put to flight all evil, confusion, and suffering; for it is impossible for a man to fall short of liberation, enlightenment, and peace, who guards with unwearying diligence the gateway of his heart.

SIXTEENTH EVENING

By constantly overcoming self, a man gains a knowledge of the subtle intricacies of his mind; and it is this divine knowledge which enables him to become established in calmness. Without self-knowledge there can be no abiding peace of mind, and those who are carried away by tempestuous passions, cannot approach the holy place where calmness reigns. The weak man is like one who, having mounted a fiery steed, allows it to run away with him, and carry him whithersoever it wills; the strong main is like one who, having mounted the steed, governs it with a masterly hand, and makes it go in whatever direction and at whatever speed he commands.

SEVENTEENTH MORNING

There is no strife, no selfishness, in the Kingdom; there is perfect harmony, equipoise, and rest. Those who live in the Kingdom of Love, have all their needs supplied by the Law of Love. As self is the root cause of all strife and suffering, so Love is the root cause of all peace and bliss.

Those who are at rest in the Kingdom, do not look for happiness in any outward possessions. They are freed from all anxiety and trouble, and resting in Love, they are the embodiment of happiness.

SEVENTEENTH EVENING

Let it not be supposed that the children of the Kingdom live in ease and indolence (these two sins are the first that have to be eradicated when the search for the Kingdom is entered upon); they live in a peaceful activity; in fact, they only truly live, for the life of self, with its train of worries, griefs, and fears, is not *real life*.

The children of the Kingdom are *known by their life,* they manifest the fruits of the Spirit— "Love, joy, peace, long-suffering, kindness, goodness, faithfulness, meekness, temperance, self-control"—under all circumstances and all vicissitudes.

EIGHTEENTH MORNING

The gospel of Jesus is a gospel of *living and doing.* If it were not this it would not voice the Eternal Truth. Its Temple is *Purified Conduct,* the entrance-door to which is *Self-Surrender.* It invites men to shake off sin, and promises, as a result, joy and blessedness and perfect peace.

The Kingdom of Heaven is perfect trust, perfect knowledge, perfect peace. . . . No sin can enter therein, no self-born thought or deed can pass its golden gates; no impure desire can defile its radiant robes. . . . All may enter it who will, but all must pay the price—*the unconditional abandonment of self.*

EIGHTEENTH EVENING

I say this—and know it to be truth—*that circumstances can only affect you in so far as you allow them to do so.* You are swayed by circumstances because you have not a right understanding of the nature, use, and power of thought. You believe (and upon this little word *belief* hang all our joys and sorrows) that outward things have the power to make or mar your life; by so doing you submit to those outward things, confess that you are their slave, and they your unconditional master. By so doing you invest them with a power which they do not of themselves possess, and you succumb, in reality not to the circumstances, but to the gloom or gladness, the fear or hope, the strength or weakness, which your thought-sphere has thrown around them.

NINETEENTH MORNING

If you are one of those who are praying for, and looking forward to, a happier world beyond the grave, here is a message of gladness for you—you may enter into and realize that happy world now; it fills the whole universe, and it is within you, waiting for you to find, acknowledge, and possess. Said one who understood the inner laws of Being—"When men shall say, lo here, or lo there, go not after them. The Kingdom of God is within you."

NINETEENTH EVENING

Heaven and hell are inward states. Sink into self and all its gratifications, and you sink into hell; rise above self into that state of consciousness which is the utter denial and forgetfulness of self and you enter Heaven.

So long as you persist in selfishly seeking for your own personal happiness, so long will happiness elude you, and you will be sowing the seeds of wretchedness. In so far as you succeed in losing yourself in the service of others, in that measure will happiness come to you, and you will reap a harvest of bliss.

TWENTIETH MORNING

Sympathy given can never be wasted.

One aspect of sympathy is that of pity—pity for the distressed or pain-stricken, with a desire to alleviate or help them in their sufferings. The world needs more of this divine quality.

> For pity makes the world
> Soft to the weak, and noble for the strong.

Another form of sympathy is that of rejoicing with others who are more successful than ourselves, as though their success were our own.

TWENTIETH EVENING

Sweet are companionships, pleasures, and material comforts, but they change and fade away. Sweeter still are Purity, Wisdom, and the knowledge of Truth, and these never change nor fade away.

He who has attained to the possession of spiritual things can never be deprived of his source of happiness; he will never have to part company with it, and wherever he goes in the whole universe, he will carry his possessions with him. His spiritual end will be the fulness of joy.

TWENTY-FIRST MORNING

Let your heart grow and expand with ever-broadening love, until, freed from all hatred, and passion, and condemnation, it embraces the whole universe with thoughtful tenderness. As the flower opens its petals to receive the morning light, so open your soul more and more to the glorious light of Truth. Soar upward on the wings of aspiration; be fearless, and believe in the loftiest possibilities.

TWENTY-FIRST EVENING

Mind clothes itself in garments of its own making.

Mind is the arbiter of life; it is the creator and shaper of conditions, and the recipient of its own results. It contains within itself both the power to create illusion and to perceive reality.

Mind is the infallible weaver of destiny; thought is the thread, good and evil deeds are the warp and woof; and the web, woven upon the loom of life, is character.

Make pure thy heart, and thou wilt make thy life
Rich, sweet, and beautiful, unmarred by strife.

TWENTY-SECOND MORNING

Cherish your visions; cherish your ideals; cherish the music that stirs in your heart, the beauty that forms in your mind, the loveliness that drapes your purest thoughts, for out of them will grow all delightful conditions, all heavenly environment; of these, if you will remain true to them, your world will at last be built.

> Guard well thy mind, and, noble, strong, and free,
> Nothing shall harm, disturb or conquer thee;
> For all thy foes are in thy heart and mind,
> There also thy salvation thou shalt find.

TWENTY-SECOND EVENING

Dream lofty dreams, and as you dream so shall you become. Your vision is the promise of what you shall one day be; your Ideal is the prophecy of what you shall at last unveil.

The greatest achievement was at first and for a time a dream. The oak sleeps in the acorn; the bird waits in the egg; and in the highest vision of the soul a waking angel stirs.

Your circumstances may be uncongenial, but they shall not long remain so when you perceive an Ideal and strive to reach it.

TWENTY-THIRD MORNING

He who has conquered doubt and fear has conquered failure. His every thought is allied with power, and all difficulties are bravely met and wisely overcome. His purposes are seasonably planted, and they bloom and bring forth fruit which does not fell prematurely to the ground.

Thought allied fearlessly to purpose becomes creative force: he who knows this is ready to become something higher and stronger than a mere bundle of wavering thoughts and fluctuating sensations; he who does this has become the conscious and intelligent wielder of his mental powers.

TWENTY-THIRD EVENING

Man's true place in the Cosmos is that of a king, not a slave, a commander under the Law of Good, and not a helpless tool in the reign of evil.

I write for men, not for babes; for those who are eager to learn, and earnest to achieve; for those who will put away (for the world's good) a petty personal indulgence, a selfish desire, a mean thought, and live on as though it were not, sans craving and regret.

Man is a master. If he were not, he could not act contrary to law.

Evil and weakness are self destructive.

The universe is girt with goodness and strength, and it protects the good and the strong.

The angry man is the weak man.

TWENTY-FOURTH MORNING

Not by learning will a man triumph over evil; not by much study will he overcome sin and sorrow. Only by conquering himself will he conquer evil; only by practising righteousness will he put an end to sorrow.

Not for the clever, nor the learned, nor the self-confident is the Life Triumphant, but for the pure, the virtuous and wise. The former achieve their particular success in life, but the latter alone achieve the great success so invincible and complete that even in apparent defeat it shines with added victory.

TWENTY-FOURTH EVENING

The true silence is not merely a silent tongue; it is a silent mind. To merely *hold one's tongue*, and yet to carry about a disturbed and rankling mind, is no remedy for weakness, and no source of power. Silentness, to be powerful, must envelop the whole mind, must permeate every chamber of the heart; it must be the silence of peace. To this broad, deep, abiding silentness a man attains only in the measure that he conquers himself.

TWENTY-FIFTH MORNING

By curbing his tongue, a man gains possession of his mind. The fool babbles, gossips, argues, and bandies words. He glories in the fact that he has had the last word, and has silenced his opponent. He exults in his own folly, is ever on the defensive, and wastes his energies in unprofitable channels. He is like a gardener who continues to dig and plant in unproductive soil.

The wise man avoids idle words, gossip, vain argument, and self-defence. He is content to appear defeated; rejoices when he is defeated; knowing that, having found and removed another error in himself he has thereby become wiser.

Blessed is he who does not strive for the last word.

TWENTY-FIFTH EVENING

Desire is *the craving for possession;* aspiration is the *hunger of the heart for peace.* The craving things leads ever farther and farther from peace, and not only ends in deprivation, but is in itself a state of perpetual want. Until it comes to an end, rest and satisfaction are impossible. The hunger for things can never be satisfied, but the hunger for peace can, and the satisfaction of peace is found—is fully possessed, when all selfish desire is abandoned. Then there is fulness of joy, abounding plenty, and rich and complete blessedness.

TWENTY-SIXTH MORNING

A man will reach the Kingdom by purifying himself, and he can only do this by pursuing a process of self-examination and self-analysis. The selfishness must be discovered and understood before it can be removed. It is powerless to remove itself, neither will it pass away of itself. Darkness ceases only when light is introduced; so ignorance can only be dispersed by knowledge, selfishness by love. A man must first of all be willing to lose himself (his self-seeking) before he can find himself (his Divine Self). He must realize that selfishness is not worth clinging to, that it is a master altogether unworthy of his service, and that divine goodness alone is worthy to be enthroned in his heart, as the supreme master of his life.

TWENTY-SIXTH EVENING

Be still my soul, and know that peace is thine.
Be steadfast, heart, and know that strength divine
Belongs to thee; cease from thy turmoil, mind,
And thou the Everlasting Rest shalt find.

If a man would have peace, let him exercise the spirit of peace; if he would find Love, let him dwell in the spirit of Love; if he would escape suffering, let him cease to inflict it; if he would do noble things for humanity, let him cease to do ignoble things for himself. If he will but quarry the mine of his own soul, he shall find there all the materials for building whatsoever he will, and he shall find there also the Central Rock on which to build in safety.

TWENTY-SEVENTH MORNING

Men go after much company, and seek out new excitements, but they are not acquainted with peace; in divers paths of pleasure they search for happiness, but they do not come to rest; through diverse ways of laughter and feverish delirium they wander after gladness and life, but their tears are many and grievous, and they do not escape death.

Drifting upon the ocean of life in search of selfish indulgences, men are caught in its storms, and only after many tempests and much privation do they fly to the Rock of Refuge which rests in the deep silence of their own being.

TWENTY-SEVENTH EVENING

Meditation centered upon divine realities is the very essence and soul of prayer. It is the silent reaching upward of the soul toward the Eternal.

Meditation is the intense dwelling, in thought, upon an idea or theme with the object of thoroughly comprehending it; and whatsoever you constantly meditate upon, you will not only come to understand, but will grow more and more into its likeness, for it will become incorporated with your very being, will become, in fact, your very self. If, therefore, you constantly dwell upon that which is selfish and debasing, you will ultimately become selfish and debased; if you ceaselessly think upon that which is pure and unselfish, you will surely become pure and unselfish.

TWENTY-EIGHTH MORNING

There is no difficulty, however great, but will yield before a calm and powerful concentration of thought, and no legitimate object but may be speedily actualized by the intelligent use and direction of one's soul forces.

Whatever your task may be, concentrate your whole mind upon it; throw into it all the energy of which you are capable. The faultless completion of small tasks leads inevitably to larger tasks. See to it that you rise by steady climbing, and you will never fall.

TWENTY-EIGHTH EVENING

He who knows that Love is at the heart of all things, and has realized the all-sufficing power of that Love, has no room in his heart for condemnation.

If you love people, and speak of them with praise, until they in some way thwart you, or do something of which you disapprove, and then you dislike them and speak of them with dispraise, you are not governed by the Love which is of God. If, in your heart, you are continually arraigning and condemning others, selfless love is hidden from you.

Train your mind in strong, impartial, and gentle thought; train your heart in purity and compassion; train your tongue to silence, and to true and stainless speech; so shall you enter the way of holiness and peace, and shall ultimately realize the immortal Love.

TWENTY-NINTH MORNING

If you would realize true prosperity, do not settle down, as many have done, into the belief that if you do right everything will go wrong. Do not allow the word "competition" to shake your faith in the supremacy of righteousness. I care not what men may say about the "laws of competition," for do not I know the Unchangeable Law which shall one day put them all to rout, and which puts them to rout even now in the heart and life of the righteous man? And knowing this law I can contemplate all dishonesty with undisturbed repose, for I know where certain destruction awaits it.

Under all circumstances do *that which you believe to be right*, and trust the Law; trust the Divine Power which is immanent in the universe, and it will never desert you, and you will always be protected.

TWENTY-NINTH EVENING

Forget yourself entirely in the sorrows of others, in ministering to others, and divine happiness will emancipate you from all sorrow and suffering. "Taking the first step with a good thought, the second with a good word, and the third with a good deed, I entered Paradise." And you also enter Paradise by pursuing the same course.

Lose yourself in the welfare of others; forget yourself in all that you do—this is the secret of abounding happiness. Ever be on the watch to guard against selfishness, and learn faithfully the divine lessons of inward sacrifice; so shall you climb the highest heights of happiness, and shall remain in the never-clouded sunshine of universal joy, clothed in the shining garment of immortality.

THIRTIETH MORNING

When the farmer has tilled and dressed his land and put in the seed, he knows that he has done all that he can possibly do, and that now he must trust to the elements, and wait patiently for the course of time to bring about the harvest, and that no amount of expectancy on his part will affect the result. Even so, he who has realized Truth, goes forth as a sower of the seeds of goodness, purity, love, and peace, without expectancy, and never looking for results, knowing that there is the Great Over-ruling Law which brings about its own harvest in due time, and which is alike the source of preservation and destruction.

THIRTIETH EVENING

The virtuous put a check upon themselves, and set a watch upon their passions and emotions; in this way they gain possession of the mind, and gradually acquire calmness; and as they acquire influence, power, greatness, abiding joy, and fulness and completeness of life.

He only finds peace who conquers himself, who strives, day by day, after greater self-possession, greater self-control, greater calmness of mind.

Where the calm mind is, there is strength and rest, there is love and wisdom; there is one who has fought successfully innumerable battles against self, who, after long toil in secret against his own failings, has triumphed at last.

THIRTY-FIRST MORNING

Sympathy bestowed increases its store in our own hearts, and enriches and fructifies our own life. Sympathy given is blessedness received; sympathy withheld is blessedness forfeited. In the measure that a man increases and enlarges his sympathy, so much nearer does he approach the ideal life, the perfect blessedness; and when his heart has become so mellowed that no hard, bitter, or cruel thought can enter and detract from its permanent sweetness, then indeed is he richly and divinely blessed.

THIRTY-FIRST EVENING

Sweet is the rest and deep the bliss of him who has freed his heart from its lusts and hatreds and dark desires; and he who, without any shadow of bitterness resting upon him, and looking out upon the world with boundless compassion and love, can breathe, in his inmost heart, the blessing:

Peace unto all living things,

making no exceptions or distinctions—such a man has reached that happy ending which can never be taken away, for this is the perfection of life, the fulness of peace, the consummation of perfect blessedness.

THROUGH THE GATE

OF GOOD

(1908)

CONTENTS

FOREWORD

The series of articles which comprise this book appeared in serial form in the third volume of "The Light of Reason," and it is in compliance with the earnest request of readers and the importunities of friends that I now reprint them in book form.

The articles are reprinted as they were originally published, with the addition of the Introduction.

—James Allen

INTRODUCTION

The genius of the present age in matters spiritual is toward simplicity, and the hunger of the human heart is for Truth, naked and uninvolved. That hunger will eventually bring about (is already bringing about) its own satisfaction, and here and there are men and women who, passing through the gateway of self-conquest, are entering into possession of the transcendent righteousness.

The closing years of the nineteenth century witnessed the culmination of formalism, and the spiritual reaction is now firmly established. Already

> *the end*
> *Of old faiths and beginning of the new*

is discernible to all who have removed from their mental vision somewhat of the textual dust of dying creeds, and have penetrated, however faintly, that sublime region of Truth which is discoverable only by practice, and which is made manifest by pure thoughts and holy deeds.

The universal decay of effete religious systems which the world is witnessing today is matter for rejoicing; it is the death which precedes life; it is the passing away of the false in order that the true may be more fully revealed. The true can, at worst, but remain hidden. It endures. It remains forever. Its invincibility cannot be qualified, and he who has had but one momentary glimpse of the true can never again be anxious for its safety. That about which men are anxious is the false, which they mistake for the true, and this, in spite of all their anxiety, must fade away at last.

In the lives of all the great teachers we see a manifestation of that universal truth, the majesty and splendor of which is as yet but dimly comprehended by mankind, but which must, during the gradual transformation and transmutation which the accumulating ages shall effect, at last become the possession of all. That Truth, as manifested by the teachers, was written by them, as it only can be written, in thoughts and deeds of the loftiest moral excellence which have been permanently impressed upon the mind of mankind by their embodiment in preceptial form. It is to the sweet lives and inspiring words of these mighty teachers that the eyes of a hungering and thirsting world are again being turned, and the light of life is being lighted up, the world over, in hearts that are ready to attune themselves to the eternal song of love and peace. What religions have failed to do, religion will accomplish: what the priest has obscured, the Spirit of truth in the heart of man will make plain, and the world is now finding spiritual healing and refreshment in turning away from traditional and historic accretions, and going back to the pure fountain of Truth as revealed so simply, clearly, and beautifully by blameless teachers, and which has its inexhaustible spring within themselves.

To aid men and women (more particularly those in Christian countries) to find this abiding Truth more speedily, these articles, setting forth the life and precepts of Jesus, were written. Formalism and self are heavy burdens to carry, and in directing the minds of men to blamelessness of conduct and purity of heart, I know I can leave the result with the supreme law, and that there are those who will read and, having read, will pass from the burdensome complexities of ignorance and formalism to the joyful simplicity of enlightenment and Truth.

—James Allen

I

THE GATE AND THE WAY

Strait *is* the gate, and narrow *is* the way, which leadeth unto life: and few there be that find it.

—JESUS

A good man out of the good treasure of the heart bringeth forth good things.

—JESUS

The supreme aim of all religions is to teach men how to live; and the learning and the living are religion itself. The purification of the human heart, the building up of a blameless life, and the perfecting of the soul, these are the great underlying and enduring factors in all religions and creeds the world over. That which is vital in every religion is the striving after and the practice of goodness; all things else are accretions, superfluities, illusions. Goodness—and by goodness I mean sinlessness—is the beautiful and imperishable form of religion, but creeds and religions are the perishable garments, woven of the threads of opinion, in which men clothe it. One after another religions come and go, but Religion, being Life itself, endures forever. Let men cease to quarrel over the garments and strive to perceive the universality and beauty of the indwelling form; thus will they become wedded to it, will become one with the supreme goodness. Religion is goodness; goodness is religion.

We know nothing higher than goodness. We can conceive of nothing more beautiful than goodness. Beholding the perfect goodness, men call it God. Seeing that goodness practiced by man, men worship him as God.

We behold Jesus as a sinless man; in him is the perfect goodness revealed, not obscurely and metaphysically, but in all his words and deeds; and it is by virtue of his sinlessness that he is accepted as an exemplar and universal teacher.

The teachers of mankind are few. A thousand years may pass by without the advent of such a one; but when the true teacher does appear, the distinguishing feature by which he is known is his life. His conduct is different from that of other men, and his teaching is never derived from any man or book, but from his own life. The teacher first lives, and then teaches others how they may likewise live. The proof and witness of his teaching is in himself, his life. Out of millions of preachers, one only is ultimately accepted by mankind as the true teacher, and the one who is thus accepted and exalted is *he who lives*. All the others are mere disquisitionaries and commentators, and as such they rapidly pass out of human ken.

Jesus, the teacher, lived, in all its perfection and in the face of the most adverse conditions, the divine life of love; he pursued the true life of good will, as distinguished from the false life of self-seeking, which the majority elect to follow. In him there was no element of selfishness, all his thoughts, words, and acts being prompted by the Spirit of love. To this Spirit of love he so entirely subjected his personality that he became one with it, so much so that he literally became divine love personified. His complete victory over the personality was accomplished by obedience to the divine law of love within himself, by virtue of which he became divine; and his whole teaching is to the effect that all who will practice the same obedience will realize the same divine life, will become consciously divine.

The unalterable meekness, undying compassion, sweet forgiveness, and unending love and patience of Jesus are the themes of a thousand hymns, the subjects of millions of heartfelt prayers; and this is so because those qualities are recognized everywhere and by all men as being distinctively divine. To make the practice of these qualities the chief object of life constitutes religion; to deny them, and to continue to live in their selfish opposites—pride, condemnation, harshness, hatred, and anger—constitutes irreligion.

Men everywhere, in their inmost hearts, though they may deny it argumentatively, know that goodness is divine; and Jesus is worshiped as God, not for any claim he made, nor because of any miraculous circumstance connected with his life, but because he never departed from the perfect goodness, the faultless love. "God is love, love is God." Man knows no God except love manifesting in the human heart and life in the form of stainless thoughts, blameless words, and deeds of gentle pity and forgiveness; and he can only know this God in the measure that he has realized love in his own heart by self-subjugation. The God which forms the subject of theological argument, and whose existence or nonexistence men are so eager to prove, is the God of hypothesis and speculation. He who, by overcoming self, has found, dwelling within him, the supreme love, knows that that love is far beyond the reach of all selfish argument and can *only be lived;* and he lives, leaving vain argument to those who wilt not come up higher.

Having, by obedience, entered into full possession of the divine life, Jesus gave to the world certain spiritual rules, by the observance of which all men could become sons of God, could live the perfect life. These rules or precepts are so simple, direct, and unmistakable that it is impossible to misunderstand them. So plain and unequivocal are they that even an unlettered child could grasp their meaning without difficulty. All of them are directly related to human conduct, and can be applied only by the individual in his own life. To carry out the spirit of these rules in one's daily conduct constitutes the whole duty of life, and lifts the individual into the full consciousness of his divine origin and nature, of his oneness with God, the Supreme Good. It is here, however, where the difficulty arises, for, although there are millions of men and women worshiping Jesus as God in a miraculous or metaphysical sense, there are really very few who believe in his precepts, and who attempt to carry them out in their lives. In the precepts themselves there can be no difficulty or misunderstanding; all this lies in the unbelief of those who read the precepts. Men do not carry out the precepts of Jesus because they do not believe it possible to do so, and so they never try; whilst there are others who, though believing it possible and necessary to carry them out, are not willing to make the personal sacrifices which those precepts demand. Yet, apart from the earnest striving to live out the teachings of Jesus there can be no true life. Merely to call Jesus "Lord" does not constitute discipleship, but to weave his words into the fabric of one's life, to put into execution his divine and self-perfecting precepts, this, and this only, constitutes discipleship.

Let it be understood thus early that with the almost innumerable creeds which have been built upon the Hebrew scriptures, I have absolutely nothing to do. I have to do entirely with the life and teaching of Jesus, and with the vital realities in the human heart to which that teaching is directed. I have to do with goodness, not with speculation; with love, not with theological theories; with self-perfection, not with fleeting opinions.

Jesus was a supremely good man; this all men know, and to know this is all-embracing and all-sufficient. He has left precepts which, if a man will guide his conduct by them, will lead him unerringly to the supreme goodness; to know this is gladdening and glorious.

A good man is the flower of humanity, and to daily grow purer, nobler, more Godlike, by overcoming some selfish tendency, is to be drawing continually nearer to the divine heart. "He that would be my disciple let him deny himself daily," is a statement which none can misunderstand or misapply, howsoever he may ignore it. Nowhere in the universe is there any substitute for goodness, and until a man has this he has nothing worthy or enduring. To the possession of goodness there is only one way, and that is *to give up all and everything that is opposed to goodness*. Every selfish desire must be eradicated; every impure thought must be yielded up; every clinging to opinion must be sacrificed; and it is the doing of this that constitutes the following of Christ. That which is above all creeds, beliefs, and opinions is a loving and self-sacrificing heart. The life of Jesus is a demonstration of this truth, and all his teaching is designed to bring about this holy and supreme consummation.

To dwell in love always and toward all is to live the true life, is to have life itself. Jesus so lived, and all men may so live if they will humbly and faithfully carry out his precepts. So long as they refuse to do this, clinging to their desires, passions, and opinions, they cannot be ranked as his disciples— they are the disciples of self. "Verily, verily, I say unto you: whosoever committeth sin is the servant of sin," is the searching declaration of Jesus. Let men cease to delude themselves with the belief that they can retain their bad tempers, their lusts, their harsh words and judgments, their personal hatreds, their petty contentions, and daring opinions, and yet have Christ. All that divides man from man, and man from goodness is not of Christ, for Christ is love. To continue to commit sin is to be a doer of sin, a follower of self, and not a doer of righteousness and a follower of Christ. Sin and Christ cannot dwell together, and he who accepts the Christ life of pure goodness ceases from sin. To follow Christ means to give up all, in our mind and conduct, that antagonizes the spirit of love; and this, we shall find as we proceed, necessitates complete self-surrender, refusing to harbor any thought that is not pure, compassionate, and gentle. The Christ Spirit of love puts an end, not only to all sin, but to all division, and contention. If I contend for an opinion, say, about the divinity of Jesus Christ, against the opinion of another as to his nondivinity, I at once create division and strife, and depart from the Christ, the spirit of love. When Christ is disputed about, Christ is lost. It is no less selfish and sinful to cling to opinion than to cling to impure desire. Knowing this, the good man gives up himself unreservedly to the Spirit of love, and dwells in love toward all, contending with none, condemning none, hating none, but loving all, seeing behind their opinions, their creeds, and their sins, into their striving, suffering, and sorrowing hearts. "He that loveth his life shall lose it." Eternal life belongs to him who will obediently relinquish his petty, narrowing, sin-loving, strife-producing personal self, for only by so doing can he enter into the large, beautiful, free, and glorious life of abounding love. Herein is the path of life; for the strait gate is the gate of goodness, and the narrow way is the way of renunciation, or self-sacrifice. So strait is the gate that no sin can pass through, and so narrow is the way that he who essays to walk it can take with him no selfish thought as his companion.

II

THE LAW AND THE PROPHETS

Therefore all things whatsoever ye would that men should do to you, do ye even so to them: for this is the law and the prophets.

—JESUS

If thou wilt enter into life, keep the commandments.

—JESUS

The commandments and precepts of Jesus were given to men to be kept. This is so simple and self-evident a truth that there ought to be no necessity to state it; yet, after the precepts of Jesus have been before the world for nearly nineteen hundred years, this necessity not only exists, but is very great, so widespread is the belief that the tasks embodied in the precepts are not only utterly impracticable, but altogether impossible of human accomplishment. This disbelief in the possibility of carrying out the divine commands is the primary delusion, due to ignorance, in which men are caught, and it is impossible for any man to comprehend spiritual things until he destroys it.

The words of Jesus are the direct outcome of an intimate knowledge of divine law, and his every utterance is in harmonious relationship with the eternal substance. This a man finds as he molds the spiritual life contained in those words into his own life—that is, as he succeeds in living the precepts.

Let us now examine these precepts and see how they are to be carried out and what they imply and involve. Most of them are embodied in the Sermon on the Mount, and all of them are directly related to individual conduct, so that there are only two possible ways of dealing with them, namely, to practice them, or to ignore them.

It is not necessary for me to refer to them all separately, as not only have my readers the Bible at their command, but each precept is based upon the same divine principle, and to learn the spirit of one is to know the spirit of them all. Indeed, seeing that not only all the precepts, but that the whole duty of life in its human and divine relationship has been embodied in the seventeen words, "all things whatsoever ye would that men should do to you, do ye even so to them," it is only necessary to refer to the other precepts in order to elucidate the carrying out of this one, for in learning this one precept, the whole range of spiritual life and knowledge is involved: "This is the law and the prophets."

The precept is extremely simple; this is why men have failed to understand it and to put it into effect. Its application, however, to the soul of the individual leaves no room for selfishness and self-compromise, and so comprehensive is it that to carry it out in its entirety means the attainment of Christlike perfection of character. But before a man can put it into practice, *he must strive to understand it*, and even this initial step necessitates a self-surrender which few are willing to make. A man can learn nothing unless he regards himself as a learner. Before a man can learn anything of the divine spirit within, he must come to the feet of Christ divested of all his desires, his opinions and views, yea, even of his cherished ideal, regarding himself as a little child, knowing nothing, blind and ignorant, seeking knowledge. Before this attitude of humility is adopted, the attainment of divine life and knowledge is impossible; but he who will adopt it will rapidly enter into the highest revelations, and the carrying out of the precept will soon become easy and natural to him.

Having clothed himself with humility the first questions a man asks himself are: "How am I acting toward others?" "What am I doing to others?" "How am I thinking of others?" "Are my thoughts of and acts toward others prompted by unselfish love, as I would theirs should be to me, or are they the outcome of personal dislike, of petty revenge, or of narrow bigotry and condemnation?" As a man, in the sacred silence of his soul, asks himself these searching questions, applying all his thoughts and acts to the spirit of the primary precept of Jesus, his understanding will become illuminated so that he will unerringly see where he has hitherto failed; and he will also see what he has to do in rectifying his heart and conduct, and the way in which it is to be done. Such a man has become a disciple of Christ at whose feet he sits, and whose commands he is prepared to carry out no matter at what sacrifice to himself.

One hour's daily meditation upon this precept, combined with a sincere wish to learn its meaning and a determination to carry it out, would rapidly lift a man above his sinful nature into the clear light and freedom of divine Truth, for it would compel him to remodel his entire life and to turn right round in his attitude toward others. Let a man, before acting, ask himself the question, "Should I like others to do this to me?" and he will soon find his way out of his spiritual darkness, for he will then begin to live for others instead of for himself; will adjust his thoughts and conduct to the principle of divine love, instead of blindly following his selfish inclinations. However others act toward him, he will begin to act toward all in a calm, quiet, forgiving spirit. If others attack his attitude, his beliefs, his religion, he will not retaliate; and will cease from attacking others, realizing that it is his supreme duty to carry out his divine Master's commands; and the carrying out of those commands will demand the readjustment, not only of his thoughts and acts, but of every detail of his life, even down to his eating and drinking and clothing. As he proceeds in this new life, the teachings of Jesus will become luminous with a new light, vital with a new life, and he will feel that every precept is for him and that he must carry them out, ceasing to accuse others because they do not carry them out. As he reads the words, "Judge not," he will know that he must cease from all harsh and unkind judgment, that he must think kindly of all, just as much so of those who are unkind to him as of those who are kind to him; that if others judge and condemn him, he must not do so to them, and, putting aside all personal considerations, must deal with them in the spirit of equity, wisdom, and love. It will thus be seen that even in carrying out the one simple precept, "Judge not," a man must necessarily rise above much that is merely personal and selfish, and will develop unusual spiritual strength. This course of conduct, diligently pursued, will lead to the observance of the precept, "Resist not evil," for if a man ceases to judge others as evil, he will cease to resist them as evil. Of late years much has been written about nonresistance to evil, but he who would comprehend the spiritual significance of this, or indeed of any precept, must not rest content with mere dialectic definitions of it, but must assiduously *practice it;* he can only find its meaning by *doing it.* And in the doing of this precept, a man will destroy in himself the eye of evil, and in its place he will learn to look through the eye of good, the eye of Truth, when he will see that evil is not worth resisting and that the practice of the good is supremely excellent.

Whilst a man is engaged in resisting evil, he is not only not practicing the good, he is actually involved in the like passion and prejudice which he condemns in another, and as a direct result of his attitude of mind, he himself is resisted by others as evil. Resist a man, a party, a law, a religion, a government as evil, and you yourself will be resisted as evil. He who considers it as a great evil that he should be persecuted and condemned, let him cease to persecute and condemn. Let him turn away from all that he has hitherto regarded as evil, and begin to look for the good, taking passion, resentment, and retaliation out of his heart, and he will very soon see that what he has all along been resisting as evil has no existence as such, and that it was merely an exaggerated and illusionary reflection of the passion and the folly which were in himself. So deep and far-reaching is this precept that the practice of it will take a man far up the heights of spiritual knowledge and attainment; and when, by following its demands, he has so far purified and over come himself as to see good and not evil in all men and all things, he will then be prepared to carry out a still higher precept (though one contained in the primary precept), namely, *"Love your enemies."*

Over none of the precepts do men stumble more than this one, and the cause for such stumbling is near at hand and very plain. It is to be expected that men who regard fighting, retaliation, and hatred toward their enemies as indications of nobility of character should look upon this precept as not only an impracticable but a very foolish command. And from their standpoint of knowledge they are right. If man be regarded as a mere animal cut off from the Divine, those fierce, destructive qualities which are esteemed noble in the beast are noble in man.

To such men, living in their animal qualities and instincts, meekness, forgiveness, and self-denying love appear as cowardice, effeminacy, and weak sentimentality. If, however, we recognize in man certain divine qualities (more active in some than in others, but possessed in a measure by all), such as love, purity, compassion, reason, wisdom, and so forth, which lift him above the animal, then the precept, "Love your enemies," not only appears practicable but is seen to represent the rightful and legitimate state of man. To the man, therefore, who says, "This is an impossible precept," I would say: "You are right; to you it is impossible; but only your unbelief in the efficacy of those qualities which constitute goodness, and your belief in the power of the animal forces, make it so; reverse your attitude of mind, and the impossibility will fade away."

No man can carry out and understand this precept who is not willing to renounce his animal nature. He who would find the Christ (the pure Spirit of truth) must cease to warp and blind his spiritual vision by flattering his feelings and passions. The source of all enmity within himself must be destroyed. Hatred is none the less hatred when it is called dislike. Personal antipathies, however natural they may be to the animal man, can have no place in the divine life. Nor can a man see spiritual things or receive spiritual truth while his mind is involved in malice, dislike, animosity, revenge, or that blind egotism which thinks "I (in my views) am right, and you are wrong." The keeping, then, of the commandment, "Love your enemies," necessitates the removal from the heart of all hatred and egotism, and as this is accomplished, the principle of divine love, which is unchangeably the same toward all—the just and the unjust, the sinful and the saintly—takes the place, in the consciousness, of those violent animal and personal loves which are continually changing, and coming and going, and which are inseparably linked with their opposite of violent hatred. It is impossible to love one's enemies whilst living in the animal personality, for that personality is of the very nature of *blind* love and hatred; it is only by deserting the personal elements that the impersonal, divine love, which does not alter with the changing attitudes of others, is found and can become the dominating factor in one's conduct; and when that is done, the disciple realizes that his true nature is divine.

The love, then, that enables a man to deal kindly with his enemies and to do to others as he would like others to do to him, irrespective of *their* attitudes of mind, is not an emotion, impulse, or preference, but a state of divine knowledge arrived at by practice; and as this knowledge is perfected in the mind, the eternal principles of the divine law of which the prophets spoke, and on which they stood, are comprehended.

He who will keep the precepts of Jesus will conquer himself and will become divinely illuminated. He who will not keep them will remain in the darkness of his lower nature, shut out from all understanding of spiritual principles and of the divine law. Herein, also, resides the infallible test of discipleship, for it was none other than Jesus the Christ who said, "He that loveth me not keepeth not my sayings," and "He that hath my commandments, and keepeth them, he it is that loveth me."

III

THE YOKE AND THE BURDEN

Take my yoke upon you, and learn of me; for I am meek and lowly in heart; and ye shall find rest unto your souls.

For my yoke *is* easy, and my burden is light.

—JESUS

Be ye therefore perfect, even as your Father which is in heaven is perfect.

—JESUS

Humanity is essentially divine. Every precept of Jesus rests upon this truth. If man were not divine, the precepts would be both worthless and meaningless, as there would be nothing within him (no divine spirit) to which they could appeal. The very fact that man is capable of loving his enemies and of returning good for evil is an attestation of his inward and essential divinity. If sin were man's natural and rightful condition, it would be right that he should remain in it and there would be no necessity to exhort him to virtue and holiness, for it would be impossible for him to act otherwise than in accordance with his original nature. Whenever men exhort their fellows to virtue, nobility of action, purity of thought, and unselfishness, they unconsciously assert and emphasize man's originally divine nature, and proclaim, though perhaps they know it not, his superiority to sin and his Godlike power to overcome it.

So long, however, has man dwelt in the habitations of sin that he has at last come to regard himself as native to it and as being cut off from the divine source, which he believes to be outside and away from him. He has thereby lost the consciousness and knowledge of his own divinity, of his essential oneness with God, the spirit of good. Humanity at present is in the position of the prodigal son, wandering in the far country of sin and attempting to live upon the swinish husks of base desires and false beliefs; and every divine precept and command is a call to man to return to his Father's house, his original innocence, and to recover and reëstablish the knowledge of his substantial oneness with the Divine.

The whole of the teaching of Jesus is an exhortation to men to do as he did, to live as he lived; he thereby recognizes and affirms the inherent equality of humanity with himself, and in declaring,

"I and my Father are one," he speaks not alone for himself but for all men. The difference between the life of Jesus and that of other men is not arbitrarily imposed, nor does it exist in essentiality; it is self-imposed and exists in individual choice. Jesus fully recognized his oneness with the Father (the divine source), and lived consciously in that oneness; other men (speaking broadly) not only do not recognize their oneness with the Divine, but do not believe it; it is therefore impossible for them, by virtue of their unbelief, to rise to the dignity and majesty of the divine life. Whilst a man regards himself as being the creature of sin, believing himself to be originally degraded, he must necessarily remain degraded, and subject to sin; but let him *realize* that he is originally divine, that he is not, never was, and never can be cut off from the Divine except in his own ignorance and willful choice, and he will at once rise above sin and begin to manifest the divine life.

Man is primarily a spiritual being, and as such is of the nature and substance of the eternal Spirit, the unchangeable reality, which men call God. Goodness, not sin, is his rightful condition; perfection, not imperfection, is his heritage, and this a man may enter into and realize *now* if he will grant the condition, which is the denial or abandonment of self, that is, of his feverish desires, his proud will, his egotism and self-seeking—all that which St. Paul calls the "natural man."

In the Sermon on the Mount, Jesus describes the way of action and thought by which the divine life is to be lived, and after having laid down the whole duty of man as a spiritual being, a son of God, he exhorts men to live as becomes their divine relationship, in the words, "Be ye therefore perfect, even as your Father which is in heaven is perfect." In sounding this high call to perfection, Jesus, far from commanding an impossibility, merely urges men to live their true life of divine perfection and to give up their false life of self-seeking and sin.

The "yoke" which Jesus calls upon men to take upon themselves is the yoke of obedience—obedience to the divine nature which is in every man, no longer obeying the lower desires and impulses; and the "burden" is the burden of a sinless life. Such a yoke is "easy," because it entails no suffering; and such a burden is "light," for it is relieved of the weight of sorrow, anxiety, and fear. It is the life of self-seeking which is so uneasy, while the burden of sin, even of the mildest forms of sin, is heavy and wearisome. To know the truth of this, a man has only to look around upon the world, and then within his own soul.

Jesus recognized the divine in all men, even those called "evil," and he dwelt upon it and reiterated it. The idea of man's being *innately* degraded, a lost creature, incapable of lifting himself to the heights of goodness and righteousness, nowhere enters into either the words, conceptions, or teaching of Jesus. On the other hand, the whole of his teaching affirms and emphasizes man's innate goodness and his unlimited capacity for practicing goodness. When he says, "Condemn not and ye shall not be condemned; forgive and ye shall be forgiven; give and it shall be given unto you; good measure pressed down, shaken together, and running over shall *men* give into your bosoms," he plainly tells us that if we will put away all resentment and treat others with kindness, forgiveness, and gentle consideration, we shall then find that men are so intrinsically good that they will heap kindnesses without number upon us. He who would find how good at heart men are, let him throw away all his ideas and suspicions about the "evil" in others, and find and practice the good within himself.

Jesus also speaks of the "righteous," of those who "hunger and thirst for righteousness," of "the meek," "the merciful," "the pure in heart," and "the peacemakers," and declares that all such are blessed. He draws our attention to the fact that those who regard themselves as evil are so far from being evil that they know how to give good gifts to their children, and that even the publicans and sinners return love for love. His testimony to the guileless innocence of little children seems to have been much overlooked and ignored by those who call themselves his followers; and in all his references to and treatment of the fallen, he looks behind and away from the surface defilement (other men regard this as the real man, and dwell upon and exaggerate its enormity), and sees and brings forth the divine beauty and goodness hidden away under the accumulation of sin.

He spoke of sinners as "captives" and "blind," and stated that it was his mission to preach deliverance and restore sight, clearly indicating that sin is foreign to man and that sinlessness is his true state; and he even declared that men shall do greater works than He did.

Nowhere in the whole range of history or inspiration is there to be found such testimony to the lofty nobility and essential purity and goodness (doubtless more or less latent) of the human heart as is found in the words and deeds of Jesus. In his divine goodness he knew the human heart, and he knew that it was good.

Man has within him the divine power by which he can rise to the highest heights of spiritual achievement; by which he can shake off sin and shame and sorrow, and do the will of the Father, the supreme good; by which he can conquer all the powers of darkness within, and stand radiant and free; by which he can subdue the world, and scale the lofty pinnacles of Truth. This can man, by choice, by resolve, and by his divine strength, accomplish; but he can accomplish it only in and by obedience; he must choose meekness and lowliness of heart, he must abandon strife for peace, passion for purity, hatred for love, self-seeking for self-sacrifice, and must overcome evil with good; for this is the holy Way of Truth; this is the safe and abiding salvation; this is the yoke and burden of the Christ.

IV

THE WORD AND THE DOER

Whosoever heareth these sayings of mine, and doeth them, I will liken him unto a wise man which built his house upon a rock: and the rain descended, and the floods came, and the wind blew, and beat upon that house; and it fell not: for it was founded upon a rock.

—JESUS

If ye continue in my word, *then* ye are my disciples indeed; and ye shall know the truth, and the truth shall make you free.

—JESUS

The Gospel of Jesus is a Gospel of *living and doing*. If it were not this, it would not voice the eternal truth. Its temple is purified conduct, the entrance door to which is self-surrender. It invites men to shake off sin, and promises, as a result, joy and blessedness and perfect peace.

There is one characteristic in the teachings of all those great souls who have been worshiped by mankind as saviors, and that is that they bring to light, and appeal directly to, the simple facts and truths of the soul and of life; and in the teaching of Jesus this feature stands out preëminently. Strictly speaking, he put forward no theory, advanced no creed, laid no claim to any particular "views," and propounded no speculative philosophy. He was content to state that which is.

Men are so taken up with their pleasures, theories, theologies, and philosophies that they cannot apprehend the simple facts of life, and it is supremely the office of the true teacher to bring men back to the simple and beautiful realities of their own souls. The false teacher, he who cannot perceive the simple truths of duty and of conduct, and does not see himself and other men as they are, when asked to point out the way of Truth will declare that it lies entirely in the acceptance of his own particular theology, and will warn the questioner against all other systems of theology. Not so, however, the true teacher, he who knows the human heart, and who sees life as it is; and particularly not so, Jesus, who, when questioned of the way of life, always told his questioner to go and *do* certain things. Never once did he refer a questioner to any views, theories, or deftly woven philosophies of his own, or indeed of other men. He referred them to duty and to purity of life and conduct, and the only things he warned them against were their own sins. And, truly, this is all that is needful.

A man either abandons sin or he clings to it; if the former, he does all and realizes the law of life; if the latter, he does nothing, and remains ignorant, blind, without understanding. Truth is contained in conduct, and not in any system of thought; and to live purely and blamelessly is infinitely superior to all wordy doctrines. Let a man carefully study every system of theology, and he will at last find that one selfless thought, one pure deed, puts them all to shame. Truth is divorced from the controversies of the creeds, but it shines with undimmed luster in the self-forgetting deed. How beautifully this is illustrated in the parables of Jesus, and how forcibly is it brought out in many of the incidents of his life; particularly in that one recorded in the 10th chapter of Luke, where the lawyer asks, "Master, what shall I do to inherit eternal life?" The answer of Jesus is to ask him to repeat the chief commandment, which being done, Jesus simply says, "This do, and thou shall live." Whereupon, the lawyer, wishing to draw Jesus into an argument in order, no doubt, to confound him, asks, "And who is my neighbor?" We then have the incomparable parable of the Good Samaritan, wherein Jesus shows in the simplest language and imagery, yet forcibly and unmistakably, that religious observances are so many vain and useless burdens unless accompanied by good deeds, and that the so-called worldly man who does unselfish deeds has already found eternal life; while the so-called religious man who shuts up his soul against mercy and unselfishness is shut out from life. To comprehend the full force of this parable it is necessary to bear in mind that the priests and the Levites were regarded by the Jews as being the highly favored and chosen of God, whereas the Samaritans were regarded as being entirely outside the pale of salvation.

Jesus recognized no religion outside conduct; and truly there is none. Pure goodness is religion, and outside it there is no religion. There are innumerable doctrines, and there is much strife and heated controversy, but a man is only truly religious when he succeeds in rising above these and this, and reaches that loving place in his heart where all hateful distinctions are burned away by the pure flames of compassion and love. And in this divine place Jesus stood, and he calls other men thither to receive rest and peace. That Jesus was meek and lowly and loving and compassionate and pure is very beautiful, but it is not sufficient; it is necessary, reader, that you also should be meek and lowly and loving and compassionate and pure. That Jesus subordinated his own will to the will of the Father, it is inspiring to know, but it is not sufficient; it is necessary that you, too, should likewise subordinate your will to that of the overruling Good. The grace and beauty and goodness that were in Jesus can be of no value to you, cannot be understood by you, unless they are also *in you;* and they can never be in you until you *practice* them; for, apart from *doing,* the qualities which constitute goodness do not, as far as you are concerned, exist. To adore Jesus for his divine qualities is a long step toward Truth, but to practice those qualities is Truth itself; and he who truly adores the perfection of another will not rest content in his own imperfection, but will fashion his soul after the likeness of that other. To us and to all there is no sufficiency, no blessedness, no peace to be derived from the goodness of another, not even the goodness of God; not until the goodness is *done* by us, not until it is, by constant effort, incorporated into our being, can we know and possess its blessedness and peace. Therefore, thou who adorest Jesus for his divine qualities, practice those qualities thyself, and thou too shalt be divine.

The teaching of Jesus brings men back to the simple truth that righteousness, or right-doing, is entirely a matter of individual conduct, and not a mystical something apart from a man's thoughts and actions, and that each must be righteous for himself; each must be a doer of the word; and it is a man's own doing that brings him peace and gladness of heart, not the doing of another.

Millions of people worship Jesus and call him Lord, but Jesus does not leave us in any difficulty or doubt as to who are his disciples, as to who have entered into life; his words are simplicity itself: "Not every one that saith unto me, Lord, Lord, shall enter into the kingdom of heaven; but he that *doeth* the will of my Father which is in Heaven;" and again, "Why call ye me Lord, Lord, and do not the things which I say?" And they are the doers of the Father's will who shape their conduct to the divine precepts.

The doer of the word demonstrates and proves its truth in his own mind and life. He thus knows the eternal rock as a substantial reality within himself, and he builds thereon the temple of righteousness which no rains of grief, no winds of temptation, and no floods of sin can destroy or undermine. It is only the *doer* of forgiveness who tastes the sweets of forgiveness; it is only he who practices love and mercy and righteousness who receives into his heart the overflowing measure of their blessedness; and none but he who dwells in peace toward all can know the boundless and immeasurable peace. Thus is the doer of the word the disciple indeed, and continuing in that word, becoming one with it in heart and mind, he knows the Truth which frees the soul from the bondage of sin.

V

THE VINE AND THE BRANCHES

I am the vine, ye *are* the branches. He that abideth in me, and I in him, the same bringeth forth much fruit: for without me ye can do nothing.

—Jesus as the Christ

Come unto me, all ye that labour and are heavy laden, and I will give you rest.

—Jesus as the Christ

The Christ is the spirit of love, which is the abiding and indwelling reality in man. Yet though its perfected temple is the human form, and it can only visibly and consciously manifest itself in and through the human personality, it is impersonal in its nature, is a universal and eternal principle, and is at once the source and the substance of life.

In this principle of love, all knowledge, intelligence, and wisdom are contained, and until a man realizes it as the one vital reality of his being, he does not fully comprehend the Christ. Such glorious realization is the crown of evolution, the supreme aim of existence. Its attainment is complete salvation, emancipation from all error, ignorance, and sin.

This principle is in all men, but is not manifested by all; and it is not known and manifested by men because they continue to cling to those personal elements which obscure its presence and power. Every personal element in human nature is changeable and perishable, and to cling to them is to embrace negations, shadows, death. In the material world, an object cannot be perceived until all intervening obstacles are removed; and in the spiritual region an abiding principle cannot be apprehended until every impermanent element is relinquished. Before a man can know love as the abiding reality within him, he must utterly abandon all those human tendencies which frustrate its perfect manifestation. By so doing he becomes one with love—becomes love itself; he then discovers that he is, and always has been, divine and one with God.

Jesus, by his complete victory over the personality, realized and manifested his oneness with the supreme spirit; and, subordinating his entire nature and life to impersonal love, he became, literally, an embodiment of the Christ. He is therefore truly called the Christ.

When Jesus said, "Without Me ye can do nothing," he spoke not of his perishable form, but of the universal spirit of love of which his conduct was a perfect manifestation; and this utterance of his is the statement of a simple truth; for the works of man are vain and worthless when they are done for personal ends, and he himself remains a perishable being, immersed in darkness and fearing death, so long as he lives in his personal gratifications. The animal in man can never respond to and know the divine; only the divine can respond to the divine. The spirit of hatred in man can never vibrate in unison with the spirit of love; love only can apprehend love and become linked with it. Man is divine; man is of the substance of love; this he may realize if he will relinquish the impure, personal elements which he has hitherto been blindly following, and will fly to the impersonal realities of the Christ Spirit; and these realities are purity, humility, compassion, wisdom, love.

Every precept of Jesus demands the unconditional sacrifice of some selfish, personal element before it can be carried out. Man cannot know the real whilst he clings to the unreal; he cannot do the work of Truth whilst he clings to error. Whilst a man cherishes lust, hatred, pride, vanity, self-indulgence, covetousness, he can do nothing, for the works of all these sinful elements are unreal and perishable. Only when he takes refuge in the Spirit of love within, and becomes patient, gentle, pure, pitiful, and forgiving, does he work the works of righteousness and bear the fruits of life. The vine is not a vine without its branches, and even then it is not complete until those branches bear fruit. Love is not complete until it is *lived* by man; until it is fully understood by him and manifested in his conduct. A man can only consciously ally himself to the vine of love by deserting all strife and hatred and condemnation and impurity and pride and self-seeking, and by thinking only loving thoughts and doing loving deeds. By so doing, he awakens within him the divine nature which he has heretofore been crucifying and denying. Every time a man gives way to anger, impatience, greed, pride, vanity, or any form of personal selfishness, he denies the Christ, he shuts himself out from love. And thus only does one deny Christ, and not by refusing to adopt a formulated creed. Christ is known only to him who by constant striving has converted himself from a sinful to a pure being, who by noble, moral effort has succeeded in relinquishing that perishable self which is the source of all suffering and sorrow and unrest, and has become rational, gentle, peaceful, loving, and pure.

Man's only refuge from sin is sinless love, flying to and dwelling in which, and abandoning all else as evanescent, unreal, and worthless, daily practicing love toward all in heart and mind and deed, harboring no injurious or impure thoughts—he discovers the imperishable principles of his being, enters fully into the knowledge of his oneness with eternal life, and receives the never-ending rest.

VI

SALVATION THIS DAY

This day is salvation come to this house.

—Jesus to Zacchæus

Behold, the kingdom of God is within you.

—Jesus

I have tried to show, in the five foregoing chapters, that the teaching of Jesus is based entirely on the perfection of conduct, and can be summed up in the one word "goodness." Jesus manifested this goodness in his life, and his teaching is vitally powerful because it is rooted in his life, his conduct. His command, "Follow me," is literal and actual, not in the sense of a slavish imitation of the external details of his life, but in scaling (as he scaled) the heights of goodness and pity and love by the conquest of self. The glory of his teaching is embodied in his precepts, as the splendor of his life is wrapped up in them; and he who adopts those precepts as the guides of his life will so perfect his conduct by purifying the inward springs of thought and action as to become a spiritualized and sinless being, fulfilling the whole duty of life and the purpose of existence. Herein also is contained complete salvation, namely, freedom from sin.

The word "salvation" is mentioned by Jesus only twice, and only one of these utterances (that to Zacchæus) can be said to have any vital significance for us; yet in that one brief statement we are fully enlightened as to its meaning by virtue of its pointed application to the altered conduct of Zacchæus. This man, we infer, had hitherto been hard, exacting, and grasping, but though he had not yet seen in person the new teacher, his message had reached his ears, and he had opened his heart to the good news that man can and should repent, and abandon selfish and sinful practices for good and sinless conduct. And this he had done, and, having proved its blessedness, no wonder that when Jesus came to his house he "received him joyfully," and told him how he had abandoned wrong-doing for right-doing; evil for good; the selfish for the unselfish life. Jesus did not inquire into the "religious views" of Zacchæus; did not impose upon him any change of view or opinion; did not demand that he believe anything about Jesus as being the Messiah, the Son of God, and so forth. Zacchæus had *changed his conduct;* had completely turned round in his attitude toward others; had abandoned greed for generosity, extortion for charity, honesty for dishonesty, selfishness for unselfishness, evil for good—and this was sufficient, as Jesus declared in the words, "This day is salvation come to this house."

The only salvation recognized and taught by Jesus is salvation from sin, and the effects of sin, *here and now;* and this must be effected by utterly abandoning sin, which, being done, the kingdom of God is realized in the heart as a state of perfect knowledge, perfect blessedness, perfect peace.

"Except a man be born again, he cannot see the kingdom of God." A man must become a "new creature," and how can he become new except by utterly abandoning the old? That man's last state is worse than his first who imagines that, though still continuing to cling to his old temper, his old opinionativeness, his old vanity, his old selfishness, he is constituted a "new creature" in some mysterious and unexplainable way by the adoption of some particular theology or religious formula. A man can be said to be born again, to be a new creature, to be saved from sin, only when he turns round on his old, natural, selfish self, and denies and abandons it. Only by putting away forever the old temper, the old opinionativeness, the old vanity, the old selfishness, the old life of self in any or every shape, only by doing this and turning to the new life of gentleness and purity and humility and unselfish love can a man be said to be saved from sin; and then he is saved indeed, for, no more practicing it, it can trouble him no more. Herein also is heaven, not a speculative heaven beyond the tomb, but a real, abiding, and ever-present heaven in the heart; a heaven from which all the hellish desires and moods and sufferings are banished, where love rules, and from which peace is never absent.

Good news indeed is that message of Jesus which reveals to man his divine possibilities; which says in substance to sin-stricken humanity, "Take up thy bed and walk;" which tells man that he need no longer remain the creature of darkness and ignorance and sin if he will but believe in goodness, and will watch and strive and conquer until he has actualized in his life the goodness that is sinless. And in thus believing and overcoming, man not only has the guide of that perfect rule which Jesus has embodied in his precepts, he has also the inward guide, the Spirit of truth in his own heart, "the light which lighteth every man that cometh into the world," which, as he follows it, will infallibly witness to the divine origin of those precepts.

He who will humbly pass through the gate of good, resolving that every element of his nature that is not pure and true and lovable shall be abandoned, that every violation of the divine precepts shall be abolished, to him, faithful, humble, true, will be revealed the sublime vision of the perfect one, and, day by day purifying his heart and perfecting his conduct in accordance with his vision, he will sooner or later rise above all the subtleties of his lower nature, will wash away every ignominious stain from his soul, and realize the perfect goodness of the eternal Christ.

THE MASTERY
OF DESTINY

(1909)

PREFACE

The discovery of the law of Evolution in the material world has prepared men for a knowledge of the law of cause and effect in the mental world. Thought is not less orderly and progressive than the material forms which embody thought; and not alone cells and atoms, but thoughts and deeds are charged with a cumulative and selective energy. In the realm of thought and deed, the *good* survives, for it is "fittest"; the *evil* ultimately perishes. To know that the "perfect law" of Causation is as all-embracing in mind as in matter, is to be relieved from all anxiety concerning the ultimate destiny of individuals and of humanity—

For man is man and master of his fate—

and the will in man which is conquering the knowledge of natural law will conquer the knowledge of spiritual law; the will which, in ignorance, chooses evil, will, as wisdom evolves and emerges, choose good. In a universe of law, the final mastery of evil by man is assured. His lesser destinies of separation and sorrow, defeat and death, are but disciplinary steps leading to the Great Destiny of triumphal mastery. He himself is unconsciously building, albeit with lacerated hands and labour-bowed form, the Temple of Glory which is to afford him an eternal habitation of peace.

In this volume I have tried to set down some words indicative of this Law and this Destiny, and the manner of its working and its building; and have so arranged the subject-matter as to make the book a companion volume to *The Life Triumphant.* The first six, and the last, chapters first appeared in *Bibby's Quarterly* and *Bibby's Annual,* and it is by kind permission of the Editor, Mr. Joseph Bibby, that they are now brought together and published in volume form, the other three chapters having been added to make the book consecutive and complete.

—JAMES ALLEN
Bryngoleu,
Ilfracombe, England
April, 1909

CONTENTS

DEEDS, CHARACTER, AND DESTINY

There is, and always has been, a wide-spread belief in Fate, or Destiny; that is, in an eternal and inscrutable Power which apportions definite ends to both individuals and nations. This belief has arisen from long observation of the facts of life. Men are conscious that there are certain occurrences which they cannot control, and are powerless to avert. Birth and death, for instance, are inevitable, and many of the incidents of life appear equally inevitable. Men strain every nerve for the attainment of certain ends, and gradually they become conscious of a Power which seems to be not of themselves, which frustrates their puny efforts, and laughs, as it were, at their fruitless striving and struggle. As men advance in life, they learn to submit, more or less, to this overruling Power which they do not understand, perceiving only its effects in themselves and the world around them, and they call it by various names, such as God, Providence, Fate, Destiny, etc.

Men of contemplation, such as poets and philosophers, step aside, as it were, to watch the movements of this mysterious Power as it seems to elevate its favourites on the one hand, and strike down its victims on the other, without reference to merit or demerit. The greatest poets, especially the dramatic poets, represent this Power in their works, as they have observed it in Nature. The Greek and Roman dramatists usually depict their heroes as having foreknowledge of their fate, and taking means to escape it; but by so doing they blindly involve themselves in a series of consequences which bring about the doom which they are trying to avert. Shakespeare's characters, on the other hand, are represented, as in Nature, with no foreknowledge (except in the form of presentiment) of their particular destiny. Thus, according to the poets, whether the man knows his fate or not, he cannot avert it, and every conscious or unconscious act of his is a step toward it.

Omar Khayyam's "Moving Finger" is a vivid expression of this idea of Fate:

The Moving Finger writes, and having writ,
Moves on: nor all thy Piety nor Wit
Shall lure it back to cancel half a line,
Nor all thy Tears wash out a Word of it.

Thus, men in all nations and times have experienced in their lives the action of this invincible Power or Law, and in our nation to-day this experience has been crystallized in the terse proverb, "Man proposes, God disposes."

But, contradictory as it may appear, there is an equally wide-spread belief in man's responsibility as a free agent.

All moral teaching is an affirmation of man's freedom to choose his course and mould his destiny; and man's patient and untiring efforts in achieving his ends are declarations of consciousness of freedom and power. This dual experience of fate on the one hand, and freedom on the other, has given rise to the interminable controversy between the believers in Fatalism and the upholders of Free-will—a controversy which was recently revived under the term "Determinism *versus* Free-will." Between apparently conflicting extremes there is always a "middle way" of balance, justice, or compensation which, while it includes both extremes, cannot be said to be either one or the other, and which brings both into harmony; and this middle way is the point of contact between two extremes. Truth cannot be a partisan, but, by its nature, is the Reconciler of extremes; and so, in the matter which we are considering, there is a "golden mean" which brings Fate and Free-will into close relationship, wherein, indeed, it is seen that these two indisputable facts in human life, for such they are, are but two aspects of one central law, one unifying and all-embracing principle, namely, *the law of causation in its moral aspect.*

Moral causation necessitates both Fate and Free-will, both individual responsibility and individual predestination, for the law of causes must also be the law of effects, and cause and effect must always be equal; the train of causation, both in matter and mind, must be eternally balanced, therefore eternally just, eternally perfect. Thus every effect may be said to be a thing *preordained,* but the predetermining power is a cause, and not the fiat of an arbitrary will.

Man finds himself involved in the train of causation. His life is made up of causes and effects. It is both a sowing and a reaping. Each act of his is a cause which must be balanced by its effects. He chooses the cause (this is Free-will), he cannot choose, alter, or avert the effect (this is Fate); thus Free-will stands for the power to initiate causes, and destiny is involvement in effects. It is therefore true that man is predestined to certain ends, but he himself has (though he knows it not) issued the mandate; that good or evil thing from which there is no escape, he has, by his own deeds, brought about.

It may here be urged that man is not responsible for his deeds, that these are the effects of his character, and that he is not responsible for the character, good or bad, which was given him at his birth. If character was "given him" at birth, this would be true, and there would then be no moral law, and no need for moral teaching; but characters are not given ready-made, they are *evolved;* they are, indeed, effects, the products of the moral law itself, that is—the products of deeds. Character is the combined result of an incalculable number of deeds, is, in reality, an accumulation of deeds which has been piled up, so to speak, by the individual during vast ages of time and through innumerable lives, by a slow process of orderly evolution. A man's birth into this life, with his complex character, to which he considers himself irresponsibly predestined, was determined by his own deeds in former lives.

Man is the doer of his own deeds; as such he is the maker of his own character; and as the doer of his deeds and the maker of his character, he is the moulder and shaper of his destiny. He has the power to modify and alter his deeds, and every time he acts he modifies his character, and with the modification of his character for good or evil, he is predetermining for himself new destinies— destinies disastrous or beneficent in accordance with the nature of his deeds. Character is destiny itself; as a fixed combination of deeds, it bears within itself the results of those deeds. These results lie hidden as moral seeds in the dark recesses of the character, awaiting their season of germination, growth, and fruitage.

Those things which befall a man are the reflections of himself; that destiny which pursued him, which he was powerless to escape by effort, or avert by prayer, was the relentless ghoul of his own wrong deeds demanding and enforcing restitution; those blessings and curses which come to him unbidden are the reverberating echoes of the sounds which he himself sent forth.

It is this knowledge of the Perfect Law working through and above all things; of the Perfect Justice operating in and adjusting all human affairs, that enables the good man to love his enemies, and to rise above all hatred, resentment, and complaining; for he knows that only his own can come to him, and that, though he be surrounded by persecutors, his enemies are but the blind instruments of a faultless retribution; and so he blames them not, but calmly receives his accounts, and patiently pays his moral debts.

But this is not all; he does not merely pay his debts; he takes care not to contract any further debts. He watches himself and makes his deeds faultless. While paying off evil accounts, he is laying up good accounts. By putting an end to his own sin, he is bringing evil and suffering to an end.

And now let us consider how the Law operates in particular instances in the outworking of destiny through deeds and character. First, we will look at this present life, for the present is the synthesis of the entire past; the net result of all that a man has ever thought and done is contained within him. It is noticeable that sometimes the good man fails and the unscrupulous man prospers—a fact which seems to put all moral maxims as to the good results of righteousness out of account—and because of this, many people deny the operation of any just law in human life, and even declare that it is chiefly the unjust that prosper. Nevertheless, the moral law exists, and is not altered or subverted by shallow conclusions. It should be remembered that man is *a changing, evolving being.* The good man was not always good; the bad man was not always bad. Even in this life (without, for the moment, going back to former lives), there was a time, in a large number of instances, when the man who is now just, was unjust; when he who is now kind, was cruel; when he who is now pure, was impure. Obversely, there was a time in this life, in a number of instances, when he who is now unjust, was just; when he who is now cruel, was kind; when he who is now impure, was pure. Thus, the good man who is overtaken with calamity to-day is reaping the result of his former evil sowing; later he will reap the happy result of his present good sowing; while the bad man is now reaping the result of his former good sowing; later he will reap the result of his present sowing of bad. But when just causes (of the effects which we see) are not apparent in this life, then they were set going in former lives; and, indeed, the entire evolution of any being, through innumerable births and deaths and ever-enlarging destinies, may be regarded as one long, extended, unbroken line of causes and effects; one indestructible, ever-growing, ever-changing, and ascending life.

Characteristics are fixed habits of mind, the results of deeds. An act repeated a large number of times becomes unconscious, or automatic—that is, it then seems to repeat itself without any effort on the part of the doer, so that it seems to him almost impossible not to do it, and then it has become a mental characteristic. Thus, the character of an individual at birth is a combination of habits which he himself has built up by his own thoughts and acts during the course of his evolution, and in accordance with his efforts in this life will his character be modified for good or evil in the future.

Here is a poor man out of work. He is honest, and is not a shirker. He wants work, and cannot get it. He tries hard, and continues to fail. Where is the justice in his lot? There was a time in this man's condition when he had plenty of work. He felt burdened with it; he shirked it, and longed for ease. He thought how delightful it would be to have nothing to do. He did not appreciate the blessedness of his lot. His desire for ease is now gratified, but the fruit for which he longed, and which he thought would taste so sweet, has turned to ashes in his mouth. The condition which he aimed for, namely, to have nothing to do, he has reached, and there he is compelled to remain till his lesson is thoroughly learned. And he is surely learning that habitual ease is degrading, that to have nothing to do is a condition of wretchedness, and that work is a noble and blessed thing. His former desires and deeds have brought him where he is; and now his present desire for work, his ceaseless searching and asking for it, will just as surely bring about its own beneficent result. No longer desiring idleness, his present condition will, as an effect, the cause of which is no longer propagated, soon pass away, and he will obtain employment; and if his whole mind is now set on work, and he desires it above all else, then when it comes he will be overwhelmed with it; it will flow in to him from all sides, and he will prosper in his industry. Then, if he does not understand the law of cause and effect in human life, he will wonder why work comes to him apparently unsought, while others who seek it strenuously fail to obtain it.

Nothing comes unbidden; where the shadow is, there also is the substance. That which comes to the individual is the product of his own deeds. As cheerful industry leads to greater industry and increasing prosperity, and labour shirked or undertaken discontentedly leads to a lesser degree of labour and decreasing prosperity, so with all the varied conditions of life as we see them—they are *the effects of deeds,* destinies wrought by the thoughts and deeds of each particular individual. So also with the vast variety of characters—they are the ripening and ripened growth of the sowing of deeds, a sowing not confined solely to this visible life, but going backward through that infinite life which traverses the portals of innumerable births and deaths, and which also will extend into the illimitable future, reaping its own harvests, eating the sweet and bitter fruits of its own deeds.

It is thus literally true that when men die they "go to heaven or hell," in accordance with their deeds. But the heaven and hell are in this world. The rich man who abused his wealth or who obtained his riches by fraud or oppression, is reborn in poverty and shame. The poor man who used the little he possessed wisely and unselfishly is reborn in plenty and honour. The cruel and unjust are reborn in the midst of harsh and untoward surroundings; the kind and just are reborn where kind hearts and gentle hands watch over and tend them. Thus, with every vice and virtue, each receives its own; each declares its own destiny.

But even those who refuse to believe in rebirth will find that even in this life men almost invariably reap what they sow; and the time is surely coming when social and political reformers will pay more attention to the development of character than the mere gaining of party issues. As the individual reaps what he sows, so the nation, being a community of individuals, reaps also what it sows. Nations become great when their leaders are just men; they fall and fade when their just men pass away. Those who are in power set an example, good or bad, for the entire nation. Great will be the peace and prosperity of a nation when there shall arise within it a line of statesmen who, having first established themselves in a lofty integrity of character, shall direct the energies of the nation toward the culture of virtue and development of character, knowing that only through personal industry, integrity, and nobility can national prosperity proceed.

Still, above all, is the Great Law, calmly and with infallible justice meting out to mortals their fleeting destinies, tear-stained or smiling, the fabric of their hands. Life is a great school for the development of character, and all, through strife and struggle, vice and virtue, success and failure, are slowly but surely learning the lessons of wisdom.

THE SCIENCE OF SELF-CONTROL

We live in a scientific age. Men of science are numbered by thousands, and they are ceaselessly searching, analyzing, and experimenting with a view to discovery and the increase of knowledge. The shelves of our libraries, both public and private, are heavy with their load of imposing volumes on scientific subjects, and the wonderful achievements of modern science are always before us—whether in our homes or in our streets, in country or town, on land or sea—there shall we have before us some marvellous device, some recent accomplishment of science, for adding to our comfort, increasing our so speed, or saving the labour of our hands.

Yet, with all our vast store of scientific knowledge, and its startling and rapidly increasing results in the world of discovery and invention, there is, in this age, one branch of science which has so far fallen into decay as to have become almost forgotten; a science, nevertheless, which is of greater importance than all the other sciences combined, and without which all science would but subserve the ends of selfishness, and aid in man's destruction—I refer to the *Science of Self-control*.

Our modern scientists study the elements and forces which are outside themselves, with the object of controlling and utilizing them. The ancients studied the elements and forces which were within themselves, with a view to controlling and utilizing them, and the ancients produced such mighty Masters of knowledge in this direction, that to this day they are held in reverence as gods, and the vast religious organizations of the world are based upon their achievements.

Wonderful as are the forces in nature, they are vastly inferior to that combination of intelligent forces which comprise the mind of man, and which dominate and direct the blind mechanical forces of nature. Therefore, it follows that, to understand, control, and direct the inner forces of passion, desire, will, and intellect, is to be in possession of the destinies of men and nations.

As in ordinary science, there are, in this divine science, degrees of attainment; and a man is great in knowledge, great in himself, and great in his influence on the world, in the measure that he is great in self-control.

He who understands and dominates the forces of external nature is the natural scientist; but he who understands and dominates the internal forces of the mind is the divine scientist; and the laws which operate in gaining a knowledge of external appearances, operate also in gaining a knowledge of internal verities.

A man cannot become an accomplished scientist in a few weeks or months, nay, not even in a few years. But only after many years of painstaking investigation can he speak with authority, and be ranked among the masters of science. Likewise, a man cannot acquire self-control, and become possessed of the wisdom and peace-giving knowledge which that self-control confers, but by many years of patient labour; a labour which is all the more arduous because it is silent, and both unrecognized and unappreciated by others; and he who would pursue this science successfully must learn to stand alone, and to toil unrewarded, as far as any outward emolument is concerned.

The natural scientist pursues, in acquiring his particular kind of knowledge, the following five orderly and sequential steps:

1. *Observation.* That is, he closely and persistently observes the facts of nature.
2. *Experiment.* Having become acquainted, by repeated observations, with certain facts, he experiments with those facts, with a view to the discovery of natural laws. He puts his facts through rigid processes of analysis, and so finds out what is useless and what of value; and he rejects the former and retains the latter.
3. *Classification.* Having accumulated and verified a mass of facts by numberless observations and experiments, he commences to classify those facts, to arrange them in orderly groups with the object of discovering some underlying law, some hidden and unifying principle, which governs, regulates, and binds together these facts.
4. *Deduction.* Thus he passes on to the fourth step of deduction. From the facts and results which are before him, he discovers certain invariable modes of action, and thus reveals the hidden laws of things.
5. *Knowledge.* Having proven and established certain laws, it may be said of such a man that he *knows.* He is a scientist, a man of knowledge.

But the attainment of scientific knowledge is not the end, great as it is. Men do not attain knowledge for themselves alone, nor to keep it locked secretly in their hearts, like a beautiful jewel in a dark chest. The end of such knowledge is use, service, the increase of the comfort and happiness of the world. Thus, when a man has become a scientist, he gives the world the benefit of his knowledge, and unselfishly bestows upon mankind the results of all his labours. Thus, beyond knowledge, there is a further step of *Use:* that is, the right and unselfish use of the knowledge acquired; the application of knowledge to invention for the common weal.

It will be noted that the five steps or processes enumerated follow in orderly succession, and that no man can become a scientist who omits any one of them. Without the first step of systematic observation, for instance, he could not even enter the realm of knowledge of nature's secrets. At first, the searcher for such knowledge has before him a universe of *things:* these things he does not understand; many of them, indeed, seem to be irreconcilably opposed one to the other, and there is apparent confusion; but by patiently and laboriously pursuing these five processes, he discovers the order, nature, and essences of things; perceives the central law or laws which bind them together in harmonious relationship, and so puts an end to confusion and ignorance.

As with the natural scientist, so with the divine scientist; he must pursue, with the same self-sacrificing diligence, five progressive steps in the attainment of self-knowledge, self-control. These five steps are the same as with the natural scientist, but *the process is reversed,* the mind, instead of being centred upon external things, is turned back upon itself, and the investigations are pursued in the realm of mind (of one's own mind) instead of in that of matter. At first, the searcher for divine knowledge is confronted with that mass of desires, passions, emotions, ideas, and intellections which he calls himself, which is the basis of all his actions, and from which his life proceeds. This combination of invisible, yet powerful, forces appears confusedly; some of them stand, apparently, in direct conflict with each other, without any appearance or hope of reconciliation; his mind in its entirety, too, with his life which proceeds from that mind, does not seem to have any equitable relation to many other minds and lives about him, and altogether there is a condition of pain and confusion from which he would fain escape. Thus, he begins by keenly realizing his state of ignorance, for no one could acquire either natural or divine knowledge, if he were convinced that without study or labour he already possessed it. With such perception of one's ignorance, there comes the desire for knowledge, and the novice in self-control enters upon the ascending pathway, in which are the following five steps:

1. *Introspection.* This coincides with the *observation* of the natural scientist. The mental eye is turned like a searchlight upon the inner things of the mind, and its subtle and ever-varying processes are observed and carefully noted. This stepping aside from selfish gratifications, from the excitements of worldly pleasures and ambitions, in order to observe, with the object of understanding, one's nature, is the beginning of self-control. Hitherto, the man has been blindly and impotently borne along by the impulses of his nature, the mere creature of things and circumstances, but now he puts a check upon his impulses and, instead of being controlled, begins to control.

2. *Self-analysis.* Having observed the tendencies of the mind, they are then closely examined, and are put through a rigid process of analysis. The evil tendencies (those that produce painful effects) are separated from the good tendencies (those that produce peaceful effects); and the various tendencies, with the particular actions they produce, and the definite results which invariably spring from these actions, are gradually grasped by the understanding, which is

at last enabled to follow them in their swift and subtle interplay and profound ramifications. It is a process of *testing and proving,* and, for the searcher, a period of being tested and proved.

3. *Adjustment.* By this time, the practical student of things divine has clearly before him every tendency and aspect of his nature, down to the profoundest promptings of his mind, and the most subtle motives of his heart. There is not a spot or corner left, which he has not explored and illuminated with the light of self-examination. He is familiar with every weak and selfish point, every strong and virtuous quality. It is considered the height of wisdom to be able to see ourselves as others see us, but the practiser of self-control goes far beyond this: he not only sees himself as others see him, he *sees himself as he is.* Thus, standing face to face with himself, not striving to hide away from any secret fault; no longer defending himself with pleasant flatteries; neither underrating nor overrating himself or his powers, and no more cursed with self-praise or self-pity, he sees the full magnitude of the task which lies before him; sees clearly ahead the heights of self-control, and knows what work he has to do to reach them. He is no longer in a state of confusion, but has gained a glimpse of the laws which operate in the world of thought, and he now begins to *adjust* his mind in accordance with those laws. This is a process of *weeding, sifting, cleansing.* As the farmer weeds, cleans, and prepares the ground for his crops, so the student removes the weeds of evil from his mind, cleanses and purifies it preparatory to sowing the seeds of righteous actions which shall produce the harvest of a well-ordered life.

4. *Righteousness.* Having adjusted his thoughts and deeds to those minor laws which operate in mental activities in the production of pain and pleasure, unrest and peace, sorrow and bliss, he now perceives that there is involved in those laws one Great Central Law which, like the law of gravitation in the natural world, is supreme in the world of mind; a law to which all thoughts and deeds are subservient, and by which they are regulated and kept in their proper sphere. This is the law of Justice or Righteousness, which is universal and supreme. To this law he now conforms. Instead of thinking and acting blindly, as the nature is stimulated and appealed to by outward things, he subordinates his thoughts and deeds to this central principle. He no longer acts from self, *but does what is right*—what is universally and eternally right. He is no longer the abject slave of his nature and circumstances, he is the master of his nature and circumstances. He is no longer carried hither and thither on the forces of his mind; he controls and guides those forces to the accomplishment of his purposes. Thus, having his nature in control and subjection, not thinking thoughts nor doing deeds which oppose the righteous law, and which, therefore, that law annuls with suffering and defeat, he rises above the dominion of sin and sorrow, ignorance and doubt, and is strong, calm, and peaceful.

5. *Pure Knowledge.* By thinking right and acting right, he proves, by experience, the existence of the divine law on which the mind is framed, and which is the guiding and unifying principle in all human affairs and events, whether individual or national. Thus, by perfecting himself in self-control, he acquires divine knowledge; he reaches the point where it may be said of him, as of the natural scientist, that he *knows.* He has mastered the science of self-control, and has brought knowledge out of ignorance, order out of confusion. He has acquired that knowledge of self which includes knowledge of all men; that knowledge of one's own life which embraces knowledge of all lives—for all minds are the same in essence (differing only in degree), are framed upon the same law; and the same thoughts and acts, by whatsoever individual they are wrought, will always produce the same results.

But this divine and peace-bestowing knowledge, as in the case of the natural scientist, is not gained for one's self alone; for if this were so, the aim of evolution would be frustrated, and it is not in the nature of things to fall short of ripening and accomplishment; and, indeed, he who thought to gain this knowledge solely for his own happiness would most surely fail. So, beyond the fifth step of Pure Knowledge, there is a still further one of *Wisdom,* which is the right application of the knowledge acquired; the pouring out upon the world, unselfishly and without stint, the result of one's labours, thus accelerating progress and uplifting humanity.

It may be said of men who have not gone back into their own nature to control and purify it, that they cannot clearly distinguish between good and evil, right and wrong. They reach after those things which they think will give them pleasure, and try to avoid those things which they believe will cause them pain. The source of their actions is self, and they only discover right painfully and in a fragmentary way, by periodically passing through severe sufferings, and lashings of conscience. But he who practises self-control, passing through the five processes, which are five stages of growth, gains that knowledge which enables him to act from the moral law which sustains the universe. He knows good and evil, right and wrong, and, thus knowing them, lives in accordance with good and right. He no longer needs to consider what is pleasant or what is unpleasant, but does what is right; his nature is in harmony with his conscience, and there is no remorse; his mind is in unison with the Great Law, and there is no more suffering and sin; for him evil is ended, and good is all in all.

CAUSE AND EFFECT IN
HUMAN CONDUCT

It is an axiom with the scientists that every effect is related to a cause. Apply this to the realm of human conduct, and there is revealed the principle of *justice*.

Every scientist knows (and now all men believe) that perfect harmony prevails throughout every portion of the physical universe, from the speck of dust to the greatest sun. Everywhere there is exquisite adjustment. In the sidereal universe, with its millions of suns rolling majestically through space and carrying with them their respective systems of revolving planets, its vast nebulæ, its seas of meteors, and its vast army of comets travelling through illimitable space with inconceivable velocity, perfect order prevails; and again, in the natural world, with its multitudinous aspects of life, and its infinite variety of forms, there are the clearly defined limits of specific laws, through the operation of which all confusion is avoided, and unity and harmony eternally obtain. If this universal harmony could be arbitrarily broken, even in one small particular, the universe would cease to be; there could be no cosmos, but only universal chaos. Nor can it be possible in such a universe of law that there should exist any personal power which is above, outside, and superior to, such law in the sense that it can defy it, or set it aside; for whatsoever beings exist, whether they be men or gods, they exist by virtue of such law; and the highest, best, and wisest among all beings would manifest his greater wisdom by his more complete obedience to that law which is wiser than wisdom, and than which nothing more perfect could be devised.

All things, whether visible or invisible, are subservient to, and fall within the scope of, this infinite and eternal law of *causation*. As all things seen obey it, so all things unseen—the thoughts and deeds of men, whether secret or open—cannot escape it

Do right, it recompenseth; do one wrong,
The equal retribution must be made.

Perfect justice upholds the universe; perfect justice regulates human life and conduct. All the varying conditions of life, as they obtain in the world today, are the result of this law reacting on human conduct. Man can (and does) choose what causes he shall set in operation, but he cannot change the nature of effects; he can decide what thoughts he shall think, and what deeds he shall do, but he has no power over the *results* of those thoughts and deeds; these are regulated by the overruling law.

Man has all power to act, but his power ends with the act committed. The result of the act cannot be altered, annulled, or escaped; it is irrevocable. Evil thoughts and deeds produce conditions of suffering; good thoughts and deeds determine conditions of blessedness. Thus man's power is limited to, and his blessedness or misery is determined by, *his own conduct.* To know this truth, renders life simple, plain, and unmistakable; all the crooked paths are straightened out, the heights of wisdom are revealed, and the open door to salvation from evil and suffering is perceived and entered.

Life may be likened to a sum in arithmetic. It is bewilderingly difficult and complex to the pupil who has not yet grasped the key to its correct solution, but once this is perceived and laid hold of, it becomes as astonishingly simple as it was formerly profoundly perplexing. Some idea of this relative simplicity and complexity of life may be grasped by fully recognizing and realizing the fact that, while there are scores, and perhaps hundreds, of ways in which a sum may be done wrong, *there is only one way by which it can be done right,* and that when that right way is found the pupil *knows it to be the right;* his perplexity vanishes, and he knows that he has mastered the problem.

It is true that the pupil, while doing his sum incorrectly, may (and frequently does) *think* he has done it correctly, but he is not sure; his perplexity is still there, and if he is an earnest and apt pupil, he will recognize his own error when it is pointed out by the teacher. So in life, men may think they are living rightly while they are continuing, through ignorance, to live wrongly; but the presence of doubt, perplexity, and unhappiness are sure indications that the right way has not yet been found.

There are foolish and careless pupils who would like to pass a sum as correct before they have acquired a true knowledge of figures, but the eye and skill of the teacher quickly detect and expose the fallacy. So in life there can be no falsifying of results; the eye of the Great Law reveals and exposes. Twice five will make ten to all eternity, and no amount of ignorance, stupidity, or delusion can bring the result up to eleven.

If one looks superficially at a piece of cloth, he sees it as a piece of cloth, but if he goes further and inquires into its manufacture, and examines it closely and attentively, he sees that it is composed of a combination of individual threads, and that, while all the threads are interdependent, each thread pursues its own way throughout, never becoming confused with its sister thread. It is this entire absence of confusion between the particular threads which constitutes the finished work *a piece of cloth;* any inharmonious commingling of the thread would result in a bundle of *waste* or a useless *rag.*

Life is like a piece of cloth, and the threads of which it is composed are individual lives. The threads, while being interdependent, are not confounded one with the other. Each follows its own course. Each individual suffers and enjoys the consequences of his own deeds, and not of the deeds of another. The course of each is simple and definite; the whole forming a complicated, yet harmonious, combination of sequences. There are action and reaction, deed and consequence, cause and effect, and the counterbalancing reaction, consequence, and effect is always in exact ratio with the initiatory impulse.

A durable and satisfactory piece of cloth cannot be made from shoddy material, and the threads of selfish thoughts and bad deeds will not produce a useful and beautiful life—a life that will wear well, and bear close inspection. Each man makes or mars his own life; it is not made or marred by his neighbour, or by anything external to himself. Each thought he thinks, each deed he does, is another thread—shoddy or genuine—woven into the garment of his life; and as he makes the garment so must he wear it. He is not responsible for his neighbour's deeds; he is not the custodian of his neighbour's actions; he is responsible only for his own deeds; he is the custodian of his own actions.

The "problem of evil" subsists in a man's own evil deeds, and it is solved when those deeds are purified. Says Rosseau:

Man, seek no longer the origin of evil; thou thyself art its origin.

Effect can never be divorced from cause; it can never be of a different nature from cause. Emerson says:

Justice is not postponed; a perfect equity adjusts the balance in all parts of life.

And there is a profound sense in which cause and effect are simultaneous, and form one perfect whole. Thus, upon the instant that a man thinks, say, a cruel thought, or does a cruel deed, that same instant he has *injured his own mind;* he is not the same man he was the previous instant; he is a little viler and a little more unhappy; and a number of such successive thoughts and deeds would produce a cruel and wretched man. The same thing applies to the contrary—the thinking of a kind thought, or doing a kind deed—an immediate nobility and happiness attend it; the man is better than he was before, and a number of such deeds would produce a great and blissful soul.

Thus individual human conduct determines, by the faultless law of cause and effect, individual merit or demerit, individual greatness or meanness, individual happiness or wretchedness. What a man thinks, that he does; what he does, that he is. If he is perplexed, unhappy, restless, or wretched, let him look to himself, for there and nowhere else is the source of all his trouble.

TRAINING OF THE WILL

Without strength of mind, nothing worthy of accomplishment can be done, and the cultivation of that steadfastness and stability of character which is commonly called "will-power" is one of the foremost duties of man, for its possession is essentially necessary both to his temporal and eternal well-being. Fixedness of purpose is at the root of all successful efforts, whether in things worldly or spiritual, and without it man cannot be otherwise than wretched, and dependent upon others for that support which should be found within himself.

The mystery which has been thrown around the subject of cultivation of the will by those who advertise to sell "occult advice" on the matter for so many dollars, should be avoided and dispelled, for nothing could be further removed from secrecy and mystery than the practical methods by which alone strength of will can be developed.

The true path of will-cultivation is only to be found in the common everyday life of the individual, and so obvious and simple is it that the majority, looking for something complicated and mysterious, pass it by unnoticed.

A little logical thought will soon convince a man that he cannot be both weak and strong at the same time, that he cannot develop a stronger will while remaining a slave to weak indulgences, and that, therefore, the direct and only way to that greater strength is to assail and conquer his weaknesses. All the means for the cultivation of the will are already at hand in the mind and life of the individual; they reside in the weak side of his character, by attacking and vanquishing which the necessary strength of will will be developed. He who has succeeded in grasping this simple, preliminary truth, will perceive that the whole science of will-cultivation is embodied in the following seven rules:

1. Break off bad habits.
2. Form good habits.
3. Give scrupulous attention to the duty of the present moment.
4. Do vigorously, and at once, whatever has to be done.
5. Live by rule.
6. Control the tongue.
7. Control the mind.

Anyone who earnestly meditates upon, and diligently practises, the above rules, will not fail to develop that purity of purpose and power of will which will enable him to successfully cope with every difficulty, and pass triumphantly through every emergency.

It will be seen that the first step is the breaking away from bad habits. This is no easy task. It demands the putting forth of great efforts, or a succession of efforts, and it is by such efforts that the will can alone be invigorated and fortified. If one refuses to take the first step, he cannot increase in will-power, for by submitting to a bad habit, because of the immediate pleasure which it affords, one forfeits the right to rule over himself, and is so far a weak slave. He who thus avoids self-discipline, and looks about for some "occult secrets" for gaining will-power at the expenditure of little or no effort on his part, is deluding himself, and is weakening the will-power which he already possesses.

The increased strength of will which is gained by success in overcoming bad habits enables one to initiate good habits; for, while the conquering of a bad habit requires merely strength of purpose, the forming of a new one necessitates the *intelligent direction of purpose*. To do this, a man must be mentally active and energetic, and must keep a constant watch upon himself. As a man succeeds in perfecting himself in the second rule, it will not be very difficult for him to observe the third, that of giving scrupulous attention to the duty of the present moment. Thoroughness is a step in the development of the will which cannot be passed over. Slipshod work is an indication of weakness. Perfection should be aimed at, even in the smallest task. By not dividing the mind, but giving the whole attention to each separate task as it presents itself, singleness of purpose and intense concentration of mind are gradually gained—two mental powers which give weight and worth of character, and bring repose and joy to their possessor.

The fourth rule—that of doing vigorously, and at once, whatever has to be done—is equally important. Idleness and a strong will cannot go together, and procrastination is a total barrier to the acquisition of purposeful action. Nothing should be "put off" until another time, not even for a few minutes. That which ought to be done now should be done now. This seems a little thing, but it is of far-reaching importance. It leads to strength, success, and peace.

The man who is to manifest a cultivated will must also live by certain fixed rules. He must not blindly gratify his passions and impulses, but must school them to obedience. He should live according to principle, and not according to passion. He should decide what he will eat and drink and wear, and what he will not eat and drink and wear; how many meals per day he will have, and at what times he will have them; at what time he will go to bed, and at what time get up. He should make rules for the right government of his conduct in every department of his life, and should religiously adhere to them. To live loosely and indiscriminately, eating and drinking and sensually indulging at the beck and call of appetite and inclination, is to be a mere animal, and not a man with will and reason. The beast in man must be scourged and disciplined and brought into subjection, and this can only be done by training the mind and life on certain fixed rules of right conduct. The saint attains to holiness by not violating his vows, and the man who lives according to good and fixed rules, is strong to accomplish his purpose.

The sixth rule, that of controlling the tongue, must be practised until one has perfect command of his speech, so that he utters nothing in peevishness, anger, irritability, or with evil intent. The man of strong will does not allow his tongue to run thoughtlessly and without check.

All these six rules, if faithfully practised, will lead up to the seventh, which is the most important of them all—namely, rightly controlling the mind. Self-control is the most essential thing in life, yet least understood; but he who patiently practises the rules herein laid down, bringing them into requisition in all his ways and undertakings, will learn, by his own experience and efforts, how to control and train his mind, and to earn thereby the supreme crown of manhood—the crown of a perfectly poised will.

THOROUGHNESS

Thoroughness consists in doing little things as though they were the greatest things in the world. That the little things of life are of primary importance, is a truth not generally understood, and the thought that little things can be neglected, thrown aside, or slurred over, is at the root of that lack of thoroughness which is so common, and which results in imperfect work and unhappy lives.

When one understands that the great things of the world and of life consist of a combination of small things, and that without this aggregation of small things the great things would be nonexistent, then he begins to pay careful attention to those things which he formerly regarded as insignificant. He thus acquires the quality of thoroughness, and becomes a man of usefulness and influence; for the possession or non-possession of this one quality may mean all the difference between a life of peace and power, and one of misery and weakness.

Every employer of labour knows how comparatively rare this quality is—how difficult it is to find men and women who will put thought and energy into their work, and do it completely and satisfactorily. Bad workmanship abounds. Skill and excellence are acquired by few. Thoughtlessness, carelessness, and laziness are such common vices that it should cease to appear strange that, in spite of "social reform," the ranks of the unemployed should continue to swell, for those who scamp their work to-day will, another day, in the hour of deep necessity, look and ask for work in vain.

The law of "the survival of the fittest" is not based on cruelty, it is based on justice; it is one aspect of that divine equity which everywhere prevails. Vice is "beaten with many stripes"; if it were not so, how could virtue be developed? The thoughtless and lazy cannot take precedence of, or stand equally with, the thoughtful and industrious. A friend of mine tells me that his father gave all his children the following piece of advice:

> Whatever your future work may be, put your whole mind upon it and do it thoroughly; you need then have no fear as to your welfare, for there are so many who are careless and negligent that the services of the thorough man are always in demand.

I know those who have, for years, tried almost in vain to secure competent workmanship in spheres which do not require exceptional skill, but which call chiefly for forethought, energy, and conscientious care. They have discharged one after another for negligence, laziness, incompetence, and persistent breaches of duty—not to mention other vices which have no bearing on this subject; yet the vast army of the unemployed continues to cry out against the laws, against society, and against Heaven.

The cause of this common lack of thoroughness is not far to seek; it lies in that thirst for pleasure which not only creates a distaste for steady labour, but renders one incapable of doing the best work, and of properly fulfilling one's duty. A short time ago, a case came under my observation (one of many such), of a poor woman who was given, at her earnest appeal, a responsible and lucrative position. She had been at her post only a few days when she began to talk of the "pleasure trips" she was going to have now she had come to that place. She was discharged at the end of a month for negligence and incompetence.

As two objects cannot occupy the same space at the same time, so the mind that is occupied with pleasure cannot also be concentrated upon the perfect performance of duty. Pleasure has its own place and time, but its consideration should not be allowed to enter the mind during those hours which should be devoted to duty. Those who, while engaged in their worldly task, are continually dwelling upon anticipated pleasures, cannot do otherwise than bungle through their work, or even neglect it when their pleasure seems to be at stake.

Thoroughness is completeness, perfection; it means doing a thing so well that there is nothing left to be desired; it means doing one's work, if not better than anyone else can do it, at least not worse than the best that others do. It means the exercise of much thought, the putting forth of great energy, the persistent application of the mind to its task, the cultivation of patience, perseverance, and a high sense of duty. An ancient teacher said, "If anything has to be done, let a man do it, let him attack it vigorously"; and another teacher said, "Whatsoever thy hand findeth to do, do it with thy might."

He who lacks thoroughness in his worldly duties, will also lack the same quality in spiritual things. He will not improve his character; will be weak and half-hearted in his religion, and will not accomplish any good and useful end. The man who keeps one eye on worldly pleasure and the other on religion, and who thinks he can have the advantage of both conditions, will not be thorough either in his pleasure-seeking or his religion, but will make a sorry business of both. It is better to be a whole-souled worldling than a half-hearted religionist; better to give the entire mind to a lower thing than half of it to a higher.

It is preferable to be thorough, even if it be in a bad or selfish direction, rather than inefficient and squeamish in good directions, for thoroughness leads more rapidly to the development of character and the acquisition of wisdom; it accelerates progress and unfoldment; and while it leads the bad to something better, it spurs the good to higher and ever higher heights of usefulness and power.

MIND-BUILDING AND LIFE-BUILDING

Everything both in nature and the works of man is produced by a process of building. The rock is built up of atoms; the plant, the animal, and man are built up of cells; a house is built of bricks, and a book is built of letters. A world is composed of a large number of forms, and a city of a large number of houses. The arts, sciences, and institutions of a nation are built up by the efforts of individuals. The history of a nation is the building of its deeds.

The process of building necessitates the alternate process of breaking down. Old forms that have served their purpose are broken up, and the material of which they are composed enters into new combinations. There is reciprocal integration and disintegration. In all compounded bodies, old cells are ceaselessly being broken up, and new cells are formed to take their place. The works of man also require to be continually renewed until they have become old and useless, when they are torn down in order that some better purpose may be served. These two processes of breaking down and building up in Nature are called *death* and *life;* in the artificial works of man they are called *destruction* and *restoration.*

This dual process, which obtains universally in things visible, also obtains universally in things invisible. As a body is built of cells, and a house of bricks, so a man's mind is built of thoughts. The various characters of men are none other than compounds of thoughts of varying combinations. Herein we see the deep truth of the saying, "As a man thinketh in his heart, so is he." Individual characteristics are *fixed processes of thought;* that is, they are fixed in the sense that they have become such an integral part of the character that they can be only altered or removed by a protracted effort of the will, and by much self-discipline. Character is built in the same way as a tree or a house is built—namely, by the ceaseless addition of new material, and that material is *thought.* By the aid of millions of bricks a city is built; by the aid of millions of thoughts a mind, a character, is built. "Rome was not built in a day," and a Buddha, a Plato, or a Shakespeare is not built in a lifetime.

Every man is a mind-builder, whether he recognizes it or not. Every man must perforce think, and every thought is another brick laid down in the edifice of mind. Such "brick-laying" is done loosely and carelessly by a vast number of people, the result being unstable and tottering characters that are ready to go down under the first little gust of trouble or temptation. Some, also, put into the building of their minds large numbers of impure thoughts; these are so many rotten bricks that crumble away as fast as they are put in, leaving always an unfinished and unsightly building, and one which can afford no comfort and no shelter for its possessor. Debilitating thoughts about one's health, enervating thoughts concerning unlawful pleasures, weakening thoughts of failure, and sickly thoughts of self-pity and self-praise are useless bricks with which no substantial mind-temple can be raised.

Pure thoughts, wisely chosen and well placed, are so many durable bricks which will never crumble away, and from which a finished and beautiful building, and one which affords comfort and shelter for its possessor, can be rapidly erected. Bracing thoughts of strength, of confidence, of duty; inspiring thoughts of a large, free, unfettered, and unselfish life, are useful bricks with which a substantial mind-temple can be raised; and the building of such a temple necessitates that old and useless habits of thought be broken down and destroyed.

> *Build thee more stately mansions, O my soul!*
> *As the swift seasons roll.*

Each man is the builder of himself. If he is the occupant of a jerry-built hovel of a mind that lets in the rains of many troubles, and through which blow the keen winds of oft-recurring disappointments, let him get to work to build a more noble mansion which will afford him better protection against those mental elements. Trying to weakly shift the responsibility for his jerry-building on to the devil, or his forefathers, or anything or anybody but himself, will neither add to his comfort, nor help him to build a better habitation.

When he wakes up to a sense of his responsibility, and an approximate estimate of his power, then he will commence to build like a true workman, and will produce a symmetrical and finished character that will endure, and be cherished by posterity, and which, while affording a never-failing protection for himself, will continue to give shelter to many a struggling one when he has passed away.

The whole visible universe is framed on a few mathematical principles. All the wonderful works of man in the material world have been brought about by the rigid observance of a few underlying principles; and all that there is to the making of a successful, happy, and beautiful life, is the knowledge and application of a few simple, root principles.

If a man is to erect a building that is to resist the fiercest storms, he must build it on a simple, mathematical principle, or law, such as the square or the circle; if he ignores this, his edifice will topple down even before it is finished.

Likewise, if a man is to build up a successful, strong, and exemplary life—a life that will stoutly resist the fiercest storms of adversity and temptation—it must be framed on a few simple, undeviating moral principles.

Four of these principles are—*Justice, Rectitude, Sincerity,* and *Kindness.* These four ethical truths are to the making of a life what the four lines of a square are to the building of a house. If a man ignores them and thinks to obtain success and happiness and peace by injustice, trickery, and selfishness, he is in the position of a builder who imagines he can build a strong and durable habitation while ignoring the relative arrangement of mathematical lines, and he will, in the end, obtain only disappointment and failure.

He may, for a time, make money, which will delude him into believing that injustice and dishonesty pay well; but in reality his life is so weak and unstable that it is ready at any moment to fall; and when a critical period comes, as come it must, his affairs, his reputation, and his riches crumble to ruins, and he is buried in his own desolation.

It is totally impossible for a man to achieve a truly successful and happy life who ignores the four moral principles enumerated, whilst the man who scrupulously observes them in all his dealings can no more fail of success and blessedness than the earth can fail of the light and warmth of the sun so long as it keeps to its lawful orbit; for he is working in harmony with the fundamental laws of the universe; he is building his life on a basis which cannot be altered or overthrown, and, therefore, all that he does will be so strong and durable, and all the parts of his life will be so coherent, harmonious, and firmly knit that it cannot possibly be brought to ruin.

In all the universal forms which are built up by the Great Invisible and unerring Power, it will be found that the observance of mathematical law is carried out with unfailing exactitude down to the most minute detail. The microscope reveals the fact that the infinitely small is as perfect as the infinitely great.

A snowflake is as perfect as a star. Likewise, in the erection of a building by man, the strictest attention must be paid to every detail.

A foundation must first be laid, and, although it is to be buried and hidden, it must receive the greatest care, and be made stronger than any other part of the building; then stone upon stone, brick upon brick is carefully laid with the aid of the plumb-line, until at last the building stands complete in its durability, strength, and beauty.

Even so it is with the life of a man. He who would have a life secure and blessed, a life freed from the miseries and failures to which so many fall victims, must carry the practice of the moral principles into every detail of his life, into every momentary duty and trivial transaction. In every little thing he must be thorough and honest, neglecting nothing.

To neglect or misapply any little detail—be he commercial man, agriculturist, professional man, or artisan—is the same as neglecting a stone or a brick in a building, and it will be a source of weakness and trouble.

The majority of those who fail and come to grief do so through neglecting the apparently *insignificant* details.

It is a common error to suppose that little things can be passed by, and that the greater things are more important, and should receive all attention; but a cursory glance at the universe, as well as a little serious reflection on life, will teach the lesson that nothing great can exist which is not made up of small details, and in the composition of which every detail is perfect.

He who adopts the four ethical principles as the law and base of his life, who raises the edifice of character upon them, who in his thoughts and words and actions does not wander from them, whose every duty and every passing transaction is performed in strict accordance with their exactions,—such a man, laying down the hidden foundation of integrity of heart securely and strongly, cannot fail to raise up a structure which shall bring him honour; and he is building a temple in which he can repose in peace and blessedness—even the strong and beautiful Temple of his life.

CULTIVATION OF CONCENTRATION

Concentration, or the bringing of the mind to a centre and keeping it there, is vitally necessary to the accomplishment of any task. It is the father of *thoroughness* and the mother of *excellence*. As a faculty, it is not an end in itself, but is an aid to all faculties, all work. Not a purpose in itself, it is yet a power which serves all purposes. Like steam in mechanics, it is a dynamic force in the machinery of the mind and the functions of life.

The faculty is a common possession, though in its perfection it is rare—just as *will* and *reason* are common possessions, though a perfectly poised will and a comprehensive reason are rare possessions—and the mystery which some modern mystical writers have thrown around it is entirely superfluous. Every successful man, in whatever direction his success may lie, practises concentration, though he may know nothing about it as a subject of study: every time one becomes absorbed in a book or task, or is rapt in devotion or assiduous in duty, concentration, in a greater or lesser degree, is brought into play.

Many books purporting to give instructions on concentration make its practice and acquisition an end in itself. Than this there is no surer nor swifter way to its destruction. The fixing of the eyes upon the tip of the nose, upon a door-knob, a picture, a mystical symbol, or the portrait of a saint; or the centring of the mind upon the navel, the pineal gland, or some imaginary point in space (I have seen all these methods seriously advised in works on this subject) with the object of acquiring concentration, is like trying to nourish the body by merely moving the jaw as in the act of eating, without taking food. Such methods prevent the end at which they aim. They lead toward dispersion and not concentration; toward weakness and imbecility rather than toward power and intelligence. I have met those who have squandered, by these practices, what measure of concentration they at first possessed, and have become the prey of a weak and wandering mind.

Concentration is an aid to the doing of something; it is not the doing of something in itself. A ladder has no value in and of itself, but only in so far as it enables us to *reach* something which we could not otherwise reach. In like manner, concentration is that which enables the mind to accomplish with ease that which it would be otherwise impossible to accomplish; but of itself it is a dead thing, and not a living accomplishment.

Concentration is so interwoven with the uses of life that it cannot be separated from duty; and he who tries to acquire it *apart from his task, his duty,* will not only fail, but will diminish, and not increase, his mental control and executive capacity, and so render himself less and less fit to succeed in his undertakings.

In the task of the hour is all the means for the cultivation of concentration—whether that task be the acquiring of divine knowledge, or the sweeping of a floor—without resorting to methods which have no practical bearing on life; for what is concentration but the bringing of a well-controlled mind to the doing of that which has to be done?

He who does his work in an aimless, a hurried, or thoughtless manner, and resorts to his artificial "concentration methods"—to his door-knob, his picture, or nasal extremity—in order to gain that which he imagines to be some kind of mystical power—but which is a very ordinary and practical quality—though he may drift toward insanity (and I knew one man who became insane by these practices), he will not increase in steadiness of mind.

The great enemy of concentration—and therefore of all skill and power—is a wavering, wandering, undisciplined mind; and it is in overcoming this that concentration is acquired. A scattered and undisciplined army would be useless. To make it effective in action and swift in victory it must be solidly concentrated and masterfully directed. Scattered and diffused thoughts are weak and worthless. Thoughts marshalled, commanded, and directed upon a given point, are invincible; confusion, doubt, and difficulty give way before their masterly approach. Concentrated thought enters largely into all successes, and informs all victories.

There is no more secret about its acquirement than about any other acquisition, for it is governed by the underlying principle of all development, namely, *practice.* To be able to do a thing, you must begin to *do it,* and keep on doing it until the thing is mastered. This principle prevails universally— in all arts, sciences, trades; in all learning, conduct, religion. To be able to paint, one must paint; to know how to use a tool skillfully, he must use the tool; to become learned, he must learn; to become wise, he must do wise things; and to successfully concentrate his mind, he must concentrate it. But the doing is not all—*it must be done with energy and intelligence.*

The beginning of concentration, then, is to go to your daily task and put your mind on it, bringing all your intelligence and mental energy to a focus upon that which has to be done; and every time the thoughts are found wandering aimlessly away, they should be brought promptly back to the thing in hand. Thus the "centre" upon which you are to bring your mind to a point, is (not your pineal gland or a point in space), but the work which you are doing every day; and your object in thus concentrating is to be able to do your work with smooth rapidity and consummate skill; for until you can thus do your work, you have not gained any degree of control over the mind; you have not acquired the power of concentration.

This powerful focussing of one's thought and energy and will upon the doing of things is difficult at first—as everything worth acquiring is difficult—but daily efforts, strenuously made and patiently followed up, will soon lead to such a measure of self-control as will enable one to bring a strong and penetrating mind to bear upon any work undertaken; a mind that will quickly comprehend all the details of the work, and dispose of them with accuracy and despatch. He will thus, as his concentrative capacity increases, enlarge his usefulness in the scheme of things, and increase his value to the world, thus inviting nobler opportunities, and opening the door to higher duties; he will also experience the joy of a wider and fuller life.

In the process of concentration there are the four following stages:

1. Attention.
2. Contemplation.
3. Abstraction.
4. Activity in Repose.

At first the thoughts are arrested, and the mind is fixed upon the object of concentration, which is the task in hand—this is *attention.* The mind is then roused into vigorous thought concerning the way of proceeding with the task—this is *contemplation.* Protracted contemplation leads to a condition of mind in which the doors of the senses are all closed against the entrance of outside distractions, the thoughts being wrapped in, and solely and intensely centred upon, the work in hand—this is *abstraction.* The mind thus centred in profound cogitation reaches a state in which the maximum of work is accomplished with the minimum of friction—this is *activity in repose.*

Attention is the first stage in all successful work. They who lack it fail in everything. Such are the lazy, the thoughtless, the indifferent and incompetent. When attention is followed by an awakening of the mind to serious thought, then the second stage is reached. To ensure success in all ordinary, worldly undertakings, it is not necessary to go beyond these two stages. They are reached, in a greater or lesser degree, by all that large army of skilled and competent workers which carries out the work of the world in its manifold departments, and only a comparatively small number reach the third stage of *abstraction;* for when abstraction is reached, we have entered the sphere of genius. In the first two stages, the work and the mind are separate, and the work is done more or less laboriously, and with a degree of friction; but in the third stage, a marriage of the work with the mind takes place, there is a fusion, a union, and the two become one: then there is a superior efficiency with less labour and friction. In the perfection of the first two stages, the mind is objectively engaged, and is easily drawn from its centre by external sights and sounds; but when the mind has attained perfection in abstraction, the *subjective* method of working is accomplished, as distinguished from the *objective.* The thinker is then oblivious to the outside world, but is vividly alive in his mental operations. If spoken to, he will not hear; and if plied with more vigorous appeals, he will bring back his mind to outside things as one coming out of a dream; indeed, this abstraction is a kind of waking dream, but its similarity to a dream ends with the subjective state: it does not obtain in the mental operations of that state, in which, instead of the confusion of dreaming, there is perfect order, penetrating insight, and a wide range of comprehension. Whoever attains to perfection in abstraction will manifest genius in the particular work upon which his mind is centred. Inventors, artists, poets, scientists, philosophers, and all men of genius, are men of abstraction. They accomplish subjectively, and with ease, that which the objective workers—men who have not yet attained beyond the second stage in concentration—cannot accomplish with the most strenuous labour.

When the fourth stage—that of *activity in repose*—is attained, then concentration in its perfection is acquired. I am unable to find a single word which will fully express this dual condition of intense activity combined with steadiness, or rest, and have therefore employed the term "activity in repose." The term appears contradictory, but the simple illustration of a spinning top will serve to explain the paradox. When a top spins at the maximum velocity, the friction is reduced to the minimum, and the top assumes that condition of perfect repose which is a sight so beautiful to the eye, and so captivating to the mind, of the schoolboy, who then says his top is "asleep." The top is apparently motionless, but it is the rest, not of inertia, but of intense and perfectly balanced activity. So the mind that has acquired perfect concentration is, when engaged in that intense activity of thought which results in productive work of the highest kind, in a state of quiet poise and calm repose. Externally, there is no apparent activity, no disturbance, and the face of a man who has acquired this power will assume a more or less radiant calmness, and the face will be more sublimely calm when the mind is most intensely engaged in active thought.

Each stage of concentration has its particular power. Thus the first stage, when perfected, leads to usefulness; the second leads to skill, ability, talent; the third leads to originality and genius; while the fourth leads to mastery and power, and makes leaders and teachers of men.

In the development of concentration, also, as in all objects of growth, the following stages embody the preceding ones in their entirety. Thus in contemplation, attention is contained; in abstraction, both attention and contemplation are embodied; and he who has reached the last stage, brings into play, in the act of contemplation, all the four stages.

He who has perfected himself in concentration is able, at any moment, to bring his thoughts to a point upon any matter, and to search into it with the strong light of an active comprehension. He can both take a thing up and lay it down with equal deliberation. He has learned how to use his thinking faculties to fixed purposes, and guide them toward definite ends. He is an intelligent doer of things, and not a weak wanderer amid chaotic thought.

Decision, energy, alertness, as well as deliberation, judgment, and gravity, accompany the habit of concentration; and that vigorous mental training which its cultivation involves, leads, through ever-increasing usefulness and success in worldly occupations, toward that higher form of concentration called "meditation," in which the mind becomes divinely illumined, and acquires the heavenly knowledge.

PRACTICE OF MEDITATION

When *aspiration* is united to *concentration,* the result is *meditation.* When a man intensely desires to reach and realise a higher, purer, and more radiant life than the merely worldly and pleasure loving life, he engages in *aspiration;* and when he earnestly concentrates his thoughts upon the finding of that life, he practises meditation.

Without intense aspiration, there can be no meditation. Lethargy and indifference are fatal to its practise. The more intense the nature of a man, the more readily will he find meditation, and the more successfully will he practise it. A fiery nature will most rapidly scale the heights of Truth in meditation, when its aspirations have become sufficiently awakened.

Concentration is necessary to worldly success: meditation is necessary to spiritual success. Worldly skill and knowledge are acquired by concentration: spiritual skill and knowledge are acquired by meditation. By concentration a man can scale the highest heights of genius, but he cannot scale the heavenly heights of Truth: to accomplish this, he must meditate. By concentration a man may acquire the wonderful comprehension and vast power of a Cæsar; by meditation he may reach the divine wisdom and perfect peace of a Buddha. The perfection of concentration is *power;* the perfection of meditation is *wisdom.* By concentration, men acquire skill in the doing of the things of life—in science, art, trade, etc.,—but by meditation, they acquire skill in *life* itself; in right living, enlightenment, wisdom, etc. Saints, sages, saviours—wise men and divine teachers—are the finished products of holy meditation.

The four stages in concentration are brought into play in meditation; the difference between the two powers being one of *direction,* and not of nature. Meditation is therefore *spiritual concentration;*

the bringing of the mind to a focus in its search for the divine knowledge, the divine life; the intense dwelling, in thought, on Truth. Thus a man aspires to know and realise, above all things else, the Truth; he then gives *attention* to conduct, to life, to self-purification: giving attention to these things, he passes into serious *contemplation* of the facts, problems, and mystery of life: thus contemplating, he comes to love Truth so fully and intensely as to become wholly absorbed in it, the mind is drawn away from its wanderings in a multitude of desires, and, solving one by one the problems of life, realises that profound union with Truth which is the state of *abstraction;* and thus absorbed in Truth, there is that balance and poise of character, that divine *action in repose,* which is the abiding calm and peace of an emancipated and enlightened mind.

Meditation is more difficult to practise than concentration because it involves a much more severe self-discipline than that which obtains in concentration. A man can practise concentration without purifying his heart and life, whereas the process of purification is inseparable from meditation. The object of meditation is divine enlightenment, the attainment of Truth, and is therefore interwoven with practical purity and righteousness. Thus while, at first, the time spent in actual meditation is short—perhaps only half an hour in the early morning—the knowledge gained in that half-hour of vivid aspiration and concentrated thought is embodied in practise during the whole day. In meditation, therefore, the entire life of a man is involved; and as he advances in its practise he becomes more and more fitted to perform the duties of life in the circumstances in which he may be placed, for he becomes stronger, holier, calmer, and wiser.

The principle of meditation is twofold, namely—

1. Purification of the heart by repetitive thought on pure things.
2. Attainment of divine knowledge by embodying such purity in practical life.

Man is a *thought-being,* and his life and character are determined by the thoughts in which he habitually dwells. By practise, association, and habit, thoughts tend to repeat themselves with greater and greater ease and frequency, and so "fix" the character in a given direction by producing that automatic action which is called "habit." By daily dwelling upon pure thoughts, the man of meditation forms the habit of pure and enlightened thinking which leads to pure and enlightened actions and well-performed duties. By the ceaseless repetition of pure thoughts, he at last becomes one with those thoughts, and is a purified being, manifesting his attainment in pure actions, in a serene and wise life.

The majority of men live in a series of conflicting desires, passions, emotions, and speculations, and there are restlessness, uncertainty, and sorrow; but when a man begins to train his mind in meditation, he gradually gains control over this inward conflict by bringing his thoughts to a focus upon a central principle. In this way the old habits of impure and erroneous thought and action are broken up, and the new habits of pure and enlightened thought and action are formed; the man becomes more and more reconciled to Truth, and there is increasing harmony and insight, a growing perfection and peace.

A powerful and lofty aspiration toward Truth is always accompanied with a keen sense of the sorrow and brevity and mystery of life, and until this condition of mind is reached, meditation is impossible. Merely musing, or whiling away the time in idle dreaming (habits to which the word meditation is frequently applied), are very far removed from meditation, in the lofty spiritual sense which we attach to that condition.

It is easy to mistake *reverie* for meditation. This is a fatal error which must be avoided by one striving to meditate. The two must not be confounded. Reverie is a loose dreaming into which a man falls; meditation is a strong, purposeful thinking into which a man rises. Reverie is easy and pleasurable; meditation is at first difficult and irksome. Reverie thrives in indolence and luxury; meditation arises from strenuousness and discipline. Reverie is first alluring, then sensuous, and then sensual. Meditation is first forbidding, then profitable, and then peaceful. Reverie is dangerous; it undermines self-control. Meditation is protective; it establishes self-control.

There are certain signs by which one can know whether he is engaging in reverie or meditation. The indications of reverie are:

1. A desire to avoid exertion.
2. A desire to experience the pleasures of dreaming.
3. An increasing distaste for one's worldly duties.
4. A desire to shirk one's worldly responsibilities.
5. Fear of consequences.
6. A wish to get money with as little effort as possible.
7. Lack of self-control.

The indications of meditation are:

1. Increase of both physical and mental energy.
2. A strenuous striving after wisdom.
3. A decrease of irksomeness in the performance of duty.
4. A fixed determination to faithfully fulfil all worldly responsibilities.
5. Freedom from fear.
6. Indifference to riches.
7. Possession of self-control.

There are certain times, places, and conditions in and under which it is impossible to meditate, others wherein it is difficult to meditate, and others wherein meditation is rendered more accessible; and these, which should be known and carefully observed, are as follows:

TIMES, PLACES, AND CONDITIONS IN WHICH MEDITATION IS IMPOSSIBLE.

1. At, or immediately after, meals.
2. In places of pleasure.
3. In crowded places.
4. While walking rapidly.
5. While lying in bed in the morning.
6. While smoking.
7. While lying on a couch or bed for physical or mental relaxation.

TIMES, PLACES, AND CONDITIONS IN WHICH MEDITATION IS DIFFICULT.

1. At night.
2. In a luxuriously furnished room.
3. While sitting on a soft, yielding seat.
4. While wearing gay clothing.
5. When in company.
6. When the body is weary.
7. If the body is given too much food.

TIMES, PLACES, AND CONDITIONS IN WHICH IT IS BEST TO MEDITATE.

1. Very early in the morning.
2. Immediately before meals.
3. In solitude.
4. In the open air or in a plainly furnished room.
5. While sitting on a hard seat.
6. When the body is strong and vigorous.
7. When the body is modestly and plainly clothed.

It will be seen by the foregoing instructions that ease, luxury, and indulgence (which induce reverie) render meditation difficult, and when strongly pronounced make it impossible; while strenuousness, discipline, and self-denial (which dispel reverie), make meditation comparatively easy. The body, too, should be neither overfed nor starved; neither in rags nor flauntingly clothed. It should not be tired, but should be at its highest point of energy and strength, as the holding of the mind to a concentrated train of subtle and lofty thought requires a high degree of both physical and mental energy.

Aspiration can often best be aroused, and the mind renewed in meditation, by the mental repetition of a lofty precept, a beautiful sentence or a verse of poetry. Indeed, the mind that is ready for meditation will instinctively adopt this practise. Mere mechanical repetition is worthless, and even a hindrance. The words repeated must be so applicable to one's own condition that they are dwelt upon lovingly and with concentrated devotion. In this way aspiration and concentration harmoniously combine to produce, without undue strain, the state of meditation.

All the conditions above stated are of the utmost importance in the early stages of meditation, and should be carefully noted and duly observed by all who are striving to acquire the practise; and those who faithfully follow the instructions, and who strive and persevere, will not fail to gather in, in due season, the harvest of purity, wisdom, bliss, and peace; and will surely eat of the sweet fruits of holy meditation.

THE POWER OF PURPOSE

Dispersion is weakness; concentration is power. Destruction is a scattering, preservation a uniting, process. Things are useful and thoughts are powerful in the measure that their parts are strongly and intelligently concentrated. Purpose is highly concentrated thought. All the mental energies are directed to the attainment of an object, and obstacles which intervene between the thinker and the object are, one after another, broken down and overcome. Purpose is the key-stone in the temple of achievement. It binds and holds together in a complete whole that which would otherwise lie scattered and useless. Empty whims, ephemeral fancies, vague desires, and half-hearted resolutions have no place in purpose. In the sustained determination to accomplish there is an invincible power which swallows up all inferior considerations, and marches direct to victory.

All successful men are men of purpose. They hold fast to an idea, a project, a plan, and will not let it go; they cherish it, brood upon it, tend and develop it; and when assailed by difficulties, they refuse to be beguiled into surrender; indeed, the intensity of the purpose increases with the growing magnitude of the obstacles encountered.

The men who have moulded the destinies of humanity have been men mighty of purpose. Like the Roman laying his road, they have followed along a well-defined path, and have refused to swerve aside even when torture and death confronted them. The Great Leaders of the race are the mental road-makers, and mankind follows in the intellectual and spiritual paths which they have carved out and beaten.

Great is the power of purpose. To know how great, let a man study it in the lives of those whose influence has shaped the ends of nations and directed the destinies of the world. In an Alexander, a Cæsar, or a Napoleon, we see the power of purpose when it is directed in worldly and personal channels; in a Confucius, a Buddha, or a Christ, we perceive its vaster power when its course is along heavenly and impersonal paths.

Purpose goes with intelligence. There are lesser and greater purposes according with degrees of intelligence. A great mind will always be great of purpose. A weak intelligence will be without purpose. A drifting mind argues a measure of undevelopment.

What can resist an unshakable purpose? What can stand against it or turn it aside? Inert matter yields to a living force, and circumstance succumbs to the power of purpose. Truly, the man of unlawful purpose will, in achieving his ends, destroy himself, but the man of good and lawful purpose cannot fail. It only needs that he daily renew the fire and energy of his fixed resolve, to consummate his object.

The weak man, who grieves because he is misunderstood, will not greatly achieve; the vain man, who steps aside from his resolve in order to please others and gain their approbation, will not highly achieve; the double-minded man, who thinks to compromise his purpose, will fail.

The man of fixed purpose who, whether misunderstandings and foul accusations, or flatteries and fair promises, rain upon him, does not yield a fraction of his resolve, is the man of excellence and achievement; of success, greatness, power.

Hindrances stimulate the man of purpose; difficulties nerve him to renewed exertion; mistakes, losses, pains, do not subdue him; and failures are steps in the ladder of success, for he is ever conscious of the certainty of final achievement.

All things at last yield to the silent, irresistible, all-conquering energy of purpose.

Out of the night that covers me,
    Black as the pit from pole to pole,
I thank whatever gods may be
    For my unconquerable soul.

In the fell clutch of circumstance
    I have not whined nor cried aloud;
Under the bludgeonings of chance
    My head is bloody but unbowed.

It matters not how strait the gate,
    How charged with punishment the scroll;
I am the master of my fate,
    I am the captain of my soul.

THE JOY OF ACCOMPLISHMENT

Joy is always the accompaniment of a task successfully accomplished. An undertaking completed, or a piece of work done, always brings rest and satisfaction. "When a man has done his duty, he is light-hearted and happy," says Emerson; and no matter how insignificant the task may appear, the doing of it faithfully and with whole-souled energy always results in cheerfulness and peace of mind.

Of all miserable men, the shirker is the most miserable. Thinking to find ease and happiness in avoiding difficult duties and necessary tasks, which require the expenditure of labour and exertion, his mind is always uneasy and disturbed, he becomes burdened with an inward sense of shame, and forfeits manliness and self-respect. "He who will not work according to his faculty, let him perish according to his necessity," says Carlyle; and it is a moral law that the man who avoids duty, and does not work to the full extent of his capacity, does actually perish, first in his character and last in his body and circumstances. Life and action are synonymous, and immediately a man tries to escape exertion, either physical or mental, he has commenced to decay.

On the other hand, the energetic increase in life by the full exercise of their powers, by overcoming difficulties, and by bringing to completion tasks which called for the strenuous use of mind or muscle.

How happy is a child when a school-lesson, long laboured over, is mastered at last! The athlete, who has trained his body through long months or years of discipline and strain, is richly blessed in his increased health and strength; and is met with the rejoicings of his friends when he carries home the prize from the field of contest. After many years of ungrudging toil, the heart of the scholar is gladdened with the advantages and powers which learning bestows. The business man, grappling incessantly with difficulties and drawbacks, is amply repaid in the happy assurance of well-earned success; and the horticulturist, vigorously contending with the stubborn soil, sits down at last to eat of the fruits of his labour.

Every successful accomplishment, even in worldly things, is repaid with its own measure of joy; and in spiritual things, the joy which supervenes upon the perfection of purpose is sure, deep, and abiding. Great is the heartfelt joy (albeit ineffable) when, after innumerable and apparently unsuccessful attempts, some ingrained fault of character is at last cast out to trouble its erstwhile victim and the world no more. The striver after virtue—he who is engaged in the holy task of building up a noble character—tastes, at every step of conquest over self, a joy which does not again leave him, but which becomes an integral part of his spiritual nature.

All life is a struggle; both without and within there are conditions against which man must contend; his very existence is a series of efforts and accomplishments, and his right to remain among men as a useful unit of humanity depends upon the measure of his capacity for wrestling successfully with the elements of nature without, or with the enemies of virtue and truth within.

It is demanded of man that he shall continue to strive after better things, after greater perfection, after higher and still higher achievements; and in accordance with the measure of his obedience to this demand, does the angel of joy wait upon his footsteps and minister unto him; for he who is anxious to learn, eager to know, and who puts forth efforts to accomplish, finds the joy which eternally sings at the heart of the universe. First in little things, then in greater, and then in greater still, must man strive; until at last he is prepared to make the supreme effort, and strive for the accomplishment of Truth, succeeding in which, he will realise the eternal joy.

The price of life is effort; the acme of effort is accomplishment; the reward of accomplishment is joy. Blessed is the man who strives against his own selfishness; he will taste in its fulness the joy of accomplishment.

ABOVE LIFE'S TURMOIL

(1910)

CONTENTS

FOREWORD

We cannot alter external things, nor shape other people to our liking, nor mould the world to our wishes but we can alter internal things,—our desires, passions, thoughts,—we can shape our liking to other people, and we can mould the inner world of our own mind in accordance with wisdom, and so reconcile it to the outer world of men and things. The turmoil of the world we cannot avoid, but the disturbances of mind we can overcome. The duties and difficulties of life claim our attention, but we can rise above all anxiety concerning them. Surrounded by noise, we can yet have a quiet mind; involved in responsibilities, the heart can be at rest; in the midst of strife, we can know the abiding peace. The twenty pieces which comprise this book, unrelated as some of them are in the letter, will be found to be harmonious in the spirit, in that they point the reader toward those heights of self-knowledge and self-conquest which, rising above the turbulence of the world, lift their peaks where the Heavenly Silence reigns.

—JAMES ALLEN

TRUE HAPPINESS

To maintain an unchangeable sweetness of disposition, to think only thoughts that are pure and gentle, and to be happy under all circumstances,—such blessed conditions and such beauty of character and life should be the aim of all, and particularly so of those who wish to lessen the misery of the world. If anyone has failed to lift *himself* above ungentleness, impurity, and unhappiness, he is greatly deluded if he imagines he can make the world happier by the propagation of any theory or theology. He who is daily living in harshness, impurity, or unhappiness is day by day adding to the sum of the world's misery; whereas he who continually lives in goodwill, and does not depart from happiness, is day by day increasing the sum of the world's happiness, and this independently of any religious beliefs which these may or may not hold.

He who has not learned how to be gentle, or giving, loving and happy, has learned very little, great though his book-learning and profound his acquaintance with the letter of Scripture may be, for it is in the process of *becoming* gentle, pure, and happy that the deep, real, and enduring lessons of life are learned. Unbroken sweetness of conduct in the face of all outward antagonism is the infallible indication of a self-conquered soul, the witness of wisdom, and the proof of the possession of Truth.

A sweet and happy soul is the ripened fruit of experience and wisdom, and it sheds abroad the invisible yet powerful aroma of its influence, gladdening the hearts of others, and purifying the world. And all who will, and who have not yet commenced, may begin *this day* if they will so resolve, to live sweetly and happily, as becomes the dignity of a true manhood or womanhood. Do not say that your surroundings are against you. A man's surroundings are *never* against him; they are there to aid him, and all those outward occurrences over which you lose sweetness and peace of mind are the very conditions necessary to your development, and it is only by meeting and overcoming them that you can learn, and grow, and ripen. The fault is in yourself.

Pure happiness is the rightful and healthy condition of the soul, and all may possess it if they will live purely and unselfishly.

Have goodwill
To all that lives, letting unkindness die,
And greed and wrath, so that your lives be made
Like soft airs passing by.

Is this too difficult for you? Then unrest and unhappiness will continue to dwell with you. Your belief and aspiration and resolve are all that are necessary to make it easy, to render it in the near future a thing accomplished, a blessed state realised.

Despondency, irritability, anxiety and complaining, condemning and grumbling—all these are thought-cankers, mind-diseases; they are the indications of a wrong mental condition, and those who suffer therefrom would do well to remedy their thinking and conduct. It is true there is much sin and misery in the world, so that all our love and compassion are needed, *but our misery is not needed*—there is already too much of that. No, it is our cheerfulness and happiness that are needed for there is too little of that. We can give nothing better to the world than beauty of life and character; without this, all other things are vain; this is pre-eminently excellent; it is enduring, real, and not to be overthrown, and it includes all joy and blessedness.

Cease to dwell pessimistically upon the wrongs around you; dwell no more in complaints about, and revolt against, the evil in others, and commence to live free from all wrong and evil yourself. Peace of mind, pure religion, and true reform lie this way. If you would have others true, be true; if you would have the world emancipated from misery and sin, emancipate yourself; if you would have your home and your surroundings happy, be happy. You can transform everything around you if you will transform yourself.

Don't bewail and bemoan . . . .
Don't waste yourself in rejection, nor bark against the bad, but chant the beauties of the good.

And this you will naturally and spontaneously do as you realise the good in yourself.

THE IMMORTAL MAN

Immortality is here and now, and is not a speculative something beyond the grave. It is a lucid state of consciousness in which the sensations of the body, the varying and unrestful states of mind, and the circumstances and events of life are seen to be of a fleeting and therefore of an illusory character.

Immortality does not belong to time, and will never be found in time; it belongs to Eternity; and just as time is here and now, so is Eternity here and now, and a man may find that Eternity and establish in it, if he will overcome the self that derives its life from the unsatisfying and perishable things of time.

Whilst a man remains immersed in sensation, desire, and the passing events of his day-by-day existence, and regards those sensations, desires, and passing events as of the essence of himself, he can have no knowledge of immortality. The thing which such a man desires, and which he mistakes for immortality, is *persistence;* that is, a continuous succession of sensations and events in time. Living in, loving, and clinging to the things which stimulate and minister to his immediate gratification, and realising no state of consciousness above and independent of this, he thirsts for its continuance, and strives to banish the thought that he will at last have to part from those earthly luxuries and delights to which he has become enslaved, and which he regards as being inseparable from himself.

Persistence is the antithesis of immortality; and to be absorbed in it is spiritual death. Its very nature is change, impermanence. It is a continual living and dying.

The death of the body can never bestow upon a man immortality. Spirits are not different from men, and live their little feverish life of broken consciousness, and are still immersed in change and mortality. The mortal man, he who thirsts for the persistence of his pleasure-loving personality, is still mortal after death, and only lives another life with a beginning and an end without memory of the past, or knowledge of the future.

The immortal man is he who has detached himself from the things of time by having ascended into that state of consciousness which is fixed and unvariable, and is not affected by passing events and sensations. Human life consists of an evermoving procession of events, and in this procession the mortal man is immersed, and he is carried along with it; and being so carried along, he has no knowledge of what is behind and before him. The immortal man is he who has stepped out of this procession, and he stands by unmoved and watches it; and from his fixed place he sees both the before, the behind, and the middle of the moving thing called life. No longer identifying himself with the sensations and fluctuations of the personality, or with the outward changes which make up the life in time, he has become the passionless spectator of his own destiny and of the destinies of men and nations.

The mortal man, also, is one who is caught in a dream, and he neither knows that he was formerly awake, nor that he will wake again; he is a dreamer without knowledge, nothing more. The immortal man is as one who has awakened out of his dream, and he knows that his dream was not an enduring reality, but a passing illusion. He is a man with knowledge, the knowledge of both states—that of persistence, and that of immortality—and is in full possession of himself.

The mortal man lives in the time or world state of consciousness which begins and ends; the immortal man lives in the cosmic or heaven state of consciousness, in which there is neither beginning nor end, but an eternal now. Such a man remains poised and steadfast under all changes, and the death of his body will not in any way interrupt the eternal consciousness in which he abides. Of such a one it is said, "He shall not taste of death," because he has stepped out of the stream of mortality, and established himself in the abode of Truth. Bodies, personalities, nations, and worlds pass away, but Truth remains, and its glory is undimmed by time. The immortal man, then, is he who has conquered himself, who no longer identifies himself with the self-seeking forces of the personality, but who has trained himself to direct those forces with the hand of a master, and so has brought them into harmony with the causal energy and source of all things.

The fret and fever of life has ceased, doubt and fear are cast out, and death is not for him who has realised the fadeless splendour of that life of Truth by adjusting heart and mind to the eternal and unchangeable verities.

THE OVERCOMING OF SELF

Many people have very confused and erroneous ideas concerning the terms *"the over-coming of self," "the eradication of desire,"* and *"the annihilation of the personality."* Some (particularly the intellectual who are prone to theories) regard it as a metaphysical theory altogether apart from life and conduct; while others conclude that it is the crushing out of all life, energy and action, and the attempt to idealise stagnation and death. These errors and confusions, arising as they do in the minds of individuals, can only be removed by the individuals themselves; but perhaps it may make their removal a little less difficult (for those who are seeking Truth) by presenting the matter in another way.

The doctrine of the overcoming or annihilation of self is simplicity itself, indeed, so simple, practical, and close at hand is it that a child of five, whose mind has not yet become clouded with theories, theological schemes and speculative philosophies, would be far more likely to comprehend it than many older people who have lost their hold upon simple and beautiful truths by the adoption of complicated theories.

The annihilation of self consists in weeding out and destroying all those elements in the soul which lead to division, strife, suffering, disease and sorrow. It does not mean the destruction of any good and beautiful and peace-producing quality. For instance, when a man is tempted to irritability or anger, and by a great effort overcomes the selfish tendency, casts it from him, and acts from the spirit of patience and love, in that moment of self-conquest he practises the annihilation of self. Every noble man practises it in part, though he may deny it in his words, and he who carries out this practice to its completion, eradicating every selfish tendency until only the divinely beautiful qualities remain, he is said to annihilated the personality (all the personal elements) and to have arrived at Truth.

The self which is to be annihilated is composed of the following ten worthless and sorrow-producing elements:

Lust
Hatred
Avarice
Self-indulgence
Self-seeking

Vanity
Pride
Doubt
Dark belief
Delusion

It is the total abandonment, the complete annihilation of these ten elements, for they comprise the body of desire. On the other hand it teaches the cultivation, practise, and preservation of the following ten divine qualities:

Purity
Patience
Humility
Self-sacrifice
Self-reliance
Fearlessness
Knowledge
Wisdom
Compassion
Love

These comprise the Body of Truth, and to live entirely in them is to be a doer and knower of the Truth, is to be an embodiment of Truth. The combination of the ten elements is called *Self* or *the Personality;* the combination of the ten qualities produces what is called Truth; the Impersonal; the abiding, real and immortal Man.

It will thus be seen that it is not the destruction of any noble, true, and enduring quality that is taught, but only the destruction of those things that are ignoble, false and evanescent. Neither is this overcoming of self the deprivation of gladness, happiness and joy, but rather is it the constant possession of these things by living in the joy-begetting qualities. It is the abandonment of the *lust* for enjoyment, but not of enjoyment itself; the destruction of the *thirst* for pleasure, but not of pleasure itself; the annihilation of the *selfish longing* for love, and power, and possessions themselves. It is the preservation of all those things which draw and bind men together in unity and concord, and, far from idealising stagnation and death, urges men to the practise of those qualities which lead to the highest, noblest, most effective, and enduring action. He whose actions proceed from some or all of the ten elements wastes his energies upon negations, and does not preserve his soul; but he whose actions proceed from some or all of the ten qualities, he truly and wisely acts and so preserves his soul.

He who lives largely in the ten earthly elements, and who is blind and deaf to the spiritual verities, will find no attraction in the doctrine of self-surrender, for it will appear to him as the complete extinction of his being; but he who is endeavouring to live in the ten heavenly qualities will see the glory and beauty of the doctrine, and will know it as the foundation of Life Eternal. He will also see that when men apprehend and practise it, industry, commerce, government, and every worldly activity will be purified; and action, purpose and intelligence, instead of being destroyed, will be intensified and enlarged, but freed from strife and pain.

THE USES OF TEMPTATION

The soul, in its journey toward perfection, passes through three distinct stages. The first is the *animal* stage, in which the man is content to live, in the gratification of his senses, unawakened to the knowledge of sin, or of his divine inheritance, and altogether unconscious of the spiritual possibilities within himself.

The second is the *dual* stage, in which the mind is continually oscillating between its animal and divine tendencies having become awakened to the consciousness of both. It is during this stage that temptation plays its part in the progress of the soul. It is a stage of continual fighting, of falling and rising, of sinning and repenting, for the man, still loving, and reluctant to leave, the gratifications in which he has so long lived, yet also aspires to the purity and excellence of the spiritual state, and he is continually mortified by an undecided choice.

Urged on by the divine life within him, this stage becomes at last one of deep anguish and suffering, and then the soul is ushered into the third stage, that of *knowledge,* in which the man rises above both sin and temptation, and enters into peace.

Temptation, like contentment in sin, is not a lasting condition, as the majority of people suppose; it is a passing phase, an experience through which the soul must pass; but as to whether a man will pass through that condition in this present life, and realise holiness and heavenly rest here and now, will depend entirely upon the strength of his intellectual and spiritual exertions, and upon the intensity and ardour with which he searches for Truth.

Temptation, with all its attendant torments can be overcome here and now, but it can only be overcome by knowledge. It is a condition of darkness or of semi-darkness. The fully enlightened soul is proof against all temptation. When a man fully understands the source, nature, and meaning of temptation, in that hour he will conquer it, and will rest from his long travail; but whilst he remains in ignorance, attention to religious observances, and much praying and reading of Scripture will fail to bring him peace.

If a man goes out to conquer an enemy, knowing nothing of his enemy's strength, tactics, or place of ambush, he will not only ignominiously fail, but will speedily fall into the hands of the enemy. He who would overcome his enemy the tempter, must discover his stronghold and place of concealment, and must also find out the unguarded gates in his own fortress where his enemy effects so easy an entrance. This necessitates continual meditation, ceaseless watchfulness, and constant and rigid introspection which lays bare, before the spiritual eyes of the tempted one, the vain and selfish motives of his soul. This is the holy warfare of the saints; it is the fight upon which every soul enters when it awakens out of its long sleep of animal indulgence.

Men fail to conquer, and the fight is indefinitely prolonged, because they labour, almost universally, under two delusions: first, that all temptations come from without; and second, that they are tempted because of their goodness. Whilst a man is held in bondage by these two delusions, he will make no progress; when he has shaken them off, he will pass on rapidly from victory to victory, and will taste of spiritual joy and rest.

Two searching truths must take the place of these two delusions, and those truths are: first, that *all temptation comes from within;* and second, that *a man is tempted because of the evil that is within him.* The idea that God, a devil, evil spirits, or outward objects are the source of temptation must be dispelled.

The source and cause of all temptation is in the *inward desire;* that being purified or eliminated, outward objects and extraneous powers are utterly powerless to move the soul to sin or to temptation. The outward object is merely the *occasion* of the temptation, *never the cause;* this is in the desire of the one tempted. If the cause existed in the object, all men would be tempted alike, temptation could never be overcome, and men would be hopelessly doomed to endless torment; but seated, as it is, in his own desires, he has the remedy in his own hands, and can become victorious over all temptation by purifying those desires. A man is tempted because there are within him certain desires or states of mind which he has come to regard as unholy. These desires may lie asleep for a long time, and the man may think that he has got rid of them, when suddenly, on the presentation of an outward object, the sleeping desire wakes up and thirsts of immediate gratification; and this is the state of temptation.

The good in a man is never tempted. Goodness destroys temptation. It is the evil in a man that is aroused and tempted. The measure of a man's temptations is the exact register of his own unholiness. As a man purifies his heart, temptation ceases, for when a certain unlawful desire has been taken out of the heart, the object which formerly appealed to it can no longer do so, but becomes dead and powerless, for there is nothing left in the heart that can respond to it. The honest man cannot be tempted to steal, let the occasion be ever so opportune; the man of purified appetites cannot be tempted to gluttony and drunkenness, though the viands and wines be the most luscious; he of an enlightened understanding, whose mind is calm in the strength of inward virtue, can never be tempted to anger, irritability or revenge, and the wiles and charms of the wanton fall upon the purified heart as empty meaningless shadows.

Temptation shows a man just where he is sinful and ignorant, and is a means of urging him on to higher altitudes of knowledge and purity. Without temptation the soul cannot grow and become strong, there could be no wisdom, no real virtue; and though there would be lethargy and death, there could be no peace and no fulness of life. When temptation is understood and conquered, perfection is assured, and such perfection may become any man's who is willing to cast every selfish and impure desire by which he is possessed, into the sacrificial fire of knowledge. Let men, therefore, search diligently for Truth, realising that whilst they are subject to temptation, they have not comprehended Truth, and have much to learn.

Ye who are tempted know, then, that ye are tempted of yourselves. "For every man is tempted when he is drawn away of his own lusts," says the Apostle James. You are tempted because you are clinging to the animal within you and are unwilling to let go; because you are living in the false mortal self which is ever devoid of all true knowledge, knowing nothing, seeking nothing, but its own immediate gratification, ignorant of every Truth, and of every divine Principle. Clinging to that self, you continually suffer the pains of three separate torments; the torment of desire, the torment of repletion, and the torment of remorse.

> *So flameth Trishna, lust and thirst of things.*
> *Eager, ye cleave to shadows, dote on dreams;*
> *A false self in the midst ye plant, and make*
> *A World around which seems;*
> *Blind to the height beyond; deaf to the sound*
> *Of sweet airs breathed from far past Indra's sky;*
> *Dumb to the summons of the true life kept*
> *For him who false puts by,*
> *So grow the strifes and lusts which make earth's war,*
> *So grieve poor cheated hearts and flow salt tears;*

So wax the passions, envies, angers, hates;
So years chase blood-stained years
With wild red feet.

In that false self lies the germ of every suffering, the blight of every hope, the substance of every grief. When you are ready to give it up; when you are willing to have laid bare before you all its self-ishness, impurity, and ignorance, and to confess its darkness to the uttermost, then will you enter upon the life of self-knowledge and self-mastery, you will become conscious of the god within you, of that divine nature which, seeking no gratification, abides in a region of perpetual joy and peace where suffering cannot come and where temptation can find no foothold. Establishing yourself, day by day, more and more firmly in that inward Divinity, the time will at last come when you will be able to say with Him whom millions worship, few understand and fewer still follow,—"The Prince of this world cometh and hath nothing in me."

THE MAN OF INTEGRITY

There are times in the life of every man who takes his stand on high moral principles when his faith in, and knowledge of, those principles is tested to the uttermost, and the way in which he comes out of the fiery trial decides as to whether he has sufficient strength to live as a man of Truth, and join the company of the free, or shall still remain a slave and a hireling to the cruel taskmaster, Self.

Such times of trial generally assume the form of a temptation to do a wrong thing and continue in comfort and prosperity, or to stand by what is right and accept poverty and failure; and so powerful is the trial that, to the tempted one, it plainly appears on the face of things as though, if he chooses the wrong, his material success will be assured for the remainder of his life, but if he does what is right, he will be ruined for ever.

Frequently the man at once quails and gives way before this appalling prospect which the Path of

Righteousness seems to hold out for him, but should he prove sufficiently strong to withstand this onslaught of temptation, then the inward seducer the spirit of self, assumes the grab of an Angel of Light, and whispers, "Think of your wife and children; think of those who are dependent upon you; will you bring them down to disgrace and starvation?"

Strong indeed and pure must be the man who can come triumphant out of such a trial, but he who does so, enters at once a higher realm of life, where his spiritual eyes are opened to see beautiful things; and then poverty and ruin which seemed inevitable do not come, but a more abiding success comes, and a peaceful heart and a quiet conscience. But he who fails does not obtain the promised prosperity, and his heart is restless and his conscience troubled.

The right-doer cannot ultimately fail, the wrong-doer cannot ultimately succeed, for

Such is the Law which moves to Righteousness
Which none at last can turn aside or stay,

and it is because justice is at the heart of things—because the Great Law is good—that the man of integrity is superior to fear, and failure, and poverty, and shame, and disgrace. As the poet further says of this Law:

The heart of its Love, the end of it
Is peace and consummation sweet-obey.

The man who fearing the loss of present pleasures or material comforts, denies the Truth within him, can be injured, and robbed, and degraded, and trampled upon, because he has first injured, robbed and degraded, and trampled upon his own nobler self; but the man of steadfast virtue, of unblemished integrity, cannot be subject to such conditions, because he has denied the craven self within him and has taken refuge in Truth. It is not the scourge and the chains which make a man a slave, but the fact that he *is* a slave.

Slander, accusation, and malice cannot affect the righteous man, nor call from him any bitter response, nor does he need to go about to defend himself and prove his innocence. His innocence and integrity alone are a sufficient answer to all that hatred may attempt against him. Nor can he ever be subdued by the forces of darkness, having subdued all those forces within himself, but he turns all evil things to good account—out of darkness he brings light, out of hatred love, out of dishonour honour; and slanders, envies, and misrepresentations only serve to make more bright the jewel of Truth within him, and to glorify his high and holy destiny.

Let the man of integrity rejoice and be glad when he is severely tried; let him be thankful that he has been given an opportunity of proving his loyalty to the noble principles which he has espoused; and let him think: "Now is the hour of holy opportunity! Now is the day of triumph for Truth! Though I lose the whole world I will not desert the right!" So thinking, he will return good for evil, and will think compassionately of the wrong-doer.

The slanderer, the backbiter, and the wrong-doer may seem to succeed for a time, but the Law of Justice prevails; the man of integrity may seem to fail for a time, but he is invincible, and in none of the worlds, visible or invisible, can there be forged a weapon that shall prevail against him.

DISCRIMINATION

There is one quality which is pre-eminently necessary to spiritual development, the quality of discrimination.

A man's spiritual progress will be painfully slow and uncertain until there opens with him the eye of discrimination, for without this testing, proving, searching quality, he will but grope in the dark, will be unable to distinguish the real from the unreal, the shadow from the substance, and will so confuse the false with the true as to mistake the inward promptings of his animal nature for those of the spirit of Truth.

A blind man left in a strange place may go grope his way in darkness, but not without much confusion and many painful falls and bruisings. Without discrimination a man is mentally blind, and his life is a painful groping in darkness, a confusion in which vice and virtue are indistinguishable one from the other, where facts are confounded with truths; opinions with principles, and where ideas, events, men, and things appear to be out of all relation to each other.

A man's mind and life should be free from confusion. He should be prepared to meet every mental, material and spiritual difficulty, and should not be inextricably caught (as many are) in the meshes of doubt, indecision and uncertainty when troubles and so-called misfortunes come along. He should be fortified against every emergency that can come against him; but such mental preparedness and strength cannot be attained in any degree without discrimination, and discrimination can only be developed by bringing into play and constantly exercising the analytical faculty.

Mind, like muscle, is developed by use, and the assiduous exercise of the mind in any given direction will develop, in that direction, mental capacity and power. The merely *critical* faculty is developed and strengthened by continuously comparing and analysing the ideas and opinions of others. But discrimination is something more and greater than criticism; it is a spiritual quality from which the cruelty and egotism which so frequently accompany criticism are eliminated, and by virtue of which a man sees things as they are, and not as he would like them to be.

Discrimination, being a spiritual quality, can only be developed by spiritual methods, namely, by questioning, examining, and analysing one's own ideas, opinions, and conduct. The critical, fault finding faculty must be withdrawn from its merciless application to the opinions and conduct of others, and must be applied, with undiminished severity, to oneself. A man must be prepared to question his every opinion, his every thought, and his every line of conduct, and rigorously and logically test them; only in this way can the discrimination which destroys confusion will be developed.

Before a man can enter upon such mental exercise, he must make himself of a *teachable* spirit. This does not mean that he must allow himself to be led by others; it means that he must be prepared to yield up any cherished thoughts to which he clings, if it will not bear the penetrating light of reason, if it shrivels up before the pure flames of searching aspirations. The man who says, "I am right!" and who refuses to question his position in order to discover whether he is right, will continue to follow the line of his passions and prejudices, and will not acquire discrimination. The man who humbly asks, "Am I right?" and then proceeds to test and prove his position by earnest thought and the love of Truth, will always be able to discover the true and to distinguish it from the false, and he will acquire the priceless possession of discrimination.

The man who is afraid to think searchingly upon his opinions, and to reason critically upon his position, will have to develop moral courage before he can acquire discrimination.

A man must be true to himself, fearless with himself, before he can perceive the Pure Principles of Truth, before he can receive the all-revealing Light of Truth.

The more Truth is inquired of, the brighter it shines; it cannot suffer under examination and analysis.

The more error is questioned, the darker it grows; it cannot survive the entrance of pure and searching thought.

To "prove all things" is to find the good and throw the evil.

He who reasons and meditates learns to discriminate; he who discriminates discovers the eternally True.

Confusion, suffering and spiritual darkness follow the thoughtless.

Harmony, blessedness and the Light of Truth attend upon the thoughtful.

Passion and prejudice are blind, and cannot discriminate: they are still crucifying *the Christ* and releasing *Barabbas*.

BELIEF: THE BASIS OF ACTION

B elief is an important word in the teachings of the wise, and it figures prominently in all religions. According to Jesus, a certain kind of belief is necessary to salvation or regeneration, and Buddha definitely taught that *right belief* is the first and most essential step in the Way of Truth, as without right belief there cannot be right conduct, and he who has not learned how to rightly govern and conduct himself, has not yet comprehended the simplest rudiments of Truth.

Belief as laid down by the Great Teachers, is not belief in any particular school, philosophy, or religion, but consists of *an altitude of mind determining the whole course of one's life.* Belief and conduct are, therefore inseparable, for the one determines the other.

Belief is the basis of all action, and, this being so, the belief which dominates the hearts or mind is shown in the life. Every man acts, thinks, lives in exact accordance with the belief which is rooted in his innermost being, and such is the mathematical nature of the laws which govern mind that it is absolutely impossible for anyone to believe in two opposing conditions at the same time. For instance, it is impossible to believe in justice and injustice, hatred and love, peace and strife, self and truth. Every man believes in one or the other of these opposites, *never in both,* and the daily conduct of every man indicates the nature of his belief. The man who believes in justice, who regards it as an eternal and indestructible Principle, never boils over with righteous indignation, does not grow cynical and pessimistic over the inequalities of life, and remains calm and untroubled through all trials and difficulties. It is impossible for him to act otherwise, for he believes that justice reigns, and that, therefore, all that is called injustice is fleeting and illusory.

The man who is continually getting enraged over the injustice of his fellow men, who talks about himself being badly treated, or who mourns over the lack of justice in the world around him, shows by his conduct, his attitude of mind, that he believes in injustice. However he may protest to the contrary, in his inmost heart he believes that confusion and chaos are dominant in the universe, the result being that he dwells in misery and unrest, and his conduct is faulty.

Again, he who believes in love, in its stability and power, *practises it under all circumstances,* never deviates from it, and bestows it alike upon enemies as upon friends. He who slanders and condemns, who speaks disparagingly of others, or regards them with contempt, believes not in love, but hatred; all his actions prove it, even though with tongue or pen he may eulogise love.

The believer in peace is known by his peaceful conduct. It is impossible for him to engage in strife. If attacked he does not retaliate, for he has seen the majesty of the angel of peace, and he can no longer pay homage to the demon of strife. The stirrer-up of strife, the lover of argument, he who rushes into self-defence upon any or every provocation, believes in strife, and will have naught to do with peace.

Further, he who believes in Truth renounces himself—that is, he refuses to centre his life in those passions, desires, and characteristics which crave only their own gratification, and by thus renouncing he becomes steadfastly fixed in Truth, and lives a wise, beautiful, and blameless life. The believer in self is known by his daily indulgences, gratifications, and vanities, and by the disappointments, sorrows, and mortifications which he continually suffers.

The believer in Truth does not suffer, for he has given up that self which is the cause of such suffering.

It will be seen by the foregoing that every man believes either in permanent and eternal Principles directing human life toward law and harmony, or in the negation of those Principles, with the resultant chaos in human affairs and in his own life.

Belief in the divine Principles of Justice, Compassion, Love, constitutes the *right belief* laid down by Buddha as being the basis of *right conduct,* and also the *belief unto salvation* as emphasised in the Christian Scriptures, for he who so believes cannot do otherwise than build his whole life upon these Principles, and so purifies his heart, and perfects his life.

Belief in the negation of this divine principle constitutes what is called in all religious *unbelief* and this unbelief is manifested as a sinful, troubled, and imperfect life.

Where there is Right Belief there is a blameless and perfect life; where there is false belief there is sin, there is sorrow, the mind and life are improperly governed, and there is affliction and unrest. "By their fruits ye shall know them."

There is much talk about, "belief in Jesus," but what does belief in Jesus mean? It means belief in his words, in the Principles he enunciated—and lived, in his commandments and in his exemplary life of perfection. He who declares belief in Jesus, and yet is all the time living in his lusts and indulgences, or in the spirit of hatred and condemnation, is self deceived. He believes not in Jesus.

He believes in his own animal self. As a faithful servant delights in carrying out the commands of his master, so he who believes in Jesus carries out his commandments, and so is saved from sin. The supreme test of belief in Jesus is this: *Do I keep his commandments?* And this test is applied by St. John himself in the following words: "He that saith. I know him (Jesus), and *keepeth not His Commandments,* is a liar, and the truth is not in him. But whoso keepeth his word, in him verily is the word of God perfected."

It will be found after a rigid and impartial analysis, that *belief* lies at the root of all human conduct. Every thought, every act, every habit, is the direct outcome of a certain fixed belief, and one's conduct alters only as one's beliefs are modified. What we cling to, in that we believe; what we practise, in that we believe. When our belief in a thing ceases, we can no longer cling to or practise it; it falls away from us as a garment out-worn. Men cling to their lusts, and lies, and vanities, because they believe in them, believe there is gain and happiness in them. When they transfer their belief to the divine qualities of purity and humility, those sins trouble them no more.

Men are saved from error by belief in the supremacy of Truth. They are saved from sin by belief in Holiness or Perfection. They are saved from evil by belief in Good, for every belief is manifested in the life. It is not necessary to inquire as to a man's theological belief, for that is of little or no account, for what can it avail a man to believe that Jesus died for him, or that Jesus is God, or that he is "justified by faith," if he continues to live in his lower, sinful nature? All that is necessary to ask is this: "How does a man live?" "How does he conduct himself under trying circumstances?" The answer to these questions will show whether a man believes in the power of evil or in the power of Good.

He who believes in the power of Good, lives a good, spiritual, or godly life, for Goodness is God, yea, verily is God Himself, and he will soon leave behind him all sins and sorrows who believes, with steadfast and unwavering faith, in the Supreme Good.

THE BELIEF THAT SAVES

It has been said that a man's whole life and character is the outcome of his *belief,* and also that his *belief* has nothing whatever to do with his life. *Both statements are true.* The confusion and contradiction of these two statements are only apparent, and are quickly dispelled when it is remembered that there are *two entirely distinct kinds of belief,* namely, *Head-belief* and *Heart-belief.*

Head, or intellectual belief, is not fundamental and causative, but it is superficial and consequent, and that it has no power in the moulding of a man's character, the most superficial observer may easily see. Take, for instance, half a dozen men from any creed. They not only hold the same theological belief, but confess the same articles of faith in every particular, and yet their characters are vastly different. One will be just as noble as another is ignoble; one will be mild and gentle, another coarse and irascible; one will be honest, another dishonest; one will indulge certain habits which another will rigidly abjure, and so on, plainly indicating that theological belief is not an influential factor in a man's life.

A man's theological belief is merely his intellectual opinion or view of the universe; God, The Bible, etc, and behind and underneath this head-belief there lies, deeply rooted in his innermost being, the hidden, silent, *secret belief of his heart,* and it is this belief which moulds and makes his whole life. It is this which makes those six men who, whilst holding the same theology, are yet so vastly at variance in their deeds—*they differ in the vital belief of the heart.*

What, then, is this heart-belief?

It is that which a man loves and clings to and fosters in his soul; for he thus loves and clings to and fosters in his heart, because he *believes* in them, and believing in them and loving them, he practises them; thus is his life the effect of his *belief,* but it has no relation to the particular creed which comprises his intellectual belief. One man clings to impure and immoral things because he believes in them; another does not cling to them because he has ceased to believe in them. A man cannot cling to anything unless he believes in it; belief always precedes action, therefore a man's deeds and life are the fruits of his belief.

The Priest and the Levite who passed by the injured and helpless man, held, no doubt, very strongly to the theological doctrines of their fathers—that was their intellectual belief,—but in their hearts they did not believe in mercy, and so lived and acted accordingly. The good Samaritan may or may not have had any theological beliefs nor was it necessary that he should have; but in his heart he believed in mercy, and acted accordingly.

Strictly speaking, there are only two beliefs which vitally affect the life, and they are, *belief in good* and *belief in evil*.

He who believes in all those things that are good, will love them, and live in them; he who believes in those things that are impure and selfish, will love them, and cling to them. The tree is known by its fruits.

A man's beliefs about God, Jesus, and the Bible are one thing; his life, as bound up in his actions, is another; therefore a man's theological belief is of no consequence; but the thoughts which he harbours, his attitude of mind toward others, and his actions, these, and these only, determine and demonstrate whether the belief of a man's heart is fixed in the false or true.

THOUGHT AND ACTION

As the fruit to the tree and the water to the spring, so is action to thought. It does not come into manifestation suddenly and without a cause. It is the result of a long and silent growth; the end of a hidden process which has long been gathering force. The fruit of the tree and the water gushing from the rock are both the effect of a combination of natural processes in air and earth which have long worked together in secret to produce the phenomenon; and the beautiful acts of enlightenment and the dark deeds of sin are both the ripened effects of trains of thought which have long been harboured in the mind.

The sudden falling, when greatly tempted, into some grievous sin by one who was believed, and who probably believed himself, to stand firm, is seen neither to be a *sudden* nor a causeless thing when the hidden process of thought which led up to it are revealed. The *falling* was merely the end, the outworking, the finished result of what commenced in the mind probably years before. The man had allowed a wrong thought to enter his mind; and a second and a third time he had welcomed it, and allowed it to nestle in his heart. Gradually he became accustomed to it, and cherished, and fondled, and tended it; and so it grew, until at last it attained such strength and force that it attracted to itself the opportunity which enabled it to burst forth and ripen into act. As falls the stately building whose foundations have been gradually undermined by the action of water, so at last falls the strong man who allows corrupt thoughts to creep into his mind and secretly under-mine his character.

When it is seen that all sin and temptation are the natural outcome of the thoughts of the indi-vidual, the way to overcome sin and temptation becomes plain, and its achievement a near possibil-ity, and, sooner or later, a certain reality, for if a man will admit, cherish, and brood upon thoughts that are pure and good, those thoughts, just as surely as the impure, will grow and gather force, and will at last attract to themselves the opportunities which will enable them to ripen into act.

"There is nothing hidden that shall not be revealed," and every thought that is harboured in the mind must, by virtue of the impelling force which is inherent in the universe, at last blossom into act good or bad according to its nature. The divine Teacher and the sensualist are both the product of their own thoughts, and have become what they are as the result of the seeds of thought which they have implanted, are allowed to fall, into the garden of the heart, and have afterwards watered, tended, and cultivated.

Let no man think he can overcome sin and temptation by wrestling with opportunity; he can only overcome them by purifying his thoughts; and if he will, day by day, in the silence of his soul, and in the performance of his duties, strenuously overcome all erroneous inclination, and put in its place thoughts that are true and that will endure the light, opportunity to do evil will give place to opportunity for accomplishing good, for a man can only attract that to him which is in harmony with his nature, and no temptation can gravitate to a man unless there is that in his heart which is capable of responding to it.

Guard well your thoughts, reader, for what you really are in your secret thoughts today, be it good or evil, you will, sooner or later, *become* in actual deed. He who unwearyingly guards the por-tals of his mind against the intrusion of sinful thoughts, and occupies himself with loving thoughts, with pure, strong, and beautiful thoughts, will, when the season of their ripening comes, bring forth the fruits of gentle and holy deeds, and no temptation that can come against him shall find him unarmed or unprepared.

YOUR MENTAL ATTITUDE

As a being of thought, your dominant mental attitude will determine your condition in life. It will also be the gauge of your knowledge and the measures of your attainment. The so-called limitations of your nature are the boundary lines of your thoughts; they are self-erected fences, and can be drawn to a narrower circle, extended to a wider, or be allowed to remain.

You are the thinker of your thoughts and as such you are the maker of yourself and condition. Thought is causal and creative, and appears in your character and life in the form of results. There are no accidents in your life. Both its harmonies and antagonisms are the responsive echoes of your thoughts. A man thinks, and his life appears.

If your dominant mental attitude is peaceable and lovable, bliss and blessedness will follow you; if it be resistant and hateful, trouble and distress will cloud your pathway. Out of ill-will will come grief and disaster; out of good-will, healing and reparation.

You imagine your circumstances as being separate from yourself, but they are intimately related to your thought world. Nothing appears without an adequate cause. Everything that happens is just. Nothing is fated, everything is formed.

As you think, you travel; as you love, you attract. You are today where your thoughts have brought you; you will be to-morrow where your thoughts take you. You cannot escape the result of your thoughts, but you can endure and learn, can accept and be glad.

You will always come to the place where your *love* (your most abiding and intense thought) can receive its measure of gratification. If your love be base, you will come to a base place; if it be beautiful, you will come to a beautiful place.

You can alter your thoughts, and so alter your condition. Strive to perceive the vastness and grandeur of your responsibility. You are powerful, not powerless. You are as powerful to obey as you are to disobey; as strong to be pure as to be impure; as ready for wisdom as for ignorance. You can learn what you will, can remain as ignorant as you choose. If you love knowledge you will obtain it; if you love wisdom you will secure it; if you love purity you will realise it. All things await your acceptance, and you choose by the thoughts which you entertain.

A man remains ignorant because he loves ignorance, and chooses ignorant thoughts; a man becomes wise because he loves wisdom and chooses wise thoughts. No man is hindered by another; he is only hindered by himself. No man suffers because of another, he suffers only because of himself.

By the noble Gateway of Pure Thought you can enter the highest Heaven; by the ignoble doorway of impure thought you can descend into the lowest hell.

Your mental attitude toward others will faithfully react upon yourself, and will manifest itself in every relation of your life. Every impure and selfish thought that you send out comes back to you in your circumstances in some form of suffering; every pure and unselfish thought returns to you in some form of blessedness. Your circumstances are *effects* of which the cause is inward and invisible. As the father-mother of your thoughts you are the maker of your state and condition. When you know yourself, you will perceive, that every event in your life is weighed in the faultless balance of equity. When you understand the law within your mind you will cease to regard yourself as the impotent and blind tool of circumstances, and will become the strong and seeing master.

SOWING AND REAPING

Go into the fields and country lanes in the spring-time, and you will see farmers and gardeners busy sowing seeds in the newly prepared soil. If you were to ask any one of those gardeners or farmers what kind of produce he expected from the seed he was sowing, he would doubtless regard you as foolish, and would tell you that he does not "expect" at all, that it is a matter of common knowledge that his produce will be of the kind which he is sowing, and that he is sowing wheat, or barley, or turnips, as the case may be, in order to reproduce that particular kind.

Every fact and process in Nature contains a moral lesson for the wise man. There is no law in the world of Nature around us which is not to be found operating with the same mathematical certainty in the mind of man and in human life. All the parables of Jesus are illustrative of this truth, and are drawn from the simple facts of Nature. There is a process of seed-sowing in the mind and life a spiritual sowing which leads to a harvest according to the kind of seed sown. Thoughts, words, and acts are seeds sown, and, by the inviolable law of things, they produce after their kind.

The man who thinks hateful thoughts brings hatred upon himself. The man who thinks loving thoughts is loved. The man whose thoughts, words and acts are sincere, is surrounded by sincere friends; the insincere man is surrounded by insincere friends. The man who sows wrong thoughts and deeds, and prays that God will bless him, is in the position of a farmer who, having sown tares, asks God to bring forth for him a harvest of wheat.

That which ye sow, ye reap; see yonder fields
The sesamum was sesamum, the corn
Was corn; the silence and the darkness knew;
So is a man's fate born.
He cometh reaper of the things he sowed.

He who would be blest, let him scatter blessings. He who would be happy, let him consider the happiness of others.

Then there is another side to this seed sowing. The farmer must scatter all his seed upon the land, and then leave it to the elements. Were he to covetously hoard his seed, he would lose both it and his produce, for his seed would perish. It perishes when he sows it, but in perishing it brings forth a great abundance. So in life, we get by giving; we grow rich by scattering. The man who says he is in possession of knowledge which he cannot give out because the world is incapable of receiving it, either does not possess such knowledge, or, if he does, will soon be deprived of it—if he is not already so deprived. To hoard is to lose; to exclusively retain is to be dispossessed.

Even the man who would increase his material wealth must be willing to part with (invest) what little capital he has, and then wait for the increase. So long as he retains his hold on his precious money, he will not only remain poor, but will be growing poorer everyday. He will, after all, lose the thing he loves, and will lose it without increase. But if he wisely lets it go; if, like the farmer, he scatters his seeds of gold, then he can faithfully wait for, and reasonably expect, the increase.

Men are asking God to give them peace and purity, and righteousness and blessedness, but are not obtaining these things; and why not? Because they are not practising them, not sowing them. I once heard a preacher pray very earnestly for forgiveness, and shortly afterwards, in the course of his sermon, he called upon his congregation to "show no mercy to the enemies of the church." Such self-delusion is pitiful, and men have yet to learn that the way to obtain peace and blessedness is to scatter peaceful and blessed thoughts, words, and deeds.

Men believe that they can sow the seeds of strife, impurity, and unbrotherliness, and then gather in a rich harvest of peace, purity and concord by merely asking for it. What more pathetic sight than to see an irritable and quarrelsome man praying for peace. Men reap that which they sow, and any man can reap all blessedness now and at once, if he will put aside selfishness, and sow broadcast the seeds of kindness, gentleness, and love.

If a man is troubled, perplexed, sorrowful, or unhappy, let him ask:

"What mental seeds have I been sowing?"

"What seeds am I sowing?"

"What have I done for others?"

"What is my attitude toward others?"

"What seeds of trouble and sorrow and unhappiness have I sown that I should thus reap these bitter weeds?"

Let him seek within and find, and having found, let him abandon all the seeds of self, and sow, henceforth, only the seeds of Truth.

Let him learn of the farmer the simple truths of wisdom.

THE REIGN OF LAW

The little party gods have had their day. The arbitrary gods, creatures of human caprice and ignorance, are falling into disrepute. Men have quarrelled over and defended them until they have grown weary of the strife, and now, everywhere, they are relinquishing and breaking up these helpless idols of their long worship.

The god of revenge, hatred and jealousy, who gloats over the downfall of his enemies; the partial god who gratifies all our narrow and selfish desires; the god who saves only the creatures of his particular special creed; the god of exclusiveness and favouritism; such were the gods (miscalled by us God) of our soul's infancy, gods base and foolish as ourselves, the fabrications of our selfish self. And we relinquished our petty gods with bitter tears and misgivings, and broke our idols with bleeding hands. But in so doing we did not lose sight of God; nay we drew nearer to the great, silent Heart of Love. Destroying the idols of self, we began to comprehend somewhat of the Power which cannot be destroyed, and entered into a wider knowledge of the God of Love, of Peace, of Joy; the

God in whom revenge and partiality cannot exist; the God of light, from whose presence the darkness of fear and doubt and selfishness cannot choose but flee.

We have reached one of those epochs in the world's progress which witnesses the passing of the false gods; the gods of human selfishness and human illusion. The new-old revelation of one universal impersonal Truth has again dawned upon the world, and its searching light has carried consternation to the perishable gods who take shelter under the shadow of self.

Men have lost faith in a god who can be cajoled, who rules arbitrarily and capriciously, subverting the whole order of things to gratify the wishes of his worshippers, and are turning, with a new light in their eyes and a new joy in their hearts, to the *God of Law*.

And to Him they turn, not for personal happiness and gratification, but for knowledge, for understanding, for wisdom, for liberation from the bondage of self. And thus turning, they do not seek in vain, nor are they sent away empty and discomfited. They find within themselves the *reign of Law,* that every thought, every impulse, every act and word brings about a result in exact accordance with its own nature; that thoughts of love bring about beautiful and blissful conditions, that hateful thoughts bring about distorted and painful conditions, that thoughts and acts good and evil are weighed in the faultless balance of the Supreme Law, and receive their equal measure of blessedness on the one hand, and misery on the other. And thus finding they enter a new Path, the Path of *Obedience to the Law*. Entering that Path they no longer accuse, no longer doubt, no longer fret and despond, for they know that God is right, the universal laws are right, the cosmos is right, and that they themselves are wrong, if wrong there is, and that their salvation depends upon themselves, upon their own efforts, upon their personal acceptance of that which is good and deliberate rejection of that which is evil. No longer merely hearers, they become doers of the Word, and they acquire knowledge, they receive understanding, they grow in wisdom, and they enter into the glorious life of liberation from the bondage of self.

"The Law of the Lord is perfect, enlightening the eyes." Imperfection lies in man's ignorance, in man's blind folly. Perfection, which is knowledge of the Perfect Law, is ready for all who earnestly seek it; it belongs to the order of things; it is yours and mine now if we will only put self-seeking on one side, and adopt the life of self-obliteration.

The knowledge of Truth, with its unspeakable joy, its calmness and quiet strength, is not for those who persist in clinging to their "rights," defending their "interests," and fighting for their "opinions"; whose works are imbued with the personal "I," and who build upon the shifting sands of selfishness and egotism. It is for those who renounce these causes of strife, these sources of pain and sorrow; and they are, indeed, Children of Truth, disciples of the Master, worshippers of the most High.

The Children of Truth are in the world today; they are thinking, acting, writing, speaking; yea, even prophets are amongst us, and their influence is pervading the whole earth. An undercurrent of holy joy is gathering force in the world, so that men and women are moved with new aspirations and hopes, and even those who neither see nor hear, feel within themselves strange yearnings after a better and fuller life.

The Law reigns, and it reigns in men's hearts and lives; and they have come to understand the reign of Law who have sought out the Tabernacle of the true God by the fair pathway of unselfishness.

God does not alter for man, for this would mean that the perfect must become imperfect; man must alter for God, and this implies that the imperfect must become perfect. The Law cannot be broken for man, otherwise confusion would ensue; man must obey the Law; this is in accordance with harmony, order, justice.

There is no more painful bondage than to be at the mercy of one's inclinations; no greater liberty than utmost obedience to the Law of Being. And the Law is that the heart shall be purified, the mind regenerated, and the whole being brought in subjection to Love till self is dead and Love is all in all, for the reign of Law is the reign of Love. And Love waits for all, rejecting none. Love may be claimed and entered into now, for it is the heritage of all.

Ah, beautiful Truth! To know that now man may accept his divine heritage, and enter the Kingdom of Heaven!

Oh, pitiful error! To know that man rejects it because of love of self!

Obedience to the Law means the destruction of sin and self, and the realisation of unclouded joy and undying peace.

Clinging to one's selfish inclinations means the drawing about one's soul clouds of pain and sorrow which darken the light of Truth; the shutting out of oneself from all real blessedness; for "whatsoever a man sows that shall he also reap."

Verily the Law reigneth, and reigneth for ever, and Justice and Love are its eternal ministers.

THE SUPREME JUSTICE

The material universe is maintained and preserved by the equilibrium of its forces.

The moral universe is sustained and protected by the perfect balance of its equivalents.

As in the physical world Nature abhors a vacuum, so in the spiritual world dishar-mony is annulled.

Underlying the disturbances and destructions of Nature, and behind the mutability of its forms, there abides the eternal and perfect mathematical symmetry; and at the heart of life, behind all its pain, uncertainty, and unrest, there abide the eternal harmony, the unbroken peace, and inviolable Justice.

Is there, then, no injustice in the universe? There is injustice, and there is not. It depends upon the kind of life and the state of consciousness from which a man looks out upon the world and judges. The man who lives in his passions sees injustice everywhere; the man who has overcome his passions, sees the operations of Justice in every department of human life. Injustice is the confused, feverish dream of passion, real enough to those who are dreaming it; Justice is the per-manent reality in life, gloriously visible to those who have wakened out of the painful nightmare of self.

The Divine Order cannot be perceived until passion and self are transcended; the Faultless Jus-tice cannot be apprehended until all sense of injury and wrong is consumed in the pure flames of all-embracing Love.

The man who thinks, "I have been slighted, I have been injured, I have been insulted, I have been treated unjustly," cannot know what Justice is; blinded by self, he cannot perceive the pure Prin-ciples of Truth, and brooding upon his wrongs, he lives in continual misery.

In the region of passion there is a ceaseless conflict of forces causing suffering to all who are involved in them. There is action and reaction, deed and consequence, cause and effect; and within and above all is the Divine Justice regulating the play of forces with the utmost mathematical accu-racy, balancing cause and effect with the finest precision. But this Justice is not perceived—cannot be perceived—by those who are engaged in the conflict; before this can be done, the fierce warfare of passion must be left behind.

The world of passion is the abode of schisms, quarrellings, wars, law-suits, accusations, con-demnations, impurities, weaknesses, follies, hatreds, revenges, and resentments. How can a man perceive Justice or understand Truth who is even partly involved in the fierce play of its blinding elements? As well expect a man caught in the flames of a burning building to sit down and reason out the cause of the fire.

In this realm of passion, men see injustice in the actions of others because, seeing only immediate appearances, they regard every act as standing by itself, undetached from cause and consequence. Having no knowledge of cause and effect in the moral sphere, men do not see the exacting and balancing process which is momentarily proceeding, nor do they ever regard their own actions as unjust, but only the actions of others. A boy beats a defenceless animal, then a man beats the defenceless boy for his cruelty, then a stronger man attacks the man for his cruelty to the boy. Each believes the other to be unjust and cruel, and himself to be just and humane; and doubtless most of all would the boy justify his conduct toward the animal as altogether necessary. Thus does ignorance keep alive hatred and strife; thus do men blindly inflict suffering upon themselves, living in passion and resentment, and not finding the true way in life. Hatred is met with hatred, passion with passion, strife with strife. The man who kills is himself killed; the thief who lives by depriving others is himself deprived; the beast that preys on others is hunted and killed; the accuser is accused, the condemner is condemned, the denouncer is persecuted.

> *By this the slayer's knife doth stab himself,*
> *The unjust judge has lost his own defender,*
> *The false tongue dooms its lie, the creeping thief*
> *And spoiler rob to render.*
> *Such is the Law.*

Passion, also has its active and passive sides. Fool and fraud, oppressor and slave, aggressor and retaliator, the charlatan and the superstitious, complement each other, and come together by the operation of the Law of Justice. Men unconsciously coöperate in the mutual production of affliction; "the blind lead the blind, and both fall together into the ditch." Pain, grief, sorrow, and misery are the fruits of which passion is the flower.

Where the passion-bound soul sees only injustice, the good man, he who has conquered passion, sees cause and effect, sees the Supreme Justice. It is impossible for such a man to regard himself as treated unjustly, because he has ceased to see injustice. He knows that no one can injure or cheat him, having ceased to injure or cheat himself. However passionately or ignorantly men may act toward him, it cannot possibly cause him any pain, for he knows that whatever comes to him (it may be abuse and persecution) can only come as the effect of what he himself has formerly sent out. He therefore regards all things as good, rejoices in all things, loves his enemies and blesses them that curse him, regarding them as the blind but beneficent instruments by which he is enabled to pay his moral debts to the Great Law.

The good man, having put away all resentment, retaliation, self-seeking, and egotism, has arrived at a state of equilibrium, and has thereby become identified with the Eternal and Universal Equilibrium. Having lifted himself above the blind forces of passion, he understands those forces, contemplates them with a calm penetrating insight, like the solitary dweller upon a mountain who looks down upon the conflict of the storms beneath his feet. For him, injustice has ceased, and he sees ignorance and suffering on the one hand and enlightenment and bliss on the other. He sees that not only do the fool and the slave need his sympathy, but that the fraud and the oppressor are equally in need of it, and so his compassion is extended toward all.

The Supreme Justice and the Supreme Love are one. Cause and effect cannot be avoided; consequences cannot be escaped.

While a man is given to hatred, resentment, anger and condemnation, he is subject to injustice as the dreamer to his dream, and cannot do otherwise than see injustice; but he who has overcome those fiery and binding elements, knows that unerring Justice presides over all, that in reality there is no such thing as injustice in the whole of the universe.

THE USE OF REASON

We have heard it said that reason is a blind guide, and that it draws men away from Truth rather than leads them to it. If this were true, it were better to remain, or to become, unreasonable, and to persuade others so to do. We have found, however, that the diligent cultivation of the divine faculty of reason brings about calmness and mental poise, and enables one to meet cheerfully the problems and difficulties of life.

It is true there is a higher light than reason; even that of the Spirit of Truth itself, but without the aid of reason, Truth cannot be apprehended. They who refuse to trim the lamp of reason will never, whilst they so refuse, perceive the light of Truth, for the light of reason is a reflection of that Light.

Reason is a purely abstract quality, and comes midway between the animal and divine consciousness in man, and leads, if rightly employed, from the darkness of one to the Light of the other. It is true that reason may be enlisted in the service of the lower, self-seeking nature, but this is only a result of its partial and imperfect exercise. A fuller development of reason leads away from the selfish nature, and ultimately allies the soul with the highest, the divine.

That spiritual Percival who, searching for the Holy Grail of the Perfect Life, is again and again

left alone,
And wearying in a land of sand and thorns,

is not so stranded because he has followed reason, but because he is still clinging to, and is reluctant to leave, some remnants of his lower nature. He who will use the light of reason as a torch to search for Truth will not be left at last in comfortless darkness.

"Come, now, and let us reason together, saith the Lord; though your sins be as scarlet, they shall be as white as snow."

Many men and women pass through untold sufferings, and at last die in their sins, *because they refuse to reason;* because they cling to those dark delusions which even a faint glimmer of the light of reason would dispel; and all must use their reason freely, fully, and faithfully, who would exchange the scarlet robe of sin and suffering for the white garment of blamelessness and peace.

It is because we have proved and know these truths that we exhort men to

tread the middle road, whose course
Bright reason traces, and soft quiet
smooths,

for reason leads away from passion and selfishness into the quiet ways of sweet persuasion and gentle forgiveness, and he will never be led astray, nor will he follow blind guides, who faithfully adheres to the Apostolic injunction, "Prove all things, and hold fast that which is good." They, therefore, who despise the light of reason, despise the Light of Truth.

Large numbers of people are possessed of the strange delusion that reason is somehow intimately connected with the denial of the existence of God. This is probably due to the fact that those who try to prove that there is no God usually profess to take their stand upon reason, while those who try to prove the reverse generally profess to take their stand on faith. Such argumentative combatants, however, are frequently governed more by prejudice than either reason or faith, their object being not to find Truth, but to defend and confirm a preconceived opinion.

Reason is concerned, not with ephemeral opinions, but with the established truth of things, and he who is possessed of the faculty of reason in its purity and excellence can never be enslaved by prejudice, and will put from him all preconceived opinions as worthless. He will neither attempt to prove nor disprove, but after balancing extremes and bringing together all apparent contradictions, he will carefully and dispassionately weigh and consider them, and so arrive at Truth.

Reason is, in reality, associated with all that is pure and gentle, moderate and just. It is said of a violent man that he is "unreasonable," of a kind and considerate man that he is "reasonable," and of an insane man that he has "lost his reason." Thus it is seen that the word is used, even to a great extent unconsciously, though none the less truly, in a very comprehensive sense, and though reason is not actually love and thoughtfulness and gentleness and sanity, it leads to and is intimately connected with these divine qualities, and cannot, except for purposes of analysis, be dissociated from them.

Reason represents all that is high and noble in man. It distinguishes him from the brute which blindly follows its animal inclinations, and just in the degree that man disobeys the voice of reason and follows his inclinations does he become brutish. As Milton says:

Reason in man obscured, or not obeyed,
Immediately inordinate desires
And upstart passions catch the government
From reason, and to servitude reduce
Man till then free.

The following definition of "reason" from Nuttall's Dictionary will give some idea of the comprehensiveness of the word:

The cause, ground, principle, or motive of anything said or done; efficient cause; final cause; the faculty of intelligence in man; especially the faculty by which we arrive at necessary truth.

It will thus be seen that "reason" is a term, the breadth of which is almost sufficient to embrace even Truth itself, and Archbishop Trench tells us in his celebrated work On the Study of Words that the terms Reason and Word "are indeed so essentially one and the same that the Greek language has one word for them both," so that the Word of God is the Reason of God; and one of the renderings of Lao-tze's "Tao" is Reason, so that in the Chinese translation of our New Testament, St. John's Gospel runs: "In the beginning was the Tao."

To the undeveloped and uncharitable mind all words have narrow applications, but as a man enlarges his sympathies and broadens his intelligence, words become filled with rich meanings and assume comprehensive proportions. Let us therefore cease from foolish quarrelings about words, and, like reasonable beings, search for principles and practise those things which make for unity and peace.

SELF-DISCIPLINE

A man does not live until he begins to discipline himself; he merely exists. Like an animal he gratifies his desires and pursues his inclinations just where they may lead him. He is happy as a beast is happy, because he is not conscious of what he is depriving himself; he suffers as the beast suffers, because he does not know the way out of suffering. He does not intelligently reflect upon life, and lives in a series of sensations, longings, and confused memories which are unrelated to any central idea or principle. A man whose inner life is so ungoverned and chaotic must necessarily manifest this confusion in the visible conditions of his outer life in the world; and though for a time, running with the stream of his desires, he may draw to himself a more or less large share of the outer necessities and comforts of life, he never achieves any real success nor accomplishes any real good, and sooner or later worldly failure and disaster are inevitable, as the direct result of the inward failure to properly adjust and regulate those mental forces which make the outer life.

Before a man accomplish anything of an enduring nature in the world he must first of all acquire some measure of success in the management of his own mind. This is as mathematical a truism as that two and two are four, for, "out of the heart are the issues of life." If a man cannot govern the forces within himself, he cannot hold a firm hand upon the outer activities which form his visible life. On the other hand, as a man succeeds, in governing himself he rises to higher and higher levels of power and usefulness and success in the world.

The only difference between the life of the beast and that of the undisciplined man is that the man has a wider variety of desires, and experiences a greater intensity of suffering. It may be said of such a man that he is dead, being truly dead to self-control, chastity, fortitude, and all the nobler qualities which constitute life. In the consciousness of such a man the crucified Christ lies entombed, awaiting that resurrection which shall revivify the mortal sufferer, and wake him up to a knowledge of the realities of his existence.

With the practice of self-discipline a man begins to live, for he then commences to rise above the inward confusion and to adjust his conduct to a steadfast centre within himself. He ceases to follow where inclination leads him, reins in the steed of his desires, and lives in accordance with the dictates of reason and wisdom. Hitherto his life has been without purpose or meaning, but now he begins to consciously mould his own destiny; he is "clothed and in his right mind."

In the process of self-discipline there are three stages namely;

Control
Purification
Relinquishment

A man begins to discipline himself by controlling those passions which have hitherto controlled him; he resists temptation and guards himself against all those tendencies to selfish gratifications which are so easy and natural, and which have formerly dominated him. He brings his appetite into subjection, and begins to eat as a reasonable and responsible being, practising moderation and thoughtfulness in the selection of his food, with the object of making his body a pure instrument through which he may live and act as becomes a man, and no longer degrading that body by pandering to gustatory pleasure. He puts a check upon his tongue, his temper, and, in fact, his every animal desire and tendency, and this he does by referring all his acts to a fixed centre within himself. It is a process of living from within outward, instead of, as formerly, from without inward. He conceives of an ideal, and, enshrining that ideal in the sacred recesses of his heart, he regulates his conduct in accordance with its exaction and demands.

There is a philosophical hypothesis that at the heart of every atom and every aggregation of atoms in the universe there is a *motionless center* which is the sustaining source of all the universal activities. Be this as it may, there is certainly in the heart of every man and woman a selfless centre without which the outer man could not be, and the ignoring of which leads to suffering and confusion. This selfless center which takes the form, in the mind, of an ideal of unselfishness and spotless purity, the attainment of which is desirable, is man's eternal refuge from the storms of passion and all the conflicting elements of his lower nature. It is the Rock of Ages, the Christ within, the divine and immortal in all men.

As a man practises self-control he approximates more and more to this inward reality, and is less and less swayed by passion and grief, pleasure and pain, and lives a steadfast and virtuous life, manifesting manly strength and fortitude. The restraining of the passions, however, is merely the initial stage in self-discipline, and is immediately followed by the process of Purification. By this a man so purifies himself as to take passion out of the heart and mind altogether; not merely restraining it when it rises within him, but preventing it from rising altogether. By merely restraining his passions a man can never arrive at peace, can never actualise his ideal; he must purify those passions.

It is in the purification of his lower nature that a man becomes strong and god-like, standing firmly upon the ideal centre within, and rendering all temptations powerless and ineffectual. This purification is effected by thoughtful care, earnest meditation, and holy aspiration; and as success is achieved confusion of mind and life pass away, and calmness of mind and spiritualized conduct ensure.

True strength and power and usefulness are born of self-purification, for the lower animal forces are not lost, but are transmuted into intellectual and spiritual energy. The pure life (Pure in thought and deed) is a life of conservation of energy; the impure life (even should the impurity not extent beyond thought) is a life of dissipation of energy. The pure man is more capable, and therefore more fit to succeed in his plans and to accomplish his purposes than the impure. Where the impure man fails, the pure man will step in and be victorious, because he directs his energies with a calmer mind and a greater definiteness and strength of purpose.

With the growth in purity; all the elements which constitute a strong and virtuous manhood are developed in an increasing degree of power, and as a man brings his lower nature into subjection, and makes his passions do his bidding, just so much will he mould the outer circumstances of his life, and influence others for good.

The third stage of self-discipline, that of Relinquishment, is a process of letting the lower desires and all impure and unworthy thoughts drop out of the mind, and also refusing to give them any admittance, leaving them to perish. As a man grows purer, he perceives that all evil is powerless, unless it receives his encouragement, and so he ignores it, and lets it pass out of his life. It is by pursuing this aspect of self-discipline that a man enters into and realises the divine life, and manifests those qualities which are distinctly divine, such as wisdom, patience, non-resistance, compassion, and love. It is here, also, where a man becomes consciously immortal, rising above all the fluctuations and uncertainties of life, and living in an intelligent and unchangeable peace.

By self-discipline a man attains to every degree of virtue and holiness, and finally becomes a purified son of God, realising his oneness with the central heart of all things.

Without self-discipline a man drifts lower and lower, approximating more and more nearly to the beast, until at last he grovels, a lost creature, in the mire of his own befoulment. By self-discipline a man rises higher and higher, approximating more and more nearly to the divine, until at last he stands erect in his divine dignity, a saved soul, glorified by the radiance of his purity. Let a man discipline himself, and he will live; let a man cease to discipline himself, and he will perish. As a tree grows in beauty, health, and fruitfulness by being carefully pruned and tended, so a man grows in grace and beauty of life by cutting away all the branches of evil from his mind, and as he tends and develops the good by constant and unfailing effort.

As a man by practise acquires proficiency in his craft, so the earnest man acquires proficiency in goodness and wisdom. Men shrink from self-discipline because in its early stages it is painful and repellent, and the yielding to desire is, at first, sweet and inviting; but the end of desire is darkness and unrest, whereas the fruits of discipline are immortality and peace.

RESOLUTION

Resolution is the directing and impelling force in individual progress. Without it no substantial work can be accomplished. Not until a man brings resolution to bear upon his life does he consciously and rapidly develop, for a life without resolution is a life without aims, and a life without aims is a drifting and unstable thing.

Resolution may of course be linked to downward tendencies, but it is more usually the companion of noble aims and lofty ideals, and I am dealing with it in this its highest use and application.

When a man makes a resolution, it means that he is dissatisfied with his condition, and is commencing to take himself in hand with a view to producing a better piece of workmanship out of the mental materials of which his character and life are composed, and in so far as he is true to his resolution he will succeed in accomplishing his purpose.

The vows of the saintly ones are holy resolutions directed toward some victory over self, and the beautiful achievements of holy men and the glorious conquests of the Divine Teachers were rendered possible and actual by the pursuit of unswerving resolution.

To arrive at the fixed determination to walk a higher path than heretofore, although it reveals the great difficulties which have to be surmounted, it yet makes possible the treading of that path, and illuminates its dark places with the golden halo of success.

The true resolution is the crisis of long thought, protracted struggle, or fervent but unsatisfied aspiration. It is no light thing, no whimsical impulse or vague desire, but a solemn and irrevocable determination not to rest nor cease from effort until the high purpose which is held in view is fully accomplished.

Half-hearted and premature resolution is no resolution at all, and is shattered at the first difficulty.

A man should be slow to form a resolution. He should searchingly examine his position and take into consideration every circumstance and difficulty connected with his decision, and should be fully prepared to meet them. He should be sure that he completely understands the nature of his resolution, that his mind is finally made up, and that he is without fear and doubt in the matter. With the mind thus prepared, the resolution that is formed will not be departed from, and by the aid of it a man will, in due time, accomplish his strong purpose.

Hasty resolutions are futile.

The mind must be fortified to endure.

Immediately the resolution to walk a higher path is made, temptation and trial begin. Men have found that no sooner have they decided to lead a truer and nobler life than they have been overwhelmed with such a torrent of new temptations and difficulties as make their position almost unendurable, and many men, because of this, relinquish their resolution.

But these temptations and trials are a necessary part of the work of regeneration upon which the man has decided and must be hailed as friends and met with courage if the resolution is to do its work. For what is the real nature of a resolution? Is it not the sudden checking of a particular stream of conduct, and the endeavour to open up an entirely new channel? Think of an engineer who decides to turn the course of a powerfully running stream or river in another direction. He must first cut his new channel, and must take every precaution to avoid failure in the carrying out of his undertaking. But when he comes to the all-important task of directing the stream into its new channel, then the flowing force, which for ages has steadily pursued its accustomed course, becomes refractory, and all the patience and care and skill of the engineer will be required for the successful completion of the work. It is even so with the man who determines to turn his course of conduct in another and higher direction. Having prepared his mind, which is the cutting of a new channel, he then proceeds to the work of redirecting his mental forces—which have hitherto flowed on uninterruptedly—into the new course. Immediately this is attempted, the arrested energy begins to assert itself in the form of powerful temptations and trials hitherto unknown and unencountered. And this is exactly as it should be; it is the law; and the same law that is in the water is in the mind. No man can improve upon the established law of things, but he can learn to understand the law instead of complaining, and wishing things were different. The man who understands all that is involved in the regeneration of his mind will "glory in tribulations," knowing that only by passing through them can he gain strength, obtain purity of heart, and arrive at peace. And as the engineer at last (perhaps after many mistakes and failures) succeeds in getting the stream to flow on peacefully in the broader and better channel, and the turbulence of the water is spent, and all dams can be removed, so the man of resolution at last succeeds in directing his thoughts and acts into the better and nobler way to which he aspires, and temptations and trials give place to steadfast strength and settled peace.

He whose life is not in harmony with his conscience and who is anxious to remedy his mind and conduct in a particular direction, let him first mature his purpose by earnest thought and self-examination, and having arrived at a final conclusion, let him frame his resolution, and having done so let him not swerve from it, let him remain true to his decision under all circumstances, and he cannot fail to achieve his good purpose; for the Great Law ever shields and protects him who, no matter how deep his sins, or how great and many his failures and mistakes, has, deep in his heart, resolved upon the finding of a better way, and every obstacle must at last give way before a matured and unshaken resolution.

THE GLORIOUS CONQUEST

Truth can only be apprehended by the conquest of self.

Blessedness can only be arrived at by overcoming the lower nature.

The way of Truth is barred by a man's self.

The only enemies that can actually hinder him are his own passions and delusions.

Until a man realises this, and commences to cleanse his heart, he has not found the Path which leads to knowledge and peace.

Until passion is transcended, Truth remains unknown. This is the Divine Law.

A man cannot keep his passions and have Truth as well.

Error is not slain until selfishness is dead.

The overcoming of self is no mystical theory, but a very real and practical thing.

It is a process which must be pursued daily and hourly, with unswerving faith and undaunted resolution if any measure of success is to be achieved.

The process is one of orderly growth, having its sequential stages, like the growth of a tree; and as fruit can only be produced by carefully and patiently training the tree even so the pure and satisfying fruits of holiness can only be obtained by faithfully and patiently training the mind in the growth of right thought and conduct.

There are five steps in the overcoming of passion (which includes all bad habits and particular forms of wrong-doing) which I will call:

Repression

Endurance

Elimination

Understanding

Victory

When men fail to overcome their sins, it is because they try to begin at the wrong end. They want to have the stage of Victory without passing through the previous four stages. They are in the position of a gardener who wants to produce good fruit without training and attending to his trees.

Repression consists in checking and controlling the wrong act (such as an outburst of temper, a hasty or unkind word, a selfish indulgence etc.), and not allowing it to take actual form. This is equivalent to the gardener nipping off the useless buds and branches from his tree. It is a necessary process, but a painful one. The tree bleeds while undergoing the process, and the gardener knows that it must not be taxed too severely. The heart also bleeds when it refuses to return passion for passion, when it ceases to defend and justify itself. It is the process of "mortifying the members" of which St. Paul speaks.

But this repression is only the beginning of self-conquest. When it is made an end in itself, and there is no object of finally purifying the heart, that is a stage of hypocrisy; a hiding of one's true nature, and striving to appear better in the eyes of others than one really is. In that case it is an evil, but when adopted as the first stage toward complete purification, it is good. Its practice leads to the second stage of *Endurance,* or forbearance, in which one silently endures the pain which arises in the mind when it is brought in contact with certain actions and attitudes of other minds toward one. As success is attained in this stage, the striver comes to see that all his pain actually arises in his own weaknesses, and not in the wrong attitudes of others toward him, these latter being merely the means by which his sins are brought to the surface and revealed to him. He thus gradually exonerates all others from blame in his falls and lapses of conduct, and accuses only himself, and so learns to love those who thus unconsciously reveal to him his sins and shortcomings.

Having passed through these two stages of self-crucifixion, the disciple enters the third, that of *Elimination,* in which the wrong thought which lay behind the wrong act is cast from the mind immediately it appears. At this stage, conscious strength and holy joy begin to take the place of pain, and the mind having become comparatively calm, the striver is enabled to gain a deeper insight into the complexities of his mind, and thus to understand the inception, growth, and outworking of sin. This is the stage of *Understanding.*

Perfection in understanding leads to the final conquest of self, a conquest so complete that the sin can no more rise in the mind even as a thought or impression; for when the knowledge of sin is complete; when it is known in its totality, from its inception as a seed in the mind to its ripened outgrowth as act and consequence, then it can no more be allowed a place in life, but it is abandoned for ever. Then the mind is at peace. The wrong acts of others no longer arouse wrong and pain in the mind of the disciple. He is glad and calm and wise. He is filled with Love, and blessedness abides with him. And this is *Victory!*

CONTENTMENT IN ACTIVITY

The confounding of a positive spiritual virtue or principle with a negative animal vice is common amongst writers even of what is called the "Advance Thought School," and much valuable energy is frequently expended in criticising and condemning, where a little calm reasoning would have revealed a greater light, and led to the exercise of a broader charity.

The other day I came across a vigorous attack upon the teaching of "Love," wherein the writer condemned such teaching as weakly, foolish, and hypocritical. Needless to say, that which he was condemning as "Love," was merely weak sentimentality and hypocrisy.

Another writer in condemning "meekness" does not know that what he calls meekness is only cowardice, while another who attacks "chastity" as "a snare," is really confusing painful and hypocritical restraint with the virtue of chastity. And just lately I received a long letter from a correspondent who took great pains to show me that "contentment" is a vice, and is the source of innumerable evils.

That which my correspondent called "contentment" is, of course *animal indifference.* The spirit of indifference is incompatible with progress, whereas the spirit of contentment may, and does, attend the highest form of activity, the truest advancement and development. Indolence is the twin sister of indifference, but cheerful and ready action is the friend of contentment.

Contentment is a virtue which becomes lofty and spiritual in its later developments, as the mind is trained to perceive and the heart to receive the guidance, in all things, of a merciful law.

To be contented does not mean to forego effort; it means to *free effort from anxiety;* it does not mean to be satisfied with sin and ignorance and folly, but to rest happily in duty done, work accomplished.

A man may be said to be content to lead a grovelling life, to remain in sin and in debt, but such a man's true state is one of indifference to his duty, his obligations, and the just claims of his fellow-men. He cannot truly be said to possess the virtue of contentment; he does not experience the pure and abiding joy which is the accompaniment of active contentment; so far as his true nature is concerned he is a sleeping soul, and sooner or later will be awakened by intense suffering, having passed through which he will find that true contentment which is the outcome of honest effort and true living.

There are three things with which a man should be content:

With whatever happens.
With his friendships and possessions.
With his pure thoughts.

Contented with whatever happens, he will escape grief; with his friends and possessions, he will avoid anxiety and wretchedness; and with his pure thoughts, he will never go back to suffer and grovel in impurities.

There are three things with which a man should not be content:

With his opinions.
With his character.
With his spiritual condition.

Not content with his opinions, he will continually increase in intelligence; not content with his character, he will ceaselessly grow in strength and virtue; and not content with his spiritual condition, he will, everyday, enter into a larger wisdom and fuller blessedness. In a word, a man should be contented, but not indifferent to his development as a responsible and spiritual being.

The truly contented man works energetically and faithfully, and accepts all results with an untroubled spirit, trusting, at first, that all is well, but afterwards, with the growth of enlightenment, *knowing* that results exactly correspond with efforts. Whatsoever material possessions come to him, come not by greed and anxiety and strife, but by right thought, wise action, and pure exertion.

THE TEMPLE OF BROTHERHOOD

Universal Brotherhood is the supreme Ideal of Humanity, and toward that Ideal the world is slowly but surely moving.

Today, as never before, numbers of earnest men and women are striving to make this Ideal tangible and real; Fraternities are springing up on every hand, and Press and Pulpit, the world over, are preaching the Brotherhood of Man.

The unselfish elements in all such efforts cannot fail to have their effect upon the race, and are with certainty urging it toward the goal of its noblest aspirations; but the ideal state has not yet manifested through any outward organisation, and societies formed for the purpose of propagating Brotherhood are continually being shattered to pieces by internal dissension.

The Brotherhood for which Humanity sighs is withheld from actuality by Humanity itself; nay, more, it is frustrated even by men who work zealously for it is a desirable possibility; and this because the purely *spiritual* nature of Brotherhood is not perceived, and the principles involved, as well as the individual course of conduct necessary to perfect unity, are not comprehended.

Brotherhood as a human organisation cannot exist so long as any degree of self-seeking reigns in the hearts of men and women who band themselves together for any purpose, as such self-seeking must eventually rend the Seamless Coat of loving unity. But although organised Brotherhood has so far largely failed, any man may realise Brotherhood in its perfection, and know it in all its beauty and completion, if he will make himself of a wise, pure, and loving spirit, removing from his mind every element of strife, and learning to practise those divine qualities without which Brotherhood is but a mere theory, opinion, or illusive dream.

For Brotherhood is at first spiritual, and its outer manifestation in the world must follow as a natural sequence.

As a spiritual reality it must be discovered by each man for himself, and in the only place where spiritual realities can be found—*within himself,* and it rests with each whether he shall choose or refuse it.

There are four chief tendencies in the human mind which are destructive of Brotherhood, and which bar the way to its comprehension, namely:

Pride
Self-love
Hatred
Condemnation

Where these are there can be no Brotherhood; in whatsoever heart these hold sway, discord rules, and Brotherhood is not realised, for these tendencies are, in their very nature, dark and selfish and always make for disruption and destruction. From these four things proceeds that serpent brood of false actions and conditions which poison the heart of man, and fill the world with suffering and sorrow.

Out of the spirit of *Pride* proceed envy, resentment, and opinionativeness. Pride envies the position, influence, or goodness of others; it thinks, "I am more deserving than this man or this woman"; it also continually finds occasion for resenting the actions of others, and says, "I have been snubbed," "I have been insulted," and thinking altogether of his own excellence, it sees no excellence in others.

From the spirit of *Self-love* proceed egotism, lust for power, and disparagement and contempt. Self-love worships the personality in which it moves; it is lost in the adoration and glorification of that "I," that "self" which has no real existence, but is a dark dream and a delusion. It desires pre-eminence over others, and thinks, "I am great," "I am more important than others"; it also disparages others, and bestows upon them contempt, seeing no beauty in them, being lost in the contemplation of its own beauty.

From the spirit of *Hatred* proceed slander, cruelty, reviling, and anger. It strives to overcome evil by adding evil to it. It says, "This man has spoken of me ill, I will speak still more ill of him and thus teach him a lesson." It mistakes cruelty for kindness, and causes its possessor to revile a reproving friend. It feeds the flames of anger with bitter and rebellious thoughts.

From the spirit of *Condemnation* proceed accusation, false pity, and false judgement. It feeds itself on the contemplation of evil, and cannot see the good. It has eyes for evil only, and finds it in almost every thing and every person. It sets up an arbitrary standard of right and wrong by which to judge others, and it thinks, "This man does not do as I would have him do, he is therefore evil, and I will denounce him." So blind is the spirit of condemnation that whilst rendering its possessor incapable of judging himself, it causes him to set himself up as the judge of all the earth.

From the four tendencies enumerated, no element of brotherliness can proceed. They are deadly mental poisons, and he who allows them to rankle in his mind, cannot apprehend the peaceful principles on which Brotherhood rests.

Then there are chiefly four divine qualities which are productive of Brotherhood; which are, as it were, the foundation stones on which it rests, namely:

Humility
Self-surrender
Love
Compassion

Wheresoever these are, there Brotherhood is active. In whatsoever heart these qualities are dominant, there Brotherhood is an established reality, for they are, in their very nature, unselfish and are filled with the revealing Light of Truth. There is no darkness in them, and where they are, so powerful is their light, that the dark tendencies cannot remain, but are dissolved and dissipated.

Out of these four qualities proceed all those angelic actions and conditions which make for unity and bring gladness to the heart of man and to the world.

From the spirit of *Humility* proceed meekness and peacefulness; from *Self-surrender* come patience, wisdom, and true judgment; from *Love* spring kindness, joy, and harmony; and from *Compassion* proceed gentleness and forgiveness.

He who has brought himself into harmony with these four qualities is divinely enlightened; he sees whence the actions of men proceed and whither they tend, and therefore can no longer live in the exercise of the dark tendencies. He has realised Brotherhood in its completion as freedom from malice; from envy, from bitterness, from contention, from condemnation. All men are his brothers, those who live in the dark tendencies, as well as those who live in the enlightened qualities, for he knows that when they have perceived the glory and beauty of the Light of Truth, the dark tendencies will be dispelled from their minds. He has but one attitude of mind toward all, that of good-will.

Of the four dark tendencies are born ill-will and strife; of the four divine qualities are born good-will and peace.

Living in the four tendencies a man is a strife-producer. Living in the four qualities a man is a peace-maker.

Involved in the darkness of the selfish tendencies, men believe that they can fight for peace, kill to make alive, slay injury by injuring, restore love by hatred, unity by contention, kindness by cruelty, and establish Brotherhood by erecting their own opinions (which they themselves will, in the course of time, abandon as worthless) as objects of universal adoration.

The wished-for Temple of Brotherhood will be erected in the world when its four foundation stones of Humility, Self-surrender, Love, and Compassion are firmly laid in the hearts of men, for Brotherhood consists, first of all, in the abandonment of self by the individual, and its after-effect is unity between man and man.

Theories and schemes for propagating Brotherhood are many, but Brotherhood itself is one and unchangeable and consists in the complete cessation from egotism and strife, and in practising good-will and peace; for Brotherhood is a practice and not a theory. Self-surrender and Good-will are its guardian angels, and peace is its habitation.

Where two are determined to maintain an opposing opinion, the clinging to self and ill-will are there, and Brotherhood is absent.

Where two are prepared to sympathise with each other, to see no evil in each other, to serve and not to attack each other, the Love of Truth and Good-will are there, and Brotherhood is present.

All strifes, divisions, and wars inhere in the proud, unyielding self; all peace, unity, and concord inhere in the Principles which the yielding up of self reveals.

Brotherhood is only practised and known by him whose heart is at peace with all the world.

PLEASANT PASTURES OF PEACE

He who aspires to the bettering of himself and humanity should ceaselessly strive to arrive at the exercise of that blessed attitude of mind by which he is enabled to put himself, mentally and sympathetically in the place of others, and so, instead of harshly and falsely judging them, and thereby making himself unhappy without adding to the happiness of those others, he will enter into their experience, will understand their particular frame of mind, and will feel for them and sympathise with them.

One of the great obstacles to the attainment of such an attitude of mind is, prejudice, and until this is removed it is impossible to act toward others as we would wish others to act toward us.

Prejudice is destructive of kindness, sympathy, love and true judgment, and the strength of a man's prejudice will be the measure of his harshness and unkindness toward others, for prejudice and cruelty are inseparable.

There is no rationality in prejudice, and, immediately it is aroused in a man he ceases to act as a reasonable being, and gives way to rashness, anger, and injurious excitement. He does not consider his words nor regard the feelings and liberties of those against whom his prejudices are directed. He has, for the time being, forfeited his manhood, and has descended to the level of an irrational creature.

While a man is determined to cling to his preconceived opinions, mistaking them for Truth, and refuses to consider dispassionately the position of others, he cannot escape hatred nor arrive at blessedness.

The man who strives after gentleness, who aspires to act unselfishly toward others, will put away all his passionate prejudice and petty opinions, and will gradually acquire the power of thinking and feeling for others, of understanding their particular state of ignorance or knowledge, and thereby entering fully into their hearts and lives, sympathising with them and seeing them as they are.

Such a man will not oppose himself to the prejudices of others by introducing his own, but will seek to allay prejudice by introducing sympathy and love, striving to bring out all that is good in men, encouraging the good by appealing to it, and discouraging the evil by ignoring it. He will realise the good in the unselfish efforts of others, though their outward methods may be very different from his own, and will so rid his heart of hatred, and will fit it with love and blessedness.

When a man is prone to harshly judge and condemn others, he should inquire how far he falls short himself, he should also reconsider those periods of suffering when he himself was misjudged and misunderstood, and, gathering wisdom and love from his own bitter experience, should studiously and self-sacrificingly refrain from piercing with anguish hearts that are as yet too weak to ignore, too immature and uninstructed to understand.

Sympathy is not required toward those who are purer and more enlightened than one's self, as the purer one lives above the necessity for it. In such a case reverence should be exercised, with a striving to lift one's self up to the purer level, and so enter into possession of the larger life. Nor can a man fully understand one who is wiser than himself, and before condemning, he should earnestly ask himself whether he is, after all, better than the man whom he has singled out as the object of his bitterness. If he is, let him bestow sympathy. If he is not, let him exercise reverence.

For thousands of years the sages have taught, both by precept and example, that evil is only overcome by good, yet still that lesson for the majority, remains unlearned. It is a lesson profound in its simplicity, and difficult to learn because men are blinded by the illusions of self. Men are still engaged in resenting, condemning, and fighting the evil in their own fellow-men, thereby increasing the delusion in their own hearts, and adding to the world's sum of misery and suffering. When they find out that their own resentment must be eradicated, and love put in its place, evil will perish for lack of sustenance.

> With burning brain and heart of hate,
> I sought my wronger, early, late,
> And all the wretched night and day
> My dream and thought was slay, and slay.
> My better self rose uppermost,
> The beast within my bosom lost
> Itself in love; peace from afar
> Shone o'er me radiant like a star.
> I slew my wronger with a deed,
> A deed of love; I made him bleed
> With kindness, and I filled for years
> His soul with tenderness and tears.

Dislike, resentment, and condemnation are all forms of hatred, and evil cannot cease until these are taken out of the heart.

But the obliterating of injuries from the mind is merely one of the beginnings in wisdom. There is a still higher and better way. And that way is so to purify the heart and enlighten the mind that, far from having to forget injuries, there will be none to remember. For it is only pride and self that can be injured and wounded by the actions and attitudes of others; and he who takes pride and self out of his heart can never think the thought, "I have been injured by another" or "I have been wronged by another."

From a purified heart proceeds the right comprehension of things; and from the right comprehension of things proceeds the life that is peaceful, freed from bitterness and suffering, calm and wise. He who thinks, "This man has injured me," has not perceived the Truth in life; falls short of that enlightenment which disperses the erroneous idea of evil as a thing to be hatefully resented. He who is troubled and disturbed about the sins of others is far from Truth; he who is troubled and disturbed about his own sins is very near to the Gate of Wisdom. He in whose heart the flames of resentment burn, cannot know Peace nor understand Truth; he who will banish resentment from his heart, will know and understand.

He who has taken evil out of his own heart cannot resent or resist it in others, for he is enlightened as to its origin and nature, and knows it as a manifestation of the mistakes of ignorance. With the increase of enlightenment, sin becomes impossible. He who sins, does not understand; he who understands does not sin.

The pure man maintains his tenderness of his heart toward those who ignorantly imagine they can do him harm. The wrong attitude of others toward him does not trouble him; his heart is at rest in Compassion and Love.

Blessed is he who has no wrongs to remember, no injuries to forget; in whose pure heart no hateful thought about another can take root and flourish.

Let those who aim at the right life, who believe that they love Truth, cease to passionately oppose themselves to others, and let them strive to calmly and wisely understand them, and in thus acting toward others they will be conquering themselves; and while sympathising with others, their own souls will be fed with the heavenly dews of kindness, and their hearts be strengthened and refreshed in the *Pleasant Pastures of Peace.*

FROM PASSION

TO PEACE

(1910)

CONTENTS

FOREWORD

The first three parts of this book—*Passion, Aspiration,* and *Temptation*—represent the common human life, with its passion, pathos, and tragedy: the last three parts—*Transcendence, Beatitude,* and *Peace*—present the Divine Life, calm, wise and beautiful, of the sage and Saviour. The middle part—*Transmutation*—is the transitional stage between the two; it is the alchemic process linking the divine with the human life. Discipline, denial, and renunciation do not constitute the Divine State; they are only the means by which it is attained. The Divine Life is established in that Perfect Knowledge which bestows Perfect Peace.

—JAMES ALLEN
Bryngoleu,
Ilfracombe, England

PASSION

The pathway of the saints and sages; the road of the wise and pure; the highway along which the Saviours have trod, and which all Saviours to come will also walk—such is the subject of this book; such is the high and holy theme which the author briefly expounds in these pages.

Passion is the lowest level of human life. None can descend lower. In its chilling swamps and concealing darkness creep and crawl the creatures of its sunless world. Lust, hatred, covetousness, pride, vanity, greed, revenge, envy, spite, retaliation, slander, backbiting, lying, theft, deceit, treachery, cruelty, suspicion, jealousy—such are the brute forces and blind, unreasoning impulses that inhabit the underworld of passion, and roam, devouring and devoured, in the rank, primeval jungles of the human mind.

There also dwell the dark shapes of remorse, and pain, and suffering; and the drooping forms of grief, and sorrow, and lamentation.

In this dark world the unwise live and die, not knowing the peace of purity, nor the joy of that Divine Light which for ever shines above them, and for them, yet shines in vain so long as it falls on unseeing eyes which look not up, but are ever bent earthward—fleshward.

But the wise look up. They are not satisfied with this passion-world, and they bend their steps toward the upper world of peace, the light and glory of which they behold, at first afar off, but nearer and with ever-increasing splendour as they ascend.

None can fall lower than passion, but all can rise higher. In that lowest place where further descent is impossible, all who move forward *must* ascend; and the ascending pathway is always at hand, near and easily accessible. It is the way of self-conquest; and he has already entered it who has begun to say "nay" to his selfishness, who has begun to discipline his desires and to control and command the unruly elements of his mind.

Passion is the arch enemy of mankind, the slayer of happiness, the opposite and enemy of peace.

From it proceeds all that defiles and destroys. It is the source of suffering, the maker of misery, and the promulgator of mischief and disaster.

The inner world of selfishness is rooted in ignorance—ignorance of Divine Law, of Divine Goodness; ignorance of the Pure Way and the Peaceful Path. Passion is dark; and it thrives and flourishes in spiritual darkness. It cannot enter the regions of spiritual light. In the enlightened mind the darkness of ignorance is destroyed; in the pure heart there is no place for passion.

Passion in all its forms is a mental thirst, a fever, a torturing unrest. As a fire consumes a magnificent building, reducing it to a heap of unsightly ashes, so are men consumed by the flames of passions; and their deeds and works fall and perish.

If one would find peace, he must come out of passion. The wise man subdues his passions, the foolish man is subdued by them. The seeker for wisdom begins by turning his back on folly. The lover of peace enters the way which leads thereto, and with every step he takes he leaves further below and behind him the dark dwelling-place of passion and despair.

The first step toward the heights of wisdom and peace is to understand the darkness and misery of selfishness; and when that is understood, the overcoming it—the coming out of it—will follow.

Selfishness, or passion, not only subsists in the gross forms of greed and glaringly ungoverned conditions of mind, it informs, also, every hidden thought which is subtly connected with the assumption and glorification of one's self; and it is most deceiving and subtle when it prompts one to dwell upon the selfishness in others, to accuse them of it and to talk about it. The man who continually dwells upon the selfishness in others will not thus overcome his own selfishness. Not by accusing others do we come out of selfishness, but by purifying ourselves. The way from passion to peace is not by hurling painful charges against others, but by overcoming one's self. By eagerly striving to subdue the selfishness of others, we remain passion-bound; by patiently overcoming our own selfishness, we ascend into freedom. He only who has conquered himself can subdue others; and he subdues them not by passion, but by love.

The foolish man accuses others and justifies himself; but he who is becoming wise justifies others and accuses himself. The way from passion to peace is not in the outer world of people; it is in the inner world of thoughts; it does not consist in altering the deeds of others, it consists in perfecting one's own deeds.

Frequently the man of passion is most eager to put others right; but the man of wisdom puts himself right. If one is anxious to reform the world, let him begin by reforming himself. The reformation of self does not end with the elimination of the sensual elements only, that is its beginning; it ends only when every vain thought and selfish aim is overcome. Short of perfect purity and wisdom, there is still some form of self-slavery or folly which needs to be conquered.

Passion is at the base of the structure of life; peace is its crown and summit. Without passion to begin with, there would be no power to work with and no achievement to end with. Passion represents power, but power misdirected, power producing hurt instead of happiness. Its forces, while being instruments of destruction in the hands of the foolish, are instruments of preservation in the hands of the wise. When curbed and concentrated and beneficently directed, they represent working energy. Passion is the flaming sword which guards the gates of Paradise. It shuts out and destroys the foolish; it admits and preserves the wise.

He is the foolish man who does not know the extent of his own ignorance; who is the slave of thoughts of self; who obeys the impulses of passion.

He is the wise man who knows his own ignorance; who understands the emptiness of selfish thoughts; who masters the impulses of passion.

The fool descends into deeper and deeper ignorance; the wise man ascends into higher and higher knowledge.

The fool desires and suffers and dies. The wise man aspires and rejoices and lives.

With mind intent on wisdom and mental gaze raised upward, the spiritual warrior perceives the upward way and fixes his attention upon the heights of Peace.

ASPIRATION

With the clear perception of one's own ignorance comes the desire for enlightenment; and thus in the heart is born Aspiration, the rapture of the saints.

On the wings of aspiration man rises from earth to heaven, from ignorance to knowledge, from the under darkness to the upper light. Without it he remains a grovelling animal, earthly, sensual, unenlightened and uninspired.

Aspiration is the longing for heavenly things: for righteousness, compassion, purity, love, as distinguished from desire, which is the longing for earthly things; for selfish possessions, personal dominance, low pleasures, and sensual gratifications.

As a bird deprived of its wings cannot soar, so a man without aspiration cannot rise above his surroundings and become master of his animal inclinations. He is the slave of passions, is subject to others, and is carried hither and thither by the changing current of events.

For one to begin to aspire means that he is dissatisfied with his low estate and is aiming at a higher condition. It is a sure sign that he is roused out of his lethargic sleep of animality and has become conscious of nobler attainments and a fuller life.

Aspiration makes all things possible. It opens the way to advancement. Even the highest state of perfection conceivable it brings near and makes real and possible; for that which can be conceived can be achieved.

Aspiration is the twin angel to inspiration. It unlocks the gates of Joy. Singing accompanies soaring. Music, poetry, prophecy and all high and holy instruments are at last placed in the hands of him whose aspirations flag not, whose spirit does not fail.

So long as animal conditions taste sweet to a man, he cannot aspire; he is so far satisfied; but when their sweetness turns to bitterness, then in his sorrow he thinks of nobler things. When he is deprived of earthly joy, he aspires to the Joy which is heavenly. It is when impurity turns to suffering that purity is sought. Truly aspiration rises, Phœnix-like, from the dead ashes of repentance, but on its powerful pinions man can reach the Heaven of heavens.

The man of aspiration has entered the way which ends in peace; and surely he will reach that end if he stays not nor turns back. If he constantly renews his mind with glimpses of the Heavenly Vision, he will reach the Heavenly State.

Man attains in the measure that he aspires. His longing to be is the gauge of what he can be. To fix the mind is to fore-ordain the achievement. As man can experience and know all low things, so he can experience and know all high things. As he has become human, so he can become divine. The turning of the mind in high and divine directions is the sole and needful task.

What is impurity but the impure thoughts of the thinker? What is purity but the pure thoughts of the thinker? One man does not do the thinking of another. Each man is pure or impure of himself alone.

If a man thinks, "It is through others, or circumstances, or heredity, that I am impure," how can he hope to overcome his errors? Such a thought will check all holy aspirations and bind him to the slavery of passion.

When a man fully perceives that his errors and impurities are his own, that they are generated and fostered by himself, that he alone is responsible for them, then he will aspire to overcome them, the way of attainment will be opened up to him, and he will see whence and whither he is travelling.

The man of passion sees no straight path before him, and behind him all is fog and gloom. He seizes the pleasure of the moment and does not strive for understanding nor think of wisdom. His way is confused, turbulent, troubled; and his heart is far from peace.

The man of aspiration sees before him the pathway up the Heavenly Heights, and behind him are the circuitous routes of passion up which he has hitherto blindly groped. Striving for understanding, with his mind set on wisdom, his way is clear and his heart already feels a foretaste of the final peace.

Men of passion strive mightily to achieve little things—things which speedily perish, and, in the place where they were, leave nothing to be remembered.

Men of aspiration strive with equal might to achieve great things—things of virtue, of knowledge, of wisdom, which do not perish, but stand as monuments of inspiration for the upliftment of mankind.

As the merchant achieves worldly success by persistent exertion, so the saint achieves spiritual success by aspiration and endeavour. One becomes a merchant, the other a saint, by the particular direction in which his mental energy is guided.

When the rapture of aspiration touches the mind, it at once refines it, and the dross of its impurities begins to fall away; yea, while aspiration holds the mind, no impurity can enter it, for the impure and the pure cannot at the same moment occupy the thought. But the effort of aspiration is at first spasmodic and shortlived. The mind falls back into its habitual error, and effort must be constantly renewed.

The lover of the pure life renews his mind daily with the invigorating glow of aspiration. He rises early and fortifies his mind with strong thoughts and strenuous endeavour. He knows that the mind is of such a nature that it cannot remain for a moment unoccupied, and that if it is not held and guided by high thoughts and pure aspirations, it will assuredly be enslaved and misguided by low thoughts and base desires.

Aspiration can be fed, fostered and strengthened by daily habit, just as is desire. It can be sought, and admitted into the mind as a divine guide; or it can be neglected and shut out. To retire for a short time each day to some quiet spot, preferably in the open air, and there call up the energies of the mind in surging waves of holy rapture, is to prepare the mind for great spiritual victories and destinies of divine import; for such rapture is the preparation for wisdom, and the prelude to peace. Before the mind can contemplate pure things it must be lifted up to them, it must rise above impure things; and aspiration is the instrument by which this is accomplished. By its aid the mind soars swiftly and surely into heavenly places, and begins to experience divine things; begins to accumulate wisdom and to learn to guide itself by an ever-increasing measure of the divine light of pure knowledge.

To thirst for righteousness; to hunger for the pure life; to rise in holy rapture on the wings of angelic aspiration—this is the right road to wisdom; this is the right striving for peace; this is the right beginning of the Way Divine.

TEMPTATION

Aspiration can carry a man into heaven, but to remain there he must learn to conform his entire mind to the heavenly conditions: to this end temptation works.

Temptation is the reversion, in thought, from purity to passion. It is a going back from aspiration to desire. It threatens aspiration until the point is reached where desire is quenched in the waters of pure knowledge and calm thought. In the early stages of aspiration, temptation is subtle and powerful, and is regarded as an enemy; but it is only an enemy in the sense that the tempted one is his own enemy; in the sense that it is the revealer of weakness and impurity, it is a friend, a necessary factor in spiritual training. It is, indeed, an accompaniment of the effort to overcome evil and apprehend Good. To be successfully conquered, the evil in a man must come to the surface and present itself, and it is in temptation that the evil hidden in the heart stands revealed and exposed.

That which temptation appeals to and arouses is unconquered desire, and temptation will again and again assail and subdue a man until he has lifted himself above the lusting impulses. Temptation is an appeal to the impure. That which is pure cannot be subject to temptation.

Temptation waylays the man of aspiration until he touches the region of the Divine Consciousness; and beyond that border temptation cannot follow him. It is when a man begins to aspire that he begins to be tempted. Aspiration rouses up all the latent good and evil, in order that the man may be fully revealed to himself, for a man cannot overcome himself unless he fully knows himself. It can scarcely be said of the merely animal man that he is tempted, for the very presence of temptation means that there is a striving for a purer state. Animal desire and gratification is the normal condition of the man who has not yet risen into aspiration; he wishes for nothing more, nothing better than his sensual enjoyments and is, for the present, satisfied. Such a man cannot be tempted to fall, for he has not yet risen.

The presence of aspiration signifies that a man has taken one step, at least, upward, and is therefore capable of being drawn back; and this backward attraction is called temptation. The allurements of temptation subsist in the impure thoughts and downward desires of the heart. The object of temptation is powerless to attract when the heart no longer lusts for it. The stronghold of temptation is within a man, not without; and until a man realises this, the period of temptation will be protracted. While a man continues to run away from outward objects, under the delusion that temptation subsists entirely in them, and does not attack and purge away his impure imaginings, his temptations will increase and his falls will be many and grievous. When a man clearly perceives that the evil is within, and not without, then his progress will be rapid, his temptations will decrease, and the final overcoming of all temptation will be well within the range of his spiritual vision.

Temptation is torment. It is not an abiding condition, but is a passage from a lower condition to a higher. The fulness and perfection of life is bliss, not torment. Temptation accompanies weakness and defeat, but a man is destined for strength and victory. The presence of torment is the signal to rise and conquer. The man of persistent and ever-renewed aspiration does not allow himself to think that temptation cannot be overcome. He is determined to be master of himself. Resignation to evil is an acknowledgment of defeat. It signifies that the battle against self is abandoned, that Good is denied, that evil is made supreme.

As the energetic man of business is not daunted by difficulties, but studies how to overcome them, so the man of ceaseless aspiration is not crushed into submission by temptations, but meditates how he may fortify his mind; for the tempter is like a coward, he only creeps in at weak and unguarded points.

The tempted one should study thoughtfully the nature and meaning of temptation, for until it is known it cannot be overcome. A wise general, before attacking the opposing force, studies the tactics of his enemy; so he who is to overcome temptation must understand how it arises in his own darkness and error, and must study, by introspection and meditation, how to disperse the darkness and supplant error by Truth.

The stronger a man's passions, the fiercer will be his temptations; the deeper his selfishness, the more subtle his temptations; the more pronounced his vanity, the more flattering and deceptive his temptations.

A man must know himself if he is to know Truth. He must not shrink from any revelation which will expose his error; on the contrary, he must welcome such revelations as aids to that self-knowledge which is the handmaid of self-conquest.

The man who cannot endure to have his errors and shortcomings brought to the surface and made known, but tries to hide them, is unfit to walk the highway of Truth. He is not properly equipped to battle with and overcome temptation. He who cannot fearlessly face his lower nature cannot climb the rugged heights of Renunciation.

Let the tempted one know this—that he himself is both tempter and tempted; that all his enemies are within; that the flatterers which seduce, the taunts which stab, and the flames which burn, all spring from that inner region of ignorance and error in which he has hitherto lived—and knowing this, let him be assured of complete victory over evil. When he is sorely tempted, let him not mourn therefore, but let him rejoice in that his strength is tried and his weakness exposed. For he who truly knows and humbly acknowledges his weakness, will not be slow in setting about the acquisition of strength.

Foolish men blame others for their lapses and sins; but let the Truth-lover blame only himself.

Let him acknowledge his complete responsibility for his own conduct, and not say, when he falls—this thing, or such and such circumstance, or that man, was to blame—for the most which others can do is to afford an opportunity for our own good or evil to manifest itself; they cannot *make* us good or evil.

Temptation is at first sore, grievous and hard to be borne; and subtle and persistent is the assailant. But if the tempted one is firm and courageous, and does not give way, he will gradually subdue his spiritual enemy and will finally triumph in the knowledge of Good.

The Adverse One is compounded of a man's own lust and selfishness and pride, and when these are put away, evil is seen to be as naught, and Good is revealed in all-victorious splendour.

TRANSMUTATION

Midway between the hell of Passion and the heaven of Peace is the purgatory of Transmutation. Not a speculative purgatory beyond the grave, but a real purgatory in the human heart. In its separating and purifying fire the base metal of error is sifted away, and only the clarified gold of Truth remains.

When temptation has culminated in sorrow and deep perplexity, then the tempted one, strenuously striving for deliverance, finds that his thraldom is entirely from himself, and that instead of fighting against outer circumstances, he must alter inner conditions. The fight against outer things is necessary at the commencement. It is the only course which can be adopted at the first, because of the prevailing ignorance of mental causation, but it never, of itself, brings about emancipation. What it does bring about is *the knowledge of the mental cause of temptation,* and the knowledge of the mental cause of temptation leads to the transmutation of thought, and the transmutation of thought leads to deliverance from the bondage of error.

The preliminary fighting is a necessary stage in spiritual development, as the crying and kicking of a helpless babe is necessary to its growth; but as the crying and kicking is not needed beyond the infant stage, so the fierce struggling with and falling under temptation ends when the knowledge of mental transmutation is acquired.

The truly wise man, he who is enlightened concerning the source and cause of temptation, does not fight against outward allurements, *he abandons all desire for them;* they thus cease to be allurements, and the power of temptation is destroyed at its source. But this abandonment of unholy desire is not a final process, it is the beginning of a regenerative and transforming power which, patiently employed, leads man to the clear and cloudless heights of spiritual enlightenment.

Spiritual transmutation consists in an entire reversal of the ordinary self-seeking attitude of mind toward men and things, and this reversal brings about an entirely new set of experiences. Thus the desire for a certain pleasure is abandoned, cut off at its source and not allowed to have any place in the consciousness. But the mental force which that desire represented is not annihilated; it is transferred to a higher region of thought, transmuted into a purer form of energy. The law of conservation of energy obtains universally in mind as in matter, and the force shut off in lower directions is liberated in higher realms of spiritual activity.

Along the saintly Way toward the divine life, the midway region of Transmutation is the Country of Sacrifice, it is the Plain of Renunciation. Old passions, old desires, old ambitions and thoughts, are cast away and abandoned, but only to reappear in some more beautiful, more permanent, more eternally satisfying form. As valuable jewels, long guarded and cherished, are thrown tearfully into the melting-pot, yet are remoulded into new and more perfect adornments, so the spiritual alchemist, at first loath to part company with long-cherished thoughts and habits, at last gives them up, to discover a little later, to his joy, that they have come back to him in the form of new faculties, rarer powers, and purer joys—spiritual jewels newly burnished, beautiful and resplendent.

In transmuting his mind from evil to good, a man comes to distinguish more and more clearly between error and Truth, and so distinguishing, he ceases to be swayed and prompted by outward things, and by the actions and attitudes of others; he acts from his knowledge of Truth. First acknowledging his errors, and then confronting them with a searching mind and a humble heart, he subdues, conquers and transmutes them.

The early stage of transmutation is painful, but brief, for the pain is soon transformed into pure spiritual joy, the brevity of the pain being measured by the intelligence and energy with which the process is pursued.

While a man thinks that the cause of his pain is in the attitude of others, he will not pass beyond it, but when he perceives that its cause is in himself, then he will pass beyond it into joy.

The unenlightened man allows himself to be disturbed, wounded, and overthrown by what he regards as the wrong attitude of others toward him; this is because the same wrong attitude is in himself. He, indeed, metes out to them, in return, the same actions, regarding as right, in himself, that which is wrong in others. Slander is given for slander, hatred for hatred, anger for anger. This is the action and reaction of evil; it is the clash of selfishness with selfishness. It is only the self, or selfish elements, within a man that can be aroused by the evil in another; the Truth, or divine characteristics in a man, cannot be approached by that evil, much less can it be disturbed and over-thrown by it.

It is the conversion, or complete reversal, of this self into Truth, that constitutes Transmutation. The enlightened man has abandoned the delusion that the evil in others has power to hurt and sub-due him, and he has grasped the profound truth that he is only overthrown by the evil in himself. He therefore ceases to blame others for his sins and sufferings, and applies himself to purifying his own heart. In this reversal of his mental attitude, he transmutes the lower selfish forces into the higher moral attributes. The base ore of error is cast into the fire of sacrifice, and there comes forth the pure gold of Truth.

Such a man stands firm and unmoved when assailed by outward things. He is self's master, not its slave. He has ceased to identify himself with the impulses of passion, and has identified himself with Truth. He has overcome evil, and has become merged in Good. He knows both error and Truth. He has abandoned error and brought himself into harmony with Truth. He returns good for evil. The more he is assailed by evil from without, the greater is his opportunity of manifesting the good from within. That which supremely differentiates the fool from the wise man is this—that the fool meets passion with passion, hatred with hatred, and returns evil for evil; whereas the wise man meets passion with peace, hatred with love, and returns good for evil.

Men inflict sufferings upon themselves through the active instrumentality of their own unpurified nature; they rise into perfect peace in the measure that they purify their hearts. The mental energy which men waste in the pursuance of dark passions is all-sufficient to enable them to reach the high-est wisdom when it is turned in the right direction. As water, when transmuted into steam, becomes a new, more definite and wide-reaching power, so passion when transmuted into intellectual and moral force becomes a new life, a new power for the accomplishment of high and unfailing purposes.

Mental forces, like molecular, have their opposite poles or modes of action; and where the nega-tive pole is, there also is the positive. Where ignorance is, wisdom is possible; where passion abounds, peace awaits; where there is much suffering, much bliss is near. Sorrow is the negation of joy; sin is the opposite of purity; evil is the denial of good. Where there is an opposite, there is that which is opposed. The adverse evil, in its denial of the good, testifies to its presence. The one thing needful, therefore, is the turning round from the negative to the positive; the conversion of the heart from impure desires to pure aspirations; the transmutation of the passional forces into moral powers.

The wise purify their thoughts; they turn from bad deeds, and do good deeds; they put error behind them, and approach Truth. Thus do they rise above the allurements of sin, above the tor-ments of temptation, above the dark world of sorrow, and enter the Divine Consciousness, the Transcendent Life.

TRANSCENDENCE

When a man passes from the dark stage of temptation to the more enlightened stage of transmutation, he has become a saint, namely—one who perceives the need of self-purification, who understands the way of self-purification, who has entered that way and is engaged in perfecting himself: but there comes a time in the process of transmutation when, with the decrease of evil and the accumulation of good, there dawns in the mind a new vision, a new consciousness, a new man; and when this is reached, the saint has become a sage; he has passed from the human life to the divine life; he is "born again," and there begins for him a new round of experiences, he wields a new power; a new universe opens out before his spiritual gaze. This is the stage of Transcendence; this I call the Transcendent Life.

When there is no more consciousness of sin; when anxiety and doubt, and grief and sorrow are ended; when lust and enmity and anger and envy no more possess the thoughts; when there remains in the mind no vestige of blame toward others for one's own condition, and when all conditions are seen to be good because the result of causes, so that no event can afflict the mind, then Transcendence is attained; then the limited human personality is outgrown, and the divine life is known; evil is transcended, and Good is all-in-all.

The divine consciousness is not an intensification of the human, it is a new form of consciousness. It springs from the old, but it is not a continuance of it. Born of the lower life of sin and sorrow, after a period of painful travail, it yet transcends that life, and has no part in it, as the perfect flower transcends the seed from which it sprang.

As passion is the keynote of the self-life, so serenity is the keynote of the transcendent life. Rising into it, man is lifted above inharmony and disturbance. When Perfect Good is realized and known, not as an opinion or an idea, but as an experience, a possession, then calm vision is acquired and tranquil joy abides through all vicissitudes. The transcendent life is ruled not by passions but by principles. It is founded not upon fleeting impulses but upon abiding laws. In its clear atmosphere the orderly sequence of all things is revealed, so that there is seen to be no room for sorrow, anxiety or regret. While men are involved in the passions of self they load themselves with cares and they trouble over many things; and more than all else do they trouble over their own little, burdened, pain-stricken personality, being anxious for its fleeting pleasures, for its protection and preservation, and for its eternal safety and continuance. Now in the life that is wise and good all this is transcended. Personal interests are replaced by universal purposes; and all cares, troubles and anxieties concerning the pleasure and fate of the personality are dispelled like the feverish dreams of a night.

Passion is blind and ignorant; it sees and knows only its own gratification. Self recognises no law; its object is to get and to enjoy. The getting is a graduated scale varying from sensual greed, through many subtle vanities, up to the desire for a personal heaven or personal immortality. But it is self still; it is the old sensual craving coming out again in a more subtle and deceptive form; it is the longing for some personal delight, along with its accompanying dread lest that delight should be lost for ever.

In the transcendent state desire and dread are ended, and the thirst for gain and the fear of loss are things that are no more; for where the universal order is seen, universal good is seen; and where perennial joy in that good is a normal condition, what is there left to desire, what remains to be feared?

He who has brought his entire nature into conformity and harmony with the law of Righteousness, who has made his thoughts pure, and his deeds blameless, he it is who has entered into liberty, he has transcended darkness and mortality, and has passed into Light and Immortality. For the transcendent state is at first a higher order of morality, then a new form of perception, and at last a comprehensive understanding of the universal moral causation. And this Morality, this Vision, and this Understanding constitute the New Consciousness, the Divine Life.

The Transcendent Man is he who is above and beyond the dominion of self; he has transcended evil, and lives in the practice and knowledge of Good. He is like a man who, having long looked upon the world with darkened eyes, is now restored to sight, and sees things as they are.

Evil is an experience, and not a power. If it were an independent power in the universe it could not be transcended by any being. But though not real as a power, it is real as a condition, an experience, for all experience is of the nature of reality. It is a state of ignorance, of undevelopment, and, as such, it recedes and disappears before the Light of Knowledge, as the intellectual ignorance of the child vanishes before the gradually accumulating learning, or as darkness dissolves before the rising light.

The painful experiences of evil pass away as the new experiences of Good enter into and possess the field of consciousness. And what are the new experiences of Good? They are many and beautiful—such as the joyful knowledge of freedom from sin; the absence of remorse; deliverance from all the torments of temptation; ineffable joy in conditions and circumstances which formerly caused deep affliction; imperviousness to hurt by the actions of others; great patience and sweetness of character; serenity of mind under all circumstances; emancipation from doubt, fear and anxiety; freedom from all dislike, envy and enmity, with the power to feel and act kindly toward those who see fit to constitute themselves one's enemies or opponents; the divine power to give blessings for curses, and to return good for evil; a deep knowledge of the human heart, with a perception of its fundamental goodness; insight into the law of moral causation and the mental evolution of beings, with a prophetic foresight of the sublime good that awaits humanity; and above all, a glad rejoicing in the limitation and impotency of evil, and in the eternal supremacy and power of Good. All these, and the calm, strong, far-reaching life that these imply and contain, are the rich experiences of the Transcendent Man, along with all the new and varied resources, the vast powers, the quickened abilities and enlarged capacities that spring to life in the New Consciousness.

Transcendence is transcendent virtue. Evil and Good cannot dwell together, and evil must be abandoned, left behind and transcended, before Good is grasped and known; and when Good is practised and fully comprehended, then all the afflictions of the mind are at an end, for that which is accompanied with pain and sorrow in the consciousness of evil is not so accompanied in the consciousness of Good. Whatsoever happens to the good man cannot cause him perplexity or sorrow, for he knows its cause and issue, knows the *good* which it is ordained to accomplish in himself, and so his mind remains happy and serene. Though the body of the good man be bound, his mind is free; though it be wounded and in pain, joy and peace abide within his heart.

A spiritual teacher had a pupil who was apt and earnest. After several years of learning and practice the pupil one day propounded a question which his master could not answer. After several days of deep meditation, the master said to his pupil, "I cannot answer the question which you have asked; have you any solution to offer?" Whereupon the pupil formulated a reply to the question which he had propounded; and the master said to him, "You have answered that which I could not. Henceforth nor I nor any man can instruct you, for now you are indeed instructed by Truth. You have soared, like the kingly eagle, where no man can follow. Your work is now to instruct others. You are no longer the pupil; you have become the master."

In looking back on the self-life which he has transcended, the divinely enlightened man sees that all the afflictions of that life were his school-masters teaching him and leading him upward, and that, in the measure that he penetrated their meaning and lifted himself above them, they departed from him. Their mission to teach him having ended, they left him triumphant master of the field; for the lower cannot teach the higher; ignorance cannot instruct wisdom; evil cannot enlighten Good; nor can the pupil set lessons for the master. That which is transcended cannot reach up to that which transcends. Evil can only teach in its own sphere where it is regarded as a master; in the sphere of Good it has no place, no authority.

The strong traveller on the highroad of Truth knows no such thing as resignation to evil; he knows only obedience to Good. He who submits to evil, saying, "Sin cannot be overcome and evil must be borne," thereby acknowledges that evil is his master; and not his master to instruct him, but to bind and oppress him. The lover of Good cannot also be a lover of evil, nor can he for one moment admit its ascendency. He elevates and glorifies Good, not evil. He loves light, not darkness.

When a man makes Truth his Master, he abandons error; and as he transcends error, he becomes more like his Master, until at last he becomes one with Truth, teaching it, as a master, by his actions, and reflecting it in his life.

Transcendence is not an abnormal condition; it belongs to the orderly process of evolution; and though, as yet, few have reached it, all will come into it in the course of the ages. And he who ascends into it, sins no more, sorrows no more, and is no more troubled; good are his thoughts, good are his actions, and good is the tranquil tenor of his way. He has conquered self, and has submitted to Truth; he has mastered evil, and has comprehended Good. Henceforth nor men nor books can instruct him, for he is instructed by the Supreme Good, even the Spirit of Truth.

BEATITUDE

When divine good is practised, life is bliss. Bliss is the normal condition of the good man; and those outer assaults, harassments and persecutions, which bring such sufferings to others, only serve to heighten his happiness, for they cause the deep fountain of Good within him to well up in greater abundance.

To have transcendent virtue is to enjoy transcendent felicity. The beatific blessedness which Jesus holds out is promised to those having the beatific virtues—to the merciful, the pure in heart, the peacemakers, and so on. The higher virtue does not merely and only lead to happiness, it *is* happiness. It is impossible for a man of transcendent virtue to be unhappy. The cause of unhappiness must be sought and found in the self-loving elements, and not in the self-sacrificing qualities. A man may have virtue, and be unhappy, but not so if he have divine virtue. Human virtue is mingled with self, and therefore with sorrow; but from divine virtue every taint of self has been purged away, and with it every vestige of misery. One comparison will suffice to illustrate this. A man may have the courage of a lion in attack and self-defence (such courage being a human virtue), but he will not thereby be rendered supremely happy; but he whose courage is of that divine kind which enables him to transcend both attack and defence, and to remain mild, serene and lovable under attack, such a man will thereby be rendered supremely happy; moreover, his assailant will be rendered more happy, in that his more powerful good will overcome and cast out the fierce and unhappy evil of the other.

The acquisition of human virtue is a great step toward Truth; but the Divine Way transcends it: Truth lies upward and beyond.

Doing good in order to gain a personal heaven or personal immortality is human virtue, but it is not unmixed with self, and not emancipated from sorrow. In the transcendent virtues all is good and good is all; there is no personal or ulterior aim. Human virtue is imperfect; it is mixed with the baser, selfish elements, and needs to be transmuted. Divine virtue is unblemished, pure; it is complete and perfect in itself.

And what are the transcendent Virtues that embody all felicity? They are—

Impartiality; the seeing so deeply into the human heart and into human actions that it becomes impossible to take sides with one man or one party against another, and therefore the power to be perfectly just.

Unlimited Kindness toward all men and all creatures, whether enemies or friends.

Perfect Patience at all times, in all circumstances, and under the severest trials.

Profound Humility; the total abnegation of self; the judging of one's own actions as though they were the actions of another.

Stainless Purity of mind and deed. Freedom from all evil thoughts and impure imaginings.

Unbroken Calmness of mind, even in the midst of outward strife, or surrounded by the turmoil of many vicissitudes.

Abiding Goodness of heart; imperviousness to evil; returning good for evil.

Compassion; deep pity for all creatures and beings in their sufferings. Shielding the weak and helpless; and protecting, out of pity, even one's enemies from injury and slander.

Abounding Love toward all living things; rejoicing with the happy and successful, and sympathising with the sorrowing and defeated.

Perfect Peace toward all things. Being at peace with all the world. A profound reconciliation to the Divine Order of the universe.

Such are the Virtues that transcend both vice and virtue. They include all that virtue embodies, while going beyond it into Divine Truth. They are the fruits of innumerable efforts to achieve; the glorious gifts of him that overcomes; they constitute the ten-jewelled crown prepared for the calm brow of him who has conquered himself. With these majestic virtues is the mind of the sage adorned. By them he is eternally shielded from sin and sorrow, from harm and hurt, from trouble and turmoil. In them he abides in a happiness, a blessedness, a bliss, so pure and tranquil, so deep and high, so far transcending all the fleeting excitements of self, as to be unknown and incomprehensible to the self-seeking consciousness.

The sage has conquered passion and has come to lasting peace. As the mighty mountain remains unmoved by the turbulent ocean that beats round its base, so the mind of the sage, towering in lofty Virtue, remains unshaken by the tempests of passion which beat unceasingly upon the shores of life. Good and wise, he is evermore happy and serene; transcendently virtuous, he lives in Beatific Bliss.

PEACE

Where passion is, peace is not; where peace is, passion is not. To know this, is to master the first letter in the Divine Language of Perfect Deeds; for to know that passion and peace cannot dwell together is to be well prepared to renounce the lesser and embrace the greater.

Men pray for peace, yet cling to passion; they foster strife, yet pray for heavenly rest: this is ignorance; profound spiritual ignorance; it is not to know the first letter in the alphabet of things divine.

Hatred and love, strife and peace, cannot dwell together in the same heart. Where one is admitted as a welcome guest, the other will be turned away as an unwelcome stranger. He who despises another will be despised by others; he who opposes his fellow-man will himself be resisted. He should not be surprised and mourn that men are divided. He should know that he is propagating strife. He should understand his lack of peace.

He is brave who conquers another, but he who conquers himself is supremely noble. He who is victorious over another may in turn be defeated, but he who overcomes himself will never be subdued.

By the way of self-conquest is the Perfect Peace achieved. Man cannot understand it, cannot approach it, until he sees the supreme necessity of turning away from the fierce fighting of things without and entering upon the noble warfare against evils within. He is already on the Saintly Way who has realised that the enemy of the world is within and not without; that his own ungoverned thoughts are the source of confusion and strife; that his own unchastened desires are the violators of his peace and of the peace of the world.

If a man has conquered lust and anger, hatred and pride, selfishness and greed, he has conquered the world; he has slain the enemies of peace; and peace remains with him.

Peace does not fight; is not a partisan; has no blatant voice. The triumph of peace is an unassailable silence.

He who is overcome by force is not thereby overcome in his heart; he may be a greater enemy than before; but he who is overcome by the spirit of peace is thereby changed at heart. He that was an enemy has become a friend. Force and strife work upon the passions and fears, but love and peace reach and reform the heart.

The pure-hearted and wise have peace in their hearts; it enters into their actions; they apply it in their lives. It is more powerful than strife; it conquers where force would fail. Its wings shield the righteous. Under its protection the harmless are not harmed. It affords a secure shelter from the heat of selfish struggle. It is a refuge for the defeated, a tent for the lost and a temple for the pure.

When peace is practised and possessed and known, then sin and remorse, grasping and disappointment, craving and temptation, desiring and grieving—all the turbulence and torment of the mind—are left behind in the dark sphere of self to which they belong, and beyond which they cannot go. Beyond where these dark spectres move, the radiant Plains of Divine Beatitude bask in Eternal Light, and to these the traveller on the High and Holy Way comes in due time. From the binding swamps of passion, through the thorny forests of many vanities, across the arid deserts of doubt and despair, he travels on, not turning back, nor staying his course, but ever moving toward his sublime destination, until at last he comes, a meek and lowly, yet strong and radiant conqueror, to the Beautiful City of Peace.

MAN: KING OF MIND, BODY, AND CIRCUMSTANCE

(1911)

Within, around, above, below,
    The primal forces burn and brood,
Awaiting wisdom's guidance; lo!
    All their material is good:
Evil subsists in their abuse;
Good, in their wise and lawful use.

FOREWORD

The problem of life consists in learning how to live. It is like the problem of addition or subtraction to the schoolboy. When mastered, all difficulty disappears, and the problem has vanished. All the problems of life, whether they be social, political, or religious, subsist in ignorance and wrong-living. As they are solved in the heart of each individual, they will be solved in the mass of men. Humanity at present is in the painful stage of "learning." It is confronted with the difficulties of its own ignorance. As men learn to live rightly, learn to direct their forces and use their functions and faculties by the light of wisdom, the sum of life will be correctly done, and its mastery will put an end to all the "problems of evil." To the wise, all such problems have ceased.

—James Allen
Bryngoleu,
Ilfracombe, England

CONTENTS

THE INNER WORLD OF THOUGHTS

Man is the maker of happiness and misery. Further, he is the creator and perpetuator of his own happiness and misery. These things are not externally imposed; they are internal conditions. Their cause is neither deity, nor devil, nor circumstance, but *Thought.* They are the effects of deeds, and deeds are the visible side of thoughts. Fixed attitudes of mind determine courses of conduct, and from courses of conduct come those reactions called *happiness* and *unhappiness.* This being so, it follows that, to alter the reactive condition, one must alter the active thought. To exchange misery for happiness, it is necessary to reverse the fixed attitude of mind and habitual course of conduct which is the cause of misery, and the reverse effect will appear in the mind and life. A man has no power to be happy while thinking and acting selfishly; he cannot be unhappy while thinking and acting unselfishly. Wheresoever the cause is, there the effect will appear. Man cannot abrogate effects, but he can alter causes. He can purify his nature; he can remould his character. There is great power in self-conquest; there is great joy in transforming oneself.

Each man is circumscribed by his own thoughts, but he can gradually extend their circle; he can enlarge and elevate his mental sphere. He can leave the low, and reach up to the high; he can refrain from harbouring thoughts that are dark and hateful, and can cherish thoughts that are bright and beautiful; and as he does this, he will pass into a higher sphere of power and beauty, will become conscious of a more complete and perfect world.

For men live in spheres low or high according to the nature of their thoughts. Their world is as dark and narrow as they conceive it to be, as expansive and glorious as their comprehensive capacity. Everything around them is tinged with the colour of their thoughts.

Consider the man whose mind is suspicious, covetous, envious. How small and mean and drear everything appears to him. Having no grandeur in himself, he sees no grandeur anywhere; being ignoble himself, he is incapable of seeing nobility in any being. Even his god is a covetous being that can be bribed, and he judges all men and women to be just as petty and selfish as he himself is, so that he sees in the most exalted acts of unselfishness only motives that are mean and base.

Consider again the man whose mind is unsuspecting, generous, magnanimous. How wondrous and beautiful is his world. He is conscious of some kind of nobility in all creatures and beings. He sees men as true, and to him they are true. In his presence the meanest forget their nature, and for the moment become like himself, getting a glimpse, albeit confused, in that temporary upliftment, of a higher order of things, of an immeasurably nobler and happier life.

That small-minded man and this large-hearted man live in two different worlds, though they be neighbours. Their consciousness embraces totally different principles. Their actions are each the reverse of the other. Their moral insight is contrary. They each look out upon a different order of things. Their mental spheres are separate, and, like two detached circles, they never mingle. The one is in hell, the other in heaven, as truly as they will ever be, and death will not place a greater gulf between them than already exists. To the one, the world is a den of thieves; to the other, it is the dwelling-place of gods. The one keeps a revolver handy, and is always on his guard against being robbed or cheated (unconscious of the fact that he is all the time robbing and cheating himself), the other keeps ready a banquet for the best. He throws open his doors to talent, beauty, genius, goodness. His friends are of the aristocracy of character. They have become a part of himself. They are in his sphere of thought, his world of consciousness. From his heart pours forth nobility, and it returns to him tenfold in the multitude of those who love him and do him honour.

The natural grades in human society—what are they but spheres of thought, and modes of conduct manifesting those spheres? The proletariat may rail against these divisions, but he will not alter or affect them. There is no artificial remedy for equalizing states of thought having no natural affinity, and separated by the fundamental principles of life. The lawless and the law-abiding are eternally apart, nor is it hatred nor pride that separates them, but states of intelligence and modes of conduct which in the moral principles of things stand mutually unrelated. The rude and ill-mannered are shut out from the circle of the gentle and refined by the impassable wall of their own mentality which, though they may remove by patient self-improvement, they can never scale by a vulgar intrusion. The kingdom of heaven is not taken by violence, but he who conforms to its principles receives the password. The ruffian moves in a society of ruffians; the saint is one of an elect brethren whose communion is divine music. All men are mirrors reflecting according to their own surface. All men, looking at the world of men and things, are looking into a mirror which gives back their own reflection.

Each man moves in the limited or expansive circle of his own thoughts, and all outside that circle is non-existent to him. He only knows that which he has *become.* The narrower the boundary, the more convinced is the man that there is no further limit, no other circle. The lesser cannot contain the greater, and he has no means of apprehending the larger minds; such knowledge comes only by growth. The man who moves in a widely extended circle of thought knows all the lesser circles from which he has emerged, for in the larger experience all lesser experiences are contained and preserved; and when his circle impinges upon the sphere of perfect manhood, when he is fitting himself for company and communion with them of blameless conduct and profound understanding, then his wisdom will have become sufficient to convince him that there are wider circles still beyond of which he is as yet but dimly conscious, or is entirely ignorant.

Men, like schoolboys, find themselves in standards or classes to which their ignorance or knowledge entitles them. The curriculum of the sixth standard is a mystery to the boy in the first; it is outside and beyond the circle of his comprehension; but he reaches it by persistent effort and patient growth in learning. By mastering and outgrowing all the standards between, he comes at last to the sixth, and makes its learning his own; and beyond still is the sphere of the teacher. So in life, men whose deeds are dark and selfish, full of passion and personal desire, cannot comprehend those whose deeds are bright and unselfish, whose minds are calm, deep, and pure, but they can reach this higher standard, this enlarged consciousness, by effort in right-doing, by growth in thought and moral comprehension. And above and beyond all lower and higher standards stand the Teachers of mankind, the Cosmic Masters, the Saviours of the world whom the adherents of the various religions worship. There are grades in teachers as in pupils, and some there are who have not yet reached the rank and position of *Master*, yet, by the sterling morality of their character, are guides and teachers; but to occupy a pulpit or rostrum does not make a man a teacher. A man is constituted a teacher by virtue of that moral greatness which calls forth the respect and reverence of mankind.

Each man is as low or high, as little or great, as base or noble, as his thoughts; no more, no less. Each moves within the sphere of his own thoughts, and that sphere is his world. In that world in which he forms his habits of thought, he finds his company. He dwells in the region which harmonizes with his particular growth. But he need not perforce remain in the lower worlds. He can lift his thoughts and ascend. He can pass above and beyond into higher realms, into happier habitations. When he chooses and wills he can break the carapace of selfish thought, and breathe the purer airs of a more expansive life.

THE OUTER WORLD OF THINGS

The world of things is the other half of the world of thoughts. The inner informs the outer. The greater embraces the lesser. Matter is the counterpart of mind. Events are streams of thought. Circumstances are combinations of thought, and the outer conditions and actions of others in which each man is involved are intimately related to his own mental needs and development. Man is a part of his surroundings. He is not separate from his fellows, but is bound closely to them by the peculiar intimacy and interaction of deeds, and by those fundamental laws of thought which are the roots of human society.

One cannot alter external things to suit his passing whims and wishes, but he can set aside his whims and wishes; he can so alter his attitude of mind toward externals that they will assume a different aspect. He cannot mould the actions of others toward him, but he can rightly fashion his actions toward them. He cannot break down the wall of circumstance by which he is surrounded, but he can wisely adapt himself to it, or find the way out into enlarged circumstances by extending his mental horizon. Things follow thoughts. Alter your thoughts, and things will receive a new adjustment. To reflect truly, the mirror must be true. A warped glass gives back an exaggerated image. A disturbed mind gives a distorted reflection of the world. Subdue the mind, organize and tranquilize it, and a more beautiful image of the universe, a more perfect perception of the world-order, will be the result.

Man has all power within the world of his own mind, to purify and perfect it, but his power in the outer world of other minds is subject and limited. This is made plain when we reflect that each finds himself in a world of men and things, a unit amongst myriads of similar units. These units do not act independently and despotically, but responsively and sympathetically. My fellow-men are involved in my actions, and they will deal with them. If what I do be a menace to them, they will adopt protective measures against me. As the human body expels its morbid atoms, so the body politic instinctively expurgates its recalcitrant members. Your wrong acts are so many wounds inflicted on this body politic, and the healing of its wounds will be your pain and sorrow. This ethical cause and effect is not different from that physical cause and effect with which the simplest is acquainted. It is but an extension of the same law; its application to the larger body of humanity. No act is aloof. Your most secret deed is invisibly reported, its good being protected in joy, its evil destroyed in pain. There is a great ethical truth in the old fable of "the Book of Life," in which every thought and deed is recorded and judged. It is because of this—that your deed belongs, not alone to yourself, but to humanity and the universe—that you are powerless to avert external effects, but are all-powerful to modify and correct internal causes; and it is also because of this that the perfecting of one's own deeds is man's highest duty and most sublime accomplishment.

The obverse of this truth—that you are powerless to obviate external things and deeds—is, that external things and deeds are powerless to injure you. The cause of your bondage as of your deliverance is within. The injury that comes to you through others is the rebound of your own deed, the reflex of your own mental attitude. *They* are the instruments, *you* are the cause. Destiny is ripened deeds. The fruit of life, both bitter and sweet, is received by each man in just measure. The righteous man is free. None can injure him; none can destroy him; none can rob him of his peace. His attitude toward men, born of understanding, disarms their power to wound him. Any injury which they may try to inflict, rebounds upon themselves to their own hurt, leaving him unharmed and untouched. The good that goes from him is his perennial fount of happiness, his eternal source of strength. Its root is serenity, its flower is joy.

The harm which a man sees in the action of another toward him—say, for instance, an act of slander—is not in the act itself, but in his attitude of mind toward it; the injury and unhappiness are created by himself, and subsist in his lack of understanding concerning the nature and power of deeds. He thinks the act can permanently injure or ruin his character, whereas it is utterly void of any such power; the reality being that the deed can only injure or ruin the doer of it. Thinking himself injured, the man becomes agitated and unhappy, and takes great pains to counteract the supposed harm to himself, and these very pains give the slander an appearance of truth, and aid rather than hinder it. All his agitation and unrest is created by his reception of the deed, and not actually by the deed itself. The righteous man has proved this by the fact that the same act has ceased to arouse in him any disturbance. He understands, and therefore ignores it. It belongs to a sphere which he has ceased to inhabit, to a region of consciousness with which he has no longer any affinity. He does not receive the act into himself, the thought of injury to himself being absent. He lives above the mental darkness in which such acts thrive, and they can no more injure or disturb him than a boy can injure or divert the sun by throwing stones at it. It was to emphasize this that Buddha, to the end of his days, never ceased to tell his disciples that so long as the thought "I have been injured," or "I have been cheated," or "I have been insulted," could arise in a man's mind, he had not comprehended the Truth.

And as with the conduct of others, so is it with external things—with surroundings and circumstances—in themselves they are neither good nor bad, it is the mental attitude and state of heart that makes them so. A man imagines he could do great things if he were not hampered by circumstances—by want of money, want of time, want of influence, and want of freedom from family ties. In reality the man is not hindered by these things at all. He, in his mind, ascribes to them a power which they do not possess, and he submits, not to them, but to his opinion about them, that is, to a weak element in his nature. The real "want" that hampers him is the *want of the right attitude of mind.* When he regards his circumstances as spurs to his resources, when he sees that his so-called "drawbacks" are the very steps up which he is to mount successfully to his achievement, then his necessity gives birth to invention, and the "hindrances" are transformed into *aids. The man* is the all-important factor. If his mind be wholesome and rightly tuned, he will not whine and whimper over his circumstances, but will rise up, and outgrow them. He who complains of his circumstances has not yet become a man, and Necessity will continue to prick and lash him till he rises into manhood's strength, and then she will submit to him. Circumstance is a severe taskmaster to the weak, an obedient servant to the strong.

It is not external things, but our thoughts about them, that bind us or set us free. We forge our own chains, build our own dungeons, take ourselves prisoners; or we loose our bonds, build our own palaces, or roam in freedom through all scenes and events. If I think that my surroundings are powerful to bind me, that thought will keep me bound. If I think that, in my thought and life, I can rise above my surroundings, that thought will liberate me. One should ask of his thoughts, "Are they leading to bondage or deliverance?" and he should abandon thoughts that bind, and adopt thoughts that set free.

If we fear our fellow-men, fear opinion, poverty, the withdrawal of friends and influence, then we are bound indeed, and cannot know the inward happiness of the enlightened, the freedom of the just; but if in our thoughts we are pure and free, if we see in life's reactions and reverses nothing to cause us trouble or fear, but everything to aid us in our progress, nothing remains that can prevent us from accomplishing the aims of our life, for then we are free indeed.

HABIT: ITS SLAVERY AND
ITS FREEDOM

Man is subject to the law of habit. Is he then free? Yes, he is free. Man did not make life and its laws; they are eternal; he finds himself involved in them, and he can understand and obey them. Man's power does not enable him to make laws of being; it subsists in discrimination and choice. Man does not create one jot of the universal conditions or laws; they are the essential principles of things, and are neither made nor unmade. He discovers, not makes, them. Ignorance of them is at the root of the world's pain. To defy them is folly and bondage. Who is the freer man, the thief who defies the laws of his country, or the honest citizen who obeys them? Who, again, is the freer man, the fool who thinks he can live as he likes, or the wise man who chooses to do only that which is right?

Man is, in the nature of things, a being of habit, and this he cannot alter; but he can alter his habits. He cannot alter the law of his nature, but he can adapt his nature to the law. No man wishes to alter the law of gravitation, but all men adapt themselves to it; they use it by bending to it, not by defying or ignoring it. Men do not run up against walls or jump over precipices in the hope that this law will alter for them. They walk alongside walls, and keep clear of precipices.

Man can no more get outside the law of habit, than he can get outside the law of gravitation, but he can employ it wisely or unwisely. As scientists and inventors master the physical forces and laws by obeying and using them, so wise men master the spiritual forces and laws in the same way. While the bad man is the whipped slave of habit, the good man is its wise director and master. Not its *maker,* let me reiterate, nor yet its arbitrary commander, but its self-disciplined user, its master by virtue of knowledge grounded on obedience. He is the bad man whose habits of thought and action are bad. He is the good man whose habits of thought and action are good. The bad man becomes the good man by transforming or transmuting his habits. He does not alter the law; he alters himself; he adapts himself to the law. Instead of submitting to selfish indulgences, he obeys moral principles. He becomes the master of the lower by enlisting in the service of the higher. The law of habit remains the same, but he is changed from bad to good by his readjustment to the law.

Habit is *repetition.* Man repeats the same thoughts, the same actions, the same experiences over and over again until they are incorporated with his being, until they are built into his character as part of himself. Faculty is fixed habit. Evolution is mental accumulation. Man, to-day, is the result of millions of repetitious thoughts and acts. He is not ready-made, he becomes, and is still becoming. His character is predetermined by his own choice. The thought, the act, which he chooses, that, by habit, he becomes.

Thus each man is an accumulation of thoughts and deeds. The characteristics which he manifests instinctively and without effort are lines of thought and action become, by long repetition, automatic; for it is the nature of habit to become, at last, unconscious, to repeat, as it were, itself without any apparent choice or effort on the part of its possessor; and in due time it takes such complete possession of the individual as to appear to render his will powerless to counteract it. This is the case with all habits, whether good or bad; when bad, the man is spoken of as being the "victim" of a bad habit or a vicious mind; when good, he is referred to as having, by nature, a "good disposition."

All men are, and will continue to be, subject to their own habits, whether they be good or bad— that is, subject to their own reiterated and accumulated thoughts and deeds. Knowing this, the wise man chooses to subject himself to good habits, for such service is joy, bliss, and freedom; while to become subject to bad habits is misery, wretchedness, slavery.

This law of habit is beneficent, for while it enables a man to bind himself to the chains of slavish practices, it enables him to become so fixed in good courses as to do them unconsciously, to do instinctively that which is right, without restraint or exertion, and in perfect happiness and freedom. Observing this automatism in life, men have denied the existence of will or freedom on man's part. They speak of him as being "born" good or bad, and regard him as the helpless instrument of blind forces.

It is true that man is the instrument of mental forces,—or to be more accurate, he is those forces,—but they are not blind, and he can direct them, and redirect them into new channels. In a word, he can take himself in hand and reconstruct his habits; for though it is also true that he is born with a given character, that character is the product of numberless lives during which it has been slowly built up by choice and effort, and in this life it will be considerably modified by new experiences.

No matter how apparently helpless a man has become under the tyranny of a bad habit, or a bad characteristic,—and they are essentially the same,—he can, so long as sanity remains, break away from it and become free, replacing it by its opposite good habit; and when the good possesses him as the bad formerly did, there will be neither wish nor need to break from that, for its dominance will be perennial happiness, and not perpetual misery.

That which a man has formed within himself, he can break up and re-form when he so wishes and wills; and a man does not wish to abandon a bad habit so long as he regards it as pleasurable. It is when it assumes a painful tyranny over him that he begins to look for a way of escape, and finally abandons the bad for something better.

No man is helplessly bound. The very law by which he has become a self-bound slave will enable him to become a self-emancipated master. To know this, he has but to act upon it,—that is, deliberately and strenuously to abandon the old lines of thought and conduct, and diligently fashion new and better lines. That he may not accomplish this in a day, a week, a month, a year, or five years, should not dishearten and dismay him. Time is required for the new repetitions to become established, and the old ones to be broken up; but the law of habit is certain and infallible, and a line of effort patiently pursued and never abandoned, is sure to be crowned with success; for if a bad condition, a mere negation, can become fixed and firm, how much more surely can a good condition, a positive principle, become established and powerful! A man is powerless to overcome the wrong and unhappy elements in himself only *so long as he regards himself as powerless.* If to the bad habit is added the thought, "I cannot," the bad habit will remain. Nothing can be overcome till the thought of powerlessness is uprooted and abolished from the mind. The great stumbling-block is not the habit itself, it is *the belief in the impossibility of overcoming it.* How can a man overcome a bad habit so long as he is convinced that it is impossible? How can a man be prevented from overcoming it when he knows that he can, and is determined to do it? The dominant thought by which man has enslaved himself is the thought, "I cannot overcome my sins." Bring this thought out into the light, in all its nakedness, and it is seen to be a belief in the power of evil, with its other pole, disbelief in the power of good. For a man to say, or believe, that he cannot rise above wrong-thinking and wrong-doing, is to submit to evil, is to abandon and renounce good.

By such thoughts, such beliefs, man binds himself; by their opposite thoughts, opposite beliefs, he sets himself free. A changed attitude of mind changes the character, the habits, the life. Man is his own deliverer. He has brought about his thraldom; he can bring about his emancipation. All through the ages he has looked, and is still looking, for an external deliverer, but he still remains bound. The Great Deliverer is within; He is the Spirit of Truth; and the Spirit of Truth is the Spirit of Good; and he is in the Spirit of Good who dwells habitually in good thoughts and their effects, good actions.

Man is not bound by any power outside his own wrong thoughts, and from these he can set himself free; and foremost, the enslaving thoughts from which he needs to be delivered are—"I cannot rise," "I cannot break away from bad habits," "I cannot alter my nature," "I cannot control and conquer myself," "I cannot cease from sin." All these "cannots" have no existence in the things to which they submit; they exist only in thought.

Such negations are bad thought-habits which need to be eradicated, and in their place should be planted the positive "I can," which should be tended and developed until it becomes a powerful tree of habit, bearing the good and life-giving fruit of right and happy living.

Habit binds us; habit sets us free. Habit is primarily in thought, secondarily in deed. Turn the thought from bad to good, and the deed will immediately follow. Persist in the bad, and it will bind you tighter and tighter; persist in the good, and it will take you into ever-widening spheres of freedom. He who loves his bondage, let him remain bound. He who thirsts for freedom, let him come and be set free.

BODILY CONDITIONS

There are to-day scores of distinct schools devoted to the healing of the body; a fact which shows the great prevalence of physical suffering, as the hundreds of religions, devoted to the comforting of men's minds, prove the universality of mental suffering. Each of these schools has its place in so far as it is able to relieve suffering, even where it does not eradicate the evil; for with all these schools of healing, the facts of disease and pain remain with us, just as sin and sorrow remain in spite of the many religions.

Disease and pain, like sin and sorrow, are too deep-seated to be removed by palliatives. Our ailments have an ethical cause deeply rooted in the mind. I do not infer by this that physical conditions have no part in disease; they play an important part as *instruments,* as factors in the chain of causation. The microbe that carried the black death was the instrument of uncleanliness, and uncleanliness is, primarily, a moral disorder. Matter is visible mind, and that bodily conflict which we call *disease* has a causal affinity to that mental conflict which is associated with sin. In his present human or self-conscious state, man's mind is continually being disturbed by violently conflicting desires, and his body attacked by morbid elements. He is in a state of mental inharmony and bodily discomfort. Animals in their wild and primitive state are free from disease because they are free from inharmony. They are in accord with their surroundings, have no moral responsibility and no sense of sin, and are free from those violent disturbances of remorse, grief, disappointment, etc., which are so destructive of man's harmony and happiness, and their bodies are not afflicted. As man ascends into the divine or cosmic-conscious state, he will leave behind and below him all these inner conflicts, will overcome sin and all sense of sin, and will dispel remorse and sorrow. Being thus restored to mental harmony, he will become restored to bodily harmony, to wholeness, health.

The body is the image of the mind, and in it are traced the visible features of hidden thoughts. The outer obeys the inner, and the enlightened scientist of the future may be able to trace every bodily disorder to its ethical cause in the mentality.

Mental harmony, or moral wholeness, makes for bodily health. I say *makes for it,* for it will not produce it magically, as it were,—as though one should swallow a bottle of medicine and then be whole and free,—but if the mentality is becoming more poised and restful, if the moral stature is increasing, then a sure foundation of bodily wholeness is being laid, the forces are being conserved and are receiving a better direction and adjustment; and even if perfect health is not gained, the bodily derangement, whatever it be, will have lost its power to undermine the strengthened and uplifted mind.

One who suffers in body will not necessarily at once be cured when he begins to fashion his mind on moral and harmonious principles; indeed, for a time, while the body is bringing to a crisis, and throwing off, the effects of former inharmonies, the morbid condition may appear to be intensified. As a man does not gain perfect peace immediately he enters upon the path of righteousness, but must, except in rare instances, pass through a painful period of adjustment; neither does he, with the same rare exceptions, at once acquire perfect health. Time is required for bodily as well as mental readjustment, and even if health is not reached, it will be approached.

If the mind be made robust, the bodily condition will take a secondary and subordinate place, and will cease to have that primary importance which so many give to it. If a disorder is not cured, the mind can rise above it, and refuse to be subdued by it. One can be happy, strong, and useful in spite of it. The statement so often made by health specialists that a useful and happy life is impossible without bodily health is disproved by the fact that numbers of men who have accomplished the greatest works—men of genius and superior talent in all departments—have been afflicted in their bodies, and to-day there are plenty of living witnesses to this fact. Sometimes the bodily affliction acts as a stimulus to mental activity, and aids rather than hinders its work. To make a useful and happy life dependent upon health, is to put matter before mind, is to subordinate spirit to body.

Men of robust minds do not dwell upon their bodily condition if it be in any way disordered—*they ignore it,* and work on, live on, as though it were not. This ignoring of the body not only keeps the mind sane and strong, but it is the best resource for curing the body. If we cannot have a perfectly sound body, we can have a healthy mind, and a healthy mind is the best route to a sound body.

A sickly mind is more deplorable than a disordered body, and it leads to sickliness of body. The mental invalid is in a far more pitiable condition than the bodily invalid. There are invalids (every physician knows them) who only need to lift themselves into a strong, unselfish, happy frame of mind to discover that their body is whole and capable.

Sickly thoughts about oneself, about one's body and food, should be abolished by all who are called by the name of *man.* The man who imagines that the wholesome food he is eating is going to injure him, needs to come to bodily vigour by the way of mental strength. To regard one's bodily health and safety as being dependent on a particular kind of food which is absent from nearly every household, is to court petty disorders. The vegetarian who says he dare not eat potatoes, that fruit produces indigestion, that apples give him acidity, that pulses are poison, that he is afraid of green vegetables, and so on, is demoralizing the noble cause which he professes to have espoused, is making it look ridiculous in the eyes of those robust meat-eaters who live above such sickly fears and morbid self-scrutinies. To imagine that the fruits of the earth, eaten when one is hungry and in need of food, are destructive of health and life is totally to misunderstand the nature and office of food. The office of food is to sustain and preserve the body, not to undermine and destroy it. It is a strange delusion,—and one that must react deleteriously upon the body,—that possesses so many who are seeking health by the way of diet, the delusion that certain of the simplest, most natural, and purest of viands are *bad of themselves,* that they have in them the elements of death, and not of life. One of these food-reformers once told me that he believed his ailment (as well as the ailments of thousands of others) was caused by eating bread; not by an excess of bread, but by the bread itself; and yet this man's bread food consisted of nutty, home-made, wholemeal loaves. Let us get rid of our sins, our sickly thoughts, our self-indulgences and foolish excesses before attributing our diseases to such innocent causes.

Dwelling upon one's petty troubles and ailments is a manifestation of weakness of character. To so dwell upon them in thought leads to frequent talking about them, and this, in turn, impresses them more vividly upon the mind, which soon becomes demoralized by such petting and pitying. It is as convenient to dwell upon happiness and health as upon misery and disease; as easy to talk about them, and much more pleasant and profitable to do so.

> *Let us live happily then, not hating those who hate us!*
> *Among men who hate us let us dwell free from hatred!*

> *Let us live happily then, free from ailments among the ailing!*
> *Among men who are ailing let us dwell free from ailments!*

> *Let us live happily then, free from greed among the greedy!*
> *Among men who are greedy let us dwell free from greed!*

Moral principles are the soundest foundations for health, as well as for happiness. They are the true regulators of conduct, and they embrace every detail of life. When earnestly espoused and intelligently understood they will compel a man to reorganize his entire life down to the most apparently insignificant detail. While definitely regulating one's diet, they will put an end to squeamishness, food-fear, and foolish whims and groundless opinions as to the harmfulness of foods. When sound moral health has eradicated self-indulgence and self-pity, all natural foods will be seen as they are—nourishers of the body, and not its destroyers.

Thus a consideration of bodily conditions brings us inevitably back to the mind, and to those moral virtues which fortify it with an invincible protection. The morally right are the bodily right. To be continually transposing the details of life from passing views and fancies, without reference to fixed principles, is to flounder in confusion; but to discipline details by moral principles is to see, with enlightened vision, all details in their proper place and order.

For it is given to moral principles alone, in their personal domain, to perceive the moral order. In them alone resides the insight that penetrates to causes, and with them only is the power to at once command all details to their order and place, as the magnet draws and polarizes the filings of steel.

Better even than curing the body is to rise above it; to be its master, and not to be tyrannized over by it; not to abuse it, not to pander to it, never to put its claims before virtue; to discipline and moderate its pleasures, and not to be overcome by its pains,—in a word, to live in the poise and strength of the moral powers, this, better than bodily cure, is yet a safe way to cure, and it is a permanent source of mental vigour and spiritual repose.

POVERTY

Many of the greatest men through all ages have abandoned riches and adopted poverty to better enable them to accomplish their lofty purposes. Why, then, is poverty regarded as such a terrible evil? Why is it that this poverty, which these great men regard as a blessing, and adopt as a bride, should be looked upon by the bulk of mankind as a scourge and a plague? The answer is plain. In the one case, the poverty is associated with a nobility of mind which not only takes from it all appearance of evil, but which lifts it up and makes it appear good and beautiful, makes it seem more attractive and more to be desired than riches and honour, so much so that, seeing the dignity and happiness of the noble mendicant, thousands imitate him by adopting his mode of life. In the other case, the poverty of our great cities is associated with everything that is mean and repulsive—with swearing, drunkenness, filth, laziness, dishonesty, and crime. What, then, is the primary evil: is it poverty, or is it sin? The answer is inevitable—it is sin. Remove sin from poverty, and its sting is gone; it has ceased to be the gigantic evil that it appeared, and can even be turned to good and noble ends. Confucius held up one of his poor disciples, Yen-hwui by name, as an example of lofty virtue to his richer pupils, yet "although he was so poor that he had to live on rice and water, and had no better shelter than a hovel, he uttered no complaint. Where this poverty would have made other men discontented and miserable, he did not allow his equanimity to be disturbed." Poverty cannot undermine a noble character, but it can set it off to better advantage. The virtues of Yen-hwui shone all the brighter for being set in poverty, like resplendent jewels set in a contrasting background.

It is common with social reformers to regard poverty as the *cause* of the sins with which it is associated; yet the same reformers refer to the immoralities of the rich as being caused by their riches. Where there is a cause its effect will appear, and were affluence the cause of immorality, and poverty the cause of degradation, then every rich man would become immoral and every poor man would come to degradation.

An evil-doer will commit evil under any circumstances, whether he be rich or poor, or midway between the two conditions. A right-doer will do right howsoever he be placed. Extreme circumstances may help to bring out the evil which is already there awaiting its opportunity, but they cannot cause the evil, cannot create it.

Discontent with one's financial condition is not the same as poverty. Many people regard themselves as poor whose income runs into several hundreds, and in some cases several thousands, of pounds a year, combined with light responsibilities. They imagine their affliction to be poverty; their real trouble is covetousness. They are not made unhappy by poverty, but by the thirst for riches. Poverty is more often in the mind than in the purse. So long as a man thirsts for more money he will regard himself as poor, and in that sense he is poor, for covetousness is poverty of mind. A miser may be a millionaire, but he is as poor as when he was penniless.

On the other hand, the trouble with so many who are living in indigence and degradation is that they *are* satisfied with their condition. To be living in dirt, disorder, laziness, and swinish self-indulgence, revelling in foul thoughts, foul words, and unclean surroundings, and to be satisfied with oneself, is deplorable. Here again, "poverty" resolves itself into a mental condition, and its solution, as a "problem," is to be looked for in the improvement of the individual from within, rather than of his outward condition. Let a man be made clean and alert within, and he will no longer be content with dirt and degradation without. Having put his mind in order, he will then put his house in order; indeed, both he and others will know that he has put himself right by the fact that he has put his immediate surroundings right. His altered heart shows in his altered life.

There are, of course, those who are neither self-deceived nor self-degraded, and yet are poor. Many such are satisfied to remain poor. They are contented, industrious, and happy, and desire nothing else; but those among them who are dissatisfied, and are ambitious for better surroundings and greater scope, should, and usually do, use their poverty as a spur to the exercise of their talents and energies. By self-improvement and attention to duty, they can rise into the fuller, more responsible life which they desire.

Devotion to duty is, indeed, not only the way out of that poverty which is regarded as restrictive, it is also the royal road to affluence, influence, and lasting joy, yea, even to perfection itself. When understood in its deepest sense it is seen to be related to all that is best and noblest in life. It includes energy, industry, concentrated attention to the business of one's life, singleness of purpose, courage and faithfulness, determination and self-reliance, and that self-abnegation which is the key to all real greatness. A singularly successful man was once asked, "What is the secret of your success?" and he replied, "Getting up at six o'clock in the morning, and minding my own business." Success, honour, and influence always come to him who diligently attends to the business of his life, and religiously avoids interfering with the duties of others.

It may here be urged—and is usually so urged—that the majority of those who are in poverty— for instance, the mill and factory workers—have not the time or opportunity to give themselves to any special work. This is a mistake. Time and opportunity are always at hand, are with everybody at all times. Those of the poor above mentioned, who are content to remain where they are, can always be diligent in their factory labour, and sober and happy in their homes, but those of them who feel that they could better fill another sphere, can prepare for it by educating themselves in their spare time. The hard-worked poor are, above all, the people who need to economize their time and energies; and the youth who wishes to rise out of such poverty must at the outset put aside the foolish and wasteful indulgences of alcohol, tobacco, sexual vice, late hours at music-halls, clubs, and gaming parties, and must give his evenings to the improvement of his mind in that course of education which is necessary to his advancement. By this method, numbers of the most influential men throughout history—some of them among the greatest—have raised themselves from the commonest poverty; a fact which proves that the time of necessity is the hour of opportunity, and not, as is so often imagined and declared, the destruction of opportunity; that the deeper the poverty, the greater is the incentive to action in those who are dissatisfied with themselves, and are bent upon achievement.

Poverty is an evil or it is not, according to the character and the condition of mind of the one that is in poverty. Wealth is an evil or not, in the same manner, Tolstoi chafed under his wealthy circumstances. To him they were a great evil. He longed for poverty as the covetous long for wealth. Vice, however, is always an evil, for it both degrades the individual who commits it, and is a menace to society. A logical and profound study of poverty will always bring us back to the individual, and to the human heart. When our social reformers condemn vice as they now condemn the rich; when they are as eager to abolish wrong-living as they now are to abolish low wages, we may look for a diminution in that form of degraded poverty which is one of the dark spots on our civilization. Before such poverty disappears altogether, the human heart will have undergone, during the process of evolution, a radical change. When that heart is purged from covetousness and selfishness; when drunkenness, impurity, indolence, and self-indulgence are driven for ever from the earth, then poverty and riches will be known no more, and every man will perform his duties with a joy so full and deep as is yet (except to the few whose hearts are already pure) unknown to men, and all will eat of the fruit of their labour in sublime self-respect and perfect peace.

MAN'S SPIRITUAL DOMINION

The kingdom over which man is destined to rule with undisputed sway is that of his own mind and life; but this kingdom, as already shown, is not separate from the universe, is not confined to itself alone; it is intimately related to entire humanity, to nature, to the current of events in which it is, for the time being, involved, and to the vast universe. Thus the mastery of this kingdom embraces the mastery of the knowledge of life; it lifts a man into the supremacy of wisdom, bestowing upon him the gift of insight into human hearts, giving him the power to distinguish between good and evil, also to comprehend that which is above both good and evil, and to know the nature and consequences of deeds.

At present men are more or less under the sway of rebellious thoughts, and the conquest of these is the supreme conquest of life. The unwise think that everything can be mastered but oneself, and they seek for happiness for themselves and others by modifying external things. The transposing of outward effects cannot bring permanent happiness, or bestow wisdom; the patching and coddling of a sin-laden body cannot produce health and well-being. The wise know that there is no real mastery until self is subdued, that when oneself is conquered, the subjugation of externals is finally assured, and they find happiness for ever springing up within them, in the calm strength of divine virtue. They put away sin, and purify and strengthen the body by rising superior to the sway of its passions.

Man can reign over his own mind; can be lord over himself. Until he does so reign, his life is unsatisfactory and imperfect. His spiritual dominion is the empire of the mental forces of which his nature is composed. The body has no causative power. The ruling of the body—that is, of appetite

and passion—is the discipline of mental forces. The subduing, modifying, redirecting, and transmuting of the antagonizing spiritual elements within, is the wonderful and mighty work which all
men must, sooner or later, undertake. For a long time man regards himself as the slave of external
forces, but there comes a day when his spiritual eyes open, and he sees that he has been a slave this
long time to none and nothing but his own ungoverned, unpurified self. In that day, he rises up,
and, ascending his spiritual throne, he no longer obeys his desires, appetites, and passions as their
slave, but henceforth rules them as his subjects. The mental kingdom through which he has been
wont to wander as a puling beggar and a whipped serf, he now discovers is his by right of lordly
self-control—his to set in order, to organize and harmonize, to abolish its dissensions and painful
contradictions, and bring it to a state of peace.

Thus rising up and exercising his rightful spiritual authority, he enters the company of those
kingly ones who in all ages have conquered and attained, who have overcome ignorance, darkness,
and mental suffering, and have ascended into Truth.

CONQUEST: NOT RESIGNATION

He who has undertaken the sublime task of overcoming himself, does not resign himself
to anything that is evil; he subjects himself only to that which is good. Resignation to
evil is the lowest weakness; obedience to good is the highest power. To resign oneself
to sin and sorrow, to ignorance and suffering, is to say in effect, "I give up; I am defeated; life is
evil, and I submit." Such resignation to evil is the reverse of religion. It is a direct denial of good; it
elevates evil to the position of supreme power in the universe. Such submission to evil shows itself
in a selfish and sorrowful life; a life alike devoid of strength against temptation, and of that joy and
calm which are the manifestation of a mind that is dominated by good.

Man is not framed for perpetual resignation and sorrow, but for final victory and joy. All the
spiritual laws of the universe are with the good man, for good preserves and shields. There are no
laws of evil. Its nature is destruction and desolation.

The conscious modification of the character away from evil and toward good, forms, at present, no part in the common course of education. Even our religious teachers have lost this knowledge and practice, and cannot, therefore, instruct concerning it. Moral growth is, so far, in the great mass of mankind, unconscious, and is brought about by the stress and struggle of life. The time will come, however, when the conscious formation of character will form an important part in the education of youth, and when no man will be able to fill the position of preacher unless he be a man of habitual self-control, unblemished integrity, and exalted purity, so as to be able to give sound instruction in the making of character, which will then be the main feature of religion.

The doctrine herein set forth by the author is the doctrine of conquest over evil; the annihilation of sin; and necessarily the permanent establishment of man in the knowledge of good, and in the enjoyment of perpetual peace. This is the teaching of the Masters of religion in all ages. Howsoever it may have been disguised and distorted by the unenlightened, it is the doctrine of all the perfect ones that were, and will be the doctrine of all the perfect ones that are to come. It is the doctrine of Truth.

And the conquest is not of an evil without; not of evil men, or evil spirits, or evil things; but of the evil within; of evil thoughts, evil desires, evil deeds; for when every man has destroyed the evil within his own heart, to where in the whole vast universe will any one be able to point, and say, "There is evil"? In that great day when all men have become good within, all traces of evil will have vanished from the earth; sin and sorrow will be unknown; and there will be universal joy for evermore.

EIGHT PILLARS OF

PROSPERITY

(1911)

He who would build both strong and high
Must first of all dig deep and low;
So rose the spire against the sky,
And so doth skill and knowledge grow.
So, with well-ordered strenuousness,
Raise thou thy structure of Success.

PREFACE

It is popularly supposed that a greater prosperity for individuals or nations can only come through a political and social reconstruction. This cannot be true apart from the practice of the moral virtues in the individuals that comprise a nation. Better laws and social conditions will always follow a higher realization of morality among the individuals of a community, but no legal enactment can give prosperity to, nay, it cannot prevent the ruin of, a man or a nation that has become lax and decadent in the pursuit and practice of virtue.

The moral virtues are the foundation and support of prosperity as they are the soul of greatness. They endure forever, and all the works of man which endure are built upon them. Without them there is neither strength, stability, nor substantial reality, but only ephemeral dreams. To find moral principles is to have found prosperity, greatness, truth, and is therefore to be strong, valiant, joyful, and free.

—JAMES ALLEN
Bryngoleu,
Ilfracombe, England

CONTENTS

SIXTH PILLAR—SINCERITY

ELEMENTS:

SEVENTH PILLAR—IMPARTIALITY

ELEMENTS:

EIGHTH PILLAR—SELF-RELIANCE

ELEMENTS:

THE TEMPLE OF PROSPERITY

THE EIGHT PILLARS

Prosperity rests upon a moral foundation. It is popularly supposed to rest upon an immoral foundation—that is, upon trickery, sharp practice, deception, and greed. One commonly hears even an otherwise intelligent man declare that "No man can be successful in business unless he is dishonest;" thus regarding business prosperity, a good thing, as the effect of dishonesty, a bad thing. Such a statement is superficial and thoughtless, and reveals a total lack of knowledge of moral causation, as well as a very limited grasp of the facts of life. It is as though one should sow henbane and reap spinach, or erect a brick house on a quagmire,—things impossible in the natural order of causation, and therefore not to be attempted. The spiritual or moral order of causation is not different in principle, but only in nature. The same law obtains in things unseen—in thoughts and deeds—as in things seen—in natural phenomena. Man sees the processes in natural objects, and acts in accordance with them, but not seeing the spiritual processes, he imagines that they do not obtain, and so he does not act in harmony with them.

Yet these spiritual processes are just as simple and just as sure as the natural processes. They are indeed the same *natural* modes manifesting in the world of mind. All the parables and a large number of the sayings of the Great Teachers are designed to illustrate this fact. The natural world is the mental world made visible. The seen is the mirror of the unseen. The upper half of a circle is in no way different from the lower half, but its sphericity is reversed. The material and the mental are not two detached arcs in the universe, they are the two halves of a complete circle. The natural and the spiritual are not at eternal enmity, but in the true order of the universe are eternally at one. It is in the *unnatural*—in the abuse of function and faculty—where division arises, and where man is wrested back, with repeated sufferings, from the perfect circle from which he has tried to depart. Every process in matter is also a process in mind. Every natural law has its spiritual counterpart.

Take any natural object, and you will find its fundamental processes in the mental sphere if you rightly search. Consider, for instance, the germination of a seed and its growth into a plant with the final development of a flower, and back to seed again. This also is a mental process. Thoughts are seeds which, falling in the soil of the mind, germinate and develop until they reach the completed stage, blossoming into deeds good or bad, brilliant or stupid, according to their nature, and ending as seeds of thought to be again sown in other minds. A teacher is a sower of seed, a spiritual agriculturist, while he who teaches himself is the wise farmer of his own mental plot. The growth of a thought is as the growth of a plant. The seed must be sown seasonably, and time is required for its full development into the plant of knowledge and the flower of wisdom.

While writing this, I pause and turn to look through my study window, and there, a hundred yards away, is a tall tree in the top of which some enterprising rook from a rookery hard by has, for the first time, built its nest. A strong northeast wind is blowing, so that the top of the tree is swayed violently to and fro by the onset of the blast; yet there is no danger to that frail thing of sticks and hair, and the mother bird, sitting upon her eggs, has no fear of the storm. Why is this? It is because the bird has instinctively built her nest in harmony with principles which ensure the maximum strength and security. First a fork is chosen as the foundation for the nest, and not a space between two separate branches, so that however great may be the swaying of the tree-top, the position of the nest is not altered, nor its structure disturbed; then the nest is built on a circular plan so as to offer the greatest resistance to any external pressure, as well as to obtain more perfect compactness within, in accordance with its purpose; and so, however the tempest may rage, the birds rest in comfort and security. This is a very simple and familiar object, and yet, in the strict obedience of its structure to mathematical law, it becomes, to the wise, a parable of enlightenment, teaching them that only by ordering one's deeds in accordance with fixed principles is perfect surety, perfect security, and perfect peace obtained amid the uncertainty of events and the turbulent tempests of life.

A house or a temple built by man is a much more complicated structure than a bird's nest, yet it is erected in accordance with those mathematical principles which are everywhere evidenced in nature. And here is seen how man, in material things, obeys universal principles. He never attempts to put up a building in defiance of geometrical proportions, for he knows that such a building would be unsafe, and that the first storm would, in all probability, level it to the ground, if, indeed, it did not fall about his ears during the process of erection. Man in his material building scrupulously obeys the fixed principles of circle, square, and angle, and aided by rule, plumb-line, and compasses, he raises a structure which will resist the fiercest storms, and afford him a secure shelter and safe protection.

All this is very simple, the reader may say. Yes, it is simple because it is true and perfect; so true that it cannot admit the smallest compromise, and so perfect that no man can improve upon it. Man, through long experience, has learned these principles of the material world, and sees the wisdom of obeying them, and I have thus referred to them in order to lead up to a consideration of those fixed principles in the mental or spiritual world which are just as simple, and just as eternally true and perfect, yet are at present so little understood by man that he daily violates them, because ignorant of their nature, and unconscious of the harm he is all the time inflicting upon himself.

In mind as in matter, in thoughts as in things, in deeds as in natural processes, there is a fixed foundation of law which, if consciously or ignorantly ignored, leads to disaster and defeat. It is, indeed, the ignorant violation of this law which is the cause of the world's pain and sorrow. In matter, this law is presented as *mathematical;* in mind, it is perceived as *moral.* But the mathematical and the moral are not separate and opposed; they are but two aspects of a united whole. The fixed principles of mathematics, to which all matter is subject, are the body of which the spirit is ethical; while the eternal principles of morality are mathematical truisms operating in the universe of mind. It is as impossible to live successfully apart from moral principles, as to build successfully while ignoring mathematical principles. Characters, like houses, only stand firmly when built on a foundation of moral law,—and they are built up slowly and laboriously, deed by deed, for in the building of character, the bricks are deeds. Businesses and all human enterprises are not exempt from the eternal order, but can only stand securely by the observance of fixed laws. Prosperity, to be stable and enduring, must rest on a solid foundation of moral principle, and be supported by the adamantine pillars of sterling character and moral worth. In the attempt to run a business in defiance of moral principles, disaster, of one kind or another, is inevitable. The permanently prosperous men in any community are not its tricksters and deceivers, but its reliable and upright men. The Quakers are acknowledged to be the most upright men in the British community, and, although their numbers are small, they are the most prosperous. The Jains in India are similar both in numbers and sterling worth, and they are the most prosperous people in India.

Men speak of "building up a business," and, indeed, a business is as much a building as is a brick house or a stone church, albeit the process of building is a mental one. Prosperity, like a house, is a roof over a man's head, affording him protection and comfort. A roof presupposes a support, and a support necessitates a foundation. The roof of prosperity, then, is supported by the following eight pillars which are cemented in a foundation of moral consistency:—

1. Energy.
2. Economy.
3. Integrity.
4. System.
5. Sympathy.
6. Sincerity.
7. Impartiality.
8. Self-Reliance.

A business built up on the faultless practice of all these principles would be so firm and enduring as to be invincible. Nothing could injure it; nothing could undermine its prosperity; nothing could interrupt its success, or bring it to the ground; but that success would be assured with incessant increase so long as the principles were adhered to. On the other hand, where these principles were all absent, there could be no success of any kind; there could not even be a business at all, for there would be nothing to produce the adherence of one part with another; but there would be that lack of life, that absence of fibre and consistency, which animates and gives body and form to any object whatsoever. Picture a man with all these principles absent from his mind, his daily life, and even if your knowledge of these principles is but slight and imperfect, yet you could not think of such a man as doing any successful work. You could picture him as leading the confused life of a shiftless tramp, but to imagine him at the head of a business, as the centre of an organization, or as a responsible and controlling agent in any department of life—this you could not do, because you realize its impossibility. The fact that no one of moderate morality and intelligence can think of such a man as commanding any success, should, to all those who have not yet grasped the import of these principles and therefore declare that morality is not a factor, but rather a hindrance, in prosperity, be a sound proof to them that their conclusion is totally wrong; for if it was right, then the greater the lack of these moral principles, the greater would be the success.

These eight principles, then, in greater or lesser degree, are the causative factors in all success of whatsoever kind. Underneath all prosperity they are the strong supports, and, howsoever appearances may be against such a conclusion, a measure of them informs and sustains every effort which is crowned with that excellence which men name success.

It is true that comparatively few successful men practice, in their entirety and perfection, all these eight principles, but there are those who do, and they are the leaders, teachers, and guides of men, the supports of human society, and the strong pioneers in the van of human evolution.

But while few achieve that moral perfection which ensures the acme of success, all lesser successes come from the partial observance of these principles which are so powerful in the production of good results that even perfection in any two or three of them alone is sufficient to ensure an ordinary degree of prosperity, and maintain a measure of local influence at least for a time, while the same perfection in two or three with partial excellence in all, or nearly all, the others, will render permanent that limited success and influence which will, necessarily, grow and extend in exact ratio with a more intimate knowledge and practice of those principles which, at present, are only partially incorporated in the character.

The boundary lines of a man's morality mark the limits of his success. So true is this that to know a man's moral status would be to know—to gauge mathematically—his ultimate success or failure. The temple of prosperity only stands in so far as it is supported by its moral pillars; as they are weakened, it becomes insecure; in so far as they are withdrawn, it crumbles away and totters to ruin.

Ultimate failure and defeat are inevitable where moral principles are ignored or defied—inevitable in the nature of things as cause and effect. As a stone thrown upward returns to the earth, so every deed, good or bad, returns upon him that sent it forth. Every unmoral or immoral act frustrates the end at which it aims, and every such succeeding act puts it further and further away as an achieved realization. On the other hand, every moral act is another solid brick in the temple of prosperity, another round of strength and sculptured beauty in the pillars which support it.

Individuals, families, nations grow and prosper in harmony with their growth in moral strength and knowledge; they fall and fail in accordance with their moral decadence.

Mentally, as physically, only that which has form and solidity can stand and endure. The unmoral is nothingness, and from it nothing can be formed. It is the negation of substance. The immoral is destruction. It is the negation of form. It is a process of spiritual denudation. While it undermines and disintegrates, it leaves the scattered material ready for the wise builder to put it into form again; and the wise builder is *Morality*. The moral is substance, form, and building power in one. Morality always builds up and preserves, for that is its nature, being the opposite of immorality which always breaks down and destroys. Morality is the Master-builder everywhere, whether in individuals or nations, whether in the world or in the universe.

Morality is invincible, and he who stands upon it to the end, stands upon an impregnable rock, so that his defeat is impossible, his triumph certain. He will be tried, and that to the uttermost, for without fighting there can be no victory, and so only can his moral powers be perfected, and it is in the nature of fixed principles, as of everything finely and perfectly wrought, to have their strength tested and proved. The steel bars which are to perform the strongest and best uses in the world must be subjected to a severe strain by the ironmaster, as a test of their texture and efficiency, before they are sent from his foundry. The brick-maker throws aside the bricks which have given way under the severe heat. So he who is to be greatly and permanently successful will pass through the strain of adverse circumstances and the fire of temptation with his moral nature not merely not undermined, but strengthened and beautified. He will be like a bar of well-wrought steel, fit for the highest use, and the universe will see, as the ironmaster his finely-wrought steel, that the use does not escape him.

Immorality is assailable at every point, and he who tries to stand upon it, sinks into the morass of desolation. Even while his efforts seem to stand, they are crumbling away. The climax of failure is inevitable. While the immoral man is chuckling over his ill-gotten gains, there is already a hole in his pocket through which his gold is falling. While he who begins with morality, yet deserts it for gain in the hour of trial, is like the brick which breaks on the first application of heat; he is not fit for use, and the universe casts him aside: yet not finally, for he is a being, not a brick; and he can live and learn, can repent and be restored.

Moral force is the life of all success, and the sustaining element in all prosperity; but there are various kinds of success, and it is frequently necessary that a man should fail in one direction that he may reach up to a greater and more far-reaching success. If, for instance, a literary, artistic, or moral genius should begin by trying to make money, it may be, and often is, to his advantage and the betterment of his genius that he should fail therein, so that he may achieve that more sublime success wherein lies his real power. Many a millionaire would doubtless be willing to barter his millions for the literary successes of a Shakespeare or the spiritual success of a Buddha, and would thereby consider that he had made a good bargain. Exceptional moral success is rarely accompanied with riches, yet financial success cannot in any way compare with it in greatness and grandeur. But I am not, in this book, dealing with the success of the saint or moral genius (such being dealt with in other of my books), but with that success which concerns the welfare, well-being, and happiness of the broadly average man and woman,—in a word, with the prosperity of the mass of mankind; a success and prosperity which, while being more or less connected with money—being present and temporal—yet is not confined thereto, but extends to and embraces all human activities, and which particularly relates to that harmony of the individual with his circumstances which produces that satisfaction called happiness and that comfort known as prosperity. To the achievement of this end, so desirable to the mass of mankind, let us now see how the eight principles operate, how the roof of prosperity is raised and made secure upon the pillars by which it is supported.

FIRST PILLAR—ENERGY

Energy is the working power in all achievement. Inert coal it converts to fire, and water it transmutes into steam; it vivifies and intensifies the commonest talent until it approaches to genius, and when it touches the mind of the dullard, it turns into a living fire that which before was sleeping in inertia.

Energy is a moral virtue, its opposing vice being laziness. As a virtue, it can be cultivated, and the lazy man can become energetic by forcibly arousing himself to exertion. Compared with the energetic man, the lazy man is not half alive. Even while the latter is talking about the difficulty of doing a thing, the former is doing it. The active man has done a considerable amount of work before the lazy man has roused himself from sleep. While the lazy man is waiting for an opportunity, the active man has gone out, met and utilized half-a-dozen opportunities. He does things while the other is rubbing his eyes.

Energy is one of the primal forces; without it nothing can be accomplished. It is the basic element in all forms of action. The entire universe is a manifestation of tireless, though inscrutable energy. Energy is, indeed, life, and without it there would be no universe, no life. When a man has ceased to act, when the body lies inert, and all the functions have ceased to act, then we say he is dead; and in so far as a man fails to act, he is so far dead. Man, mentally and physically, is framed for action, and not for swinish ease. Every muscle of the body (being a lever for exertion) is a rebuke to the lazy man. Every bone and nerve is fashioned for resistance; every function and faculty is there for a legitimate use. All things have their end in action; all things are perfected in use.

This being so, there is no prosperity for the lazy man, no happiness, no refuge, and no rest; for him, there is not even the ease which he covets, for he at last becomes a homeless outcast, a troubled, harried, despised man, so that the proverb wisely puts it that, "The lazy man does the hardest work," in that, avoiding the systematic labour of skill, he brings upon himself the hardest lot.

The man of energy exerts himself to the accomplishment of some end, or ends. The end may be a good one or a bad one; but if a bad one, that is the abuse of energy which reacts destructively on the doer, like one striking a wall with his fist, and only injures his own hand. Energy is always good, but it is only useful when applied to good ends, and those ends, when reached, constitute happiness, success, prosperity.

Yet energy misapplied is better than no energy at all. This is powerfully put by St. John in the words: "I would have you either hot or cold; if you are lukewarm I will spew you out of my mouth." The extremes of heat and cold here symbolize the transforming agency of energy, in its good and bad aspects. The lukewarm stage is colourless, lifeless, useless; it can scarcely be said to have either virtue or vice, and is merely barren, empty, fruitless. The man who applies his abounding energy to bad ends, has, at least, one saving virtue, the virtue of exertion, and the very power with which he strives to acquire his selfish ends, will bring upon him such difficulties, pains, and sorrows, that will compel him to learn by experience, and so at last to refashion his base of action. At the right moment, when his mental eyes open to better purposes, he will turn round and cut new and proper channels for the outflow of his power, and will then be just as strong in good as he formerly was in evil. This truth is beautifully crystallized in the old proverb, "The greater the sinner, the greater the saint."

Energy is power, and without it there will be no accomplishment; there will not even be virtue, for virtue does not only consist of not doing evil, but also, and primarily, of doing good. There are those who try, yet fail through insufficient energy. Their efforts are too feeble to produce positive results. Such are not vicious, and because they never do any deliberate harm, are usually spoken of as good men that fail. But to lack the initiative to do harm is not to be good; it is only to be weak and powerless. He is the truly good man who, having the power to do evil, yet chooses to direct his energies in ways that are good. Without a considerable degree of energy, therefore, there will be no moral power. What good there is, will be latent and sleeping; there will be no going forth of good, just as there can be no mechanical motion without the motive power.

Energy is the informing power in all doing in every department of life, and whether it be along material or spiritual lines. The call to action which comes not only from the soldier but from the lips or pen of every teacher in every grade of thought, is a call to men to rouse their sleeping energy, and to do vigorously the task in hand. Even the men of contemplation and meditation never cease to rouse their disciples to exertion in meditative thought. Energy is alike needed in all spheres of life, and not only are the rules of the soldier, the engineer and the merchant rules of action, but nearly all the precepts of the saviours, sages, and saints are precepts of *doing*.

The advice of one of the Great Teachers to his disciples, "Keep wide awake," tersely expresses the necessity for tireless energy if one's purpose is to be accomplished, and is equally good advice to the salesman as to the saint. "Eternal vigilance is the price of liberty," and liberty is the reaching of one's fixed end. It was the same Teacher who said: "If anything is to be done, let a man do it at once; let him attack it vigorously!" The wisdom of this advice is seen when it is remembered that action is creative, that increase and development follow upon legitimate use. To get more energy we must use to the full that which we already possess. Only to him that hath is given. Only to him that puts his hand vigorously to some task do power and freedom come.

But energy to be productive must not only be directed toward good ends, it must be carefully controlled and conserved. "The conservation of energy" is a modern term expressive of that principle in nature by which no energy is wasted or lost, and the man whose energies are to be fruitful in results must work intelligently upon this principle. Noise and hurry are so much energy running to waste. "More haste, less speed." The maximum of noise usually accompanies the minimum of accomplishment. With much talk there is little doing. Working steam is not heard. It is the escaping steam which makes a great noise. It is the concentrated powder which drives the bullet to its mark.

In so far as a man intensifies his energies by conserving them and concentrating them upon the accomplishment of his purpose, just so far does he gain in quietness and silence, in repose and calmness. It is a great delusion that noise means power. There is no greater baby than the blustering boaster. Physically a man, he is but an infant mentally, and having no strength to do anything, and no work to show, he tries to make up for it by loudly proclaiming what he has done, or could do.

"Still waters run deep," and the great universal forces are inaudible. Where calmness is, there is the greatest power. Calmness is the sure indication of a strong, well-trained, patiently disciplined mind. The calm man knows his business, be sure of it. His words are few, but they tell. His schemes are well planned, and they work true, like a well-balanced machine. He sees a long way ahead, and makes straight for his object. The enemy, Difficulty, he converts into a friend, and makes profitable use of him, for he has studied well how to "agree with his adversary while he is in the way with him." Like a wise general, he has anticipated all emergencies. Indeed, he is *the man who is prepared before-hand.* In his meditations, in the counsels of his judgment, he has conferred with causes, and has caught the bent of all contingencies. He is never taken by surprise; is never in a hurry, is safe in the keeping of his own steadfastness, and is sure of his ground. You may think you have got him, only to find, the next moment, that you have tripped in your haste, and that he has got you; or rather that you, wanting calmness, have hurried yourself into the dilemma which you had prepared for him. Your impulse cannot do battle with his deliberation, but is foiled at the first attack; your uncurbed energy cannot turn aside the wisely directed stream of his concentrated power. He is "armed at all points." By a mental Jiu-Jitsu acquired through self-discipline, he meets opposition in such a way that it destroys itself. Upbraid him with angry words, and the reproof hidden in his gentle reply searches to the very heart of your folly, and the fire of your anger sinks into the ashes of remorse. Approach him with a vulgar familiarity, and his look at once fills you with shame, and brings you back to your senses. As he is prepared for all events, so he is ready for all men; though no men are ready for him. All weaknesses are betrayed in his presence, and he commands by an inherent force which calmness has rendered habitual and unconscious.

Calmness, as distinguished from the dead placidity of languor, is the acme of concentrated energy. There is a focused mentality behind it. In agitation and excitement the mentality is dispersed. It is irresponsible, and is without force or weight. The fussy, peevish, irritable man has no influence. He repels, and not attracts. He wonders why his "easy-going" neighbour succeeds, and is sought after, while he, who is always hurrying, worrying, and troubling (he miscalls it *striving*), fails, and is avoided. His neighbour, being a calmer man, not more easy-going but more deliberate, gets through more work, does it more skilfully, and is more self-possessed and manly. This is the reason of his success and influence. His energy is controlled and used, while the other man's energy is dispersed and abused.

Energy, then, is the first pillar in the temple of prosperity, and without it, as the first and most essential equipment, there can be no prosperity. No energy means no capacity; there is no aptitude for work, and therefore no manly self-respect and independence. Amongst the unemployed will be found many who are unemployable through sheer lack of this first essential of work—energy. The man that stands many hours a day at a street corner with his hands in his pockets and a pipe in his mouth, waiting for someone to treat him to a glass of beer, is little likely to find employment, or to accept it should it come to him. Physically flabby and mentally inert, he is every day becoming more so, is making himself more unfit to work, and therefore unfit to live. The energetic man may pass through temporary periods of unemployment and suffering, but it is impossible for him to become one of the permanently unemployed. He will either find work or make it, for inertia is painful to him, and work is a delight; and he who delights in work will not long remain unemployed.

The lazy man does not wish to be employed. He is in his element when doing nothing. His chief study is how to avoid exertion. To vegetate in semi-torpor is his idea of happiness. He is unfit and unemployable. Even the extreme Socialist, who places all unemployment at the door of the rich, would discharge a lazy servant, and so add one more to the army of the unemployed; for laziness is one of the lowest vices, repulsive to all active, right-minded men.

But energy is a composite power. It does not stand alone. Involved in it are qualities which go to the making of vigorous character and the production of prosperity. Mainly, these qualities are contained in the four following characteristics:—

1. Promptitude.
2. Vigilance.
3. Industry.
4. Earnestness.

The pillar of energy is therefore a concrete mass composed of these four tenacious elements. They are tough, enduring, and are calculated to withstand the wildest weather of adversity. They all make for life, power, capacity, and progress.

Promptitude is a valuable possession. It begets reliability. People who are alert, prompt, and punctual are relied upon. They can be trusted to do their duty, and to do it vigorously and well. Masters who are prompt are a tonic to their employees, and a whip to those who are inclined to shirk. They are a means of wholesome discipline to those who would not otherwise discipline themselves. Thus while aiding their own usefulness and success, they contribute to the usefulness and success of others. The perfunctory worker, who is ever procrastinating, and is always behind time, becomes a nuisance, if not to himself, to others, and his services come to be regarded as of little economic value. Deliberation and despatch, handmaids of promptitude, are valuable aids in the achievement of prosperity. In ordinary business channels, alacrity is a saving power, and promptness spells profit. It is doubtful whether a confirmed procrastinator ever succeeded in business. I have not yet met one such, though I have known many who have failed.

Vigilance is the guard of all the faculties and powers of the mind. It is the detective that prevents the entrance of any violent and destructive element. It is the close companion and protector of all success, liberty, and wisdom. Without this watchful attitude of mind, a man is a fool, and there is no prosperity for a fool. The fool allows his mind to be ransacked and robbed of its gravity, serenity, and judgment, by mean thoughts and violent passions as they come along to molest him. He is never on his guard, but leaves open the doors of his mind to every nefarious intruder. He is so weak and unsteady as to be swept off his balance by every gust of impulse that overtakes him. He is an example to others of what they should not be. He is always a failure, for the fool is an offence to all men, and there is no society that can receive him with respect. As wisdom is the acme of strength, so folly is the other extreme of weakness.

The lack of vigilance is shown in thoughtlessness, and in a general looseness in the common details of life. Thoughtlessness is but another name for folly. It lies at the root of a great deal of failure and misery. No one who aims at any kind of usefulness and prosperity (for usefulness in the body politic and prosperity to oneself cannot be severed), can afford to be asleep with regard to his actions and the effect of those actions on others and reactively on himself. He must, at the outset of his career, wake up to a sense of his personal responsibility. He must know that wherever he is—in the home, the counting-house, the pulpit, the store, in the schoolroom or behind the counter, in company or alone, at work or at play—his conduct will materially affect his career for good or bad; for there is a subtle influence in behaviour which leaves its impress on every man, woman, and child that it touches, and that impress is the determining factor in the attitude of persons toward one another. It is for this reason that the cultivation of good manners plays such an important part in all coherent society. If you carry about with you a disturbing or disagreeable mental defect, it needs not to be named and known to work its poison upon your affairs. Its corrosive influence will eat into all your efforts, and disfigure your happiness and prosperity, as a powerful acid eats into and disfigures the finest steel. On the other hand, if you carry about an assuring and harmonious mental excellence, it needs not that those about you understand it, to be influenced by it. They will be drawn toward you in good-will, often without knowing why, and that good quality will be the most powerful support in all your affairs, bringing you friends and opportunities, and greatly aiding in the success of all your enterprises. It will even right your mistakes, and largely neutralize the bad effects of your minor incapacities, covering a multitude of faults.

Thus we receive at the hands of the world according to the measure of our giving. For bad, bad; for good, good. For defective conduct, indifferent influence and imperfect success; for superior conduct, lasting power and consummate achievement. We act, and the world responds. When the foolish man fails, he blames others, and sees no error in himself; but the wise man watches and corrects himself, and so is assured of success.

The man whose mind is vigilant and alert, has thereby a valuable equipment in the achievement of his aims; and if he be fully alive and wide awake on all occasions, to all opportunities, and against all marring defects of character, what event, what circumstance, what enemy shall overtake him and find him unprepared? What shall prevent him from achieving the legitimate end at which he aims?

Industry brings cheerfulness and plenty. Vigorously industrious people are the happiest members of the community. They are not always the richest, if by riches is meant a superfluity of money; but they are always the most light-hearted and joyful, and the most satisfied with what they do and have, and are therefore the richer, if by richer we mean more abundantly blessed. Active people have no time for moping and brooding, or for dwelling selfishly upon their ailments and troubles.

Things most used are kept the brightest, and people most employed best retain their brightness and buoyancy of spirit. Things unused tarnish quickest; and the time-killer is attacked with ennui and morbid fancies. To talk of having to "kill time" is almost like a confession of imbecility; for who, in the short life at his disposal, and in a world so flooded with resources of knowledge and usefulness, can have too much time? People with sound heads and good hearts can fill up every moment of every day usefully and happily, and if they refer to time at all, it is to the effect that it is all too short to enable them to do all that they would like to do.

Industry, too, promotes health and well-being. The active man goes to bed tired every night; his rest is sound and sweet, and he wakes up early in the morning, fresh and strong for another day's delightful toil. His appetite and digestion are good. He has an excellent sauce in recreation, and a good tonic in toil. What companionship can such a man have with moping and melancholy? Such morbid spirits hang around those who do little and dine excessively. People who make themselves useful to the community, receive back from the community their full share of health, happiness, and prosperity. They brighten the daily task, and keep the world moving. They are the gold of the nation and the salt of the earth.

"*Earnestness*," said a Great Teacher, "is the path of immortality. They who are in earnest do not die; they who are not in earnest are as if dead already." Earnestness is the dedication of the entire mind to its task. We live only in what we do. Earnest people are dissatisfied with anything short of the highest excellence in whatever they do, and they always reach that excellence. There are so many that are careless and half-hearted, so satisfied with a poor performance, that the earnest ones shine apart, as it were, in their excellence. There are always plenty of "vacancies" in the ranks of usefulness and service for earnest people. There never was, and never will be, a deeply earnest man or woman who did not fill successfully some suitable sphere. Such people are scrupulous, conscientious, and painstaking, and cannot rest in ease until the very best is done, and the whole world is always on the lookout to reward the best. It always stands ready to pay the full price, whether in money, fame, friends, influence, happiness, scope, or life, for that which is of surpassing excellence, whether it be in things material, intellectual, or spiritual. Whatever you are,—whether shopkeeper or saintly teacher,—you can safely give the very best to the world without any doubt or misgiving. If the indelible impress of your earnestness be on your goods in one case, or on your words in the other, your business will flourish, or your precepts will live.

Earnest people make rapid progress both in their work and their character. It is thus that they live, and "do not die," for stagnation only is death, and where there is incessant progress and ever-ascending excellence, stagnation and death are swallowed up in activity and life.

Thus are the making and masonry of the First Pillar explained. He who builds it well, and sets it firm and straight, will have a powerful and enduring support in the business of his life.

SECOND PILLAR—ECONOMY

I t is said of Nature that she knows no vacuum. She also knows no waste. In the divine economy of Nature everything is conserved and turned to good account. Even excreta are chemically transmuted, and utilized in the building up of new forms. Nature destroys every foulness, not by annihilation, but by transmutation, by sweetening and purifying it, and making it serve the ends of things beautiful, useful, and good.

That economy which, in nature, is a universal principle, is in man a moral quality, and it is that quality by which he preserves his energies, and sustains his place as a working unit in the scheme of things.

Financial economy is merely a fragment of this principle, or rather it is a material symbol of that true economy which is purely mental, and its transmutations spiritual. The financial economist exchanges coppers for silver, silver for gold, gold for notes, and the notes he converts into the figures of a bank account. By these conversions of money into more readily transmissible forms he is the gainer in the financial management of his affairs. The spiritual economist transmutes passions into intelligence, intelligence into principles, principles into wisdom, and wisdom is manifested in actions which are few but of powerful effect. By all these transmutations he is the gainer in character, and in the management of his life.

True economy is the middle way in all things, whether material or mental, between waste and undue retention. That which is wasted, whether money or mental energy, is rendered powerless; that which is selfishly retained and hoarded up, is equally powerless. To secure power, whether of capital or mentality, there must be concentration, but concentration must be followed by legitimate use. The gathering up of money or energy is only a means; the end is *use;* and it is use only that produces power.

An all-round economy consists in finding the middle way in the following seven things: *Money, Food, Clothing, Recreation, Rest, Time,* and *Energy.*

Money is the symbol of exchange, and represents purchasing power. He who is anxious to acquire financial wealth,—as well as he who wishes to avoid debt,—must study how to apportion his expenditure in accordance with his income, so as to leave a margin of ever-increasing working capital, or to have a little store ready in hand for any emergency. Money spent in thoughtless expenditure—in worthless pleasures or harmful luxuries—is money wasted and power destroyed; for, although a limited and subordinate power, the means and capacity for legitimate and virtuous purchase is, nevertheless, a power, and one that enters largely into the details of our everyday life. The spendthrift can never become rich, but, if he begin with riches, must soon become poor. The miser, with all his stored-away gold, cannot be said to be rich, for he is in want, and his gold, lying idle, is deprived of its power of purchase. The thrifty and prudent are on the way to riches, for while they spend wisely they save carefully, and gradually enlarge their sphere as their growing means allow.

The poor man who is to become rich must begin at the bottom, and must not wish, nor try, to appear affluent by attempting something far beyond his means. There is always plenty of room and scope at the bottom, and it is a safe place from which to begin, as there is nothing below, and everything above. Many a young business man comes at once to grief by swagger and display which he foolishly imagines are necessary to success, but which, deceiving no one but himself, lead quickly to ruin. A modest and true beginning, in any sphere, will better ensure success than an exaggerated advertisement of one's standing and importance. The smaller the capital, the smaller should be the sphere of operations. Capital and scope are hand and glove, and they should fit. Concentrate your capital within the circle of its working power, and, however circumscribed that circle may be, it will continue to widen and extend as the gathering momentum of power presses for expression.

Above all, take care always to avoid the two extremes of parsimony and prodigality.

Food represents life, vitality, and both physical and mental strength. There is a middle way in eating and drinking, as in all else. The man who is to achieve prosperity must be well nourished, but not overfed. The man that starves his body, whether through miserliness or asceticism (both forms of false economy), diminishes his mental energy, and renders his body too enfeebled to be the instrument for any strong achievement. Such a man courts sickly-mindedness, a condition conducive only to failure.

The glutton, however, destroys himself by excess. His bestialized body becomes a stored-up reservoir of poisons which attract disease and corruption, while his mind becomes more and more brutalized and confused, and therefore more incapable. Gluttony is one of the lowest and most animal vices, and is obnoxious to all who pursue a moderate course.

The best workers and most successful men are they who are most moderate in eating and drinking. By taking enough nourishment, but not too much, they attain the maximum physical and mental fitness. Being thus well equipped by moderation, they are enabled vigorously and joyfully to fight the battle of life.

Clothing is covering and protection for the body; though it is frequently wrested from this economic purpose, and made a means of vain display. The two extremes to be avoided here are negligence and vanity. Custom cannot, and need not, be ignored; and cleanliness is all-important. The ill-dressed, unkempt man or woman invites failure and loneliness. A man's dress should harmonize with his station in life, and it should be of good quality, and be well-made and appropriate. Clothing should not be cast aside while comparatively new, but should be well worn. If a man be poor, he will not lose in either self-respect or the respect of others by wearing threadbare clothing, if it be clean, and his whole body be clean and neat. But vanity, leading to excessive luxury in clothing, is a vice which should be studiously avoided by virtuous people. I knew a lady who had forty dresses in her wardrobe; also a man who had twenty walking-sticks, about the same number of hats, and some dozen mackintoshes; while another had some twenty or thirty pairs of boots. Rich people who thus squander money on piles of superfluous clothing, are courting poverty; for it is waste, and waste leads to want. The money so heedlessly spent could be better used, for suffering abounds and charity is noble.

An obtrusive display in clothing and jewellery bespeaks a vulgar and empty mind. Modest and cultured people are modest and becoming in their dress, and their spare money is wisely used in further enhancing their culture and virtue. Education and progress are of more importance to them than vain and needless apparel; and literature, art, and science are encouraged thereby. A true refinement is in the mind and behaviour, and a mind adorned with virtue and intelligence cannot add to its attractiveness (though it may detract from it) by an ostentatious display of the body. Time spent in uselessly adorning the body could be more fruitfully employed. Simplicity in dress, as in other things, is the best. It touches the point of excellence in usefulness, comfort, and bodily grace, and bespeaks true taste and cultivated refinement.

Recreation is one of the necessities of life. Every man and woman should have some definite work as the main object of life, and to which a considerable amount of time should be devoted, and he should only turn from it at given and limited periods for recreation and rest. The object of recreation is greater buoyancy of both body and mind, with an increase of power in one's serious work. It is, therefore, a means, not an end; and this should ever be borne in mind, for, to many, some forms of recreation—innocent and good in themselves—become so fascinating, that they are in danger of making them the end of life, and of thus abandoning duty for pleasure. To make of life a ceaseless round of games and pleasures, with no other object in life, is to turn living upside-down, as it were, and it produces monotony and enervation. People who do it are the most unhappy of mortals, and suffer from languor, ennui, and peevishness. As sauce is an aid to digestion, and can only produce sickness if taken as food, so recreation is a refreshment in the intervals of labour, and can only lead to misery when made the work of life. When a man has done his day's duty he can turn to his recreation with a freed mind and a light heart, and both his work and his pleasure will be to him a source of happiness.

It is a true economy in this particular neither to devote the whole of one's time to work nor to recreation, but to apportion to each its time and place; and so fill out life with those changes which are necessary to a long life and a fruitful existence.

All agreeable change is recreation, and the mental worker will gain both in the quality and quantity of his work by laying it down at the time appointed for restful and refreshing recreation; while the physical worker will improve in every way by turning to some form of study as a hobby or means of education.

As we do not spend all our time in eating, or sleeping, or resting, neither should we spend it in exercise or pleasure, but should give recreation its proper place as a natural tonic in the economic scheme of our life.

Rest is for recuperation after toil. Every self-respecting human being should do sufficient work every day to make his sleep restful and sweet, and his rising up fresh and bright.

Enough sleep should be taken, but not too much. Over-indulgence on the one hand, or deprivation on the other, are both harmful. It is an easy matter to find out how much sleep one requires. By going to bed early, and getting up early (rising a little earlier every morning if one has been in the habit of spending long hours in bed), one can very soon accurately gauge and adjust the number of hours he or she requires for complete recuperation. It will be found as the sleeping hours are shortened that the sleep becomes more and more sound and sweet, and the waking up more and more alert and bright. People who are to prosper in their work must not give way to ignoble ease and over-indulgence in sleep. Fruitful labour, and not ease, is the true end of life, and ease is only good in so far as it subserves the ends of work. Sloth and prosperity can never be companions, can never even approach each other. The sluggard will never overtake success, but failure will speedily catch up with him, and leave him defeated. Rest is to fit us for greater labour, and not to pamper us in indolence. When the bodily vigour is restored, the end of rest is accomplished. A perfect balance between labour and rest contributes considerably to health, happiness, and prosperity.

Time is that which we all possess in equal measure. The day is not lengthened for any man. We should therefore see to it that we do not squander its precious minutes in unprofitable waste. He who spends his time in self-indulgence and the pursuit of pleasure, presently finds himself old, and nothing has been accomplished. He who fills full with useful pursuits the minutes as they come and go, grows old in honour and wisdom, and prosperity abides with him. Money wasted can be restored; health wasted can be restored; but time wasted can never be restored.

It is an old saying that "time is money." It is, in the same way, health, and strength, and talent, and genius, and wisdom, in accordance with the manner in which it is used; and to properly use it, the minutes must be seized upon as they come, for once they are past they can never be recalled. The day should be divided into portions, and everything—work, leisure, meals, recreation—should be attended to in its proper time; and the time of *preparation* should not be overlooked or ignored. Whatever a man does, he will do it better and more successfully by utilizing some small portion of the day in preparing his mind for his work. The man who gets up early in order to think and plan, that he may weigh and consider and forecast, will always manifest greater skill and success in his particular pursuit than the man who lies in bed till the last moment, and only gets up just in time to begin breakfast. An hour spent in this way before breakfast will prove of the greatest value in making one's efforts fruitful. It is a means of calming and clarifying the mind, and of focussing one's energies so as to render them more powerful and effective. The best and most abiding success is that which is made before eight o'clock in the morning. He who is at his business at six o'clock, will always—all other conditions being equal—be a long way ahead of the man who is in bed at eight. The lie-a-bed heavily handicaps himself in the race of life. He gives his early-rising competitor two or three hours' start every day. How can he ever hope to win with such a self-imposed tax upon his time? At the end of a year that two or three hours' start every day is shown in a success which is the synthesis of accumulated results. What, then, must be the difference between the efforts of these two men at the end, say, of twenty years! The lie-a-bed, too, after he gets up is always in a hurry trying to regain lost time, which results in more loss of time, for hurry always defeats its own end. The early riser, who thus economizes his time, has no need to hurry, for he is always ahead of the hour, is always well up with his work; he can well afford to be calm and deliberate, and to do carefully and well whatever is in hand, for his good habit shows itself at the end of the day in the form of a happy frame of mind, and in bigger results in the shape of work skilfully and successfully done.

In the economizing of time, too, there will be many things which a man will have to eliminate from his life; some of the things and pursuits which he loves, and desires to retain, will have to be sacrificed to the main purpose of his life. The studied elimination of non-essentials from one's daily life is a vital factor in all great achievement. All great men are adepts in this branch of economy, and it plays an important part in the making of their greatness. It is a form of economy which also enters into the mind, the actions, and the speech, eliminating from them all that is superfluous, and that impedes, and does not subserve, the end aimed at. Foolish and unsuccessful people talk carelessly and aimlessly, act carelessly and aimlessly, and allow everything that comes along—good, bad, and indifferent—to lodge in their mind. The mind of the true economist is a sieve which lets everything fall through except that which is of use to him in the business of his life. He also employs only necessary words, and does only necessary actions, thus vastly minimizing friction and waste of power.

To go to bed betime and to get up betime, to fill in every working minute with purposeful thought and effective action, this is the true economy of time.

Energy is economized by the formation of good habits. All vices are a reckless expenditure of energy. Sufficient energy is thoughtlessly wasted in bad habits to enable men to accomplish the greatest success, if conserved and used in right directions. If economy be practised in the six points already considered, much will be done in the conservation of one's energies; but a man must go still further, and carefully husband his vitality by the avoidance of all forms of vice; and by vice is meant not only all forms of physical self-indulgences and impurities, but also all those mental vices such as hurry, worry, excitement, despondency, anger, complaining and envy—which deplete the mind and render it unfit for any important work or admirable achievement. They are common forms of mental dissipation which a man of character should study how to avoid and overcome. The energy wasted in frequent fits of bad temper would, if controlled and properly directed, give a man strength of mind, force of character, and much power to achieve. The angry man is a strong man made weak by the dissipation of his mental energy. He needs self-control to manifest his strength. The calm man is always his superior in any department of life, and will always take precedence of him, both in his success, and in the estimation of others. No man can afford to disperse his energies in fostering bad habits and bad tendencies of mind. Every vice, however apparently small, will tell against him in the battle of life. Every harmful self-indulgence will come back to him in the form of some trouble or weakness. Every moment of riot or of pandering to his lower inclinations will make his progress more laborious, and will hold him back from scaling the high heaven of his wished-for achievement. On the other hand, he who economizes his energies, and bends them toward the main task of his life, will make rapid progress, and nothing will prevent him from reaching the golden city of success.

It will be seen that economy is something far more profound and far-reaching than the mere saving of money. It touches every part of our nature and every phase of our life. The old saying, "Take care of the pence, and the pounds will take care of themselves," may be regarded as a parable, for the lower passions of men are not bad of themselves when regarded as native energy; it is the abuse of that energy that is bad, and if this passional energy be taken care of and stored up and transmuted, it reappears as force of character. To waste this valuable energy in the pursuit of vice is like wasting the pence, and so losing the pounds; but to take care of it for good uses is to store up the pence of passions, and so gain the golden pounds of good. Take care, therefore, of the lower energies, and the higher achievements will take care of themselves.

The Pillar of Economy, when soundly built, will be found to be composed largely of these four qualities:—

1. Moderation.
2. Efficiency.
3. Resourcefulness.
4. Originality.

Moderation is the strong core of economy. It avoids extremes, finding the middle way in all things. It also consists in abstaining from the unnecessary and the harmful. There can be no such thing as moderation in that which is evil, for that would be excess. A true moderation abstains from evil. It is not a moderate use of fire to put our hands into it, but to warm them by it at a safe distance. Evil is a fire that will burn a man though he but touch it. A harmful luxury is best left severely alone. Smoking, snuff-taking, alcoholic drinking, gambling, and other such common vices, although they have dragged thousands down to ill-health, misery, and failure, have never helped one toward health, happiness, and success. The man who eschews them will always be ahead of the man that pursues them, their talents and opportunities being equal. Healthy, happy, and long-lived people are always moderate and abstemious in their habits. By moderation the life-forces are preserved; by excess they are destroyed. Men, also, who carry moderation into their thoughts, allaying their passions and feelings, avoiding all unwholesome extremes and morbid sensations and sentiments, add knowledge and wisdom to happiness and health, and thereby attain to the highest felicity and power. The immoderate destroy themselves by their own folly. They weaken their energies and stultify their capabilities, and instead of achieving an abiding success, reach only, at best, a fitful and precarious prosperity.

Efficiency proceeds from the right conservation of one's forces and powers. All skill is the use of concentrated energy. Superior skill, as talent and genius, is a higher degree of concentrated force. Men are always skillful in that which they love, because the mind is almost ceaselessly centred upon it. Skill is the result of that mental economy which transmutes thought into invention and action. There will be no prosperity without skill, and one's prosperity will be in the measure of one's skill. By a process of natural selection, the inefficient fall into their right places among the badly paid or unemployed; for who will employ a man who cannot, or will not, do his work properly? An employer may occasionally keep such a man out of charity; but this will be exceptional, as places of business, offices, households, and all centres of organized activity, are not charitable institutions, but industrial bodies which stand or fall by the fitness and efficiency of their individual members. Skill is gained by thoughtfulness and attention. Aimless and inattentive people are usually out of employment, to wit, the lounger at the street corner. They cannot do the simplest thing properly, because they will not rouse up the mind to thought and attention. Recently an acquaintance of mine employed a tramp to clean his windows, but the man had refrained from work and systematic thought for so long that he had become incapable of both, and could not even clean a window. Even when shown how to do it, he could not follow the simple instructions given. This is an instance, too, of the fact that the simplest thing requires a measure of skill in the doing. Efficiency largely determines a man's place among his fellows, and leads one on by steps to higher and higher positions as greater powers are developed. The good workman is skillful with his tools, while the good man is skillful with his thoughts. Wisdom is the highest form of skill. Aptitude is incipient wisdom. There is *one* right way of doing everything, even the smallest, and a thousand wrong ways. Skill consists in finding the one right way, and adhering to it. The inefficient bungle confusedly about among the thousand wrong ways, and do not adopt the right even when it is pointed out to them. They do this in some cases because they think, in their ignorance, that they know best, thereby placing themselves in a position where it becomes impossible to learn, even though it be only to learn how to clean a window or sweep a floor. Thoughtlessness and inefficiency are all too common. There is plenty of room in the world for thoughtful and efficient people. Employers of labour know how difficult it is to get the best workmanship. The good workman, whether with tools or brain, whether with speech or thought, will always find a place for the exercise of his skill.

Resourcefulness is the outcome of efficiency. It is an important element in prosperity, for the resourceful man is never confounded. He may have many falls, but he will always be equal to the occasion, and will be on his feet again immediately. Resourcefulness has its fundamental cause in the conservation of energy. It is energy transmuted. When a man cuts off certain mental or bodily vices which have been depleting him of his energy, what becomes of the energy so conserved? It is not destroyed or lost, for energy can never be destroyed or lost. *It becomes productive energy.* It reappears in the form of fruitful thought. The virtuous man is always more successful than the vicious man because he is teeming with resources. His entire mentality is alive and vigorous, abounding with stored-up energy. What the vicious man wastes in vicious indulgence, the virtuous man uses in fruitful industry. A new life and a new world, abounding with all fascinating pursuits and pure delights, opens up to the man who shuts himself off from the old world of animal vice, and his place will be assured by the resources which will well up within him. Barren seed perishes in the earth; there is no place for it in the fruitful economy of nature. Barren minds sink in the struggle of life. Human society makes for good, and there is no room in it for the emptiness engendered by vice. But the barren mind will not sink forever. When it wills, it can become fruitful, and regain itself. By the very nature of existence, by the eternal law of progress, the vicious man *must* fall; but having fallen, he can rise again. He can turn from vice to virtue, and stand, self-respecting and secure, upon his own resources.

The resourceful men invent, discover, initiate. They cannot fail, for they are in the stream of progress. They are full of new schemes, new methods, new hopes, and their life is so much fuller and richer thereby. They are men of supple minds. When a man fails to improve his business, his work, his methods, he falls out of the line of progress, and has begun to fail. His mind has become stiff and inert like the body of an aged man, and so fails to keep pace with the rapidly moving ideas and plans of resourceful minds. A resourceful mind is like a river which never runs dry, and which affords refreshment, and supplies new vigour in times of drought. Men of resources are men of new ideas, and men of new ideas flourish where others fade and decay.

Originality is resourcefulness ripened and perfected. Where there is originality there is genius, and men of genius are the lights of the world. Whatever work a man does, he should fall back upon his own resources in the doing it. While learning from others he should not slavishly imitate them, but should put himself into his work, and so make it new and original. Original men get the ear of the world. They may be neglected at first, but they are always ultimately accepted, and become patterns for mankind. Once a man has acquired the knack of originality, he takes his place as a leader among men in his particular department of knowledge and skill. But originality cannot be forced; it can only be developed; and it is developed by proceeding from excellence to excellence, by ascending in the scale of skill by the full and right use of one's mental powers. Let a man consecrate himself to his work, let him, so consecrated, concentrate all his energies upon it, and the day will come when the world will hail him as one of its strong sons; and he, too, like Balzac, who after many years of strenuous toil one day exclaimed, "I am about to become a genius!" will at last discover, to his joy, that he has joined the company of original minds, the gods who lead mankind into newer, higher, and more beneficent ways.

The composition of the Second Pillar is thus revealed. Its building awaits the ready workman who will skilfully apply his mental energies.

THIRD PILLAR—INTEGRITY

There is no striking a cheap bargain with prosperity. It must be purchased, not only with intelligent labour, but with moral force. As the bubble cannot endure, so the fraud cannot prosper. He makes a feverish spurt in the acquirement of money, and then collapses. Nothing is ever gained, ever can be gained, by fraud. It is but wrested for a time, to be again returned with heavy interest. But fraud is not confined to the unscrupulous swindler. All who are getting, or trying to get, money without giving an equivalent are practicing fraud, whether they know it or not. Men who are anxiously scheming how to get money without working for it, are frauds, and mentally they are closely allied to the thief and swindler under whose influence they come, sooner or later, and who deprives them of their capital. What is a thief but a man who carries to its logical extreme the desire to possess without giving a just return—that is, unlawfully? The man that courts prosperity must, in all his transactions, whether material or mental, study how to give a just return for that which he receives. This is the great fundamental principle in all sound commerce, while in spiritual things it becomes the doing to others that which we would have them do to us, and applied to the forces of the universe, it is scientifically stated in the formula, "Action and reaction are equal."

Human life is reciprocal, not rapacious, and the man who regards all others as his legitimate prey will soon find himself stranded in the desert of ruin, far away from the path of prosperity. He is too far behind in the process of evolution to cope successfully with honest men. The fittest, the best, always survive, and he, being the worst, cannot therefore continue. His end, unless he change in time, is sure—it is the jail, the filthy hovel, or the place of the deserted outcast. His efforts are destructive, and not constructive, and he thereby destroys himself.

It was Carlyle who, referring to Mohammed being then universally regarded by Christians as an impostor, exclaimed, "An impostor found a religion! An impostor couldn't build a brick house!" An impostor, a liar, a cheat—the man of dishonesty—cannot build, as he has neither tools nor material with which to build. He can no more build up a business, a character, a career, a success, than he can found a religion or build a brick house. He not only does not build, but all his energies are bent on undermining what others have built, but this being impossible, he undermines himself.

Without integrity, energy and economy will at last fail, but aided by integrity, their strength will be greatly augmented. There is not an occasion in life in which the moral factor does not play an important part. Sterling integrity tells wherever it is, and stamps its hall-mark on all transactions; and it does this because of its wonderful coherence and consistency, and its invincible strength. For the man of integrity is in line with the fixed laws of things—not only with the fundamental principles on which human society rests, but with the laws which hold the vast universe together. Who shall set these at naught? Who then shall undermine the man of unblemished integrity? He is like a strong tree whose roots are fed by perennial springs, and which no tempest can lay low.

To be complete and strong, integrity must embrace the whole man, and extend to all the details of his life; and it must be so thorough and permanent as to withstand all temptations to swerve into compromise. To fail in one point is to fail in all, and to admit, under stress, a compromise with falsehood, howsoever necessary and insignificant it may appear, is to throw down the shield of integrity, and to stand exposed to the onslaughts of evil.

The man who works as carefully and conscientiously when his employer is away as when his eye is upon him, will not long remain in an inferior position. Such integrity in duty, in performing the details of his work, will quickly lead him into the fertile regions of prosperity.

The shirker, on the other hand, he who does not scruple to neglect his work when his employer is not about—thereby robbing his employer of the time and labour for which he is paid—will quickly come to the barren region of unemployment, and will look in vain for needful labour.

There will come a time, too, to the man who is not deeply rooted in integrity, when it will seem necessary to his prospects and prosperity that he should tell a lie or do a dishonest thing—I say, to the man who is not deeply rooted in this principle, for a man of fixed and enlightened integrity knows that lying and dishonesty can never under any circumstance be necessary, and therefore he neither needs to be tempted in this particular, nor can he possibly be tempted—but the one so tempted must be able to cast aside the subtle insinuation of falsehood which in a time of indecision and perplexity arises within him, and he must stand firmly by the principle, being willing to lose and suffer rather than sink into obliquity. In this way only can he become enlightened concerning this moral principle, and discover the glad truth that integrity does not lead to loss and suffering, but to gain and joy; that honesty and deprivation are not, and cannot be, related as cause and effect.

It is this willingness to sacrifice rather than be untrue that leads to enlightenment in all spheres of life; and the man who, rather than sacrifice some selfish aim, will lie or deceive, has forfeited his right to moral enlightenment, and takes his place lower down among the devotees of deceit, among the doers of shady transactions, and men of no character and no reputation.

A man is not truly armoured with integrity until he has become incapable of lying or deceiving either by gesture, word, or act; until he sees, clearly, openly, and freed from all doubt, the deadly effects of such moral turpitude. The man so enlightened is protected from all quarters, and can no more be undermined by dishonest men than the sun can be pulled down from heaven by madmen, and the arrows of selfishness and treachery that may be poured upon him will rebound from the strong armour of his integrity and the bright shield of his righteousness, leaving him unarmed and untouched.

A lying tradesman will tell you that no man can thrive and be honest in these days of keen competition. How can such a man know this, seeing that he has never tried honesty? Moreover, such a man has no knowledge of honesty, and his statement is, therefore, a statement of ignorance, and ignorance and falsehood so blind a man that he foolishly imagines all are as ignorant and false as himself. I have known such tradesmen, and have seen them come to ruin. I once heard a business man make the following statement in a public meeting: "No man can be entirely honest in business; he can only be approximately honest." He imagined that his statement revealed the condition of the business world; it did not; *it revealed his own condition.* He was merely telling his audience that he was a dishonest man, but his ignorance, moral ignorance, prevented him from seeing this. Approximate honesty is only another term for dishonesty. The man who deviates a little from the straight path, will deviate more. He has no fixed principle of right, and is only thinking of his own advantage. That he persuades himself that *his* particular dishonesty is of a white and harmless kind, and that he is not so bad as his neighbour, is only one of the many forms of self-delusion which ignorance of moral principles creates.

Right-doing between man and man in the varied relations and transactions of life is the very soul of integrity. It includes, but is more than, honesty. It is the backbone of human society, and the support of human institutions. Without it there would be no trust, no confidence between men, and the business world would topple to its fall.

As the liar thinks all men are liars, and treats them as such, so the man of integrity treats all men with confidence. He trusts them, and they trust him. His clear eye and open hand shame the creeping fraud so that he cannot practice his fraud on him. As Emerson has so finely put it: "Trust men and they will be true to you, even though they make an exception in your favour to all their rules of trade."

The upright man by his very presence commands the morality of those about him, making them better than they were. Men are powerfully influenced by one another, and, as good is more powerful than evil, the strong and good man both shames and elevates, by his contact, the weak and bad.

The man of integrity carries about with him an unconscious grandeur which both awes and inspires. Having lifted himself above the petty, the mean, and the false, these coward vices slink from his presence in confusion. The highest intellectual gift cannot compare with this lofty moral grandeur. In the memory of men and the estimation of the world the man of integrity occupies a higher place than the man of genius. Buckminster says, "The moral grandeur of an independent integrity is the sublimest thing in nature." It is the quality in man which produces heroes. The man of unswerving rectitude is intrinsically always a hero. It only needs the occasion to bring out the heroic element. He is always, too, possessed of a permanent happiness. The man of genius may be very unhappy, but not so the man of integrity. Nothing—nor sickness, nor calamity, nor death—can deprive him of that permanent satisfaction which inheres in uprightness.

Rectitude leads straight to prosperity by four successive steps. First, the upright man wins the confidence of others. Second, having gained their confidence, they put trust in him. Third, this trust, never being violated, produces a good reputation; and fourth, a good reputation spreads further and further, and so brings about success.

Dishonesty has the reverse effect. By destroying the confidence of others, it produces in them suspicion and mistrust, and these bring about a bad reputation which culminates in failure.

The Pillar of Integrity is held together by these four virile elements:—

1. Honesty.
2. Fearlessness.
3. Purposefulness.
4. Invincibility.

Honesty is the surest way to success. The day at last comes when the dishonest man repents in sorrow and suffering; but no man ever needs to repent of having been honest. Even when the honest man fails—as he does sometimes through lacking other of these pillars, such as energy, economy, or system—his failure is not the grievous thing it is to the dishonest man, for he can always rejoice in the fact that he has never defrauded a fellow-being. Even in his darkest hour he finds repose in a clear conscience.

Ignorant men imagine that dishonesty is a short cut to prosperity. This is why they practice it.

The dishonest man is morally short-sighted. Like the drunkard who sees the immediate pleasure of his habit, but not the ultimate degradation, he sees the immediate effect of a dishonest act—a larger profit—but not its ultimate outcome; he does not see that an accumulated number of such acts must inevitably undermine his character, and bring his business toppling about his ears in ruin. While pocketing his gains, and thinking how cleverly and successfully he is imposing on others, he is all the time imposing on himself, and every coin thus gained *must* be paid back with added interest, and from this just retribution there is no possible loophole of escape. This moral gravitation is as sure and unvarying as the physical gravitation of a stone to the earth.

The tradesman who demands of his assistants that they shall lie, and misrepresent his goods to customers, is surrounding himself on all hands with suspicion, mistrust, and hatred. Even the moral weaklings who carry out his instructions despise him while defiling themselves with his unclean work. How can success thrive in such a poisonous atmosphere? The spirit of ruin is already in such a business, and the day of its fall is ordained.

An honest man may fail, but not because he is honest, and his failure will be honourable, and will not injure his character and reputation. His failure, too, resulting doubtless from his incapacity in the particular direction of his failure, will be a means of leading him into something more suited to his talents, and thus to ultimate success.

Fair dealing is admired by all; even the dishonest admire it in others, and he who deals justly with others in all his business transactions, who speaks the truth, and abides by his contracts even when they turn out to his own loss, such a man need fear no evil, for his actions can only result in good to himself and all with whom he is concerned.

Fearlessness accompanies honesty. The honest man has a clear eye and an unflinching gaze. He looks his fellow-men in the face, and his speech is direct and convincing. The liar and cheat hangs his head; his eye is muddy and his gaze oblique. He cannot look another man in the eye, and his speech arouses mistrust, for it is ambiguous and unconvincing.

When a man has fulfilled his obligations, he has nothing to fear. All his business relations are safe and secure. His methods and actions will endure the light of day. Should he pass through a difficult time, and get into debt, everybody will trust him and be willing to wait for payment, and all his debts will be paid. Dishonest people try to avoid paying their debts, and they live in fear; but the honest man tries to avoid getting into debt, but when debt overtakes him, he does not fear, but, redoubling his exertions, his debts are paid.

The dishonest are always in fear. They do not fear debt, but fear that they will have to pay their debts. They fear their fellow-men, fear the established authorities, fear the results of all that they do, and they are in constant fear of their misdeeds being revealed, and the consequences which may at any moment overtake them.

The honest man is rid of all this burden of fear. He is light-hearted, and walks erect among his fellows; not assuming a part and skulking and cringing, but being himself, and meeting eye to eye. Not deceiving or injuring any, there are none to fear, and anything said against him can only redound to his advantage.

And this fearlessness is, in itself, a tower of strength in a man's life, supporting him through all emergencies, enabling him to battle manfully with difficulties, and in the end securing for him that success of which he cannot be dispossessed.

Purposefulness is the direct outcome of that strength of character which integrity fosters. The man of integrity is the man of direct aims and strong and intelligent purposes. He does not guess, and work in the dark. All his plans have in them some of that moral fibre of which his character is wrought. A man's work will always in some way reflect himself, and the man of sound integrity is the man of sound plans. He weighs and considers and looks ahead, and so is less likely to make serious mistakes, or to bungle into a dilemma from which it is difficult to escape. Taking a moral view of all things, and always considering moral consequences, he stands on a firmer and more exalted ground than the man of mere policy and expedience; and while commanding a more extended view of any situation, he wields the greater power which a more comprehensive grasp of details, with the principles involved, confers upon him. Morality always has the advantage of expediency. Its purposes always reach down far below the surface, and are therefore more firm and secure, more strong and lasting. There is a native directness, too, about integrity, which enables the man to go straight to the mark in whatever he does, and which makes failure almost impossible.

Strong men have strong purposes, and strong purposes lead to strong achievements. The man of integrity is above all men *strong,* and his strength is manifested in that thoroughness with which he does the business of his life; a thoroughness which commands respect, admiration, and success.

Invincibility is a glorious protector, but it only envelopes the man whose integrity is perfectly pure and unassailable. Never to violate, even in the most insignificant particular, the principle of integrity, is to be invincible against all the assaults of innuendo, slander, and misrepresentation. The man who has failed in one point is vulnerable, and the shaft of evil, entering that point, will lay him low, like the arrow in the heel of Achilles. Pure and perfect integrity is proof against all attack and injury, enabling its possessor to meet all opposition and persecution with dauntless courage and sublime equanimity. No amount of talent, intellect, or business acumen can give a man that power of mind and peace of heart which come from an enlightened acceptance and observance of lofty moral principles. Moral force is the greatest power. Let the seeker for a true prosperity discover this force, let him foster and develop it in his mind and in his deeds, and as he succeeds he will take his place among the strong leaders of the earth.

Such is the strong and adamantine Pillar of Integrity. Blessed and prosperous above all men will be he who builds its incorruptible masonry into the temple of his life.

FOURTH PILLAR—SYSTEM

System is that principle of order by which confusion is rendered impossible. In the natural and universal order everything is in its place, so that the vast universe runs more perfectly than the most perfect machine. Disorder in space would mean the destruction of the universe; and disorder in a man's affairs destroys his work and his prosperity.

All complex organizations are built up by system. No business or society can develop into large dimensions apart from system, and this principle is pre-eminently the instrument of the merchant, the business man, and the organizer of institutions.

There are many departments in which a disorderly man may succeed—although attention to order would increase his success—but he will not succeed in business, unless he can place the business entirely in the hands of a systematic manager, who will thereby remedy his own defect.

All large business concerns have been evolved along definitely drawn systematic lines, any violation of which would be disastrous to the efficiency and welfare of the business. Complex business or other organizations are built up like complex bodies in nature, by scrupulous attention to details. The disorderly man thinks he can be careless about everything but the main end, but by ignoring the means he frustrates the end. By the disarrangement of details, organisms perish, and by the careless neglect of details, the growth of any work or concern is prevented.

Disorderly people waste an enormous amount of time and energy. The time frittered away in hunting for things is sufficient, were it conserved by order, to enable them to achieve any success, for slovenly people never have a place for anything, and have to hunt, frequently for a long time, for any article which they require. In the irritation, bad humour, and chagrin which this daily hunting for things brings about, as much energy is dissipated as would be required to build up a big business, or scale the highest heights of achievement in any direction.

Orderly people conserve both their time and energy. They never lose anything, and therefore never have to find anything. Everything is in its place, and the hand can be at once placed upon it, though it be in the dark. They can well afford to be cool and deliberate, and so use their mental energies in something more profitable than irritation, bad temper, and accusing others for their own lack of order.

There is a kind of genius in system which can perform apparent wonders with ease. A systematic man can get through so great a quantity of work in such a short time, and with such freedom from exhaustion, as to appear almost miraculous. He scales the heights of success while his slovenly competitor is wallowing hopelessly in the bogs of confusion. His strict observance of the law of order enables him to reach his ends swiftly and smoothly, without friction or loss of time.

The demands of system, in all departments of the business world, are as rigid and exacting as the holy vows of a saint, and cannot be violated in the smallest particular but at the risk of one's financial prospects. In the financial world, the law of order is an iron necessity, and he who faultlessly observes it, saves time, temper, and money.

Every enduring achievement in human society rests upon a basis of system; so true is this, that were system withdrawn, progress would cease. Think, for instance, of the vast achievements of literature—the works of classic authors and of great geniuses; the great poems, the innumerable prose works, the monumental histories, the soul-stirring orations; think also of the social intercourse of human society, of its religions, its legal statutes, and its vast fund of book-knowledge—think of all these wonderful resources and achievements of language, and then reflect that they all depend for their origin, growth, and continuance on the systematic arrangement of twenty-six letters, an arrangement having inexhaustible and illimitable results by the fact of its rigid limitation within certain fixed rules.

Again, all the wonderful achievements of mathematics have come from the systematic arrangement of ten figures; while the most complex piece of machinery, with its thousands of parts working together smoothly and almost noiselessly to the achievement of the end for which it was designed, was brought forth by the systematic observance of a few mechanical laws.

Herein we see how system simplifies that which is complex; how it makes easy that which was difficult; how it relates an infinite variety of details to the one central law of order, and so enables them to be dealt with and accounted for with perfect regularity, and with an entire absence of confusion.

The scientist names and classifies the myriad details of the universe, from the microscopic rotifer to the telescopic star, by his observance of the principle of system, so that out of many millions of objects, reference can be made to any one object in, at most, a few minutes. It is this faculty of speedy reference and swift dispatch which is of such overwhelming importance in every department of knowledge and industry, and the amount of time and labour thus saved to humanity is so vast as to be incomputable. We speak of religious, political, and business systems; of systems of thought, education, travel, government, and so on, indicating that all things in human society are welded together by the adhesive qualities of order.

System is, indeed, one of the great fundamental principles in progress, and in the binding together, in one complete whole, of the world's millions of human beings while they are at the same time each striving for a place, and are competing with one another in opposing aims and interests.

We see here how system is allied with greatness, for the many separate units whose minds are untrained to the discipline of system, are kept in their places by the organizing power of the comparatively few who perceive the urgent, the unescapable, necessity for the establishment of fixed and inviolable rules, whether in business, law, religion, science, or politics—in fact, in every sphere of human activity; for immediately two human beings meet together, they need some common ground of understanding for the avoidance of confusion; in a word, some *system* to regulate their actions.

Life is too short for confusion; and knowledge grows and progress proceeds along avenues of system which prevent retardation and retrogression, so that he who systematizes his knowledge or business, simplifies and enhances it for his successor, enabling him to begin, with a free mind, where he left off.

Every large business has its system which renders its vast machinery workable, enabling it to run like a well-balanced and well-oiled machine. A remarkable business man, a friend of mine, once told me that he could leave his huge business for twelve months, and it would run on without a hitch till his return; and he does occasionally leave it for several months, while travelling, and on his return, every man, boy, and girl; every tool, book, and machine; every detail down to the smallest, is in its place doing its work as when he left; and no trouble, no difficulty, no confusion has arisen.

There can be no marked success apart from a love of regularity and discipline, and the avoidance of friction, along with the restfulness and efficiency of mind which spring from such regularity. People who abhor discipline, whose minds are ungoverned and anarchic, and who are careless and irregular in their thinking, their habits, and the management of their affairs, cannot be highly successful and prosperous, and they fill their lives with numerous worries, troubles, difficulties, and petty annoyances, all of which would disappear under a proper regulation of their lives.

An unsystematic mind is an untrained mind, and it can no more cope with well-disciplined minds in the race of life than an untrained athlete can successfully compete with a carefully trained competitor in athletic races. The ill-disciplined mind, that thinks anything will do, rapidly falls behind the well-disciplined minds—who are convinced that only the best will do—in the strenuous race for the prizes of life, whether they be material, mental, or moral prizes. The man who, when he comes to do his work, is unable to find his tools, or to balance his figures, or to find the key of his desk, or the key to his thoughts, will be struggling in his self-made toils while his methodical neighbour will be freely and joyfully scaling the invigorating heights of successful achievement. The business man whose method is slovenly, or cumbersome, or behind the most recent developments of skilled minds, should only blame himself if his prospects are decadent, and should wake up to the necessity for more highly specialized and effective methods in his concern. He should seize upon everything—every invention and idea—that will enable him to economize time and labour, and aid him in thoroughness, deliberation, and dispatch.

System is the law by which everything—every organism, business, character, nation, empire—is built. By adding cell to cell, department to department, thought to thought, law to law, and colony to colony in orderly sequence and classification, all things, concerns, and institutions grow in magnitude and evolve to completeness. The man who is continually improving his methods, is gaining in building power; it therefore behooves the business man to be resourceful and inventive in the improvement of his methods, for the builders—whether of cathedrals or characters, businesses or religions—are the strong ones of the earth, and the protectors and pioneers of humanity. The systematic builder is a creator and preserver, while the man of disorder demolishes and destroys; and no limit can be set to the growth of a man's powers, the completeness of his character, the influence of his organization, or the extent of his business, if he but preserve intact the discipline of order, and have every detail in its place, keep every department to its special task, and tabulate and classify with such efficiency and perfection as to enable him at any moment to bring under examination or into requisition the remotest detail in connection with his special work.

In System are contained these four ingredients:—

1. Readiness.
2. Accuracy.
3. Utility.
4. Comprehensiveness.

Readiness is *aliveness*. It is that spirit of alertness by which a situation is immediately grasped and dealt with. The observance of system fosters and develops this spirit. The successful general must have the power of readily meeting any new and unlooked-for move on the part of the enemy; so every business man must have the readiness to deal with any unexpected development affecting his line of trade; and so also must the man of thought be able to deal with the details of any new problem which may arise. Dilatoriness is a vice that is fatal to prosperity, for it leads to incapability and stupidity. The men of ready hands, ready hearts, and ready brains, who know what they are doing, and do it methodically, skilfully, and with smooth yet consummate despatch, are the men who need to think little of prosperity, as an end, for it comes to them whether they seek it or not; success runs after them, and knocks at their door; and they unconsciously command it by the superb excellence of their faculties and methods.

Accuracy is of supreme importance in all commercial concerns and enterprises, but there can be no accuracy apart from system, and a system which is more or less imperfect will involve its originator in mistakes more or less disastrous until he improves it.

Inaccuracy is one of the commonest failings, because accuracy is closely allied to self-discipline, and self-discipline, along with that glad subjection to external discipline which it involves, is an indication of high moral culture to which the majority have not yet attained. If the inaccurate man will not willingly subject himself to the discipline of his employer or instructor, but thinks he knows better, his failing can never be remedied, and he will thereby bind himself down to an inferior position if in the business world; or to imperfect knowledge if in the world of thought.

The prevalence of the vice of inaccuracy (and in view of its disastrous effects it must be regarded as a vice, though perhaps one of the lesser vices) is patent to every observer in the way in which the majority of people relate a circumstance or repeat a simple statement of fact. It is nearly always made untrue by more or less marked inaccuracies. Few people, perhaps (not reckoning those who deliberately lie), have trained themselves to be accurate in what they say, or are so careful as to admit and state their liability to error, and from this common form of inaccuracy many untruths and misunderstandings arise.

More people take more pains to be accurate in what they do than in what they say, but even here inaccuracy is very common, rendering many inefficient and incompetent, and unfitting them for any strenuous and well-sustained endeavour. The man who habitually uses up a portion of his own or his employer's time in trying to correct his errors, or for the correction of whose mistakes another has to be employed, is not the man to maintain any position in the work-a-day world; much less to reach a place among the ranks of the prosperous.

There never yet lived a man who did not make some mistakes on his way to his particular success, but he is the capable and right-minded man who perceives his mistakes and quickly remedies them, and who is glad when they are pointed out to him. It is habitual and persistent inaccuracy which is a vice; and he is the incapable and wrong-minded man who will not see or admit his mistakes, and who takes offence when they are pointed out to him.

The progressive man learns by his own mistakes as well as by the mistakes of others. He is always ready to test good advice by practice, and aims at greater and ever greater accuracy in his methods, which means higher and higher perfection; for accuracy is perfection, and the measure of a man's accuracy will be the measure of his uniqueness and perfection.

Utility, or usefulness, is the direct result of method in one's work. Labour arrives at fruitful and profitable ends when it is systematically pursued. If the gardener is to gather in the best produce, he must not only sow and plant, but he must sow and plant at the right time; and if any work is to be fruitful in results, it must be done seasonably, and the time for doing a thing must not be allowed to pass by.

Utility considers the practical end, and employs the best means to reach that end. It avoids side issues, dispenses with theories, and retains its hold only on those things which can be appropriated to good uses in the economy of life.

Unpractical people burden their minds with useless and unverifiable theories, and court failure by entertaining speculations which, by their very nature, cannot be applied in practice. The man whose powers are shown in what he does, and not in mere talking and arguing, avoids metaphysical quibblings and quandaries, and applies himself to the accomplishment of some good and useful end.

That which cannot be reduced to practice should not be allowed to hamper the mind. It should be thrown aside, abandoned, and ignored. A man recently told me that if his theory should be proved to have no useful end, he should still retain his hold upon it as a beautiful theory. If a man chooses to cling to so-called "beautiful" theories which are proved to have no use in life, and no substantial basis of reality, he must not be surprised if he fail in his worldly undertakings, for he is an unpractical man.

When the powers of the mind are diverted from speculative theorizing to practical doing, whether in material or moral directions, skill, power, knowledge, and prosperity increase. A man's prosperity is measured by his usefulness to the community, and a man is useful in accordance with what he does, and not because of the theories which he entertains.

The carpenter fashions a chair; the builder erects a house; the mechanic produces a machine; and the wise man moulds a perfect character. Not the schismatics, the theorists, and the controversialists, but the workers, the makers, and the doers, are the salt of the earth.

Let a man turn away from the mirages of intellectual speculation, and begin to *do* something, and to do it with all his might, and he will thereby gain a special knowledge, wield a special power, and reach his own unique position and prosperity among his fellows.

Comprehensiveness is that quality of mind which enables a man to deal with a large number of related details, to grasp them in their entirety, along with the single principle which governs them and binds them together. It is a masterly quality, giving organizing and governing power, and is developed by systematic attention to details. The successful merchant holds in his mind, as it were, all the details of his business, and regulates them by a system adapted to his particular form of trade. The inventor has in his mind all the details of his machine, along with their relation to a central mechanical principle, and so perfects his invention. The author of a great poem or story relates all his characters and incidents to a central plot, and so produces a composite and enduring literary work. Comprehensiveness is analytic and synthetic capacity combined in the same individual. A capacious and well-ordered mind, which holds within its silent depths an army of details in their proper arrangement and true working order, is the mind that is near to genius, even if it has not already arrived. Every man cannot be a genius, nor does he need to be, but he can be gradually evolving his mental capacity by careful attention to system in his thoughts and business, and as his intellect deepens and broadens, his powers will be intensified and his prosperity accentuated.

Such, then, are the four corner Pillars in the Temple of Prosperity, and of themselves they are sufficient permanently to sustain it without the addition of the remaining four. The man who perfects himself in Energy, Economy, Integrity, and System will achieve an enduring success in the work of his life, no matter what the nature of that work may be. It is impossible for one to fail who is full of energy, who carefully economizes his time and money and virtuously husbands his vitality, who practises unswerving integrity, and who systematizes his work by first systematizing his mind.

Such a man's efforts will be rightly directed, and that, too, with concentrated power, so that they will be effective and fruitful. In addition he will reach a manliness and an independent dignity which will unconsciously command respect and success, and will strengthen weaker ones by its very presence in their midst. "Seest thou a man diligent in business; he shall stand before kings, he shall not stand before mean men," says a scripture of such a one. He will not beg, or whimper, or complain, or cynically blame others, but will be too strong and pure and upright a man to sink himself so low. And so, standing high in the nobility and integrity of his character, he will fill a high place in the world and in the estimation of men. His success will be certain and his prosperity will endure. "He will stand and not fall in the battle of life."

FIFTH PILLAR—SYMPATHY

The remaining pillars are the four central pillars in the temple of prosperity. They give it greater strength and stability, and add both to its beauty and utility. They contribute greatly to its attractiveness, for they belong to the highest moral sphere, and therefore to great beauty and nobility of character. They, indeed, make a man great, and place him among the comparatively few whose minds are rare, and that shine apart in sparkling purity and bright intelligence.

Sympathy should not be confounded with that maudlin and superficial sentiment which, like a pretty flower without root, presently perishes and leaves behind neither seed nor fruit. To fall into hysterical weeping when parting with a friend, or on hearing of some suffering abroad, is not sympathy. Neither are bursts of violent indignation against the cruelties and injustices of others any indication of a sympathetic mind. If one is cruel at home—if he badgers his wife, or beats his children, or abuses his servants, or stabs his neighbours with shafts of bitter sarcasm—what hypocrisy is in his profession of love for suffering people who are outside the immediate range of his influence! What shallow sentiment informs his bursts of indignation against the injustices and hard-heartedness in the world around him!

Says Emerson of such: "Go love thy infant; love thy wood-chopper: be good-natured and modest: have that grace; and never varnish your hard, uncharitable ambition with this incredible tenderness for black folk a thousand miles off. Thy love afar is spite at home." The test of a man is in his immediate acts, and not in his ultra sentiments; and if those acts are consistently informed with selfishness and bitterness,—if those at home hear his steps with dread, and feel a joyful relief on his departure,—how empty are his expressions of sympathy for the suffering or down-trodden! How futile his membership of a philanthropic society!

Though the well of sympathy may feed the spring of tears, that spring more often draws its supply from the dark pool of selfishness, for when selfishness is thwarted it spends itself in tears.

Sympathy is a deep, silent, inexpressible tenderness which is shown in a consistently self-forgetful, gentle character. Sympathetic people are not gushing and spasmodic, but are permanently self-restrained, firm, quiet, unassuming and gracious. Their undisturbed demeanour where the suffering of others is concerned is frequently mistaken for indifference by shallow minds, but the sympathetic and discerning eye recognizes, in their quiet strength and their swiftness to aid while others are weeping and wringing their hands, the deepest, soundest sympathy.

Lack of sympathy is shown in cynicism, ill-natured sarcasm, bitter ridicule, taunting and mockery, and anger and condemnation, as well as in that morbid and false sentiment which is a theoretical and assumed sympathy, having no basis in practice.

Lack of sympathy arises in egotism; sympathy arises in love. Egotism is involved in ignorance; love is allied to knowledge. It is common with men to imagine themselves as separate from their fellows, with separate aims and interests; and to regard themselves as right and others wrong in their respective ways. Sympathy lifts a man above this separate and self-centred life, and enables him to live in the hearts of his fellows, and to think and feel with them. He puts himself in their place, and becomes, for the time being, as they are. As Whitman, the hospital hero, expresses it: "I do not ask the wounded person how he feels; I myself become the wounded person." It is a kind of impertinence to question a suffering creature. Suffering calls for aid and tenderness, and not for curiosity; and the sympathetic man or woman feels the suffering, and ministers to its alleviation.

Nor can sympathy boast, and wherever self-praise enters in, sympathy passes out. If one speaks of his many deeds of kindness, and complains of the ill-treatment he has received in return, he has not done kindly deeds, but has yet to reach that self-forgetful modesty which is the sweetness of sympathy.

Sympathy, in its real and profound sense, is oneness with others in their strivings and sufferings, so that the man of sympathy is a composite being; he is, as it were, a number of men, and he views a thing from a number of different sides, and not from one side only, and that his own particular side. He sees with other men's eyes, hears with their ears, thinks with their minds, and feels with their hearts. He is thus able to understand men who are vastly different from himself; the meaning of their lives is revealed to him, and he is united to them in the spirit of goodwill. Said Balzac: "The poor fascinate me; their hunger is my hunger; I am with them in their homes; their privations I suffer; I feel the beggar's rags upon my back; I for the time being become the poor and despised man." It reminds us of the saying of one greater than Balzac, that a deed done for a suffering little one was done for him.

And so it is; sympathy leads us to the hearts of all men, so that we become spiritually united to them, and when they suffer we feel the pain; when they are glad we rejoice with them; when they are despised and persecuted, we spiritually descend with them into the depths, and take into our hearts their humiliation and distress; and he who has this binding, uniting spirit of sympathy, can never be cynical and condemnatory, can never pass thoughtless and cruel judgments upon his fellows, because in his tenderness of heart he is ever with them in their pain.

But to have reached this ripened sympathy, it must needs be that one has loved much, suffered much, and sounded the dark depths of sorrow. It springs from acquaintance with the profoundest experiences, so that a man has had conceit, thoughtlessness, and selfishness burnt out of his heart. No man can have true sympathy who has not been, in some measure at least, "a man of sorrows, and acquainted with grief," but the sorrow and grief must have passed, must have ripened into a fixed kindness and habitual calm.

To have suffered so much in a certain direction that the suffering is finished, and only its particular wisdom remains, enables one, wherever that suffering presents itself, to understand and deal with it by pure sympathy; and when one has been "perfected by suffering" in many directions, he becomes a centre of rest and healing for the sorrowing and broken-hearted who are afflicted with the afflictions which he has experienced and conquered. As a mother feels the anguish of her suffering child, so the man of sympathy feels the anguish of suffering men.

Such is the highest and holiest sympathy, but a sympathy much less perfect is a great power for good in human life, and a measure of it is everywhere and every day needed. While rejoicing in the fact that in every walk in life there are truly sympathetic people, one also perceives that harshness, resentment, and cruelty are all too common. These hard qualities bring their own sufferings, and there are those who fail in their business, or particular work, entirely because of the harshness of their disposition. A man who is fiery and resentful, or who is hard, cold, and calculating, with the springs of sympathy dried up within him, even though he be otherwise an able man, will, in the end, scarcely avoid disaster in his affairs. His heated folly in the one case, or cold cruelty in the other, will gradually isolate him from his fellows and from those who are immediately related to him in his particular avocation, so that the elements of prosperity will be eliminated from his life, leaving him with a lonely failure, and perhaps a hopeless despair.

Even in ordinary business transactions, sympathy is an important factor, for people will always be attracted to those who are of a kindly and genial nature, preferring to deal with them rather than with those who are hard and forbidding. In all spheres where direct personal contact plays an important part, the sympathetic man with average ability will always take precedence of the man of greater ability but who is unsympathetic.

If a man be a minister or a clergyman, a cruel laugh or an unkind sentence from him will seriously injure his reputation and influence, but particularly his influence, for even they who admire his good qualities will, through his unkindness, unconsciously have a lower regard for him in their personal esteem.

If a business man profess religion, people will expect to see the good influence of that religion on his business transactions. To profess to be a worshipper of the gentle Jesus on Sunday, and all the rest of the week be a hard, grasping worshipper of Mammon, will injure his trade, and detract considerably from his prosperity.

Sympathy is a universal spiritual language which all, even the animals, instinctively understand and appreciate, for all beings and creatures are subject to suffering, and this sameness of painful experience leads to that unity of feeling which we call sympathy.

Selfishness impels men to protect themselves at the expense of others: but sympathy impels them to protect others by the sacrifice of self; and in this sacrifice of self there is no real and ultimate loss, for while the pleasures of selfishness are small and few, the blessings of sympathy are great and manifold.

It may be asked, "How can a business man, whose object is to develop his own trade, practice self-sacrifice?" *Every man can practice self-sacrifice just where he is, and in the measure that he is capable of understanding it.* If one contends that he cannot practise a virtue because of his circumstances, he will never practise it, for were his circumstances different, he would still have the same excuse. Diligence in business is not incompatible with self-sacrifice, for devotion to duty, even though that duty be trade, is not selfishness, but may be an unselfish devotion. I know a business man who, when a competitor who had tried to "cut him out" in business, cut himself out and failed set that same competitor up in business again. Truly a beautiful act of self-sacrifice; and the man that did it is, to-day, one of the most successful and prosperous of business men.

The most prosperous commercial traveller I have ever known, was overflowing with exuberant kindness and geniality. He was as innocent of all "tricks of trade" as a new-born infant, but his great heart and manly uprightness won for him fast friends wherever he went. Men were glad to see him come into their office or shop or mill, and not alone for the good and bracing influence he brought with him, but also because his business was sound and trust-worthy. This man was successful through sheer sympathy, but sympathy so pure and free from policy, that he himself would probably have denied that his success could be attributed to it. Sympathy can never hinder success. It is selfishness that blights and destroys. As goodwill increases, man's prosperity will increase. All interests are mutual, and stand or fall together, and as sympathy expands the heart, it extends the circle of influence, making blessings, both spiritual and material, more greatly to abound.

Fourfold are the qualities which make up the great virtue of sympathy, namely:—

1. Kindness.
2. Generosity.
3. Gentleness.
4. Insight.

Kindness, when fully developed, is not a passing impulse but a permanent quality. An intermittent and unreliable impulse is not kindness, though it often goes under that name. There is no kindness in praise if it be followed by abuse. The love which seems to prompt the spontaneous kiss will be of little account if it be associated with a spontaneous spite. The gift which seemed so gracious will lose its value should the giver afterwards wish its value in return. To have one's feelings aroused to do a kind action toward another by some external stimulus pleasing to oneself, and shortly afterwards to be swayed to the other extreme toward the same person by an external event unpleasing to oneself, should be regarded as weakness of character; and it is also a selfish condition, for to do a kind action only toward one who pleases us, and when he pleases us, is to be thinking of oneself only. A true kindness is unchangeable, and needs no external stimulus to force it into action. It is a well from which thirsty souls can always drink, and it never runs dry. Kindness, when it is a strong virtue, is bestowed not only on those who please us, but also upon those whose actions go contrary to our wish and will, and it is a constant and never-varying glow of genial warmth.

There are some actions of which men repent; such are all unkind actions. There are other actions of which men do not repent, and such are all kind actions. The day comes when men are sorry for the cruel things they said and did; but the day of gladness is always with them for the kindly things they have said and done.

Unkindness mars a man's character, it mars his face as time goes on, and it mars that perfection of success which he would otherwise reach.

Kindness beautifies the character, it beautifies the face with the growth of the years, and it enables a man to reach that perfection of success to which his intellectual abilities entitle him. A man's prosperity is mellowed and enriched by the kindliness of his disposition.

Generosity goes with a large-hearted kindness. If kindness be the gentle sister, Generosity is the strong brother. A free, open-handed, and magnanimous character is always attractive and influential. Stinginess and meanness always repel; they are dark, cramped, narrow, and cold. Kindness and generosity always attract; they are sunny, genial, open, and warm. That which repels makes for isolation and failure; that which attracts makes for union and success.

Giving is as important a duty as getting; and he who gets all he can, and refuses to give, will at last be unable to get; for it is as much a spiritual law that we cannot get unless we give, as that we cannot give unless we get.

Giving has always been taught as a great and important duty by all the religious teachers. This is because giving is one of the highways of personal growth and progress. It is a means by which we attain to greater and greater unselfishness, and by which we prevent the falling back into selfishness. It implies that we recognize our spiritual and social kinship with our fellowmen, and are willing to part with a portion of that we have earned or possess, for the good and well-being of others. The greedy man who, the more he gets, hungers for more still, and refuses to loosen his grasp upon his accumulating store, like a wild beast with its prey, is retrogressing; he is shutting himself out from all the higher and joy-giving qualities, and from free and life-giving communion with unselfish, happy human hearts. Dickens's Scrooge in "A Christmas Carol" represents the condition of such a man with graphic vividness and dramatic force.

Our public men in England to-day (probably also in America) are nearly all (I think I might say all, for I have not yet met an exception) great givers. These men,—Lord Mayors, Mayors, Magistrates, Town and City Councillors, and all men filling responsible public offices,—being men who have been singularly successful in the management of their own private affairs, are considered the best men for the management of public affairs, and numerous noble institutions throughout the land are perpetual witnesses to the munificence of their gifts. Nor have I been able to find any substantial truth in the accusation, so often hurled against such men by the envious and unsuccessful, that their riches are made unjustly. Without being perfect men, they are an honourable class of manly, vigorous, generous, and successful men who have acquired riches and honour by sheer industry, ability, and uprightness.

Let a man beware of greed, of meanness, of envy, of jealousy, of suspicion, for these things, if harboured, will rob him of all that is best in life, aye, even all that is best in material things, as well as all that is best in character and happiness. Let him be liberal of heart and generous of hand, magnanimous and trusting, not only giving cheerfully and often of his substance, but allowing his friends and fellow-men freedom of thought and action—let him be thus, and honour, plenty, and prosperity will come knocking at his door for admittance as his friends and guests.

Gentleness is akin to divinity. Perhaps no quality is so far removed from all that is coarse, brutal, and selfish as gentleness, so that when one is becoming gentle, he is becoming divine. It can only be acquired after much experience and through great self-discipline. It only becomes established in a man's heart when he has controlled and brought into subjection his animal passions. Its external signs are a low-pitched, clear voice, a distinct, firm, but quiet enunciation, and freedom from excitement, vehemence, or resentment in peculiarly aggravating circumstances.

If there is one quality which, above all others, should distinguish the religious man, it is the quality of gentleness, for it is the hall-mark of spiritual culture. The rudely aggressive man is an affront to cultivated minds and unselfish hearts. Our word *gentleman* has not altogether departed from its original meaning. It is still applied to one who is modest and self-restrained, and is considerate for the feelings and welfare of others. A gentle man—one whose good behaviour is prompted by thoughtfulness and kindliness—is always loved, whatever may be his origin. Quarrelsome people make a display—in their bickerings and recriminations—of their ignorance and lack of culture. The man who has perfected himself in gentleness never quarrels. He never returns the hard word; he leaves it alone, or meets it with a gentle word which is far more powerful than wrath. Gentleness is wedded to wisdom, and the wise man has overcome all anger in himself, and so understands how to overcome it in others. The gentle man is saved from most of the disturbances and turmoils with which uncontrolled men afflict themselves. While they are wearing themselves out with wasteful and needless strain, he is quiet and composed, and such quietness and composure are strong to win in the battle of life.

Insight is the gift of sympathy. The sympathetic mind is the profoundly perceiving mind. We understand by experience, and not by argument. Before we can know a thing or being, our life must touch its or his life. Argument analyzes the outer skin, but sympathy reaches to the heart. The cynic sees the hat and coat, and thinks he sees the man. The sympathetic seer sees the man, and is not concerned with the hat and coat. In all kinds of hatred there is a separation by which each misjudges the other. In all kinds of love there is a mystic union by which each knows the other. Sympathy, being the purest form of love, sees to the heart of men and things. Shakespeare is the greatest poet because he has the largest heart. No other figure in all literature has shown such a profound knowledge of the human heart, and of nature, both animate and inanimate. The *personal* Shakespeare is not to be found in his works; he is merged, by sympathy, into his characters. The wise man and the philosopher; the madman and the fool; the drunkard and the harlot—these he, for the time being, became; he stood where they stood; he entered into their particular experiences, and knew them better than they knew themselves. Shakespeare has no partiality, no prejudice; his sympathy embraces all, from the lowest to the highest.

Prejudice is the great barrier to sympathy and knowledge. It is impossible to understand those against whom one harbours a prejudice. We only see men and things as they are when we divest our minds of partial judgments. We become seers as we become sympathisers. Sympathy has knowledge for her companion.

Inseparable are the feeling heart and the seeing eye. The man of pity is the man of prophecy. He whose heart beats in tune with all hearts, to him the contents of all hearts are revealed. Nor are past and future any longer insoluble mysteries to the man of sympathy. His moral insight apprehends the perfect round of human life.

Sympathetic insight lifts a man into the consciousness of freedom, gladness, and power. His spirit inhales joy as his lungs inhale air. There are no longer any fears of his fellow-men—of competition, hard times, enemies, and the like. These groveling illusions have disappeared, and there has opened up before his awakened vision a realm of greatness and grandeur.

SIXTH PILLAR—SINCERITY

Human society is held together by its sincerity. A universal falseness would beget a universal mistrust which would bring about a universal separation, if not destruction. Life is made sane, wholesome, and happy by our deep-rooted belief in one another. If we did not trust men, we could not transact business with them, could not even associate with them. Shakespeare's Timon shows us the wretched condition of a man who, through his own folly, has lost all faith in the sincerity of human nature. He cuts himself off from the company of all men, and finally commits suicide. Emerson has something to the effect that if the trust system were withdrawn from commerce, society would fall to pieces; that system being an indication of the universal confidence men place in each other. Business, commonly supposed by the shortsighted and foolish to be all fraud and deception, is based on a great trust—a trust that men will meet and fulfil their obligations. Payment is not asked until the goods are delivered; and the fact of the continuance of this system for ages, proves that most men do pay their debts, and have no wish to avoid such payment.

Back of all its shortcomings, human society rests on a strong basis of truth. Its fundamental note is sincerity. Its great leaders are all men of superlative sincerity; and their names and achievements are not allowed to perish—a proof that the virtue of sincerity is admired by all the race.

It is easy for the insincere to imagine that everybody is like themselves, and to speak of the "rottenness of society,"—as though a rotten thing could endure age after age,—for is not everything yellow to the jaundiced eye? People who cannot see anything good in the constitution of human society, should overhaul themselves. Their trouble is near home. They call good, evil. They have dwelt cynically and peevishly on evil till they cannot see good, and everything and everybody appear evil. "Society is rotten from top to bottom," I heard a man say recently; and he asked me if I did not think so. I replied that I should be sorry to think so; that while society had many blemishes, it was sound at the core, and contained within itself the seeds of perfection.

Society, indeed, is so sound that the man who is playing a part for the accomplishment of entirely selfish ends cannot long prosper, and cannot fill any place as an influence. He is soon unmasked and disgraced; and the fact that such a man can, for even a brief period, batten on human credulity, speaks well for the trustfulness of men, if it reveals their lack of wisdom.

An accomplished actor on the stage is admired, but the designing actor on the stage of life brings himself down to ignominy and contempt. In striving to appear what he is not, he becomes as one having no individuality, no character, and he is deprived of all influence, all power, all success.

A man of profound sincerity is a great moral force, and there is no force—not even the highest intellectual force—that can compare with it. Men are powerful in influence according to the soundness and perfection of their sincerity. Morality and sincerity are so closely bound up together, that where sincerity is lacking, morality, as a power, is lacking also, for insincerity undermines all the other virtues, so that they crumble away and become of no account. Even a little insincerity robs a character of all its nobility, and makes it common and contemptible. Falseness is so despicable a vice that it cannot co-exist with character and influence, and no man of moral weight can afford to dally with pretty compliments, or play the fool with trivial and conventional deceptions. Let a man resort to deception, howsoever light, in order to please, and he is no longer strong and admirable, but is become a shallow weakling whose mind has no deep well of power from which men can draw, and no satisfying richness to stir in them a worshipful regard.

Even they who are for the moment flattered with the painted lie, or pleased with the deftly woven deception, will not escape those permanent undercurrents of influence which move the heart and shape the judgment to fixed and final issues, while these designed delusions create but momentary ripples on the surface of the mind.

"I am very pleased with his attentions," said a woman of an acquaintance, "but I would not marry him." "Why not?" she was asked. "He doesn't ring true," was the reply.

Ring true! a term full of meaning. It has reference to the coin which, when tested by its ring, emits a sound which reveals the sterling metal throughout, without the admixture of any base material. *It comes up to the standard,* and will pass anywhere and everywhere for its full value.

So with men. Their words and actions emit their own peculiar influence. There is in them an inaudible sound which all other men inwardly hear and instinctively detect. They know the false ring from the true, yet know not how they know. As the outer ear can make the most delicate distinctions in sounds, so the inner ear can make equally subtle distinctions between souls. None are ultimately deceived but the deceiver. It is the blind folly of the insincere that, while flattering themselves upon their successful simulations, they are deceiving none but themselves. Their actions are laid bare before all hearts. There is at the heart of man a tribunal whose judgments do not miscarry. If the senses faultlessly detect, shall not the soul infallibly know! This inner infallibility is shown in the collective judgment of the race. This judgment is perfect; so perfect that in literature, art, science, invention, religion—in every department of knowledge—it divides the good from the bad, the worthy from the unworthy, the true from the false, zealously guarding and preserving the former, and allowing the latter to perish. The works, words, and deeds of great men are the heirlooms of the race, and the race is not careless of their value. A thousand men write a book, and one only is a work of original genius, yet the race singles out that one, elevates and preserves it, while it consigns the nine hundred and ninety-nine copyists to oblivion. Ten thousand men utter a sentence under a similar circumstance, and one only is a sentence of divine wisdom, yet the race singles out that saying for the guidance of posterity, while the other sentences are heard no more. It is true that the race slays its prophets, but even that slaying becomes a test which reveals the true ring, and men detect its trueness. The slain one has come up to the standard, and the deed of his slaying is preserved as furnishing infallible proof of his greatness.

As the counterfeit coin is detected, and cast back into the melting pot, while the sterling coin circulates among all men, and is valued for its worth, so the counterfeit word, deed, or character is perceived, and is left to fall back into the nothingness from which it emerged, a thing unreal, powerless, dead.

Spurious things have no value, whether they be bric-a-brac or men. We are ashamed of imitations that try to pass for the genuine article. Falseness is cheap. The masquerader becomes a byword: he is less than a man; he is a shadow, a spook, a mere mask. Trueness is valuable. The sound-hearted man becomes an exemplar: he is more than a man; he is a reality, a force, a moulding principle. By falseness all is lost—even individuality dissolves—for falseness is nonentity, nothingness. By trueness, everything is gained, for trueness is fixed, permanent, real.

It is all-important that we be real; that we harbour no wish to appear other than what we are; that we simulate no virtue, assume no excellency, adopt no disguise. The hypocrite thinks he can hoodwink the world and the eternal law of the world. There is but one person that he hoodwinks, and that is himself, and for that the law of the world inflicts its righteous penalty. There is an old theory that the excessively wicked are annihilated. I think to be a pretender is to come as near to annihilation as a man can get, for there is a sense in which the man is gone, and in his place there is but a mirage of shams. The hell of annihilation which so many dread, he has descended into; and to think that such a man can prosper is to think that shadows can do the work of entities, and displace real men.

If any man thinks he can build up a successful career on pretences and appearances, let him pause before sinking into the abyss of shadows; for in insincerity there is no solid ground, no substance, no reality; there is nothing on which anything can stand, and no material with which to build; but there are loneliness, poverty, shame, confusion, fears, suspicions, weepings, groanings, and lamentations; for if there is one hell lower, darker, fouler than all others, it is the hell of insincerity.

Four beautiful traits adorn the mind of the sincere man: they are:—

1. Simplicity.
2. Attractiveness.
3. Penetration.
4. Power.

Simplicity is naturalness. It is simple being, without fake or foreign adornment. Why are all things in nature so beautiful? Because they are natural. We see them as they are, not as they might wish to appear, for in sooth they have no wish to appear otherwise. There is no hypocrisy in the world of nature outside of human nature. The flower which is so beautiful in all eyes would lose its beauty if it could pretend. Looking upon nature we look upon reality, and its beauty and perfection gladden and amaze us. We cannot find anywhere a flaw, and are conscious of our incapacity to improve upon anything, even to the most insignificant. Everything has its own peculiar perfection, and shines in the beauty of unconscious simplicity.

One of the modern social cries is "Back to nature." It is generally understood to mean a cottage in the country, and a piece of land to cultivate. It will be of little use to go into the country if we take our shams with us; and any veneer which may cling to us can as well be washed off just where we are. It is good that they who feel burdened with the conventions of society should fly to the country, and court the quiet of nature, but it will fail if it be anything but a means to that inward redemption which will restore us to the simple and the true.

But though humanity has wandered from the natural simplicity of the animal world, it is moving toward a higher, a divine simplicity. Men of great genius are such because of their spontaneous simplicity. They do not feign; they *are*. Lesser minds study style and effect. They wish to cut a striking figure on the stage of the world, and by that unholy wish they are doomed to mediocrity. Said a man to me recently, "I would give twenty years of my life to be able to write an immortal hymn." With such an ambition a man cannot write a hymn. He wants to pose. He is thinking of himself, of his own glory. Before a man can write an immortal hymn, or create any immortal work, he must give, not twenty years of his life to ambition, but his whole life to humanity. He must forget that he can do anything great, and must sing, paint, write, out of ten thousand bitter experiences, ten thousand failures, ten thousand conquests, ten thousand joys. He must know Gethsemane; he must work with blood and tears.

Retaining his intellect and moral powers, and returning to simplicity, a man becomes great. He forfeits nothing real. Only the shams are cast aside, revealing the standard gold of character. Where there is sincerity there will always be simplicity—a simplicity of the kind that we see in nature, the beautiful simplicity of truth.

Attractiveness is the direct outcome of simplicity. This is seen in the attractiveness of all natural objects, to which we have referred, but in human nature it is manifested as *personal influence*. Of recent years certain pseudo-mystics have been advertising to sell the secret of "personal magnetism" for so many dollars, by which they purport to show vain people how they can make themselves attractive to others by certain "occult" means, as though attractiveness can be bought and sold, and put on and off like powder and paint. Nor are people who are anxious to be thought attractive, likely to become so, for their vanity is a barrier to it. The very desire to be thought attractive is, in itself, a deception, and it leads to the practice of numerous deceptions. It infers, too, that such people are conscious of lacking the genuine attractions and graces of character, and are on the lookout for a substitute; but there is no substitute for beauty of mind and strength of character. Attractiveness, like genius, is lost by being coveted, and possessed by those who are too solid and sincere of character to desire it. There is nothing in human nature—not talent, nor intellect, nor affection, nor beauty of feature,—that can compare in attractive power to that soundness of mind and wholeness of heart which we call sincerity. There is a perennial charm about a sincere man or woman, and they draw about themselves the best specimens of human nature. There can be no personal charm apart from sincerity. Infatuation there may be, and is, but this is a kind of disease, and is vastly different from the indissoluble bond by which sincere people are attached. Infatuation ends in painful disillusion, but as there is nothing hidden between sincere souls, and they stand upon that solid ground of reality, there is no illusion to be dispelled.

Leaders among men attract by the power of their sincerity, and the measure of their sincerity is the measure of their attractive influence. Howsoever great may be a man's intellect, he can never be a permanent leader and guide of men unless he be sincere. For a time he may sail jauntily upon the stream of popularity, and believe himself secure, but it is only that he may shortly fall the lower in popular odium. He cannot long deceive the people with his painted front. They will soon look behind, and find of what spurious stuff he is made. He is like a woman with a painted face. She thinks she is admired for her complexion, but all know it is paint, and despise her for it. She has one admirer—herself, and the hell of limitation to which all the insincere commit themselves is the hell of self-admiration.

Sincere people do not think of themselves—of their talent, their genius, their virtue, their beauty,—and because they are so unconscious of themselves they attract all, and win their confidence, affection, and esteem.

Penetration belongs to the sincere. All shams are unveiled in their presence. All simulators are transparent to the searching eye of the sincere man. With one clear glance he sees through all their flimsy pretences. Tricksters wither under his strong gaze, and want to get away from it. He who has rid his heart of all falseness, and entertains only that which is true, has gained the power to distinguish the false from the true in others. He is not deceived who is not self-deceived.

As men looking round on the objects of nature, infallibly distinguish them—such as a snake, a bird, a horse, a tree, a rose, and so on—so the sincere man distinguishes between the variety of characters. He perceives in a movement, a look, a word, an act, the nature of the man, and acts accordingly. He is on his guard without being suspicious. He is prepared for the pretender without being mistrustful. He acts from positive knowledge, and not from negative suspicion. Men are open to him, and he reads their contents. His penetrative judgment pierces to the centre of actions, and enables him to deal with them as they are. His direct and unequivocal conduct strengthens in others the good, and shames the bad, and he is a staff of strength to those who have not yet attained to his soundness of heart and head.

Power goes with penetration. An understanding of the nature of actions is accompanied with the power to meet and deal with all actions in the right and best way. Knowledge is always power, but knowledge of the nature of actions is superlative power, and he who possesses it, becomes a Presence to all hearts, and modifies their actions for good. Long after his bodily presence has passed away, he is still a moulding force in the world, and is a spiritual reality working subtly in the minds of men, and shaping them toward sublimer ends. At first his power is local and limited, but the circle of righteousness which he has set moving continues to extend and extend till it embraces the whole world, and all men are influenced by it.

The sincere man stamps his character upon all that he does, and also upon all people with whom he comes in contact. He speaks a word in season and some one is impressed; the influence is communicated to another, and another, and presently some despairing soul ten thousand miles away hears it and is restored. Such a power is prosperity in itself, and its worth is not to be valued in coin. Money cannot purchase the priceless jewels of character, but labour in right-doing can, and he who makes himself sincere, who acquires a robust soundness throughout his entire being, will become a man of singular success and rare power.

Such is the strong Pillar of Sincerity. Its supporting power is so great that, once it is completely erected, the Temple of Prosperity is secure. Its walls will not crumble; its rafters will not decay; its roof will not fall in. It will stand while the man lives, and when he has passed away it will continue to afford a shelter and a home for others through many generations.

SEVENTH PILLAR—IMPARTIALITY

To get rid of prejudice is a great achievement. Prejudice piles obstacles in a man's way—obstacles to health, success, happiness, and prosperity, so that he is continually running up against imaginary enemies who, when prejudice is removed, are seen to be friends. Life is, indeed, a sort of obstacle race to the man of prejudice, a race wherein the obstacles cannot be negotiated and the goal is not reached; whereas to the impartial man life is a day's walk in a pleasant country, with refreshment and rest at the end of the day.

To acquire impartiality, a man must remove that innate egotism which prevents him from seeing anything from any point of view other than his own. A great task, truly, but a noble one, and one that can be well begun now, even if it cannot be finished. Truth can "remove mountains," and prejudice is a range of mental mountains beyond which the partisan does not see, and of which he does not believe there is any beyond. These mountains removed, however, there opens to the view the unending vista of mental variety blended in one glorious picture of light and shade, of colour and tone, gladdening beholding eyes.

By clinging to stubborn prejudice what joys are missed, what friends are sacrificed, what happiness is destroyed, and what prospects are blighted! And yet freedom from prejudice is a rare thing. There are few men who are not prejudiced partisans upon the subjects which are of interest to them. One rarely meets a man that will dispassionately discuss his subject from both sides, considering all the facts and weighing all the evidence so as to arrive at truth on the matter. Each partisan has his own case to make out. He is not searching for truth, for he is already convinced that his own conclusion is the truth, and that all else is error; but he is defending his own case, and striving for victory. Neither does he attempt to prove that he has the truth by a calm array of facts and evidence, but defends his position with more or less heat and agitation.

Prejudice causes a man to form a conclusion, sometimes without any basis of fact or knowledge, and then to refuse to consider anything which does not support that conclusion; and in this way prejudice is a complete barrier to the attainment of knowledge. It binds a man down to darkness and ignorance, and prevents the development of his mind in the highest and noblest directions. More than this, it also shuts him out from communion with the best minds, and confines him to the dark and solitary cell of his own egotism.

Prejudice is a shutting up of the mind against the entrance of new light, against the perception of more beauty, against the hearing of diviner music. The partisan clings to his little, fleeting, flimsy opinion, and thinks it the greatest thing in the world. He is so in love with his own conclusion (which is only a form of self-love) that he thinks all men ought to agree with him, and he regards men as more or less stupid who do not see as he sees, while he praises the good judgment of those who are one with him in his view. Such a man cannot have knowledge, cannot have truth. He is confined to the sphere of opinion (to his own self-created illusions) which is outside the realm of reality. He moves in a kind of self-infatuation which prevents him from seeing the commonest facts of life, while his own theories—usually more or less groundless—assume, in his mind, overpowering proportions. He fondly imagines that there is but one side to everything, and that side his own. There are at least two sides to everything, and he it is who finds the truth in a matter who carefully examines both sides with all freedom from excitement, and without any desire for the predominance of one side over another.

In its divisions and controversies the world at large is like two lawyers defending a case. The counsel for the prosecution presents all the facts which prove his side, while counsel for the defence presents all the facts which support his contention, and each belittles or ignores or tries to reason away the facts of the other. The judge in the case, however, is like the impartial thinker among men; having listened to all the evidence on both sides, he compares and sifts it so as to form an impartial summing up in the cause of justice.

Not that this universal partiality is a bad thing, for as in all other extremes, nature here reduces the oppositions of conflicting parties to a perfect balance; moreover, it is a factor in evolution; it stimulates men to think who have not yet developed the power to rouse up vigorous thought at will, and it is a phase through which all men have to pass. But it is only a byway,—and a tangled, confused, and painful one—toward the great highway of Truth. It is the arc of which impartiality is the perfect round. The partisan sees a portion of the truth, and thinks it the whole, but the impartial thinker sees the whole truth which includes all sides. It is necessary that we first see truth in sections, as it were, until, having gathered up all the parts, we may piece them together and form the perfect circle; and the forming of such circle is the attainment of impartiality.

The impartial man examines, weighs, and considers, with freedom from prejudice and from likes and dislikes. His one wish is to discover the truth. He abolishes preconceived opinions, and lets facts and evidence speak for themselves. He has no case to make out for himself, for he knows that truth is unalterable, that his opinions can make no difference to it, and that it can be investigated and discovered. He thereby escapes a vast amount of friction and nervous wear and tear to which the feverish partisan is subject; and in addition, he looks directly upon the face of Reality, and so becomes tranquil and peaceful.

So rare is freedom from prejudice that wherever the impartial thinker may be, he is sure, sooner or later, to occupy a very high position in the estimation of the world, and in the guidance of its destiny. Not necessarily an office in worldly affairs, for that is improbable, but an exalted position in the sphere of influence. There may be such a one now, and he may be a carpenter, a weaver, a clerk;

he may be in poverty or in the home of a millionaire; he may be short or tall, or of any complexion, but whatever and wherever he may be, he has, though unknown, already begun to move the world, and will one day be universally recognized as a new force and creative centre in evolution.

There was one such some nineteen hundred years ago. He was only a poor, unlettered carpenter; he was regarded as a madman by his own relatives, and he came to an ignominious end in the eyes of his countrymen; but he sowed the seeds of an influence which has altered the whole world.

There was another such in India some twenty-five centuries ago. He was accomplished, highly educated, and was the son of a capitalist and landed proprietor—a petty king. He became a penniless, homeless mendicant, and to-day one-third of the human race worship at his shrine, and are restrained and elevated by his influence.

"Beware when the great God lets loose a thinker on this planet," says Emerson; and a man is not a thinker who is bound by prejudice; he is merely the strenuous upholder of an opinion. Every idea must pass through the medium of his particular prejudice, and receive its colour, so that dispassionate thinking and impartial judgment are rendered impossible. Such a man sees everything only in its relation, or imagined relation, to his opinion, whereas the thinker sees things as they are. The man who has so purified his mind of prejudice and of all the imperfections of egotism as to be able to look directly upon reality, has reached the acme of power; he holds in his hands, as it were, the vastest influence, and he will wield this power whether he knows it or not; it will be inseparable from his life, and will go from him as perfume from the flower. It will be in his words, his deeds, in his bodily postures and the motions of his mind, even in his silence and the stillness of his frame. Wherever he goes, even though he should fly to the desert, he will not escape this lofty destiny, for a great thinker is the centre of the world; by him all men are held in their orbits, and all thought gravitates toward him.

The true thinker lives above and beyond the seething whirlpool of passion in which mankind is engulfed. He is not swayed by personal considerations, for he has grasped the import of impersonal principles, and being thus a non-combatant in the clashing warfare of egotistic desires, he can, from the vantage ground of an impartial, but not indifferent watcher, see both sides equally, and grasp the cause and meaning of the fray.

Not only the Great Teachers, but the greatest figures in literature, are those who are free from prejudice, who, like true mirrors, reflect things impartially. Such are Whitman, Shakespeare, Balzac, Emerson, Homer. These minds are not local, but universal. Their attitude is cosmic and not personal. They contain within themselves all things and beings, all worlds and laws. They are the gods who guide the race, and who will bring it at last out of its fever of passion into their own serene land.

The true thinker is the greatest of men, and his destiny is the most exalted. The altogether impartial mind has reached the divine, and it basks in the full daylight of Reality.

The four great elements of impartiality are:—

1. Justice.
2. Patience.
3. Calmness.
4. Wisdom.

Justice is the giving and receiving of equal values. What is called "striking a hard bargain" is a kind of theft. It means that the purchaser gives value for only a portion of his purchase, the remainder being appropriated as clear gain. The seller also encourages it by closing the bargain.

The just man does not try to gain an advantage; he considers the true values of things, and moulds his transactions in accordance therewith. He does not let "what will pay" come before "what is right," for he knows that the right pays best in the end. He does not seek his own benefit to the disadvantage of another, for he knows that a just action benefits, equally and fully, both parties to a transaction. If "one man's loss is another man's gain," it is only that the balance may be adjusted later on. Unjust gains cannot lead to prosperity, but are sure to bring failure. A just man could no more take from another an unjust gain by what is called a "smart transaction" than he could take it by picking his pocket. He would regard the one as dishonest as the other.

The bargaining spirit in business is not the true spirit of commerce. It is the selfish and thieving spirit which wants to get something for nothing. The upright man purges his business of all bargaining, and builds it on the more dignified basis of justice. He supplies "a good article" at its right price, and does not alter. He does not soil his hands with any business which is tainted with fraud. His goods are genuine and they are properly priced.

Customers who try to "beat down" a tradesman in their purchases, are degrading themselves. Their practice assumes one or both of two things; namely, that either the tradesman is dishonest and is overcharging (a low, suspicious attitude of mind), or that they are eager to cajole him out of his profit (an equally base attitude) and so benefit by his loss. The practice of "beating down" is altogether a dishonest one, and the people who pursue it most assiduously are those who complain most of being "imposed on"; and this is not surprising, seeing that they themselves are all the time trying to impose upon others.

On the other hand, the tradesman who is anxious to get all he can out of his customers, irrespective of justice and the right values of things, is a kind of robber, and is slowly poisoning his success, for his deeds will assuredly come home to him in the form of financial ruin.

Said a man of fifty to me the other day, "I have just discovered that all my life I have been paying fifty per cent more for everything than I ought to." A just man cannot feel that he has ever paid too much for anything, for he does not close with any transaction which he considers unjust; but if a man is eager to get everything at half-price, then he will be always meanly and miserably mourning that he is paying double for everything. The just man is glad to pay full value for everything, whether in giving or receiving, and his mind is untroubled and his days are full of peace.

Let a man above all avoid meanness, and strive to be ever more and more perfectly just, for if not just, he can be neither honest, nor generous, nor manly, but is a kind of disguised thief trying to get all he can, and give back as little as possible. Let him eschew all bargaining, and teach bargainers a better way by conducting his business with that exalted dignity which commands a large and meritorious success.

Patience is the brightest jewel in the character of the impartial man. Not a particular patience with a particular thing—like a girl with her needlework, or a boy building his toy engine—but an unswerving considerateness, a sweetness of disposition at all times and under the most trying circumstances, an unchangeable gentle strength which no trial can mar and no persecution can break. A rare possession, it is true, and one not to be expected for a long time yet from the bulk of mankind, but a virtue that can be reached by degrees; and even a partial patience will work wonders in a man's life and affairs, as a confirmed impatience will work devastation. The irascible man is courting speedy disaster, for who will care to deal with a man who is continually going off like gunpowder when some small spark of complaint or criticism falls upon him! Even his friends will one by one desert him, for who would court the company of a man who rudely assaults him with an impatient and fiery tongue over every little difference or misunderstanding!

A man must begin wisely to control himself, and to learn the beautiful lessons of patience, if he is to be highly prosperous, if he is to be a man of use and power. He must learn to think of others, to act for their good, and not alone for himself; to be considerate, forbearing, and long-suffering. He must study how to have a heart at peace with men who differ from him on those things which he regards as most vital. He must avoid quarrelling as he would avoid drinking a deadly poison. Discords from without will be continually overtaking him, but he must fortify himself against them; he must study how to bring harmonies out of them by the exercise of patience.

Strife is common: it pains the heart and distorts the mind. Patience is rare: it enriches the heart and beautifies the mind. Every cat can spit and fume; it requires no effort, but only a looseness of behaviour. It takes a *man* to keep his moorings through all events, and to be painstaking and patient with the shortcomings of humanity. But patience wins. As soft water wears away the hardest rock, so patience overcomes all opposition. It gains the hearts of men. It conquers and controls.

Calmness accompanies patience. It is a great and glorious quality. It is the peaceful haven of emancipated souls after their long wanderings on the tempest-riven ocean of passion. It marks the man who has suffered much, endured much, experienced much, and has finally conquered.

A man cannot be impartial who is not calm. Excitement, prejudice, and partiality spring from disturbed passions. When personal feeling is thwarted, it rises and seethes like a stream of water that is dammed. The calm man avoids this disturbance by directing his feeling from the personal to the impersonal channel. He thinks and feels for others as well as for himself. He sets the same value on other men's opinions as on his own. If he regards his own work as important, he sees also that the work of other men is equally important. He does not contend for the merit of his own against the demerit of that of others. He is not overthrown, like Humpty-dumpty, with a sense of self-importance. He has put aside egotism for truth, and he perceives the right relations of things. He has conquered irritability, and has come to see that there is nothing in itself that should cause irritation. As well be irritable with a pansy because it is not a rose, as with a man because he does not see as you see. Minds differ, and the calm man recognizes the differences as facts in human nature.

The calm, impartial man is not only the happiest man, he also has all his powers at his command. He is sure, deliberate, executive, and swiftly and easily accomplishes in silence what the irritable man slowly and laboriously toils through with much noise. His mind is purified, poised, concentrated, and is ready at any moment to be directed upon a given work with unerring power. In the calm mind all passions are tranquillized, all conflicts are harmonized, all contradictions are reconciled, and there is radiant gladness and perpetual peace. As Emerson puts it, "Calmness is joy fixed and habitual."

One should not confound indifference with calmness, for it is at the opposite extreme. Indifference is lifelessness, while calmness is glowing life and full-orbed power. The calm man has partly or entirely conquered self, and having successfully battled with the selfishness within, he knows how to meet and overcome it successfully in others. In any moral contest the calm man is always the victor. So long as he remains calm, defeat is impossible.

Self-control is better than riches, and calmness is a perpetual benediction.

Wisdom abides with the impartial man. Her counsels guide him; her wings shield him; she leads him along pleasant ways to happy destinations.

Wisdom is many-sided. The wise man adapts himself to others. He acts for their good, yet never violates the moral virtues or the principles of right conduct. The foolish man cannot adapt himself to others; he acts for himself only, and continually violates the moral virtues and the principles of right conduct. There is a degree of wisdom in every act of impartiality, and once a man has touched and experienced the impartial zone, he can recover it again and again, until he finally establishes himself in it.

Every thought, word, or act of wisdom tells on the world at large, for it is fraught with greatness. Wisdom is a well of knowledge and a spring of power. It is profound and comprehensive, and is so exact and all-inclusive as to embrace the smallest details. In its spacious greatness it does not overlook the small. The wise mind is like the world: it contains all things in their proper place and order, and is not burdened thereby. Like the world, also, it is free, and unconscious of any restrictions; yet it is never loose, never erring, never sinful and repentant. Wisdom is the steady, grown-up being of whom folly was the crying infant. It has outgrown the weakness and dependence, the errors and punishments of infantile ignorance, and is erect, poised, strong, and serene.

The understanding mind needs no external support. It stands of itself on the firm ground of knowledge; not book knowledge, but ripened experience. It has passed through all minds, and therefore knows them. It has traveled with all hearts, and knows their journeyings in joy and sorrow.

When wisdom touches a man, he is lifted up and transfigured. He becomes a new being, with new aims and powers, and he inhabits a new universe in which to accomplish a new and glorious destiny.

Such is the Pillar of Impartiality which adds its massive strength and incomparable grace to support and beautify the Temple of Prosperity.

EIGHTH PILLAR—SELF-RELIANCE

Every young man ought to read Emerson's essay on "Self-Reliance." It is the manliest, most virile essay that was ever penned. It is calculated to cure alike those two mental maladies common to youth; namely, self-depreciation and self-conceit. It is almost as sure to reveal to the prig the smallness and emptiness of his vanity, as it is to show the bashful man the weakness and ineffectuality of his diffidence. It is a new revelation of manly dignity: as much a revelation as any that was vouchsafed to ancient seer and prophet, and perhaps a more practical, eminently suited to this mechanic age, coming as it does from a modern prophet of a new type and cradled in a new race; and its chief merit is its powerfully tonic quality.

Let not self-reliance be confounded with self-conceit, for as high and excellent as is the one, just so low and worthless is the other. There cannot be anything mean in self-reliance, while in self-conceit there cannot be anything great.

The man that never says "no" when questioned on subjects of which he is entirely ignorant, to avoid, as he imagines, being thought ignorant, but confidently puts forward guesses and assumptions as knowledge, will be known for his ignorance and ill-esteemed for his added conceit. An honest confession of ignorance will command respect where a conceited assumption of knowledge will elicit contempt.

The timid, apologetic man who seems almost afraid to live, who fears that he will do something not in the approved way, and will subject himself to ridicule, is not a full man. He must needs imitate others, and have no independent action. He needs that self-reliance which will compel him to fall back on his own initiative, and so become a new example instead of the slavish follower of an old one. As for ridicule—he who is hurt by it is no man. The shafts of mockery and sarcasm cannot pierce the strong armour of the self-reliant man, they cannot reach the invincible citadel of his honest heart to sting or wound it. The sharp arrows of irony may rain upon him, but he laughs as they are deflected by the strong breastplate of his confidence and fall harmless about him.

"Trust thyself," says Emerson; "every heart vibrates to that iron string." Throughout the ages men have so far leaned, and do still lean, upon external makeshifts instead of standing upon their own native simplicity and original dignity. The few who have had the courage so to stand, have been singled out and elevated as heroes; and he is indeed the true hero who has the hardihood to let his nature speak for itself, who has that strong metal which enables him to stand upon his own intrinsic worth.

It is true that the candidate for such heroism must endure the test of strength. He must not be shamed from his ground by the bugbears of an imitative conventionalism. He must not fear for his reputation or position, or for his standing in the Church or his prestige in local society. He must learn to act and live as independently of these considerations as he does of the current fashions in the antipodes. Yet when he has endured this test, and slander and odium have failed to move or afflict him, he has become a man indeed, one that society will have to reckon with, and finally accept on his own terms.

Sooner or later all men turn for guidance to the self-reliant man, and while the best minds do not make a prop of him, they respect and value his work and worth, and recognize his place among the gods that have gone before.

It must not be thought an indication of self-reliance to scorn to learn. Such an attitude is born of a stubborn superciliousness which has the elements of weakness, and is prophetic of a fall, rather than the elements of strength and the promise of high achievement which are characteristic of self-reliance. Pride and vanity must not be associated with self-reliance. Those degrade, while this ennobles. Pride rests upon incidentals and appurtenances—on money, clothing, property, prestige, position—and these lost, all is lost. Self-reliance rests upon essentials and principles—on worth, probity, purity, sincerity, character, truth—and whatever may be lost is of little account, for these are never lost. Pride tries to hide its ignorance by ostentation and assumption, and is unwilling to be thought a learner in any direction. It stands, during its little fleeting day, on ignorance and appearance, and the higher it is lifted up today, the lower will it be cast down to-morrow. Self-reliance has nothing to hide, and is willing to learn; and while there can be no humility where pride is, self-reliance and humility are compatible, nay more, they are complementary, and the sublimest form of self-reliance is only found associated with the profoundest humility. "Extremes meet," says Emerson, "and there is no better example than the haughtiness of humility. No aristocrat, no prince born to the purple, can begin to compare with the self-respect of the saint. Why is he so lowly, but that he knows that he can well afford it, resting on the largeness of God in him?" It was Buddha who, in this particular, said: "Those who, either now or after I am dead, shall be a lamp unto themselves, relying upon themselves only and not relying upon any external help, but holding fast to the truth as their lamp, and seeking their salvation in the truth alone, shall not look for assistance to any one besides themselves, it is they, among my disciples, who shall reach the very topmost height! But they must be willing to learn." In this saying, the repeated insistence on the necessity for relying upon oneself alone, coupled with the final exhortation to be eager to learn, is the wisest utterance on self-reliance that I know. In it, the Great Teacher comprehends that perfect balance between self-trust and humility which the man of truth must acquire.

"Self-trust is the essence of heroism." All great men are self-reliant, and we should use them as teachers and exemplars, and not as props and perambulators. A great man comes who leans upon no one, but stands alone in the solitary dignity of truth, and straightway the world begins to lean upon him, begins to make him an excuse for spiritual indolence and a destructive self-abasement. Better than cradling our vices in the strength of the great would it be newly to light our virtues at their luminous lamp. If we rely upon the light of another, darkness will overtake us, but if we rely upon our own light we have but to keep it burning. We may both draw light from another and communicate it, but to think it sufficient while our own lamp is rusting in neglect, is shortly to find ourselves abandoned in darkness. Our own inner light is the light which never fails us.

What is the "inner light" of the Quakers but another name for self-reliance? We should stand upon what we are, not upon what another is. "But I am so small and poor," you say: well, stand upon that smallness, and presently it will become great. A babe must needs suckle and cling, but not so a man. Henceforth he goes upon his own limbs. Men pray to God to put into their hands that which they are framed to reach out for; to put into their mouths the food for which they should strenu-ously labour. But men will outgrow this spiritual infancy. The time will come when men will no more pay a priest to pray for them and preach to them.

Man's chief trouble is a mistrust of himself, so that the self-trusting man becomes a rare and singular spectacle. If a man look upon himself as a "worm," what can come out of him but an ineffectual wriggling! Truly, "He that humbleth himself shall be exalted" but not he that degradeth himself. A man should see himself as he is, and if there is any unworthiness in him, he should get rid of it, and retain and rely upon that which is of worth. A man is only debased when he debases himself; he is exalted when he lives an exalted life.

Why should a man, with ceaseless iterations, draw attention to his fallen nature? There is a false humility which takes a sort of pride in vice. If one has fallen, it is that he may rise and be the wiser for it. If a man falls into a ditch, he does not lie there and call upon every passer-by to mark his fallen state; he gets up and goes on his way with greater care. So if one has fallen into the ditch of vice, let him rise and be cleansed, and go on his way rejoicing.

There is not a sphere in life wherein a man's influence and prosperity will not be considerably increased by even a measure of self-reliance, and to the teacher—whether secular or religious—to organizers, managers, overseers, and all in positions of control and command, it is an indispensable quality.

The four grand qualities of self-reliance are:—

1. Decision.
2. Steadfastness.
3. Dignity.
4. Independence.

Decision makes a man strong. The waverer is the weakling. A man who is to play a speaking part, howsoever small, in the drama of life must be decisive and know what he is about. Whatever he doubts, he must not doubt his power to act. He must know his part in life, and put all his energy into it. He must have some solid ground of knowledge from which to work, and stand securely on that. It may be only the price and quality of stock, but he must know his work thoroughly, and know that he knows it. He must be ready at any time to answer for himself when his duty is impugned. He should be so well grounded upon his particular practice as not to be afflicted with hesitation on any point or in any emergency. It is a true saying that "the man that hesitates is lost." No one believes in him who does not believe in himself, who doubts, halts, and wavers, and cannot extricate himself from the tangled threads of two courses. Who would deal with a tradesman who did not know the price of his own goods, or was not sure where to find them? A man must know his business. If he does not know his own, who shall instruct him? He must be able to give a good report of the truth that is in him, must have that decisive touch which skill and knowledge only can impart.

Certainty is a great element in self-reliance. To have weight, a man must have some truth to impart, and all skill is a communication of truth. He must "speak with authority, and not as the scribes." He must master something, and know that he has mastered it, so as to deal with it lucidly and understandingly, in the way of a master, and not to remain always an apprentice.

Indecision is a disintegrating factor. A minute's faltering may turn back the current of success. Men who are afraid to decide quickly for fear of making a mistake, nearly always make a mistake when they do act. The quickest, in thought and action, are less liable to blunder, and it is better to act with decision and make a mistake than to act with indecision and make a mistake, for in the former case there is but error, but in the latter, weakness is added to error.

A man should be decided always, both where he knows and where he does not know. He should be as ready to say no as yes, as quick to acknowledge his ignorance as to impart his knowledge. If he stands upon fact, and acts from the simple truth, he will find no room for halting between two opinions.

Make up your mind quickly, and act decisively. Better still, have a mind that is already made up, and then decision will be instinctive and spontaneous.

Steadfastness arises in the mind that is quick to decide. It is, indeed, a final decision upon the best course of conduct and the best path in life. It is the vow of the soul to stand firmly by its principles whatever betide. It is neither necessary nor unnecessary that there be any written or spoken vow, for unswerving loyalty to a fixed principle is the spirit of all vows.

The man without fixed principles will not accomplish much. Expediency is a quagmire and a thorny waste, in which a man is continually sticking in the shifting mud of his own moral looseness, and is pricked and scratched with the thorns of his self-created disappointments.

One must have some solid ground on which to stand among one's fellows. We cannot stand on the bog of concession. Shiftiness is a vice of weakness, and the vices of weakness do more to undermine character and influence than the vices of strength. The man that is vicious through excess of animal strength takes a shorter cut to truth—when his mind is made up—than he who is vicious through lack of virility, and whose chief vice consists in not having a mind of his own upon anything. When one understands that power is adaptable to both good and bad ends, it will not surprise him that the drunkards and harlots should reach the kingdom of heaven before the diplomatic religionists. They are at least thorough in the course which they have adopted, vile though it be, and thoroughness is strength. It only needs that strength to be turned from bad to good, and lo! the loathed sinner has become the lofty saint!

A man should have a firm, fixed, determined mind. He should decide upon those principles which are best to stand by in all issues, and which will most safely guide him through the maze of conflicting opinions, and inspire him with unflinching courage in the battle of life. Having adopted his principles, they should be more to him than gain or happiness, more even than life itself, and if he never deserts them, he will find that they will never desert him; they will defend him from all enemies, deliver him safely from all dangers, light up his pathway through all darkness and difficulties. They will be to him a light in darkness, a resting-place from sorrow, and a refuge from the conflicts of the world.

Dignity clothes, as with a majestic garment, the steadfast mind. He who is as unyielding as a bar of steel when he is expected to compromise with evil, and as supple as a willow wand in adapting himself to that which is good, carries about with him a dignity that calms and uplifts others by its presence.

The unsteady mind, the mind that is not anchored to any fixed principles, that is stubborn where its own desires are threatened, and yielding where its own moral welfare is at stake, has no gravity, no balance, no calm composure.

The man of dignity cannot be down-trodden and enslaved, because he has ceased to tread upon and enslave himself. He at once disarms, with a look, a word, a wise and suggestive silence, any attempt to demean him. His mere presence is a wholesome reproof to the flippant and the unseemly, while it is a rock of strength to the lover of the good.

But the chief reason why the dignified man commands respect is, not only that he is supremely self-respecting, but that he graciously treats all others with a due esteem. Pride loves itself, and treats those beneath it with supercilious contempt, for love of self and contempt for others are always found together in equal degrees, so that the greater the self-love, the greater the arrogance. True dignity arises, not from self-love, but from self-sacrifice—that is, from unbiased adherence to a fixed central principle. The dignity of the judge arises from the fact that in the performance of his duty he sets aside all personal considerations and stands solely upon the law; his little personality, impermanent and fleeting, becomes nothing, while the law, enduring and majestic, becomes all. Should a judge, in deciding a case, forget the law and fall into personal feeling and prejudice, his dignity would be gone. So with the man of stately purity of character, he stands upon the divine law, and not upon personal feeling; for immediately a man gives way to passion he has sacrificed dignity, and takes his place as one of the multitude of the unwise and uncontrolled.

Every man will have composure and dignity in the measure that he acts from a fixed principle. It only needs that the principle be right, and therefore unassailable. So long as a man abides by such a principle and does not waver or descend into the personal element, attacking passions, prejudices, and interests, howsoever powerful, will be weak and ineffectual before the unconquerable strength of an incorruptible principle, and will at last yield their combined and unseemly confusion to his single and majestic right.

Independence is the birthright of the strong and well-controlled man. All men love and strive for liberty. All men aspire to some sort of freedom.

A man should labour for himself or for the community. Unless he is a cripple, a chronic invalid, or is mentally irresponsible, he should be ashamed to depend upon others for all he has, giving nothing in return. If one imagines that such a condition is freedom, let him know that it is one of the lowest forms of slavery. The time will come when, to be a drone in the human hive, even (as matters are now) a respectable drone and not a poor tramp, will be a public disgrace and will be no longer respectable.

Independence, freedom, glorious liberty, come through labour and not from idleness, and the self-reliant man is too strong, too honourable, too upright to depend upon others, like a sucking babe, for his support. He earns, with hand or brain, the right to live as becomes a man and a citizen; and this he does whether born rich or poor, for riches are no excuse for idleness; rather are they an opportunity to labour, with the rare facilities which they afford, for the good of the community.

Only he who is self-supporting is free, self-reliant, independent.

Thus is the nature of the Eight Pillars explained. On what foundation they rest, the manner of their building, their ingredients, the fourfold nature of the material of which each is composed, what positions they occupy, and how they support the Temple,—all is made clear, so that he who knew not how to build, may now build; and he who knew but imperfectly, may know more perfectly; and he who knew perfectly may rejoice in this systematization and simplification of the moral order in Prosperity. Let us now consider the Temple itself, that we may know the might of its Pillars, the strength of its walls, the endurance of its roof, and the architectural beauty and perfection of the whole.

THE TEMPLE OF PROSPERITY

The reader who has followed the course of this book with a view to obtaining information on the details of money-making, business transactions, profit and loss in various undertakings, prices, markets, agreements, contracts, and other matters connected with the achievement of prosperity, will have noted an entire absence of any instruction on these matters of detail. The reason for this is fourfold, namely:—

First—Details cannot stand alone, but are powerless to build up anything unless intelligently related to principles.

Second—Details are infinite and are ceaselessly changing, while principles are few and are eternal and unchangeable.

Third—Principles are the coherent factors in all details, regulating and harmonizing them, so that to have right principles is to be right in all the subsidiary details.

Fourth—A teacher of truth in any direction *must* adhere rigidly to principles, and must not allow himself to be drawn away from them into the ever-changing maze of private particulars and personal details, because such particulars and details have only a local right and are only necessary for certain individuals, while principles are universally right and are necessary for all men.

He who grasps the principles of this book so as to be able intelligently to practice them, will be able to reach the heart of this fourfold reason. The details of a man's affairs are important, but they are *his* details, or the details of his particular branch of industry, and all outside that branch are not concerned with them; but moral principles are the same for all men, they are applicable to all conditions and govern all particulars.

The man who works from fixed principles does not need to harass himself over the complications of numerous details. He will grasp, as it were, the entire details in one single thought, and will see them through and through, illumined by the light of the principle to which they stand related, and this without friction, and with freedom from anxiety and strain.

Until principles are grasped, details are regarded, and dealt with, as primary matters, and so viewed they lead to innumerable complications and confused issues. In the light of principles, they are seen to be secondary facts, and so seen, all difficulties connected with them are at once overcome and annulled by a reference to principles.

He who is involved in numerous details without the regulating and synthesizing element of principles is like one lost in a forest, with no direct path along which to walk amid the mass of objects. He is swallowed up by the details, while the man of principles contains all details within himself: he stands outside them, as it were, and grasps them in their entirety, while the other man can only see the few that are nearest to him at the time.

All things are contained in principles. They are the laws of things, and all things observe their own law. It is an error to view things apart from their nature. Details are the letter of which principles are the spirit. It is as true in art, science, literature, commerce, as in religion that "the letter killeth, the spirit giveth life." The body of a man, with its wonderful combinations of parts, is important, but only in its relation to the spirit. The spirit being withdrawn, the body is useless and is put away. The body of a business, with all its complicated details, is important, but only in its relation to the vivifying principles by which it is controlled. These withdrawn, the business will perish.

To have the body of prosperity—its material presentation—we must first have the spirit of prosperity, and the spirit of prosperity is the quick spirit of moral virtue. Moral blindness prevails. Men see money, property, pleasure, leisure, etc., and, mistaking them for prosperity, strive to get them for their own enjoyment; but, when obtained, they find no enjoyment in them.

Prosperity is at first a spirit, an attitude of mind, a moral power, a life, which manifests outwardly in the form of plenty, happiness, joy. Just as a man cannot become a genius by writing poems, essays, plays, but must develop and acquire the soul of genius,—when the writing will follow as effect to cause,—so one cannot become prosperous by hoarding up money, and by gaining property and possessions, but must develop and acquire the soul of virtue,—when the material accessories will follow as effect to cause,—for the spirit of virtue is the spirit of joy, and it contains within itself all abundance, all satisfaction, all fulness of life.

There is no joy in money, there is no joy in property, there is no joy in material accumulations or in any material thing of itself. These things are dead and lifeless. The spirit of joy must be in the man or it is nowhere. He must have within him the capacity for happiness. He must have the wisdom to know how to use these things, and not merely hoard them. He must possess them, and not be possessed by them. They must be dependent upon him, and not he upon them. They must follow him, and not he forever be running after them; and they will inevitably follow him, if he have the moral elements within to which they are related.

Nothing is absent from the kingdom of heaven; it contains all good, true, and necessary things, and "the kingdom of God is within you." I know rich people who are supremely happy, because they are generous, magnanimous, pure, and joyful; but I also know rich people who are very miserable, and these are they who looked to money and possessions for their happiness, and have not developed the spirit of good and of joy within themselves.

How can it be said of a wretched man that he is "prosperous," even if his income be ten thousand pounds a year? There must be fitness, and harmony, and satisfaction in a true prosperity. When a rich man is happy, it is that he brought the spirit of happiness to his riches, and not that the riches brought happiness to him. He is a full man with full material advantages and responsibilities, while the miserable rich man is an empty man looking to riches for that fulness of life which can only be evolved from within.

Thus prosperity resolves itself into a moral capacity, and in the wisdom to use rightfully and enjoy lawfully the material things which are inseparable from our earthly life. If one would be free without, let him first be free within, for if he be bound in spirit by weakness, selfishness, or vice, how can the possession of money liberate him! Will it not rather become, in his hands, a ready instrument by which further to enslave himself?

The visible effects of prosperity, then, must not be considered alone, but in their relation to the mental and moral cause. There is a hidden foundation to every building; the fact that it continues to stand is proof of that. There is a hidden foundation to every form of established success; its permanence proves that it is so. Prosperity stands on the foundation of *character*, and there is not, in all the wide universe, any other foundation. True wealth is weal, welfare, well-being, soundness, wholeness, and happiness. The wretched rich are not truly wealthy. They are merely encumbered with money, luxury, and leisure, as instruments of self-torture. By their possessions they are self-cursed.

The moral man is ever blessed, ever happy, and his life viewed as a whole is always a success. To this there is no exception, for whatever failures he may have in detail, the finished work of his life will be sound, whole, complete; and through all he will have a quiet conscience, an honourable name, and all manifold blessings which are inseparable from richness of character, and without this moral richness, financial riches will not avail or satisfy.

Let us briefly recapitulate, and again view the Eight Pillars in their strength and splendour.

1. *Energy:* Rousing oneself up to strenuous and unremitting exertion in the accomplishment of one's task.
2. *Economy:* Concentration of power; the conservation of both capital and character, the latter being mental capital, and therefore of the utmost importance.
3. *Integrity:* Unswerving honesty; keeping inviolate all promises, agreements, and contracts, apart from all considerations of loss or gain.
4. *System:* Making all details subservient to order, and thereby relieving the memory and the mind of superfluous work and strain by reducing many to one.
5. *Sympathy:* Magnanimity, generosity, gentleness, and tenderness; being open-handed, free, and kind.
6. *Sincerity:* Being sound and whole, robust and true; and therefore not being one person in public and another in private, and not assuming good actions openly while doing bad actions in secret.
7. *Impartiality:* Justice; not striving for self, but weighing both sides, and acting in accordance with equity.
8. *Self-Reliance:* Looking to oneself only for strength and support by standing on principles which are fixed and invincible, and not relying upon outward things which at any moment may be snatched away.

How can any life be other than successful which is built on these Eight Pillars? Their strength is such that no physical or intellectual strength can compare with it; and to have built all the eight perfectly would render a man invincible. It will be found, however, that men are often strong in one or several of these qualities, and weak in others; and it is this weak element that invites the ignorant to attribute, for instance, a man's failure in business to his honesty. It is impossible for honesty to produce failure. The cause of failure must be looked for in some other direction,—in the lack, and not the possession, of some good and necessary quality. Moreover, such attribution of failure to honesty is a slur on the integrity of commerce, and a false indictment of those men, numerous enough, who are honourably engaged in trade. A man may be strong in Energy, Economy, and System, but comparatively weak in the other five. Such a man will just fail of complete success by lacking one of the four corner pillars, namely, Integrity. His Temple will give way at that weak corner, for the first four Pillars *must* be well built before the Temple of Prosperity can stand secure. They are the first qualities to be acquired in a man's moral evolution, and without them the second four cannot be possessed. Again, if a man be strong in the first three, and lack the fourth, the absence of order will invite confusion and disaster into his affairs; and so on with any partial combination of these qualities, especially of the first four; for the second four are of so lofty a character that at present men can but possess them, with rare exceptions, in a more or less imperfect form. The man of the world, then, who wishes to secure an abiding success in any branch of commerce, or in one of the many lines of industry in which men are commonly engaged, *must* build into his character, by practice, the first four Moral Pillars. By these fixed principles he must regulate his thoughts, his conduct, and his affairs; consulting them in every difficulty, making every detail serve them, and above all, *never deserting them under any circumstance to gain some personal advantage or to save some personal trouble;* for so to desert them is to make oneself vulnerable to the disintegrating elements of evil, and to become assailable to accusations from others. He who so abides by these four principles will achieve a full measure of success in his own particular work, whatever it may be; his Temple of Prosperity will be well built and well supported, and it will stand secure. The perfect practice of these four principles is within the scope of all men who are willing to study them with that object in view, for they are so simple and plain that a child could grasp their meaning, and their perfection in conduct does not call for an unusual degree of self-sacrifice, though it demands some self-denial and personal discipline without which there can be no success in this world of action. The second four Pillars, however, are principles of a more profound nature, are more difficult to understand and practice, and call for the highest degree of self-sacrifice and self-effacement. Few, at present, can reach that detachment from the personal element which their perfect practice demands; but the few who accomplish this in any marked degree will vastly enlarge their powers and enrich their life, and will adorn their Temple of Prosperity with a singular and attractive beauty which will gladden and elevate all beholders long after they have passed away.

But those who are beginning to build their Temple of Prosperity in accordance with the teaching of this book, must bear in mind that a building requires time to erect, and that it must be patiently raised up, brick upon brick and stone upon stone, and the Pillars must be firmly fixed and cemented, and labour and care will be needed to make the whole complete. And the building of this inner mental Temple is none the less real and substantial because invisible and noiseless, for in the raising up of this Temple, as of Solomon's—which was "seven years in building"—it can be said, "there was neither hammer nor axe nor any tool of iron heard in the house, while it was in the building."

Even so, O reader! construct thy character, raise up the house of thy life, build up thy Temple of Prosperity. Be not as the foolish who rise and fall upon the uncertain flux of selfish desires; but be at peace in thy labour, crown thy career with completeness, and so be numbered among the wise who, without uncertainty, build upon a fixed and secure foundation—even upon the Principles of Truth which endure forever.

LIGHT ON LIFE'S DIFFICULTIES

(1912)

I, Truth, am thy Redeemer, come to Me;
*   Lay doom thy sin and pain and wild unrest;*
And I will calm thy spirit's stormy sea,
*   Pouring the oil of peace upon thy breast:*
Friendless and lone—lo, I abide with thee.

Defeated and deserted, cast away,
*   What refuge hast thou? Whither canst thou fly?*
Upon my changeless breast thy burdens lay;
*   I am thy certain refuge, even I:*
All things are passing; I alone can stay.

Lo I, the Great Forsaken, am the Friend
*   Of the forsaken; I, whom men despise,*
The weak, the helpless, and despised defend;
*   I gladden aching hearts and weeping eyes;*
Rest thou in Me, I am thy sorrow's end.

Lovers and friends and wealth, pleasures and fame—
*   These fail and change, and pass into decay;*
But My Love does not change; and in thy blame
*   I blame thee not, nor turn my face away:*
In My calm bosom hide thy sin and shame.

FOREWORD

When a man enters a dark room he is not sure of his movements; he cannot see the objects around, or properly locate them, and is liable to hurt himself by coming into sudden contact with them; but let a light be introduced, and immediately all confusion disappears, every object is seen, and there is no more danger of being hurt.

To the majority life is such a dark room, and their frequent hurts—their disappointments, perplexities, sorrows, and pains—are caused by sudden contact with principles which they do not see, and are therefore not prepared to deal with; but when the light of wisdom is introduced into the darkened understanding, confusion vanishes, difficulties are dissolved, all things are seen in their true place and proportion, and henceforth the man walks, open-eyed and unhurt, in the clear light of a wise comprehension.

—JAMES ALLEN
Bryngoleu,
Ilfracombe, England

CONTENTS

THE LIGHT THAT LEADS
TO PERFECT PEACE

This book is intended to be a strong and kindly companion, as well as a source of spiritual renewal and inspiration to those who aim at a life well-lived and made strong and serene. It will help its readers to transform themselves into the ideal character thy would wish to be, and to make their life here that blessed thing which the majority only hope for in some future life.

Our life is what we make it by our own thoughts and deeds. It is our own state and attitude of mind which determine whether we are happy or unhappy, strong or weak, sinful or holy, foolish or wise. If one is unhappy, that state of mind belongs to himself, and is originated within himself; it is a state which responds to certain outward happenings, but its *cause* lies within, and not in those outward occurrences. If one is weak in will, he has brought himself to, and remains in, that condition by the course of thought and action which he has chosen and is still choosing. If one is sinful, it is because he has committed, and continues to commit, sinful acts. If he is foolish, it is because he himself does foolish things.

A man has no character, no soul, no life apart from his thoughts and deeds. What they are, that he is. As they are modified, so does he change. He is endowed with will, and can modify his character. As the carpenter changes the block of wood into a beautiful piece of furniture, so can the erring and sin-stricken man change himself into a wise and truth-loving being.

Each man is responsible for the thoughts which he thinks and the acts which he does, for his state of mind, and the life which he lives. No power, no event, no circumstance can compel a man to evil and unhappiness. He himself is his own compeller. He thinks and acts by his own volition. No being, however wise and great—not even the Supreme—can make him good and happy. He himself must choose the good, and thereby find the happy.

And because of this—*that when a man wishes and wills* he can find the Good and the True, and enjoy its bliss and peace—there is eternal gladness in the Courts of Truth, and holy joy amongst the Perfect Ones.

The Gates of Heaven are forever open, and no one is prevented from entering by any will or power but his own; but no one can enter the Kingdom of Heaven so long as he is enamored of, and chooses, the seductions of hell, so long as he resigns himself to sin and sorrow.

There is a larger, higher, nobler, diviner life than that of sinning and suffering, which is so common—in which, indeed, nearly all are immersed—a life of victory over sin, and triumph over evil; a life wise and happy, benign and tranquil, virtuous and peaceful. This life can be found and lived now, and he who lives it is steadfast in the midst of change; restful among the restless; peaceful, though surrounded by strife. Should death confront him, he is calm; though assailed by persecution, he knows no bitterness, and his heart is compassionate and filled with rejoicing. In this supremely beautiful life there is no evil, sin and sorrow are ended, and aching hearts and weeping eyes are no more.

This life of triumph is not for those who are satisfied with any lower conditions; it is for those who thirst of it and are willing to achieve it; who are as eager for righteousness as the miser is for gold. It is always at hand, and is offered to all, and blessed are they who accept and embrace it; they will enter the World of Truth; they will find the Perfect Peace.

LIGHT ON FACTS AND HYPOTHESES

When freedom of thought and freedom of expression abound, there is much controversy and much confusion, yet it is from such controversial confusion that the simple facts of life emerge, attracting us with their eternal uniformity and harmony, and appealing forcibly to us with their invisible simplicity and truth.

We are living in such an age of freedom and mental conflict. Never were religious sects so numerous. Schools—philosophical, occult, and otherwise—abound, and each is eager for the perpetuation and dominance of its own explanation of the universe. The world is in a condition of mental ferment. Contradiction has reached the point of confusion, so that the earnest seeker for Truth can find no solid rock of refuge in the opposing systems which are presented to him, and is thereby thrown back upon himself, upon those incontrovertible facts of his own being which are ever with him,—which are, indeed, himself, his life.

Controversy is ranged around hypotheses, not around facts. Fact is fixed and final; hypothesis is variable and vanishing. In his present stage of development, man is not alive to the beautiful simplicity of facts, nor to the power of satisfaction which is inherent in them; he does not perceive the intrinsic loveliness of truth, but must add something to it; hence, when a fact is named, the question almost invariably arises, "How can you explain the fact?" and then follows a hypothesis which leads to another hypothesis, and so on and on until the fact is altogether lost sight of amid a mass of contradictory suppositions. Thus arise the sects and controversial schools.

The clear perception of one fact will lead to the perception of other facts, but a supposition, while appearing to elucidate a fact, does in reality cover it up. We cannot realize the stately splendor of Truth while playing with the gaudy and attractive toys of pretty hypotheses. Truth is not an opinion, nor can any opinion enlarge or adorn it. Fact and supposition are eternally separate, and the cleverest intellectual jugglery—while it may entertain and deceive even the elect—cannot in the slightest degree alter a fact or affect the nature of things-as-they-are. Because of this, the true teacher abandons the devious path of hypothesis, and deals only with the simple facts of life, fixing the attention of men upon these, instead of increasing confusion and intensifying wordy warfare by foisting another assumption upon a world already lost and bewildered in a maze of hypotheses.

The facts of life are ever before us, and can be understood and known if we but abandon our egotism and the blinding delusions which that egotism creates. Man need not go beyond his own being to find wisdom, and the facts of that being afford a sufficient basis on which to erect a temple of knowledge of such beauty and dimensions that it shall at once emancipate and glorify.

Man is; and as he thinks, so he is. A perception and realization of these two facts alone—of man's being and thinking—lead into a vast avenue of knowledge which cannot stop short of the highest wisdom and perfection. One of the reasons why men do not become wise is that they occupy themselves with interminable speculations about a *soul* separate from themselves—that is, from their own mind—and so blind themselves to their actual nature and being. The supposition of a separate soul veils the eyes of man so that he does not see himself, does not know his mentality, is unaware of the nature of his thoughts without which he would have no conscious life.

Man's life is actual; his thoughts are actual; his life is actual. To occupy ourselves with the investigation of things that are, is the way of wisdom. Man considered as above, beyond, and separate from mind and thought, is speculative and not actual, and to occupy ourselves with the study of things that are not, is the way of folly.

Man cannot be separated from his mind; his life cannot be separated from his thoughts. Mind, thought, and life are as inseparable as light, radiance, and color, and are no more in need of another factor to elucidate them than are light, radiance, and color. The facts are all-sufficient, and contain within themselves the groundwork of all knowledge concerning them.

Man as mind is subject to change. He is not something "made" and finally complete, but has within him the capacity for progress. By the universal law of evolution he has *become* what he is, and is becoming that which he will be. His being is modified by every thought he thinks. Every experience affects his character. Every effort he makes changes his mentality. Herein is the secret of man's degradation, and also of his power and salvation if he but utilize this law of change in the right choice of thought.

To live is to think and act, and to think and act is to change. While man is ignorant of the nature of thought, he continues to change for better or worse; but, being acquainted with the nature of thought, he intelligently accelerates and directs the process of change, and only for the better.

What the sum total of a man's thoughts are, that he is. From the sameness of thought with man there is not the slightest fractional deviation. There is a change of result with the addition and subtraction of thought, but the mathematical law is an invariable quantity.

Seeing that man is mind, that mind is composed of thought, and that thought is subject to change, it follows the deliberately to change the thought is to change the man.

All religions work upon the heart, the thought of man, with the object of directing it into purer and higher channels; and success in this direction, whether partial or complete, is called "salvation"—that is, deliverance from one kind of thought, one condition of mind, by the substitution of another thought, another condition. It is true that the dispensers of religion to-day do not know this because of the hypothetical veil which intervenes between the fact and their consciousness; but they *do* it without knowing it, and the Great Teachers who founded the various religions, built upon this fact, as their precepts plainly show. The chief things upon which these Teachers lay such stress, and so constantly reiterate—such as the purification of the heart, the thinking of right thoughts, and the doing of good deeds—what are they but calls to a higher, nobler mode of thought-energizing forces urging men to effort in the choosing of thoughts which shall lift them into realms of greater power, greater good, greater bliss?

Aspiration, meditation, devotion—these are the chief means which men in all ages employ to reach up to higher modes of thought, wide airs of peace, vaster realms of knowledge, for "as he thinketh in his heart, so is he"; he is saved from himself—from his own folly and suffering—by creating within new habits of thoughts, by becoming a new thinker, a new man.

Should a man by a supreme effort succeed in thinking as Jesus thought—not by imitation, but by a sudden realization of his indwelling power—he would be as Jesus. In the Buddhistic records there is an instance of a man, not the possessor of great piety or wisdom, who asked Buddha how one might attain the highest wisdom and enlightenment, and Buddha replied, "by ceasing from all desire"; and it is recorded that the man let go all personal desires and at once realized the highest wisdom and enlightenment. One of the sayings of Buddha runs, "The only miracle with which a wise man concerns himself is the transformation of a sinner into a saint," and Emerson referred to this transforming power of change of thought when he said:—

"It is as easy to be great as to be small,"

which is closely akin to that other great and oft-repeated but little understood saying:—

"Be ye therefore perfect, even as your Father which is in Heaven is perfect."

And, after all, what is the fundamental difference between a great man and a small one? It is one of thought, of mental attitude. True, it is one of knowledge, but then, knowledge cannot be separated from thought; and every substitution of a better for a worse thought is a transforming agency which marks an important advance in knowledge. Throughout the whole range of human life, from the lowest savage to the highest type of man, thought determines character, condition, knowledge.

The mass of humanity moves slowly along the evolutionary path urged by the blind impulse of its dominant thoughts as they are stimulated and called forth by external things; but the true thinker, the sage, travels swiftly and intelligently along a chosen path of his own. The multitudes, unenlightened concerning their spiritual nature, are the slaves of thought, but the sage is the master of thought. They follow blindly; he chooses intelligently. They obey the impulse of the moment, thinking of their immediate pleasure and happiness; he commands and subdues impulse, resting upon that which is permanently right. They, obeying blind impulse, violate the law of righteousness; he, conquering impulse, obeys the law of righteous. The sage stands face to face with the facts of life. He knows the nature of thought. He understands and obeys the law of his being.

But the sorrow-burdened victim of blind impulse can open his mental eyes and see the true nature of things when he wishes to do so. The sage—intelligent, radiant, calm—and the fool—confused, darkened, disturbed—are one in essence, and are divided only by the nature of their thoughts; when the fool turns away from and abandons his foolish thoughts and chooses and adopts wise thoughts, lo! he becomes a sage.

Socrates saw the essential oneness of virtue and knowledge, and so every sage sees. Learning may aid and accompany wisdom, but it does not lead to it. Only the choosing of wise thoughts, and necessarily, the doing of wise deeds, leads to wisdom. A man may be learned in the schools, but foolish in the school of life. Not the committing of words to memory, but the establishing oneself in purer thoughts, nobler thinking, leads to the peace-giving revelations of true knowledge.

Folly and wisdom, ignorance and enlightenment, are not merely the result of thought, they are thought itself. Both cause and effect—effort and result—are contained in thought.

All that we are is the result of what we have thought.
It is founded on our thoughts; it is made up of our thoughts.

Man is not a being possessing a soul, another self. He himself is soul. He himself is the thinker and doer, actor and knower. His composite mentality is himself. His spiritual nature is rounded by his sphere of thought. He it is that desires and sorrows, enjoys and suffers, loves and hates. The mind is not the instrument of a metaphysical, superhuman soul. Mind is soul; mind is being; mind is men.

Man can find himself. He can see himself as he is. When he is prepared to turn from the illusory and self-created world of hypothesis in which he wanders, and to stand face to face with actuality, then will be known himself as he is; moreover, he can picture himself as he would wish to be and can create within him the new thinker, the new man; for every moment is the time of choice—and every hour is destiny.

LIGHT ON THE LAW OF CAUSE
AND EFFECT IN HUMAN LIFE

How frequently people associate the word "law" with hardness and cruelty! It seems to embody, for them, nothing but an inflexible tyranny. This arises partly from their inability to perceive principles apart from persons, and partly from the idea that the office of law is solely to punish. Viewed from such an attitude of mind, the term *law* is hazily regarded as some sort of indefinite personality whose business it is to hunt transgressors and crush them with overwhelming punishments.

Now while law punishes, its primary office is to *protect*. Even the laws which man makes, are framed by him to protect himself from his own baser passions. The law of our country is instituted for the protection of life and property, and it only comes into operation as a punishing factor when it is violated. Offenders against it probably think of it as cruel, and doubtless regard it with terror, but to them that obey it, it is an abiding protector and friend, and can hold for them no terror.

So with the Divine Law which is the stay of the Universe, the heart and life of the Cosmos—it is that which protects and upholds, and it is no less protective in its penalties than in its peaceful blessings; it is, indeed, an eternal protection which is never for one moment withheld, and it shields all beings against themselves by bringing all violations of itself, whether ignorant or willful, through pain to nothingness.

Law cannot be partial. It is an unvarying mode of action, disobeying which, we are hurt; obeying, we are made happy. Neither protestation nor supplication can alter it, for if it could be altered or annulled the universe would collapse and chaos would prevail.

It is not less kind that we should suffer the penalty of our wrong-doing than that we should enjoy the blessedness of our right-doing. If we could escape the effects of our ignorance and sin, all security would be gone, and there would be no refuge, for we could then be equally doubtful of the result of our wisdom and goodness. Such a scheme would be one of caprice and cruelty, whereas law is a method of justice and kindness.

Indeed, the supreme law is the principle of eternal kindness, faultless in working, and infinite in application. It is none other than that.

Eternal Love, forever full,
Forever flowing free.

of which the Christian sings; and the "Boundless Compassion" of Buddhistic precepts and poetry. The law which punishes us is the law which preserves us. When in their ignorance men would destroy themselves, its everlasting arms are thrown about them in loving, albeit sometimes painful, protection. Every pain we suffer brings us nearer to the knowledge of the Divine Wisdom. Every blessing we enjoy speaks to us of the perfection of the Great Law, and of the fulness of bliss that shall be man's when he has come to his heritage of Divine Knowledge. We progress by learning, and we learn, up to a certain point, by suffering. When the heart is mellowed by love, the law of love is perceived in all its wonderful kindness; when wisdom is acquired, peace is assured.

We cannot alter the law of things, which is of sublime perfection, but we can alter ourselves so as to comprehend more and more of that perfection, and make its grandeur ours. To wish to bring down the perfect to the imperfect is the height of folly, but to strive to bring the imperfect up to the perfect is the height of wisdom.

Seers of the Cosmos do not mourn over the scheme of things. They see the universe as a perfect whole, and not as an imperfect jumble of parts. The Great Teachers are men of abiding joy and heavenly peace.

The blind captive of unholy desire may cry:

Ah! Love; could you and I with him conspire
To grasp this sorry scheme of things entire.
Would we not shatter it to bits, and then
Remould it nearer to the heart's desire?

This is the wish of the voluptuary, the wish to enjoy unlawful pleasures to any extent, and not reap any painful consequences. It is such men who regard the universe as a "sorry scheme of things." They want the universe to bend to their will and desire; want lawlessness, not law; but the wise man bends his will and subjects his desires to the Divine Order, and he sees the universe as the glorious perfection of an infinitude of parts.

Buddha always referred to the moral law of the universe as the Good Law, and indeed it is not rightly perceived if it is thought of as anything but good; for in it there can be no grain of evil, no element of unkindness. It is no iron-hearted monster crushing the weak and destroying the igno-rant, but a soothing love and brooding compassion shielding the tenderest from harm, and protect-ing the strongest from a too destructive use of their strength. It destroys all evil, it preserves all good. It enfolds the tiniest seedling in its care, and it destroys the most colossal wrong with a breath. To perceive it, is the beatific vision; to know it, is the beatific bliss; and they who perceive and know it are at peace; they are glad forever more.

Such is the law which moves to righteousness,
Which none at last can turn aside or stay;
The heart of it is love; the end of it
Is peace and consummation sweet: obey.

LIGHT ON VALUES—SPIRITUAL
AND MATERIAL

It is an old-time axiom that "everything has its price." Everybody knows this commercially, but how few know it spiritually. Business consists of a mutual interchange of equitable values. The customer gives money and receives goods, and the merchant gives goods and receives money. This method is universal, and is regarded by all as just. In spiritual things the method is the same, but the form of interchange is different. For material things a material thing is given in exchange, but for spiritual things a spiritual thing is given in exchange. Now these two forms of exchange cannot be transposed; they are of reverse natures, and remain eternally separate. Thus a man may take a sovereign to a shop and ask for a pound's worth of food, or clothing, or literature, and he will receive goods to the value of his sovereign; but if he were to take a sovereign to a teacher of Truth, and ask to be supplied with a pound's worth of religion, or righteousness, or wisdom, he would be told that those things cannot be purchased with money, that their spiritual nature excludes them from material business transactions. The wise teacher, however, would also tell him that these spiritual necessities *must* be purchased, that though money cannot buy them, yet they have their price, that something must be parted with before they can be received, that, in a word, instead of offering money he must offer up self, or selfishness. For so much selfishness given up, so much religion, righteousness, and wisdom would be immediately received, and this without fail, and with perfect equity, for if a man is sure of receiving perishable material food and clothing for the money he puts down, how much more surely will he receive the imperishable spiritual sustenance and protection for the selfishness which he lays down! Shall the law operate in the lesser, and fail in the greater? Man may fail to observe the law, but the law is infallible.

A man may love his money, but he must part with it before he can receive the material comforts of life. Likewise a man may love his selfish gratifications, but he must give them up before he can receive the spiritual comforts of religion.

Now when a tradesman gives goods for money, it is not that he may keep the money, but that he may give it in exchange for other goods. The primary function of business is not to enable everybody to hoard up money, but to facilitate the interchange of commodities. The miser is the greatest of all failures, and he may die of starvation and exposure while being a millionaire, because he is a worshipper of the letter of money, and an ignorer of its spirit—the spirit of mutual interchange.

Money is a means, not an end; its exchange is a sign that goods are being justly given and received. Thus commerce, with all its innumerable ramifications of detail, is reducible to one primary principle, namely:

Mutual interchange of the material necessities of life.

Now let us follow this principle into the spiritual sphere, and trace there its operation. When a religious man gives spiritual things—kindness, sympathy, love—and receives happiness in return, it is not that he may hoard and hug to himself that happiness, but that he may give it to others, and so receive back spiritual things. The primary function of religion is not to enable all to hoard up personal pleasure, but to render actual the interchange of spiritual blessings. The most selfish man—he whose chief object is the getting of happiness for himself—is a spiritual miser, and his mind may perish of spiritual destitution though he be surrounded with the objects which he has obtained to pander to his pleasure, because he is worshipping the letter of happiness, and is ignoring its spirit—the spirit of unselfish interchange. The object of selfishness is the getting of personal pleasure, or happiness; the object of religion is the diffusion of virtue. Thus religion, with all its innumerable creeds, may be resolved into one primary principle, namely:

Mutual interchange of spiritual blessings.

What, then, are the spiritual blessings? They are kindness, brotherliness, goodwill, sympathy, forbearance, patience, trustfulness, peacefulness, love unending, and compassion unlimited. These blessings, these necessities for the starving spirit of man, can be obtained, but their price *must* be paid; unkindness, uncharitableness, ill-will, hardness, ill-temper, impatience, suspicion, strife, hatred, and cruelty—all these, along with the happiness, the personal satisfaction, which they give must be yielded up. These spiritual coins, dead in themselves, must be parted with, and when parted with, there will be immediately received their spiritual counterparts, the living and imperishable blessings to which they are a means and of which they are a sign.

To conclude, when a man gives money to a merchant, and receives goods in return, he does not wish to have his money again. He has willingly parted with it forever, and is satisfied with the exchange. So when a man gives up unrighteousness in exchange for righteousness, he does not wish to have his selfish pleasures back again. He has given them up forever, and is satisfied and in peace.

Thus also, when one bestows a gift, even though it be a material gift, he does not look for the receiver to send him back its value in money, because it is a religious deed, and not a business transaction. The material thing thus given represents the interchange of a spiritual blessing, and its accompanying bliss, the bliss of a gift bestowed, and that of a gift received.

"Are not two sparrows sold for a farthing?" Everything in the universe—every object and every thought—is valued. Material things have a material value, spiritual things have a spiritual value, and to confound these values is not wise. To seek to purchase spiritual blessings with money, or material luxuries with virtue, is the way of selfishness and folly. It is to confound barter with religion, and to make a religion of barter. Sympathy, kindness, love cannot be bought and sold, they can only be given and received. When a gift is paid for, it ceases to be a gift.

Because everything has a value, that which is freely given is gained with accumulation. He who gives up the lesser happiness of selfishness, gains the greater happiness of unselfishness. The universe is just, and its justice is so perfect that he who has once perceived it can no more doubt or be afraid, he can only wonder and be glad.

LIGHT ON THE SENSE OF PROPORTION

In a nightmare there is no relation of one thing to another; all things are haphazard, and there is general confusion and misery. Wise men have likened the self-seeking life to a nightmare; and there is a close resemblance between a selfish life, in which the sense of proportion is so far lost that things are only seen as they affect one's own selfish aims, and in which there are feverish excitements and overwhelming troubles and disasters, and that state of troubled sleep known as nightmare.

In a nightmare, too, the controlling will and perceiving intelligence are asleep; and in a selfish life the better nature and spiritual perceptions are locked in profound slumber.

The uncultivated mind lacks the sense of proportion. It does not see the right relation of one natural object to another, and is therefore dead to the beauty and harmony with which it is surrounded.

And what is this sense of proportion but the faculty of *seeing things as they are!* It is a faculty which needs cultivating, and its cultivation, when applied to natural objects, embraces the entire intelligence and refines the moral nature. It enters, however, into spiritual things as well as things natural, and here is more lacking, and more greatly needed; for to see things as they are in the spiritual sphere, is to find no ground for grief, no lodging place for lamentation.

Whence spring all this grief and anxiety, and fear and trouble? Is it not because things are not as men wish them to be? Is it not because the multiplicity of desires prevents them from seeing things in their true perspective and right proportion?

When one is overwhelmed with grief, he sees nothing but his loss, its nearness to him blots out the whole view of life. The thing in itself may be small, but to the sufferer it assumes a magnitude which is out of all proportion to the surrounding objects of life.

All who have passed the age of thirty, can look back over their lives at times when they were perplexed with anxiety, overwhelmed with grief, or even, perhaps, on the verge of despair, over incidents which, seen now in their right proportion, are known to be very small.

If the would-be suicide will to-day stay his hand, and wait, he will at the end of ten years marvel at his folly over so comparatively small a matter.

When the mind is possessed by passion or paralyzed with grief, it has lost the power of judgment, it cannot weigh and consider, it does not perceive the relative values and proportions of the things by which it is disturbed; awake and acting, it yet moves in a nightmare which holds its faculties in thrall.

The passionate partisan lacks this sense of proportion to such an extent, that to him his own side or view appears all that is right and good, and his opponent's all that is bad and wrong. To this partiality his reason is chained, so that whatever reason he may bring to bear upon the matter, is enlisted in the service of bias, and is not exercised in order to find the just relation which exists between the two sides. He is so convinced that his own party is all right, and the other, equally intelligent, party is all wrong, that it is impossible for him to be impartial and just. The only thing he understands as justice is that of getting his own way, or placing some ruling power in the hands of his party.

Just as the sense of proportion in things material puts an end to the spirit of repugnance, so in things spiritual it puts an end to the spirit of strife. The true artist does not see ugliness anywhere, he sees only beauty. That which is loathsome to others, fills, to him, its rightful place in nature, and it appears in his picture as a thing of beauty. The true seer does not see evil anywhere, he sees universal good. That which is hateful to others, he sees in its rightful place in the scheme of evolution, and it is held dispassionately in his mind as an object of contemplation.

Men worry, and grieve, and fight, because they lack this sense of proportion, because they do not see things in their right relations. The objects of their turbulence are not things-in-themselves, but their own opinions about things, self-created shadows, the unreal creations of an egoistic nightmare.

The cultivation and development of the ethical sense of proportion converts the heated partisan into the gentle peacemaker, and gives the calm and searching eye of the prophet to the hitherto blind instrument in the clashing play of selfish forces.

The spiritual sense of proportion gives sanity; it restores the mind to calmness; it bestows impartiality and justice, and reveals a universe of faultless harmony.

LIGHT ON ADHERENCE TO PRINCIPLE

The man of Truth never departs from the divine principles which he has espoused. He may be threatened with sickness, poverty, pain, loss of friends and position, yea, even with immediate death, yet he does not desert the principles which he knows to be eternally true. To him, there is one thing more grievous, more to be feared and shunned than all the above evils put together, and that is—*the desertion of principle.* To turn coward in the hour of trial, to deny conscience, to join the rabble of passions, desires, and fears, in turning upon, accusing, and crucifying the Eternal Christ of Divine Principle, because, forsooth, that principle has not given him personal health, affluence and ease—this, to the man of Truth, is the evil of evils, the sin of sins.

We cannot escape sickness and death. Though we avoid them for a long time, in the end they will overtake us. But we can escape wrong-doing, we can avoid fear and cowardice; and when we eschew wrong-doing and cast out fear, the evils of life will not subdue us when they overtake us, for we shall have mastered them; instead of avoiding them for a season we shall have conquered them on their own ground.

There are those who teach that it is right to do wrong when that wrong is to protect another; that it is good, for instance, to tell a lie when its object is the well-being of another—that is, that it is right to desert the principle of truthfulness under severe trial. Such teaching has never emanated from the lips of the Great Teachers. It has not been uttered even by those lesser, yet superbly noble men, the prophets, saints, and martyrs, for these divinely illuminated men knew full well that no circumstance can make a wrong a right, and that a lie has no saving and protective power. Wrong-doing is a greater evil than pain, and a lie is more deadly and destructive than death. Jesus rebuked Peter for trying to shield his Master's life by wrong-doing, and no right-minded person would accept life at the expense of the moral character of another when it appeared possible to do so.

All men admire and revere the martyrs, those steadfast men and women who feared wrong, cowardice, and lying, but who did not fear pain and death; who were steadfast and calm in their adherence to principle even when brought to the utmost extremity of trial, yea, even when the taunts and jeers of enemies assailed them, and the tears and agonies of loved ones appealed to them, they flinched not nor turned back, knowing that the future good and salvation of the whole world depended upon their firmness in that supreme hour; and for this, they stand through all time as monuments of virtue, centres of saving and uplifting power for all humankind. But he who lied to save himself, or for the sake of the two or three beings whom he personally loved, is rarely heard of, for in that hour of desertion of principle, his power was gone; and if he *is* heard of, he is not loved for that lie; he is always looked upon as one who fell when the test was applied; as an example of the highest virtue he is rejected by all men in all times.

Had all men believed that an untruth was right under extreme circumstances, we should have had no martyrs and saints, the moral fibre of humanity would have been undermined, and the world left to grope in ever deepening darkness.

The attitude which regards wrong-doing for the sake of others as the right thing to do, is based on the tacit assumption that wrong and untruth are inferior evils to unhappiness, pain, and death; but the man of moral insight knows that wrong and untruth are the greater evils, and so he never commits them, even though his own life or the lives of others appear to be at stake.

It is easy for a man in the flowery time of ease or the heyday of prosperity to persuade himself that he is staunchly adhering to principle, but when pain overtakes him, when the darkness of misfortune begins to settle down upon him, and the pressure of circumstances hems him in—then he is on his trial, then he has come to his testing time; in that season it will be brought to the light whether he clings to self or adheres to Truth.

Principles are for our salvation in the hour of need. If we desert them in that hour, how can we be saved from the snares and pains of self?

If a man does wrong to his conscience, thinking thereby to avoid some immediate pain or pressing evil, he does but increase pain and evil. The good man is less anxious to avoid pain than wrong-doing.

There is neither wisdom nor safety in deserting permanent and protective principles when our happiness seems to be at stake. If we desert the true for the pleasant, we shall lose both the pleasant and the true; but if we desert the pleasant for the true, the peace of truth will soothe away our sorrow. If we barter the higher for the lower, emptiness and anguish will overtake us, and then, having abandoned the Eternal, where is our rock of refuge? But if we yield up the lower for the higher, the strength and satisfaction of the higher will remain with us, fulness of joy will overtake us, and we shall find in truth a rock of refuge from the evils and sorrows of life.

To find the permanent amid all the changes of life, and, having found it, adhere to it under all circumstances—this only is true happiness, this only is salvation and lasting peace.

LIGHT ON THE SACRIFICE
OF THE SELF

Self-sacrifice is one of the fundamental principles in the teaching of all the Great Spiritual Masters. It consists in yielding up self, or selfishness, so that Truth may become the source of conduct. Self is not an entity that has to be cast out, but a condition of mind that has to be converted. The renunciation of self is not the annihilation of intelligent being, but the annihilation of every dark and selfish desire. Self is the blind clinging to perishable things and transient pleasures as distinguished from the intelligent practice of virtue and righteousness. Self is the lusting, coveting, desiring of the heart, and it is this that must be yielded up before Truth can be known, with its abiding calm and endless peace.

To give up *things* will not avail; *it is the lust for things* that must be sacrificed. Though a man sacrifice wealth, position, friends, fame, home, wife, child—yea, and life also—it will not avail if self is not renounced. Buddha renounced the world and all that it held dear to him, but for six years he wandered and searched and suffered, and not till he yielded up the desires of his heart did he become enlightened and arrive at peace.

By giving up only the *objects* of self-indulgence, no peace will ensue, but torment will follow. It is self-indulgence, *the desire for the object,* that must be abandoned—then peace enters the heart.

Sacrifice is painful so long as there is any vestige of self remaining in the heart. While there remains in the heart a lurking desire for an unworthy object or pleasure that has been sacrificed, there will be periods of intense suffering, and fierce temptation; but when the *desire* for the unworthy object or pleasure is put away forever from the mind, and the sacrifice is complete and perfect, then, concerning that particular object or pleasure, there can be no more suffering or temptation. So when self in its entirety is sacrificed, sacrifice, in its painful aspect, is at an end, and perfect knowledge and perfect peace are reached.

Hatred is self; covetousness is self; envy and jealousy are self; malice is self; pride and superciliousness are self; vanity and boasting are self; gluttony and sensuality are self; lying and deception are self; speaking evil of one's neighbor is self; anger and revenge are self. Self-sacrifice consists in yielding up all these dark conditions of mind and heart. The process is a painful one in its early stages, but soon a divine peace descends at intervals upon the pilgrim; later, this peace remains longer with him, and finally, when the rays of Truth begin to be shed abroad in the heart, remains with him.

This sacrifice leads to peace; for in the perfect life of Truth, there is no more sacrifice, and no more pain and sorrow; for where there is no more self there is nothing to be given up; where there is no clinging of the mind to perishable things there is nothing to be renounced; where all has been laid upon the altar of Truth, selfish love is swallowed up in divine love; and in divine love there is no thought of self, for there is the perfection of insight, enlightenment, and immortality, and therefore perfect peace.

LIGHT ON THE MANAGEMENT
OF THE MIND

Following the last chapter a few hints on the management of one's mind will doubtless be opportune. Before a man can see even the necessity for thorough and complete self-government, he will have to throw off a great delusion in which so many are involved—the delusion of believing that his lapses of conduct are due to those about him, and not entirely to himself. "I could make far greater progress if I were not hindered by others," or "It is impossible for me to make any headway, seeing that I live with such irritable people," are commonly expressed complaints which spring from the error of imagining that others are responsible for one's own folly.

The violent or irritable man always blames those about him for his fits of anger, and by continually living in this delusion, he becomes more and more confirmed in his rashness and perturbations, for how can a man overcome—nay, how can he even try to overcome, his weakness if he convinces himself that it springs entirely from the actions of others? Moreover, firmly believing this, as he does, he vents his anger more and more upon others in order to try and make matters better for himself, and so becomes completely lost to all knowledge of the real origin of his unhappy state.

Men cast the blame of their unprosperous acts
Upon the abettors of their own resolve,
Or anything but their weak guilty selves.

All a man's weaknesses and sins and falls take their rise in his own heart, and he alone is responsible for them. It is true there are tempters and provokers, but temptations and provocations are powerless to him who refuses to respond to them. Tempters and provokers are but foolish men, and he who gives way to them has become a willing co-operator in their folly; he is unwise and weak, and the source of his troubles is in himself. The pure man cannot be tempted; the wise man cannot be provoked.

Let a man fully realize that he is absolutely responsible for his every action, and he has already gone a considerable distance along the path which leads to wisdom and peace, for he will then commence to utilize temptation as a means of growth, and the wrong conduct of others he will regard as a test of his own strength.

Socrates thanked the gods for the gift of a shrewish wife in that it enabled him the better to cultivate the virtue of patience; and it is a simple and easily perceived truth that we can the better grow patient by living with the impatient, better grow unselfish by living with the selfish. If a man is impatient with the impatient, he is himself impatient; if he is selfish with the selfish, then he is himself selfish. The test and measure of virtue is trial, and, like gold and precious stones, the more it is tested the brighter it shines. If a man thinks he has a virtue, yet gives way when its opposing vice is presented to him, let him not delude himself, he has not yet attained to the possession of that virtue.

If a man would rise and become a man indeed, let him cease to think the weak and foolish thought, "I am hindered by others," and let him set about to discover that he is hindered only by himself; let him realize that the giving way to another is but a revelation of his own imperfection, and lo! upon him will descend the light of wisdom, and the door of peace will open unto him, and he will soon become the conqueror of self.

The fact that a man is continually troubled and disturbed by close contact with others, is an indication that he requires such contact to impel him onward to a clearer comprehension of himself, and toward a higher and more steadfast state of mind. The very things which he regards as insurmountable hindrances will become to him the most valuable aids when he fully realizes his moral responsibility and his innate power to do right. He will then cease to blame others for his unmanly conduct, and will commence to live steadfastly under all circumstances; the scales of self-delusion will quickly fall from his eyes, and he will then see that ofttimes when he imagined himself provoked by others, he himself was really the provoker; and as he rises above his own mental perturbations, the necessity for coming in contact with the same conditions in others will cease, and he will pass, by a natural process, into the company of the good and pure, and will then awaken in others the nobility which he has arrived at in himself.

Be noble! and the nobleness that lies
In other men, sleeping, but never dead,
Will rise in majesty to meet thine own.

LIGHT ON SELF-CONTROL:
THE DOOR OF HEAVEN

The foremost lesson which the world has to learn on its way to wisdom, is the lesson of self-control. All the bitter punishments which men undergo in the school of experience are inflicted because they have failed to learn this lesson. Apart from self-control, salvation is a meaningless word, and peace is an impossibility; for how can a man be saved from any sin whilst he continues to give way to it? or how can he realize abiding peace until he has conquered and subdued the troubles and perturbations of his mind?

Self-control is the Door of Heaven; it leads to light and peace. Without it a man is already in hell; he is lost in darkness and unrest. Men inflict upon themselves far-reaching sufferings, and pass through indescribable torments, both of body and soul, through lack of self-control; and not until they resort to its practice can their sufferings and torments pass away, for it has no substitute, nothing can take its place, and there is no power in the universe that can do for a man that which he, sooner or later, *must* do for himself, by entering upon the practice of self-control.

By self-control a man manifests his divine power and ascends toward divine wisdom and perfection. Every man can practice it. The weakest man can begin now, and until he does begin, his weakness will remain, or he will become weaker still. Calling or not calling upon God or Jesus, Brahma or Buddha, Spirits or Masters, will not avail men who refuse to govern themselves and to purify their hearts. Believing or disbelieving that Jesus is God, that Buddha is omniscient, or the Spirits or Masters guide human affairs, cannot help men who continue to cling to the elements of strife and ignorance and corruption within themselves.

What theological affirmation or denial can justify, or what outward power put right, the man who refuses to abandon a slanderous or abusive tongue, or give up an angry temper, or to sacrifice his impure imaginings? The flower reaches the upper light by first contending with the under darkness, and man can only reach the Light of Truth by striving against the darkness within himself.

The vast importance of self-control is not realized by men, its absolute necessity is not apprehended by them, and the spiritual freedom and glory to which it leads are hidden from their eyes. Because of this, men are enslaved and misery and suffering ensue. Let a man contemplate the violence, impurity, disease, and suffering which obtain upon earth, and consider how much of it is due to want of self-control, and he will gradually come to realize the great need there is for self-control.

I say again, that self-control is the Gate of Heaven, for without it neither happiness nor love nor peace can be realized and maintained. In the degree that it is lacked by a man, in just that measure will his mind and life be given over to confusion, and it is because such a large number of individuals have not yet learned to practice it that the enforced restraint of national laws is required for the maintenance of order and the prevention of a destructive confusion. Self-control is the beginning of virtue, and it leads to the acquisition of every noble attribute; it is the first essential quality in a well-ordered and truly religious life, and it leads to calmness, blessedness, and peace. Without it, although there may be theological belief or profession, there can be no true religion, for what is religion but enlightened conduct? and what is spirituality but the triumph over the unruly tendencies of the mind?

When men both depart from and refuse to practice self-control, then they fall into the great and dark delusion of separating religion from conduct; then they persuade themselves that religion consists, not in overcoming self and living blamelessly, but in holding a certain belief about Scripture, and in worshipping a certain Saviour in a particular way; hence arise the innumerable complications and confusions of letter-worship, and the violence and bitter strife into which men fall in defence of their own formulated religion. But true religion cannot be formulated; it is purity of mind, a loving heart, a soul at peace with the world. It needs not to be defended, for it is Being and Doing and Living. A man begins to practice religion when he begins to control himself.

LIGHT ON ACTS AND
THEIR CONSEQUENCES

One of the commonest excuses for wrong-doing is that if right were done calamity would ensue. Thus the foolish concern themselves, not with the act, but with the consequence of the act, a foreknowledge of which is assumed. The desire to secure pleasant results, and to escape unpleasant consequences, is at the root of that confusion of mind which renders men incapable of distinguishing between good and evil, and prevents them from practising the one and abandoning the other. Even when it is claimed that the wrong thing is done, not for one's self, but in order to secure the happiness of others, the delusion is the same, only it is more subtle and dangerous.

The wise concern themselves with the act, and not with its consequences. They consider, not what is pleasant or unpleasant, but *what is right*. Thus doing what is right only, and not straining after results, they are relieved of all burdens of doubt, desire, and fear. Nor can one who so acts ever become involved in an inextricable difficulty, or be troubled with painful perplexity. His course is so simple, straight, and plain that he can never be confused with misgivings and uncertainties. Those who so act are said by Krishna to act "without regard to the fruits of action," and he further declares that those who have thus renounced results are supremely good, supremely wise.

Those who work for pleasant results only, and who depart from the right path when their, or others', happiness appears to be at stake, cannot escape doubt, difficulty, perplexity, and pain. Ever forecasting probable consequences, they act in one way to-day, and in another way to-morrow; unstable, and blown about by the changing winds of circumstance, they become more and more bewildered, and the consequences about which they trouble do not accrue.

But they who work for righteousness only, who are careful to do the right act, putting away all selfish considerations, all thought of results, they are steadfast, unchanging, untroubled and in peace amid all vicissitudes, and the fruits of their acts are ever sweet and blessed.

Even the knowledge, which only the righteous possess, that wrong acts can never produce good results, and that right acts can never bring about bad results, is in itself fraught with sweet assurance and peace. For whether the fruits of acts are sought or unsought, they cannot be escaped.

They who sow to self, and, ignorant of the law of Truth, think they can make their own results, reap the bitter fruits of self.

They who sow to righteousness, knowing themselves to be the reapers, *and not the makers of consequences,* reap the sweet fruits of righteousness.

Right is supremely simple, and is without complexity. Error is interminably complex, and involves the mind in confusion.

To put away self and passion, and establish one's self in right-doing, this is the highest wisdom.

LIGHT ON THE WAY OF WISDOM

The Path of Wisdom is the highest way, the way in which all doubt and uncertainty are dispelled and knowledge and surety are realized.

Amid the excitements and pleasures of the world and the surging whirlpools of human passions, Wisdom—so calm, so silent and so beautiful—is indeed difficult to find, difficult, not because of its incomprehensible complexity, but because of its unobtrusive simplicity, and because self is so blind and rash, and so jealous of its rights and pleasures.

Wisdom is "rejected of men" because it always comes right home to one's self in the form of wounding reproof, and the lower nature of man cannot bear to be reproved. Before Wisdom can be acquired, self must be wounded to the death, and because of this, because Wisdom is the enemy of self, self rises in rebellion, and will not be overcome and denied.

The foolish man is governed by his passions and personal cravings, and when about to do anything he does not ask "Is this right?" but only considers how much pleasure or personal advantage he will gain by it. He does not govern his passions and act from fixed principles, but is the slave of his inclinations and follows where they lead.

The wise man governs his passions and puts away all personal cravings. He never acts from impulse and passion, but dispassionately considers what is right to be done, and does it. He is always thoughtful and self-possessed, and guides his conduct by the loftiest moral principles. He is superior to both pleasure and pain.

Wisdom cannot be found in books or travel, in learning or philosophy, it is *acquired by practice only.* A man may read the precepts of the greatest sages continually, but if he does not purify and govern himself he will remain foolish. A man may be intimately conversant with the writings of the greatest philosophers, but so long as he continues to give way to his passions he will not attain to wisdom.

Wisdom is right action, right doing; folly is wrong action, wrong-doing. All reading, all study, all learning is vain if a man will not see his errors and give them up. Wisdom says to the vain man, "Do not praise yourself," to the proud man, "Humble yourself," to the gossip, "Govern your tongue," to the angry man, "Subdue your anger," to the resentful man, "Forgive your enemy," to the self-indulgent man, "Be temperate," to the impure man, "Purge your heart of lust," and to all men, "Beware of small faults, do your own duty faithfully, and never intermeddle with the duty of another."

These things are very simple; the doing of them is simple, but as it leads to the annihilation of self, the selfish tendencies in man object to them and rise up in revolt against them, loving their own life of turbulent excitement and feverish pleasure, and hating the calm and beautiful silence of Wisdom. Thus men remain in folly.

Nevertheless, the Way of Wisdom is always open, is always ready to receive the tread of the pilgrim who has grown weary of the thorny and intricate ways of folly. No man is prevented from becoming wise but by himself; no man can acquire Wisdom but by his own exertions; and he who is prepared to be honest with himself, to measure the depths of his ignorance, to come face to face with his errors, to recognize and acknowledge his faults, and at once to set about the task of his own regeneration, such a man will find the way of Wisdom, walking which with humble and obedient feet, he will in due time come to the sweet City of Deliverance.

LIGHT ON DISPOSITION

I cannot help it, it is my disposition." How often one hears this expression as an excuse for wrong-doing. What does it imply? This, that the person who utters it believes that he has no choice in the matter, that he cannot alter his character. He believes that he must go on doing the wrong thing to the end of his days because he was "born so," or because his father or grandfather was like it; or, if not these, then some one along the family line a hundred, or two or three hundred years ago must have been afflicted, and therefore he is and must remain so. Such a belief should be uprooted, destroyed, and cast away, for it is not only without reason, it is a complete barrier to all progress, to all growth in goodness, to all development of character and noble expansion of life. Character is not permanent; it is, indeed, one of the most changeable things in nature. If not changed by a conscious act of the will, it is being continually modified and re-formed by the pressure of circumstances. Disposition is not fixed, except in so far as one fixes it by continuing to do the same thing, and by persistence in the stubborn belief that he "cannot help it." Immediately one gets rid of that belief he will find that he *can* help it; further, he will find that intelligence and will are instruments which can mould disposition to any extent, and that, too, with considerable rapidity if one is in earnest.

What is disposition but a habit formed by repeating the same thing over and over again? Cease repeating (doing) the thing, and lo! the disposition is changed, the character is altered. To cease from an old habit of thought or action is, I know, difficult at first, but with each added effort the difficulty decreases, and finally disappears, and then the new and good habit is formed and the disposition is changed from bad to good, the character is ennobled, the mind is delivered from torment and is lifted into joy.

There is no need for any one to remain the slave of a disposition which causes him unhappiness, and which he himself regards as undesirable. He can abandon it. He can break away from the slavery. He can deliver himself and be free.

LIGHT ON INDIVIDUAL LIBERTY

Within the sphere of his own mind man has all power, but in the sphere of other minds and outside things, his power is extremely limited. He can command his own mind, but he cannot command the mind of others. He can choose what he shall think, but he cannot choose what others shall think. He cannot control the weather as he wills, but he can control his mind, and decide what his mental attitude toward the weather shall be.

A man can reform the dominion of his own mind, but he cannot reform the outer world because that outer world is composed of other minds having the same freedom of choice as himself. A pure being cannot cleanse the heart of one less pure, but by his life of purity and by elucidating his experience in the attainment of purity, he can, as a teacher, act as a guide to others, and so enable them more readily and rapidly to purify themselves. But even then those others have all power to decide whether they shall accept or reject such guidance, so complete is man's choice.

It is because of this dual truth—that man has no power in the outer realm of others' minds and yet has all power over his own mind, that he cannot avoid the consequences of his own thoughts and acts. Man is altogether powerless to alter or avert consequences, but he is altogether powerful in his choice of causative thought. Having chosen his thoughts, he must accept their full consequences; having acted, he cannot escape the full results of his act.

Law reigns universally, and there is perfect individual liberty. A man can do as he likes, but all other men can do as they like. A man has power to steal, but others have power to protect themselves against the thief. Having sent out his thought, having acted his purpose, a man's power over that thought and purpose is at an end; the consequences are certain and cannot be escaped, and they will be of the nature of the thought and act which produced them—painful or blessed.

Seeing that a man can think and do as he chooses, and that all others have the like liberty, a man has to learn, sooner or later, to reckon with other minds, and until he does this he will be ceaselessly involved in suffering. To think and act apart from the consideration of others is both an abuse of power and an infringement of liberty. Such thoughts and acts are annulled and brought to nought by the harmonizing Principle of Liberty itself, and such annulling and bringing to nought is felt by the individual as suffering. When the mind, rising above ignorance, recognizes the magnitude of its power within its own sphere and, ceasing to antagonize itself against others, it harmonizes itself to those other minds, acknowledging their freedom of choice, then is realized spiritual plenitude and the cessation of suffering.

Selfishness, egotism, and despotism are, from the spiritual standpoint, transferable terms; they are one and the same thing. Every selfish thought or act is a manifestation of egotism, is an effort of despotism, and it is met with suffering and defeat: it is annulled because the Law of Liberty cannot, in the smallest particular, be annulled. If selfishness could conquer, Liberty would be non-existent, but selfishness fails of all results but pain, because Liberty is supreme. An act of selfishness contains two elements of egotism: namely, (1) the denial of the liberty of others, and (2) the assertion of one's own liberty beyond its legitimate sphere. It thereby destroys itself. Despotism is death.

Man is not the creature of selfishness, he is the maker of it; it is an indication of his power—his power to disobey even the law of his being. Selfishness is power without wisdom; it is energy wrongly directed. A man is selfish because he is ignorant of his nature and power as a mental being; such ignorance and selfishness entail suffering, and by repeated suffering and age-long experience he at last arrives at knowledge and the legitimate exercise of his power. The truly enlightened man cannot be selfish: he cannot accuse others of selfishness, or try to coerce them into being unselfish.

The selfish man is eager to bend others to his own way and will, believing it to be the only right way for all; he thereby ignorantly wastes himself in trying to check in others the power which he freely exercises himself, namely—the power to choose their own way and exercise their own will. By so doing, he places himself in direct antagonism with the like tendencies and freedom of other minds, and brings into operation the instruments of his own suffering. Hence the ceaseless inter-play of conflicting forces; the unending conflagration of passion; the turmoil, strife, and woe. Selfishness is misapplied power.

The unselfish man is he who, ceasing from all personal interference, abandoning the "I" as the source of judgment, and having recognized his illimitable freedom through the abandonment of all egotism even in thought, refrains from encroachment upon the boundless freedom of others, realizing the legitimacy of their choice and their right to the free employment of their power. However others may choose to act toward such a man, it can never cause him any trouble or suffering, because he is perfectly willing that they should so choose to act, and he harbors no wish that they should act in any other way. He realizes that his sole duty, as well as his entire power, *lies in acting rightly toward them,* and that he is in no way concerned with their actions toward him; that is both their choice and their business. To the unselfish man, therefore, malice, envy, backbiting, jealousy, accusation, condemnation, and persecution have passed away. Having ceased to practice these things, he is not disturbed when they are hurled at him. Thus liberation from sin is liberation from suffering. The selfless man is free; he has made the thraldom of sin impossible; he has broken every bond.

LIGHT ON THE BLESSING
AND DIGNITY OF WORK

That "labor is life" is a principle pregnant with truth, and one which cannot be too often repeated, or too closely studied and practised. Labor is so often regarded as an irksome and even degrading means of obtaining ease and pleasure, and not as what it really is—a thing happy and noble in itself, that the lesson contained in the maxim needs to be taken to heart and more and more thoroughly learned.

Activity, both mental and physical, is the essence of life. The complete cessation of activity is death, and death is immediately followed by corruption. Ease and death are closely associated. The more there is of activity, the more abounding is life. The brain-worker, the original thinker, the man of unceasing mental activity, is the longest-lived man in the community; the agricultural laborer, the gardener, the man of unceasing physical activity, comes next with length of years.

Pure-hearted, healthy-minded people love work, and are happy in their labors. They never complain of being "overworked." It is very difficult, almost impossible, for a man to be overworked if he lives a sound and pure life. It is worry, bad habits, discontent and idleness that kill—especially idleness, for if labor is life, then idleness must be death. Let us get rid of sin before we talk about being overworked.

There are those who are afraid of work, regarding it as an enemy, and who fear a breakdown by doing too much. They have to learn what a health-bestowing friend work is. Others are ashamed of work, looking upon it as a degrading thing to be avoided. The "pure in heart and sound in head" are neither afraid nor ashamed of work, and they dignify whatsoever they undertake. No necessary work can be degrading, but if a man regard his work as such, he is already degraded, not by his task, but by his slavish vanity.

Man hath his daily work of body and mind
Appointed, which declares his dignity.

The idle man who is afraid of work, and the vain man who is ashamed of it, are both on the way to poverty, if they are not already there. The industrious man, who loves work, and the man of true dignity, who glorifies work, are both on their way to affluence, if they are not already there. The lazy man is sowing the seeds of poverty and crime; the vain man is sowing the seeds of humiliation and shame. The industrious man is sowing the seeds of affluence and virtue; the dignified worker is sowing the seeds of victory and honor. Deeds are seeds, and the harvest will appear in due season.

There is a common desire to acquire riches with as little effort as possible, which is a kind of theft. To try to obtain the fruits of labor without laboring is to take the fruits of another man's labor; to try to get money without giving its equivalent is to take that which belongs to another and not to one's self. What is theft but this frame of mind carried to its logical extreme?

Let us rejoice in our work; let us rejoice that we have the strength and capacity for work, and let us increase that strength and capacity by unremitting labor. Whatever our work may be, it is noble, and will be perceived by the world as noble, if we perform it in a noble spirit. The virtuous do not despise any labor which falls to their lot; and he who works and faints not, who is faithful, patient, and uncomplaining even in the time of poverty, he will surely at last eat of the sweet fruits of his labor; yea, even while he labors and seems to fail, happiness will be his constant companion, for, "Blessed is the man that has found his work; let him ask no other blessedness."

LIGHT ON GOOD MANNERS AND REFINEMENT

Move upward, working out the beast,
And let the ape and tiger die.

All culture is getting away from the beast. Evolution itself is a refining process, and the unwritten laws of society inhere in the evolutionary law.

Education is intellectual culture. The scholar is engaged in purifying and perfecting his intellect; the religious devotee is engaged in purifying and perfecting his heart.

When a man aspires to nobler heights of achievement, and sets about the realization of his ideal, he commences to refine his nature; and the more pure a man makes himself within, the more refined, gracious, and gentle will be his outward demeanor.

Good manners have an ethical basis, and cannot be divorced from religion. To be ill-mannered is to be imperfect, for what are ill manners but the outward expression of inward defects? What a man does, that he is. If he acts rudely, he is a rude man; if he acts foolishly, he is a foolish man; if he acts gently, he is a gentleman. It is a mistake to suppose that a man can have a gentle and refined mind behind a rough and brutal exterior (though such a man may possess some strong animal virtues), as the outer is an expression of the inner.

One of the steps in the noble Eightfold Path to perfection as expounded by Buddha is—Right Conduct or Good Behavior, and it should be plain to all that the man who has not yet learned how to conduct himself toward others in a kindly, gracious, and unselfish spirit, has not yet entered the pathway of a holy life.

If a man refines his heart, he will refine his behavior; if he refines his behavior, it will help him to refine his heart.

To be coarse, brutish, and snappish may be natural to a beast, but the man who aspires to be even an endurable member of society (not to mention the higher manhood), will at once purge away any such bestial traits that may possess him.

All those things which aid in man's refinement—such as music, painting, poetry, manners—are servants and messengers of progress. Man degrades himself when he imitates the brute. Let us not mistake barbarism for simplicity, or vulgarity for honesty.

Unselfishness, kindliness, and consideration for others will always be manifested outwardly as gentleness, graciousness, and refinement. To affect these graces by simulating them may seem to succeed, but it does not. Affectation and hypocrisy are soon divulged; every man's eye, sooner or later, pierces through their flimsiness, and ultimately none but the actors of them are deceived. As Emerson says:—

> *What is done for effect, is seen to be done for effect; and what is done for love,*
> *is felt to be done for love.*

Children who are well-bred are taught always to consider the happiness of others before their own: to offer them the most comfortable seat, the choicest fruit, the best tidbit, and so on; and also to do everything, even the most trivial acts, in the right way. And these two things—*unselfishness and right action*—are at the basis, not only of good manners, but of all ethics, religion, and true living: they represent power and skill. The selfish man is weak and unskilful in the exercise of thought;

the vulgar man is weak and unskilful in his actions. Unselfishness is the right way of thinking; good manners are the right way of acting. As Emerson, again, says:—

There is always a best way of doing everything, if it be to boil an egg. Manners are
the happy way of doing things right.

It is a frequent error among men to imagine that the Higher Life is an ideal something quite above and apart from the common details of life, and that to neglect these or to perform them in a slovenly manner is an indication that the mind is occupied on "higher things." Whereas it is an indication that the mind is becoming inexact, dreamy, and weak, instead of exact, wide awake, and strong. No matter how apparently trivial the thing is which has to be done, there is a right way and a wrong way of doing it, and to do it in the right way saves friction, time, and trouble, conserves power, and develops grace, skill, and happiness.

The artisan has a variety of tools with which to ply his particular craft, and he is taught (and also finds by experience) that each tool must be applied to its special use, and never under any circumstances must one tool be made to do service for another. By using every tool in its proper place and in the right way, the maximum of dexterity and power is attained. Should a boy in learning a trade refuse instruction, and persist in using the tools in his own way, making one tool do service for another, he would never become anything better than a clumsy bungler, and would be a failure in his trade.

It is the same throughout the whole life. If a man opens himself to receive instruction, and studies how to do everything rightly and lawfully, he becomes strong and skilful and wise, master of himself, his thoughts and actions; but if he persists in following his momentary impulses, in doing everything as he feels prompted, not exercising thoughtfulness, and rejecting instruction, such a man will attain to nothing better than a slovenly and bungling life.

Confucius paid the strictest attention to dress, eating, deportment, passing speech—to all the so-called trivialities of life, as well as to the momentous affairs of state and the lofty moral principles which he expounded; and he taught his disciples that it is the sign of a vulgar and foolish mind to regard anything as "trivial" that is necessary to be done, that the wise man pays attention to all his duties, and does everything wisely, thoughtfully, and rightly.

It is not an arbitrary edict of society that the man who persists in eating with his knife shall be rejected, for a knife is given to cut with, and a fork to eat with, and to put things to wrong and slovenly uses—even in the passing details of life—does not make for progress, but is retrogressive and makes for confusion.

It is not a despotic condition in the law of things that so long as a man persists in thinking and acting unkindly of and toward others he shall be shut out from Heaven, and shall remain in the outer pain and unrest, for selfishness is disruption and disorder. The universe is sustained by exactness, it rests on order, it demands right doing, and the searcher for wisdom will watch all his ways. He will think purely, speak gently, and act graciously, refining his entire nature, both in the letter and the spirit.

LIGHT ON DIVERSITIES OF CREEDS

Those who depart from the common track in matters of faith, and strike out independently in search of the Higher Life as distinguished from the letter of religious dogma, are apt to sink into a pitfall which awaits them at the first step, namely, the pitfall of *pride*. Attacking "creeds," and speaking contemptuously of "the orthodox" (as though orthodoxy were synonymous with evil) are not uncommon practices among those who fondly imagine they are in possession of greater spiritual light. Departure from orthodoxy does not by any means include departure from sin; indeed, it is not infrequently accompanied with increased bitterness and contempt. Change of opinion is one thing, change of heart is quite another. To withdraw one's adherence from creeds is easy; to withdraw one's self from sin is more difficult.

Hatred and pride, and not necessarily orthodoxy and conformity, are the things to be avoided. One's own sin, and not another man's creed, is the thing to be despised. The right-minded man cannot plume himself on being "*broader*" than others, or assume that he is on a "higher plane" than others, or think with pharisaical contempt of those who still cling to some form of letter worship which he has abandoned. Applying the words "narrow," "bigoted," and "selfish" to others, is not the indication of an enlightened mind. No person would wish these terms to be applied to himself, and he who is becoming truly religious, does not speak of others in words which would wound him were they directed toward himself.

Those who are learning how to exercise humility and compassion are becoming truly enlightened. Thinking lowly of themselves and kindly of others; condemning their own sins with merciless logic, and thinking with tender pity of the sins of others, they develop that insight into the nature and law of things which enables them to see the truth that is in others, and in the religions of others, and they do not condemn their neighbor because he holds a different faith, or because he adheres to a formal creed. Creeds must be, and he who performs faithfully his duty in his particular creed, not interfering with or condemning his neighbor in the performance of his duty, is bringing the world nearer to perfection and peace.

Amid all the diversities of creeds there is the unifying power of undying and unalterable Love— and he who has Love has entered into sympathetic union with all.

He who has acquired the true spirit of Religion, who has attained to pure insight and deep charity of heart, will avoid all strife and condemnation, and will not fall into the delusion of praising his own sect (should he belong to one) and trying to prove that it alone is right, and of dispraising other sects, and trying to prove that they are false. As the true man does not speak in praise of himself or his own work, so the man of humility, charity, and wisdom does not speak of his own sect as being superior to all others, nor seek to elevate his own particular religion by picking holes in forms of faith which are held as sacred by others.

Nothing more explicit and magnanimous has ever been uttered, in reference to this particular phase of the practice of charity, than is to be found in the twelfth Edict of Asoka, the great Indian Ruler and Saint who lived some two or three centuries previous to the Christian era, and whose life, devoted to the spread of Truth, testified to the beauty of his words: the edict runs thus:—

> There should be no praising of one's own sect and decrying of other sects; but, on the contrary, a rendering of honor to other sects for whatever cause honor may be due. By so doing, both one's own sect may be helped forward, and other sects will be benefited; by acting otherwise, one's own sect will be destroyed in injuring others. Whosoever exalts his own sect by decrying others, does so doubtless out of love for his own sect, thinking to spread abroad the fame thereof. But, on the contrary, he inflicts the more an injury upon his own sect.

These are wise and holy words; the breath of charity is in them, and they may be well pondered upon by those who are anxious to overthrow, not the religions of other men, but their own shortcomings.

It is a dark and deep-seated delusion that causes a man to think he can best advance the cause of his own religion by exposing what he regards as the "evils" of other religions; and the most pitiful part of it is, that while such a one rejoices in the thought that by continually belittling other sects he will perhaps at last wipe them out, and win all men to his side, he is all the time engaged in the sad work of bringing into disrepute, and thereby destroying, his own sect.

Just as every time a man slanders another, he inflicts lasting injury upon his own character and prospects, so every time one speaks evil of another sect, he soils and demeans his own. And the man who is prone to attack and condemn other religions is the one who suffers most when his own is attacked and condemned. If a man does not like that his own religion should be denounced as evil and false, he should carefully guard himself that he does not condemn other religions as such. If it pleases him when his own cause is well spoken of and helped, he should speak well of and help other causes which, while differing from his own in method, have the same good end in view. In this way he will escape the errors and miseries of sectarian strife, and will perfect himself in divine charity.

The heart that has embraced gentleness and charity avoids all those blind passions which keep the fires of party strife, violence, persecution, and bitterness burning from age to age. It dwells in thoughts of pity and tenderness, scorning nothing, despising nothing, not stirring up enmity; for he who acquires gentleness, gains that clear insight into the Great Law which cannot be obtained in any other way, he sees that there is good in all sects and religions, and he makes that good his own.

Let the truth-seeker avoid divisions and invidious distinctions, and let him strive after charity; for charity does not slander, backbite, or condemn; it does not think of trampling down another's, and elevating its own.

Truth cannot contradict itself. The nature of Truth is exactness, reality, undeviating certitude. Why, then, the ceaseless conflict between the religions and creeds? Is it not because of error? Contradiction and conflict belong to the domain of error, for error, being confusion, is in the nature of self-contradiction. If the Christian says, "My religion is true and Buddhism is false," and if the Buddhist says, "Christianity is false and Buddhism is true," we are at once confronted with an irreconcilable contradiction, for these two religions cannot be both true and false. Such a contradiction cannot spring from Truth, and must therefore spring from error. But if both these religious partisans should now say, or think, "Yes, truly the contradiction springs from error, but the error is in the other man and his religion, and not in me and mine," this does but intensify the contradiction. Whence, then, springs the error, and where is Truth? Does not the very attitude of mind which these men adopt toward each other constitute the error? and were they to reverse that attitude, exchanging antagonism for good-will, would they not perceive the Truth which does not stand in conflict with itself?

The man who says, "My religion is true, and my neighbor's is false," has not yet discovered the truth in his own religion, for when a man has done that, he will see Truth in all religions. As behind all the universal phenomena there is but one Truth, so behind all the religions and creeds there is but one religion, for every religion contains the same ethical teaching, and all the Great Teachers taught exactly the same thing.

The precepts of the Sermon on the Mount are to be found in all religions, and the life which those precepts demand was lived by all the Great Teachers and many of their disciples, for the Truth is a pure heart and a blameless life, and not a set of dogmas and opinions. All religions teach purity of heart, holiness of life, compassion, love, and good-will; they teach the doing of good deeds and the giving up of selfishness and sin. These things are not dogmas, theologies, and opinions, they are things to be done, to be practised, to be lived. Men do not differ about these things, for they are the acknowledged verities in every sect. What, then, do they differ about? About their opinions, their speculations, their theologies.

Men differ about that which is unreal, not that which is real; they fight over error, and not over Truth. The very essential of all religion (and religions) is that before a man can know anything of Truth, he must cease from fighting his fellow-man, and shall learn to regard him with good-will and love; and how can a man do this while he is convinced that his neighbor's religion is false, and that it is his duty to do all that he can to undermine and overthrow it? This is not doing unto others as we would that they should do to us.

That which is true and real is true and real everywhere and always. There is no distinction between the pious Christian and the pious Buddhist. Purity of heart, piety of life, holy aspirations, and the love of Truth are the same in the Buddhist as the Christian. The good deeds of the Buddhist are not different from the good deeds of the Christian. Remorse for sin and sorrow for wrong thoughts and deeds spring in the hearts, not only of Christians, but men of all religions. Great is the need of sympathy. Great is the need of love.

All religions are the same in that they teach the same fundamental verities, but men, instead of practising these verities, engage in opinions and speculations about things which are outside the range of knowledge and experience, and it is in defending and promulgating their own particular speculations that men become divided and engage in conflict with each other.

Condemnation is incipient persecution. The thought, "I am right and you are wrong," is a seed prolific of hatred. It was out of this seed that the Spanish Inquisition grew. He who would find the universal Truth must abandon egotism, must quench the hateful flames of condemnation, and, taking out of his heart the baneful thought, "All others are wrong," must think the illuminating thought, "It is I who am wrong," and having thus thought, he will cease from sin, and will live in love and good-will toward all, making no distinctions, engaging in no divisions, a peacemaker and not a partisan. Thus living charitably disposed toward all, he will become one with all, and will comprehend the Universal Truth, the Eternal Religion; for while error refutes error and selfishness divides, Truth demonstrates Truth and Religion unifies.

LIGHT ON LAW AND MIRACLE

The love of the wonderful is an element in human nature, which, like passions and desires, requires to be curbed, directed, and finally transmuted; otherwise superstition and the obscuration of reason and insight cannot be avoided. The idea of miracle must be transcended before the orderly, eternal, and beneficent nature of law can be perceived, and that peace and certainty which a knowledge of law bestows can be enjoyed.

Just as a child when its eyes are opened to the phenomena of this world becomes involved in wonder, and revels in tales of giants and fairies, so when a man first opens his mental eyes to spiritual things does he become involved in stories of marvels and miracles; and as the child at last becomes a man and leaves behind him the crudities of childhood, understanding more accurately the relative nature of the phenomena around him, so with a fuller spiritual development and greater familiarity with the inner realities, a man at last leaves behind him the era of childish wonderment, comes into touch with the laws of things, and governs his life by principles that are fixed and invariable.

Law is universal and eternal, and, although vast areas of knowledge are waiting to be revealed, cause and effect will ever prevail, and every new discovery, every truth revealed, will serve to bring men nearer to a realization of the beauty, stability, and supremacy of law. And very gladdening it is to know that law is inviolable and eternal throughout every department of nature, for then we know that the operations of the universe are ever the same, and can therefore be discovered, understood, and obeyed. This is a ground of certainty, and therefore of great hope and joy. The idea of miracle is a denial of law and the substitution of an arbitrary and capricious power.

It is true that around the lives of the Great Teachers of humanity stories of miracle have grown, but they have emanated from the undeveloped minds of the people, and not from the Teachers themselves. Lao-Tze expounded the Supreme Law, or Reason, which admits of no miracle, yet his religion has, to-day, become so corrupted with the introduction of the marvellous as to be little better than a mass of superstition. Even Buddhism, whose founder declared that, "Seeing that the Law of Karma (cause and effect) governs all things, the disciple who aims at performing miracles does not understand the doctrine," and that "The desire to perform miracles arises either from covetousness or vanity," has surrounded, in its corrupted form, the life of its Great Master with a number of miracles. Even during the lifetime of Ramakrishna, the Hindu teacher who died in 1886, and who is regarded by his disciples as an incarnation of Deity to this age, all sorts of miracles were attributed to him by the people, and are now associated with his name; yet, according to Max Müller, these miracles are without any foundation of evidence or fact, and Ramakrishna himself ridiculed and repudiated miracle.

As men become more enlightened, miracles and wonder-working will be expunged from religion, and the orderly beauty of Law and the ethical grandeur of obedience to Law will become revealed and known. No man who desires to perform miracles or astral or psychological wonders, who is curious to see invisible or supernatural beings, or who is ambitious to become a "Master" or an "Adept," can attain a clear perception of Truth and the living of the highest life. Childish wonderment about things must be supplanted by knowledge of things, and vanity is a complete barrier to the entrance of the true path which demands of the disciple lowliness of heart, humility. He is on the true path who is cultivating kindliness, forbearance, and a loving heart; and the marks of the true Master are not miracles and wonder-working, but infinite patience, boundless compassion, spotless purity, and a heart at peace with all.

LIGHT ON WAR AND PEACE

War springs from inward strife. "War in heaven" precedes war on earth. When the inward spiritual harmony is destroyed by division and conflict, it will manifest itself outwardly in the form of war. Without this inward conflict war could not be, nor can war cease until the inward harmony is restored.

War consists of aggression and resistance, and after the fight has commenced both combatants are alike aggressors and resisters. Thus the effort to put an end to war by aggressive means produces war. "I have set myself stubbornly against the war spirit," said a man a short time ago. He did not know that he was, by that attitude of mind, practising and fostering the war spirit.

To fight against war is to produce war. It is impossible to fight for peace, because all fighting is the annihilation of peace. To think of putting an end to war by denouncing and fighting it is the same as if one should try to quench fire by throwing straw upon it. He, therefore, who is truly a man of peace, does not resist war, but practises peace. He who takes sides and practises attack and defence, is responsible for war, for he is always at war in his mind. He cannot know the nature of peace, for he has not arrived at peace in his own heart. The true man of peace is he who has put away from his mind the spirit of quarreling and party strife, who neither attacks others nor defends himself, and whose heart is at peace with all. Such a man has already laid in his heart the foundations of the empire of peace; he is a peace maker, for he is at peace with the whole world and practises the spirit of peace under all circumstances.

Very beautiful is the spirit of peace, and it says, "Come and rest." Bickerings, quarrellings, party divisions—these must be forever abandoned by him who would establish peace.

War will continue so long as men will allow themselves, individually, to be dominated by passion, and only when men have quelled the inward tumult will the outward horror pass away.

Self is the great enemy, the producer of all strife, and the maker of many sorrows; he, therefore, who will bring about peace on earth, let him overcome egotism, let him subdue his passions, let him conquer himself.

LIGHT ON THE BROTHERHOOD OF MAN

There is no lack of writing and preaching about "universal brotherhood," and it has been adopted as a leading article of faith by many newly formed societies; but what is so urgently needed to begin with, is not universal brotherhood, but *particular Brotherhood,* that is, the adoption of a magnanimous, charitable, and kindly spirit toward those with whom we come in immediate contact; toward those who contradict, oppose and attack us, as well as toward those who love and agree with us.

I make a very simple statement of truth when I say that until such particular brotherhood is practised, universal brotherhood will remain a meaningless term, for universal brotherhood is an end, a goal, and the way to it is by particular brotherhood; the one is a sublime and far-reaching consummation, the other is the means by which that consummation must be realized.

I remember on one occasion reading a paper devoted largely to the teaching of universal brotherhood, and the leading article—a long and learned one—was an exposition of this subject; but on turning over a few more pages, I found another piece by the same writer in which he accused of misrepresentation, lying, and selfishness, not his enemies, but the brethren of his own Society, who bear, at least as far as such sins are concerned, stainless reputations.

A scriptural writer has asked the question, "If a man love not his brother whom he hath seen, how can he love God whom he hath not seen?" In the same manner, if a man does not love the brother whom he knows, how can he love men of all creeds and all nations whom he does not know?

To write articles on universal brotherhood is one thing; to live in peace with one's relations and neighbors and to return good for evil is quite another.

To endeavor to propagate universal brotherhood while fostering in our heart some sparks of envy, spite, resentment, malice, or hatred, is to be self-deluded; for thus shall we be all the time hindering and denying, by our actions, that which we eulogize by our words; but so subtle is such self-delusion, that, until the very heights of love and wisdom are reached, we are all liable at any moment to fall into it.

It is not because our fellow-men do not hold our views, or follow our religion, or see as we see, that universal brotherhood remains unrealized, but because of the prevalence of ill-will; and if we hate, avoid, and condemn others because they differ from us, or treat selfishly and harshly those who are near to us, all that we may say or do in the cause of universal brotherhood will be only another snare to our feet, a mockery to our aspirations, and a farce to the world at large.

Let us, then, remove all hatred and malice from our hearts; let us be filled with good-will toward those who try and test us by their immediate nearness; let us love them that hate us, and think magnanimously of those who condemn us or our doctrine—in a word, let us take the first step toward universal brotherhood, by practising brotherhood in the place where we now are, and toward those with whom we associate, which is the place where it is most needed; and as we succeed in being brotherly in these important particulars, universal brotherhood will be found to be not far distant.

LIGHT ON LIFE'S SORROWS

There is great sorrow in the world. This is one of the supreme facts of life. Grief and afflic-tion visit every heart, and many that are to-day revelling in hilarious joy or sinful riot, will to-morrow be smitten low with sorrow. Suddenly, and with swift and silent certainty, comes its poignant arrow, entering the human heart, slaying its joy, laying low its hopes, and shat-tering all its earthly plans and prospects. Then the humbled, smitten soul reflects, and enters deeply and sympathetically into the hidden meanings of human life.

In the dark times of sorrow, men approach very near to Truth. When in one brief hour the builded hopes of many years of toil fall like a toy palace, and all earthly pleasures burst and vanish like petty bubbles in the grasp, then the crushed spirit, bewildered, tempest-tossed, and without a refuge, gropes in dumb anguish for the Eternal, and seeks its abiding peace.

"Blessed are they that mourn," said the Teacher of the West, and the Teacher of the East declared that "Where there is great suffering there is great bliss." Both these sayings express the truth that sorrow is a teacher and a purifier. Sorrow is not the end of life—though it is, in its consummation, the end of the worldly life—but it is the beginning of the heavenly life; it leads the bewildered spirit into rest and safety; for the end of sorrow is joy and peace.

Strong searcher for Truth! Strenuous fighter against self and passion! seasons of sorrow must be your portion for a time. While any vestige of self remains, temptations will assail you, and the veil of illusion will cloud your spiritual vision, producing sorrow and unrest; and when heavy clouds settle down upon your spirit, accept the darkness as your own, and pass through it bravely into the cloudless light beyond.

Bear well in mind that nothing can overtake you that does not belong to you and that is not for your eternal good. As the poet has truly sung—

Nor space nor time, nor deep nor high Can keep my own away from me.

And not alone are the bright things of life yours; the dark things are yours also. When difficulties and troubles gather thickly about you; when failures come and friends fall away; when the tongue that sweetly praised you, bitterly blames; when beloved lips that pressed upon your lips the soft, warm kisses of love, taunt and mock you in the lonely hour of your solitary grief; or when you lay beneath the sod the cold casket of clay that but yesterday held the responsive spirit of your beloved,—when these things overtake you, remember that the hour of your Gethsemane has come, that the cup of anguish is yours to drink. Drink it silently and murmur not, for in that hour of oppressive darkness and blinding pain no prayer will save you, no cry to heaven will bring you sweet relief; but faith and patience only will give you the strength to endure, and to go through your crucifixion with a meek and gentle spirit, not complaining, blaming no one, but accepting it as your own.

When one has reached the lowest point of sorrow; when, weak and exhausted, and overcome with a sense of powerlessness, he cries to God for help, and there comes no answering comfort and no succor—then, discovering the painfulness of sorrow and the insufficiency of prayer alone, he is ready to enter the path of self-renunciation, ready to purify his heart, ready to practice self-control, ready to become a spiritual athlete, and to develop that divine and invincible strength which is born of self-mastery.

He will find the cause of sorrow in his own heart, and will remove it. He will learn to stand alone; not craving sympathy from any, but giving it to all. Not thoughtlessly sinning and remorsefully repenting, but studying how not to commit sin. Humbled by innumerable defeats, and chastened by many sufferings, he will learn how to act blamelessly toward others, how to be gently and strong, kind and steadfast, compassionate and wise.

Thus he will gradually rise above sorrow, and at last Truth will dawn upon his mind, and he will understand the meaning of abiding peace. His mental eye will open to perceive the Cosmic Order. He will be blessed with the Vision of the Law, and will receive the Beatific Bliss.

When the true order of things is perceived, sorrow is transcended. When the contracted personal self which hugs its own little fleeting pleasures and broods over its own petty disappointments and dissatisfactions is broken up and cast away, then the larger life of Truth enters the mind, bringing bliss and peace; and the Universal Will takes the place of self. The individual becomes one with humanity. He forgets self in his love for all. His sorrow is swallowed up in the bliss of Truth.

Thus when you have, by experience, entered completely into the sorrow that is never lifted from the heart of mankind; when you have reaped and eaten all the bitter fruits of your own wrong thoughts and deeds—then divine compassion for all suffering beings will be born in your heart, healing all your wounds and drying all your tears. You will rise again into a new and heavenly life, where the sting of sorrow cannot enter, for there is no self there. After the crucifixion comes the transfiguration; the sorrowless state is reached through sorrow, and "the wise do not grieve."

Ever remember this—in the midst of sin and sorrow there abides the world of Truth. Redemption is at hand. The troubled may find peace; the impure may find purity. Healing awaits the broken-hearted; the weak will be adorned with strength, and the downtrodden will be lifted up and glorified.

LIGHT ON LIFE'S CHANGES

The tendency of things to advance from a lower to a higher level, and from high to higher still, is universal. The worlds exist in order that beings may experience, and by experiencing, acquire knowledge and increase in wisdom.

Evolution is only another word for progress. It signifies perpetual change, but a purposeful change, a change accompanied by growth. Evolution does not mean the creation of a new being from a being of a different order; it means the modification of beings by experience and change; and such modification is progress.

The fact of change is ever before us. Nothing can escape it. Plants, animals, and men germinate, reach maturity, and pass into decay. Even the lordly suns and their attendant worlds rolling through illimitable spaces, although their life is reckoned in millions of years, at last decay and perish after having passed through innumerable changes. We cannot say of any being or object—"This will remain forever as it is," for even while we are saying it, the being or object would be undergoing change.

Sadness and suffering accompany this change; and beings mourn for that which has departed, for the things which are lost and gone. Yet in reality change is good, for it is the open door to all achievement, advancement and perfection.

Mind, as well as matter, is subject to the same change. Every experience, every thought, every deed, changes a man. There is little resemblance between the old man and his period of childhood and youth.

An eternally fixed, unchangeable being is not known. Such a being may be assumed, but it is a postulate only. It is not within the range of human observation and knowledge. A being not subject to change would be a being outside progress.

There is a teaching which declares that man has a spiritual soul that is eternally pure, eternally unchanged, eternally perfect, and that the sinning, suffering, changing man as we see him is an illusion—that, indeed, the spiritual soul is *the* man, and the other is an unreality.

There is another teaching that affirms that man is eternally imperfect, that stainless purity can never be reached, and that perfection is an impossibility, an illusion.

It will be found that these two extremes have no relation to *human experience*. They are both of the nature of speculative metaphysics which stand in opposition to the *facts of life*; so much so that the adherents of these two extremes deny the existence of the commonest every-day facts of human experience. That which is assumed is regarded as real; the facts of life are declared to be unreal.

It is well to avoid both these extremes, and find the middle way of human experience. It is well to avoid opinions and speculations of our own or others, it is well to *refer to the facts of life*. We see that man passes through birth and growth and old age, that he experiences sin, sickness, and death; that he sorrows and suffers, aspires and rejoices; and that he is ever looking forward to greater purity and striving toward perfection. These are not opinions, speculations, or metaphysics—they are universal facts.

If man were already perfect, there were no need for him to be perfected, and all moral teaching would be useless and ridiculous. Moreover, a perfect being could not be subject to illusion and unreality.

On the other hand, if a man could never attain to purity and perfection, his aspirations and strivings would be useless. They would indeed be mockeries; and the heavenly perfection of saintly and divine men would have to be belittled and denied.

We see around us sin and sorrow and suffering; and we see before us, in the lives of the great teachers, the sinless, sorrowless, divine state. Therefore, we know that man is an imperfect being, yet capable of, and destined for, perfection. The divine state toward which he aspires, he will reach. The fact that he so ardently desires it, means that he can reach it, even if the fact were not demonstrated in those great ones who have already attained.

Man is not a compound of two beings, one real and perfect, the other unreal and imperfect. He is one and real, and his experiences are real. His imperfection is apparent, and his advancement and progress are also apparent.

The realities of life claim men in spite of their metaphysics, and all come under the same law of change and progress. He who affirms the eternal sinlessness and perfection of man, should not, to be logical and consistent, ever speak of sins and faults, of disease and death; yet he refers to these things as matters to be dealt with. Thus in theory he denies the existence of that which he habitually recognizes in practice.

He also who denies the possibility of perfection, should not aspire or strive; yet we find him practising self-denial and striving ceaselessly toward perfection.

Holding to the theoretical does not absolve men from the inevitable. The teacher of the unreality of sickness, old age, and death is at last caught in the toils of disease, succumbs to age, and disappears in death.

Change is not only inevitable, it is constant and unvarying law. Without it, everything would remain forever as it is, and there could be neither growth nor progress.

The strenuous struggle of all life is a prophecy of its perfection. The lookings upward of all beings is evidence of their ceaseless ascension. Aspirations, ideals, moral aims, while they denote man's imperfection, assuredly point to his future perfection. They are neither unnecessary nor aimless, but are woven into the fabric of things; they belong to the vital essence of the universe.

Whatsoever a man believes or disbelieves, what theories he holds or does not hold, one thing is certain—he is found in the stream of life, and *must* think and act; and to think and act is to experience; and to experience is to change and develop.

That man is conscious of sin, means that he can become pure; that he abhors evil, signifies that he can reach up to Good; that he is a pilgrim in the land of error, assures us, without doubt, that he will at last come to the beautiful city of Truth.

LIGHT ON THE TRUTH
OF TRANSITORINESS

I t is well sometimes to meditate deeply and seriously on the truth of Transitoriness. By meditation we will come to perceive how all compounded things must pass away; yea, how even while they remain they are already in process of passing away. Such meditation will soften the heart, deepen the understanding, and render one more fully conscious of the sacred nature of life.

What is there that does not pass away, among all the things of which a man says, "This will be mine to-morrow"? Even the mind is continually changing. Old characteristics die and pass away, and new ones are formed. In the midst of life all things are dying. Nothing endures; nothing can be retained. Things appear and then disappear; they become, and then they pass away.

The ancient sages declared the visible universe to be Mâyâ, illusion, meaning thereby that impermanency is the antithesis of Reality. Change and decay are in the very nature of visible things, and they are unreal—illusory—in the sense that they pass away forever.

He who would ascend into the realm of Reality, who would penetrate into the world of Truth, must first perceive, with no uncertain vision, the transitory nature of the things of life; he must cease to delude himself into believing that he can retain his hold on his possessions, his body, his pleasures and objects of pleasure; for as the flower fades and as the leaves of the tree fall and wither, so must these things, in their season, pass away for ever.

The perception of the Truth of Transitoriness is one of the first great steps in wisdom, for when it is fully grasped, and its lesson has sunk deeply into the heart, the clinging to perishable things which is the cause of all sorrow, will be yielded up, and the search for the Truth which abides will be accelerated.

Anguish is rife because men set their hearts on the acquisition of things that perish, because they lust for the possession of those things which even when obtained cannot be retained.

There is no sorrow that would not vanish if the clinging to evanescent things were given up; there is no grief that would not be dispersed if the desire to have and to hold those things which in their very nature cannot endure, were taken out of the heart.

Tens of thousands of grief-stricken hearts are to-day bewailing the loss of some loved object which they called theirs in days that are past, are weeping over that which is gone forever and cannot be restored.

Men are slow to learn the lessons of experience and to acquire wisdom, and unnumbered griefs and pains and sorrows have failed to impress them with the Truth of Transitoriness. He who clings to that which is impermanent, cannot escape sorrow, and the intensity of his sorrow will be measured by the strength of his clinging. He who sets his heart on perishable things embraces the companionship of grief and lamentation.

Men cannot find wisdom because they will not renounce the clinging to things, because they believe that the clinging to perishable objects is the source of happiness, and not the cause of sorrow; they cannot escape unrest and enter into the life of peace because desire is difficult to quench, and the immediate and transitory pleasure which gratified desire affords is mistaken for abiding joy.

It is because the true order of things is not understood that grief is universal; it is ignorance of the fleeting nature of things that lies at the root of sorrow.

The sting of anguish will be taken out of life when the lust to hold and to preserve the things of decay is taken out of the heart.

Sorrow is ended for him who sees things as they are; who, realizing the nature of transiency, detaches his heart and mind from the things that perish.

There is a right use for perishable things, and when they are rightly used, and not doted upon for themselves alone, their loss will cause no sorrow.

If a rich man thinks in his heart, "My riches and possessions are no part of me, nor can I call them mine, seeing that when I am summoned to depart from this world, I cannot take them with me; they are entrusted to me to use rightly, and I will employ them to the best of my ability for the good of men and for the world," such a man, though surrounded by luxuries and responsibilities, will be lifted above sorrow, and will draw near to Truth. On the other hand, if the poor man does not covet riches and possessions, his condition will cause him no anxiety and unrest.

He who by a right understanding of life rids his heart of all selfish grasping and clinging, who uses everything wisely and in its proper place, and who, with chastened heart, and mind clarified of all thirsty desires, remains serene and self-contained in the midst of all changes, such a man will find Truth, he will stand face to face with Reality.

For in the midst of all error there abides the Truth; at the heart of transiency there reposes the Permanent; and illusion does but veil the eternal and unchanging Reality.

The nature of that Reality it is not my purpose to deal with here; let it suffice that I indicate that it is only found by abandoning, in the heart, all that is not of Love and Compassion and Wisdom and Purity. In these things there is no element of transitoriness, no sorrow, and no unrest.

When the truth of Transitoriness is well perceived, and when the lesson contained in the truth of Transitoriness is well learned, then does a man set out to find the abiding Truth; then does he wean his heart from those selfish elements which are productive of sorrow.

He whose treasure is Truth, who fashions his life in accordance with Wisdom, will find the Joy which does not pass away, will leave behind him the land of lamentation, and, crossing the wide ocean of illusion, will come to the Sorrowless Shore.

THE LIGHT THAT NEVER GOES OUT

Amid the multitude of conflicting opinions and theories, and caught in the struggle of existence, whither shall the confused truthseeker turn to find the path that leads to peace unending? To what refuge shall he fly from the uncertainties and sorrows of change?

Will he find peace in pleasure? Pleasure has its place, and in its place it is good; but as an end, as a refuge, it affords no shelter, and he who seeks it as such does but increase the anguish of life; for what is more fleeting than pleasure, and what is more empty than the heart that seeks satisfaction in so ephemeral a thing? There is, therefore, no abiding refuge in pleasure.

Will he find peace in wealth and worldly success? Wealth and worldly success have their place, but they are fickle and uncertain possessions, and he who seeks them for themselves alone will be burdened with many anxieties and cares; and when the storms of adversity sweep over his glittering yet frail habitation, he will find himself helpless and exposed. But even should he maintain such possessions throughout life, what satisfaction will they afford him in the hour of death? There is no abiding refuge in wealth and worldly success.

Will he find peace in health? Health has its place, and it should not be thrown away or despised, but it belongs to the body which is destined for dissolution, and is therefore perishable. Even should health be maintained for a hundred years, the time will come when the physical energies will decline and debility and decay will overtake them. There is no abiding refuge in health.

Will he find refuge in those whom he dearly loves? Those whom he loves have their place in his life. They afford him means of practising unselfishness, and therefore of arriving at Truth. He should cherish them with loving care, and consider their needs before his own; but the time will come when they will be separated from him, and he will be left alone. There is no abiding refuge in loved ones.

Will he find peace in this Scripture or that? Scripture fills an important place. As a guide it is good, but it cannot be a refuge, for one may know the Scripture by heart, and yet be in sore conflict and unrest. The theories of men are subject to successive changes, and no limit can be set to the variety of textual interpretations. There is no abiding refuge in Scripture.

Will he find rest in this teacher or that? The teacher has his place, and as an instructor he renders good service. But teachers are numerous, and their differences are many; though one may regard his particular teacher as in possession of Truth, that teacher will one day be taken from him. There is no abiding refuge in a teacher.

Will he find peace in solitude? Solitude is good and necessary in its place, but he who courts it as a lasting refuge will be like one perishing of thirst in a waterless desert. He will escape men and the turmoil of the city, but he will not escape himself and the unrest of his heart. There is no abiding rest in solitude.

If, then, the seeker can find no refuge in pleasure, in success, in health, in friends, in Scripture, in the teacher, or in solitude, whither shall he turn to find that sanctuary which shall afford abiding peace?

Let him take refuge in righteousness; let him fly to the sanctuary of a purified heart. Let him enter the pathway of a blameless, stainless life, and walk it meekly and patiently until it brings him to the eternal temple of Truth in his own heart.

He who has taken refuge in Truth, even in the habitation of a wise understanding and a loving and steadfast heart, is the same whether in pleasure or pain; wealth or poverty; success or failure; health or sickness; with friends or without; in solitude or noisy haunts; and he is independent of bibles and teachers, for the Spirit of Truth instructs him. He perceives, without fear or sorrow, the change and decay which are in all things. He has found peace; he has entered the abiding sanctuary; he knows the Light that will never go out.

FOUNDATION STONES
TO HAPPINESS
AND SUCCESS

(1913)

More Good is the recompense of Good;
More Virtue is the reward of Virtue;
More capacity is the crown of Use.
In Goodness, Virtue, and the wise use of all our powers is all happiness.
Other forms of happiness are fleeting,
But this abides, and does not pass away.

FOREWORD

How does a man begin the building of a house? He first secures a plan of the proposed edifice, and then proceeds to build according to the plan, scrupulously following it in every detail, beginning with the foundation. Should he neglect the beginning—the beginning on a mathematical plan—his labor would be wasted, and his building, should it reach completion without tumbling to pieces, would be insecure and worthless. The same law holds good in any important work: the right beginning and first essential is *a definite mental plan on which to build*.

Nature will have no slipshod work, no slovenliness, and she annihilates confusion, or rather, confusion is in itself annihilated. Order, definiteness, purpose, eternally prevail, and he who in his operations ignores these mathematical elements at once deprives himself of substantiality, completeness, happiness, and success.

—James Allen

EDITOR'S PREFACE

This is one of the last manuscripts written by James Allen. Like all his works it is eminently practical. He never wrote *theories*, or for the sake of writing; but he wrote when he had a message, and it became a message *only when he had lived it out in his own life*, and knew that it was good. Thus he wrote *facts*, which he had proven by practice.

To live out the teaching of this book faithfully in every detail of life will lead one to more than happiness and success—even to Blessedness, Satisfaction, and Peace.

—LILY L. ALLEN
Bryngoleu,
Ilfracombe, England

CONTENTS

RIGHT PRINCIPLES

It is wise to know what comes first, and what to do first. To begin anything in the middle or at the end is to make a muddle of it. The athlete who began by breaking the tape would not receive the prize. He must begin by facing the starter and toeing the mark, and even then a good start is important if he is to win. The pupil does not begin with algebra and literature, but with counting and A B C. So in life—the business men who begin at the bottom, achieve the more enduring success; and the religious men who reach the highest heights of spiritual knowledge and wisdom are they who have stooped to serve a patient apprenticeship to the humbler tasks, and have not scorned the common experiences of humanity, or overlooked the lessons to be learned from them.

The first things in a sound life—and therefore in a truly happy and successful life—are *right principles*. Without right principles to begin with, there will be wrong practices to follow with, and a bungled and wretched life to end with. All the infinite variety of calculations which tabulate the commerce and science of the world, come out of the ten figures; all the hundreds of thousands of books which constitute the literature of the world, and perpetuate its thought and genius, are built up from the twenty-six letters. The greatest astronomer cannot ignore the ten simple figures. The profoundest man of genius cannot dispense with the twenty-six simple characters. The fundamentals in all things are few and simple; yet without them there is no knowledge and no achievement. The fundamentals—the basic principles—in life, or true living, are also few and simple, and to learn them thoroughly, and study how to apply them to all the details of life, is to avoid confusion, and to secure a substantial foundation for the orderly building up of an invincible character and a permanent success; and to succeed in comprehending those principles in their innumerable ramifications in the labyrinth of conduct, is to become a Master of Life.

The first principles in life are principles of conduct. To name them is easy. As mere words they are on all men's lips, but as fixed sources of action, admitting of no compromise, few have learned them. In this short talk I will deal with five only of these principles. These five are among the simplest of the root principles of life, but they are those that come nearest to the every-day life, for they touch the artisan, the business man, the householder, the citizen, at every point. Not one of them can be dispensed with but at severe cost, and he who perfects himself in their application will rise superior to many of the troubles and failures of life, and will come into these springs and currents of thought which flow harmoniously toward the regions of enduring success. First among these principles is—

Duty. A much-hackneyed word, I know, but it contains a rare jewel for him who will seek it by assiduous application. The principle of duty means strict adherence to one's own business, and just as strict non-interference in the business of others. The man who is continually instructing others, gratis, how to manage their affairs, is the one who most mismanages his own.

Duty also means undivided attention to the matter in hand, intelligent concentration of the mind on the work to be done; it includes all that is meant by thoroughness, exactness, and efficiency. The details of duties differ with individuals, and each man should know his own duty better than he knows his neighbor's, and better than his neighbor knows his; but although the working details differ, the principle is always the same. Who has mastered the demands of duty?

Honesty is the next principle. It means not cheating or overcharging another. It involves the absence of all trickery, lying and deception by word, look or gesture. It includes sincerity, the saying what you mean, and the meaning what you say. It scorns cringing policy and shining compliment. It builds up good reputations, and good reputations build up good businesses, and bright joy accompanies well-earned success. Who has scaled the heights of Honesty?

Economy is the third principle. The conservation of one's financial resources is merely the vestibule leading toward the more spacious chambers of true economy. It means, as well, the husbanding of one's physical vitality and mental resources. It demands the conservation of energy by the avoidance of enervating self-indulgences and sensual habits. It holds for its follower, strength, endurance, vigilance, and capacity to achieve. It bestows great power on him who learns it well. Who has realized in all its force the supreme strength of Economy?

Liberality follows economy. It is not opposed to it. Only the man of economy can afford to be generous. The spendthrift, whether in money, vitality, or mental energy, wastes so much on his own miserable pleasures as to have none left to bestow upon others. The giving of money is the smallest part of liberality. There is a giving of thoughts, and deeds, and sympathy, the bestowing of good-will, the being generous toward calumniators and opponents. It is a principle that begets a noble, far-reaching influence. It brings loving friends and stanch comrades, and is the foe of loneliness and despair. Who has measured the breadth of Liberality?

Self-control is the last of these five principles, yet the most important. Its neglect is the cause of vast misery, innumerable failures, and tens of thousands of financial, physical, and mental wrecks.

Show me the business man who loses his temper with a customer over some trivial matter, and I will show you a man who, by that condition of mind, is doomed to failure. If all men practised even the initial stages of self-control, anger, with its consuming and destroying fire, would be unknown. The lessons of patience, purity, gentleness, kindness and steadfastness which are contained in the principle of self-control, are slowly learned by men, yet until they are truly learned, a man's character and success are uncertain and insecure. Where is the man who has perfected himself in self-control? Wherever he may be, he is a Master indeed.

The five principles are five practices, five avenues to achievement, and five sources of knowledge. It is an old saying and a good rule that "Practice makes perfect," and he who would make his own the wisdom which is inherent in those principles, must not merely have them on his lips, they must be established in his heart. To know them, and receive what they alone can bring, he must *do* them, and give them out in his actions.

SOUND METHODS

From the five foregoing Right Principles, when they are truly apprehended and practised, will issue *Sound Methods*. Right principles are manifested in harmonious action, and method is to life what law is to the universe. Everywhere in the universe there is the harmonious adjustment of parts, and it is this symmetry and harmony that reveals a cosmos, as distinguished from chaos. So in human life, the difference between a true life and a false, between one purposeful and effective and one purposeless and weak, is one of method. The false life is an incoherent jumble of thoughts, passions, and actions; the true life is an orderly adjustment of all its parts. It is all the difference between a mass of lumber and a smoothly working efficient machine. A piece of machinery in perfect working order is not only a useful, but an admirable and attractive thing; but when its parts are all out of gear, and refuse to be readjusted, its usefulness and attractiveness are gone, and it is thrown on the scrap-heap. Likewise a life perfectly adjusted in all its parts so as to achieve the highest point of efficiency, is not only a powerful, but an excellent and beautiful thing; whereas a life confused, inconsistent, discordant, is a deplorable exhibition of wasted energy.

If life is to be truly lived, method must enter into, and regulate, every detail of it, as it enters and regulates every detail of the wondrous universe of which we form a part. One of the distinguishing differences between a wise man and a foolish is, that the wise man pays careful attention to the smallest things, while the foolish man slurs over them, or neglects them altogether. Wisdom consists in maintaining things in their right relations, in keeping all things, the smallest as well as the greatest, in their proper places and times. To violate order is to produce confusion and discord, and *unhappiness* is but another name for discord.

The good business man knows that system is three parts of success, and that disorder means failure. The wise man knows that disciplined, methodical living is three parts of happiness, and that looseness means misery. What is a fool but one who thinks carelessly, acts rashly and lives loosely? What is a wise man but one who thinks carefully, acts calmly, and lives consistently!

The true method does not end with the orderly arrangement of the material things and external relations of life; this is but its beginning; it enters into the adjustment of the mind—the discipline of the passions, the elimination and choice of words in speech, the logical arrangement of the thoughts, and the selection of right actions.

To achieve a life rendered sound, successful, and sweet by the pursuance of sound methods, one must begin, not by neglect of the little every-day things, but by assiduous attention to them. Thus the hour of rising is important, and its regularity significant; as also are the time of retiring to rest, and the number of hours given to sleep. Between the regularity and irregularity of meals, and the care and carelessness with which they are eaten, is all the difference between a good and bad digestion (with all that this implies) and an irritable or comfortable frame of mind, with its train of good or bad consequences, for, attaching to these meal-times and meal-ways are matters of both physiological and psychological significance. The due division of hours for business and for play, not confusing the two, the orderly fitting in of all the details of one's business, times for solitude, for silent thought and for effective action, for eating and for abstinence—all these things must have their lawful place in the life of him whose "daily round" is to proceed with the minimum degree of friction, who is to get the most of usefulness, influence, and joy out of life.

But all this is but the beginning of that comprehensive method which embraces the whole life and being. When this smooth order and logical consistency is extended to the words and actions, to the thoughts and desires, then wisdom emerges from folly, and out of weakness comes power sublime. When a man so orders his mind as to produce a beautiful working harmony between all its parts, then he reaches the highest wisdom, the highest efficiency, the highest happiness.

But this is the end; and he who would reach the end must begin at the beginning. He must systematize and render logical and smooth the smallest details of his life, proceeding step by step toward the finished accomplishment. But each step will yield its own particular measure of strength and gladness.

To sum up, method produces that smoothness which goes with strength and efficiency. Discipline is method applied to the mind. It produces that calmness which goes with power and happiness. Method is *working* by rule; discipline is *living* by rule. But working and living are not separate; they are but two aspects of character, of life.

Therefore, be orderly in work; be accurate in speech; be logical in thought. Between these and slovenliness, inaccuracy, and confusion, is the difference between success and failure, music and discord, happiness and misery.

The adoption of sound methods of working, acting, thinking,—in a word, of *living*, is the surest and safest foundation for sound health, sound success, sound peace of mind. The foundation of unsound methods will be found to be unstable, and to yield fear and unrest even while it appears to succeed; when failure comes, it is grievous indeed.

TRUE ACTIONS

Following on Right Principles and Methods, come True Actions. One who is striving to grasp true principles and work with sound methods will soon come to perceive that details of conduct cannot be overlooked,—that, indeed, those details are fundamentally distinctive or creative, according to their nature, and are, therefore, of deep significance and comprehensive importance; and this perception and knowledge of the nature and power of passing actions will gradually open and grow within him as an added vision, a new revelation. As he acquires this insight, his progress will be more rapid, his pathway in life more sure, his days more serene and peaceful; in all things he will go the true and direct way, unswayed and untroubled by the external forces that play around and about him. Not that he will be indifferent to the welfare and happiness of those about him; that is quite another thing; but he will be indifferent to their opinions, to their ignorance, to their ungoverned passions. By *True Actions*, indeed, is meant acting rightly toward others, and the right-doer knows that actions in accordance with truth are but for the happiness of those about him, and he will do them even though an occasion may arise when some one near to him may advise or implore him to do otherwise.

True actions may easily be distinguished from false by all who wish so to distinguish in order that they may avoid false action, and adopt true. As in the material world we distinguish things by their form, color, size, etc., choosing those things which we require, and putting by those things which are not useful to us, so in the spiritual world of deeds, we can distinguish between those that are bad and those that are good by their nature, their aim, and their effect, and can choose and adopt those that are good, and ignore those that are bad.

In all forms of progress, *avoidance of the bad* always precedes *acceptance and knowledge of the good*, just as a child at school learns to do its lessons right by having repeatedly pointed out to it how it has done them wrong. If one does not know what is wrong and how to avoid it, how can he know what is right and how to practice it? Bad, or untrue, actions are those that spring from a consideration of one's own happiness only, and ignore the happiness of others, that arise in violent disturbances of the mind and unlawful desires, or that call for concealment in order to avoid undesirable complications. Good, or true, actions are those that spring from a consideration for others, that arise in calm reason and harmonious thought framed on moral principles, or that will not involve the doer in shameful consequences if brought into the full light of day.

The right-doer will avoid those acts of personal pleasure and gratification which by their nature bring annoyance, pain, or suffering to others, no matter how insignificant those actions may appear to be. He will begin by putting away these; he will gain a knowledge of the unselfish and true by first sacrificing the selfish and untrue. He will learn not to speak or act in anger, or envy, or resentment, but will study how to control his mind, and will restore it to calmness before acting; and, most important of all, he will avoid, as he would the drinking of deadly poison, those acts of trickery, deceit, double-dealing in order to gain some personal profit or advantage, and which lead, sooner or later, to exposure and shame for the doer of them. If a man is prompted to do a thing which he needs to conceal, and which he would not lawfully and frankly defend if it were examined of witness, he should know by that, that it is a wrong act, and therefore to be abandoned without one further moment of consideration.

The carrying out of this principle of honesty and sincerity of action, too, will further lead him into such a path of thoughtfulness in right-doing as will enable him to avoid doing those things which would involve him in the deceptive practices of other people. Before signing papers, or entering into verbal or written arrangements, or engaging himself to others in any way at their request, particularly if they be strangers, he will first inquire into the nature of the work or undertaking, and so, enlightened, he will know exactly what to do, and will be fully aware of the import of his action. To the right-doer, *thoughtlessness* is a crime. Thousands of actions done with good intent lead to disastrous consequences because they are acts of thoughtlessness, and it is well said that "the way to hell is paved with good intentions." The man of true actions is, above all things, thoughtful; "Be ye therefore wise as serpents and harmless as doves."

The term *Thoughtlessness* covers a wide field in the realm of deeds. It is only by increasing in thoughtfulness that a man can come to understand the nature of actions, and, can, thereby, acquire the power of *always doing that which is right*. It is impossible for a man to be thoughtful and act foolishly. Thoughtfulness embraces wisdom.

It is not enough that an action is prompted by a good impulse or intention; it must arise in *thoughtful consideration* if it is to be a true action; and the man who wishes to be permanently happy in himself and a power for good to others must concern himself only with true actions. "I did it with the best of intentions" is a poor excuse from one who has thoughtlessly involved himself in the wrong-doing of others. His bitter experience should teach him to act more thoughtfully in the future.

True actions can only spring from a true mind; and therefore while a man is learning to distinguish and choose between the false and the true, he is correcting and perfecting his mind, and is thereby rendering it more harmonious and felicitous, more efficient and powerful. As he acquires the "inner eye" to clearly distinguish the right in all the details of life, and the faith and knowledge to do it, he will realize that he is building the house of his character and life upon a rock which the winds of failure and the storms of persecution can never undermine.

TRUE SPEECH

Truth is known by practice only. Without sincerity there can be no knowledge of Truth; and true speech is the beginning of all sincerity. Truth in all its native beauty and original simplicity consists in abandoning and not doing all those things which are untrue, and in embracing and doing all those things which are true. True speech is therefore one of the elementary beginnings in the life of Truth. Falsehood, and all forms of deception; slander and all forms of evil-speaking—these must be totally abandoned and abolished before the mind can receive even a small degree of spiritual enlightenment. The liar and slanderer is lost in darkness; so deep is his darkness that he cannot distinguish between good and evil, and he persuades himself that his lying and evil-speaking are necessary and good, that he is thereby protecting himself and other people.

Let the would-be student of "higher things" look to himself and beware of self-delusion. If he is given to uttering words that deceive, or to speaking evil of others—if he speaks in insincerity, envy, or malice—then he has not yet begun to study higher things. He may be studying metaphysics, or miracles, or psychic phenomena, or astral wonders—he may be studying how to commune with invisible beings, to travel invisibly during sleep, or to produce curious phenomena—he may even study spirituality theoretically and as a mere book study, but if he is a deceiver and a back-biter, the higher life is hidden from him. For the higher things are these—*uprightness, sincerity, innocence, purity, kindness, gentleness, faithfulness, humility, patience, pity, sympathy, self-sacrifice, joy, goodwill, love*—and he who would study them, know them, and make them his own, must *practice* them, there is no other way.

Lying and evil-speaking belong to the lowest forms of spiritual ignorance, and there can be no such thing as spiritual enlightenment while they are practised. Their parents are selfishness and hatred.

Slander is akin to lying, but it is even more subtle, as it is frequently associated with indignation, and by assuming more successfully the appearance of truth, it ensnares many who would not tell a deliberate falsehood. For there are two sides to slander—there is *the making or repeating of it*, and there is *the listening to it and acting upon it*. The slanderer would be powerless without a listener. Evil words require an ear that is receptive to evil in which they may fall, before they can flourish; therefore he who listens to a slander, who believes it, and allows himself to be influenced against the person whose character and reputation are defamed, is in the same position as the one who framed or repeated the evil report. The evil-speaker is a positive slanderer; the evil-listener is a passive slanderer. The two are co-operators in the propagation of evil.

Slander is a common vice and a dark and deadly one. An evil report begins in ignorance, and pursues its blind way in darkness. It generally takes its rise in a misunderstanding. Some one feels that he, or she, has been badly treated, and, filled with indignation and resentment, unburdens himself to his friends and others in vehement language, exaggerating the enormity of the supposed offence on account of the feeling of injury by which he is possessed; his listeners, without hearing *the other person's* version of what has taken place, and on no other proof than the violent words of an angry man or woman, become cold in their attitude toward the one spoken against, and repeat to others what they have been told, and as such repetition is always more or less inaccurate, a distorted and altogether untrue report is soon passing from mouth to mouth.

It is because slander is such a common vice that it can work the suffering and injury that it does. It is because so many (not deliberate wrong-doers, and unconscious of the nature of the evil into which they so easily fall) are ready to allow themselves to be influenced against one whom they have hitherto regarded as honorable, that an evil report can do its deadly work. Yet its work is only amongst those who have not altogether acquired the virtue of true speech, the cause of which is a truth-loving mind. When one who has not entirely freed himself from repeating or believing an evil report about another, hears of an evil report about himself, his mind becomes aflame with burning resentment, his sleep is broken and his peace of mind is destroyed. He thinks the cause of all his suffering is in the other man and what that man has said about him, and is ignorant of the truth that *the root and cause of his suffering lies in his own readiness to believe an evil report about another*. The virtuous man—he who has attained to true speech, and whose mind is sealed against even the appearance of evil-speaking—cannot be injured and disturbed about any evil reports concerning himself; and although his reputation may for a time be stained *in the minds of those who are prone to suggestions of evil*, his integrity remains untouched and his character unsoiled; for no one can be stained by the evil deeds of another, but only by his own wrong-doing. And so, through all misrepresentation, misunderstanding, and contumely, he is untroubled and unrevengeful; his sleep is undisturbed, and his mind remains in peace.

True speech is the beginning of a pure, wise and well-ordered life. If one would attain to purity of life, if he would lessen the evil and suffering of the world, let him abandon falsehood and slander in thought and word, let him avoid even the appearance of these things, for there are no lies and slanders so deadly as those which are half-truths, and let him not be a participant in evil-speaking by listening to it. Let him also have compassion on the evil-speaker, knowing how such a one is binding himself to suffering and unrest; for no liar can know the bliss of Truth; no slanderer can enter the kingdom of peace.

By the words which he utters is a man's spiritual condition declared; by these also is he finally and infallibly adjudged, for as the Divine Master of the Christian world has declared:—"By thy words shalt thou be justified, and by thy words shalt thou be condemned."

EQUAL-MINDEDNESS

To be equally minded is to be peacefully minded, for a man cannot be said to have arrived at peace who allows his mind to be disturbed and thrown off the balance by occurrences.

The man of wisdom is dispassionate, and meets all things with the calmness of a mind in repose and free from prejudice. He is not a partisan, having put away passion, and he is always at peace with himself and the world, not taking sides nor defending himself, but sympathizing with all.

The partisan is so convinced that his own opinion and his own side are right, and all that goes contrary to them is wrong, that he cannot think there is any good in the other opinion and the other side. He lives in a continual fever of attack and defence, and has no knowledge of the quiet peace of an equal mind.

The equal-minded man watches himself in order to check and overcome even the appearance of passion and prejudice in his mind, and by so doing he develops sympathy for others, and comes to understand their position and particular state of mind; and as he comes to understand others, he perceives the folly of condemning them and opposing himself to them. Thus there grows up in his heart a divine charity which cannot be limited, but which is extended to all things that live and strive and suffer.

When a man is under the sway of passion and prejudice he is spiritually blind. Seeing nothing but good in his own side, and nothing but evil in the other, he cannot see anything as it really is, not even his own side; and not understanding himself, he cannot understand the hearts of others, and thinks it is right that he should condemn them. Thus there grows up in his heart a dark hatred for those who refuse to see with him and who condemn him in return, he becomes separated from his fellow-men, and confines himself to a narrow torture-chamber of his own making.

Sweet and peaceful are the days of the equal-minded man, fruitful in good, and rich in manifold blessings. Guided by wisdom, he avoids those pathways which lead down to hatred and sorrow and pain, and takes those which lead up to love and peace and bliss. The occurrences of life do not trouble him, nor does he grieve over those things which are regarded by mankind as grievous, but which must befall all men in the ordinary course of nature. He is neither elated by success nor cast down by failure. He sees the events of his life arrayed in their proper proportions, and can find no room for selfish wishes or vain regrets, for vain anticipations and childish disappointments.

And how is this equal-mindedness—this blessed state of mind and life—acquired? Only by over-coming one's self, only by purifying one's own heart, for the purification of the heart leads to unbiassed comprehension, unbiassed comprehension leads to equal-mindedness, and equal-mindedness leads to peace. The impure man is swept helplessly away on the waves of passion; the pure man guides himself into the harbor of rest. The fool says, "I have an opinion"; the wise man goes about his business.

GOOD RESULTS

A considerable portion of the happenings of life come to us without any *direct* choosing on our part, and such happenings are generally regarded as having no relation to our will or character, but as appearing fortuitously, as occurring without a cause. Thus one is spoken of as being "lucky," and another "unlucky," the inference being that each has received something which he never earned, never caused. Deeper thought and a clearer insight into life convince us, however, that nothing happens without a cause, and that cause and effect are always related in perfect adjustment and harmony. This being so, every happening directly affecting us is intimately related to our own will and character, is, indeed, an effect justly related to a cause having its seat in our consciousness. In a word, involuntary happenings of life are the results of our own thoughts and deeds. This, I admit, is not apparent on the surface, but what fundamental law, even in the physical universe, *is* so apparent? If thought, investigation, and experiment are necessary to the discovery of the principles which relate one material atom to another, even so are they imperative to the perception and understanding of the mode of action which relate one mental condition to another; and such modes, such laws, are known by the right-doer, by him who has acquired an understanding mind by the practice of true actions.

We reap as we sow. Those things which come to us, though not by our own *choosing*, are by our *causing*. The drunkard did not choose the delirium tremens or insanity which overtook him, but he caused it by his own deeds. In this case the law is plain to all minds, but where it is not so plain, it is none the less true. Within ourselves is the deep-seated cause of all our sufferings, the spring of all our joys. Alter the inner world of thoughts, and the outer world of events will cease to bring you sorrow; make the heart pure, and to you all things will be pure, all occurrences happy and in true order.

> *Within yourselves deliverance must be sought,*
> *Each man his prison makes.*
> *Each hath such lordship as the loftiest ones;*
> *Nay, for with Powers above, around, below*
> *As with all flesh and whatsoever lives,*
> *Act maketh joy or woe.*

Our life is good or bad, enslaved or free, according to its causation in our thoughts, for out of these thoughts spring all our deeds; and from these deeds come equitable results. We cannot seize good results violently, like a thief, and claim and enjoy them, but we can bring them to pass by setting in motion the causes within ourselves.

Men strive for money, sigh for happiness, and would gladly possess wisdom, yet fail to secure these things, while they see others to whom these blessings appear to come unbidden. The reason is that they have generated causes which prevent the fulfilment of their wishes and efforts.

Each life is a perfectly woven net-work of causes and effects, of efforts (or lack of efforts) and results, and good results can only be reached by initiating good efforts, good causes. The doer of true actions, who pursues sound methods grounded on right principles, will not need to strive and struggle for good results; they will be there as the effects of his righteous rule of life. He will reap the fruit of his own actions and the reaping will be in gladness and peace.

This truth of sowing and reaping in the moral sphere is a simple one, yet men are slow to understand and accept it. We have been told by a Wise One that "the children of darkness are wiser in their day than the children of light," and who would expect, in the material world, to reap and eat where he had not sown and planted? Or who would expect to reap wheat in the field where he had sown tares, and would fall to weeping and complaining if he did not? Yet this is just what men do in the spiritual field of mind and deed. They do evil, and expect to get from it good, and when the bitter harvesting comes in all its ripened fulness, they fall into despair, and bemoan the hardness and injustice of their lot, usually attributing it to the evil deeds of others, refusing even to admit the possibility of its cause being hidden in themselves, in their own thoughts and deeds. The children of light—those who are searching for the fundamental principles of right living with a view to making themselves into wise and happy beings—must train themselves to observe this law of cause and effect in thought, word and deed, as implicitly and obediently as the gardener obeys the law of sowing and reaping. He does not even question the law; he recognizes and obeys it. When the wisdom which he instinctively practises in his garden, is practised by men in the garden of their minds—when the law of the sowing of deeds is so fully recognized that it can no longer be doubted or questioned—then it will be just as faithfully followed by the sowing of those actions which will bring about a reaping of happiness and well-being for all. As the children of matter obey the laws of matter, so let the children of spirit obey the laws of spirit, for the law of matter and the law of spirit are one; they are but two aspects of one thing; the outworking of one principle in opposite directions.

If we observe right principles or causes, wrong effects cannot possibly accrue. If we pursue sound methods, no shoddy thread can find its way into the web of our life, no rotten brick enter into the building of our character to render it insecure; and if we do true actions, what but good results can come to pass; for to say that good causes can produce bad effects is to say that nettles can be reaped from a sowing of corn.

He who orders his life along the moral lines thus briefly enunciated, will attain to such a state of insight and equilibrium as to render him permanently happy and perennially glad; all his efforts will be seasonably planted; all the issues of his life will be good, and though he may not become a millionaire—as indeed he will have no desire to become such—he will acquire the gift of peace, and true success will wait upon him as its commanding master.

JAMES ALLEN'S BOOK
OF MEDITATIONS
FOR EVERY DAY
IN THE YEAR

(1913)

He who does not find
The way of Meditation cannot reach
Emancipation and enlightenment.
But thou wilt find the way of Holy Thought;
With mind made calm and steadfast, thou wilt see
The Permanent amid the mutable,
The Truth eternal in the things that change:
Thou wilt behold the Perfect Law: Cosmos
From Chaos rises when the conquered self
Lies underneath man's heel: Love be thy strength;
Look on the passion-tortured multitudes,
And have compassion on them; know their pain
By thy long sorrow ended. Thou will come
To perfect peace, and so wilt bless the world,
Leading unto the High and Holy Way
The feet of them that seek.—And now I go
To my Abode; go thou unto thy work.

EDITOR'S PREFACE

James Allen may truly be called the Prophet of Meditation. In an age of strife, hurry, religious con-troversy, heated arguments, ritual and ceremony, he came with his message of Meditation, calling men away from the din and strife of tongues into the peaceful paths of stillness within their own souls, where "the Light that lighteth every man that cometh into the world" ever burns steadily and surely for all who will turn their weary eyes from the strife *without* to the quiet *within*. Many of the Meditations were written as he came down from the Cairn in the early morning, where he spent those precious hours alone with God while the world slept. Others are gleaned from his many writ-ings, published and *unpublished*, and are arranged for daily readings at his request, and, we believe, under his spiritual guidance. The book must ever be a stronghold of Spiritual Truth and blessing to all who read it, and especially to those who use it for daily meditation. Its great power lies in that it is the very heart of a good man *who lived every word he wrote*. The beautiful half-tone portrait is a speaking likeness of the Author. It was taken only six weeks before his translation, and has not been published before.

We are indebted to Messrs. Putnam's Sons (London and New York), and to Messrs. Wm. Rider and Son, Limited (London), for their cordial expressions of pleasure that some of the Meditations should be culled from the books published by them, viz., *The Mastery of Destiny*, and *Above Life's Turmoil* (Putnam), and *From Passion to Peace*, and *Man: King of Mind, Body, and Circumstance* (Rider).

—Lily L. Allen
Bryngoleu,
Ilfracombe, England

January First.

Frequently the man of passion is most eager to put others right; but the man of wisdom puts himself right. If one is anxious to reform the world, let him begin by reforming himself. The reformation of self does not end with the elimination of the sensual elements only; that is its beginning. It ends only when every vain thought and selfish aim is overcome. Short of perfect purity and wisdom, there is still some form of self-slavery or folly which needs to be conquered.

On the wings of aspiration man rises from earth to heaven, from ignorance to knowledge, from the under darkness to the upper light. Without it he remains a grovelling animal, earthly, sensual, unenlightened, and uninspired.

The way from passion to peace is by overcoming one's self.

Aspiration is the longing for heavenly things.

January Second.

Let first things be put first; work before play; duty before enjoyment; and others before self: this is an excellent rule which cannot lead astray. To make a right beginning is half-way to victory. The athlete who makes a bad start may lose his prize; the merchant who makes a false start may lose his reputation; and the Truth-seeker who makes a wrong start may forego the crown of Righteousness. To begin with pure thoughts, sterling rectitude, unselfish purpose, noble aims, and an incorruptible conscience—this is to start right; this it is to put first things first, so that all other things will follow in harmonious order, making life simple, beautiful, successful, and peaceful.

Where is peace to be found! Where is the hiding-place of truth!

The soul will cry out for its lost heritage.

January Third.

So long as animal conditions taste sweet to a man, he cannot aspire: he is so far satisfied; but when their sweetness turns to bitterness, then in his sorrow he thinks of nobler things. When he is deprived of earthly joy, he aspires to the joy which is heavenly. It is when impurity turns to suffering that purity is sought. Truly aspiration rises, phoenix-like, from the dead ashes of repentance, but on its powerful pinions man can reach the heaven of heavens.

The man of aspiration has entered the way which leads to peace; and surely he will reach that end if he stays not nor turns back. If he constantly renews his mind with glimpses of the heavenly vision, he will reach the heavenly state.

If one would find peace, he must come out of passion.

That which can be conceived can be achieved.

JANUARY FOURTH.

Man attains in the measure that he aspires. His longing to be is the gauge of what he can be. To fix the mind is to fore-ordain the achievement. As man can experience and know all low things, so he can experience and know all high things. As he has become human, so he can become divine. The turning of the mind in high and divine directions is the sole and needful task.

Our life is what we make it by our own thoughts and deeds.

There is a life of victory over sin, and triumph over evil.

What is impurity but the impure thoughts of the thinker? What is purity but the pure thoughts of the thinker? One man does not do the thinking of another. Each man is pure or impure of himself alone. The man of aspiration sees before him the pathway up the heavenly heights, and his heart already experiences a foretaste of the final peace.

JANUARY FIFTH.

The Gates of Heaven are for ever open, and no one is prevented from entering by any will or power but his own; but no one can enter the Kingdom of Heaven so long as he is enamoured of, and chooses, the seductions of hell, so long as he resigns himself to sin and sorrow.

When a man wishes and wills he can find the good and the true.

Every moment is the time of choice; every hour is destiny.

There is a larger, higher, nobler, diviner life than that of sinning and suffering, which is so common—in which, indeed, nearly all are immersed—a life of victory over sin, and triumph over evil; a life wise and happy, benign and tranquil, virtuous and peaceful. This life can be found and lived now, and he who lives it is steadfast in the midst of change; restful among the restless; peaceful, though surrounded by strife.

JANUARY SIXTH.

As the energetic man of business is not daunted by difficulties, but studies how to overcome them, so the man of ceaseless aspiration is not crushed into submission by temptations, but meditates how he may fortify his mind; for the tempter is like a coward, he only creeps in at weak and unguarded points. The tempted one should study thoughtfully the nature and meaning of temptation, for until it is known it cannot be overcome. He who is to overcome temptation must understand how it arises in his own darkness and error, and must study, by introspection and meditation, how to disperse the darkness and supplant error by truth.

The lover of the pure life renews his mind daily.

Engage daily in holy meditation on Truth and its attainment.

A man must know himself if he is to know truth. Self-knowledge is the handmaid of self-conquest.

JANUARY SEVENTH.

Every step upward means the leaving of something behind and below. The high is reached only at the sacrifice of the low. The good is secured only by abandoning the evil. Knowledge is acquired only by the destruction of ignorance. Every acquisition has its price, which must be paid "to the uttermost farthing." Every animal, every creeping thing, possesses some gift, some power, which man, in his upward march, has laid down, which he has exchanged for some higher gift, or power. What great good men forfeit by clinging to old selfish habits! Behind every humble sacrifice a winged angel waits to bear us up the heights of knowledge and wisdom.

Let him who has attained guard against falling back. Let him be careful in little things, and be well fortified against the entrance of sin.

As errors and impurities are revealed, purge them away.

Aim, with ardour, for the attainment of a perfect life.

JANUARY EIGHTH.

All the varied activities of human life are rooted in, and draw their vitality from, one common source—the human heart. The cause of all suffering and all happiness resides, not in the outer activities of human life, but in the inner activities of the heart and mind; and every external agency is sustained by the life which it derives from human conduct.

The man who cannot endure to have his errors and shortcomings brought to the surface and made known, but tries to hide them, is unfit to walk the highway of Truth. He is not properly equipped to battle with and overcome temptation. He who cannot fearlessly face his lower nature cannot climb the rugged heights of renunciation.

The strife of the world in all its forms has its origin in one common cause, namely, individual selfishness.

Each man comes under the laws of his own being, never under the laws of another.

JANUARY NINTH.

Do not despair because of failure. From your particular failure there is a special greatness, a peculiar wisdom, to be gained; and no teacher can lead you to that greatness, that wisdom, more surely and swiftly than your experience of failure. In every mistake you make, in every fall you encounter, there is a lesson of vital import if you will but search it out; and he who will stoop to discover the good in that which appears to be disastrous will rise superior to every event, and will utilise his failures as winged steeds to bear him to a final and supreme success.

When the soul is most tried, its need is greatest.

Where temptation is powerful, the greater and more enduring will be the victory.

Foolish men blame others for their lapses and sins, but let the truth-lover blame only himself. Let him acknowledge his complete responsibility for his own conduct.

JANUARY TENTH.

The old must pass away before the new can appear. The old cottage must be demolished before the new mansion can appear upon its site. The old error must be destroyed before the new truth can come. . . . The old self must be renounced before the new man can be born. When the old self of temper, impatience, envy, pride, and impurity has perished, then in its place will appear the new man of gentleness, patience, goodwill, humility, and purity. Let the old life of sin and sorrow pass; let the new life of Righteousness and Joy come in. . . . Then all that was old and ugly will be made new and beautiful.

The great need of the soul is the need of that permanent Principle called Righteousness.

A life of virtue is noble and excellent.

It is in the realisation of this Principle where the Kingdom of Heaven, the abiding home of the soul, resides, and which is the source and storehouse of every permanent blessing.

JANUARY ELEVENTH.

The deplorable failure of many outward and isolated reforms is traceable to the fact that their devotees pursue them as an end in themselves, failing to see that they are merely steps toward ultimate, individual perfection.

It matters little what is without, for it is all a reflection of your own consciousness.

It matters everything what you are within, for everything without will be mirrored and coloured accordingly.

All true reform *must come from within*, in a changed heart and mind. The giving up of certain foods and drinks, and the breaking away from certain outward habits, are good and necessary beginnings; but they are only beginnings, and to end there is to fall far short of a true spiritual life. It is good, therefore, to cleanse the heart, to correct the mind, and to develop the understanding, for we know that the one thing needed is a regenerate heart.

JANUARY TWELFTH.

The days are lengthening. Each day now the sun rises a little higher, and the light lingers a little longer. So each day we can strengthen our character; each day we can open our heart a little more to the light of Truth, and allow the Sun of Righteousness to shine more highly in our mind. The sun does not increase in volume or intensity, but the earth turns toward it, and receives more as it turns. All that there is of Truth and Good is now. It does not increase or diminish, but as we turn toward it we receive of its radiance and beneficence in ever-increasing abundance and power.

Renew your resolution daily, and in the hour of temptation do not depart from the right path.

You can acquire Truth only by practice.

As the artisan acquires skill in fashioning the articles of his craft by daily and diligent practice with his tools, so do you acquire skill in fashioning good deeds by daily and diligent practice of the Truth.

January Thirteenth.

Every day is a new birth in time, holding out new beginnings, new possibilities, new achievements. The ages have witnessed the stars in their orbits, but this day hath no age witnessed. It is a new appearance, a new reality. It heralds a new life—yea, a new order, a new society, a new age. It holds out new hopes, new opportunities, to all men. In it you can become a new man, a new woman. For you it can be the day of regeneration, renewal, rebirth. From the old past with its mistakes, failures, and sorrows, you can rise a new being, endued with power and purpose, and radiant with the inspiration of a new ideal.

The wise purify their thoughts.

Be upright, gentle, and pure-hearted.

Be chaste in mind and body. Abandon sensual pleasures. Purge the mind of selfishness, and live a life of exalted purity.

January Fourteenth.

Victory of all kinds is preceded by a season of preparation. It can no more appear spontaneously and erratically than can a flower or a mountain. Like them, it is the culminating point in a process of growth, in a series of causes and effects. No mere wishing, no magic word, will produce worldly success; it must be achieved by an orderly succession of well-directed efforts. No spiritual victory will be achieved by him who imagines that it does not begin until the hour of temptation arrives. All spiritual triumphs are gained in the silent hour of meditation, and through a series of successes in lesser trials. The time of great temptation is the climax of a conquest that long preparation has made certain and complete.

Exert yourself ceaselessly in decreasing evil and accumulating good.

Fix your minds on the practice of virtue, and the comprehension and application of fixed and noble principles.

January Fifteenth.

As the falling rain prepares the earth for the future crops of grain and fruit, so the rains of many sorrows showering upon the heart prepare and mellow it for the coming of that wisdom that perfects the mind and gladdensthe heart. As the clouds darken the earth but to cool and fructify it, so the clouds of grief cast a shadow over the heart to prepare it for nobler things. The hour of sorrow is the hour of reverence. It puts an end to the shallow sneer, the ribald jest, the cruel calumny; it softens the heart with sympathy, and enriches the mind with thoughtfulness. Wisdom is mainly recollection of all that was learned by sorrow.

Do not think that your sorrow will remain; it will pass away like a cloud.

The Never-Ending Gladness awaits your Homecoming.

Where self ends, grief passes away.

January Sixteenth.

There is no greater happiness than to be occupied with good, whether it be good thoughts, good actions, or good employment; for every good thing is fraught with bliss, and evil cannot enter the heart or house that is tenanted by all that is good. The mind whose doors are guarded by good shuts out unhappiness as the well-sentried garrison shuts out the foe. Unhappiness can only enter through unguarded doors, and even then its power over the tenant is not complete unless it find him occupied with evil. Not to entertain evil thoughts; not to do bad actions; not to engage in worthless or questionable employment, but to resort to good in all things—this is the source of supreme happiness.

Live sweetly and happily, as becomes the dignity of a true manhood and womanhood.

Pure happiness is the rightful and happy condition of the soul.

January Seventeenth.

Do not trouble about results, or be anxious as to the future; but be troubled about personal shortcomings, and be anxious to remove them; for know this simple truth—wrong does not result from right, and a good present cannot give birth to a bad future. You are the custodian of your deeds, but not of the results which flow from them. The deeds of to-day bring the happiness or sorrow of to-morrow. Be therefore concerned about what you think and do, rather than about what may or may not come to you; for he whose deeds are good does not concern himself about results, and is freed from fear of future ill.

All things are orderly and sequential, being governed by the law of causation.

Verily the Law reigneth, and reigneth for ever, and Justice and Love are its eternal ministers.

January Eighteenth.

The storm may rage without, but it cannot affect us if there is peace within. As by the fireside there is security from the fiercest storm, so the heart that is steadfast in the knowledge of Truth abides in peace, though all around be strife and perturbation. The bitter opposition of men and the unrest of the world cannot make us bitter and restless unless we enter into and co-operate with it. Rather, if we have peace in our heart, will the outer turmoil cause our peace to deepen, to take firmer root, and to show forth more abundantly in works of peace for the softening of human hearts and the enlightening of human minds.

Blessed is he who has no wrongs to remember, no injuries to forget, in whose pure heart no hateful thought about another can take root and flourish.

Speak only words which are truthful and sincere.

He who speaks evil of another cannot find the way of peace.

January Nineteenth.

When a storm has subsided, and all is calm again, observe how all nature seems to pause in a restorative silence. A restful quiet pervades all things, so that even inanimate objects seem to participate in the recuperative repose. So when a too violent eagerness or a sudden burst of passion has spent itself, there comes a period of reflective thought, a time of calm, in which the mind is restored, and things are seen in their true outlines and right proportions. It is wise to take advantage of this quiet time by gaining a truer knowledge of one's self, and forming a more kindly judgment of others. The hour of calm is the hour of restoration.

Joy comes and fills the self-emptied heart; it abides with the peaceful; its reign is with the pure.

Purification is necessarily severe. All becoming is painful.

Make your every thought, word, and deed sweet and pure.

January Twentieth.

When the tears flow, and the heart aches, remember then the sorrow of the world. When sorrow has overtaken you, remember then that it overtakes all; that none escape it; that it is the great fact in human life that makes religion a necessity. Think not that your pain is isolated and unjustly inflicted. It is but a fragment of the great pain of the world. It is the common experience of all. Perceiving this, let sorrow gently lead you into a deeper religion, a wider compassion, a tenderer regard for all men and all creatures. Let it bring you into greater love and deeper peace.

Bear well in mind that nothing can overtake you that does not belong to you, and that is not for your eternal good.

In the dark times of sorrow, men approach very near to Truth.

The end of sorrow is joy and peace.

January Twenty-first.

As light displaces darkness, and quiet follows storm, so gladness displaces sorrow, and peace comes after pain. The deeper wisdom which flows from acquaintance with sorrow brings with it a holier and more abiding joy than that shallow excitement that preceded sorrow. Between the lesser joys of the senses and the greater joy of the spirit lies the dark vale of sorrow through which all earthly pilgrims pass, and having passed through it, the Heavenly Joy, the Abiding Gladness, is henceforth our companion. They who have passed from the earthly to the heavenly pilgrimage have lifted the dark veil of sorrow from the radiant face of Truth.

The sorrowless state is reached through sorrow.

He whose treasure is Truth, who fashions his life in accordance with Wisdom, will find the Joy which does not pass away; crossing the wide ocean of illusion, he will come to the sorrowless Shore.

JANUARY TWENTY-SECOND.

In happiness and unhappiness, in joy and sorrow, in success and failure, in victory and defeat; in religion, business, circumstances; in all the issues of life, the determining factor is character. In the mentality of individuals lie the hidden causes of all that pertains to their outward life. Character is both cause and effect. It is the doer of deeds and the recipient of results. Heaven, hell, purgatory, are contained within it. The character that is impure and vicious will experience a life from which the elements of happiness and beauty are lacking, wheresoever they may be placed; but a pure and virtuous character will show forth a life that is happy and beautiful. As you make your character, so will you shape your life.

All outward oppression is but the shadow and effect of the real oppression within.

To put away self and passion, and establish one's self in right doing, this is the highest wisdom.

JANUARY TWENTY-THIRD.

When great difficulties arise, and troubles beset, regard your perplexity as a call to deeper thought and more vigorous action. Nothing will attack you that you are not capable of overcoming; no problem will vex you that you cannot solve. The greater your trial, the greater your test of strength, and the more complete and triumphant your victory. However complicated your maze of confusion may be, there is a way out of it, and the finding of that way will exercise your powers to the utmost, and will bring out all your latent skill, energy, and resource. When you have mastered that which threatens to master you, you will rejoice in a new-found strength.

Not departing from the path of holiness, but surmounting all difficulties and continuing to the end—whosoever does this will comprehend Truth.

Knowing the Truth by practice, and being at one with Truth, you will be invincible, for Truth cannot be confounded or overthrown.

JANUARY TWENTY-FOURTH.

We advance by a series of efforts. We gather strength, whether mental or physical, by a succession of strivings in given directions. Exertion, oft repeated, leads to power. It is by obeying this law that the athlete trains himself to accomplish wonderful feats of speed or endurance.

When the exertion is along intellectual lines, it leads to unusual talent, or genius; and when in spiritual channels, it leads to wisdom, or transcendent greatness. We should not mourn when circumstances are driving us to greater efforts and more protracted exertion. Events are only evil to the mind that makes them so. They are good to him that accepts their discipline as salutary.

Look not outside thee nor behind thee for the light and blessedness of Truth, but look within.

Thou wilt find Truth within the narrow sphere of thy duty, even in the humble and hidden sacrifices of thine own heart.

January Twenty-fifth.

Despondency, anxiety, worry, and irritability cannot cure the ills against which they are directed. They only add more misery to the troubles that prompt them. The cultivation of a steadfast and serene spirit cannot be overlooked if life is to yield any measure of usefulness and happiness. The trifles, and even greater troubles, which annoy would soon dissolve and disappear if confronted with a temper that refuses to be ruffled and disturbed. Personal aims, wishes, schemes, and pleasures will meet with checks, rebuffs, and obstacles; and it is in learning to meet these reverses in a wise and calm spirit that we discover the true and abiding happiness within our heart.

There is no blessedness anywhere until impatience is sacrificed.

When impatience and irritability are put away, then is realised and enjoyed the blessedness of a strong, quiet, and peaceful mind.

January Twenty-sixth.

We are becoming wise when we know and realise that happiness abides in certain habits of mind, or mental characteristics, rather than in material possessions, or in certain combinations of circumstances. It is a common delusion to imagine that if one only possessed this or that—a little more money, a little more leisure, this man's talent, or that man's opportunities; or if one had better friends, or more favourable surroundings—one would be happy with a perfect felicity. Alas! discontent and misery lie in such vain wishes. If happiness is not already found within, it will never be found without. The happiness of a wise mind abides through all vicissitudes.

The greatest blessedness comes to him who infuses into his mind the purest and noblest thoughts.

Your whole life is a series of effects, having their cause in thought—in your own thought.

January Twenty-seventh.

There is an infinite patience in nature which it is profitable to contemplate. A comet may take a thousand years to complete its orbit; the sea may occupy ten thousand years in wearing away the land; the complete evolution of the human race may occupy millions of years. This should make us ashamed of our hurry, fussiness, discontent, disappointments, and ridiculous self-importance over trifling things of an hour or a day. Patience is conducive to the highest greatness, the most far-reaching usefulness, and the profoundest peace. Without it, life will lose much of its power and influence, and its joy will be largely destroyed.

> So with well-ordered strenuousness
>   Raise thou thy structure of Success.

A sweet and happy soul is the ripened fruit of experience and wisdom.

He who fills with useful pursuits the minutes as they come and go grows old in honour and wisdom, and prosperity abides with him.

January Twenty-eighth.

If to-day is cold and gloomy, is that a cause for despair? Do we not know that there are warm, bright days ahead? Already the birds are beginning to sing, and the tremulous trill in their little throats is prophetic of the approaching love of a new spring, and of the bounty of a summer that as yet is but a sleeping germ in the womb of this gloomy day, but whose birth is sure, and its full growth certain. No effort is vain. The spring of all your aspirations is near—very near; and the summer of your unselfish deeds will surely come to pass.

> Self shall depart, and Truth shall take its place;
>   The Changeless One, the Indivisible,
> Shall take up His abode in me, and cleanse
>   The White Robe of the Heart Invisible.

No pure thought, no unselfish deed, can fall short of its felicitous results, and every such result is a happy consummation.

Go to your task with love in your heart, and you will go to it light-hearted and cheerful.

January Twenty-ninth.

By earnest self-examination strive to realise, and not merely hold as a theory, that evil is a passing phase, a self-created shadow; that all your pains, sorrows, and misfortunes have come to you by a process of undeviating and absolutely perfect law; have come to you because you deserve and require them, and that by first enduring, and then understanding them, you may be made stronger, wiser, nobler. When you have fully entered into this realisation, you will be in a position to mould your own circumstances, to transmute all evil into good, and to weave, with a master hand, the fabric of your destiny.

All evil is corrective and remedial, and is therefore not permanent.

Cease to be a disobedient child in the school of experience, and begin to learn, with humility and patience, the lessons that are set for your ultimate perfection.

January Thirtieth.

Tell me what that is upon which you most frequently and intensely think, that to which, in your silent hours, your soul most naturally turns, and I will tell you to what place of pain or peace you are travelling, and whether you are growing into the likeness of the divine or the bestial. There is an unavoidable tendency to become literally the embodiment of that quality upon which one most constantly thinks. Let, therefore, the object of your meditation be above and not below, so that every time that you revert to it in thought you will be lifted up; let it be pure and unmixed with any selfish element; so shall your heart become purified and drawn nearer to Truth, and not defiled and dragged more hopelessly into error.

Meditation centred upon divine realities is the very essence and soul of prayer.

Meditation is the secret of all growth in spiritual life and knowledge.

January Thirty-first.

If you are daily praying for wisdom, for peace, for loftier purity, and a fuller realisation of Truth, and that for which you pray is still far from you, it means that you are praying for one thing, whilst living out in thought and act another. If you will cease from such waywardness, taking your mind off those things, the selfish clinging to which debars you from the possession of the stainless realities for which you pray; if you will no longer ask God to grant you that which you do not deserve, or to bestow upon you that love and compassion which you refuse to bestow upon others, but will commence to think and act in the spirit of Truth, you will day by day be growing into those realities, so that ultimately you will become one with them.

If you ceaselessly think upon that which is pure and unselfish, you will surely become pure and unselfish.

Enter the path of Meditation, and let the supreme object of your meditation be Truth.

February First.

Is there no way of escape from pain and sorrow? Are there no means by which the bonds of evil may be broken? Is permanent happiness and abiding peace a foolish dream? No, there is a way—and I speak it with gladness—by which evil may be slain for ever; there is a process by which every adverse condition or circumstance can be put on one side for ever, never to return; and there is a practice by which unbroken and unending peace and bliss can be partaken of and realised. And the

Unrest and pain and sorrow are the shadows of life.

Men remain in evil because they are not willing or prepared to learn the lesson which it came to teach them.

beginning of the way which leads to this glorious realisation is *the acquirement of a right understanding of the nature of evil.* It is not sufficient to deny or ignore evil; it must be understood.

February Second.

Evil, when rightly understood, is found to be, not an unlimited power or principle in the universe, but a passing phase of human experience, and it therefore becomes a teacher to those who are willing to learn. Evil is not an abstract something outside yourself; it is an experience in your own heart, and by patiently examining and rectifying your heart you will be gradually led into the discovery of the origin and nature of evil, which will necessarily be followed by its complete eradication. . . . There is no evil in the universe which is not the result of ignorance, and which would not, if we were ready and willing to learn its lesson, lead us to higher wisdom, and then vanish away.

You must get outside yourself, and must begin to examine and understand yourself.

Every soul attracts its own, and nothing can possibly come to it that does not belong to it.

February Third.

All that you positively know is contained in your own experience; all that you ever will know must pass through the gateway of experience, and so become part of yourself. Your own thoughts, desires, and aspirations comprise your world, and, to you, all that there is in the universe of beauty, and joy, and bliss, or of ugliness, and sorrow, and pain, is contained within yourself. By your own thoughts you make or mar your life, your world, your universe. As you build within by the power of thought, so will your outward life and circumstances shape themselves accordingly. Whatsoever you harbour in the inmost chambers of your heart will, sooner or later, by the inevitable law of reaction, shape itself in your outward life.

What you are, so is your world.

Every soul is a complex combination of gathered experiences and thoughts, and the body is but an improvised vehicle for its manifestation.

February Fourth.

He who clings to self is his own enemy, and is surrounded by enemies. He who relinquishes self is his own saviour, and is surrounded by friends like a protecting belt. Before the divine radiance of a pure heart all darkness vanishes and all clouds melt away, and he who has conquered self has conquered the universe. Come, then, out of your pov-

To them that seek the highest Good All things subserve the wisest ends.

All glory and all good await The coming of Obedient feet.

erty; come out of your pain; come out of your troubles, and sighings, and complainings, and heartaches, and loneliness *by coming out of yourself.* Let the old tattered garment of your petty selfishness fall from you, and put on the new garment of universal Love. You will then realise the inward heaven, and it will be reflected in all your outward life.

February Fifth.

When the thought-forces are directed in harmony with the over-ruling Law, they are up-building and preservative, but when subverted they become disintegrating and self-destructive. To adjust all your thoughts to a perfect and unswerving faith in the omnipotence and supremacy of Good is to co-operate with that Good, and to realise within yourself the solution and destruction of all evil. *Believe and ye shall live.* And here we have the true meaning of salvation; salvation from the darkness and negation of evil, by entering into and realising the living light of the Eternal Good.

All men's accomplishments were first wrought out in thought, and then objectivised.

It is the silent and conquering thought-forces which bring all things into manifestation.

February Sixth.

There is no difficulty, however great, but will yield before a calm and powerful concentration of thought, and no legitimate object but may be speedily actualised by the intelligent use and direction of one's soul-forces.

Not until you have gone deeply and searchingly into your inner nature, and have overcome many enemies that lurk there, can you have any approximate conception of the subtle power of thought, of its inseparable relation to outward and material things, or of its magical potency, when rightly poised and directed, in re-adjusting and trans-forming the life-conditions. Every thought you think is a force sent out, and in accordance with its nature and intensity will it go out to seek a lodgment in minds receptive to it, and will react upon yourself for good or evil.

There is nothing that a strong faith and an unflinching purpose may not accomplish.

Think good thoughts, and they will quickly become actualised in your outward life in the form of good conditions.

February Seventh.

If you would acquire overcoming power, you must cultivate poise and passivity. You must be able to stand alone. All power is associated with immovability. The mountain, the massive rock, the storm-tried oak, all speak to us of power, because of their combined solitary grandeur and defiant fixity; while the shifting sand, the yielding twig, and the waving reed speak to us of weakness, because they are movable and non-resistant, and are utterly useless when detached from their fellows. He is the man of power who, when all his fellows are swayed by some emotion or passion, remains calm and unmoved. The hysterical, the fearful, the thoughtless and frivolous, let such seek company, or they will fall for lack of support; but the calm, the fearless, the thoughtful and grave, let such seek solitude, and to their power more power will be added.

He only is fitted to command and control who has succeeded in commanding and controlling himself.

Be of single aim. Have a legitimate and useful purpose, and devote yourself unreservedly to it.

February Eighth.

If you would realise true prosperity, do not settle down, as many have done, into the belief that if you do right everything will go wrong. Do not allow the word *competition* to shake your faith in the supremacy of righteousness. I care not what man may say about the laws of competition, for do I not know the Unchangeable Law, which shall one day put them all to rout, and which puts them to rout even now in the heart and life of the righteous man? And knowing this Law I can contemplate all dishonesty with undisturbed repose, for I know where certain destruction awaits it. Those who have wandered from the highway of righteousness guard themselves against competition; those who always pursue the right need not to trouble about such defence.

Self-seeking is self-destruction.

Under all circumstances do that which you believe to be right, and trust the Law; trust the Divine Power, and you will always be protected.

February Ninth.

The wisely loving heart commands without exercising any authority. All things and all men obey him who obeys the Highest. He thinks, and lo! he has already accomplished! He speaks, and behold! a world hangs upon his simple utterances! He has harmonised his thoughts with the Imperishable and Unconquerable Forces, and for him weakness and uncertainty are no more. His every thought is a purpose; his every act an accomplishment; he moves with the Great Law, not setting his puny personal will against it, and he thus becomes a channel through which the Divine Power can flow in unimpeded and beneficent expression. He has thus become Power itself.

Perfect Love is Perfect Power.

Perfect Love is Perfect Wisdom.

February Tenth.

At the outset, meditation must be distinguished from *idle reverie*. There is nothing dreamy and unpractical about it. It is *a process of searching and uncompromising thought which allows nothing to remain but the simple and naked truth.* Thus meditating you will no longer strive to build yourself up in your prejudices, but, forgetting self, you will remember only that you are seeking the Truth. And so you will remove, one by one, the errors which you have built around yourself in the past, and will patiently wait for the revelation of Truth which will come when your errors have been sufficiently removed.

If you really seek Truth, you will be willing to make the effort necessary for its achievement.

Let the supreme object of your meditation be Truth.

February Eleventh.

Spiritual meditation and self-discipline are inseparable; you will, therefore, commence to meditate upon yourself so as to try and understand yourself, for, remember, the great object you will have in view will be the complete removal of all your errors in order that you may realise Truth. You will begin to question your motives, thoughts, and acts, comparing them with your ideal, and endeavouring to look upon them with a calm and impartial eye. In this manner you will be continually gaining more of that mental and spiritual equilibrium without which men are but helpless straws upon the ocean of life.

As the flower opens its petals to receive the morning light, so open your soul more and more to the glorious light of Truth.

Soar upward on the wings of aspiration; be fearless, and believe in the loftiest possibilities.

February Twelfth.

The nature of an initial impulse will always determine the body of its results. A beginning also presupposes an ending, a consummation, achievement, or goal. A gate leads to a path, and the path leads to some particular destination; so a beginning leads to results, and results lead to a completion.

A beginning is a cause, and as such it must be followed by an effect.

The effect will always be of the same nature as the cause.

There are right beginnings and wrong beginnings, which are followed by effects of a like nature. You can, by careful thought, avoid wrong beginnings and make right beginnings, and so escape evil results and enjoy good results. In aiming at the life of Blessedness, one of the simplest beginnings to be considered and rightly made is that which we all make every day—namely, the beginning of each day's life.

February Thirteenth.

Everything in the universe is made of little things, and the perfection of the great is based upon the perfection up of the small. If any detail of the universe were imperfect, the whole would be imperfect. If any particle were omitted, the aggregate would cease to be. Without a grain of dust there would be no world, and the whole is perfect because the grain of dust is perfect. Neglect of the small is confusion of the great. The snowdrop is as perfect as the star; the dewdrop is as symmetrical as the planet; the microbe is not less mathematically proportioned than the man. By laying stone upon stone, plumbing and fitting each with perfect adjustment, the temple at last stands forth in all its architectural beauty.

Wisdom inheres in the common details of everyday existence.

When the parts are made perfect, the Whole will be without blemish.

February Fourteenth.

The great man knows the vast value that inheres in moments, words, greetings, meals, apparel, correspondence, rest, work, detached efforts, fleeting obligations, in the thousand-and-one little things which press upon him for attention—briefly, in the common details of life. He sees everything as divinely apportioned, needing only the application of dispassionate thought and action on his part to render life blessed and perfect. He neglects nothing, does not hurry, seeks to escape nothing but error and folly; attends to every duty as it is presented to him, and does not postpone and regret. By giving himself unreservedly to his nearest duty, he attains to that combined childlike simplicity and unconscious power which is greatness.

To neglect small tasks, or to execute them in a perfunctory manner, is a mark of weakness and folly.

There is no way to strength and wisdom but by acting strongly and wisely in the present moment.

February Fifteenth.

The foolish man thinks that little faults, little indulgences, little sins, are of no consequence; he persuades himself that so long as he does not commit flagrant immoralities he is virtuous, and even holy; but he is thereby deprived of virtue and holiness, and the world knows him accordingly; it does not reverence, adore, and love him; it passes him by; he is reckoned of no account; his influence is destroyed. The efforts of such a man to make the world virtuous, his exhortations to his fellow men to abandon great vices, are empty of substance and barren of fruitage. The insignificance which he attaches to his small vices permeates his whole character, and is the measure of his manhood.

He who masters the small becomes the rightful possessor of the great.

He who regards his smallest delinquencies as of the gravest nature becomes a saint.

February Sixteenth.

As the year consists of a given number of sequential moments, so a man's character and life consists of a given number of sequential thoughts and deeds, and the finished whole will bear the impress of the parts.

Little kindnesses, generosities, and sacrifices make up a kind and generous character. The truly honest man is honest in the minutest details of his life. The noble man is noble in every little thing he says and does. You do not live your life in the mass; you live it in fragments, and from these the mass emerges. You can will to live each fragment nobly if you choose, and, this being done, there can be no particle of baseness in the finished whole.

Truth is wrapped up in infinitesimal details.

Thoroughness is genius.

February Seventeenth.

Truth is the one Reality in the universe, the inward Harmony, the perfect Justice, the eternal Love. Nothing can be added to it, nor taken from it. It does not depend upon any man, but all men depend upon it. You cannot perceive the beauty of Truth while you are looking out from the eyes of self. If you are vain, you will colour everything with your own vanities. If lustful, your heart and mind will be clouded with the smoke and flames of passion, and everything will appear distorted through them. If proud and opinionative, you will see nothing in the whole universe except the magnitude and importance of your own opinions. The humble Truth-lover has learned to distinguish between *opinion* and *Truth*.

Truth in its very nature is ineffable and can only be lived.

He who has most of Charity has most of Truth.

February Eighteenth.

You may easily know whether you are a child of Truth or a worshipper of self, if you will silently examine your mind, heart, and conduct. Do you harbour thoughts of suspicion, enmity, envy, lust, pride; or do you strenuously fight against these? If the former, you are chained to self, no matter what religion you may profess; if the latter, you are a candidate for Truth, even though outwardly you may profess no religion. Are you passionate, self-willed, ever seeking to gain your own ends, self-indulgent, and self-centred; or are you gentle, mild, unselfish, quit of every form of self-indulgence, and are ever ready to give up your own? If the former, self is your master; if the latter, Truth is the object of your affection.

There is but one religion, the religion of Truth.

The signs by which the Truth-lover is known are unmistakable

February Nineteenth.

Temptation waylays the man of aspiration until he touches the region of the divine consciousness, and beyond that border temptation cannot follow him. It is when a man begins to aspire that he begins to be tempted. Aspiration rouses up all the latent good and evil, in order that the man may be fully revealed to himself, for a man cannot overcome himself unless he fully knows himself. It can scarcely be said of the merely animal man that he is tempted, for the very presence of temptation means that there is a striving for a purer state. Animal desire and gratification is the normal condition of the man who has not yet risen into aspiration; he wishes for nothing more, nothing better, than his sensual enjoyments, and is, for the present, satisfied. Such a man cannot be tempted to fall, for he has not yet risen.

That which temptation appeals to and arouses is unconquered desire.

Aspiration can carry a man to heaven.

February Twentieth.

Let the tempted one know this: that he himself is both tempter and tempted; that all his enemies are within; that the flatterers which seduce, the taunts which stab, and the flames which burn, all spring from that inner region of ignorance and error in which he has hitherto lived; and knowing this, let him be assured of complete victory over evil. When he is sorely tempted, let him not mourn, therefore, but let him rejoice in that his strength is tried and his weakness exposed. For he who truly knows and humbly acknowledges his weakness will not be slow in setting about the acquisition of strength.

A man must know himself, if he is to know Truth.

He who cannot fearlessly face his lower nature cannot climb the rugged heights of renunciation.

February Twenty-first.

The giving up of self is not merely the renunciation of outward things. It consists of the renunciation of the inward sin, the inward error. Not by giving up vain clothing; not by relinquishing riches; not by abstaining from certain foods; not by speaking smooth words; not by merely doing these things is the Truth found. But by giving up the spirit of vanity; by relinquishing the desire for riches; by abstaining from the lust of self-indulgence; by giving up all hatred, strife, condemnation, and self-seeking, and becoming gentle and pure at heart, by doing these things is the Truth found.

Seek diligently the path of holiness.

The renunciation of self is the way of Truth.

February Twenty-second.

A Man commences to develop power when, checking his impulses and selfish inclinations, he falls back upon the higher and calmer consciousness within him, and begins to steady himself upon a principle.

The realisation of unchanging principles in consciousness is at once the source and secret of the highest power.

When, after much searching, and suffering, and sacrificing, the light of an eternal principle dawns upon the soul, a divine calm ensues and joy unspeakable gladdens the heart.

He who has realised such a principle ceases to wander, and remains poised and self-possessed.

He who ceases to be passion's slave becomes a master-builder in the Temple of Destiny.

Only that work endures that is built upon an indestructible principle.

February Twenty-third.

It is easy for a man, so long as he is left in the enjoyments of his possessions, to persuade himself that he believes in and adheres to the principles of Peace, Brotherhood, and Universal Love; but if, when his enjoyments are threatened, or he imagines they are threatened, he begins to clamour loudly for war, he shows that he believes in and stands upon, not Peace, Brotherhood, and Love, but strife, selfishness, and hatred.

He who does not desert his principles when threatened with the loss of every earthly thing, even to the loss of reputation and life, is the man of power, is the man whose every word endures, is the man whom the after-world honours, reveres, and worships.

Men and women of real power and influence are few.

There is no way to the acquirement of spiritual power except by that inward illumination and enlightenment.

February Twenty-fourth.

Man's essential being is inward, invisible, spiritual, and as such it derives its life, its strength, from within not from without. Outward things are channels through which its energies are expended, but for renewal it must fall back on the inward silence. In so far as man seeks to drown this silence in the noisy pleasures of the senses, and endeavours to live in the conflicts of outward things, just so much does he reap the experiences of pain and sorrow, which, becoming at last intolerable, drive him back to the feet of the inward Comforter, to the shrine of the peaceful solitude within.

All pain and sorrow is spiritual starvation, and aspiration is the cry for food.

It is in solitude only that a man can be truly revealed to himself.

February Twenty-fifth.

Take the principle of Divine Love, and quietly and diligently meditate upon it with the object of arriving at a thorough understanding of it. Bring its searching light to bear upon all your habits, your actions, your speech and intercourse with others, your every secret thought and desire. As you persevere in this course, the Divine Love will become more and more perfectly revealed to you, and your own shortcomings will stand out in more and more vivid contrast, spurring you on to renewed endeavour; and having once caught a glimpse of the incomparable majesty of that imperishable principle, you will never again rest in your weakness, your selfishness, your imperfection, but will pursue that Love until you have relinquished every discordant element, and have brought yourself into perfect harmony with it.

Inward harmony is spiritual power.

Make no stay, no resting-place, until the inmost garment of your soul is bereft of every stain.

February Twenty-sixth.

Just as the body requires rest for the recuperation of its forces, so the spirit requires solitude for the renewal of its energies. Solitude is as indispensable to man's spiritual welfare as sleep is to his bodily well-being; and pure thought, or meditation, which is evoked in solitude, is to the spirit what activity is to the body. As the body breaks down when deprived of the needful rest and sleep, so do the spirits of men break down when deprived of the necessary silence and solitude. Man, as a spiritual being, cannot be maintained in strength, uprightness, and peace except he periodically withdraw himself from the outer world of perishable things, and reach inwardly toward the abiding and imperishable realities.

In solitude a man gathers strength to meet the difficulties and temptations of life.

He who loves Truth, who desires and seeks wisdom, will be much alone.

February Twenty-seventh.

Men, clinging to self, and to the comfortless shadows of evil, are in the habit of thinking of Divine Love as something belonging to a God who is out of reach; as something outside themselves, and that must for ever remain outside. Truly, the Love of God is ever beyond the reach of self, but when the heart and mind are emptied of self then the selfless Love, the supreme Love, the Love that is of God, or Good, becomes an inward and abiding reality.

Human loves are reflections of the Divine Love.

Divine Love knows neither sorrow nor change.

And this inward realisation of holy Love is none other than the Love of Christ, that is so much talked about, and so little comprehended; the Love that not only saves the soul from sin, but lifts it also above the power of temptation.

FEBRUARY TWENTY-EIGHTH.

If a man can find no peace within himself, where shall he find it? If he dreads to be alone with himself, what steadfastness shall he find in company? If he can find no joy in communion with his own thoughts, how shall he escape misery in his contact with others? The man who has yet found nothing within himself upon which to stand will nowhere find a place of constant rest. Without is change, and decay, and insecurity; within is all surety and blessedness. The soul is sufficient of itself. Where the need is, there is the abundant supply. Your eternal dwelling-place is within.

Let a man learn to stand alone.

Be rich in yourself, be complete in yourself.

FEBRUARY TWENTY-NINTH.

Until you can stand alone, looking for guidance neither to spirits nor mortals, gods nor men, but guiding yourself by the light of the truth within you, you are not unfettered and free, not altogether blessed. But do not mistake pride for self-reliance. To attempt to stand upon the crumbling foundation of pride is to be already fallen. No man depends upon others more than the proud man. His happiness is entirely in the hands of others. But the self-reliant man stands, not upon personal pride, but on an abiding law, principle, ideal, reality, within himself. Upon this he poises himself, refusing to be swept from his strong foothold either by the waves of passion within or the storms of opinion without.

Find your centre of balance and succeed in standing alone.

Find the joy that results from well-earned freedom, the peace that flows from wise self-possession, the blessedness that inheres in native strength.

MARCH FIRST.

As the heart, so is the life. The within is ceaselessly becoming the without. Nothing remains unrevealed. That which is hidden is but for a time; it ripens and comes forth at last. Seed, tree, blossom, and fruit is the fourfold order of the universe. From the state of a man's heart proceed the conditions of his life; his thoughts blossom into deeds, and his deeds bear the fruitage of character and destiny.

Life is ever unfolding from within, and revealing itself to the light, and thoughts engendered in the heart at last reveal themselves in words, actions, and things accomplished.

As the fountain from the hidden spring, so issues man's life from the secret recesses of his heart.

Mind clothes itself in garments of its own making.

March Second.

Let man realise that life in its totality proceeds from the mind, and lo, the way of blessedness is opened to him. For he will then discover that he possesses the power to rule his mind, and to fashion it in accordance with his ideal. So will he elect to strongly and steadfastly walk those pathways of thought and action which are altogether excellent; to him life will become beautiful and sacred; and, sooner or later, he will put to flight all evil, confusion, and suffering; for it is impossible for a man to fall short of liberation, enlightenment, and peace who guards with unwearying diligence the gateway of his heart.

There is no nobler work or higher science than that of self-perfection.

He who aims at the possession of a calm, wise, and seeing mind engages in the most sublime task that man can undertake.

March Third.

It is in the nature of the mind to acquire knowledge by the repetition of its experiences. A thought which it is very difficult, at first, to hold and to dwell upon, at last becomes, by constantly being held in the mind, a natural and habitual condition. Just as a boy, when commencing to learn a trade, cannot even handle his tools aright, much less use them correctly, but after long repetition and practice plies them with perfect ease and consummate skill, so a state of mind at first apparently impossible of realisation is, by perseverance and practice, at last acquired and built into the character as a natural and spontaneous condition.

A thought constantly repeated at last becomes a fixed habit.

When the heart is pure all outward things are pure.

In this power of the mind to form and reform its habits, its conditions, is contained the basis of man's salvation, and the open door to perfect liberty by the mastery of self.

March Fourth.

A man's life, in its totality, proceeds from his mind, and his mind is a combination of habits, which he can, by patient effort, modify to any extent, and over which he can gain complete ascendancy and control. Let a man realise this, and he has at once obtained possession of the key which shall open the door to his complete emancipation.

Every sin may be overcome.

The Higher Life is a higher living in thought, word, and deed.

But emancipation from the ills of life (which are the ills of one's mind) is a matter of steady growth from within, and not a sudden acquisition from without. Hourly and daily must the mind be trained to think stainless thoughts, and to adopt right and dispassionate attitudes, until he has wrought out of it the Ideal of his holiest dreams.

MARCH FIFTH.

All duty should be regarded as sacred, and its faithful and unselfish performance one of the leading rules of conduct. All personal and selfish considerations should be extracted and cast away from the doing of one's duty; and when this is done, Duty ceases to be irksome, and becomes joyful. Duty is only irksome to him who craves some selfish enjoyment or benefit for himself. Let the man who is chafing under the irksomeness of his duty look to himself, and he will find that his wearisomeness proceeds, not from the duty itself, but from his selfish desire to escape it. He who neglects duty, be it great or small, or of a public or private nature, neglects Virtue; and he who in his heart rebels against Duty rebels against Virtue.

Without the right performance of Duty, the higher virtues cannot be known.

The virtuous man concentrates his mind on the perfect doing of his own duty.

MARCH SIXTH.

Those things which befall a man are the reflections of himself; that destiny which pursued him, which he was powerless to escape by effort, or avert by prayer, was the relentless ghoul of his own wrong deeds demanding and enforcing restitution; those blessings and curses which come to him unbidden are the reverberating echoes of the sounds which he himself sent forth.

Man is the doer of his own deeds; as such he is the maker of his own character.

Character is destiny.

Man finds himself involved in the train of causation. His life is made up of causes and effects. It is both a sowing and a reaping. Each act of his is a cause which must be balanced by its effects. He chooses the cause (this is Free-will), he cannot choose, alter, or avert the effect (this is Fate); thus Free-will stands for the power to initiate causes, and destiny is involvement in effects.

MARCH SEVENTH.

All sin is ignorance. It is a condition of darkness and undevelopment. The wrong-thinker and the wrong-doer is in the same position in the school of life as is the ignorant pupil in the school of learning. He has yet to learn how to think and act correctly, that is, in accordance with Law. The pupil in learning is not happy so long as he does his lessons wrongly, and unhappiness cannot be escaped while sin remains unconquered.

Every form of unhappiness springs from a wrong condition of mind.

Happiness is mental harmony.

Life is a series of lessons. Some are diligent in learning them, and they become pure, wise, and altogether happy. Others are negligent, and do not apply themselves, and they remain impure, foolish, and unhappy.

MARCH EIGHTH.

Selfishness, or passion, not only subsists in the gross forms of greed and glaringly ungoverned conditions of mind; it informs also every hidden thought which is subtly connected with the assumption and glorification of one's self; and it is most deceiving and subtle when it prompts one to dwell upon the selfishness of others, to accuse them of it and to talk about it. The man who continually dwells upon the selfishness in others will not thus overcome his own selfishness. Not by accusing others do we come out of selfishness, but by purifying ourselves. The way from passion to peace is not by hurling painful charges against others, but by overcoming one's self. By eagerly striving to subdue the selfishness of others, we remain passion-bound; by patiently overcoming our own selfishness we ascend into freedom.

If one would find peace, he must come out of passion.

The ascending pathway is always at hand. It is the way of self-conquest.

MARCH NINTH.

On the wings of aspiration man rises from earth to heaven, from ignorance to knowledge, from the under darkness to the upper light. Without it he remains a grovelling animal, earthly, sensual, unenlightened, and uninspired.

Aspiration is the longing for heavenly things—for righteousness, compassion, purity, love—as distinguished from desire, which is the longing for earthly things—for selfish possessions, personal dominance, low pleasures, and sensual gratifications. For one to begin to aspire means that he is dissatisfied with his low estate, and is aiming at a higher condition. It is a sure sign that he is roused out of his lethargic sleep of animality, and has become conscious of nobler attainments and a fuller life.

Aspiration—the rapture of the saints.

Aspiration makes all things possible.

MARCH TENTH.

When the rapture of aspiration touches the mind it at once refines it, and the dross of its impurities begins to fall away; yea, while aspiration holds the mind, no impurities can enter it, for the impure and the pure cannot at the same moment occupy the thought. But the effort of aspiration is at first spasmodic and short-lived. The mind falls back into its habitual error and must be constantly renewed.

The man of aspiration sees before him the pathway up to the heavenly heights.

The lover of the pure life renews his mind daily with the invigorating glow of aspiration.

To thirst for righteousness; to hunger for the pure life; to rise in holy rapture on the wings of angelic aspiration—this is the right road to wisdom; this is the right striving for peace; this is the right beginning of the way divine.

MARCH ELEVENTH.

Spiritual transmutation consists in an entire reversal of the ordinary self-seeking attitude of mind toward men and things, and this reversal brings about on entirely new set of experiences. Thus the desire for a certain pleasure is abandoned, cut off at its source, and not allowed to have any place in the consciousness; but the mental force which that desire represented is not annihilated, it is transferred to a higher region

Error is sifted away. The Gold of Truth remains.

The clear and cloudless heights of spiritual enlightenment.

of thought, transmuted into a purer form of energy. The law of conservation of energy obtains universally in mind as in matter, and the force shut off in lower directions is liberated in higher realms of spiritual activity.

MARCH TWELFTH.

Along the Saintly Way toward the divine life, the midway region of Transmutation is the Country of Sacrifice, it is the Plain of Renunciation. Old passions, old desires, old ambitions and thoughts, are cast away and abandoned, but only to reappear in some more beautiful, more permanent, more eternally satisfying form. As valuable jewels, long guarded and cherished, are thrown tearfully into the melting-pot, yet are remoulded into new and perfect adornments, so the spiritual alchemist, at first loth to part company with long-cherished thoughts and habits, at last gives them up, to discover, a little later, to his joy, that they have come back to him in the form of new faculties, rarer powers, and purer joys, spiritual jewels newly burnished, beautiful, and resplendent.

The early stage of transmutation is painful but brief, for the pain is soon transformed into pure spiritual joy.

The wise man meets passion with peace, hatred with love, and returns good for evil.

MARCH THIRTEENTH.

It is this knowledge of the Perfect Law working through and above all things; of the Perfect Justice operating in and adjusting all human affairs, that enables the good man to love his enemies, and to rise above all hatred, resentment, and complaining; for he knows that only his own can come to him, and that, though he be surrounded by persecutors, his enemies are but the blind instruments of a faultless retribu-

The present is the synthesis of the entire past; the net result of all that a man has ever thought and done is contained within him.

Characteristics are fixed habits of mind, the results of deeds.

tion; and so he blames them not, but calmly receives his accounts, and patiently pays his moral debts. But this is not all; he does not merely pay his debts; he takes care not to contract any further debts. He watches himself and makes his deeds faultless.

March Fourteenth.

Nothing comes unbidden; where the shadow is, there also is the substance. That which comes to the individual is the product of his own deeds. As cheerful industry leads to greater industry and increasing prosperity, and labour shirked or undertaken discontentedly leads to a lesser degree of labour and decreasing prosperity, so with all the varied conditions of life as we see them—they are *the effects of deeds,* destinies wrought by the thoughts and deeds of each particular individual. So also with the vast variety of characters—they are the ripening and ripened growth of the sowing of deeds, a sowing not confined solely to this visible life, but going backward through that infinite life which traverses the portals of innumerable births and deaths, and which also will extend into the illimitable future, reaping its own harvests, eating the sweet and bitter fruits of its own deeds.

Heaven and hell are in this world.

Life is a great school for the development of character.

March Fifteenth.

Man is a *thought-being,* and his life and character are determined by the thoughts in which he habitually dwells. By practice, association, and habit, thoughts tend to repeat themselves with greater and greater ease and frequency, and so "fix" the character in a given direction by producing that automatic action which is called "habit." By daily dwelling upon pure thoughts, the man of meditation forms the habit of pure and enlightened thinking which leads to pure and enlightened actions, and well-performed actions. By the ceaseless repetition of pure thoughts, he at last becomes one with those thoughts, and is a purified being, manifesting his attainment in pure actions.

Purification of the heart by repetitive thought on pure things.

Attainment of divine knowledge by embodying such purity in practical life.

March Sixteenth.

Blessed is that day, and not to be forgotten, when a man discovers that he himself is his own undoer and his own saviour. That within himself is the cause of all his suffering and lack of knowledge, and that also within is the source of all peace, enlightenment, and Godliness. Selfish thoughts, impure desires, and acts not shaped by Truth are the baneful

He who will control himself will put an end to all his sufferings.

He who will deny himself will find the holy place where calmness lives.

seeds from which all suffering springs; while selfless thoughts, pure aspirations, and the sweet acts of Truth are the seeds from which all blessedness grows.

MARCH SEVENTEENTH.

He who governs his tongue is greater than a successful disputant in the arena of intellectualism; he who controls well his mind is more powerful than the king of many nations; and he who holds himself in entire subjection is more than gods and angels. When a man who is enslaved by self realises that he must work out his own salvation, in that moment he will rise up in the dignity of his divine manhood and say, "Henceforward I will be a master in Israel, and not a slave in the House of Bondage."

Not until a man realises this, and commences to patiently purify his inner life, can he find the way which leads to lasting peace.

He who will purify himself will destroy all his ignorance.

A life of perfect peace and blessedness by means of self-government and self-enlightenment.

MARCH EIGHTEENTH.

You will be greatly helped if you devote at least *one hour* every day to quiet meditation on lofty moral subjects and their application to everyday life. In this way you will cultivate a calm, quiet strength, and will develop right perception and correct judgment. Do not be anxious to hurry matters. Do your duty to the very uttermost; live a disciplined and self-denying life; conquer impulse, and guide your actions by moral and spiritual Principles, as distinguished from your *feelings,* firmly believing that your object will be, in its own time, completely accomplished.

Impatience is a handmaid of impulse, and never helped any man.

Still go on becoming, and as you grow more perfect you will make fewer mistakes and will suffer less.

MARCH NINETEENTH.

In every heart there are two kings, but one is a usurper and tyrant; he is named self, and his thoughts and deeds are those of lust, hatred, passion, and strife; the other, the rightful monarch, is named Truth, and his thoughts and deeds are those of purity and love, meekness and peace. Brother, sister, to what monarch dost thou bow? What king hast thou crowned in thy heart? Well is it with thy soul if Thou canst say: "I bow down to the Monarch of Truth; in my inmost heart I have crowned the King of Peace." Blessed indeed and immortal shall he be who shall find in the inward and heavenly places the King of Righteousness, and shall bow his heart to Him.

The diadem of the King of Truth is a righteous life, his sceptre is the sceptre of peace, and his throne is in the hearts of mankind.

Power resides in blamelessness of heart. All earthly things are symbols.

MARCH TWENTIETH.

"The peace which passeth understanding" is a peace which no event or circumstance can shake or mar, because it is not merely a passing calm between two storms, but is an abiding peace that is born of knowledge. Men have not this peace, because they do not understand, because they do not *know,* and they do not understand and know because they are blinded and rendered ignorant by their own errors and impurities; and whilst they are unwilling to give these up, they cannot but remain entirely ignorant of impersonal Principles.

It is by the eradication of the inward errors and impurities alone that a knowledge of Truth can be gained. There is no other way to wisdom and peace.

Whilst a man loves his lusts he cannot love wisdom.

MARCH TWENTY-FIRST.

Are our sufferings and troubles entirely the result of our own ignorance and wrong-doing, or are they partly or wholly brought about by others, and by outward conditions?

Our sufferings *are* just, and are entirely the result of our own ignorance, error, and wrong-doing.

"Ye suffer from yourselves, none else compels." If this were not so, if a man could commit an evil deed and escape, the consequences of that deed being visited upon an innocent person, then there would be no Law of Justice, and without such a Law the universe could not, even for a single moment, exist. All would be chaos. Upon the surface, men *appear* to suffer through others, but it is only an appearance—an appearance which a deeper knowledge dispels.

If we could suffer, even partly, through others, our sufferings would be unjust.

Man is not the result of outward conditions; outward conditions are the result of man.

MARCH TWENTY-SECOND.

Men suffer because they love self, and do not love righteousness, and loving self they love their delusions, and it is by these that they are bound. There is one supreme liberty of which no man can be deprived by any but himself—*the liberty to love and to practice righteousness.* This includes all other liberties. It belongs to the whipped and chained slave equally as to the king, and he who will enter into this liberty will cast from him every chain. By this the slave will walk out from the presence of his oppressor, who will be powerless to stay him. By this the king will cease to be defiled by his surrounding luxuries, and will be a king indeed.

In the knowledge of truth there is freedom.

No outward oppressor can burden the righteous heart.

MARCH TWENTY-THIRD.

The wise man knows. For him anxiety, fear, disappointment, and unrest have ceased, and under whatever condition or circumstance he may be placed his calmness will not be broken, and he will bend and adjust everything with capacity and wisdom. Nothing will cause him grief. When friends yield up the body of flesh, he knows that they still *are,* and does not sorrow over the shell they have discarded. None can injure him, for he has identified himself with that which is unaffected by change.

Joy is to the sinless!

Peace is to the pure.

The knowledge which brings peace, then, is the knowledge of unchangeable Principles arrived at by the practice of pure goodness, righteousness, becoming one with which a man becomes immortal, unchangeable, indestructible.

MARCH TWENTY-FOURTH.

The flesh flatters; the Spirit reproves.

The flesh blindly gratifies; the Spirit wisely disciplines.

The flesh loves secrecy; the Spirit is open and clear.

The flesh remembers the injury of a friend; the Spirit forgives the bitterest enemy.

The flesh is noisy and rude; the Spirit is silent and gracious.

The flesh is subject to moods; the Spirit is always calm.

The flesh incites to impatience and anger; the Spirit controls with patience and serenity.

The flesh is thoughtless; the Spirit is thoughtful.

Love, meekness, gentleness, self-accusation, forgiveness, patience, compassion, reproof—these are the works of the Spirit.

Hatred, pride, harshness, accusing others, revenge, anger, cruelty, and flattery—these are the works of the flesh.

MARCH TWENTY-FIFTH.

A Truth is first perceived, and afterwards realised. The perception may be instantaneous, the realisation is almost invariably a process of gradual unfoldment. You will have to *learn* to love, regarding yourself as a child; and as you make progress in learning, the Divine will unfold within you. You can only learn to love by constantly meditating upon Love as a divine principle, and by adjusting, day by day, all your thought, and words, and acts to it. Watch yourself closely, and when you think, or say, or do anything which is not born of pure unselfish

You can only help others in so far as you have uplifted and purified yourself.

When love is perfected and revealed in the heart, Christ is known.

love, resolve that you will henceforth guard yourself in that direction. By so doing you will every day grow purer, tenderer, holier, and soon you will find it easy to love, and will realise the Divine within you.

MARCH TWENTY-SIXTH.

It is well to become conscious of your shortcomings, for, having realised them, and feeling the necessity of overcoming them, you will, sooner or later, rise above them into the pure atmosphere of duty and unselfish love. You should not picture dark things in the future, but if you think of the future at all, think of it as bright. Above all, do your duty each day, and do it cheerfully and unselfishly, and then each day will bring its own measure of joy and peace, and the future will hold much happiness for you. The best way to overcome your faults is to perform all your duties faithfully, without thinking of any gain to yourself, and to do all you can to make others happy; speaking kindly to all, doing kind things when you can, and not retaliating when others do or say unkind things.

Follow faithfully where the inward light leads you.

Put your whole heart into the present, living it, minute by minute, hour by hour, and day by day, self-governed and pure.

MARCH TWENTY-SEVENTH.

The righteous man, having nothing to hide, committing no acts which require stealth, and harbouring no thoughts and desires which he would not like others to know, is fearless and unashamed. His step is firm, his body upright, and his speech direct, and without ambiguity. He looks everybody in the face. How can he fear any, who wrongs none? How can he be ashamed before any, who deceives none? And ceasing from all wrong, he can never be wronged; ceasing from all deceit, he can never be deceived. It is impossible for evil to overcome good, so the righteous man can never be brought low by the unrighteous.

The righteous man is invincible. No enemy can possibly overcome him.

He cannot be afflicted by weariness and unrest whose heart is at peace with all.

MARCH TWENTY-EIGHTH.

There is that outburst of passion which is called "righteous indignation," and it appears to be righteous, but looked at from a higher conception of conduct it is seen to be *not* righteous. There is a certain stamp of nobility about indignation at wrong or injustice, and it is certainly far higher and nobler than *indifference*, but there is a loftier nobility still, by which it is seen that indignation is never necessary, and where love and gentleness take its place, they overcome the wrong much more effectually. A person that is apparently wronged requires our pity, but

It is better to love than to accuse and denounce.

When divine compassion is perceived in its fullness and beauty, indignation and all forms of passion cease to exercise any influence over us.

the one who wrongs requires still more our compassion, for he is ignorantly laying up for himself a store of suffering: *he must reap the wrong he is sowing.*

MARCH TWENTY-NINTH.

The term *Goodness* does not mean sickly sentiment, but *inward virtue, the direct result of which is strength and power;* therefore, the good man is not weak, the weak man is not good.

If a man would do a noble thing, and does not do it, he is not exalted thereby, but debased.

An exalted being apart front an exalted life is inconceivable and cannot be.

We should not judge the souls of others in the spirit of condemnation; but we can judge of our own life and conduct by *results.* There is nothing more certain than this, the evil doer speedily *proves* that his evil produces misery; the good man *demonstrates* that his goodness results in happiness.

It is a fact that one may "flourish like a green bay tree" and yet be unrighteous, but we should also remember that the bay tree at last perishes, or is cut down, and such is the fate of the unrighteous.

MARCH THIRTIETH.

The Teachers of mankind are few. A thousand years may pass by without the advent of such a one; but when the true Teacher does appear, the distinguishing feature by which he is known is *his life.* His *conduct* is different from other men, and his teaching is never derived from any man or book, but *from his own life.* The Teacher *first lives,* and then teaches others how they may likewise live. The proof and witness of his teaching is in himself, his life. Out of millions of preachers, one only is ultimately accepted by mankind as the true Teacher, and the one who is thus accepted and exalted is *he who lives.*

We know nothing higher than Goodness.

The supreme aim of all religions is to teach men how to live.

MARCH THIRTY-FIRST.

Jesus gave to the world a code of rules, by the observance of which all men could become sons of God, could live the Perfect Life. These rules or precepts are so simple, direct, and unmistakable that it is impossible to misunderstand them. So plain and unequivocal are they that even an unlettered child could grasp their meaning without difficulty. All of them are directly related to human conduct, and can be applied only by the individual in his own life. To carry out the spirit of these rules in

Love is far beyond the reach of all selfish argument and can only be lived.

Men everywhere, in their inmost hearts, know that Goodness is divine.

one's daily conduct constitutes the whole duty of life, and lifts the individual into the full consciousness of his divine origin and nature, of his oneness with God, the Supreme Good.

April First.

Each man is responsible for the thoughts which he thinks and the acts which he does, for his state of mind, and the life which he lives. No power, no event, no circumstance, can compel a man to evil and unhappiness. He himself is his own compeller. He thinks and acts by his own volition. No being, however wise and great—not even the Supreme—can make him good and happy. He himself must choose the good, and thereby find the happy.

A man has no character, no soul, no life, apart from his thoughts and deeds.

There is a larger, higher, nobler, diviner life than that of sinning and suffering.

   This life of triumph is not for those who are satisfied with any lower conditions; it is for those who thirst for it and are willing to achieve it; who are as eager for righteousness as the miser is for gold. It is always at hand, and is offered to all, and blessed are they who accept and embrace it; they will enter the world of Truth; they will find the Perfect Peace.

April Second.

Man's life is actual; his thoughts are actual; his deeds are actual. To occupy ourselves with the investigation of things that are, is the way of wisdom. Man, considered as above, beyond, and separate from, mind and thought, is speculative and not actual, and to occupy ourselves with the study of things that are not, is the way of folly.

Man is; and as he thinks, so he is.

To live is to think and act, and to think and act is to change.

   Man cannot be separated from his mind; his life cannot be separated from his thoughts. Mind, thought, and life are as inseparable as light, radiance, and colour. The facts are all-sufficient, and contain within themselves the ground-work of all knowledge concerning them.

April Third.

The purification of the heart, the thinking of right thoughts, and the doing of good deeds—what are they but calls to a higher, nobler mode of thought—energising forces urging men to effort in the choosing of thoughts which shall lift them into realms of greater power, greater good, greater bliss?

Man as mind is subject to change. He is not something "made" and finally completed, but has within him the capacity for progress.

Man's being is modified by every thought he thinks. Every experience affects his character.

   Aspiration, meditation, devotion—these are the chief means which men in all ages employ to reach up to higher modes of thought, wider airs of peace, vaster realms of knowledge, for "as he thinketh in his heart, so is he"; he is saved from himself—from his own folly and suffering—by creating within, new habits of thought; by becoming a new thinker, a new man.

April Fourth.

The multitudes, unenlightened concerning their spiritual nature, are the slaves of thought, but the sage is the master of thought. They follow blindly; he chooses intelligently. They obey the impulse of the moment, thinking of their immediate pleasure and happiness; he commands and subdues impulse, resting upon that which is permanently right. They, obeying blind impulse, violate the law of rightousness; he, conquering impulse, obeys the law of righteousness. The sage stands face to face with the facts of life. He knows the nature of thought. He understands and obeys the law of his being.

Only the choosing of wise thoughts, and, necessarily the doing of wise deeds, leads to wisdom.

Thought determines character, condition, knowledge.

April Fifth.

It is not less kind that we should suffer the penalty of our wrong-doing than that we should enjoy the blessedness of our right-doing. If we could escape the effects of our ignorance and sin, all security would be gone, and there would be no refuge, for we could then be equally deprived of the result of our wisdom and goodness. Such a scheme would be one of caprice and cruelty, whereas law is a method of justice and kindness.

Indeed, the supreme law is the principle of eternal kindness, faultless in working, and infinite in application. It is none other than that

Law cannot be partial. It is an unvarying mode of action, disobeying which, we are hurt; obeying, we are made happy.

Every pain we suffer brings us nearer to the knowledge of the Divine Wisdom.

> *Eternal Love, for ever full,*
> *For ever flowing free,*

of which the Christian sings; and the "Boundless Compassion" of Buddhistic precept and poetry.

April Sixth.

Buddha always referred to the moral law of the universe as the Good Law, and indeed it is not rightly perceived if it is thought of as anything but good, for in it there can be no grain of evil, no element of unkindness. It is no iron-hearted monster crushing the weak and destroying the ignorant, but a soothing love and brooding compassion shielding the tenderest from harm, and protecting the strongest from a too destructive use of their strength. It destroys all evil, it preserves all good. It enfolds the tiniest seedling in its care, and it destroys the most colossal wrong with a breath. To perceive it, is the beatific vision; to know it, is the beatific bliss; and they who perceive and know it are at peace; they are glad for ever more.

Seers of the Cosmos do not mourn over the scheme of things.

The wise man bends his will and subjects his desire to the Divine Order.

April Seventh.

There comes a time in the process of transmutation when, with the decrease of evil and the accumulation of good, there dawns in the mind a new vision, a new consciousness, a new man. And when this is reached, the saint has become a sage; he has passed from the human life to the divine life. He is "born again," and there begins for him a new round of experiences; he wields a new power; a new universe opens out before his spiritual gaze. This is the stage of Transcendence; this I call the Transcendent Life.

When Transcendence is attained, then the limited personality is outgrown, and the divine life is known; evil is transcended, and Good is all-in-all.

Rise above the allurements of sin, and enter the Divine Consciousness, the Transcendent Life.

As passion is the keynote of the self-life, so serenity is the keynote of the transcendent life.

April Eight.

The transcendent life is ruled, not by passions, but by principles. It is founded, not upon fleeting impulses, but upon abiding laws. In its clear atmosphere, the orderly sequence of all things is revealed, so that there is seen to be no more room for sorrow, anxiety, or regret. While men are involved in the passions of self, they load themselves with cares, and trouble over many things; and more than all else do they trouble over their own little, burdened, pain-stricken personality, being anxious for its fleeting pleasures, for its protection and preservation, and for its eternal safety and continuance. Now in the life that is wise and good all this is transcended. Personal interests are replaced by universal purposes, and all cares, troubles, and anxieties concerning the pleasure and fate of the personality are dispelled like the feverish dreams of a night.

When Perfect Good is realised and known, then calm vision is acquired.

Universal Good is seen.

April Eleventh.

By the way of self-conquest is the Perfect Peace achieved. Man cannot understand it, cannot approach it, until he sees the supreme necessity of turning away from the fierce fighting of things without, and entering upon the noble warfare against evils within. He is already on the Saintly Way who has realised that the enemy of the world is within, and not without; that his own ungoverned thoughts are the source of confusion and strife; that his own unchastened desires are the violaters of his peace, and of the peace of the world.

If a man has conquered lust and anger, hatred and pride, selfishness and greed, he has conquered the world.

He is brave who conquers another: but he who conquers himself is supremely noble.

He who is victorious over another may in turn be defeated; but he who overcomes himself will never be subdued.

April Twelfth.

He who is overcome by force is not thereby overcome in his heart: he may be a greater enemy than before; but he who is overcome by the spirit of peace is thereby changed at heart. He that was an enemy has become a friend.

The pure-hearted and wise have peace in their hearts; it enters into their actions; they apply it in their lives. It is more powerful than strife; it conquers where force would fail. Its wings shield the righteous. Under its protection, the harmless are not harmed. It affords a secure shelter from the heat of selfish struggle. It is a refuge for the defeated, a tent for the lost, and a temple for the pure.

Force and strife work upon the passions and fears, but love and peace reach and reform the heart.

When divine good is practised, life is bliss. Bliss is the normal condition of the good man.

April Thirteenth.

And this Love, this Wisdom, this Peace, this tranquil state of mind and heart, may be attained to, may be realised, by all who are willing and ready to yield up self, and who are prepared to humbly enter into a comprehension of all that the giving up of self involves. There is no arbitrary power in the universe, and the strongest chains of fate by which men are bound are self-forged. Men are chained to that which causes suffering because they desire to be so, because they love their chains, because they think their little dark prison of self is sweet and beautiful, and they are afraid that if they desert that prison they will lose all that is real and worth having.

He who has realised the Love that is divine has become a new man.

To the divinely wise, knowledge and Love are one and inseparable.

Ye suffer from yourselves, none else compels, None other holds ye that ye live and die.

April Fourteenth.

As the shadow follows the form, and as smoke comes after fire, so effect follows cause, and suffering and bliss follow the thoughts and deeds of men. There is no effect in the world around us but has its hidden or revealed cause, and that cause is in accordance with absolute justice. Men reap a harvest of suffering because in the near or distant past they have sown the seeds of evil; they reap a harvest of bliss also as a result of their own sowing of the seeds of good. Let a man meditate upon this, let him strive to understand it, and he will then begin to sow only seeds of good, and will burn up the tares and weeds which he has formerly grown in the garden of his heart.

The world does not understand the Love that is selfless because it is engrossed in the pursuit of its own pleasures.

It is toward the complete realisation of this divine Love that the whole world is moving.

April Fifteenth.

The world is, and will be for many years to come, shut out from that Golden Age which is the realisation of selfless Love. You, if you are willing, may enter it now, by rising above your selfish self; if you will pass from prejudice, hatred, and condemnation to gentle and forgiving love.

Where hatred, dislike, and condemnation are, selfless Love does not abide. It resides only in the heart that has ceased from all condemnation.

He who knows that Love is at the heart of all things, and has realised the all-sufficing power of that Love, has no room in his heart for condemnation.

He who purifies his own heart is the world's greatest benefactor.

Let men and women take this course, and lo! the Golden Age is at hand.

April Sixteenth.

He whose heart is centred in the supreme Love does not brand and classify men; does not seek to convert men to his own views, nor to convince them of the superiority of his methods. Knowing the Law of Love, he lives it, and maintains the same calm attitude of mind and sweetness of heart toward all. The debased and the virtuous, the foolish and the wise, the learned and the unlearned, the selfish and the unselfish, receive alike the benediction of his tranquil thought.

You can only attain to this supreme knowledge, this divine Love, by unremitting endeavour in self-discipline, and by gaining victory after victory over yourself.

Only the pure in heart see God.

Enter into the New Birth, and the Love that does not die will be awakened within you, and you will be at peace.

April Seventeenth.

Train your mind in strong, impartial, and gentle thought; train your heart in purity and compassion; train your tongue to silence and to true and stainless speech; so shall you enter the way of holiness and peace, and shall ultimately realise the immortal Love. So living, without seeking to convert, you will convince; without arguing, you will teach; not cherishing ambition, the wise will find you out; and without striving to gain men's opinions, you will subdue their hearts. For Love is all-conquering, all-powerful; and the thoughts, and deeds, and words of Love can never perish.

Where there is pure spiritual knowledge, Love is perfected and fully realised.

This is the realisation of selfless Love.

April Eighteenth.

We have opened our eyes, and the dark night of terror is no more. Long have we slept in matter and sensation; long did we struggle in the painful nightmare of evil; but now we are awake in Spirit and Truth: We have found the Good, and the struggle with evil is ended.

Rejoice! for the morning has dawned: The Truth has awakened us.

How beautiful is Truth! How glorious is the realm of reality! How ineffable is the bliss of Holiness!

We slept, yet knew not that we slept. We suffered, yet knew not that we suffered. We were troubled in our dreaming, yet none could awake us, for all were dreaming like ourselves. Yet there came a pause in our dreaming; our sleep was stayed. Truth spoke to us, and we heard; and lo! we opened our eyes, and saw. We slumbered, and saw not; we slept, and knew not; but now we are awake and see. Yea, we know we are awake because we have seen Holiness, and we love sin no more.

April Nineteenth.

To sin is to dream, and to love sin is to love darkness. They who love darkness are involved in the darkness; they have not yet seen the light. He who has seen the light does not choose to walk in darkness. To see the Truth is to love it, and, in comparison, error has no beauty. The dreamer is now in pleasure, now in pain; this hour in confidence, the next in fear. He is without stability, and has no abiding refuge. When the monsters of remorse and retribution pursue him, whither can he fly? There is no place of safety unless he awake. Let the dreamer struggle with his dream; let him strive to realise the illusory nature of all self-seeking desire, and lo! he will open his spiritual eyes upon the world of Light and Truth. He will be happy, sane, and peaceful, seeing things as they are.

Abandon error for Truth, and illusion for Reality.

Truth is the Light of the universe, the day of the mind.

April Twentieth.

When all else fails, Truth does not fail. When the heart is desolate and the world affords no shelter, Truth provides a peaceful refuge and a quiet rest. The cares of life are many, and its path is beset with difficulties; but Truth is greater than care, and is superior to all difficulties. Truth lightens our burdens; it lights up our pathway with the radiance of joy. Loved ones pass away, friends fail, and possessions disappear. Where then is the voice of comfort? Where is the whisper of consolation? Truth is the comforter of the comfortless, and the consoler of them that are deserted. Truth does not pass away, nor fail, nor disappear. Truth bestows the consolation of abiding peace. Be alert, and listen, that ye may hear the call of Truth, even the voice of the Great Awakener.

The Knowledge of Truth is an abiding consolation.

Truth removes the sting from affliction, and disperses the clouds of trouble.

April Twenty-first.

Truth brings joy out of sorrow, and peace out of perturbation; it points the selfish to the Way of Good, and sinners to the Path of Holiness. Its spirit is the doing of Righteousness. To the earnest and faithful it brings consolation; upon the obedient it bestows the crown of peace. I take refuge in Truth: Yea, in the Spirit of Good, in the knowledge of Good, and in the doing of Good I abide. And I am reassured and comforted. It is to me as though malice were not, and hatred had vanished away. Lust is confined to the nethermost darkness, it hath no way in Truth's transcendent Light. Pride is broken up and dissolved, and vanity is melted away as a mist. I have set my face toward the Perfect Good, and my feet in the Blameless Way; and because of this I am consoled.

He who clings to his delusions, loving self and sin, cannot find the Truth.

I am strengthened and comforted, having found refuge in Truth.

April Twenty-second.

Our good deeds remain with us, they save and protect us. Evil deeds are error. Our evil deeds follow us, they overthrow us in the hour of temptation. The evil doer is not protected from sorrow; but the good doer is shielded from all harm. The fool says unto his evil deed, "Remain thou hidden, be thou unexposed"—but his evil is already published, and his sorrow is sure. If we are in evil, what shall protect us? What keep us from misery and confusion? Nor man nor woman, nor wealth nor power, nor heaven nor earth, shall keep us from confusion. From the results of evil there is no escape; no refuge and no protection. If we are in Good, what shall overtake us? What bring us to misery and confusion? Nor man nor woman, nor poverty nor sickness, nor heaven nor earth, shall bring us to confusion.

A pure heart and a blameless life avail. They are filled with joy and peace.

There is a straight way and a quiet rest.

April Twenty-third.

Disciple: Teacher of teachers, instruct Thou me.

   Master: Ask, and I will answer.

   Disciple: I have read much, but am ignorant still; I have studied the doctrines of the schools, but have not become wise thereby; I know the scriptures by heart, but peace is hidden from me. Point out to me, O Master! the way of knowledge. Reveal to me the highway of divine wisdom; lead Thou Thy child into the path of peace.

Master: The way of knowledge, O Disciple! is by searching the heart; the highway of wisdom is by the practice of righteousness; and by a sinless life is found the way of peace.

Be glad and not sorrowful, all ye who love Truth!
For your sorrows shall pass away, like the mists of the morning.

Behold where Love Eternal rests concealed!
(The deathless Love that seemed so far away!)
E'en in the lowly heart; it stands revealed
To him who lives the sinless life to-day.

April Twenty-fourth.

Disciple: Lead me, O Master! for my darkness is very great! Will the darkness lift, O Master? Will trial end in victory, and will there be an end to my many sorrows?

Master: When thy heart is pure the darkness will disappear. When thy mind is freed from passion, thou wilt reach the end of trial, and when the thought of self-preservation is yielded up, there will be no more cause for sorrow. Thou art now upon the way of discipline and purification; all my disciples must walk that way. Before thou canst enter the white light of knowledge, before thou canst behold the full glory of Truth, all thy impurities must be purged away, thy delusions all dispelled, and thy mind fortified with endurance. Relax not thy faith in Truth; forget not that Truth is eternally supreme; remember that I, the Lord of Truth, am watching over thee.

Great is the conquest which thou hast entered upon, even the mighty conquest of thyself; be faithful and thou shalt overcome.

Be faithful, and endure, and I will teach thee all things.

April Twenty-fifth.

Disciple: What are the greater and the lesser powers?

Master: Hear me again, O Disciple! Walking faithfully the path of discipline and purification, not abandoning it, but submitting to its austerities, thou wilt acquire the three lesser powers of discipleship; thou wilt also receive the three greater powers. And the greater and the lesser powers will render thee invincible. *Self-control, Self-reliance,* and *Watchfulness*—these are the three lesser powers. *Steadfastness, Patience, Gentleness*—these are the three greater powers. When thy mind is well-controlled, and in thy keeping; when thou reliest upon no external aid, but upon Truth alone; and when thou art ceaselessly watchful over thy thoughts and actions—then thou wilt approach the Supreme Light.

Blessed is he who obeys the Truth, he shall not remain comfortless.

Thy darkness will pass away for ever, and joy and light will wait upon thy footsteps.

APRIL TWENTY-SIXTH.

By these four things is the heart defiled—the craving for pleasure, the clinging to temporal things, the love of self, the lust for personal continuance; from these four defilements spring all sins and sorrows. Wash thou thy heart; put away sensual cravings; detach thy mind from the wish for possessions; abandon self-defence and self-importance. Thus putting away all cravings, thou wilt attain to satisfaction; detaching thy mind from the love of perishable things, thou wilt acquire wisdom; abandoning the thought of self, thou wilt come to peace. He who is pure is free from desire; he does not crave for sensual excitements; he sets no value on perishable things; he is the same in riches and poverty, in success or failure, in victory or defeat, in life or death. His happiness remains, his rest is sure.

Be strenuous in effort, patient in endurance, strong in resolution.

Hold fast to love, and let it shape thy doing.

APRIL TWENTY-SEVENTH.

The unrighteous man is swayed by his feelings; likes and dislikes are his masters; prejudices and partialities blind him; desiring and suffering, craving and sorrowing, self-control he knows not, and great is his unrest. The righteous man is master of his moods; likes and dislikes he has abandoned as childish things; prejudice and partiality he has put away. Desiring nothing, he does not suffer; not craving enjoyment, sorrow does not overtake him; perfect in self-control, great peace abides with him.

Instruct me in the doing which is according to the Eternal, so that I may be watchful, and fail not.

Be thoughtful and wise, strong and kindhearted.

    Do not condemn, resent, or retaliate; do not argue, or become a partisan. Maintain thy calmness with all sides; be just, and speak the truth. Act in gentleness, compassion, and charity. Be infinitely patient. Hold fast to love, and let it shape thy doing. Have goodwill to all without distinction. Think equally of all, and be disturbed by none.

APRIL TWENTY-EIGHTH.

Think of thyself as abolished. In all thy doing think of the good of others and of the world, and not of pleasure or reward to thyself. Thou art no longer separate and divided from men, thou art one with all. No longer strive against others for thyself, but sympathise with all. Regard no man as thine enemy, for thou art the friend of all men. Be at peace with all. Pour out compassion on all living things, and let boundless

Be watchful, that no thought of self creep in again and stain thee.

Open thine eyes to the Eternal Light.

charity adorn thy words and deeds. Such is the glad way of Truth; such is the doing which is according to the Eternal. Filled with joy is the right-doer; he acts from principles which do not change and pass away. He is one with the Eternal, and has passed beyond unrest. The peace of the righteous man is perfect; it is not disturbed by change and impermanence. Freed from passion, he is equal-minded, calm, and does not sorrow; he sees things as they are, and is no more confused.

April Twenty-ninth.

Increase thy strength and self-reliance; make
The spectres of thy mind obey thy will;
See thou command thyself, nor let no mood,
No subtle passion nor no swift desire
Hurl thee to baseness; but, shouldst thou be hurled,
Rise, and regain thy manhood, taking gain
Of lowliness and wisdom from thy fall.
Strive ever for the mastery of thy mind,
And glean some good from every circumstance
That shall confront thee; make thy store of strength
Richer for ills encountered and o'ercome.
Submit to naught but nobleness; rejoice
Like a strong athlete straining for the prize,
When thy full strength is tried.

Knowledge is for him who seeks;
Wisdom crowneth him who
strives;
Peace in sinless silence speaks:
All things perish, Truth
survives.

Follow where Virtue leads
High and still higher;
Listen where Pureness pleads,
Quench not her fire.
Lo! he shall see
Reality,
Who cometh upward, cleansed
from all desire.

April Thirtieth.

Be not the slave
Of lusts and cravings and indulgences,
Of disappointments, miseries, and griefs,
Fears, doubts, and lamentations, but control
Thyself with calmness: master that in thee
Which masters others, and which heretofore
Has mastered thee: let not thy passions rule,
But rule thy passions; subjugate thyself
Till passion is transmuted into peace,
And wisdom crown thee; so shalt thou attain
And, by attaining, know.

Look thou within. Lo! In the midst of change
Abides the Changeless; at the heart of strife

Deliverance shall him entrance
who strives with sins and
sorrows, tears and pains,
Till he attains.

I am ignorant, yet strive to
know; nor will I cease to
strive till I attain.

The Perfect Peace reposes. At the root
Of all the restless striving of the world
Is passion. Whoso follows passion findeth pain,
But whoso conquers passion findeth peace.

May First.

Eolaus: *I know that sorrow follows passion; know*
That grief and emptiness, and heartaches wait
Upon all earthly joys; so am I sad;
Yet Truth must be, and being, can be found;
And though I am in sorrow, this I know—
I shall be glad when I have found the Truth.
Prophet: *There is no gladness like the joy of Truth.*
The pure in heart swim in a sea of bliss
That evermore nor sorrow knows, nor pain;
For who can see the Cosmos and be sad?
To know is to be happy; they rejoice
Who have attained Perfection; these are they
Who live, and know, and realise the Truth.

Comfort ye! The heights of
Blessed Vision ye shall reach.

He findeth Truth who findeth
self-control.

May Second.

Every soul, consciously or unconsciously, hungers for righteousness, and every soul seeks to gratify that hunger in its own particular way, and in accordance with its own particular state of knowledge. The hunger is one, and the righteousness is one, but the pathways by which righteousness is sought are many. They who seek consciously are blessed, and shall shortly find that final and permanent satisfaction of soul which righteousness alone can give, for they have come into a knowledge of the true path. They who seek unconsciously, although for a time they may bathe in a sea of pleasure, are not blessed, for they are carving out for themselves pathways of suffering, over which they must walk with torn and wounded feet, and the soul will cry out for its lost heritage—the eternal heritage of the righteous.

Not in any of the three worlds
can the soul find lasting satis-
faction, apart from the realisa-
tion of righteousness.

Blessed are they who earnestly
and intelligently seek.

May Third.

The journey to the Kingdom may be a long and tedious one, or it may be short and rapid. It may occupy a minute, or it may take a thousand ages. Everything depends on the faith and belief of the searcher. The majority cannot "enter in because of their unbelief"; for how can men realise righteousness when they do not believe in it, nor in the possibility of its accomplishment? Neither is it necessary to leave the outer world, and one's duties therein. Nay, it can only be found through the unselfish performance of one's duty. But all who believe, and aspire to achieve, will sooner or later arrive at victory, if, amid all their worldly duties, they faint not, nor lose sight of the Ideal Goodness, and continue, with unshaken resolve, to "press on to Perfection."

Glorious, radiant, free, detached from the tyranny of self!

The outward life harmonises itself with the inward music.

May Fourth.

The whole journey from the Kingdom of Strife to the Kingdom of Love resolves itself into a process which may be summed up in the following words:—The regulation and purification of conduct. Such a process must, if assiduously pursued, necessarily lead to perfection. It will also be seen that as the man obtains the mastery over certain forces within himself, he arrives at a knowledge of all the laws which operate in the realm of all these forces, and by watching the ceaseless working of cause and effect within himself, until he understands it, he then understands it in its universal adjustments in the body of humanity.

The process is also one of simplification of the mind, a sifting away of all but the essential gold in character.

The regulation and purification of conduct.

He lives no longer for himself, he lives for others: and so living, he enjoys the highest bliss, the deepest peace.

May Fifth.

A GOOD man is the flower of humanity, and to daily grow purer, nobler, more Godlike, by overcoming some selfish tendency, is to be continually drawing nearer to the Divine Heart. "He that would be My disciple, let him deny himself daily," is a statement which none can misunderstand or misapply, howsoever he may ignore it. Nowhere in the universe is there any substitute for Goodness; and until a man has this, he has nothing worthy or enduring. To the possession of Goodness there is only one way, and that is, *to give up all and everything that is opposed to Goodness.* Every selfish desire must be eradicated; every impure thought must be yielded up; every clinging to opinion must be sacrificed; and it is in the doing of this that constitutes the following of Christ.

Apart from the earnest striving to live out the teachings of Jesus there can be no true life.

That which is above all creeds, beliefs, and opinions is a loving and self-sacrificing heart.

May Sixth.

Jesus so lived, and all men may so live, if they will humbly and faithfully carry out His precepts. So long as they refuse to do this, clinging to their desires, passions, and opinions, they cannot be ranked as His disciples; they are the disciples of self. "Verily, verily, I say unto you: whosoever committeth sin is the servant of sin," is the searching declaration of Jesus. Let men cease to delude themselves with the belief that they can retain their bad tempers, their lusts, their harsh words and judgments, their personal hatreds, their petty contentions and darling opinions, and yet have Christ. All that divides man from man, and man from Goodness, is not of Christ, for Christ is Love.

To dwell in love always and toward all is to live the true life, is to have Life itself.

Sin and Christ cannot dwell together, and he who accepts the Christ-life of pure Goodness ceases from sin.

May Seventh.

It is no less selfish and sinful to cling to opinion than to cling to impure desire. Knowing this, the good man gives up himself unreservedly to the Spirit of Love, and dwells in Love toward all, contending with none, condemning none, hating none, but loving all, seeing behind their opinions, their creeds, and their sins, into their striving, suffering, and sorrowing hearts. "He that loveth his life shall lose it." Eternal life belongs to him who will obediently relinquish his petty, narrowing, sin-loving, strife-producing personal self, for only by so doing can he enter into the large, beautiful, free, and glorious life of abounding Love. Herein is the Path of Life; for the Straight Gate is the Gate of Goodness.

When Christ is disputed about, Christ is lost.

The narrow way is the Way of Renunciation, or self-sacrifice.

May Eighth.

"How am I acting toward others?" "What am I doing for others?" "How am I thinking of others?" "Are my thoughts of, and acts toward others, prompted by unselfish love, as I would theirs should be to me; or are they the outcome of personal dislike, of petty revenge, or of narrow bigotry and condemnation?" As a man, in the sacred silence of his soul, asks himself these searching questions, applying all his thoughts and acts to the spirit of the primary precept of the Christ, his understanding will become illuminated, so that he will unerringly see where he has hitherto failed; and he will see what he has got to do in rectifying his heart and conduct, and the way in which it is to be done.

A man can learn nothing unless he regards himself as a learner.

Evil is not worth resisting. The practice of the good is supremely excellent.

MAY NINTH.

Whilst a man is engaged in resisting evil, he is not only not practising the good, he is actually involved in the like passion and prejudice which he condemns in another; and as a direct result of his attitude of mind, he himself is resisted by others as evil. Resist a man, a party, a religion, a government, as evil, and you yourself will be resisted as evil. He who considers it as a great evil that he should be persecuted and condemned, let him cease to persecute and condemn. Let him turn away from all that he has hitherto regarded as evil, and begin to look for the good. So deep and far-reaching is this precept that the practice of it will take a man far up the heights of spiritual knowledge and attainment.

Personal antipathies, however natural they may be to the animal man, can have no place in the divine life.

He who will keep the precepts of Jesus will conquer himself, and will become divinely illuminated.

MAY TENTH.

So long has man dwelt in the habitations of sin that he has at last come to regard himself as native to it, and as being cut off from the Divine Source, which he believes to be outside and away from him. Man is primarily a spiritual being, and as such, is of the nature and substance of the Eternal Spirit, the Unchangeable Reality, which men call God. Goodness, not sin, is his rightful condition; perfection, not imperfection, is his heritage, and this a man may enter into and realise *now* if he will grant the condition, which is the denial or abandonment of self, that is, of his feverish desires, his proud will, his egotism and self-seeking—all that which St. Paul calls the "natural man."

Humanity is essentially divine.

Jesus, in His divine goodness, knew the human heart, and He knew that it was good.

MAY ELEVENTH.

Man has within him the divine power by which he can rise to the highest heights of spiritual achievement; by which he can shake off sin and shame and sorrow, and do the will of the Father, the Supreme Good; by which he can conquer all the powers of darkness within, and stand radiant and free; by which he can subdue the world, and scale the lofty pinnacles of God. This can man, by choice, by resolve, and by his divine strength, accomplish; but he can only accomplish it in and by *obedience*; he must choose meekness and lowliness of heart; he must abandon strife for peace; passion for purity; hatred for love; self-seeking for self-sacrifice, and must overcome evil with good.

He who would find how good at heart men are, let him throw away all his ideas and suspicions about the "evil" in others, and find and practice the good within himself.

This is the holy way of Truth; this is the safe and abiding salvation; this is the yoke and burden of the Christ.

MAY TWELFTH.

That Jesus was meek, and lowly, and loving, and compassionate, and pure is very beautiful, but it is not sufficient; it is necessary that you also should be meek, and lowly, and loving, and compassionate, and pure. That Jesus subordinated His own will to the will of the Father, it is inspiring to know, but it is not sufficient; it is necessary that you, too, should likewise subordinate your will to that of the overruling Good. The grace and beauty and goodness that were in Jesus can be of no value to you, cannot be understood by you, unless they are also *in you,* and they can never be in you until you *practice* them, for, apart from *doing,* the qualities which constitute Goodness do not, as far as you are concerned, exist.

The Gospel of Jesus is a Gospel of living and doing.

Pure Goodness is religion, and outside it there is no religion.

MAY THIRTEENTH.

To us and to all there is no sufficiency, no blessedness, no peace to be derived from the goodness of another, not even the goodness of God; not until the goodness is *done* by us, not until it is, by constant effort, incorporated into our being, can we know and possess its blessedness and peace. Therefore, thou who adorest Jesus for His divine qualities, practice those qualities thyself, and thou too shalt be divine.

They are the doers of the Father's will who shape their conduct to the Divine precepts.

It is only the doer of forgiveness who tastes the sweets of forgiveness.

The teaching of Jesus brings men back to the simple truth that righteousness, or *right-doing,* is entirely a matter of individual conduct, and not a mystical something apart from a man's thoughts and actions, and that each must be righteous for himself; each must be a *doer* of the word, and it is a man's *own* doing that brings him peace and gladness of heart, not the doing of another.

MAY FOURTEENTH.

When Jesus said, "Without Me ye can do nothing," He spoke not of His perishable form, but of the Universal Spirit of Love, of which His conduct was a perfect manifestation; and this utterance of His is the statement of a simple truth; for the works of men are vain and worthless when they are done for personal ends, and he himself remains a perishable being, immersed in darkness and fearing death, so long as

The Christ is the Spirit of Love.

In this Principle of Love, all Knowledge, Intelligence, and Wisdom are contained.

he lives in his personal gratifications. The animal in man can never respond to and know the divine; only the divine can respond to the divine. The spirit of hatred in man can never vibrate in unison with the Spirit of Love; Love only can apprehend Love, and become linked with it. Man is divine; man is of the substance of Love; this he may realise if he will relinquish the impure, personal elements which he has hitherto been blindly following, and will fly to the impersonal Realities of the Christ Spirit.

May Fifteenth.

Every precept of Jesus demands the unconditional sacrifice of some selfish, personal element, before it can be carried out. Man cannot know the Real whilst he clings to the unreal; he cannot do the work of Truth whilst he clings to error. Whilst a man cherishes lust, hatred, pride, vanity, self-indulgence, covetousness, he can do nothing, for the works of all these sinful elements are unreal and perishable. Only when he takes refuge in the Spirit of Love within, and becomes patient, gentle, pure, pitiful, and forgiving, does he the works of Righteousness, and bears the fruits of Life. The vine is not a vine without its branches, and even then it is not complete until those branches *bear fruit.*

Love is not complete until it is lived by man.

Man's only refuge from sin is sinless Love.

Daily practising love toward all in heart and mind and deed, harbouring no injurious or impure thoughts, he discovers the imperishable Principles of his being.

May Sixteenth.

A man can only consciously ally himself to the Vine of Love by deserting all strife, and hatred, and condemnation, and impurity, and pride, and self-seeking, and by thinking and doing loving deeds. By so doing he awakens within him the divine nature which he has heretofore been crucifying and denying. Every time a man gives way to anger, impatience, greed, pride, vanity, or any form of personal selfishness, he denies the Christ, he shuts himself out from Love. And thus only is Christ denied, and not by refusing to adopt a formulated creed. Christ is only known to him who by constant striving has converted himself from a sinful to a pure being, who by noble, moral effort has succeeded in relinquishing that perishable self, which is the source of all suffering and sorrow and unrest, and has become rational, gentle, peaceful, loving, and pure.

Before a man can know Love as the abiding Reality within him, he must utterly abandon all time human tendencies which frustrate its perfect manifestation.

Such glorious realisation is the crown of evolution, the supreme aim of existence.

May Seventeenth.

Those who are at rest in the Kingdom do not look for happiness in any outward possession. They see that all such possessions are mere transient effects that come when they are required, and, after their purpose is served, pass away. They never think of these things (money, clothing, food, etc.) except as mere accessories and *effects* of the true Life. They are, therefore, freed from all anxiety and trouble, and, resting in Love, they are the embodiment of Happiness. Standing upon the imperishable Principles of Purity, Compassion, Wisdom, and Love, they are immortal, and know they are immortal; they are one with God, the Supreme Good, and know they are one with God. Seeing the realities of things, they can find no room anywhere for condemnation.

As self is the root cause of all strife and suffering, so Love is the root cause of all peace and bliss.

All men are essentially divine, though unaware of their divine nature.

May Eighteenth.

Let it not be supposed that the children of the Kingdom live in ease and indolence (these two sins are the first that have to be eradicated when the search for the Kingdom is entered upon); they live in a peaceful activity; in fact, *they only* truly live, for the life of self, with its train of worries, griefs, and fears, is not *real* life. They perform all their duties with the most scrupulous diligence, apart from thoughts of self, and employ all their means, as well as powers and faculties, which are greatly intensified, in building up the Kingdom of Righteousness in the hearts of others, and in the world around them. This is their work, first by example, then by precept. They sorrow no more, but live in perpetual gladness, for, though they see the suffering in the world, they also see the final Bliss and the Eternal Refuge.

All so-called evil is seen to be rooted in ignorance.

Whosoever is ready may come now.

May Nineteenth.

The only salvation recognised and taught by Jesus is salvation from sin, and the effects of sin, *here and now*; and this must be effected by utterly abandoning sin, which, having done, the Kingdom of God is realised in the heart as a state of perfect knowledge, perfect blessedness, perfect peace.

"Except a man be born again, he cannot see the Kingdom of God." A man must become a new creature, and how can he become new except by utterly abandoning the old? That man's last state is worse than his first who imagines that, though still continuing to cling to his old temper, his old opinionativeness, his old vanity, his old selfishness, he is constituted a "new creature" in some mysterious and unexplainable way by the adoption of some particular theology or religious formula.

Heaven is not a speculative thing beyond the tomb but a real, ever-present Heaven in the heart.

Heaven is where Love rules, and where Peace is never absent.

May Twentieth.

Good news indeed is that message of Jesus which reveals to man His divine possibilities; which says in substance to sin-stricken humanity, "Take up thy bed and walk"; which tells man that he need no longer remain the creature of darkness and ignorance and sin, if he will but believe in *Goodness*, and will watch and strive and conquer until he has actualised in his life the Goodness that is sinless. And in thus believing and overcoming, man has not only the guide of that Perfect Rule which Jesus has embodied in His precepts, he has also the inward Guide, the Spirit of Truth in his own heart, "The Light that lighteth every man that cometh into the world," which, as he follows it, will infallibly witness to the divine origin of those precepts.

To the faithful, humble, and true will be revealed the sublime Vision of the Perfect One.

Realise the perfect Goodness of the Eternal Christ.

May Twenty-first.

The children of the Kingdom *are known by their life*. They manifest the fruits of the Spirit—"love, joy, peace, long-suffering, kindness, goodness, faithfulness, meekness, temperance, self-control"—under all circumstances and vicissitudes. They are entirely free from anger, fear, suspicion, jealousy, caprice, anxiety, and grief. Living in the Righteousness of God, they manifest qualities which are the very reverse of those which obtain in the world, and which are regarded by the world as foolish. They demand no *rights*; they do not defend themselves; do not retaliate; do good to those who attempt to injure them; manifest the same gentle spirit toward those who oppose and attack them, as toward those who agree with them; do not pass judgment on others; condemn no man and no system, and live at peace with all.

The Kingdom of Heaven is perfect trust, perfect knowledge, perfect peace.

That Kingdom is in the heart of every man and woman.

May Twenty-second.

The Temple of Righteousness is built, and its four walls are the four Principles—Purity, Wisdom, Compassion, Love. Peace is its roof, its floor is Steadfastness, its entrance door is Selfless Duty, its atmosphere is Inspiration, and its music is the Joy of the perfect. It cannot be shaken, and, being eternal and indestructible, there is no more need to seek protection in taking thought for the things of the morrow. And the Kingdom of Heaven being established in the heart, the obtaining of the material necessities of life is no more considered, for, having found the Highest, all these things are added as effect to cause, the struggle for existence has ceased, and the spiritual, mental, and material needs are daily supplied from the Universal Abundance.

Find the Kingdom by daily effort and patient work.

Pay the price . . . the unconditional abandonment of self.

May Twenty-third.

Now is the reality in which time is contained. It is more and greater than time; it is an ever-present reality. It knows neither past nor future, and is eternally potent and substantial. Every minute, every day, every year is a dream as soon as it has passed, and exists only as an imperfect and unsubstantial picture in the memory, if it be not entirely obliterated.

Past and future are dreams; *now is* a reality. All things are now; all power, all possibility, all action is now. Not to act and accomplish now is not to act and accomplish at all. To live in thoughts of what you might have done, or in dreams of what you mean to do, this is folly; but to put away regret, to anchor anticipation, and to do and to work *now,* this is wisdom.

All things are possible now, and only now.

Man has all power now.

MAY TWENTY-FOURTH.

Man has all power now; but not knowing this, he says, "I will be perfect next year, or, in so many years, or in so many lives." The dwellers in the Kingdom of God, who live only in the now, say, "I am perfect now," and refraining from all sin now, and ceaselessly guarding all the portals of the mind, not looking to the past nor to the future, nor turning to the left or right, they remain eternally holy and blessed. "Now is the accepted time, now is the day of salvation." Say to yourself, "I will live in my Ideal now; I will be my Ideal now; and all that tempts me away from my Ideal I will not listen to; I will listen only to the voice of my Ideal." Thus resolving, and thus doing, you shall not depart from the Highest, and shall eternally manifest the Truth.

Cease to tread every byway that tempts thy soul into the shadow-land.

Manifest thy native and divine strength now.

MAY TWENTY-FIFTH.

In the hour of temptation do not depart from the right path. Avoid excitement. When passions are aroused, restrain and subdue them. When the mind would wander, bring it back to rest on higher things. Do not think—"I can get Truth from the Teacher, or from the books." You can acquire Truth only by practice. The teacher and the books can do no more than give instructions; and you must apply them. Those only who practice faithfully the rules and lessons given, and rely entirely upon their own efforts, will become enlightened. The Truth must be earned. Do not be led away by phenomenal appearances, or seek communications with spirits, or the dead; but attain to virtue, wisdom, and knowledge of the Supreme Law by the practice of Truth. Trust the Teacher; trust the Law; trust the path of Righteousness.

Be resolute. Be of single purpose. Renew your resolution daily.

Put away all wavering and doubt, and practice the lessons of wisdom with unlimited faith.

MAY TWENTY-SIXTH.

Speak only words which are truthful and sincere. Do not deceive either by word, look, or gesture. Avoid slander as you would a deadly snake, lest you be caught in its toils. He who speaks evil of another cannot find the way of peace. Put away all dissipations of idle gossip. Do not talk about the private affairs of others, or discuss the ways of Society, or criticise the eminent. Do not recriminate, or accuse others of offences, but meet all offences with blameless conduct. Do not condemn those who are not walking in the righteous path, but protect them with compassion, walking the path yourself. Quench the flame of anger with the pure water of Truth. Be modest in your words, and do not utter, or participate in, coarse, frivolous, or unseemly jests. Gravity and reverence are marks of purity and wisdom.

Avoid exaggerations. The Truth is sufficient.

Do not dispute about Truth, but live it.

May Twenty-seventh.

Do your duty with the utmost faithfulness, putting away all thought of reward. Let no thought of pleasure or self entice you from your duty. Do not interfere with the duties of others. Be upright in all things. Under the most severe trial, though your happiness and life should seem to be at stake, do not swerve from the right. The man of unconquerable integrity is invincible; he cannot be confounded, and he escapes from the painful mazes of doubt and bewilderment. If one should abuse or accuse, or speak ill of you, remain silent and self-controlled, striving to understand that the wrong-doer cannot injure you unless you retaliate, and allow yourself to be carried away by the same wrong condition of mind. Strive, also, to meet the evil-doer with compassion, seeing how he is injuring himself.

Abstinence, sobriety, and self-control are good.

The pure-minded cannot think, "I have been injured by another." They know no enemy but self.

May Twenty-eighth.

Bear no ill-will. Subdue anger and overcome hatred. Think of all, and act toward all, with the same unalterable kindness and compassion. Do not, under the severest trial, give way to bitterness, or words of resentment; but meet anger with calmness, mockery with patience, and hatred with love. Do not be a partisan, but be a peacemaker. Do not increase division between man and man, or promote strife by taking sides with one party against another, but give equal justice, equal love, equal good-will to all. Do not disparage other teachers, other religions, or other schools of thought. Do not set up barriers between rich and poor, employer and employed, governor and governed, master and servant, but be equal-minded toward all, perceiving their several duties. By constantly controlling the mind, subduing bitterness and resentment, and striving to acquire a steadfast kindness, the spirit of good-will will at last be born.

Let your charity increase and extend till self is swallowed up in kindness.

Be strong, energetic, steadfast.

MAY TWENTY-NINTH.

Bring reason to bear on all things. Test all things. Be eager to know and understand. Be logical in thought. Be consistent in word and action. Bring the searchlight of knowledge to bear on your condition of mind, in order to simplify it and remove its errors. Question yourself with searching scrutiny. Let go of belief, hearsay, and speculation, and lay hold on knowledge. He who stands upon knowledge acquired by practice is filled with a sublime yet lowly confidence, and is able to speak the word of Truth with power. Master the task of discrimination. Learn to distinguish between good and evil; to perceive the facts of life, and understand them in their relation one to another. Awake the mind to see the orderly sequence of cause and effect in all things, both mental and material. Thus will be revealed the worthlessness of pleasure-seeking and sin, and the glory and gladness of a life of sublime virtue and spotless purity.

Be right-minded, intelligent, and clear-seeing.

Truth is. There is no chaos.

MAY THIRTIETH.

Then you will see, not with fleshly eyes, but with the pure and single eye of Truth. You will then understand your nature—perceiving how, as a mental being, you have evolved through countless ages of experience, how you have risen, through an unbroken line of lives, from low to high, and from high to higher still—how the ever-changing tendencies of the mind have been built up by thought and action—how your deeds have made you what you are. Thus, understanding your own nature, you will understand the nature of all beings, and will dwell always in compassion. You will understand the Great Law, not only universally and in the abstract, but also in its particular application to individuals. Then self will be ended. It will be dispersed like a cloud, and Truth will be all in all.

Train your mind to grasp the Great Law of Causation which is unfailing justice.

Find no room for hatred, no room for self, no room for sorrow.

MAY THIRTY-FIRST.

Folly and wisdom, weakness and strength, are within a man, and not in any external thing, neither do they spring from any external cause. A man cannot be strong for another, he can only be strong for himself; he cannot overcome for another, he can only overcome for himself. You may learn of another, but you must accomplish for yourself. Put away all external props, and rely upon the Truth within you. A creed will not

Be self-reliant, but let thy self-reliance be saintly and not selfish.

Goodness is the aim of all religions.

bear a man up in the hour of temptation; he must possess the inward Knowledge which slays temptation. A speculative philosophy will prove a shadowy thing in the time of calamity; a man must have the inward Wisdom which puts an end to grief.

The Unfailing Wisdom is found only by constant practice in pure thinking and well-doing; by harmonising one's mind and heart to those things which are beautiful, lovable, and true.

June First.

The spirit of love does not decrease when a man realises that perfect justice obtains in the spiritual government of the world; on the other hand, it is increased and intensified, for he knows that men suffer *because they do not understand,* because they err in ignorance. "The comfortably conditioned" are frequently involved in greater suffering than the poor, and, like others, are garnering their own mixed harvest of happiness and suffering. This teaching of Absolute Justice is not more encouraging for the rich than for the poor, for while it tells the rich, who are selfish and oppressive, or who misuse their wealth, that they must reap the results of all their actions, it also tells the suffering and oppressed that, as they are now reaping what they have formerly sown, they may, and surely will, by sowing the good seeds of purity, love, and peace, shortly also reap a harvest of good, and so rise above their present woes.

The incentive to self-sacrificing labour does not reside in any theory about the universe, but in the spirit of love and compassion.

This painful consequences of all self-seeking must be met and passed through.

June Second.

Fixed attitudes of mind determine courses of conduct, and from courses of conduct come those reactions called happinesses and unhappinesses. This being so, it follows that, to alter the reactive condition, one must alter the active thought. To exchange misery for happiness it is necessary to reverse the fixed attitude of mind and habitual course of conduct which is the cause of misery, and the reverse effect will appear in the mind and life. A man has no power to be happy while thinking and acting selfishly; he cannot be unhappy while thinking and acting unselfishly. Wheresoever the cause is, there the effect will appear. Man cannot abrogate effects, but he can alter causes. He can purify his nature; he can remould his character. There is great power in self-conquest; there is great joy in transforming oneself.

Man is the maker of happiness and misery.

Each man is circumscribed by his own thoughts.

June Third.

Consider the man whose mind is suspicious, covetous, envious. How small and mean and drear everything appears to him. Having no grandeur in himself, he sees no grandeur anywhere, being ignoble himself, he is incapable of seeing nobility in any being; selfish as he himself is, he sees in the most exalted acts of unselfishness only motives that are mean and base.

Consider again the man whose mind is unsuspecting, generous, magnanimous. How wondrous and beautiful is his world. He sees men as true, and to him they are true. In his presence the meanest forget their nature, and for the moment become like himself, getting a glimpse, albeit confused, in that temporary upliftment of a higher order of things, of an immeasurably nobler and happier life.

Men live in spheres low or high according to the nature of their thoughts.

Refrain from harbouring thoughts that are dark and hateful, and cherish thoughts that are bright and beautiful.

June Fourth.

The kingdom of heaven is not taken by violence, but he who conforms to its principles receives the password. The ruffian moves in a society of ruffians; the saint is one of an elect brotherhood whose communion is divine music. All men are mirrors reflecting according to their own surface. All men, looking at the world of men and things, are looking into a mirror which gives back their own reflection.

Each man moves in the limited or expansive circle of his own thoughts, and all outside that circle is non-existent to him. He only knows that which he has *become*. The narrower the boundary, the more convinced is the man that there is no further limit, no other circle. The lesser cannot contain the greater, and he has no means of apprehending the larger minds; such knowledge comes only by growth.

The small-minded man and the large-hearted man live in two different worlds though they be neighbours.

Men, like schoolboys, find themselves in standards or classes to which their ignorance or knowledge entitles them.

June Fifth.

The inner informs the outer. The greater embraces the lesser. Matter is the counterpart of mind. Events are streams of thoughts. Circumstances are combinations of thought, and the outer conditions and actions of others in which each man is involved, are intimately related to his own mental needs and development. Man is a part of his surroundings. He is not separate from his fellows, but is bound closely to them by the peculiar intimacy and interaction of deeds, and by those fundamental laws of thought which are the roots of human society.

The world of things is the other half of the world of thoughts.

Things follow thoughts. Alter your thoughts, and things will receive a new adjustment.

One cannot alter external things to suit his passing whims and wishes, but he can set aside his whims and wishes; he can so alter his attitude of mind towards externals, that they will assume a different aspect. He cannot mould the actions of others toward him, but he can rightly fashion his actions toward them.

June Sixth.

The cause of your bondage as of your deliverance is within. The injury that comes to you through others is the rebound of your own deed, the reflex of your own mental attitude. *They* are the instruments, *you* are the cause. Destiny is ripened fruits. The fruit of life, both bitter and sweet, is received by each man in just measure. The righteous man is free. None can injure him; none can destroy him; none can rob him of his peace. His attitude toward men, born of understanding, disarms their power to wound him. Any injury which they may try to inflict rebounds upon themselves to their own hurt, leaving him unharmed and untouched. The good that goes from him is his perennial fount of happiness, his eternal source of strength. Its root is serenity, its flower is joy.

The perfecting of one's own deeds is man's highest duty and most sublime accomplishment.

External things and deeds are powerless to injure you.

June Seventh.

A man imagines he could do great things if he were not hampered by circumstances—by want of money, want of time, want of influence, and want of freedom from family ties. In reality the man is not hindered by these things at all. He, in his mind, ascribes to them a power which they do not possess, and he submits, not to them, but to his opinions about them, that is, to a weak element in his nature. The real "want" that hampers him is *the want of the right attitude of mind.* When he regards his circumstances as spurs to his resources, when he sees that his so-called "drawbacks" are the very steps up which he is to mount successfully to his achievement, then his necessity gives birth to invention, and the "hindrances" are transformed into aids.

The man is the all-important factor.

He who complains of his circumstances has not yet become a man.

June Eighth.

Man's power subsists in discrimination and choice. Man does not create one jot of the universal conditions or laws; they are the essential principles of things, and are neither made nor unmade. He discovers, not makes, them. Ignorance of them is at the root of the world's pain. To defy them is folly and bondage. Who is the freer man, the thief who defies the laws of his Country, or the honest citizen who obeys them? Who, again, is the freer man, the fool who thinks he can live as he likes, or the wise man who chooses to do only that which is right?

Nothing can prevent us from accomplishing the aims of our life.

He is the good man whose habits of thought and action are good.

Man is, in the nature of things, a being of habit, and this he cannot alter; but he can alter his habits. He cannot alter the law of his nature, but he can adapt his nature to the law.

JUNE NINTH.

Man repeats the same thoughts, the same actions, the same experiences over and over again, until they are incorporated with his being, until they are built into his character as part of himself. Evolution is mental accumulation. Man to-day is the result of millions of repetitious thoughts and acts. He is not ready-made, he becomes, and is still becoming. His character is pre-determined by his own choice. The thought, the act, which he chooses, that, by habit, he becomes.

He becomes the master of the lower by enlisting in the service of the higher.

Habit is repetition. Faculty is fixed habit.

Thus each man is an accumulation of thoughts and deeds. The characteristics which he manifests instinctively and without effort are lines of thought and action become, by long repetition, automatic; for it is the nature of habit to become, at last, unconscious, to repeat, as it were, itself without any apparent choice or effort on the part of its possessor; and in due time it takes such complete possession of the individual as to appear to render his will powerless to counteract it.

JUNE TENTH.

It is true that man is the instrument of mental forces—or to be more accurate, he is those forces—but they are not blind, and he can direct them into new channels. In a word, he can take himself in hand and reconstruct his habits; for though it is also true that he is born with a given character, that character is the product of numberless lives during which it has been slowly built up by choice and effort, and in this life it will be considerably modified by new experiences.

By thoughts man binds himself.

A changed attitude of mind changes the character, the habits, the life.

No matter how apparently helpless a man has become under the tyranny of a bad habit, or a bad characteristic—and they are essentially the same—he can, so long as sanity remains, break away from it and become free.

JUNE ELEVENTH.

One who suffers in body will not necessarily at once be cured when he begins to fashion his mind on moral and harmonious principles; indeed, for a time, while the body is bringing to a crisis, and throwing off the effects of former inharmonies, the morbid condition may appear to be intensified. As a man does not gain perfect peace imme-

The body is the image of the mind.

Mental harmony, or moral wholeness, makes for bodily health.

diately he enters upon the path of righteousness, but must, except in rare instances, pass through a painful period of adjustment, neither does he, with the same rare exception, at once acquire perfect health. Time is required for bodily as well as mental readjustment, and even if health is not reached, it will be approached. If the mind be made robust, the bodily condition will take a secondary and subordinate place, and will cease to have that primary importance which so many give to it.

June Twelfth.

Whilst vainly imagining that the pleasures of earth are real and satisfying, pain and sorrow continually remind man of their unreal and unsatisfying nature. Ever striving to believe that complete satisfaction is to be found in material things, he is conscious of an inward and persistent revolt against this belief, which revolt is at once a refutation of his essential mortality, and an inherent and imperishable proof that only in the immortal, the eternal, the infinite, can he find abiding satisfaction and unbroken peace.

Reach out into a comprehension of the Infinite.

The common ground of faith—the root and spring of all religion—the heart of Love!

Man is essentially and spiritually divine and eternal, and, immersed in mortality and troubled unrest, he is striving to enter into a consciousness of his real nature.

June Thirteenth.

The spirit of man is inseparable from the Infinite, and can be satisfied with nothing short of the Infinite, and the burden of pain will continue to weigh upon man's heart, and the shadows of sorrow to darken his pathway, until, ceasing from wanderings in the dream-world of matter, he comes back to his home in the reality of the Eternal.

The restful Reality of the Eternal Heart.

To become one with the Infinite is the goal of man.

As the smallest drop of water detached from the ocean contains all the qualities of the ocean, so man, detached in consciousness from the Infinite, contains within himself its likeness; and as the drop of water must, by the law of nature, ultimately find its way back to the ocean and lose itself in its silent depths, so must man, by the unfailing law of his nature, at last return to his source, and lose himself in the heart of the Infinite.

June Fourteenth.

This divine state is, and must ever be, incomprehensible to the merely personal. Personality, separateness, selfishness, are one and the same, and are the antithesis of wisdom and divinity. By the unqualified surrender of the personality, separateness and selfishness cease, and man enters into the possession of his divine heritage of immortality and infinity.

Such surrender of the personality is regarded by the worldly and selfish mind as the most grievous of all calamities, the most irreparable loss, yet it is the one supreme and incomparable blessing, the only real and lasting gain. The mind unenlightened upon the inner laws of being and upon the nature and destiny of its own life clings to transient appearances, things which have in them no enduring substantiality, and so clinging, perishes, for the time being, amid the shattered wreckage of its own illusions.

Enter into perfect harmony with the Eternal Law, which is Wisdom, Love, and Peace.

Love is universal, supreme, and all-sufficing. This is the realisation of selfless love.

June Fifteenth.

Men cling to and gratify the flesh as though it were going to last for ever, and though they try to forget the nearness and inevitably of its dissolution, the dread of death and of the loss of all that they cling to clouds their happiest hours, and the chilling shadow of their own selfishness follows them like a remorseless spectre.

And with the accumulation of temporal comforts and luxuries, the divinity within men is drugged, and they sink deeper and deeper into materiality, into the perishable life of the senses; and where there is sufficient intellect, theories concerning the immortality of the flesh come to be regarded as infallible truths.

When a man's soul is clouded with selfishness in any or every form, he loses the power of spiritual discrimination, and confuses the temporal with the eternal.

The perishable in the universe can never become permanent; the permanent can never pass away.

June Sixteenth.

All nature in its myriad forms of life is changeable, impermament, unenduring. Only the informing Principle of nature endures. Nature is many, and is marked by separation. The informing Principle is one, and is marked by unity. By overcoming the senses and the selfishness within, which is the overcoming of nature, man emerges from the chrysalis of the personal and illusory, and wings himself into the glorious light of the impersonal, the region of Truth, out of which all perishable forms come.

Man cannot immortalize the flesh.

Only by realising the God state of consciousness does man enter into immortality.

Let men, therefore, practice self-denial; let them conquer their animal inclinations; let them refuse to be enslaved by luxury and pleasure; let them practice virtue, and grow daily into higher and ever higher virtue, until at last they grow into the Divine.

June Seventeenth.

Whoever fights ceaselessly against his own selfishness, and strives to supplant it with all-embracing love, is a saint, whether he live in a cottage or in the midst of riches and influence; or whether he preaches or remains obscure.

This only is true service—to forget oneself in love toward all.

Only the work that is impersonal can live.

To the worldling, who is beginning to aspire toward higher things, the saint, such as a sweet St. Francis of Assisi, or a conquering St. Anthony, is a glorious and inspiring spectacle; to the saint, an equally enrapturing sight is that of the sage, sitting serene and holy, the conqueror of sin and sorrow, no more tormented by regret and remorse, and whom even temptation can never reach; and yet even the sage is drawn on by a still more glorious vision, that of the Saviour actively manifesting His knowledge in selfless works, and rendering His divinity more potent for good by sinking Himself in the throbbing, sorrowing heart of mankind.

June Eighteenth.

It is given to the world to learn one great and divine lesson—the lesson of absolute unselfishness. The saints, sages, and saviours of all time are they who have submitted themselves to this task, and have learned and lived it. All the scriptures of the world are framed to teach this one lesson, all the great teachers reiterate it. It is too simple for the world which, scorning it, stumbles along in the complex ways of selfishness.

Where duties, howsoever humble, are done without self-interest, and with joyful sacrifice, there is true service and enduring work.

A pure heart is the end of all religion and the beginning of divinity.

To search for this righteousness is to walk the Way of Truth and Peace, and he who enters this Way will soon perceive that Immortality which is independent of birth and death, and will realise that in the divine economy of the universe the humblest effort is not lost. The world will not have finished its long journey until every soul has entered into the blissful realisation of its own divinity.

June Nineteenth.

As there are depths in the ocean which the fiercest storm cannot reach, so there are silent, holy depths in the heart of man which the storms of sin and sorrow can never disturb. To reach this silence and to live consciously in it is peace.

Discord is rife in the outward world, but unbroken harmony holds sway at the heart of the universe. The human soul reaches blindly toward the harmony of the sinless state, and to reach this state and to live consciously in it is peace. Come away, for a while, from external things, from the pleasure of the senses, from the arguments of the intellect, from the noise and the excitements of the world, and withdraw yourself into the inmost chamber of your heart, and there, free from the sacrilegious intrusion of all selfish desires, you will find a holy calm, a blissful repose; the faultless eye of Truth will open within you, and you will see things as they really are.

In the external universe there is ceaseless turmoil, change, and unrest; at the heart of all things there is undisturbed repose; in this deep silence dwelleth the Eternal.

Become as little children.

June Twentieth.

Men cry peace! peace! where there is no peace, but, on the contrary, discord, disquietude, and strife. Apart from that wisdom which is inseparable from self-renunciation, there can be no real and abiding peace.

Hatred severs human lives, fosters persecution, and hurls nations into ruthless war.

The peace which results from social comfort, passing gratification, or worldly victory is transitory in its nature, and is burnt up in the heat of fiery trial. Only the Peace of Heaven endures through all trial, and only the selfless heart can know the Peace of Heaven.

This inward peace, this silence, this harmony, this love is the Kingdom of Heaven.

Holiness alone is undying peace. Self-control leads to it, and the ever-increasing Light of Wisdom guides the pilgrim on his way. It is partaken of in a measure as soon as the path of virtue is entered upon, but it is only, realised in its fullness when self disappears in the consummation of a stainless life.

June Twenty-first.

If, O reader! you would realise the Joy that never ends, and the tranquillity that cannot be disturbed; if you would leave behind for ever your sins, your sorrows, your anxieties, and perplexities; if, I say, you would partake of this salvation, this supremely glorious Life, then conquer yourself. Bring every thought, every impulse, every desire into perfect obedience; to the divine power resident within you. There is no other way to peace but this; and if you refuse to walk it, your much praying and your strict adherence to ritual will be fruitless and unavailing, and neither gods nor angels can help you. Only to him that overcometh is given the white stone of the regenerate life, on which is written the New and Ineffable Name.

Realise the Light that never fades!

The holy place within you is your real and eternal self: it is the divine within you.

June Twenty-second.

The schoolmaster never attempts to teach his pupils the abstract principles of mathematics at the commencement; he knows that by such a method teaching would be vain, and learning impossible. He first places before them a very simple sum, and, having explained it, leaves them to *do it*. When, after repeated failures and ever-renewed effort, they have succeeded in doing it correctly, a more difficult task is set them, and then another and another; and not until the pupils have, through many years of diligent application, mastered all the lessons in arithmetic does he attempt to unfold to them the underlying mathematical principles.

Spiritual Principles can only be acquired after long discipline in the pursuit and practice of Virtue.

Thus practice ever precedes knowledge even in the ordinary things of the world, and in spiritual things, in the living of the higher life, this law is rigid in its exactions.

June Twenty-third.

In a properly governed household the child is first taught to be obedient, and to conduct itself properly under all circumstances. The child is not even told why it must do this, but is commanded to do it, and only after it has so far succeeded in doing what is right and proper is it told *why* it should do it. No father would attempt to teach his child the principles of ethics before exacting from it the practice of filial duty and social virtue.

Virtue can only be known by *doing*, and the knowledge of Truth can only be arrived at by perfecting oneself in the practice of Virtue; and to be complete in the practice and acquisition of Virtue is to be complete in the knowledge of Truth.

Truth can only be arrived at by daily and hourly doing the lessons of Virtue.

Undaunted by failure, and made stronger by difficulties.

June Twenty-fourth.

Where Love is, God is, and where Goodness lives
There Christ abides; and he who daily strives
'Gainst self and selfishness, shaping his mind
For Truth and Purity, shall surely find
The Master's presence in his inmost heart.
God shall be one with him (and not apart)
Who overcomes himself, and makes his life
Godlike and holy; banishing all strife
Far from him; letting hate and anger die,
And greed and pride and fleshly lusts that lie
To God and Goodness: great shall be his peace,
Happy and everlasting his release
From pain and sorrow who doth conquer sin.
To the pure heart comes God and dwells therein:

Learn the lessons of Virtue, and thus build up in the strength of knowledge, destroying ignorance and the ills of life.

Make pure thy heart, and thou wilt make thy life Rich, sweet, and beautiful, unmarred by strife.

He only who the Path of Good hath trod
Hath found the Life that's "hid with Christ in God."

JUNE TWENTY-FIFTH.

It will be seen that the first step in the discipline of the mind is the overcoming of indolence. This is the easiest step, and until it is perfectly accomplished the other steps cannot be taken. The clinging to indolence constitutes a complete barrier to the Path of Truth. Indolence consists in giving the body more ease and sleep than it requires, in procrastinating, and in shirking and neglecting those things which should receive immediate attention. This condition of laziness must be overcome by rousing up the body at an early hour, giving it just the amount of sleep it requires for complete recuperation, and by doing, promptly and vigorously, every task and duty, no matter how small, as it comes along.

Stimulate the mind to watchfulness and reflection.

The heart must be purified of sensual and gustatory lust.

JUNE TWENTY-SIXTH.

Success is rooted in a subtle mental brooding along a given line. It subsists in an individual characteristic, or combination of characteristics, and not in a particular circumstance, or set of circumstances. The circumstances appear, it is true, and form part of the success, but these would be useless without the mind that can penetrate and utilise them.

At the root of every success there is some form of well-husbanded and well-directed energy. There has been some persistent brooding of the mind upon a project. Success is like a flower: it may appear more or less suddenly, but it is the finished product of a long series of efforts, of preparatory stages. Men see the success, but the preparation for it, the innumerable mental processes that led up to it, are hidden from them.

A listless mind could not achieve any kind of success.

Without exertion nothing can be accomplished.

JUNE TWENTY-SEVENTH.

Pressing forward persistently along a given way is sure to lead to a destination that is definitely associated with that way. Frequent going aside, or turning back, will render effort fruitless; no destination will be reached; success will remain afar off.

Effort, and the more effort, and then effort again, is the keynote of success. As the simple old saying has it:

If at first you don't succeed, Try again.

In order to achieve the higher forms of success, a man must give up anxiety, hurry, and fussiness.

Transmute the energy that wears and breaks down into that deeper and less obtrusive kind that preserves and builds up.

All the precepts of successful business men are precepts of *doing*; all the precepts of the wise teachers are precepts of *doing*. To cease to do is to cease to be of any use in the economy of life. Doing means effort, exertion.

June Twenty-eighth.

When a man exchanges coppers for silver, and silver for gold, he does not thereby give up the use of money; he exchanges a heavy mass for one that is lighter and smaller but more valuable. So when a man exchanges hurry for deliberation, and deliberation for calmness, he does not give up effort, he merely exchanges a diffusive and more or less ineffective energy for a more highly concentrated, effective, and valuable form.

The silent, calm people will manifest a more enduring form of success than those who are noisy and restless.

The root of success is in character.

Yet even the crudest forms of effort are necessary at first, for without them to begin with the higher forms could not be acquired. The child must crawl before it can walk; it must babble before it can talk; it must talk before it can compose. Man begins in weakness and ends in strength, but from beginning to end he advances by the efforts he makes, by the exertion he puts forth.

June Twenty-ninth.

When in their ignorance men would destroy themselves, its everlasting arms are thrown about them in loving, albeit sometimes painful, protection. Every pain we suffer brings us nearer to the knowledge of the Divine Wisdom. Every blessedness we enjoy speaks to us of the perfection of the Great Law, and of the fullness of bliss that shall be man's when he has come to his heritage of divine knowledge. We progress by learning, and we learn, up to a certain point, by suffering. When the heart is mellowed by love, the law of love is perceived in all its wonderful kindness; when wisdom is acquired, peace is assured.

The law which punishes us is the law which preserves us.

To wish to bring down the perfect to the imperfect is the crown of folly, but to strive to bring the imperfect up to the perfect is the height of wisdom.

We cannot alter the law of things, which is of sublime perfection, but we can alter ourselves so as to comprehend more and more of that perfection, and make its grandeur ours.

June Thirtieth.

Seers of the Cosmos see the universe as a perfect whole, and not as an imperfect jumble of parts. The Great Teachers are men of abiding joy and heavenly peace.

The blind captive of unholy desire may cry:

Ah! Love, could you and I with Him conspire
To grasp this sorry scheme of things entire,
Would we not shatter it to bits, and then
Remould it nearer to the heart's desire?

Seers of the Cosmos do not mourn over the scheme of things.

To perceive it, is the beatific vision; to know it, is the beatific bliss.

This is the wish of the voluptuary, the wish to enjoy unlawful pleasures to any extent, and not reap any painful consequences. It is such men who regard the universe as a "sorry scheme of things." They want the universe to bend to their will and desire; want lawlessness, not law; but the wise man bends his will and subjects his desires to the Divine Order, and he sees the universe as the glorious perfection of an infinitude of parts.

JULY FIRST.

In whatever condition a man finds himself, he can always find the True; and he can find it only by so utilising his present condition as to become strong and wise. The effeminate hankering after rewards, and the craven fear of punishment, let them be put away for ever, and let a man joyfully bend himself to the faithful performance of all his duties, forgetting himself and his worthless pleasures, and living strong and

Wisdom is the aim of every philosophy.

Canst thou mend a broken vase by weeping over it?

pure and self-contained; so shall he surely find the Unfailing Wisdom, the God-like Patience and Strength. "The situation that has not its Duty, its Ideal, was never yet occupied by man." All that is beautiful and blessed is in thyself, not in thy neighbour's wealth. Thou art poor? Thou art poor indeed if thou art not stronger than thy poverty! Thou hast suffered calamities? Tell me, wilt thou cure calamity by adding anxiety to it? There is no evil but will vanish if thou wilt wisely meet it.

JULY SECOND.

The man who conquers another by force is strong; the man who con-quers himself by Meekness is mighty. He who conquers another by force will himself likewise be conquered; he who conquers himself by Meekness will never be overthrown, for the human cannot overcome the divine. The meek man is triumphant in defeat. Socrates lives the

The might of meekness!

Meekness is a divine quality, and as such is all powerful.

more by being put to death; in the crucified Jesus the risen Christ is revealed; and Stephen, in receiving his stoning, defies the hurting power of stones. That which is real cannot be destroyed, but only that which is unreal. When a man finds that within him which is real, which is constant, abiding, changeless, and eternal, he enters into that Reality, and becomes meek. All the powers of darkness will come against him, but they will do him no hurt, and will at last depart from him.

July Third.

Into the cause of causes shalt thou penetrate, and lifting, one after another, every veil of illusion, shalt reach at last the inmost Heart of Being. Thus becoming one with Life, thou shalt know all life, and, seeing into causes, and knowing realities, thou shalt be no more anxious about thyself, and others, and the world, but shalt see that all things that are, are engines of the Great Law. Canopied with gentleness, thou shalt bless where others curse; love where others hate; forgive where others condemn; yield where others strive; give up where others grasp; lose where others gain. And in their strength they shall be weak; and in thy weakness thou shalt be strong; yea, thou shalt mightily prevail. "Therefore, when Heaven would save a man, it enfolds him with gentleness."

Nothing is hidden from him who overcomes himself.

He that hath not unbroken gentleness hath not Truth.

July Fourth.

The righteous man is invincible. No enemy can possibly overcome or confound him; and he needs no other protection than that of his own integrity and holiness. As it is impossible for evil to overcome Good, so the righteous man can never be brought low by the unrighteous. Slander, envy, hatred, malice can never reach him, nor cause him any suffering, and those who try to injure him only succeed ultimately in bringing ignominy upon themselves.

How can he fear any who wrongs none?

Ceasing from all wrong you can never be wronged; ceasing from all deceit you can never be deceived.

The righteous man having nothing to hide, committing no acts which require stealth, and harbouring no thoughts and desires which he would not like others to know, is fearless and unashamed. His step is firm, his body upright, and his speech direct and without ambiguity. He looks everybody in the face. How can he be ashamed before any who deceives none?

July Fifth.

The Children of Light who abide in the Kingdom of Heaven see the universe, and all that it contains, as the manifestation of one Law—the Law of Love. They see Love as the moulding, sustaining, protecting, and perfecting Power immanent in all things animate and inanimate. To them Love is not merely and only a rule of life, it is the Law of life,

The universe is preserved because Love is at the Heart of it.

Love is the only preserving power.

it is Life itself. Knowing this, they order their whole life in accordance with Love, not regarding their own personality. By thus practising obedience to the Highest, to divine Love, they become conscious partakers of the power of Love, and so arrive at perfect Freedom as Masters of Destiny. Love is Perfect Harmony, pure bliss, and contains, therefore, no element of suffering. Let a man think no thought and do no act that is not in accordance with pure Love, and suffering shall no more trouble him.

July Sixth.

If a man would know Love, and partake of its undying bliss, he must practice it in his heart; he must become Love. He who always acts from the spirit of Love is never deserted, is never left in a dilemma or difficulty, for Love (impersonal Love) is both Knowledge and Power. He who has learned how to Love has learned how to master every difficulty, how to transmute every failure into success, how to clothe every event and condition in garments of blessedness and beauty.

The way to Love is by self-mastery, and, travelling that way, a man builds himself up in Knowledge as he proceeds. Arriving at Love, he enters into full possession of body and mind, by right of the divine Power which he has earned. "Perfect Love casteth out fear."

To know Love is to know that there is no harmful power in the whole universe.

Perfect Love is perfect Harmlessness. And he who has destroyed in himself all thoughts of harm, and all desire to harm, receives the universal protection.

July Seventh.

There is no bondage in the Heavenly Life. There is Perfect Freedom. This is its great glory. This Supreme Freedom is gained only by obedience. He who obeys the Highest co-operates with the Highest, and so masters every force within himself and every condition without. A man may choose the lower and neglect the Higher, but the Higher is never overcome by the lower: herein lies the revelation of Freedom. Let a man choose the Higher and abandon the lower; he shall then establish himself as an overcomer, and shall realise Perfect Freedom.

To give the reins to inclination is the only slavery; to conquer oneself is the only freedom. The slave to self loves his chains, and will not have one of them broken for fear he would be depriving himself of some cherished delight. He thus defeats and enslaves himself.

By self-enlightenment is Perfect Freedom found.

The Land of Perfect Freedom lies through the Gate of Knowledge.

July Eighth.

All outward oppression is but the shadow and effect of the real oppression within. For ages the oppressed have cried for liberty, and a thousand man-made statutes have failed to give it to them. They can give it only to themselves; they shall find it only in obedience to the Divine Statutes which are inscribed upon their hearts. Let them resort to the inward Freedom, and the shadow of oppression shall no more darken the earth. Let men cease to oppress themselves, and no man shall oppress his brother. Men legislate for an *outward* freedom, yet continue to render such freedom impossible of achievement by fostering an inward condition of enslavement. They thus pursue a shadow without, and ignore the substance within. All outward forms of bondage and oppression will cease to be when man ceases to be the willing bond-slave of passion, error, and ignorance.

Man will be free when he is freed from self.

Freedom is to the free!

July Ninth.

The great man is always the good man; he is always simple. He draws from, nay, lives in, the inexhaustible fountain of divine Goodness within; he inhabits the Heavenly Places; communes with the vanished great ones; lives with the Invisible: he is inspired, and breathes the airs of Heaven.

   He who would be great, let him learn to be good. He will therefore become great by not seeking greatness. Aiming at greatness, a man arrives at nothingness; aiming at nothingness he arrives at greatness. The desire to be great is an indication of littleness, of personal vanity and obtrusiveness. The willingness to disappear from gaze, the utter absence of self-aggrandisement, is the witness of greatness. Littleness seeks and loves authority. Greatness is never authoritative, and it thereby becomes the authority to which the after ages appeal.

The True, the Beautiful, the Great is always childlike, and is perennially fresh and young.

Be thy simple self, thy better self, the impersonal self, and lo! thou art great!

July Tenth.

Wouldst thou preach the living Word? Thou shalt forgo thyself, and become that Word. Thou shalt know one thing—*that the human heart is good, is divine*; thou shalt live one thing—Love. Thou shalt love all, seeing no evil, believing no evil; then, though thou speak but little, thy every act shall be a power, thy every word a precept. By thy pure thought, thy selfless deed, though it appear hidden, thou shalt preach, down the ages, to untold multitudes of aspiring souls.

   To him who chooses Goodness, sacrificing all, is given that which includes all. He becomes the possessor of the Best, communes with the Highest, and enters the company of the Great.

The greatness that is flawless, rounded, and complete is above and beyond all art.

It is Perfect Goodness in manifestation: therefore the greatest souls are always Teachers.

JULY ELEVENTH.

Thoughts are seeds, which, falling in the soil of the mind, germinate and develop until they reach the completed stage, blossoming into deeds good or bad, brilliant or stupid, according to their nature, and ending as seeds of thought to be again sown in other minds. A teacher is a sower of seed, a spiritual agriculturist, while he who teaches himself is the wise farmer of his own mental plot. The growth of a thought is as the growth of a plant. The seed must be sown seasonally, and time is required for its full development into the plant of knowledge and the flower of wisdom.

Every natural law has its spiritual counterpart.

The seen is the mirror of the unseen.

JULY TWELFTH.

The advice of one of the Great Teachers to his disciples, "Keep wide awake," tersely expresses the necessity for tireless energy if one's purpose is to be accomplished, and is equally good advice to the salesman as to the saint. "Eternal vigilance is the price of liberty," and liberty is the reaching of one's fixed ends. It was the same Teacher who said: "If anything is to be done, let a man do it at once; let him attack it vigorously!" The wisdom of this advice is seen when it is remembered that action is creative, that increase and development follow upon legitimate use. To get more energy we must use to the full that which we already possess. Only to him that puts his hand vigorously to some task do power and freedom come.

Energy to be productive must not only be directed toward good ends, it must be carefully controlled and conserved.

Noise and hurry are so much energy running to waste

JULY THIRTEENTH.

Where calmness is, there is the greatest power. Calmness is the sure indication of a strong, well-trained, patiently disciplined mind. The calm man knows his business, be sure of it. His words are few, but they tell. His schemes are well planned, and they work true, like a well-balanced machine. He sees a long way ahead, and makes straight for his object. The enemy, Difficulty, he converts into a friend, and makes profitable use of him, for he has studied well how to "agree with his adversary while he is in the way with him." Like a wise general, he has anticipated all emergencies. Indeed, he is *the man who is prepared beforehand*. In his meditations, in the counsels of his judgment, he has conferred with

It is a great delusion that noise means power.

Working steam is not heard. It is the escaping steam which makes a great noise.

causes, and has caught the bent of all contingencies. He is never taken by surprise; is never in a hurry; is safe in the keeping of his own steadfastness; and is sure of his ground.

July Fourteenth.

Calmness, as distinguished from the dead placidity of languor, is the acme of concentrated energy. There is a focused mentality behind it. In agitation and excitement the mentality is dispersed. It is irresponsible, and is without force or weight. The fussy, peevish, irritable man has no influence. He repels, not attracts. He wonders why his "easy-going" neighbour succeeds, and is sought after, while he, who is always hurrying, worrying, and troubling (he miscalls it *striving),* fails, and is avoided. His neighbour, being a calmer man, not more easygoing but more deliberate, gets through more work, does it more skilfully, and is more self-possessed and manly. This is the reason of his success and influence. His energy is controlled and used, while the other man's energy is dispersed and abused.

Energy is the first pillar in the temple of prosperity.

No energy means no capacity.

July Fifteenth.

The poor man who is to become rich must begin at the bottom, and must not wish, or try, to appear affluent by attempting something far beyond his means. There is always plenty of room and scope at the bottom, and it is a safe place from which to begin, as there is nothing below, and everything above. Many a young business man comes at once to grief by swagger and display, which he foolishly imagines are necessary to success, but which, deceiving no one but himself, lead quickly to ruin. A modest and true beginning, in any sphere, will better ensure success than an exaggerated advertisement of one's standing and importance.

The spendthrift can never become rich, but, if he begin with riches, must soon become poor.

The thrifty and prudent are on the way to riches.

July Sixteenth.

An obtrusive display in clothing and jewellery bespeaks a vulgar and empty mind. Modest and cultured people are modest and becoming in their dress, and their spare money is wisely used in further enhancing their culture and virtue. Education and progress are of more importance to them than needless, vain apparel; and literature, art, and science are encouraged thereby. A true refinement is in the mind and behaviour, and a mind adorned with virtue and intelligence cannot add to its attractiveness (though it may detract from it) by an ostentatious display of the body.

Vanity leading to excessive luxury in clothing is a vice which should be studiously avoided by virtuous people.

Simplicity in dress, as in other things, is the best.

July Seventeenth.

The man who gets up early in order to think and plan, that he may weigh and consider and forecast, will always manifest greater skill and success in his particular pursuit than the man who lies in bed till the last moment, and only gets up in time to begin breakfast. An hour spent in this way before breakfast will prove of the greatest value in making one's efforts fruitful. It is a means of calming and clarifying the mind, and of focusing one's energies so as to render them more powerful and effective. The best and most abiding success is that which is made before eight o'clock in the morning. He who is at his business at six o'clock will always—all other conditions being equal—be a long way ahead of the man who is in bed at eight.

Money wasted can be restored; health wasted can be restored; but time wasted can never be restored.

The day is not lengthened for any man.

July Eighteenth.

There is *one* right way of doing every thing, even the smallest, and a thousand wrong ways. Skill consists in finding the one right way, and adhering to it. The inefficient bungle confusedly about among the thousand wrong ways, and do not adopt the right one when it is pointed out to them. They do this in some cases because they think, in their ignorance, that they know best, thereby placing themselves in a position where it becomes impossible to learn, even though it be only to learn how to clean a window or sweep a floor. Thoughtlessness and inefficiency are all too common. There is plenty of room in the world for thoughtful and efficient people. Employers of labour know how difficult it is to get the best workmanship. The good workman, whether with tools or brains, whether with speech or thought, will always find a place for the exercise of his skill.

Wisdom is the highest form of skill.

Skill is gained by thoughtfulness and attention.

July Nineteenth.

As the bubble cannot endure, so the fraud cannot prosper. He makes a feverish spurt in the acquirement of money, and then collapses. Nothing is ever gained, ever can be gained, by fraud. It is but wrested for a time, to be again returned with heavy interest. But fraud is not confined to the unscrupulous swindler. All who are getting, or trying to get, money without giving an equivalent are practising fraud, whether they know it or not. Men who are anxiously scheming how to get money

There is no striking a cheap bargain with prosperity.

Prosperity must be purchased, not only with intelligent labour, but with moral force.

without working for it are frauds, and mentally they are closely allied to the thief and swindler under whose influence they come, sooner or later, and who deprives them of their capital.

July Twentieth.

To be complete and strong, integrity must embrace the whole man, and extend to all the details of his life; and it must be so thorough and permanent as to withstand all temptations to swerve into compromise. To fail in one point is to fail in all, and to admit, under stress, a compromise with falsehood, howsoever necessary and insignificant it may appear, is to throw down the shield of integrity, and to stand exposed to the onslaughts of evil.

The man who works as carefully and conscientiously when his employer is away as when his eye is on him, will not long remain in an inferior position. Such integrity in duty, in performing the details of his work, will quickly lead him into the fertile regions of prosperity.

Sterling integrity tells wherever it is, and stamps its hall-mark on all transactions.

The man of integrity is in line with the fixed law of things. He is like a strong tree whose roots are fed by perennial springs, and which no tempest can lay low.

July Twenty-first.

Honesty is the surest way to success. The day at last comes when the dishonest man repents in sorrow and suffering; but no man ever needs to repent of having been honest. Even when the honest man fails— as he does sometimes through lacking other of those pillars, such as energy, economy, or system—his failure is not the grievous thing that it is to the dishonest man, for he can always rejoice in the fact that he has never defrauded a fellow-being. Even in his darkest hour he finds repose in a clear conscience.

Ignorant men imagine that dishonesty is a short cut to prosperity.

The dishonest man is morally short-sighted.

July Twenty-second.

Invincibility is a glorious protector, but it only envelops the man whose integrity is perfectly pure and unassailable. Never to violate, even in the most insignificant particular, is to be invincible against all the assaults of innuendo, slander, and misrepresentation. The man who has failed in one point is vulnerable, and the shaft of evil, like the arrow in the heel of Achilles, will lay him low. Pure and perfect integrity is proof against all attack and injury, enabling its possessor to meet all opposition and persecution with dauntless courage and sublime equanimity. No amount of talent, intellect, or business acumen can give a man that

Strong men have strong purposes, and strong purposes lead to strong achievements.

Moral force is the greatest power.

power of mind and peace of heart which come from an enlightened acceptance and observance of lofty moral principles.

July Twenty-third.

Sympathy should not be confounded with that maudlin and superficial sentiment which, like a pretty flower without root, presently perishes and leaves behind neither seed nor fruit. To fall into hysterical weeping when parting with a friend, or on hearing of some suffering abroad, is not sympathy. Neither are bursts of violent indignation against the cruelties and injustices of others any indication of a sympathetic mind. If one is cruel at home—if he badgers his wife, or beats his children, or abuses his servants, or stabs his neighbours with shafts of sarcasm— what hypocrisy is in his profession of love for suffering people who are outside the immediate range of his influence! What shallow sentiment informs his bursts of indignation against the injustices and hard-heartedness in the world around him!

The test of a man is in his immediate acts, and not in his ultra sentiments.

Sympathy is a deep, inexpressible tenderness which is shown in a consistently self-forgetful, gentle character.

July Twenty-fourth.

Sympathy leads us to the hearts of all men, so that we become spiritually united to them, and when they suffer we feel the pain; when they are glad, we rejoice with them; when they are despised and persecuted, we spiritually descend with them into the depths, and take into our hearts their humiliation and distress; and he who has this binding, uniting spirit of sympathy can never be cynical and condemnatory, can never pass thoughtless and cruel judgments upon his fellows, because in his tenderness of heart he is ever with them in their pain.

Lack of sympathy arises in egotism; sympathy arises in love.

Sympathy, in its real and profound sense, is oneness with others in their strivings and sufferings.

But to have reached this ripened sympathy, it must needs be that he has loved much, suffered much, and sounded the dark depths of sorrow. It springs from acquaintance with the profoundest experiences, so that a man has had conceit, thoughtlessness, and selfishness burnt out of his heart.

July Twenty-fifth.

Let a man beware of greed, of meanness, of envy, of jealousy, of suspicion, for these things, if harboured, will rob him of all that is best in life, aye, even all that is best in material things, as well as all that is best in character and happiness. Let him be liberal of heart and generous of

Gentleness is the hall-mark of spiritual culture.

Gentleness is akin to divinity.

hand, magnanimous and trusting, not only giving cheerfully and often of his substance, but allowing his friends and fellow-men freedom of thought and action—let him be thus, and honour, plenty, and prosperity will come knocking at his door for admittance as his friends and guests.

July Twenty-sixth.

The man who has perfected himself in gentleness never quarrels. He never returns the hard word; he leaves it alone, or meets it with a gentle word, which is far more powerful than wrath. Gentleness is wedded to wisdom, and the wise man has overcome all anger in himself, and so understands how to overcome it in others. The gentle man is saved from most of the disturbances and turmoils with which uncontrolled men afflict themselves. While they are wearing themselves out with wasteful and needless strain, he is quiet and composed, and such quietness and composure are strong to win in the battle of life.

A gentle man—one whose good behaviour is prompted by thoughtfulness and kindliness—is always loved, whatever may be his origin.

Argument analyses the outer skin, but sympathy reaches to the heart.

July Twenty-seventh.

It is all-important that we be real; that we harbour no wish to appear other than what we are; that we simulate no virtue, assume no excellency, adopt no disguise. The hypocrite thinks he can hoodwink the world and the eternal law of the world. There is but one person that he hoodwinks, and that is himself, and for that the law of the world inflicts its righteous penalty. There is an old theory that the excessively wicked are annihilated. I think to be a pretender is to come as near to annihilation as a man can get, for there is a sense in which a man is gone, and in his place there is but a mirage of shams.

Spurious things have no value, whether they be bric-a-brac or men.

The sound-hearted man becomes an exemplar: he is, more than a man; he is a reality, a force, a moulding principle.

July Twenty-eighth.

The painful experiences of evil pass away as the new experiences of good enter into and possess the field of consciousness. And what are the new experiences of good? They are many and beautiful—such as the joyful knowledge of freedom from sin; the absence of remorse; deliverance from all the torments of temptation; ineffable joy in conditions and circumstances which formerly caused deep affliction; imperviousness to hurt by the actions of others; great patience and sweetness

Evil is an experience, and not a power.

Evil is a state of ignorance, of undevelopment, and as such it recedes and disappears before the light of knowledge.

of character; serenity of mind under all circumstances; emancipation from doubt, fear, and anxiety; freedom from all dislike, envy, and enmity.

JULY TWENTY-NINTH.

To have transcendent virtue is to enjoy transcendent felicity. The beatific blessedness which Jesus holds out is promised to those having the beatific virtues—to the merciful, the pure in heart, the peacemakers, and so on. The higher virtue does not merely and only lead to happiness, it *is* happiness. It is impossible for a man of transcendent virtue to be unhappy. The cause of unhappiness must be sought and found in the self-loving elements, and not in the self-sacrificing qualities. A man may have virtue and be unhappy, but not so if he have divine virtue. Human virtue is mingled with self, and therefore with sorrow; but from divine virtue every taint of self has been purged away, and with it every vestige of misery.

When divine good is practised, life is bliss.

Truth lies upward and beyond.

JULY THIRTIETH.

Men pray for peace, yet cling to passion; they foster strife, yet pray for heavenly rest. This is ignorance, profound spiritual ignorance; it is not to know the first letter in the alphabet of things divine.

Hatred and love, strife and peace, cannot dwell together in the same heart. Where one is admitted as a welcome guest, the other will be turned away as an unwelcome stranger. He who despises another will be despised by others; he who opposes his fellow-men will himself be resisted. He should not be surprised, and mourn, that men are divided. He should know that he is propagating strife. He should understand his lack of peace.

Where passion is, peace is not; where peace is, passion is not.

By the way of self-conquest is the Perfect Peace achieved.

JULY THIRTY-FIRST.

If men only understood
That their wrong can never smother
The wrong doing of another;
That by hatred hate increases,
And by Good all evil ceases,
They would cleanse their hearts and actions,
Banish thence all vile detractions—
   If they only understood

If men only understood
That the wrong act of a brother
Should not call from them another.

If they only understood.
   How Love conquers . . .
. . . They would ever
Live in Love, in hatred never—
   If they only understood.

If men only understood
That the heart that sins must *sorrow,*
That the hateful mind to-morrow
Reaps its barren harvest, weeping,
Starving, resting not, nor sleeping,
Tenderness would *fill their being,*
They would see with Pity's seeing—
If they only understood.

AUGUST FIRST.

"Goodwill gives insight," and only he who has so conquered his personality that he has but one attitude of mind, that of goodwill, is possessed of divine insight, and is capable of distinguishing the true from the false. The supremely good man is, therefore, the wise man, the divine man, the enlightened seer, the knower of the Eternal. Where you find unbroken gentleness, enduring patience, sublime lowliness, graciousness of speech, self-control, self-forgetfulness, and deep and abounding sympathy, look there for the highest wisdom, seek the company of such a one, for he has realised the Divine, he lives with the Eternal, he has become one with the Infinite. Those who are spiritually awakened have alone comprehended the Universal Reality where all appearances are dispersed and dreaming and delusion are destroyed.

Let a man abandon self, let him overcome the world, let him deny the personal; by this pathway only can he enter into the heart of the Infinite.

To centre one's life in the Great Law of Love is to enter into rest, harmony, peace.

AUGUST SECOND.

To refrain from all participation in evil and discord; to cease from all resistance to evil, and from the omission of that which is good, and to fall back upon unswerving obedience to the holy calm within, is to enter into the inmost heart of things, is to attain to a living, conscious experience of that eternal and infinite principle which must ever remain a hidden mystery to the merely perceptive intellect. Until this principle is realised, the soul is not established in peace, and he who so realises is truly wise; not wise with the wisdom of the learned, but with the simplicity of a blameless heart and of a divine manhood.

To enter into a realisation of the Infinite and Eternal is to rise superior to time.

To realise this Law, this Unity, this Truth, is to enter into the Infinite, is to become one with the Eternal.

There is one Great Law which exacts unconditional obedience, one unifying principle which is the basis of all diversity, one eternal Truth wherein all the problems of earth pass away like shadows.

AUGUST THIRD.

Entering into the Infinite is not a mere theory or sentiment. It is a vital experience which is the result of assiduous practice in inward purification. When the body is no longer to be, even remotely, the real man; when all appetites and desires are thoroughly subdued and purified; when the emotions are rested and calm; and when the oscillation of the intellect ceases and perfect poise is secured, then, and not till then, does consciousness become one with the Infinite; not till then is childlike wisdom and profound peace secured.

Men grow weary and grey over the dark problems of life, and finally pass away and leave them unsolved because they cannot see their way out of the darkness of the personality, being too much engrossed in its limitations.

Become established in Immortality, Heaven, and the Spirit, which make up the Empire of Light.

Seeking to save his personal life, man forfeits the greater impersonal Life of Truth; clinging to the perishable, he is shut out from a knowledge of the Eternal.

AUGUST FOURTH.

Error is involved in the darkness of unfathomable complexity, but eternal simplicity is the glory of Truth.

Love of self shuts men out from Truth, and seeking their own personal happiness they lose the deeper, purer, and more abiding bliss. Says Carlyle, "There is in man a higher than happiness. He can do without happiness, and instead thereof find blessedness. . . . Love not pleasure, love God. This is the Everlasting Yea, wherein all contradiction is solved; wherein whoso walks and works, it is well with him."

He who has yielded up that self, that personality that most men love, and to which they cling with such fierce tenacity, has left behind him all perplexity, and has entered into a simplicity so profoundly simple as to be looked upon by the world, involved as it is in a network of error, as foolishness.

Self and error are synonymous.

At rest in the Infinite.

AUGUST FIFTH.

When a man has yielded up his lusts, his errors, his opinions and prejudices, he has entered into possession of the knowledge of God, having slain the selfish desire for heaven, and along with it the ignorant fear of hell; having relinquished even the love of life itself, he has gained supreme bliss and Life Eternal, the Life which bridges life and death,

The region of Reality. Unchanging principle.

By the surrender of self all difficulties are overcome.

and knows its own immortality. Having yielded up all without reservation, he has gained all, and rests in peace on the bosom of the Infinite.

Only he who has become so free from self as to be equally content to be annihilated as to live, or to live as to be annihilated, is fit to enter into the Infinite. Only he who, ceasing to trust his perishable self, has learned to trust in boundless measure the Great Law, the Supreme Good, is prepared to partake of undying bliss.

August Sixth.

The spirit of Love which is manifested as a perfect and rounded life is the crown of being and the supreme end of knowledge upon this earth.

There is no more regret, nor disappointment, nor remorse, where all selfishness has ceased.

How does a man act under trial and temptation? Many men boast of being in possession of Truth who are continually swayed by grief, disappointment, and passion, and who sink under the first little trial that comes along. Truth is nothing if not unchangeable, and in so far as a man takes his stand upon Truth does he become steadfast in virtue, does he rise superior to his passions and emotions and changeable personality.

He who is patient, calm, and forgiving under all circumstances manifests the Truth.

Men formulate perishable dogmas, and call them Truth. Truth cannot be formulated; it is ineffable, and ever beyond the reach of intellect. It can only be experienced by practice; it can only be manifested in a stainless heart and a perfect life.

August Seventh.

Truth will never be proved by wordy arguments and learned treatises, for if men do not perceive the Truth in infinite patience, undying forgiveness, and all-embracing compassion, no words can ever prove it to them.

Practice heart-virtue, and search humbly and diligently for the Truth.

It is an easy matter for the passionate to be calm and patient when they are in the midst of calmness, or when they are alone. It is equally easy for the uncharitable to be gentle and kind when they are dealt kindly with, but he who retains his patience and calmness under all

There is one great all-embracing Law which is the foundation of the universe, the Law of Love.

trial, who remains sublimely meek and gentle under the most trying circumstances, he, and he alone, is possessed of the spotless Truth. And this is so because such lofty virtues belong to the Divine, and can only be manifested by one who has attained to the highest wisdom, who has relinquished his passionate and self-seeking nature, who has realised the supreme and unchangeable Law, and has brought himself into harmony with it.

AUGUST EIGHTH.

It is because of the effort of the soul to realise this Law that men come again and again to live, to suffer, and to die; and when realised, suffering ceases, personality is dispersed, and the fleshly life and death are destroyed, for consciousness becomes one with the Eternal.

The Law is absolutely impersonal, and its highest manifested expression is that of Service. When the purified heart has realised Truth, it is then called upon to make the last, the greatest, and holiest sacrifice, the sacrifice of the well-earned enjoyment of Truth. It is by virtue of this sacrifice that the divinely-emancipated soul comes to dwell amongst the lowliest and least, and to be esteemed the servant of all mankind.

To become possessed of a knowledge of the Law of Love, to enter into conscious harmony with it, is to become immortal, invincible, indestructible.

The Spirit of Love is alone singled out as worthy to receive the unstinted worship of posterity.

AUGUST NINTH.

The glory alike of the saint, the sage, and the saviour is this—that he has realised the most profound lowliness, the most sublime unselfishness; having given up all, even his own personality, all his works are holy and enduring, for they are freed from every taint of self. He gives, yet never thinks of receiving; he works, yet without regretting the past or anticipating the future, and never looks for reward.

When the farmer has tilled and dressed his land and put in the seed, he knows that he has done all that he can possibly do, and that now he must trust to the elements, and wait patiently for the course of time to bring about the harvest, and that no amount of expectancy on his part will affect the result. Even so, he who has realised the Truth goes forth as a sower of the seeds of goodness, purity, love, and peace, without expectancy, and never looking for results, knowing that there is the Great Over-ruling Law which brings about its own harvest in due time, and which is alike the source of preservation and destruction.

Truth cannot be limited.

Every holy man became such by unremitting perseverance in self-sacrifice.

AUGUST TENTH.

What the saints, sages, and saviours have accomplished, you likewise may accomplish if you will only tread the way which they trod and pointed out, the way of self-sacrifice, of self-denying service.

Truth is very simple. It says, "Give up self," "Come unto Me" (away from all that defiles) "and I will give you rest." All the mountains of commentary that have been piled upon it cannot hide it from the heart

He who enters upon the holy way begins by restraining his passions.

Saintship is the beginning of holiness.

that is earnestly seeking for righteousness. It does not require learning; it can be known in spite of learning. Disguised under many forms by erring, self-seeking men, the beautiful simplicity and clear transparency of Truth remains unaltered and undimmed, and the unselfish heart enters into and partakes of its shining radiance. Not by weaving complex theories, not by building up speculative philosophies, is Truth realised; but by weaving the web of inward purity, by building up the Temple of a stainless life, is Truth realised.

August Eleventh.

The divine within is the abode of peace, the temple of wisdom, the dwelling-place of immortality. Apart from this inward resting-place, this Mount of Vision, there can be no true peace, no knowledge of the Divine, and if you can remain there for one minute, one hour, or one day, it is possible for you to remain there always.

Only when you identify yourself with the Divine can you be said to be "clothed and in your right mind."

All your sins and sorrows, your fears and anxieties, are your own, and you can cling to them or you can give them up. Of your own accord you cling to your unrest; of your own accord you can come to abiding peace. No one else can give up sin for you; you must give it up yourself.

Give up all self-seeking; give up self, and lo! the Peace of God is yours.

The greatest Teacher can do no more than walk the way of Truth for himself, and point it out to you; you yourself must walk it for yourself. You can obtain freedom and peace alone by your own efforts, by yielding up that which binds the soul, and which is destructive of peace.

August Twelfth.

O thou who wouldst teach men of Truth!
Hast thou passed through the desert of doubt?
Art thou purged by the fires of sorrow? hath truth
The fiends of opinion cast out.
Of thy human heart? Is thy soul so fair
That no false thought can ever harbour there?

Come out of the storms of sin and anguish.

Enter the inward resting-place.

O thou who wouldst teach men of Love!
Hast thou passed through the place of despair?
Hast thou wept through the dark night of grief? does it move
(Now freed from its sorrow and care)
Thy human heart to pitying gentleness,
Looking on wrong, and hate, and ceaseless stress?

O thou who wouldst teach men of Peace!

Hast thou crossed the wide ocean of strife?
Hast thou found on the Shores of the Silence release
From all the wild unrest of life?
From thy human heart hath all striving gone,
Leaving but Truth, and Love, and Peace alone?

AUGUST THIRTEENTH.

Think of your servants with kindness, consider their happiness and comfort, and never demand of them that extremity of service which you yourself would not care to perform were you in their place, Rare and beautiful is that humility of soul by which a servant entirely forgets himself in his master's good; but far rarer, and more beautiful with a divine beauty, is that nobility of soul by which a man, forgetting his own happiness, seeks the happiness of those who are under his authority, and who depend upon him for their bodily sustenance. And such a man's happiness is increased tenfold, nor does he need to complain of those whom he employs. Said a well-known and extensive employer of labour, who never needs to dismiss an employee: "I have always had the happiest relations with my work-people. If you ask me how it is to be accounted for, I can only say that it has been my aim from the first to do to them as I would wish to be done by."

Make yourself pure and lovable, and you will be loved by all.

Be friendly toward others, and friends will soon flock round you.

AUGUST FOURTEENTH.

As the rising sun puts to rout the helpless shadows, so are all the impotent forces of evil put to flight by the searching rays of positive thought which shine forth from a heart made strong in purity and faith.

Where there is sterling faith and uncompromising purity there is health, there is success, there is power. In such a one, disease, failure, and disaster can find no lodgment, for there is nothing on which they can feed.

Even physical conditions are largely determined by mental states, and to this truth the scientific world is rapidly being drawn. The old, materialistic belief that a man is what his body makes him is rapidly passing away, and is being replaced by the inspiring belief that man is superior to his body, and that his body is what he makes it by the power of thought.

To dwell continually in good thoughts is to throw around oneself a psychic atmosphere of sweetness and power which leaves its impress upon all who come in contact with it.

There is no evil in the universe but has its root and origin in the mind.

AUGUST FIFTEENTH.

If you are given to anger, worry, jealousy, greed, or any other inharmonious state of mind, and expect perfect physical health, you are expecting the impossible, for you are continually sowing the seeds of disease in your mind. Such conditions of mind are carefully shunned by the wise man, for he knows them to be far more dangerous than a bad drain or an infected house.

If you would be free from all physical aches and pains, and would enjoy perfect physical harmony, then put your mind in order, and harmonise your thoughts. Think joyful thoughts; think loving thoughts; let the elixir of goodwill course through your veins, and you will need no other medicine. Put away your jealousies, your suspicions, your worries, your hatreds, your selfish indulgences, and you will put away your dyspepsia, your biliousness, your nervousness and aching joints.

Renounce.

If you would secure health, you must learn to work without friction.

AUGUST SIXTEENTH.

Pour the oil of tranquillity upon the turbulent waters of the passions and prejudices, and the tempests of misfortune, however they may threaten, will be powerless to wreck the barque of your soul, as it threads its way across the ocean of life. And if that barque be piloted by a cheerful and never-failing faith, its course will be doubly sure, and many perils will pass it by which would otherwise attack it. By the power of faith every enduring work is accomplished. Faith in the Supreme; faith in the over-ruling Law; faith in your work, and in your power to accomplish that work—here is the rock upon which you must build if you would achieve, if you would stand and not fall.

Order your thoughts and you will order your life.

Follow, under all circumstances, the highest promptings within you.

AUGUST SEVENTEENTH.

Cultivate a pure and unselfish spirit, and combine with purity and faith singleness of purpose, and you are evolving from the elements enduring success of greatness and power.

If your present position is distasteful to you, and your heart is not in your work, nevertheless perform your duties with scrupulous diligence; and whilst resting your mind in the idea that the better position and greater opportunities are waiting for you, ever keep an active mental outlook for budding possibilities, so that when the critical moment arrives, and the new channel presents itself, you will step into it with your mind fully prepared for the undertaking, and with that intelligence and foresight which is born of mental discipline.

Whatever your task may be, concentrate your whole mind upon it, throw into it all the energy of which you are capable. The faultless completion of small tasks leads inevitably to larger tasks.

Let your heart grow large and loving and unselfish, and great and lasting will be your influence and success.

Learn by constant practice how to husband your resources, and to concentrate them, at any moment, upon a given point.

AUGUST EIGHTEENTH.

When that young man, whom I knew, passing through continual reverses and misfortunes, was mocked by his friends and told to desist from further effort, and he replied, "The time is not far distant when you will marvel at my good fortune and success," he showed that he was possessed of that silent and irresistible power which has taken him over innumerable difficulties, and crowned his life with success.

If you have not this power, you may acquire it by practice, and the beginning of power is likewise the beginning of wisdom. You must commence by overcoming those purposeless trivialities to which you have hitherto been a willing victim. Boisterous and uncontrolled laughter, slander and idle talk, and joking merely to raise a laugh—all these things must be put on one side as so much waste of valuable energy.

Passion is not power; it is the abuse of power, the dispersion of power.

Be of single aim; have a legitimate and useful purpose, and devote yourself unreservedly to it.

AUGUST NINETEENTH.

The satisfaction which results from gratified desire is brief and illusionary, and is always followed by an increased demand for gratification. Desire is insatiable as the ocean, and clamours louder and louder as its demands are attended to. It claims ever-increasing service from its deluded devotees, until at last they are struck down with physical or mental anguish, and are hurled into the purifying fires of suffering. Desire is the region of hell, and all torments are centred there. The giving up of desire is the realisation of heaven, and all delights await the pilgrim there.

Happiness is that inward state of perfect satisfaction which is joy and peace.

Heaven and hell are inward states.

> *I sent my soul through the invisible,*
> *Some letter of that after life to spell,*
> *And by and by my soul returned to me,*
> *And whispered, "I myself am heaven and hell."*

AUGUST TWENTIETH.

Sink into self and all its gratifications, and you sink into hell; rise above self into that state of consciousness which is the utter denial and forgetfulness of self, and you enter heaven. Self is blind, without judgment, not possessed of true knowledge, and always leads to suffering. Correct perception, unbiased judgment, and true knowledge belong only to the divine state, and only in so far as you realise this divine consciousness can you know what real happiness is. So long as you persist in selfishly seeking for your own happiness, so long will happiness elude you, and you will be sowing the seeds of wretchedness. In so far as you succeed in losing yourself in the service of others, in that measure will happiness come to you, and you will reap a harvest of bliss.

To seek selfishly is only to lose happiness

Abiding happiness will come to you when, ceasing to selfishly cling, you are willing to give up.

AUGUST TWENTY-FIRST.

Spiritual meditation is the pathway to Divinity. It is the mystic ladder which reaches from earth to heaven, from error to Truth, from pain to peace. Every saint has climbed it; every sinner must sooner or later come to it, and every weary pilgrim that turns his back upon self and the world, and sets his face resolutely toward the Father's Home, must plant his feet upon its golden rounds. Without its aid you cannot grow into the divine state, the divine likeness, the divine peace, and the fadeless glories and unpolluting joys of Truth will remain hidden from you.

Whatsoever you constantly meditate upon you will not only come to understand, but will grow more and more into its likeness.

If you constantly dwell upon that which is selfish and debasing, you will ultimately become selfish and debased.

AUGUST TWENTY-SECOND.

Select some portion of the day in which to meditate, and keep that period sacred to your purpose. The best time is the very early morning when the spirit of repose is upon everything. All natural conditions will then be in your favour; the passions, after the long bodily fast of the night, will be subdued, the excitements and worries of the previous day will have died away, and the mind, strong and yet restful, will be receptive to spiritual instruction. Indeed, one of the first efforts you will be called upon to make will be to shake off lethargy and indulgence, and if you refuse you will be unable to advance, for the demands of the spirit are imperative.

If you would enter into possession of profound and abiding peace, come now and enter the path of meditation.

The sluggard and the self-indulgent can have no knowledge of Truth.

AUGUST TWENTY-THIRD.

If you are given to hatred or anger, you will meditate upon gentleness and forgiveness, so as to become acutely alive to a sense of your harsh and foolish conduct. You will then begin to dwell in thoughts of love, of gentleness, of abounding forgiveness; and as you overcome the lower by the higher, there will gradually, silently steal into your heart a knowledge of the divine Law of Love with an understanding of its bearing upon all the intricacies of life and conduct. And in applying this knowledge to your every thought, word, and act, you will grow more and more gentle, more and more loving, more and more divine. And thus with every error, every selfish desire, every human weakness; by the power of meditation is it overcome; and as each sin, each error, is thrust out, a fuller and clearer measure of the Light of Truth illumines the pilgrim soul.

The direct outcome of your meditations will be a calm, spiritual strength.

Great is the overcoming power of holy thought.

August Twenty-fourth.

As, by the power of meditation, you grow in wisdom, you will relinquish, more and more, your selfish desires which are fickle, impermanent, and productive of sorrow and pain; and will take your stand, with increasing steadfastness and trust, upon unchangeable principles, and will realise heavenly rest.

The use of meditation is the requirement of a knowledge of eternal principles, and the power which results from meditation is the ability to rest upon and trust those principles, and so become one with the Eternal. The end of meditation is, therefore, direct knowledge of Truth, God, and the realisation of divine and profound peace.

Strive to rise, by the power of meditation, above all selfish clinging to partial gods or party creeds; above dead formalities and lifeless ignorance.

Meditation will enrich the soul with saving remembrance in the hour of strife, of sorrow, or of temptation.

Remember that you are to grow into Truth by steady perseverance.

August Twenty-fifth.

So believing, so aspiring, so meditating, divinely sweet and beautiful will be your spiritual experiences, and glorious the revelations that will enrapture your inward vision. As you realise the divine Love, the divine Justice, the Perfect Law of Good, or God, great will be your bliss and deep your peace. Old things will pass away, and all things will become new. The veil of the material universe, so dense and impenetrable to the eye of error, so thin and gauzy to the eye of Truth, will be lifted and the spiritual universe will be revealed. Time will cease, and you will live only in Eternity. Change and mortality will no more cause you anxiety and sorrow, for you will become established in the unchangeable, and will dwell in the very heart of immortality.

Believe that a life of perfect holiness is possible.

He who believes climbs rapidly the heavenly hills.

AUGUST TWENTY-SIXTH.

Upon the battlefield of the human soul two masters are ever contending for the crown of supremacy, for the kingship and dominion
of the heart; the master of self, called also the "Prince of this world,"
and the master of Truth, called also the Father God. The master self
is that rebellious one whose weapons are passion, pride, avarice, vanity, self-will, implements of darkness; the master Truth is that meek
and lowly one whose weapons are gentleness, patience, purity, sacrifice,
humility, love, instruments of Light.

Where self is, Truth is not;
where Truth is, self is not.

You cannot perceive the beauty
of Truth while you are looking
out through the eyes of self.

In every soul the battle is waged, and as a soldier cannot engage at once in two opposing armies, so
every heart is enlisted either in the ranks of self or of Truth. There is no half-and-half course. Jesus, the
manifested Christ, declared that "No man can serve two masters; for either he will hate the one and love the
other; or else he will hold to the one and despise the other. Ye cannot serve God and Mammon."

AUGUST TWENTY-SEVENTH.

Do you seek to know and to realise Truth? Then you must be prepared to
sacrifice, to renounce to the uttermost, for Truth in all its glory Can only
be perceived and known when the last vestige of self has disappeared.

The lovers of Truth worship
Truth with the sacrifice of self.

As you let self die, you will be
reborn in Truth.

The eternal Christ declared that he who would be His disciple must
"deny himself daily." Are you willing to deny yourself, to give up your lusts,
your prejudices, your opinions? If so, you may enter the narrow way of
Truth, and find that peace from which the world is shut out. The absolute denial, the utter extinction of self is
the perfect state of Truth, and all religions and philosophies are but so many aids to this supreme attainment.

AUGUST TWENTY-EIGHTH.

When men, lost in the devious ways of error and self, have forgotten the
"heavenly birth," the state of holiness and Truth, they set up artificial
standards by which to judge one another, and make acceptance of, and
adherence to, their own particular theology the test of Truth; and so
men are divided one against another, and there is ceaseless enmity and
strife, and unending sorrow and suffering.

Every holy man is a saviour of
mankind.

To be in the world and yet not of
the world is the highest perfection.

Reader, do you seek to realise the birth into Truth? There is only one way: *Let self die.* All those lusts, appetites, desires, opinions, limited conceptions, and prejudices to which you have hitherto so tenaciously clung,

let them fall from you. Let them no longer hold you in bondage, and Truth will be yours. Cease to look upon your own religion as superior to all others, and strive humbly to learn the supreme lesson of charity.

August Twenty-ninth.

A thorough understanding of this Great Law which permeates the universe leads to the acquirement of that state of mind known as *obedience*. To know that justice, harmony, and love are supreme in the universe is likewise to know that all adverse and painful conditions are the result of our own disobedience to that Law. Such knowledge leads to strength and power, and it is upon such knowledge alone that a true life and an enduring success and happiness can be built. To be patient under all circumstances, and to accept all circumstances as necessary factors in your training, is to rise superior to all painful conditions, and to overcome them with an overcoming which is sure, and which leaves no fear of their return, for by the power of obedience to law they are utterly slain.

The cause of all power, as of all weakness, is within.

There is no progress apart from unfoldment within.

August Thirtieth.

Perhaps the chains of poverty hang heavily upon you, and you are friendless and alone, and you long with an intense longing that your load may be lightened; but the load continues, and you seem to be enveloped in an ever-increasing darkness. Perhaps you complain, you bewail your lot, you blame your birth, your parents, your employer, or the unjust Powers who have bestowed upon you so undeservedly poverty and hardship, and upon another affluence and case. Cease your complaining and fretting; none of these things which you blame are the cause of your poverty; the cause is within yourself, and where the cause is, there is the remedy.

There is no sure foothold in prosperity or peace except by orderly advancement in knowledge.

There is no room for a complainer in a universe of law, and worry is soul-suicide.

August Thirty-first.

The world around, both animate and inanimate, wears the aspect with which your thoughts clothe it. "All that we are is the result of what we have thought; it is founded on our thoughts; it is made up of our thoughts." Thus said Buddha, and it therefore follows that if a man is happy, it is because he dwells in happy thoughts; if miserable, because he dwells in despondent and debilitating thoughts. Whether one be fearful or fearless, foolish or wise, troubled or serene, within that soul

What your thoughts are, that is your real self.

You are swayed by circumstances because you have not a right understanding of the nature, use, and power of thought.

lies the cause of its own state or states, and never without. And now I seem to hear a chorus of voices exclaim, "But do you really mean to say that outward circumstances do not affect our minds?" I do not say that, but I say this, and know it to be an infallible truth, *that circumstances can only affect you in so far as you allow them to do so.*

SEPTEMBER FIRST.

Men of robust minds do not dwell upon their bodily condition if it be in any way disordered—*they ignore it,* and work on, live on, as though it were not. This ignoring of the body not only keeps the mind sane and strong, but it is the best resource for curing the body. If we cannot have a perfectly sound body, we can have a healthy mind, and a healthy mind is the best route to a sound body.

A sickly mind is more deplorable than a disordered body, and it leads to sickness of body. The mental invalid is in a far more pitiable condition than the bodily invalid. There are invalids (every physician knows them) who only need to lift themselves into a strong, unselfish, happy frame of mind to discover that their body is whole and capable.

To make a useful and happy life dependent upon health is to put matter before mind, is to subordinate spirit to body.

Moral principles are the soundest foundations for health, as well as for happiness.

SEPTEMBER SECOND.

Where there is a cause its effect will appear; and were affluence the cause of immorality, and poverty the cause of degradation, then every rich man would become immoral, and every poor man would come to degradation.

An evil-doer will commit evil under any circumstances, whether he be rich or poor, or midway between the two conditions. A right-doer will do right howsoever he be placed. Extreme circumstances may help to bring out the evil which is already there awaiting its opportunity, but they cannot cause the evil, cannot create it.

Poverty is more often in the mind than in the purse. So long as a man thirsts for more money he will regard himself as poor, and in that sense he is poor, for covetousness is poverty of mind.

Men are not made unhappy by poverty, but by the thirst for riches.

A miser may be a millionaire, but he is as poor as when he was penniless.

SEPTEMBER THIRD.

Wonderful as are the forces in nature, they are vastly inferior to that combination of intelligent forces which comprise the mind of man, and which dominate and direct the blind mechanical forces of nature. Therefore, it follows that to understand, control, and direct the inner forces of passion, desire, will, and intellect, is to be in possession of the destinies of men and nations.

He who understands and dominates the forces of external nature is the natural scientist; but he who understands and dominates the internal forces of the mind is the divine scientist; and the laws which operate in gaining a knowledge of external appearances operate also in gaining a knowledge of internal verities.

A man is great in knowledge, great in himself, and great in his influence in the world, in the measure that he is great in self-control.

The end of knowledge is use, service, the increase of the comfort and happiness of the world.

September Fourth.

Perfect justice upholds the universe; perfect justice regulates human life and conduct. All the varying conditions of life, as they obtain in the world to-day, are the results of this law reacting on human conduct. Man can (and does) choose what causes he shall set in operation, but he cannot change the nature of effects; he can decide what thoughts he shall think, and what deeds he shall do, but he has no power over the *results* of those thoughts and deeds; these are regulated by the over-ruling law.

Man has all power to act, but his power ends with the act committed. The result of the act cannot be altered, annulled, or escaped; it is irrevocable.

All things, whether visible or invisible, are subservient to, and fall within the scope of, the infinite and eternal law and causation.

Evil thoughts and deeds produce conditions of suffering; good thoughts and deeds determine conditions of blessedness.

September Fifth.

Life may be likened to a sum in arithmetic. It is bewilderingly difficult and complex to the pupil who has not yet grasped the key to its correct solution, but once this is perceived and laid hold of it becomes as astonishingly simple as it was formerly profoundly perplexing. Some idea of this relative simplicity and complexity of life may be grasped by fully recognising and realising the fact that, while there are scores, and perhaps hundreds, of ways in which a sum may be done wrong, *there is only one way by which it can be done right,* and that when the right way is found *the pupil knows it to be right*; his perplexity vanishes, and he knows that he has mastered the problem.

Man's power is limited to, and his blessedness or misery is determined by, his own conduct.

In life there can be no falsifying of results; the eye of the Great Law reveals and exposes.

September Sixth.

Life is like a piece of cloth, and the threads of which it is composed are individual lives. The threads, while being independent, are not confounded one with the other. Each follows its own course. Each individual suffers and enjoys the consequences of his own deeds, and not the deeds of another. The course of each is simple and definite; the whole forming a complicated, yet harmonious, combination of sequences. There are action and reaction, deed and consequence, cause and effect, and the counterbalancing reaction, consequence, and effect is always in exact ratio with the initiatory impulse.

Selfish thoughts and bad deeds will not produce a useful and beautiful life.

Each man makes or mars his own life.

September Seventh.

The "problem of evil" subsists in a man's own evil deeds, and it is solved when those deeds are purified. Says Rousseau:

"Man, seek no longer the origin of evil; thou thyself art its origin."

Effect can never be divorced from cause; it can never be of a different nature from cause. Emerson says:

"Justice is not postponed; a perfect equity adjusts the balance in all parts of life."

And there is a profound sense in which cause and effect are simultaneous, and form one perfect whole. Thus, upon the instant that a man thinks, say, a cruel deed, that same instant *he has injured his own mind*; he is not the same man he was the previous instant; he is a little viler and a little more unhappy; and a number of successive thoughts and deeds would produce a cruel and wretched man.

Man is responsible only for his own deeds; he is the custodian of his own actions.

An immediate nobility and happiness attend the thinking of a kind thought, or doing a kind deed.

September Eighth.

The cultivation of that steadfastness and stability of character which is commonly called "will-power" is one of the foremost duties of man, for its possession is essentially necessary both to his temporal and external well-being. Fixedness of purpose is at the root of all successful efforts, whether in things worldly or spiritual, and without it man cannot be otherwise than wretched, and dependent upon others for that support which should be found within himself.

The true path of will-cultivation is only to be found in the common everyday life of the individual, and so obvious and simple is it that the majority, looking for something complicated and mysterious, pass it by unnoticed.

Without strength of mind, nothing worthy of accomplishment can be done.

The direct and only way to greater strength is to assail and conquer weaknesses.

SEPTEMBER NINTH.

He who has succeeded in grasping this simple, preliminary truth will perceive that the whole science of will-cultivation is embodied in the following seven rules:

1. Break off bad habits.
2. Form good habits.
3. Give scrupulous attention to the duty of the present moment.
4. Do vigorously, and at once, whatever has to be done.
5. Live by rule.
6. Control the tongue.
7. Control the mind.

In the training of the will the first step is the breaking away from bad habits

Anyone who earnestly meditates upon, and diligently practises, the above rules will not fail to develop that purity of purpose and power of will which will enable him to successfully cope with every difficulty, and pass triumphantly through every emergency.

SEPTEMBER TENTH.

He who thus avoids self-discipline, and looks about for some "occult secrets" for gaining will-power at the expenditure of little or no effort on his part, is deluding himself, and is weakening the willpower which he already possesses.

The strength of will which is gained by success in overcoming bad habits enables one to initiate good habits; for, while the conquering of a bad habit requires merely strength of purpose, the forming of a new one necessitates the *intelligent direction of purpose*. To do this, a man must be mentally active and energetic, and must keep a constant watch upon himself.

By submitting to a bad habit one forfeits the right to rule over himself.

Thoroughness is a step in the development of the will which cannot be passed over. Slip-shod work is an indication of weakness.

SEPTEMBER ELEVENTH.

By not dividing the mind, but giving the whole attention to each separate task as it presents itself, singleness of purpose and intense concentration of mind are gradually gained—two mental powers which give weight and worth of character, and bring repose and joy to their possessor.

Doing vigorously, and at once, whatever has to be done is equally important. Idleness and a strong will cannot go together, and procras-

Perfection should be aimed at, even in the smallest task.

Live according to principle, and not according to passion.

tination is a total barrier to the acquisition of purposeful action. Nothing should be "put off" until another time, not even for a few minutes. That which ought to be done now should be done now. This seems a little thing, but it is of far-reaching importance. It leads to strength, success, and peace.

SEPTEMBER TWELFTH.

That the little things of life are of primary importance is a truth not generally understood, and the thought that little things can be neglected, thrown aside, or slurred over is at the root of that lack of thoroughness which is so common, and which results in imperfect work and unhappy lives.

Thoroughness consists in doing little things as though they were the greatest things in the world.

He who acquires the quality of thoroughness becomes a man of usefulness and influence.

When one understands that the great things of the world and of life consist of a combination of small things, and that without this aggregation of small things the great things would be non-existent, then he begins to pay careful attention to those things which he formerly regarded as insignificant.

SEPTEMBER THIRTEENTH.

Every employer of labour knows how difficult it is to find men and women who will put thought and energy into their work, and do it completely and satisfactorily. Bad workmanship abounds. Skill and excellence are acquired by few. Thoughtlessness, carelessness, and laziness are such common vices that it should cease to appear strange that, in spite of "social reform," the ranks of the unemployed should continue to swell, for those who scamp their work to-day will, another day, in the hour of deep necessity, look and ask for work in vain.

The cause of the common lack of thoroughness lies in the thirst for pleasure.

The mind that is occupied with pleasure cannot also be concentrated upon the perfect performance of duty.

The law of "the survival of the fittest" is not based on cruelty, it is based on justice; it is one aspect of that divine equity which everywhere prevails. Vice is "beaten with many stripes"; if it were not so, how could virtue be developed? The thoughtless and lazy cannot take precedence of, or stand equally with, the thoughtful and industrious.

SEPTEMBER FOURTEENTH.

Thoroughness is completeness, perfection; it means doing a thing so well that there is nothing left to be desired; it means doing one's work, if not better than anyone else can do it, at least not worse than the best that others do. It means the exercise of much thought, the putting forth of great energy, the persistent application of the mind to its task, the cultivation of patience, perseverance, and a high sense of duty. An ancient teacher said, "If anything has to be done, let a man do it, let him attack it vigorously"; and another teacher said, "Whatsoever thy hand findeth to do, do it with thy might."

He who lacks thoroughness in his worldly duties will also lack the same in spiritual things.

It is better to be a whole-souled worldling than a half-hearted religionist.

September Fifteenth.

Despondency, irritability, anxiety, complaining, condemning, and grumbling—all these are thought-cankers, mind-diseases; they are the indications of a wrong mental condition, and those who suffer there-from would do well to remedy their thinking and conduct. It is true there is much sin and misery in the world, so that all our love and compassion are needed, *but our misery is not needed*—there is already too much of that. No, it is our cheerfulness and our happiness that are needed, for there is too little of that. We can give nothing better to the world than beauty of life and character; without this, all other things are vain; this is pre-eminently excellent; it is enduring, real, and not to be overthrown, and it includes all joy and blessedness.

He who has not learned how to be gentle, loving, and happy has learned very little.

A man's surroundings are never against him; they are there to aid him.

September Sixteenth.

Unbroken sweetness of conduct in the face of all outward antagonism is the infallible indication of a self-conquered soul, the witness of wisdom, and the proof of the possession of Truth.

A sweet and happy soul is the ripened fruit of wisdom, and it sheds abroad the invisible aroma of its influence, gladdening the hearts of others, and purifying the world.

If you would have others true, be true; if you would have the world emancipated from misery and sin, emancipate yourself; if you would have your home and your surroundings happy, be happy.

And this you will naturally and spontaneously do as you realise the good in yourself.

You can transform everything around you if you will transform yourself.

Commence to live free from all wrong and evil. Peace of mind and true reform lie this way.

September Seventeenth.

Immortality does not belong to time, and will never be found in time: it belongs to Eternity; and just as time is here and now, so is Eternity here and now, and a man may find that Eternity and establish himself in it, if he will overcome the self that derives its life from the unsatisfying and perishable things of time.

Whilst a man remains immersed in sensation, desire, and the passing events of his day-by-day existence, and regards those sensations, desires, and passing events as of the essence of himself, he can have no knowledge of immortality. The thing which such a man desires, and which he mistakes for immortality, is *persistence;* that is, a continuous succession of sensations and events of time.

Immortality is here and now, and is not a speculative something beyond the grave.

Persistence is the antithesis of immortality.

September Eighteenth.

Spirits are not different from men, and live their little feverish life of broken consciousness, and are still immersed in change and mortality. The mortal man, he who thirsts for the persistence of his pleasure-loving personality, is still mortal after death, and only lives another life with a beginning and an end, without memory of the past or knowledge of the future.

The death of the body can never bestow upon a man immortality.

The immortal man is in full possession of himself.

The immortal man is he who has detached himself from the things of time by having ascended into that state of consciousness which is fixed and unvariable, and is not affected by passing events and sensations. He is as one who has awakened out of his dream, and he knows that his dream was not an enduring reality, but a passing illusion. He is a man with knowledge, the knowledge of both states—that of persistence, and that of immortality.

September Nineteenth.

The immortal man remains poised and steadfast under all changes, and the death of his body will not in any way interrupt the eternal consciousness in which he abides. Of such a one it is said, "He shall not taste of death," because he has stepped out of the stream of mortality, and established himself in the abode of Truth. Bodies, personalities, nations, and worlds pass away, but Truth remains, and its glory is undimmed by time. The immortal man, then, is he who has conquered himself; who no longer identifies himself with the self-seeking forces of the personality, but who has trained himself to direct those forces with the hand of a master, and so has brought them into harmony with the causal energy and source of all things.

The mortal man lives in the time or world state of consciousness which begins and ends.

The immortal man lives in the cosmic or heaven state of consciousness, in which there is neither beginning nor end, but an eternal now.

September Twentieth.

The doctrine of the overcoming or annihilation of self is simplicity itself; indeed, so simple, practical, and close at hand is it that a child of five, whose mind has not yet become clouded with theories, theological schemes, and speculative philosophies, would be far more likely to comprehend it than many older people who have lost their hold upon simple and beautiful truths by the adoption of complicated theories.

The annihilation of self consists in weeding out and destroying all those elements in the soul which lead to division, strife, suffering, disease, and sorrow. It does not mean the destruction of any good and beautiful and peace-producing quality.

The overcoming of self is the annihilation of all the sorrow-producing elements.

The overcoming of self is the cultivation of all the divine qualities.

September Twenty-first.

Temptation, with all its attendant torments, *can* be overcome here and now, but it can only be overcome with knowledge. It is a condition of darkness, or of semi-darkness. The fully enlightened soul is proof against all temptation. When a man fully understands the source, nature, and meaning of temptation, in that hour he will conquer it, and will rest from his long travail; but whilst he remains in ignorance, attention to religious observances and much praying and reading of Scripture will fail to bring him peace.

He who would overcome his enemy the tempter must discover his stronghold and place of concealment, and must also find out the unguarded gates in his own fortress where the enemy effects so easy an entrance.

This is the holy warfare of the saints.

September Twenty-second.

Men fail to conquer, and the fight is indefinitely prolonged, because they labour, almost universally, under two delusions; first, that all temptations come from without; and second, that they are tempted because of their goodness. Whilst a man is held in bondage by these delusions, he will make no progress; when he has shaken them off, he will pass on rapidly from victory to victory, and will taste of spiritual joy and rest.

The source and cause of all temptation is in the *inward desire*; that being purified and eliminated, outward objects and extraneous powers are utterly powerless to move the soul to sin or to temptation. The outward object is merely the *occasion* of the temptation, *never the cause*; this is in the desire of the one tempted.

All temptation comes from within.

A man is tempted because there are certain desires or states of mind which he has come to regard as unholy.

September Twenty-third.

It is the evil in a man that is aroused and tempted. The measure of a man's temptations is the exact register of his own unholiness. As a man purifies his heart, temptation ceases, for when a certain unlawful desire has been taken out of the heart the object which formerly appealed to it can no longer do so, but becomes dead and powerless, for there is nothing left in the heart that can respond to it. The honest man cannot be tempted to steal, let the occasion be ever so opportune; the man of purified appetites cannot be tempted to gluttony and drunkenness; he whose mind is calm in the strength of inward virtue can never be tempted to anger, and the wiles and charms of the wanton fall upon the purified heart as empty, meaningless shadows.

The good in a man is never tempted. Goodness destroys temptation.

Temptation shows a man just where he is.

SEPTEMBER TWENTY-FOURTH.

The man who, fearing the loss of present pleasures or material comforts, denies the truth within him can be injured, and robbed, and degraded, and trampled upon, because he has first injured, robbed, and degraded, and trampled upon his own nobler self; but the man of steadfast virtue, of unblemished integrity, cannot be subject to such conditions, because he has denied the craven self within him and has taken refuge in Truth. It is not the scourge and the chains which make a man a slave, but the fact that he *is* a slave.

The Great Law is good—the man of integrity is superior to fear, and failure, and poverty, and shame, and disgrace.

Slander, accusation, and malice cannot affect the righteous man, nor call from him any bitter response, nor does he need to go about to defend himself and prove his innocence. Innocence and integrity alone are a sufficient answer to all that hatred may attempt.

SEPTEMBER TWENTY-FIFTH.

Let the man of integrity rejoice and be glad when he is severely tried; let him be thankful that he has been given an opportunity of proving his loyalty to the noble principles which he has espoused; and let him think, "Now is the hour of holy opportunity! Now is the day of triumph for Truth! Though I lose the whole world, I will not desert the right!" So thinking, he will return good for evil, and will think compassionately of the wrong-doer.

The man of integrity turns all evil things to good account.

The man of integrity can never be subdued by the forces of darkness, having subdued all those forces within himself.

The slanderer, the backbiter, and the wrongdoer may seem to succeed for a time, but the Law of Justice prevails; the man of integrity may seem to fail for a time, but he is invincible, and in none of the worlds, visible or invisible, can there be a forged weapon that shall prevail against him.

SEPTEMBER TWENTY-SIXTH.

A man's mind and life should be free from confusion. He should be prepared to meet every mental, material, and spiritual difficulty, and should not be intricately caught (as many are) in the meshes of doubt, indecision, and uncertainty when troubles and so-called misfortunes come along. He should be fortified against every emergency that can come against him; but such mental preparedness and strength cannot be attained in any degree without discrimination, and discrimination can only be developed by bringing into play and constantly exercising the analytical faculty.

Without discrimination a man is mentally blind.

Mind, like muscle, is developed by use.

SEPTEMBER TWENTY-SEVENTH.

The man who is afraid to think searchingly upon his opinions, and to reason critically upon his position, will have to develop moral courage before he can acquire discrimination.

A man must be true to himself, fearless with himself, before he can perceive the pure principles of Truth, before he can receive the all-revealing Light of Truth.

The more Truth is inquired of, the brighter it shines; it cannot suffer under examination and analysis.

The more error is questioned, the darker it grows; it cannot survive the entrance of pure and searching thought.

To "prove all things" is to find the good and to throw away the evil.

He who reasons and meditates learns to discriminate; he who discriminates discovers the eternally True.

Confusion, suffering, and spiritual darkness follow the thoughtless.

Harmony, blessedness, and the Light of Truth attend upon the thoughtful

SEPTEMBER TWENTY-EIGHTH.

Belief is the basis of all action, and, this being so, the belief which dominates the heart or mind is shown in the life. Every man acts, thinks, lives in exact accordance with the belief which is rooted in his innermost being, and such is the mathematical nature of the laws which govern mind that it is absolutely impossible for anyone to believe in two opposing conditions at the same time. For instance, it is impossible to believe in justice and injustice, hatred and love, peace and strife, self and truth. Every man believes in one or the other of these opposites, *never in both,* and the daily conduct of every man indicates the nature of his belief.

Belief is an attitude of mind determining the whole course of one's life.

Belief and conduct are inseparable, for the one determines the other.

SEPTEMBER TWENTY-NINTH.

The man who is continually getting enraged over the injustice of his fellow men, who talks about himself being badly treated, or who mourns over the lack of justice in the world around him, shows by his conduct, his attitude of mind, that he believes in injustice. However he may protest to the contrary, in his inmost heart he believes that confusion and chaos are dominant in the universe, the result being that he dwells in misery and unrest, and his conduct is faulty.

Again, he who believes in love, in its stability and power, *practises it under all circumstances,* never deviates from it, and bestows it alike upon enemies as upon friends.

Justice reigns, and all that is called injustice is fleeting and illusory.

The man who believes in justice remains calm through all trials and difficulties.

September Thirtieth.

Men are saved from error by belief in the supremacy of Truth. They are saved from sin by belief in Holiness or Perfection. They are saved from evil by belief in Good, for every belief is manifested in the life. It is not necessary to inquire as to a man's theological belief, for that is of little or no account, for what can it avail a man to believe that Jesus died for him, or that Jesus is God, or that he is "justified by faith," if he continues to live in his lower, sinful nature? All that is necessary to ask is this: "How does a man live?" "How does he conduct himself under trying circumstances?" The answer to these questions will show whether a man believes in the power of evil or in the power of Good.

Every thought, every act, every habit, is the direct outcome of belief.

When our belief in a thing ceases, we can no longer cling to or practice it.

October First.

He who believes in all those things that are good will love them, and live in them; he who believes in those things that are impure and selfish will love them, and cling to them. The tree is known by its fruits.

A man's beliefs about God, Jesus, and the Bible are one thing; his life, as bound up in his actions, is another; therefore a man's theological belief is of no consequence; but the thoughts which he harbours, his attitude of mind toward others, and his actions—these, and these only, determine and demonstrate whether the belief of a man's heart is fixed in the false or the true.

A man cannot cling to anything unless he believes in it; belief always precedes action, therefore a man's deeds and life are the fruits of his belief.

There are only two beliefs which vitally affect the life, and they are: belief in good and belief in evil.

October Second.

The sudden falling, when greatly tempted, into some grievous sin by one who was believed, and who believed himself, to stand firm, is seen neither to be a *sudden* nor a causeless thing when the hidden processes of thought which led up to it are revealed. The *falling* was merely the end, the outworking, the finished result of what commenced in the mind probably years before. The man had allowed a wrong thought to enter his mind; and a second and a third time he had welcomed it, and allowed it to nestle in his heart. Gradually he became accustomed to it, and cherished and fondled, and tended it; and so it grew until at last it attained such strength and force that it attracted to itself the opportunity which enabled it to burst forth and ripen into act.

As the fruit to the tree and the water to the spring, so is action to thought.

All sin and temptation are the natural outcome of the thoughts of the individual.

OCTOBER THIRD.

"There is nothing hidden that shall not be revealed," and every thought that is harboured in the mind must, by virtue of the impelling force which is inherent in the universe, at last blossom into act good or bad, according to its nature. The divine Teacher and the sensualist are both the product of their own thoughts, and have become what they are as the result of the seeds of thought which they have implanted, or allowed to fall, into the garden of the heart, and have afterwards watered, tended, and cultivated.

Let no man think he can overcome sin and temptation by wrestling with opportunity; he can only overcome them by purifying his thoughts.

Guard well your thoughts, reader, for what you really are in your secret thoughts to-day you will become in actual deed.

A man can only attract that to him which is in harmony with his nature.

OCTOBER FOURTH.

You are the thinker of your thoughts, and as such you are the maker of your self and condition. Thought is causal and creative, and appears in your character and life in the form of *results*. There are no accidents in your life. Both its harmonies and antagonisms are the responsive echoes of your thoughts. A man thinks, and his life appears.

If your dominant mental attitude is peaceable and lovable, bliss and blessedness will follow you; if it be resistant and hateful, trouble and distress will cloud your pathway. Out of ill-will will come grief and disaster; out of good-will, healing and reparation.

As a being of thought, your dominant mental attitude will determine your condition in life.

The boundary lines of your thoughts are self-erected fences.

OCTOBER FIFTH.

Where the passion-bound soul sees only injustice, the good man, he who has conquered passion, sees cause and effect, sees the Supreme Justice. It is impossible for such a man to regard himself as treated unjustly, because he has ceased to see injustice. He knows that no one can injure or cheat him, having ceased to injure or cheat himself. However passionately or ignorantly men may act toward him, it cannot possibly cause him any pain, for he knows that whatever comes to him (it may be abuse and persecution) can only come as the effect of what he himself has formerly sent out. He therefore regards all things as good, rejoices in all things, loves his enemies, blesses them that curse him, regarding them as the blind but beneficent instruments by which he is enabled to pay his moral debts to the Great Law.

Pain, grief, sorrow, and misery are the fruits of which passion is the flower.

The Supreme Justice and the Supreme Love are one.

October Sixth.

As a body is built of cells, and a house of bricks, so a man's mind is built of thoughts. The various characters of men are none other than compounds of thoughts of varying combinations. Herein we see the deep truth of the saying, "As a man thinketh in his heart, so is he." Individual characteristics are *fixed processes of thought;* that is, they are fixed in the sense that they have become an integral part of the character, that they can be only altered or removed by a protracted effort of the will, and by much self-discipline. Character is built in the same way as a tree or a house is built—namely, by the ceaseless addition of new material, and that material is *thought.*

The history of a nation is the building of its deeds.

By the aid of millions of bricks a city is built; by the aid of millions of thoughts a character, a mind, is built.

October Seventh.

Pure thoughts, wisely chosen and well placed, are so many durable bricks which will never crumble away, and from which a finished and beautiful building, and one which affords comfort and shelter for its possessor, can be rapidly erected. Bracing thoughts of strength, of confidence, of duty; inspiring thoughts of a large, free, unfettered, and unselfish life, are useful bricks with which a substantial mind temple can be raised; and the building of such a temple necessitates that old and useless habits of thought be broken down and destroyed.

Every man is a mind-builder.

Each man is the builder of himself.

Build thee more stately mansions, O my soul, As the swift seasons roll.

October Eighth.

If a man is to build up a successful strong, and exemplary life—a life that will stoutly resist the fiercest storms of adversity and temptation—it must be framed on a few, simple, undeviating moral principles.

Four of these principles are: *Justice, Rectitude, Sincerity,* and *Kindness.* These four ethical truths are to the making of a life what the four lines of a square are to the building of a house. If a man ignores them and thinks to obtain success and happiness by injustice, trickery, and selfishness, he is in the position of a builder who imagines he can build a strong and durable habitation while ignoring the relative arrangement of mathematical lines, and he will, in the end, obtain only disappointment and failure.

Build like a true workman.

Working in harmony with the fundamental laws of the universe.

OCTOBER NINTH.

He who adopts the four ethical principles as the law and base of his life, who raises the edifice of character upon them, who in his thoughts and words and actions does not wander from them, whose every duty and every passing transaction is performed in strict accordance with their exactions, such a man, laying down the hidden foundations of integrity of heart securely and strongly, cannot fail to raise up a structure which shall bring him honour; and he is building a temple in which he can repose in peace and blessedness-even the strong and beautiful Temple of his life.

It is a common error to suppose that little things can be passed by, and that the greater things are more important.

He who would have a life secure and blessed must carry the practice of the moral principles into every detail of it.

OCTOBER TENTH.

When a man intensely desires to reach and realise a higher, purer, and more radiant life than the merely worldly and pleasure-loving life, he engages in *aspiration*; and when he earnestly concentrates his thoughts upon the finding of that life, he practises meditation.

Without intense aspiration there can be no meditation. Lethargy and indifference are fatal to its practice. The more intense the nature of the man, the more readily will he find meditation and the more successfully will he practice it. A fiery nature will most rapidly scale the heights of Truth in meditation, when its aspirations have become sufficiently awakened.

When aspiration is united to concentration, the result is meditation.

Meditation is necessary to spiritual success.

OCTOBER ELEVENTH.

By concentration a man can scale the highest heights of genius, but he cannot scale the heavenly heights of Truth; to accomplish this he must meditate. By concentration a man may acquire the wonderful comprehension and vast power of a Cæsar; by meditation he may reach the divine wisdom and perfect peace of a Buddha. The perfection of concentration is *power*; the perfection of meditation is *wisdom*. By concentration men acquire skill in the doing of the things of life—in science, art, trade, etc.—but by meditation they acquire skill in *life* itself; in right living, enlightenment, wisdom, etc. Saints, sages, saviours—wise men and divine teachers—are the finished products of holy meditation.

When a man aspires to know and realise the Truth, he gives attention to conduct, to self-purification.

Love Truth so fully and intensely as to become wholly absorbed in it.

October Twelfth.

While, at first, the time spent in actual meditation is short—perhaps only half an hour in the early morning—the knowledge gained in that half-hour of vivid aspiration and concentrated thought is embodied in practice during the whole day. In meditation, therefore, the entire life of a man is involved; and as he advances in its practice he becomes more and more fitted to perform the duties of life in the circumstances in which he may be placed, for he becomes stronger, holier, calmer, and wiser.

The object of meditation is divine enlightenment.

Man is a thought-being, and his life and character are determined by the thoughts in which he habitually dwells.

The principle of meditation is twofold, namely:

1. Purification of the heart by repetitive thought on pure things.
2. Attainment of divine knowledge by embodying such purity in practical life.

October Thirteenth.

By daily dwelling upon pure thoughts, the man of meditation forms the habit of pure and enlightened thinking which leads to pure and enlightened actions and well-performed duties. By the ceaseless repetition of pure thoughts, he at last becomes one with those thoughts, and is a purified being, manifesting his attainment in pure actions, in a serene and wise life.

By practice, association, and habit, thoughts tend to repeat themselves.

It is easy to mistake reverie for meditation.

The majority of men live in a series of conflicting desires, passions, emotions, and speculations, and there are restlessness, uncertainty, and sorrow; but when a man begins to train his mind in meditation, he gradually gains control over this inward conflict by bringing his thoughts to a focus upon a central principle.

October Fourteenth.

The rich and the poor alike suffer for *their* own *selfishness*; and none escape. The rich have their particular sufferings as well as the poor. Moreover, the rich are continually losing their riches; the poor are continually acquiring them. The poor man of to-day is the rich man of to-morrow, and *vice versa*. Fear, also, follows men like a great shadow, for the man who obtains and holds by selfish force will always be haunted by a feeling of insecurity, and will continually fear its loss; whilst the poor man, who is selfishly seeking or coveting material riches, will be harassed by the fear of destitution. And one and all who live in this under-world of strife are overshadowed by one great fear-the fear of death.

Selfishness, the root of the tree of evil and of all suffering, derives its nourishment from the dark soil of ignorance.

Each individual suffers by virtue of his own selfishness.

October Fifteenth.

A man must pass through *three Gateways of Surrender.* The first is *the Surrender of Desire*; the second is *the Surrender of Opinion*; the third is *the Surrender of Self.* Entering into meditation, he will commence to examine his desires, tracing them out in his mind, and following up their effects in his life and upon his character; and he will quickly perceive that, without the renunciation of desire, a man remains a slave both to himself and to his surroundings and circumstances. Having discovered this, the first Gate, that of *the Surrender of Desire,* is entered. Passing through this Gate, he adopts a process of self-discipline which is the first step in the purification of the soul.

The spirit is strengthened and renewed by meditation upon spiritual things.

The lamp of faith must be continually fed and assiduously trimmed.

October Sixteenth.

Let a man, therefore, press on courageously, heeding neither the revilings of his friends without, nor the clamourings of his enemies within; aspiring, searching, striving; looking ever toward his Ideal with eyes of holy love; day by day ridding his mind of selfish motive, his heart of impure desire; stumbling sometimes, sometimes falling, but ever travelling onward and rising higher; and recording each night in the silence of his own heart the journey of the day, let him not despair if but each day, in spite of all its failures and falls, records some holy battle fought, though lost, some silent victory attempted, though unachieved.

The loss of to-day will add to the gain of to-morrow for him whose mind is set on the conquest of self.

Learn to distinguish between the real and the unreal, the shadow and the substance.

October Seventeenth.

Clothing his soul with the colourless Garment of Humility, a man bends all his energies to the uprooting of those opinions which he has hitherto loved and cherished. He now learns to distinguish between Truth, which is one and unchangeable, and his own and others' opinions about Truth, which are many and changeable. He sees that his *opinions* about Goodness, Purity, Compassion, and Love, are very distinct from those qualities themselves, and that he must stand upon those divine Principles, and not on his own opinions. Hitherto he has regarded his own opinions as of great value, but now he ceases so to elevate his own opinions, and to defend them against those of others, and comes to regard them as utterly worthless.

Acquire the priceless possession of spiritual discernment.

Stand upon the divine Principles of Purity, Wisdom, Compassion, and Love.

OCTOBER EIGHTEENTH.

He who resolves that he will not rest satisfied with appearances, shadows, illusions shall, by the piercing light of that resolve, disperse every fleeting phantasy, and shall enter into the substance and reality of life. He shall learn how to live, and he shall *live.* He shall be the slave of no passion, the servant of no opinion, the votary of no fond error. Finding the Divine Centre within his own heart, he shall be pure and calm and strong and wise, and will ceaselessly radiate the Heavenly Life in which he lives—which is himself.

Find the Divine Centre within.

Not to know that within you that is changeless, and defiant of time and death, is not to know anything, but is to play vainly with unsubstantial reflections in the Mirror of Time.

OCTOBER NINETEENTH.

Men love their desires, for gratification seems sweet to them, but its end is pain and vacuity; they love the argumentations of the intellect, for egotism seems most desirable to them, but the fruits thereof are humiliation and sorrow. When the soul has reached the end of gratification and reaped the bitter fruits of egotism, it is ready to receive the Divine Wisdom and to enter into the Divine Life. Only the crucified can be transfigured; only by the death of self can the Lord of the heart rise again into the Immortal Life, and stand radiant upon the Olivet of Wisdom.

Having betaken himself to the Divine Refuge within, and remaining there, a man is free from sin. No doubt shall shake his trust, no uncertainty shall rob him of repose.

Where self is not, there is the Garden of the Heavenly Life.

OCTOBER TWENTIETH.

Let the impure turn to Purity, and they shall be pure; let the weak resort to Strength, and they shall be strong; let the ignorant fly to Knowledge, and they shall be wise. All things are man's, and he chooses that which he will have. To-day he chooses in ignorance, to-morrow he shall choose in wisdom. He shall "work out his own salvation," whether he believe it or not, for he cannot escape himself, nor transfer to another the eternal responsibility of his own soul. By no theological subterfuge shall he trick the Law of his being, which shall shatter all his selfish makeshifts and excuses for right thinking and right doing. Nor shall God do for him that which it is destined his soul shall accomplish for itself.

Life is more than motion, it is Music; more than rest, it is Peace; more than work, it is Duty; more than labour, it is Love.

Life is more than enjoyment, it is Blessedness.

OCTOBER TWENTY-FIRST.

Men fly from creed to creed, and find unrest; they travel in many lands, and discover—disappointment; they build themselves beautiful mansions, and plant pleasant gardens, and reap—ennui and discomfort. Not until a man falls back upon the Truth within himself does he find rest and satisfaction; not until he builds the inward Mansion of Faultless Conduct does he find the endless and incorruptible Joy, and, having obtained that, he will infuse it into all his doings and possessions.

He who would find Blessedness, let him find himself.

The spiritual Heart of man is the Heart of the universe.

When a man can no longer carry the weight of his many sins, let him fly to the Christ, whose throne is the centre of his own heart, and he shall become light-hearted, entering the glad company of the Immortals.

OCTOBER TWENTY-SECOND.

Whilst a man is dwelling upon the past or future he is missing the present; he is forgetting to live now. All things are possible now, and *only* now. Without wisdom to guide him, and mistaking the unreal for the real, a man says, "If I had done so-and-so last week, last month, or last year, it would have been better with me to-day"; or, "I know what is best to be done, and I will do it to-morrow." The selfish cannot comprehend the vast importance and value of the present, and fail to see it

All power, all possibility, all action is now.

To put away regret, to anchor anticipation, to do and work now, this is wisdom.

as the substantial reality of which past and future are the empty reflections. It may truly be said that past and future do not exist except as negative shadows, and to live in them-that is, in the regretful and selfish contemplation of them—is to miss the reality in life.

OCTOBER TWENTY-THIRD.

Cease to tread every byway of dependence, every winding sideway that tempts thy soul into the shadowland of the past and the future, and manilest thy native and divine strength now. Come out into "the open road."

That which you would be, and hope to be, you may be now. Non-accomplishment resides in your perpetual postponement, and, having the power to postpone, you also have the power to accomplish— to perpetually accomplish; realise this truth, and you shall be to-day, and every day, the ideal man of whom you dreamed.

Act now, and lo! all things are done; live now, and behold! thou art in the midst of Plenty; *be now, and know* that thou art perfect.

Virtue consists in fighting sin day after day.

+==

Holiness consists in leaving sin, unnoticed and ignored, to die by the wayside.

October Twenty-fourth.

To-morrow is too late for anything, and he who sees help and salvation in to-morrow shall continually fail and fall to-day.

Thou didst fall yesterday! Didst sin grievously! Having realised this, leave it instantly and forever, and watch that thou sinnest not now. The while thou art bewailing the past every gate of thy soul remains unguarded against the entrance of sin now.

The foolish man, loving the boggy side of procrastination rather than the firm highway of Present Effort, says, "I will rise early to-morrow; I will get out of debt to-morrow; I will carry out my intentions to-morrow." But the wise man, realising the momentous import of the Eternal Now, rises early to-day; keeps out of debt to-day; carries out his intentions to-day; and so never departs from strength and peace and ripe accomplishment.

Say not unto thy soul, "Thou shalt be purer to-morrow"; but rather say, "Thou shalt be pure now."

+==

Thou shalt not rise by grieving over the irremediable past, but by remedying the present.

October Twenty-fifth.

It is wisdom to leave that which has not arrived, and to attend to that which is; and to attend to it with such a consecration of soul and concentration of effort as shall leave no loophole for regret to creep in.

A man's spiritual comprehension being clouded by the illusions of self, he says, "I was born on such a day, so many years ago, and shall die at my allotted time." But he was not born, neither will he die, for how can that which is immortal, which eternally is, be subject to birth and death? Let a man throw off his illusions, and then he will see that the birth and death of the *body* are the mere incidents of a journey, and not its beginning and end.

Looking back to happy beginnings, and forward to mournful endings, a man's eyes are blinded so that he beholds not his own immortality.

+==

The universe, with all that it contains, is now.

October Twenty-sixth.

Let life cease to be lived as a fragmentary thing, and let it be lived as a perfect Whole; the simplicity of the Perfect will then be revealed. How shall the fragment comprehend the Whole? Yet how simple that the

Whole should comprehend the fragment. How shall sin perceive Holiness? Yet how plain that Holiness should understand sin. He who would become the Greater let him abandon the lesser. In no form is the circle contained, but in the circle all forms are contained. In no colour is the radiant light imprisoned, but in the radiant light all colours are embodied. Let a man destroy all the forms of self, and he shall apprehend the Circle of Perfection.

Let a man put away egotism, and he will see the universe in all the beauty of its pristine simplicity.

When a man succeeds in entirely forgetting (annihilating) his personal self, he becomes a mirror in which the universal Reality is faultlessly reflected.

October Twenty-seventh.

Sink thyself compassionately in the heart of humanity, and thou shalt reproduce the harmonies of Heaven; lose thyself in unlimited love toward all, and thou shalt work enduring works and shalt become one with the eternal Ocean of Bliss.

Man evolves outward to the periphery of complexity, and then involves backward to the Central Simplicity. When a man discovers that it is mathematically impossible for him to know the universe before knowing himself, he then starts upon the Way which leads to Original Simplicity. He begins to unfold from within, and as he unfolds himself, he enfolds the universe.

In the perfect chord of music the single note, though forgotten, is indispensably contained, and the drop of water becomes of supreme usefulness by losing itself in the ocean.

Cease to speculate about God, and find the all-embracing Good within thee.

October Twenty-eighth.

He who will not give up his secret lust, his covetousness, his anger, his opinion about this or that, can see nor know; nothing; he will remain a dullard in the school of Wisdom, though he be accounted learned in the colleges.

If a man would find the key of Knowledge, let him find himself. Thy sins are not thyself; they are not any part of thyself; they are diseases which thou hast come to love. Cease to cling to them, and they will no longer cling to thee. Let them fall away, and thyself shall stand revealed. Thou shalt know thyself as Comprehensive Vision, Invincible Principle, Immortal Life, and Eternal Good.

The pure man knows himself as pure being.

Purity is extremely simple, and needs no argument to support it.

October Twenty-ninth.

Meekness, Patience, Love, Compassion, and Wisdom—these are the dominant qualities of Original Simplicity; therefore the imperfect cannot understand it. Wisdom only can apprehend Wisdom, therefore the fool says, "No man is wise." The imperfect man says, "No man can be perfect," and he therefore remains where he is. Though he live with a perfect man all his life, he shall not behold his perfection. Meekness he will call cowardice; Patience, Love, Compassion he will see as weakness; and Wisdom will appear to him as folly. Faultless discrimination belongs to the Perfect Whole, and resides not in any part, therefore men are exhorted to refrain from judgment until they have themselves manifested the Perfect Life.

Truth lives itself.

A blameless life is the only witness of Truth.

OCTOBER THIRTIETH.

Knowing the Divine Heart within, all hearts are known, and the thoughts of all men become his who has become master of his own thoughts; therefore the good man does not defend himself, but moulds the minds of others to his own likeness.

As the problematical transcends crudity, so Pure Goodness transcends the problematical. All problems vanish when Pure Goodness is reached; therefore the Good man is called "The Slayer of illusions." What problem can vex where sin is not? O thou who strivest loudly and resteth not! retire into the holy silence of thine own being, and live therefrom. So shalt thou, finding Pure Goodness, rend in twain the Veil of the Temple of Illusion, and shalt enter into the Patience, Peace, and transcendent Glory of the Perfect, for Pure Goodness and Original Simplicity are one.

He who has found the indwelling Reality of his own being has found the original and universal Reality.

So extremely simple is Original Simplicity that a man must let go his hold of everything before he can perceive it.

OCTOBER THIRTY-FIRST.

To detach oneself from every outward thing, and to rest securely upon the inward virtue, this is the Unfailing Wisdom. Having this Wisdom, a man will be the same whether in riches or poverty. The one cannot add to his strength, nor the other rob him of his serenity. Neither can riches defile him who has washed away all the inward defilement, nor the lack of them degrade him who has ceased to degrade the temple of his soul.

To refuse to be enslaved by any outward thing or happening, regarding all such things and happenings as for your use, for your education, this is Wisdom. To the wise all occurrences are *good,* and, having no eye for evil, they grow wiser every day. They utilise all things, and thus put all things under their feet. They see all their mistakes as soon as made, and accept them as lessons of intrinsic value, knowing that there are no mistakes in the Divine Order.

Great will be his pain and unrest who seeks to stand upon the approbation of others.

To love where one is not loved; herein lies the strength which shall never fail a man.

NOVEMBER FIRST.

All strength and wisdom and power and knowledge a man will find within himself, but he will not find it in egotism; he will only find it in obedience, submission, and willingness to learn. He must obey the higher and not glorify himself in the lower. He who stands upon egotism, rejecting reproof, instruction, and the lessons of experience, will surely fall; yea, he is already fallen. Said a great teacher to his disciples, "Those who shall be a lamp unto themselves, relying upon themselves only, and not relying upon any external help, but holding fast to the Truth as their lamp, and, seeking their salvation in the Truth alone, shall not look for assistance to any beside themselves, it is they among my disciples who shall reach the very topmost height! *But they must be willing to learn.*"

The wise man is always anxious to learn, but never anxious to teach.

The true Teacher is in the heart of every man.

NOVEMBER SECOND.

Things are useful and thoughts are powerful in the measure that their parts are strongly and intelligently concentrated. Purpose is highly concentrated thought. All the mental energies are directed to the attainment of an object, and obstacles which intervene between the thinker and the object are, one after another, broken down and overcome. Purpose is the keystone in the temple of achievement. It binds and holds together in a complete whole that which would otherwise lie scattered and useless. Empty whims, ephemeral fancies, vague desires, and half-hearted resolutions have no place in purpose. In the sustained determination to accomplish there is an invincible power which swallows up all inferior considerations and marches direct to victory.

Dispersion is weakness; concentration is power.

All successful men are men of purpose.

NOVEMBER THIRD.

Doubt, anxiety, and worry are unsubstantial shades in the underworld of self, and shall no more trouble him who will climb the serene altitudes of his soul. Grief, also, will be for ever dispelled by him who will comprehend the Law of his being. He who so comprehends shall find the Supreme Law of Life, and he shall find that it is Love, that it is imperishable Love. He shall become one with Love, and loving all, with mind freed from all hatred and folly, he shall receive the invincible protection which Love affords. Claiming nothing, he shall suffer no loss; seeking no pleasure, he shall find no grief; and employing all his powers as instruments of service, he shall evermore live in the highest state of blessedness and bliss.

Know this—thou makest and unmakest thyself.

Thou art a slave if thou preferrest to be; thou art a master if thou wilt make thyself one.

November Fourth.

The mountain bends not to the fiercest storm, but it shields the fledgling and the lamb; and though all men tread upon it, yet it protects them, and bears them up upon its deathless bosom. Even so is it with the meek man who, though shaken and disturbed by none, yet compassionately bends to shield the lowliest creature, and, though he may be despised, lifts up all men, and lovingly protects them.

He who has found Meekness has found divinity.

The meek man has realised the divine consciousness and knows himself as divine.

As glorious as the mountain in its silent might is the divine man in his silent Meekness; like its form, his loving compassion is expansive and sublime. Truly his body, like the mountain's base, is fixed in the valleys and the mists; but the summit of his being is eternally bathed in cloudless glory, and lives with the Silence.

November Fifth.

The meek man shines in darkness, and flourishes in obscurity. Meekness cannot boast, nor advertise itself, nor thrive on popularity. It is *practised,* and is seen and not seen; being a spiritual quality it is perceived only by the eye of the spirit. Those who are not spiritually awakened see it not, nor do they love it, being enamoured of, and blinded by, worldly shows and appearances. Nor does history take note of the meek man. Its glory is that of strife and self-aggrandisement; his is the glory of peace and gentleness. History chronicles the earthly, not the heavenly acts. Yet though he lives in obscurity, he cannot be hidden

He who lives in Meekness is without fear, knowing the Highest, and having the lowest under his feet.

The meek man is found in the time of trial; when other men fall he stands.

(how can light be hid?); he continues to shine after he has withdrawn himself from the world, and is worshipped by the world which knew him not.

November Sixth.

He who imagines he can be injured by others, and who seeks to justify and defend himself against them, does not understand Meekness, does not comprehend the essence and meaning of life. "He abused me, he beat me, he defeated me, he robbed me. In those who harbour such thoughts hatred will never cease . . . for hatred ceases not by hatred at any time; hatred ceases by love." What sayest thou? Thy neighbour has spoken thee falsely? Well, what of that? Can a falsity hurt thee? That

The meek man resists none, and thereby conquers all.

Take all evil out of thine own heart, then shalt thou see the folly of resisting it in another.

which is false is false, and there is an end of it. It is without life, and without power to hurt any but him who seeks to be hurt by it. It is nothing to thee that thy neighbour should speak falsely of thee, but it is much to thee that thou shouldst resist him, and seek to justify thyself, for, by so doing, thou givest life and vitality to thy neighbour's falseness, so that thou art injured and distressed.

NOVEMBER SEVENTH.

Purpose goes with intelligence. There are lesser and greater purposes, according with degrees of intelligence. A great mind will always be great of purpose. A weak intelligence will be without purpose, A drifting mind argues a measure of undevelopment.

Great is the power of purpose.

Inert matter yields to a living force, and circumstance succumbs to the power of purpose.

The men who have moulded the destinies of humanity have been men mighty of purpose. Like the Roman laying his road, they have followed along a well-defined path, and have refused to swerve aside even when torture and death confronted them. The Great Leaders of the race are the mental road-makers, and mankind follows in the intellectual and spiritual paths which they have carved out and beaten.

NOVEMBER EIGHTH.

The weak man, who grieves because he is misunderstood, will not greatly achieve; the vain man, who steps aside from his resolve in order to please others and gain their approbation, will not highly achieve; the double-minded man, who thinks to compromise his purpose, will fail.

All things at last yield to the silent, irresistible all-conquering energy of purpose.

The intensity of the purpose increases with the growing magnitude of the obstacles encountered.

The man of fixed purpose who, whether misunderstandings and foul accusations, or flatteries and fair promises, rain upon him, does not yield a fraction of his resolve is the man of excellence and achievement; of success, greatness, and power.

Hindrances stimulate a man of purpose; difficulties nerve him to renewed exertion; mistakes, losses, pains, do not subdue him; and failures are steps in the ladder of success, for he is ever conscious of the certainty of final achievement.

NOVEMBER NINTH.

Of all miserable men, the shirker is the most miserable. Thinking to find ease and happiness in avoiding difficult tasks, which require the expenditure of labour and exertion, his mind is always uneasy and disturbed, he becomes burdened with an inward sense of shame, and forfeits manliness and self-respect. "He who will not work according to his faculty, let him perish according to his necessity," says Carlyle; and it is a moral law that the man who avoids duty, and does not work to the full extent of his capacity, does actually perish, first in his character, and last in his body and circumstances. Life and action are synonymous, and immediately a man tries to escape exertion, either physical or mental, he has commenced to decay.

Joy is always the accompaniment of a task successfully accomplished.

An undertaking completed, or a piece of work done, always brings rest and satisfaction.

November Tenth.

Every successful accomplishment, even in worldly things, is repaid with its own measure of joy; and in spiritual things the joy which supervenes upon the perfection of purpose is sure, deep, and abiding. Great is the heartfelt joy (albeit ineffable) when, after innumerable and apparently unsuccessful attempts, some ingrained fault of character is at last cast out, to trouble its erstwhile victim and the world no more. The striver after virtue—he who is engaged in the holy task of building up a noble character—tastes, at every step of conquest over self, a joy which does not leave him again, but which becomes an integral part of his spiritual nature.

The price of life is effort.

The reward of accomplishment is joy.

November Eleventh.

As you think, you travel; as you love, you attract. You are to-day where your thoughts have brought you; you will be to-morrow where your thoughts take you. You cannot escape the results of your thoughts, but you can endure and learn, can accept and be glad.

You will always come to the place where your *love* (your most abiding and intense thought) can receive its measure of gratification. If your love be base, you will come to a base place; if it be beautiful, you will come to a beautiful place.

You can alter your thoughts, and so alter your condition. You are powerful, not powerless.

Everything that happens is just.

Nothing is fated, everything is formed.

November Twelfth.

Every fact and process in Nature contains a moral lesson for the wise man. There is no law in the world which is not to be found operating with the same mathematical certainty in the mind of man and in human life. All the parables of Jesus are illustrative of this truth, and are drawn from the simple facts of Nature. There is a process of seed-sowing

The man whose thoughts, words, and acts are sincere is surrounded by sincere friends; the insincere man is surrounded by insincere friends.

in the mind and life, a spiritual sowing which leads to a harvest according to the kind of seed sown. Thoughts, words, and acts are seeds sown, and, by the inviolable law of things, they produce after their kind.

The man who thinks hateful thoughts brings hatred upon himself. The man who thinks loving thoughts is loved

When you know yourself you will perceive that every event in your life is weighed in the faultless balance of equity.

NOVEMBER THIRTEENTH.

The farmer must scatter all his seed upon the land, and then leave it to the elements. Were he to covetously hoard his seed, he would lose both it and his produce, for his seed would perish. It perishes when he sows it, but in perishing it brings forth a greater abundance. So in life, we get by giving; we grow rich by scattering. The man who says he is in possession of knowledge which he cannot give out because the world is incapable of receiving it either does not possess such knowledge, or, if he does, will soon be deprived of it—if he is not already deprived of it. To hoard is to lose; to exclusively retain is to be dispossessed.

He who would be blessed, let him scatter blessings.

He who would be happy, let him consider the happiness of others.

NOVEMBER FOURTEENTH.

If a man is troubled, perplexed, sorrowful, or unhappy, let him ask:

"What mental seeds have I been sowing?"

"What seeds *am* I sowing?"

"What is my attitude toward others?"

"What seeds of trouble and sorrow and unhappiness have I sown that I should thus reap these bitter weeds?"

Let him seek within and find, and having found, let him abandon all the seeds of self, and sow, henceforth, only the seeds of Truth.

Let him learn of the farmer the simple truths of wisdom, and sow broadcast the seeds of kindness, gentleness, and love.

Men reap that which they sow.

The way to obtain peace and blessedness is to scatter peaceful and blessed thoughts, words, and deeds.

NOVEMBER FIFTEENTH.

We have reached one of those epochs in the world's progress which witnesses the passing of the false gods; the gods of human selfishness and human illusion. The new-old revelation of one universal impersonal Truth has again dawned upon the world, and its searching light has carried consternation to the perishable gods who take shelter under the shadow of self.

Destroying the idols of self, we draw nearer to the great, silent Heart of Love.

Enter the Path of obedience to the Law.

Men have lost faith in a god who can be cajoled, who rules arbitrarily and capriciously, subverting the whole order of things to gratify the wishes of his worshippers, and are turning, with a new light in their hearts, to the *God of Law.* And to Him they turn, not for personal happiness and gratification, but for knowledge, for understanding, for wisdom, for liberation from the bondage of self.

November Sixteenth.

Entering that Path—the Path of the Supreme Law—men no longer accuse, no longer doubt, no longer fret and despond, for they know now that God is right, the universal laws are right, the cosmos is right, and that they *themselves* are wrong, if wrong there is, and that their salvation depends upon themselves, upon their own efforts, upon their personal acceptance of that which is good, and deliberate rejection of that which is evil. No longer merely hearers, they become *doers* of the Word, and they acquire knowledge, they receive understanding, they grow in wisdom, and they enter into the glorious life of liberation from the bondage of self.

Perfection, which is knowledge of the Perfect Law, is ready for all who earnestly seek it.

Adopt the life of self-obliteration.

November Seventeenth.

The Children of Truth are in the world to-day; they are thinking, writing, speaking, acting; yea, even prophets are amongst us, and their influence is pervading the whole earth. An undercurrent of holy joy is gathering force in the world, so that men and women are moved with new aspirations and hopes, and even those who neither see nor hear, feel within them strange yearnings after a better and fuller life.

The Law reigns, and it reigns in men's hearts and lives; they have come to understand the reign of Law who have sought out the Tabernacle of the true God by the fair pathway of unselfishness.

God does not alter for man, for this would mean that the perfect must become imperfect; man must alter for God.

The Law cannot be broken for man, otherwise confusion would ensue; this is in accordance with harmony, order, justice.

November Eighteenth.

The Law is that the heart shall be purified, the mind regenerated, and the whole being brought in subjection to Love, till self be dead and Love is all in all, for the reign of Law is the reign of Love. And Love waits for all, rejecting none. Love may be claimed and entered into now, for it is the heritage of all.

Ah, beautiful Truth! To know that *now* man may accept his divine heritage, and enter the Kingdom of Heaven!

There is no more painful bondage than to be at the mercy of one's inclinations.

There is no greater liberty than utmost obedience to the Law of Being.

Oh, pitiful error! To know that man rejects it because of love of self!

Obedience to one's selfish inclinations means the drawing about one's soul clouds of pain and sorrow which darken the light of Truth; the shutting out of oneself from all real blessedness; for "whatsoever a man sows that shall he also reap."

November Nineteenth.

Is there, then, no injustice in the universe? There is injustice, and there is not. It depends upon the kind of life and the state of consciousness from which a man looks out upon the world and judges. The man who lives in his passions sees injustice everywhere; the man who has overcome his passions, sees the operations of Justice in every department of human life.

Injustice is the confused feverish dream of passion, real enough to those who are dreaming it; Justice is the permanent reality in life, gloriously visible to those who have wakened out of the painful nightmare of self.

The moral universe is sustained and protected by the perfect balance of its equivalents.

As in the physical world Nature abhors a vacuum, so in the spiritual world disharmony is annulled.

November Twentieth.

The man who thinks, "I have been slighted, I have been injured, I have been insulted, I have been treated unjustly," cannot know what justice is; blinded by self, he cannot perceive the pure Principles of Truth, and, brooding upon his wrongs, he lives in continual misery.

In the region of passion there is a ceaseless conflict of forces causing suffering to all who are involved in them. There is action and reaction, deed and consequence, cause and effect; and within and above all is the divine Justice regulating the play of forces with the utmost mathematical accuracy, balancing cause and effect with the finest precision.

The Divine Order cannot be perceived until passion and self are transcended.

Justice is not perceived—cannot be perceived—by those who are engaged in conflict.

November Twenty-first.

Men blindly inflict suffering upon themselves, living in passion and resentment, and not finding the true way of life. Hatred is met with hatred, passion with passion, strife with strife. The man who kills is himself killed; the thief who lives by depriving others, is himself deprived; the beast that preys on others is hunted and killed; the accuser is accused, the condemner is condemned, the denouncer is persecuted.

Having no knowledge of cause and effect in the moral sphere, men do not see the exacting process which is momentarily proceeding.

Ignorance keeps alive hatred and strife.

By this the slayer's knife doth stab himself,
The unjust judge has lost his own defender,
The false tongue dooms its lie, the creeping thief
And spoiler rob to render.
Such is the Law.

November Twenty-second.

The good man, having put away all resentment, retaliation, self-seeking, and egotism, has arrived at a state of equilibrium, and has thereby become identified with the Eternal and Universal Equilibrium. Having lifted himself above the blind forces of passion, he understands those forces, contemplates them with a calm penetrating insight, like the solitary dweller on a mountain who looks down upon the conflict of the storms beneath his feet. For him, injustice has ceased, and he sees ignorance and suffering on the one hand, and enlightenment and bliss on the other. He sees that not only do the fool and the slave need his sympathy, but that the fraud and the oppressor are equally in need of it, and so his compassion is extended toward all.

Cause and effect cannot be avoided; consequence cannot be escaped.

Unerring Justice presides over all.

November Twenty-third.

He who will use the light of reason as a torch to search for Truth, will not be left at last in comfortless darkness.

"Come now, and let us reason together, saith the Lord; though your sins be as scarlet, they shall be as white as snow."

Many men and women pass through untold sufferings, and at last die in their sins, *because they refuse to reason*; because they cling to those dark delusions which even a faint glimmer of the light of reason would dispel; and all must use their reason freely, fully, and faithfully, who would exchange the scarlet robe of sin and suffering for the white garment of blessedness and peace.

They who refuse to trim their lamps of reason will never perceive the Light of Truth.

They who despise the light of reason, despise the Light of Truth.

November Twenty-fourth.

Before a man can accomplish anything of an enduring nature in the world he must first of all acquire some measure of success in the management of his own mind. This is as mathematical a truism as that two and two are four, for "out of the heart are the issues of life." If a man cannot govern the forces within himself, he cannot long hold a firm hand upon the outer activities which form the visible life. On the other

A man does not live until he begins to discipline himself; he merely exists.

With the practice of self-discipline a man begins to live.

hand, as a man succeeds in governing himself he rises to higher and higher levels of power and usefulness and success in the world. Hitherto his life has been without purpose or meaning, but now he begins to consciously mould his own destiny; he is "clothed and in his right mind."

November Twenty-fifth.

A man begins to discipline himself by controlling those passions which have hitherto controlled him; he resists temptation, and guards himself against all those tendencies to selfish gratifications which are so easy and natural, and which have formerly dominated him. He brings his appetite into subjection, and begins to eat as a reasonable and responsible being, practising moderation and thoughtfulness in the selection of his food, with the object of making his body a pure instrument through which he may live and act as becomes a man, and no longer degrading that body by pandering to gustatory pleasure. He puts a check upon his tongue, his temper, and, in fact, his every animal desire and tendency.

In the process of self-discipline there are three stages—control, purification, and relinquishment.

There is in the heart of every man and woman a selfless centre.

November Twenty-sixth.

As a man practises self-control he approximates more and more to the inward reality, and is less and less swayed by passion and grief, pleasure and pain, and lives a steadfast and virtuous life, manifesting manly strength and fortitude. The restraining of the passions, however, is merely the initial stage in self-discipline, and is immediately followed by the process of *Purification.* By this a man so purifies himself as to take passion out of the heart and mind altogether; not merely restraining it when it rises within him, but preventing it from rising altogether. By merely restraining his passions a man can never arrive at peace, can never actualise his ideal; he must purify these passions.

The Rock of Ages, the Christ within, the divine and immortal in all men!

It is in the purification of his lower nature that a man becomes strong and godlike.

November Twenty-seventh.

True strength and power and usefulness are born of self-purification, for the lower animal forces are not lost, but are transmuted into intellectual and spiritual energy. The pure life (pure in thought and deed) is a life of conservation of energy; the impure life (even should the impurity not extend beyond thought) is a life of dissipation of energy. The pure man is more capable, and therefore more fit to succeed in his plans and to accomplish his purposes than the impure. Where the

Purification is effected by thoughtful care, earnest meditation, and holy aspiration.

With the growth in purity, all the elements which constitute a strong and virtuous manhood are developed.

impure man fails, the pure man will step in and be victorious, because he directs his energies with a calmer mind and a greater definiteness and strength of purpose.

NOVEMBER TWENTY-EIGHTH.

As a man grows purer, he perceives that all evil is powerless, unless it receives his encouragement, and so he ignores it, and lets it pass out of his life. It is by pursuing this aspect of self-discipline that a man enters into and realises the divine life, and manifests those qualities which are distinctly divine, such as wisdom, patience, non-resistance, compassion, and love. It is here, also, where a man becomes consciously immortal, rising above all the fluctuations and uncertainties of life, and living in an intelligent and unchangeable peace.

By self-discipline a man rises higher and higher, approximating more and more nearly to the divine.

By self-discipline a man attains to every degree of virtue and holiness, and finally becomes a purified son of God, realising his oneness with the central heart of all things.

NOVEMBER TWENTY-NINTH.

When a man makes a resolution, it means that he is dissatisfied with his condition, and is commencing to take himself in hand, with a view to producing a better piece of workmanship out of the mental materials of which his character and life are composed, and in so far as he is true to his resolution he will succeed in accomplishing his purpose.

The vows of the saintly ones are holy resolutions directed toward some victory over self, and the beautiful achievements of holy men and the glorious conquests of the Divine Teachers were rendered possible and actual by unswerving resolution.

A life without resolution is a life without aims, and a life without aims is a drifting and unstable thing.

Resolution—the companion of noble aims and lofty ideals.

NOVEMBER THIRTIETH.

Half-hearted and premature resolution is no resolution at all, and is shattered at the first difficulty.

A man should be slow to form a resolution. He should searchingly examine his position and take into consideration every circumstance and difficulty with his decision, and should be fully prepared to meet them. He should be sure that he completely understands the nature of his resolution, that his mind is finally made up, and that he is without doubt in the matter. With the mind thus prepared, the resolution that is formed will not be departed from, and by the aid of it a man will, in due time, accomplish his strong purpose.

True resolution is the crisis of long thought.

Hasty resolutions are futile.

DECEMBER FIRST.

Contentment is a virtue which becomes lofty and spiritual, as the mind is trained to perceive and the heart to receive the guidance, in all things, of a merciful law.

Indolence is the twin sister of indifference, but ready action is the friend of contentment.

To be contented does not mean to forgo effort; it means to *free effort from anxiety*; it does not mean to be satisfied with sin and ignorance and folly, but to rest happily in duty done, and work accomplished.

True contentment is the outcome of honest effort and true living.

A man may be said to be content to lead a grovelling life, to remain in sin and in debt, but such a man's true state is one of indifference to his duty, his obligations, and the just claims of his fellow-men. He cannot truly be said to possess the virtue of contentment; he does not experience the pure and abiding joy which is the accompaniment of active achievement.

DECEMBER SECOND.

There are three things with which a man should be content: With whatever happens; with his friendships and possessions; and with his pure thoughts. Contented with whatever happens, he will escape grief; with his friendships and possessions, he will avoid anxiety and wretchedness; and with his pure thoughts, he will never go back to suffer and grovel in impurities.

The truly contented man works energetically and faithfully, and accepts all results with an untroubled spirit.

Results exactly correspond with efforts.

There are three with which a man should not be content: With his opinions; with his character; and with his spiritual condition. Not content with his opinions, he will continually increase in intelligence; not content with his character, he will ceaselessly grow in strength and virtue; and not content with his spiritual condition, he will, every day, enter into a larger wisdom and a fuller blessedness.

DECEMBER THIRD.

Brotherhood as a human organisation cannot exist so long as any degree of self-seeking reigns in the hearts of men and women who band themselves together for any purpose, as such self-seeking must eventually rend the Seamless Coat of loving unity. But although organised Brotherhood has so largely failed, any man may realise Brotherhood in its perfection, and know if in all its beauty and completion, if he will make himself a wise, pure, loving spirit, removing from his mind every

Universal Brotherhood is the supreme Ideal of Humanity: and toward that Ideal the world is slowly but surely moving.

In whatsoever heart discord rules, Brotherhood is not realised.

element of strife, and learning to practice those divine qualities without which Brotherhood is but a mere theory, opinion, or illusive dream.

December Fourth.

From the spirit of Humility proceed meekness and peacefulness; from Self-surrender come patience, wisdom, and true judgment; from Love spring kindness, joy, harmony; and from Compassion proceed gentleness and forgiveness.

Brotherhood is at first spiritual, and its outer manifestation in the world must follow as a natural result.

He who has brought himself into harmony with these four qualities is divinely enlightened; he sees whence the actions of men proceed and whither they tend, and therefore can no longer live in the exercise of the dark tendencies. He has realised Brotherhood in its completion, as freedom from malice, from envy, from bitterness, from contention, from condemnation. All men are his brothers, those who live in the dark tendencies as well as those who live in the enlightening qualities. He has but one attitude of mind toward all, that of goodwill.

Where pride, self-love, hatred, and condemnation are, there can be no Brotherhood.

December Fifth.

Theories and schemes for propagating Brotherhood are many, but Brotherhood itself is one and unchangeable, and consists in the complete cessation from egotism and strife, and in practising good-will and peace; for Brotherhood is a practice and not a theory. Self-surrender and Good-will are its guardian angels, and peace is its habitation.

Brotherhood consists, first of all, in the abandonment of self by the individual.

Where two are determined to maintain an opposing opinion, the clinging of self and ill-will are there, and Brotherhood is absent.

Brotherhood is only practised and known by him whose heart is at peace with all the world.

Where two are prepared to sympathise with each other, to see no evil in each other, to serve and not to attack each other, the love of Truth and Good-will are there and Brotherhood is present.

December Sixth.

Sympathy is not required toward those who are purer and more enlightened than one's self, as the purer one lives above the necessity for it. In such a case reverence should be exercised, with a striving to lift one's self up to the purer level, and so enter possession of the larger life. Nor can a man fully understand one who is wiser than himself, and before condemning, he should earnestly ask himself whether he is, after all, better than the man whom he has singled out as the object of his bitterness. If he is, let him bestow sympathy. If he is not, let him exercise reverence.

Prejudice and cruelty are inseparable.

When a man is prone to harshly judge and condemn others, he should inquire how far he falls short himself.

DECEMBER SEVENTH.

The obliterating of injuries from the mind is merely one of the beginnings in wisdom. There is a still higher and better way. And that way is to purify the heart and enlighten the mind that, far from having to forget injuries, there will be none to remember. For it is only pride and self that can be injured and wounded by the actions and attitudes of others; and he who takes pride and self out of his heart can never think the thought, "I have been injured by another," or, "I have been wronged by another."

From a purified heart proceeds the right comprehension of things; and from the right comprehension of things proceeds the life that is peaceful, freed from bitterness and suffering, calm and wise.

Dislike, resentment, and condemnation are all forms of hatred, and evil cannot cease until these are taken out of the heart.

He who is troubled and disturbed about the sins of others is far front the Truth.

DECEMBER EIGHTH.

He in whose heart the flames of resentment burn, cannot know peace nor understand Truth; he who will banish resentment from his heart, will know and understand.

He who has taken evil out of his own heart, cannot resent or resist it in others, for he is enlightened as to its origin and nature, and knows it as a manifestation of the mistakes of ignorance. With the increase of enlightenment, sin becomes impossible. He who sins, does not understand; he who understands, does not sin.

The pure man maintains his tenderness of heart toward those who ignorantly imagine that they can do him harm. The wrong attitude of others toward him does not trouble him; his heart is at rest in Compassion and Love.

He who is troubled and disturbed about his own sins is very near to the Gate of Wisdom.

Let those who aim at the right life, calmly and wisely understand.

DECEMBER NINTH.

The deeds and thoughts that lead to suffering are those that spring from self-interest and self-seeking; the thoughts and deeds that produce blessedness are those that spring from Truth. The process by which the mind is thus changed and transmuted is two-fold; it consists of *meditation and practice.* By silent meditation, the ground and reason of right conduct is sought, and by practice, right-doing is accomplished in daily life.

A pure heart and a righteous life are the great and all-important things.

Truth is not something that can be gleaned from a book; it can be learned and known by practice only.

For Truth is not a matter of book learning, or subtle reasoning, or disputation, or controversial skill; it consists in right-doing.

DECEMBER TENTH.

He who wishes to acquire Truth must practice it. He must begin at the very first lesson in self-control, thoroughly master it, and then pass on to the next and the next, until he attains to the moral perfection at which he aims. It is common with men to imagine that Truth consists in holding certain ideas or opinions. They read a number of treatises, and then form an opinion which they call "Truth," and then they go about disputing with their fellow-men in order to try to prove that their opinion is the Truth. In worldly matters men are wise, for they *do* things in order to achieve their ends, but in spiritual things they are foolish, for they merely read, and do not do things, and then imagine they have acquired Truth.

He only has Truth who has found it by practice.

He only has Truth whose life shows it forth in pure and blameless conduct.

DECEMBER ELEVENTH.

By its very nature, Love can never be the exclusive possession of any religion, sect, school, or brotherhood. The common claim, therefore, of such sections of the community to the exclusive possession of Truth in their particular religious doctrine is a denial of Love. Truth is a spirit and a life, and though it may manifest through manifold doctrines, it can never be confined to any one particular form of doctrine. Love is a winged angel that refuses to be chained to any letter doctrine whatsoever. Love is above and beyond, outside and greater than all the opinions, doctrines, and philosophies of men; yet Love includes all—the righteous and the unrighteous, the fair and foul, the clean and the unclean. He whose Love is so deep and wide as to envelop all men of all creeds is he who has most of religion, and most of wisdom, and also most of insight, for he knows and sees men as they are.

Love, all inclusive.

Hatred is absence of Love, and therefore absence of all that is included in Love.

DECEMBER TWELFTH.

The way of Love is the way of Life—Immortal Life—and the beginning of that way consists in getting rid of our carpings, quarrellings, fault-findings, and suspicions. If these petty vices possess us, let us not deceive ourselves, but let us confess that we have not Love. To be thus honest with ourselves is to be prepared to find Love; but to be self-deceived is to be shut out from Love. If we are to grow in Love, we must begin at the beginning, and remove from our minds all mean and suspicious thoughts about our fellow-workers and fellow-men. We must learn to treat them with large-hearted freedom, and to perceive the right reason for their actions, to excuse them on grounds of personal right and personal freedom when their opinions, methods, or actions are contrary to us; thus shall we come at last to love them with that Love of which St. Paul speaks, a Love that is a permanent principle.

Love broadens and expands the mind of a man until it embraces in its kindly folds all mankind without distinction.

He who has Love—of whatsoever creed or none—is enlightened with the Light of Truth.

DECEMBER THIRTEENTH.

It is the wrong deeds of men which bring all the unhappiness into the world. It will be right deeds which will transform all its misery into happiness. By wrong deeds we come to sorrow; by right deeds we come to bliss.

But a man must not think the thought: "It is the wrong deeds of others which have made me unhappy," for such a thought produces bitterness toward others and increases hatred. He must understand that his unhappiness is from something wrong within himself; he must regard it as a sign that he is yet imperfect, that there is some weak spot within which must be strengthened. He must never accuse others for his lapses of conduct, or for his troubles, but must gain more steadfastness of heart, must establish himself more firmly in the Truth.

The Life of Truth is that in which wrong-thinking and wrong-doing are abandoned, and right-thinking and right-doing are embraced.

Walk with lowly footsteps the holy way of Truth.

DECEMBER FOURTEENTH.

The principles of Truth were discovered by searching and practice, and are so stated and arranged as to make the path plainer for other feet to tread; and it is the path along which every being has travelled who has passed from sin to sinlessness, from error to Truth. It is the ancient Way along which every saint, every Buddha, every Christ has walked to divine perfection, and along which every imperfect being in the future will pass to reach this glorious goal. It matters not what religion a man professes, if he is daily striving with his own sins, and purifying his heart, he is walking this path; for while opinions, theologies, and religions differ, sin does not differ, the overcoming of sin does not differ, and Truth does not differ.

The principles of Truth are fixed and eternal, and cannot be made or unmade by anyone.

Religions change from age to age, but the principles of divine virtue are eternally the same.

DECEMBER FIFTEENTH.

We have sat at the feet of all the Great Teachers, and have learned of them. Unspeakable has been our rejoicing to have found, in the lives and precepts of gentle Indian and Chinese Teachers, the same divine qualities and the same preceptive truths which adorn the character of Jesus Christ. To us they are all wonderful and adorable, and so great and good and wise that we can but reverence and learn of them. They have also had the same marvellous influence for good over the various races among which they have appeared, and have all equally called forth the undying worship of millions of human beings.

Truth is one, though it has a variety of aspects, and is adaptable to men in various stages of growth.

Great Teachers are perfected flowers of humanity, types of what all men will one day be.

December Sixteenth.

There is a distinction between a worldly life and a religious life. He who is daily following his impure inclinations, with no wish to give them up, is irreligious; while he who is daily controlling and purging away his impure inclinations is religious.

The religious man should curb his passions and the indulgence of his desires, for that is what constitutes religion. He must learn to see men and things *as they are,* and must perceive that they are living in accordance with their nature, and their right of choosing their path as intelligent human beings. He must never intrude his rules of life upon them; and never presume to be, or even think of himself as being, on a "higher plane" than they are. He must learn to put himself in their place, and to see from their standpoint.

Perfect purity of heart is a condition of emancipation from all the cravings and indulgences of self.

A lover of Truth must be a lover of all men. He must let his love go out without restraint or stint.

December Seventeenth.

The unceasing change, the insecurity and the mystery of life make it necessary to find some basis of certainty on which to rest if happiness and peace of mind are to be maintained. This basic principle, a knowledge of which the whole race will ultimately acquire, is best represented by the term *Divine Justice.* Human justice differs with every man according to his own light or darkness, but there can be no variation in that Divine Justice by which the universe is eternally sustained. Divine Justice is spiritual mathematics. As with figures and objects, so with the thoughts and deeds of men, two and two equally make four.

The ground of certainty on which we can securely rest amid all the incidents of life, is the mathematical exactitude of the moral law.

Given the same cause, there will always be the same effect.

December Eighteenth.

Given the same thought or deed in a like circumstance, the result will always be the same. Without this fundamental ethical justice there could be no human society, for it is the just reactions of the deeds of individuals which prevents society from tottering to its fall.

It thus follows that the inequalities of life, as regards the distribution of happiness and suffering, are the outworking of moral forces operating along lines of flawless accuracy. This flawless accuracy, this perfect law, is the one great fundamental certainty in life, the finding of which insures a man's perfection, makes him wise and enlightened, and fills him with rejoicing and peace.

All the spiritual laws with which men are acquainted have, and must have, the same infallibility in their operations.

The moral order of the universe is not, cannot be disproportionate, for if it were, the universe would fall.

December Nineteenth.

Take away a belief in this certainty from a man's consciousness, and he is adrift on a self-created ocean of chance, without rudder, chart, or compass. He has no ground on which to build a character or life, no incentive for noble deeds, no centre for moral action; he has no island of peace and no harbour of refuge. Even the crudest idea of God as of a great man whose mind is perfect, who cannot err, and who has "no variableness nor shadow of turning," is a popular expression of a belief in this basic principle of Divine Justice.

Nothing can transcend right.

Man cannot suffer for something which he has never done, or never left undone, for this would be an effect without a cause.

According to this principle there is neither favour nor chance, but unerring and unchangeable right. Thus all the sufferings of men are right as *effects,* their causes being the mistakes of ignorance; but as effects they will pass away.

December Twentieth.

The process of growth is seen in the flower, but though not seen in the mental growth, it is nevertheless there.

I said the process of mental growth was not seen; but this is only true in a general sense. The true thinker and sage does see, with his spiritual eye, the process of spiritual growth. Just as the natural scientist has made himself acquainted with natural causes and effects—as, indeed, the ordinary observer is so acquainted—so he has made him-

Talent, genius, goodness, greatness, are not launched upon the world ready-made. They are the result of a long train of causes and effects.

Nothing appears ready-made. There is always a changing, a growing, a becoming.

self familiar with spiritual causes and effects. He sees the process by which characters, like plants, come into being; and when he sees the flowers of genius and virtue appear, he knows from what mental seeds they sprang, and how they gradually came to perfection through long periods of silent growth.

December Twenty-first.

As a man cannot live in two countries at the same time, but must leave the one before he can settle in the other, so a man cannot inhabit two spiritual countries at the same time, but must leave behind the land of sin before he can live at peace in the land of truth. When one leaves his native land, that he may begin anew in an adopted country, he leaves behind all beloved associations, sweet companionships, dear friends and relatives, yea, all upon which his heart has been ever set must be parted with and left behind. So when one resolves to live in the new world of Truth, the old world of error, with its loved pleasures, cherished sins, and vain associations, must be renounced. By such renunciation the individual gains, humanity gains, and the universe becomes a brighter and more beautiful habitation.

An awakened vision calls us to a nobler life.

We must shake the mud of the valley from our feet if we are to commune with the mountain silence.

December Twenty-second.

That is the right mental attitude which seeks the good in all the occurrences of life, and extracts strength, knowledge, and wisdom from them. Right thoughts are thoughts of cheer, of joy, of hope, of confidence, of courage, of constant love, of large generosity, of abounding faith and trust. These are the affirmations that make strong characters and useful and noble lives, and that build up those personal successes which make the progress of the world. Such thoughts are inevitably followed by right action, by the putting forth of energy and effort in work, in the accomplishment of some legitimate object; and as the climber at last reaches the hill-top, so the earnest, cheerful, and untiring worker at last accomplishes his end.

Right thoughts spring from a right mental attitude, and lead to right actions.

All the successful people, through all time, have reached their particular success by labouring for it.

December Twenty-third.

To inflict suffering upon others is to become more deeply involved in ignorance; but to suffer ourselves is to come nearer to enlightenment. Pain teaches men how to be kind and compassionate. It at last makes

Suffering is a purifying and perfecting process. "We become obedient by the things which we suffer."

them tender-hearted and thoughtful for the sufferings of others. When a man does a cruel deed, he thinks, in his ignorance, that that is the end of it, but it is only the beginning. Attached to the deed is a train of consequences which will plunge him in a tormenting hell of pain. For every wrong thought we think, or unkind deed we do, we must suffer some form of mental or bodily pain; and the kind of pain will be in accordance with the initiative thought or act.

By acquainting man with suffering, it enables him to feel for the sufferings of others.

December Twenty-fourth.

Just as the strong doing of small tasks leads to greater strength, so the doing of those tasks weakly leads to greater weakness. What a man is in his fractional duties that he is in the aggregate of his character. Weakness is as great a source of suffering as sin, and there can be no true blessedness until some measure of strength of character is evolved. The weak man becomes strong by attaching value to little things and doing them accordingly. The strong man becomes weak by falling into looseness and neglect concerning small things, thereby forfeiting his simple wisdom and squandering his energy.

Every resource is already with you and within you.

There is no way to strength and wisdom but by acting strongly and wisely in the present moment.

December Twenty-fifth.

The past is dead and unalterable; let it sink into oblivion, but extract and retain its divine lessons; let those lessons be strength to you now, and make them the starting-points of a nobler, purer, more perfect life in the coming years. Let all thoughts of hatred, resentment, strife, and ill-will die with the dying years; erase from the tablet of your heart all malicious memories, all unholy grudges. Let the cry, "Peace on earth and good-will to men!" which at this season re-echoes through the world from myriads of lips, be to you something more than an oft-reiterated platitude. Let its truth be practised by you; let it dwell in your heart; and do not mar its harmony and peace by thoughts of ill-will.

The year is passing, and blessed are they who can let its mistakes, its injuries, and wrongs pass away for ever, and be remembered no more.

Blessed is he who has no wrongs to remember, no injuries to forget; in whose pure heart no hateful thought about another can take root and flourish.

December Twenty-sixth.

Do not regard your difficulties and perplexities as portentous of ill; by so doing you will make them ill; but regard them as prophetic of good, which, indeed, they are. Do not persuade yourself that you can evade them:

you cannot. Do not try to run away from them; this is impossible, for wherever you go they will still be there with you—but meet them calmly and bravely; confront them with all the dispassion and dignity which you can command; weigh up their proportions; measure their strength; understand them; attack them, and finally vanquish them. Thus will you develop strength and intelligence; thus will you enter one of those byways of blessedness which are hidden from the superficial gaze.

No man can be confronted with a difficulty which he has not the strength to meet and subdue.

There is no peace in sin, no rest in error, no final refuge but in Wisdom.

December Twenty-seventh.

What heavy burden is a man weighted with which is not made heavier and more unendurable by weak thoughts or selfish desires? If your circumstances are "trying" it is because you need them, and can evolve the strength to meet them. They are trying because there is some weak spot in you, and they will continue to be trying until that spot is eradicated. Be glad that you have the opportunity of becoming stronger and wiser. No circumstances can be trying to wisdom; nothing can weary love. Stop brooding over your own trying circumstances and contemplate the lives of some of those about you.

Go to your task with love in your heart and you will go to it light-hearted and cheerful.

The duty which you shirk is your reproving angel; the pleasure which you race after is your flattering enemy.

December Twenty-eighth.

There are little selfish indulgences, some of which appear harmless, and are commonly fostered; but no selfish indulgence can be harmless, and men and women do not know what they lose by repeatedly and habitually succumbing to effeminate and selfish gratifications. If the God in man is to rise strong and triumphant, the beast in man must perish. The pandering to the animal nature, even when it appears innocent and seems sweet, leads away from truth and blessedness. Each time you give way to the animal within you, and feed and gratify him, he waxes stronger and more rebellious, and takes firmer possession of your mind, which should be in the keeping of Truth.

Animal indulgence is alien to the perception of Truth.

Live superior to the craving for sense-excitement, and you will live neither vainly nor uncertainly.

December Twenty-ninth.

Whatever others may say of you, whatever they may do to you, *never take offence.* Do not return hatred with hatred. If another hates you perhaps you have, consciously or unconsciously, failed somewhere in your conduct, or there may be some misunderstanding which the exercise of a little gentleness and reason may remove; but under all circumstances "Father, forgive them" is infinitely better than "I will have nothing more to do with them." Hatred is so small and poor, so blind and wretched. Love is so great and rich, so far-seeing and blissful.

Sacrifice all hatred, slay it upon the altar of devotion—devotion to others.

Open the floodgates of your heart for the inpouring of that sweet, great, beautiful love which embraces all.

December Thirtieth.

Knowing this—that selfishness leads to misery, and unselfishness to joy, not merely for one's self alone—for if this were all how unworthy would be our endeavours!—but for the whole world, and because all with whom we live and come in contact will be the happier and the truer for unselfishness; because Humanity is one, and the joy of one is the joy of all—knowing this, let us scatter flowers and not thorns in the common ways of life—yea, even in the highway of our enemies let us scatter the blossoms of unselfish love—so shall the pressure of their footprints fill the air with the perfume of holiness and gladden the world with the aroma of joy.

Inside the gateway of unselfishness lies the elysium of Abiding Joy.

Seek the highest Good, and you will taste the deepest, sweetest joy.

December Thirty-first.

Happy in the Eternal Happiness is he who has come to that Life from which the thought of self is abolished. Already, even now and in this life, he has entered the Kingdom of Heaven. He is at rest on the bosom of the Infinite.

Sweet is the rest and deep the bliss of him who has freed his heart from its lusts and hatreds and dark desires; and he who, without any shadow of bitterness or selfishness, can breathe, in his heart, the blessing:

The universe has no favorites; it is supremely just, and gives to every man his rightful earnings.

Man can find the right way in life, and, having found it, can rejoice and be glad.

Peace unto all living things, making no exceptions or distinctions—such a man has reached that happy ending which can never be taken away, the fullness of peace, the consummation of Perfect Blessedness.

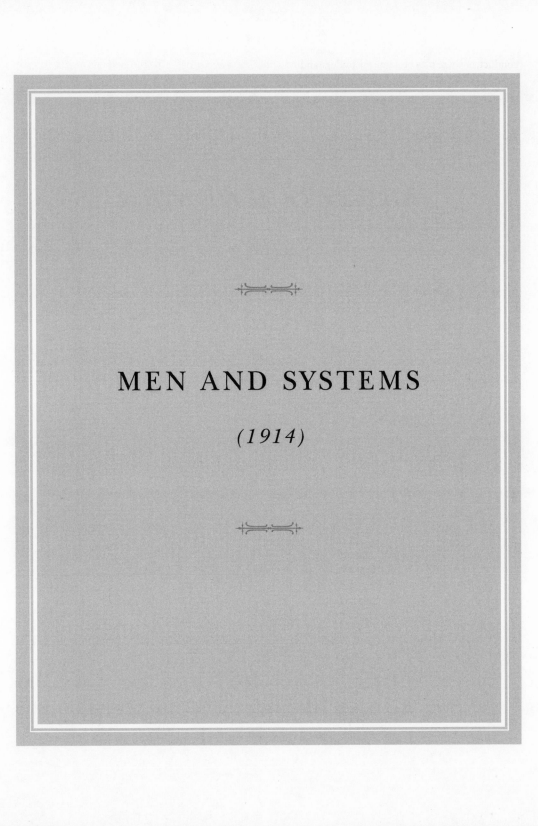

MEN AND SYSTEMS

(1914)

CONTENTS

INTRODUCTION

The unceasing change, the insecurity and the mystery of life make it necessary to find some basis of certainty on which to rest if happiness and peace of mind are to be maintained. All science, philosophy, and religion are so many efforts in search of this permanent basis; all interpretations of the universe, whether from the material or spiritual side, are so many attempts to formulate some unifying principle or principles by which to reconcile the fluctuations and contradictions of life.

It has been said that mathematics is the only exact science; that is, the only science that eternally works out true without a single exception. Yet mathematics is but the body of which ethics is the spirit. There is not a mathematical problem but has its ethical counterpart, and the spirit of ethics is as eternally exact as the form of mathematics.

It is being discovered that all natural sciences are fundamentally mathematical. Even music—popularly considered to be as far removed from mathematics as possible—is now known to be strictly mathematical. The science of harmony revealed certain fixed tones which never vary in their relative proportions, and all of which can be numerically resolved. These tones, like the numbers which represent them, are eternally fixed, and though their combinations—also like the combinations of numbers—are infinite, a given combination will always produce the same result.

This mathematical foundation in all things is the keystone in the temple of science, and when sciences are perfected they will be found to be in strict accordance with mathematical laws.

In religion also there are this same mathematical certainty and exactitude, and this mathematical certainty constitutes the "rock of ages," and the "great peace," on which and in which the saints and sages have ever found rest from the stress and turmoil of life.

Human life and evolution at present is the learning of those preliminary lessons which are leading the race toward the mastery and understanding of this basic or divine knowledge; for without such a permanent, exact, mathematical basis, no lesson could be learned. When human beings are spoken of as learning the lessons of God or of life, two things are inferred, namely—(1) a state of ignorance on the part of the learner, and (2) that there is some definite knowledge which he has to acquire. This is seen plainly in a child at school. Its lessons imply that there is a permanent principle of knowledge toward which it is progressing. Without such knowledge there could be no lessons.

Thus when one speaks of erring men as learning the lessons of life, he infers, whether he realizes it or not, the existence of a permanent basis of knowledge toward the possession of which all men are moving.

This basic principle, a knowledge of which the whole race will ultimately acquire, is best represented by the term *Divine Justice.* Human justice differs with every man according to his own light or darkness, but there can be no variation in that Divine Justice by which the universe is eternally sustained. Divine Justice is spiritual mathematics. As with figures and objects, whether simple or complex, there is a right and unvarying result, and no amount of ignorance or deliberate falsification can ever make it otherwise, so with every combination of thoughts or deeds, whether good or bad, there is an unvarying and inevitable consequence which nothing can avert.

If this were not so; if we could have effect without cause, or consequence unrelated to act, experience could never lead to knowledge, there would be no foundation of security, and no lessons could be learned.

Thus every effect has a cause, and cause and effect are in such intimate relationship as to leave no room for injustice to creep in. Nevertheless, there is ignorance, and, through ignorance, the doing of life's lessons wrongly, and this doing of life's sums wrongly is that error, or sin, which is the source of man's sufferings. How often the child at school weeps because it cannot do its sums correctly! and older children in the school of life do the same thing when the sum of their actions has worked out in the form of suffering instead of happiness.

The ground of certainty, then, on which we can securely rest amid all the incidents of life, is *the mathematical exactitude of the moral law.* The moral order of the universe is not, cannot, be disproportionate, for if it were, the universe would fall to pieces. If a brick house cannot stand unless it be built in accordance with certain geometrical proportions, how could a vast universe, with all its infinite complexities of form and motion, proceed in unbroken majesty from age to age unless guided by unerring and infallible justice?

All the physical laws with which men are acquainted never vary in their operations. Given the same cause, there will always be the same effect. All the spiritual laws with which men are acquainted have, and must have, the same infallibility in their operations. Given the same thought or deed in a like circumstance, and the result will always be the same. Without this fundamental ethical justice there could be no human society, for it is the just reactions of the deeds of individuals which prevent society from tottering to its fall.

It thus follows that the inequalities of life, as regards the distribution of happiness and suffering, are the outworking of moral forces operating along lines of flawless accuracy. This flawless accuracy, this perfect law, is the one great fundamental certainty in life, the finding of which insures a man's perfection, makes him wise and enlightened, and fills him with rejoicing and peace.

Take away a belief in this certainty from a man's consciousness, and he is adrift on a self-created ocean of chance, without rudder, chart, or compass. He has no ground on which to build a character or life, no incentive for noble deeds, no center for moral action; he has no island of peace and no harbor of refuge. Even the crudest idea of God as of a great man whose mind is perfect, who cannot err, and who has "no variableness nor shadow of turning," is a popular expression of a belief in this basic principle of Divine Justice.

According to this principle there is neither favor nor chance, but unerring and unchangeable right. Thus all the sufferings of men are right *as effects*, their causes being the mistakes of ignorance; but as effects they will pass away. Man cannot suffer for something which he has never done, or never left undone, for this would be an effect without a cause.

Man suffers through and of himself. Where the effect is there is the cause. Its seat is within, not without. The things which men are reaping to-day are of the same kind which they formerly sowed. The good man of to-day may be reaping the results of past evil; the bad man of to-day may be reaping the results of past good. Seen thus, this divine principle throws an illuminating light on those cases (common enough) where the good suffer and fail, and the bad enjoy and prosper. Things as they are did not spring into existence without a cause. They have behind them a long train of causes and effects, and another such train will follow them in the future. In viewing the objects in a landscape we allow for perspective; we must do the same in viewing events.

This principle of Divine Justice is not distinct from Divine Law. It is the same. Partial men separate justice from love, and even regard them as antagonistic, but in the divine life they blend into one.

Nothing can transcend right. Nothing can be more loving than that we should experience the consequences of ignorance and error, and so become "perfected through suffering." In this Divine Love, which never alters, never errs, never passes over a single deed, we have a sure rock of salvation, for that which could shift and change could afford no foothold. Only in the unchangeable, the eternally true, is there permanent peace and safety. Resorting to this divine principle, abandoning all evil, and clinging to good, we come to a knowledge and realization of that basis of certainty on which we can firmly stand through all life's changes; we have found the rock of ages and the refuge of the saints.

—JAMES ALLEN
Bryngoleu,
Ilfracombe, England

THEIR CORRELATIONS AND
COMBINED RESULTS

There is to-day a widespread revolt against those modes of human activity designated "Systems," and these systems are almost invariably referred to as something distinct from, and yet directing, controlling or tyrannizing over humanity itself. Thus, the leaders in the revolt referred to, speak of the "commercial system," the "social system," the "competitive system," the "political system," and so on; and the particular system condemned is made responsible for—made the cause of—certain widespread evils, such as poverty, vice, etc., as though "systems" were some sort of discarnate and gigantic despots, enslaving and crushing an innocent and unwilling humanity.

Such an arbitrary and external form of system has no existence; it is a delusion. Human systems cannot be separated from human desires and needs; they are, indeed, the visible outworking of those desires and needs. A system is none other than the combined and concerted mode of action of the community; it signifies a tacit agreement on the part of all, or nearly all, that things should be thus and so; it is a method in which human kind *agree to act;* and as men act, so systems appear, as they cease to act, so they disappear.

And let it be understood that such *agreement to act* has no reference to, or bearing upon, a man's attitude toward a system—whether for or against—but depends upon his actions. A man may violently condemn a system with his lips, yet show that he is in agreement with it in his heart by the fact that he continues to act in accordance with it, to follow it out in his daily life. We are all aware of that form of religious hypocrisy (nearly always unconscious) that continues to commit the sin which it violently denounces; thus showing, in practice, a fundamental agreement with that which, superficially and in theory, is opposed; and this form of unconscious inconsistency is not confined to religion, it is a pronounced factor in all moral activities, and is nowhere more strongly in evidence than in those directions where the reform of "existing systems" is, theoretically at any rate, the primary aim. Thus, when I had asked some socialists, who condemn the present capitalist system as a system of getting rich on the labor of the poor, why they themselves live on dividends—that is, on the fruits of other men's labor—thus propagating every day that which they denounce as an evil—the reply almost invariably has been, "You should blame the system, not me." This reply shows that such people regard themselves as the helpless victims of a tyrannical something which exists external to, and independent of, themselves and their actions, and which they call a "system." But a little reflection will show that that which they denounce as the "system" is none other than the viewing as evil certain actions *in others* which they regard as good *in themselves.*

Such people being, by their concerted action with others, in agreement with the thing which they denounce, are not merely *accessories* to the "system" which they regard as evil, *they are themselves that system,* and doubtless to many a rampant denouncer of the slayer of the wage-earning lambs might justly be brought the charge—"Thou art the man!"

Human systems are human modes of action which are dependent for their continuance on a fundamental tacit agreement among men to continue to act in the same way; and such agreement implies that those who continue to enact any particular system must be prepared to meet and to accept its disadvantages, as well as its advantages; for in the struggle for advantage there must always be the corresponding disadvantage; in the battle of human interests there must always be both victory and defeat.

Viewed in this light, the term "innocent victims of the system," so much in vogue, is seen to be shallow and delusive. There are no innocent victims of a system in which *all* engage either in the letter or the spirit; if guilt there be, then all are guilty, and the innocence is superficial and apparent, not fundamental and real. In reality, however, there is neither innocence nor guilt attached to a human system which has evolved through long processes of struggle and time. There is merely the victory and happiness on the one hand, and the defeat and misery on the other; and the defeated are not the innocent, nor the victorious the guilty, for both these conditions in social life are the just effects of men's actions, as victory and defeat attach to a battle or a race.

To make this more plain, let us take a simple illustration. Here are ten men who mutually agree to engage, among themselves, in certain forms of gambling. Now, the object of each of these men is to win, and so increase his wealth, yet they all know that there is also the possibility of losing; know, indeed, that some *must* lose, for such is the unavoidable hazard of the game. Immediately these men commence to act by laying down their stakes, they have created a system which might be called "the gambling system," and the advantages and disadvantages of such a system soon become apparent. There is ceaseless fluctuation of their combined wealth—some winning and becoming rich, and then again losing and becoming poor; but ultimately some lose all they possess and have to retire defeated, while others acquire the loser's part and become rich on their gains.

Now, it cannot be said of the winners that they are guilty of exploiting and crushing down the losers; nor can it be said of the losers that they are the innocent victims of the system of gambling in which they are engaged. In the mental attitude and actions of these ten men there is neither innocence nor guilt, but a mutual engagement in a method, with its inevitable results, namely, the reaping of its advantages on the one hand, the suffering from its disadvantages on the other.

In like manner, of the various systems in which men have involved themselves, there are no innocent victims, no guilty tyrants. Victims there are, if men choose to apply that term to the defeated, or to those who, for the time being, are suffering loss, but they are the victims of their own deeds, and not of an overruling and compelling injustice outside themselves. Of the ten men who engage in gambling, none are victimized, none can possibly be victimized, but themselves. Those outside the system—that is, those who do not encourage and propagate it by their acts—remain untouched, uninjured by it. So if our present commercial system should be a "system of greed," as many social reformers style it, then not by any possibility whatever could any but the greedy be injured by it.

Doubtless there is much greed in the world, for in its present stage of evolution, humanity is learning its lessons largely along selfish paths; but greed can never have any existence in an external "system," it can only exist in human hearts, nor can greed injure any but the greedy. Commercialism is free from greed in the hands of those who have destroyed greed in themselves. But they who are greedy will taint everything—even religion—with their own impure condition.

Industrialism, the outworking of a nation's energies and abilities, is wholesome and noble; it is covetousness which produces woe, and the sole sufferers from covetousness are the covetous themselves.

I will here anticipate the common query—"What of the innocent victims of the rapacious company promoter?"—by replying (and this reply will be found adaptable to all human conditions and systems), they are not innocent, but have the same attitude of mind as the unscrupulous company promoter—namely, the desire to obtain money, and as much of it as possible, without laboring for it. The company promoter is the instrument through whom they reap the results of their own greed, and fall victims to their own covetousness.

Social reformers may denounce the system of "capitalism" or "commercialism," but so long as they themselves continue to enact that side of commercialism which is most akin to covetousness, namely, its speculative as distinguished from its industrial side, by keeping a keen eye to "good investments," and following up increased "dividends" with avidity, just so long will that which they call "a system of greed" (and indeed to them it is such) continue.

Those who are striving to live by speculation, on the fruits of another's labors, or who have the spirit so to do should the opportunity arise (and the number of those who are anxious to acquire money without giving its equivalent is very large), should not bemoan the existence of want and poverty, but should perceive and receive such conditions as the inevitable disadvantages of the method which they are acting out, as luxury and riches are its advantages.

The hope of one day becoming suddenly rich without working for it, and living ever after a life of unbroken ease, is a common chimera among the poor. While covetousness continues to sway the human mind, want and poverty will continue.

Men desire, and then they act, and their combined acts constitute what men call "systems." The ten gamblers desired to increase their wealth without laboring for it, and at each other's loss, and they acted accordingly. Their combined actions constituted the system with its combination of results. Systems are, therefore, deeds, the deeds, combined and reciprocal, of a number of individuals; and the so-called evils in the world which men attribute to systems as distinguished from men, are the reactions upon individuals of their own deeds.

A system cannot be "unjust," because men inevitably reap the just effects of their own deeds. The evils which prevail in the world are indications of justice, not injustice. Poverty and want are the natural disadvantages of the present social life, or system—that is, of the way in which men agree to act. There is suffering, but there is no injustice. It could not be said of those among the ten gamblers who were reduced to poverty, that they were treated unjustly by the winners, or that they were the innocent victims of the system of gambling. Their lot was just; their poverty being the inevitable result of their own actions.

Recently a socialist friend of mine was somewhat violently condemning landlords and landlordism, and I pulled him up by saying—"But why do you condemn landlords, seeing that you are one yourself; have you not, only a few weeks ago, added another piece of land to that which you already possessed?" He replied—"It's the system, not me. So long as the present system lasts I shall have to work with it; but, when it is altered, I shall be willing to give up my land."

If a gambler were continually condemning the "system" of gambling as a bad one, and yet continued to gamble, we should justly say that he was confused both in his morals and perceptions; and he is equally confused who, while condemning any other system, social, political, or whatsoever, yet continues to act it out. Such a man does not, in his heart, regard the system as bad, but as good and just; this is evidenced by the fact that he continues to propagate it by his actions.

Systems are to men as light to the sun, rain to the clouds, or thoughts to the mind. They are both men and the deeds of men. To regard them as separate from men is confusion of thought and principle. Nor can there possibly be any injustice in their outworking, for the reaction of ignorant deeds is certain; the recompense of enlightened deeds is sure.

I see no evil in systems; I see evil in ignorance and wrong-doing. All systems are legitimate, for men have liberty to act in their own way. The ten gamblers who mutually agree to enrich and impoverish each other, have nobody to blame but themselves; and if the winners are satisfied with their gains, the losers should be equally satisfied with their losses; if they are not, then they should look to themselves and remedy their deeds. Their poverty is good discipline, in that it is driving them to seek a better way of action.

If a man regards a system as bad, he should withdraw from it in practice, and should bend his actions in another direction; for immediately two men act in concert, a system is formed, and the good and the bad which lurk in their actions will soon be manifested in the system which they have launched forth.

In the life of humanity, in systems, in what are called *good* and *bad*, is visible the outworking of the combined results of men's deeds; and in all, through all, and over all, justice reigns eternally triumphant.

WORK, WAGES AND WELL-BEING

Activity is a necessity of existence, and usefulness is the object of being. Nature at once cuts off that which has become useless. Her economy is faultless, and she will not be burdened with things which have ceased to be of service in her progressive workshop. Nor does she allow her handy tools to lie unused, nor her bright things to rust. Wheresoever there is ability, there also are scope and opportunity; where there is energy, there also are legitimate channels for its exercise; where there is a soaring mind, the means of achievement are ready to hand. As the field waits for the plow, the sea for the ship, and the port for produce, so Nature in all her departments, whether material or mental, stands ready to coöperate with man in all his labors, and to reward him according to his diligence and industry. The statement "There is no scope for my abilities" is either an expression of vanity, an excuse for negligence, or a confession of lack of resource, or of inability to utilize opportunity. Ability need never lie unused for a moment. There is unlimited scope for all abilities. All that is required is the capacity for work.

Of all abilities, the capacity for work is the most useful and necessary, and its possession is a glorious power; and this men discover when they are disabled, or stricken down with sickness. When they are thus forcibly prevented from engaging in wholesome invigorating labor, what would they not give to have once again the spirited and glowing use of brain or muscle, or to spend exuberant strength in healthful exertion?

Work is of two kinds—it is either *loving labor* or *enforced slavery*. The man whose sole object is to get through his work in order to draw his pay, who has no love for, and no interest in, his work beyond what it represents in cash, is a slave and not a true worker. He labors only under the compulsion of necessity. His entire interest is in *getting* instead of in *doing*. He gives his labor irksomely and perfunctorily, but receives his pay with eagerness, striving, when he thinks he safely can, to give less and less labor, and get more and more wages. "Less work and more pay" is the cry of slaves and not of men.

On the contrary, the man whose heart is centered in his work, who aims at the perfect performance of his duty, is a true worker whose usefulness and influence are cumulative and progressive, carrying him on from success to greater and greater success, from low spheres of labor to higher and higher still. Thinking little or nothing of the wages, and much of the work; caring not for the gaining of reward, but eager and willing in service, he is sealed by Nature as one of her chosen sons, fitted by virtue of his unselfish labors to receive the greater excellence and the fuller reward.

For while full recompense may, and frequently does, escape the man who covetously seeks it, it cannot be withheld from him who ignores it in his work. For the true recompense is never withheld, but, in the selfish desire to secure the recompense without giving its equivalent, disappointment is the pay received, and the expected reward does not appear.

The wages of work are sure. In the universal economy no man is cheated; he cannot be defrauded of his just earnings, for every effort receives its proportionate result; first work as the cause, and then wages as the effect. But while wages is the result, it is not the end; it is only a means to a still greater and more far-reaching result and end, namely, the progress and increased happiness both of the individual and the race, in a word, to *well-being*.

The receiving of so much money for work done does not represent wages in its entirety; it is, indeed, only a small portion of the actual wages of true work; while the man who considers that the end of work is reached when he has received the money due, receives all he bargains for, he does not derive complete satisfaction from his labors, nor comprehend or enter the higher spheres of knowledge and usefulness, which are reserved for the devotees of unselfish duty.

It is a day of definitely marked progress in the life of a man when, by the illumination of spirit which proceeds from the development of a higher sense of duty, he passes from the burdensome sphere of slavery to the happy world of work; when he leaves behind him the grasping and bartering, the drudgery and humiliation, and, accepting his place among his fellows, becomes a cheerful coöperator with humanity, and a willing and happy instrument in the economy of things.

Such a man receives the completion of wages in its sevenfold fullness as follows:

1. Money
2. Usefulness
3. Excellence
4. Power
5. Independence

6. Honor

7. Happiness

First, he receives the full amount of money of which his work is the equivalent; but in addition to this, his *usefulness* to the world is increased, and continues to increase in an ever-ascending degree; and this greater usefulness is one of the pure delights of labor, for one of the chief rewards of use is to be of greater use. To the slave, idleness is coveted as the reward of labor; but the worker rejoices in more work still.

This accumulating usefulness leads to the wages of *excellence*—skill, a growing perfection in the work undertaken; and every child that has learned its lesson, and every man and woman that has mastered a problem or a language, or surmounted a great difficulty, is acquainted with the happiness which is the sure accompaniment of such success; although, not until later do they realize the full significance of all that is involved in such success in relation to their career.

For a point of excellence is at last reached which merges into *power*—knowledge, mastery. The man who is devoted to his work, becomes at last a master in that work, whatever it may be. He becomes a teacher, a guide, and instructor to others who are treading the lower levels of the path up which he has climbed. He is sought out by others for the knowledge which he has acquired through practice and experience. He is relied upon, and takes his proper place among those who lead and serve mankind. Power is a form of wages received as the result of long and arduous labor. It is received only by him who has built it up, so to speak, who has earned it. The sowing of earnest and unselfish toil leads to the reaping of power.

Associated with power is *independence.* The true worker takes his place among his fellows as a useful citizen. The fearless flash of honesty is in his eyes, the ring of worth is in his voice, and the steadfastness of self-reliance is in his gait. He is not a drone in the human hive, but stands out in shining contrast to the skulking shirker who imagines that the highest good in life is to get something without working for it. The slave who goes to his hated work only because he is whipped to it by necessity, comes down to beggary and shame and is despised and neglected; but the true worker ascends into independence and honor, and is admired and sought.

Honor—this is one of the higher forms of wages, and it comes unerringly and unsought to all who are energetic and faithful in the work of their life. It may be, and often is, late in coming, but come it must and does, and always at its own proper time; for while money is the first and smallest item in wages, honor is one of the last and greatest; and the greater the honor, the longer and harder is the course of labor by which it is earned. There are degrees of honor according to the measure of usefulness, and the greatest men receive the greatest honor.

They who receive the fullness of wages, receive the fullness of *happiness,* for true work as surely brings about happiness, as idleness and enforced labor are paid in the coin of unhappiness. From the perfection of happiness proceeds well-being—a quiet conscience, a satisfied heart, a tranquil mind, and the consciousness of having increased the happiness, and aided in the progress of man-kind through the full and faithful exercise of one's abilities.

First work, and then wages; but well-being only follows when the work is of the true kind, when it is loved for its own sake, and when the money received for such work is utilized for further work and better achievement instead of being squandered in folly and self-indulgence. Even he who only works for the pay in coin will derive just the measure of well-being which that pay can purchase if he spends it carefully, and will thus aid, in a small measure, industrial progress; but he can also, by a foolish use of his wages, make it an instrument of ill-being, and reduce himself to a dead and useless limb on the tree of life.

It is demanded by the law of things that every man shall receive the equivalent of what he gives. If he gives idleness he receives inactivity—death; if he gives stinted and unwilling service he receives stinted and hardly secured pay; if he gives loving and generous labor, he receives generous recom-pense in a life replete with blessedness.

It may here be asked, "But what about the toiling masses? What you say may be, and doubtless is, true of certain favored individuals, but how can it apply to the vast army of mill-workers and factory hands whose toil is long and hard and almost purely mechanical?"

It applies with equal force to them. There are no favored individuals; and there was a time when those who now occupy the high places stood in the low. There is no reason why the mill-worker should not be unselfish in his labor, and faithful and conscientious in duty; and there is every reason why he should economize his entire financial, physical and mental resources, using his money for the improvement of his home and surroundings and his evenings and spare time in the culture of his intellectual and moral powers. He will thus be preparing himself for higher spheres of usefulness and power, which will not be withheld from him when he is sufficiently equipped and strengthened to deal with intricate matters and carry weighty responsibilities; while the process of preparation itself will be one of ever-increasing knowledge, strength and happiness.

Work, wages and well-being are three broad stages in individual and racial evolution; and the polit-ical economy of the future will take into account those higher mental and spiritual forms of wages which it now ignores, but which are still the most powerful factors in the well-being of men and nations.

Well, indeed, will it be for that nation which is the first to realize and wisely utilize the fact that its prosperity and happiness are not limited to its material resources, but that in the mental and spiritual material of its inhabitants it possesses inexhaustible mines of living resources, which, when worked with the tools of suitably-evolved educational methods, will afford rich yields of prosperity and peace; that the surest and swiftest way to even material success—as well as to all the higher and nobler successes—is by the assiduous cultivation of character.

THE SURVIVAL OF THE FITTEST
AS A DIVINE LAW

Nature and Spirit were at one time universally considered to be at enmity, and even to-day the majority of people regard them as opposed to each other; but a fuller knowledge of the Cosmos reveals the sublime fact that the natural and the spiritual are two aspects of One Eternal Truth.

Nature is the Spirit made visible and tangible. The seen is the expressed form and letter of the unseen. We search in trackless deserts of speculation to find the real, while all the time it stands before us. The return, from those weary and fruitless wanderings, to Truth is a coming back to the simple and obvious; but whereas we went out with sealed eyes, we come back with them unsealed: we look upon Nature with a vision clarified from ignorance and egotism, and lo! the unclean has become clean, the mortal has become immortal, the natural is seen to be also the spiritual.

Thus, when the physical scientist reveals a natural law, he, at the same time, makes known to the understanding mind—whether he himself knows it or not—a spiritual law. The whole universe is spiritual, and every physical law is the letter of a moral principle. When the moral nature of the Cosmos is apprehended, all controversies about matter and spirit—as things opposed—are at an end, and the assiduous worker in physical realms—often spoken of contemptuously as a "materialist"— is seen to be a *revealer,* as well as the worker in spiritual realms, the two phases of the universe being, as we have pointed out, but two arcs of one perfect whole.

When Charles Darwin made known the law of "the survival of the fittest," he revealed the working of Divine Justice in Nature. The almost universal prejudice and passionate opposition among religious people which the announcement of his discovery aroused was based, not on the fact itself, but upon a total misunderstanding of that law. That opposition has to-day nearly died out; but even yet one frequently hears this law referred to as a "cruel law," and the belief in it denounced as tending to destroy pity and love.

Such people always think of this law as "the survival of the cruelest," or "the survival of the strongest," and here is where the misunderstanding arises. The correct term, "The Survival of the *Fittest,*" must not be lost sight of; for the fittest are never the cruelest, and rarely the strongest. The strongest and cruelest creatures have long since passed away, and have given place to weaker, but *more intelligent,* creatures and beings. Think of the numberless insects, and of the many powerful enemies which beset them on every hand. Yet these wonderful and beautiful creatures continue to flourish, and they owe their continuance to their intelligence, which is greater, better, and more fitted to survive than the strength and cruelty of their enemies. For what is the survival of the fittest but the survival of *the best?* In a world of continual progress, it must needs be that the best of every period takes precedence of the worst—the good of the bad, the fit of the unfit. This, indeed, is the very meaning of progress. When we think of progress, we at once think of something, by its superiority—its greater fitness to the time and occasion—taking precedence of something which is inferior and has fallen out of the line of advancement; and this progress, this advancement, this survival of the fittest, resolves itself into a moral principle, into a Divine Law.

Opponents of this teaching tacitly assume that the most selfish are the fittest to survive, and they thereupon condemn the teaching as callous, and accuse Darwin of making selfishness supreme. But the error is theirs, their's and not Darwin's or the law's. In their prejudice they wrest his meaning to a false issue, and attack that. Their error consists in assuming that the fittest to survive are the most selfish; whereas such are the worst specimens, and not the best. When we realize that the unselfish are more fitted to survive than the selfish, this law assumes an aspect the very opposite from that which its opponents have given it, and we at once see that in it are involved the profoundest moral principles, namely, the principles of Justice and Love.

Remembering that it is the *fittest* that survive, what, then—in this universe of law and order—constitutes the fittest? It is evident that the fittest are *the most advanced specimens of any given species.* Not the strongest, not the cruelest, not the most selfish, not even the finest physically; but *the most advanced,* those most in line with the order of evolution.

The fittest at one period are not the fittest at another. There was a time when brute force was dominant; but that was when nothing higher had been evolved. Yet even in that long distant period—ten million years back, when gigantic monsters held sway upon the earth—something higher was being evolved. Already, intelligence, yea, and unselfish love, were beginning to make themselves felt; for those great beasts loved and protected their young, and so all who most unselfishly shield their offspring, be they beasts or men, will be most protected, while, obviously, any species that neglected its offspring would rapidly perish.

Thus, long, long ages ago, the fragile babe of intelligence was born in the manger of brute force, and since then, through all the ages of struggle, it has been gradually but surely overcoming brutal strength and terror; so that to-day intelligence has conquered, or almost conquered; for the strongest brutes have passed away forever, having given place to beings physically weaker and smaller, but better and more morally perfect.

Without the operation of such a law man could never have come into existence; for man is, up to the present, the crown and summit of a process of struggle, selection, and progress which began many millions of years ago when the first of life appeared upon the earth. Man is the product of the law of the survival of the fittest operating through millions of years, perhaps millions of ages; yet in brute strength he is far inferior to many animals. He rules the earth to-day because of the principle of intelligence within him. But there is being evolved in man a higher principle and intelligence, namely, *Divine Love*, which is as much higher and more powerful than intelligence as intelligence is higher and more powerful than brute force. I use the term *"Divine Love"* in order to distinguish it from human affection and from that intermittent kindly impulse which are both spoken of as love. Intelligence may aid selfishness, but not so Love: in Love all selfishness is swallowed up and brute force is no more, both being transmuted into gentleness.

The beginnings of this Divine Love are already in the world. We see its wonderful operation in the few men in whom it has been perfected, namely, the Great Spiritual Teachers who, by their precepts and the example of their lives, rule the world to-day; and selfish men worship them as God. We see in these men the prophecy of what Love will do in the distant future, when a large number of men possess it in an advanced degree; how selfishness and selfish men will submit to it and be governed by it, as the brutes now submit to man's intelligence and are ruled by it. And this Love is making its appearance not only in the Great Teachers, but in men less evolved; and though in these it is, as yet, in a more or less rudimentary form, nevertheless, the stirrings of its gentleness and joy are being felt in many human hearts.

A common argument against the survival of the fittest is that were men to put it into practice, they would kill off all their weaklings and invalids, preserving only the strong, and thus destroying all pity and love and humanity. This argument is a demonstration of the error to which we have already referred. It is ludicrously self-contradictory; for, while it admits that the best elements are pity and love and humanity, it asserts that these would perish if the fittest, or best, survived. And here we are at the heart of the whole matter. *The best does survive,* and, therefore, pity, compassion, and love cannot be overthrown by selfishness and force, because they are superior qualities and will survive when selfishness is forever annihilated.

Speaking of human beings, it is plain that the fittest to survive are not the selfish and the cruel, but those who have developed the finest characteristics of kindness, compassion, justice, and love; in a word, the most moral, the purest, and wisest.

To talk about putting this law "into practice" shows ignorance of its nature; for it is independent in its operation, and is always in activity, and all men and creatures obey it; and should ever a race of men, under the mistaken notion that they were practicing it, do it such violence as to "kill off their weaklings and invalids," the law would not cease to operate in their case, and they, by virtue of that very law, would soon exterminate themselves.

With the ceaseless march of human progress, cruelty is becoming less and less fitted to survive against the growing intelligence and gentleness. The cruel races have nearly all died out, only disorganized remnants of them remaining. The fierce animals of prey are becoming fewer, and brutal men are now regarded as a menace to society. Gradually and inevitably, also, selfish and aggressive men will come to have less and less power in the world, will become more out of harmony with the growing environment of peace and good-will, till at last they will pass away from the earth alto-gether, as the gigantic brutes have passed away, no longer fitted to survive in a world conquered by Love, in which righteousness and truth become triumphant.

Thus this law, as represented by Darwin, is the aspect, in Nature, of the operation of Justice, or Love; for in the Light of Truth, Justice and Love are seen to be one. The spiritual aspect of the law was intimately known by all the Great Teachers, and men have overlooked the fact that these Teachers embodied it in their teaching. Thus the precept of Jesus, "The meek shall inherit the earth," is none other than a simple but Divine statement of the survival of the fittest.

JUSTICE IN EVIL

To-day we frequently meet with the assertion "All is good." Pope in his famous essay on man, said—

Whatever is, is right,

and nearly all are familiar with Browning's oft-quoted line—

God's in his heaven, all's right with the world.

In the face of these statements, the questions naturally arise:—Are war and famine good? Are sickness and poverty good? Are sorrow and suffering good? These things belong to the category of the great facts of human life; are they good? Again, are sin and selfishness right? Are drunkenness and brutality right? Are crime and violence right? Are accidents by sea and land right? Are catas-trophes involving hundreds of thousands of lives right? These things, like the former, are everyday facts. They are real, and cause wide-spread suffering; are they right?

Many persons must have questioned thus during the past years of unprecedented catastrophes in the form of volcanic eruptions, earthquakes, floods, famines, wars, and various forms of crimes and violence.

Are these things right? If so, why are men so eager to escape them? Even those who are given to quoting "Whatever is, is right" will, in the next breath, refer to certain "evils" and propose some method of being rid of them.

It is plain that in the sense of adding to human happiness, these things *are not right,* for they conduce to human misery. Even those who deny the existence of evil in theory recognize it in practice, in their efforts to conquer it.

Nevertheless, those statements as to the Universal Good and the rightness of all things, are true. It is all a matter of relativity. The recognition of evil, and the statement that all is good, are not contradictory. When the events of life are related to human happiness, then some are recognized as "good" and some as "evil," but when they are related to the fundamental and eternal principle of Justice, then all things are seen to be good, right, in harmony with the Great Law of inviolable Equity.

Take a simple example—that of physical pain. When we are considering human happiness, bodily pain is an evil, but when we consider the principle of Life itself, and its protection and continuance, then physical pain is seen to be good, as it is a warning monitor urging man to the protection of his body from hurt and extinction.

And it is with mental pain as with physical—with sorrow, remorse, loneliness and grief,—it is evil because it destroys happiness; but as the effect of ignorance and wrong-doing it is just, and therefore good, as it urges men to seek the paths of wisdom and right-doing.

The prophet Isaiah says:

I form the light and create darkness; I make peace and create evil; I the Lord do all these things.

He thus recognizes the justice of evil, that it has its place in the moral universe as the opposite of good, just as darkness has its place in the physical universe as the opposite of light.

The prophet Amos expresses the same thing when he says:

Shall there be evil in a city, and the Lord hath not done it?

The writings of the Hebrew prophets in the Old Testament teem with statements of the truth that evil is rooted in justice, not in injustice; that all the afflictions and calamities which overtake men spring from some violation, on man's part, of the moral law. So pronounced are they upon this point that they even attribute the suffering caused by purely external occurrences—such as floods, storms, earthquakes, drought, and dearth of food—to man's inward unrighteousness and his consequent departure from the Divine Order.

And, indeed, a profound acquaintance with the human heart and with human life does reveal the great truth—a truth never apparent on the surface, and therefore hidden from the shallow and unthinking—that all tragedy is the culminating point in the conflict of human passions. Where there are no violent passions there can be no tragedy, no disaster, no catastrophe. When humanity has attained to inward harmony and peace, it will be free from all those forms of violence which now devastate the world and scourge humankind with grief and lamentation.

Maeterlinck perceives this truth clearly, for in his *"Wisdom and Destiny,"* he says:

Fatality shrinks back abashed from the soul that has more than once conquered her; there are certain disasters she dare not send forth when this soul is near.

. . . The mere presence of the sage suffices to paralyze destiny; and of this we find proof in the fact that there exists scarce a drama wherein a true sage appears; when such is the case, the event must needs halt before reaching bloodshed and tears. Not only is there no drama wherein sage is in conflict with sage, but, indeed, there are very few whose action revolves round a sage. And, truly, can we imagine that an event shall turn into tragedy between men who have earnestly striven to gain knowledge of self? . . . It is rarely indeed that tragic poets will allow a sage to appear on the scene, though it be for an instant. They are afraid of a lofty soul, for they know that events are no less afraid; and were there heroes to soar to the height the real hero would gain, their weapons would fall to the ground, and the drama itself become peace—the peace of enlightenment.

It is a significant fact that, while Shakespeare depicted nearly every type of character, he never brought a sage into his dramas. The truth is that his tragedies could not have taken place in the presence of a sage. Their outward violence stands related as *effect* to the hidden *cause* of disordered and conflicting passions. The sage has lifted himself above such disorder and conflict, and such is the power of his harmonious and tranquil spirit that, in his presence the passions of others will be calmed and subdued, and their approaching tragic issue averted.

It is a mighty truth, and one which stands clearly revealed in the mind of the sage and the prophet, that all the evils of humanity spring from the ignorance, and, therefore, from the mistakes, the wrongdoing of humanity itself. It is, therefore, just and right. But though just and right, it is not desirable; it is evil, and needs to be transcended. It is just and right, as imprisonment is just and right for the thief, in that it teaches man, and ultimately brings him to the feet of wisdom. As physical pain is a protector of man's body, so mental pain is a protector of his mind and of his life.

From man's ignorance of the Divine Law—of the Moral Order of the universe—arise those thoughts and passions—inward conditions—which are the source of tragedy, disaster, catastrophe.

Envy, ill-will, jealousy, produce strife and quarreling, and ultimately bring about wars in which thousands are killed and disabled, and hundreds of homes are filled with mourning. Greediness, self-indulgence, and the thirst for pleasure lead through gluttony, indolence, and drunkenness to disease, poverty, and plague. Covetousness, lust and selfishness in all its forms cause men to practice deception, lying and dishonesty, and to strive against others in the blind pursuance of their petty plans and pleasures; thus leading to deprivation, loss and ruin; and where there are excessively violent passions there is always a violent life ending in a premature and violent death.

Man, by his ignorance, his selfishness, his darkness of mind, is the maker of sorrow, and the cause of catastrophe. His sufferings are indications that the Divine Law has been arrested, and is now asserting itself. The tragic darkness of his life is the outcome of that same Justice from which his joyful light proceeds. If every suicide, every ruin, every woe, even every accident, could be traced to its original cause in the moral constitution of things, its justice would be found to be without blemish.

And that which applies to individuals applies in the same way to nations. Widespread selfishness leads inevitably to widespread disaster; national corruption is followed by wholesale catastrophe, and by national disaster and ruin.

And not alone poverty, disease, and famine, but even earthquakes, volcanic eruptions, floods, and all such external happenings would be found, in their original cause, to be intimately related to men's moral life. That external accidents have a moral cause is plainly seen in the case of violent persons bringing about fatal accidents to themselves through folly and recklessness.

Man's body, both by chemical and gravitational affinity, is a portion of the earth, as his mind, both spiritually and ethically, is a portion of the Moral Order of the universe. His life and being are interwoven with, and are inseparable from, the very nature and constitution of things, and, being a moral entity, and therefore a reasonable agent, it is within the domain of his power to discover and work with the Divine Law instead of striving against it.

All man's pains, afflictions, disasters, calamities, are the shock resulting from running, either percipiently or blindly, against the Moral Law, as a reckless rider or blind man is hurt when he runs up against a wall; and these sorrows are not the arbitrary visitations and punishments of an offended Deity, but are matters of cause and effect, just as the pain of burning is the effect of coming into too close contact with fire.

In these days of social, political, and theological conflicts; and with wars, famines, floods, crimes, conflagrations, and volcanic and seismic catastrophes taking place on every hand, a return to the study of the Hebrew prophets—burning, as they are, with the fire of Truth on national matters and local catastrophes—would prove, not only scientifically enlightening, but would help considerably toward unveiling, in the mind of man, the revelation of the beauty and order of the Cosmos, and the perfect justice of human life.

The evils of life are right because of the causes which man has created; but man, having created causes which produce evil, can also create causes which produce good; and when the inward passions are tamed and subdued the outward violence will disappear, or will be powerless to hurt mankind.

Between the inward violence of surging passions and the outward violence of Nature there is such a close correspondence as to render them, in the inner order of things, of one indivisible essence. As the prophet Amos again puts it:

> For they know not to do right, saith the Lord, who store up violence and robbery in their palaces. Therefore, thus saith the Lord God; an adversary there shall be round about the land; and he shall bring down thy strength from thee, and thy palaces shall be spoiled.

The outward "adversary" is necessary to nullify the inward violence, is brought into existence by it. When a nation becomes corrupt, it is conquered and swallowed up. When cities become morally bankrupt, they fall to pieces, or are destroyed by some outward force.

JUSTICE AND LOVE

One frequently hears justice referred to as being opposed to love. Such an error arises out of lack of understanding of the profound and comprehensive significance of these two principles; for two divine laws cannot stand in opposition or contradiction to each other. Two basic laws, both admittedly good, *must* harmonize, otherwise one would be evil, for good cannot oppose good. The antagonism which men place between justice and love does not exist in reality; it is an error arising from ignorance of the true nature and right application of the principles involved.

The element of kindness is never absent from justice; if it were, it would be cruelty and not justice. The element of severity is never absent from love; if it were, it would be weak emotionalism and not love. There is often more love in a severe reproof than in a yielding acquiescence. The father who has little love for his child, though he may not treat it cruelly, will not take pains to train it properly; but the father who has great love for his child will train it with a firm yet gentle hand. He will be just to his child because he loves it. He will administer correction and reproof when necessary, that his child may profit thereby.

Justice is not separate from love; love is not separate from justice. The essential oneness of the two principles is simply expressed in the divine edict—"Whatsoever a man soweth, that shall he also reap." It is in accordance both with perfect love and perfect justice that man should reap the good results of his good deeds, and the bad results of his bad deeds. All men admit this, theoretically, though the majority refuse to recognize the operation of such a law in the universe, arguing, when overtaken with trouble, that in their case they are not reaping what they have sown, as they have never done anything to call for such misfortune, but are suffering innocently (unjustly), or are afflicted through the wrong-doing of others.

Such a law, however, obtains, and those who will search long enough, and look deep below the surface of things, will find it and be able to trace, with precision, its faultless working. Nor would a right-minded man wish it to be otherwise. He would know that the kindest thing that could be done to him would be that he should suffer the full penalty of all his mistakes and wrong-doing, so that he might thereby grow more rapidly in virtue and wisdom. Petitions to Deity to abrogate the just punishment of sins committed are without avail, and can only spring from an immature moral sense. Woe indeed would descend upon man if the law of justice could thus be set aside.

Self-afflicted and torn with sorrow as he now is, there is hope in the law which bestows no special favors and is unfailingly just; but if man, by offering up a prayer could escape the effects of his bad deeds, then justice would be non-existent, and as for love, where would it be? For if one could thus be deprived of his *bad* earnings, what assurance could he have of not being robbed of his good earnings? Thus the ground of salvation would be cut away, and caprice and despotism would take the place of love and justice.

As a coin, which is one, has two distinct sides, so love and justice are two aspects of the same thing. Men do not perceive the love that is hidden in justice, nor the justice that is hidden in love, because they perceive only one side, and do not take pains to turn these principles round, as it were, and see them in their completion.

Justice, being a divine principle, cannot contain any element of cruelty. All its apparent harshness is the chastening fire of love. Man himself, and not the law *per se,* has brought about all the afflictions which are working for his ultimate happiness and good. Love reigns supreme in the universe because justice is supreme. A tender and loving hand administers the rod of chastisement. Man is protected even against himself. Love and justice are one.

SELF-PROTECTION

Animal, Human and Divine

Many and wonderful are the means and methods of self-protection in this world of combat! Natural history has revealed the fact that even plants employ means of self-protection; and when we come to the animal world, the methods adopted to avoid annihilation in the struggle for life are so numerous and remarkable as to call forth our admiration and wonder. Nor, in this fight for life is "the battle to the fierce and the race to the strong" in all cases. Indeed, the weak things of Nature exhibit such ingenuity in the means which they adopt to escape their enemies, that they are equally successful in holding their own with the fiercest creatures that have few enemies to fear. The insects, weakest of all creatures, have developed this self-protective ingenuity to a remarkable degree, even to imitating in color and form the twigs upon which they rest, adopting the hue of the soil or the dead or living leaves among which they live, and in some cases, through long experience, they have so closely imitated in color and form certain flowers which they habitually haunt that their enemies, the birds, keen as is their sight, pass them by; and even man, with all his intelligence, cannot distinguish them from the flowers unless he has had some experience as an observant naturalist. The smallest fishes adopt similar means of concealing themselves, although they are in the lowest class of animal life.

When we come to the quadrupeds, (although the weaker and smaller among them, those most hunted by the larger, adopt ruses similar to those which prevail among the insects and fishes) brute strength largely takes the place of stratagem. The beast has developed powerful weapons of defense, such as horns, fangs, claws, etc., combined with an iron or lithe muscularity, with which he maintains his place on the earth, and defies extinction. Endurance, speed, strength and ferocity are the means of self-protection among the brutes.

Animal self-protection reaches its highest excellence in the superb strength and cunning of the lion and the tiger, yet it appears weak and clumsy when compared with the means of self-protection adopted by man; for self-preservation, although it is not all-powerful in the human as in the animal world, is still a dominant impulse among human beings.

Man is possessed of the entire animal nature, and the animal impulses and instincts are strong within him, but there is, along with this animal life, an added intelligence and moral sense,—a self-consciousness—by virtue of which his self-protective scope and power are greatly enlarged and intensified. He is still an animal, with endurance, speed, strength and ferocity, but he is also something more and greater—he is an intelligent, self-conscious being.

Among men of low order of intelligence, the animal methods still largely obtain. In the struggle of life, the savage relies on brute strength. Even among civilized communities, there are still thousands of admirers of "the noble art of self-defense," which can only be noble in the sense that we speak of the ferocity of the lion as being noble, and is devoid of art, being compounded entirely of brute force and cunning. Indeed, this practice is so closely allied to the beast that it has long ceased to be a means of self-defense among civilized men, and has become merely a vulgar pastime for the few.

Working along physical lines, and still following the well-worn track of animal instinct, man has invented numerous implements of destruction by which to annihilate his enemy and preserve himself, and upon these, with increasing ingenuity and subtlety, he continues to improve. Working along the new path of pure intelligence—which is pre-eminently the human, as distinguished from the animal sphere of activity—he discovers means of adding to his physical comforts and for the peaceful protection of his body, and asserts his right and power to live, not by brute force, but by toil of hand and keenness of brain. The basic struggle here, indeed, is not directly a fight for food and life, but for the artificial means by which food is procured and life maintained, namely, money. The fierce animal struggle has evolved into the more kindly human one; in place of the bloody strife with tooth and claw there is the more amicable combat of wit and skill. Man has discovered— though he has as yet only partially learned this—that there are better methods of self-protection than that of attacking, killing and despoiling others, that by such a method he endangers his own comfort, happiness, and even life, and that it is better to engage in a bloodless competition for supremacy and leave every person to take his place in life according to the measure of his mental capacity. Right has begun to take the place of might, and although the struggle is largely one for money, it is not altogether so, but is surely evolving into one for the securing of those mental qualities which increase man's nobility, and better fit him as an instrument of life and progress; such are the intellectual qualities of reason, judgment, tact, foresight, ingenuity, resource, inventiveness; and the moral qualities of kindness, forbearance, sympathy, forgiveness, reverence, honesty, justice. Human education at present is almost entirely along these intellectual and moral lines. The instruments by which man struggles with man for the capacity to live and to endure are faculties, not fangs; talents, not talons.

Intellectual and moral excellence constitute the passport to existence in the human world.

The intellectually vigorous and the morally upright take the lead in the race of life. Nevertheless, the weaker ones take their place, and have scope and opportunity for development. Slowly man is learning that in the protection of others—the weak, the suffering and the afflicted—he is affording a surer protection for himself.

In such methods of self-protection we perceive an enormous advance upon the savage instinct of the brute. Commerce, crafts, and games take the place of plunder and destruction; and limited animal affection is enlarged to benevolence and philanthropy. In human competition the brute still lurks, but its ferocity is subdued, its nature is largely transmuted into something better, more beneficent; its dark horror is lightened up with the warm rays of kindness; its harshness is softened by the gentleness of a larger and ever-increasing love.

But high as is human over animal self-protection, there is another form of self-protection that is as high above the human as that is above the animal, and that is divine, or spiritual protection. By this method the man does not fight with others physically, after the manner of the brute, he does not struggle with others mentally, as does the human being; he fights with the brute within himself, in order to annihilate it; he struggles with the greed in his own nature, that he may fit himself to live the higher, nobler, more enduring life of peace, good-will and wisdom.

In divine protection, the fierce struggle with others is at an end, the competition of self-interest is no more, and the weapons employed are self-sacrifice and non-resistance. And these weapons can only be understood and employed by him whose moral elevation is such as to gain him admittance to the World of Divine Things. Just as the fanged and taloned brute cannot grasp and use those mental weapons of resource and inventiveness which the more highly endowed and talented human being employs with such ease and power, so the self-seeking man cannot comprehend and wield those instruments of self-sacrifice and non-resistance with which the divine man not merely shields himself, but protects the whole world.

Self-interest, resistance to, and competition with others are the most powerful factors in the purely human life, but in the divine life, self-obliteration and deep-felt sympathy with and compassion for others are the dominant motives.

The divine man conquers by non-retaliation, and by yielding where others enter into selfish strife; and his gentle powers are so invincible that the lesser selfish powers, great and potent as those are when compared with the merely animal equipments, dissolve away in ineffectual weakness. As bestial instincts cannot vie with human powers, so human powers cannot stand against divine principles, and the divine man stands upon, and acts upon, such principles. In him the human qualities mentioned are merged into the divine principles of Patience, Humility, Purity, Compassion and Love.

Both the animal and the human are concerned only with the protection and preservation of the body which is temporal, but the divine man's preservation is concerned with the spirit which is eternal, like the principles upon which he stands. In a word, divine preservation consists in preserving the mind from passion and selfishness, and imbuing it with pureness and wisdom.

We get a glimpse into the vast power inherent in self-sacrifice and non-resistance when we contemplate the lives and characters of the few divine men who practiced these principles—in Jesus,

Buddha, and others. All men, broadly speaking, yield and bow down to these great Masters in Divine Things. Men who have reached the greatest heights in worldly achievement—monarchs, conquerors, successful generals, statesmen, orators, financiers—bow in humble reverence and awe before the names of those Great Ones, recognizing intuitively that their own conquests and achievements, with all their worldly glory, are as nothing compared with that supreme self-conquest, that mighty spiritual achievement which those gentle teachers of mankind exhibited. To-day some five hundred millions of people bow down to Buddha as their Guide and Master, and some three hundred millions likewise bend before Jesus as their Savior and the Keeper of their lives.

In these three methods of self-protection—animal, human, and spiritual—we perceive the fundamental forces which are at work in the evolution of sentient beings; an evolution beginning with the lowest creature and extending to the divinest being of whom we have any direct knowledge. We also see that there is no inherent evil in any of these methods, that all are equally legitimate, and belong to the cosmic order of things. Each in its own sphere is right and necessary, leading to higher and higher intelligence, and deeper and deeper knowledge. The animal defends itself in accordance with its nature and the limits of its knowledge; the human being protects itself likewise in harmony with the dictates of his human nature; and the divine being eternally preserves himself in peace and blessedness by virtue of his clearer insight and deeper wisdom.

Nor is any measure of force lost during the process of evolution. The brute passion is, in man, transmuted into intellectual and moral energy, and in the divine man both are merged into control and equanimity.

AVIATION AND THE
NEW CONSCIOUSNESS

Dr. Bucke in his work, *"Cosmic Consciousness,"* published some ten years ago, stated that aërial navigation would become an accomplished fact in the near future, and that it would revolutionize the social and economic conditions of the world.

So far as the advent of the new means of travel is concerned, he has proved to be a true prophet, and I am convinced that his prophecy of its revolutionizing aspect will shortly begin to be proved true. Of this great revolution in its completion Dr. Bucke says:

> Before aërial navigation boundaries, tariffs, and, perhaps, distinctions of language will fade out. Great cities will no longer have reason for being and will melt away. The men who now dwell in cities will inhabit in summer the mountains and the seashores; building often in airy and beautiful spots, now almost or quite inaccessible, commanding the most extensive and magnificent views. In the winter they will probably dwell in communities of moderate size. As the herding together, as now, in great cities, so the isolation of the worker of the soil will become a thing of the past. Space will be practically annihilated, there will be no crowding together and no enforced solitude.

The above is a beautiful picture of the result upon human society, of the discovery of aviation, and it will no doubt prove true. Not that such a condition will be brought about rapidly. It will at least require several hundred years, and it is highly probable that it will be several thousand years before it is fully realized. As yet we are only in the crudest beginnings of flying, and the mastery of the air as a medium of human transit affords more scope for improvement and invention than any of the mechanical modes of locomotion hitherto employed. Invention will follow upon invention, through a long period of time, until men will be able to propel themselves through the air with a swiftness, a safety, and a skill perhaps equal to that of the migratory birds of the swiftest type. It was Edison who long years ago declared that the ultimate and perfected flying-machine would be built on the principle of the bird. While conforming more or less to this principle, the present machines are more on the principle of the kite, the motor-driving power taking the place of the string. In his book, *"The Coming Race,"* Lord Lytton describes the individuals of that race as each possessing a pair of mechanical wings which were under the complete control of the operator, and by means of which he soared into the air and propelled himself gracefully through space. Doubtless this will be the form which the perfected flying-machine will take, and it conforms to that "principle of the bird" referred to by Edison.

But the phase of aviation with which we are here concerned is that which connects it with the evolving consciousness of man; for out of that self-consciousness, which is now man's dominant condition, and which is inevitably connected with struggle and suffering, with labor and sorrow, the beginnings of a higher, diviner form of consciousness are making their appearances. From man's present state of imperfection, combined with ceaseless aspiration toward a better, but as yet undefined, state, there is surely coming, as from a matrix, a new order of life, a more blessed condition, a greatly evolved form of consciousness hitherto unknown to man except in a few isolated cases.

Invention is allied to progress, is, indeed, an outward manifestation of inward growth. All man's inventions are adaptations to his expanding consciousness, and they definitely mark important turning points in the evolution of the race. At the moment of man's necessity, the new and needed thing appears. Just as the human intellect was preparing to break from the bonds of old superstitions, and sally forth in joyous and untrammeled freedom, the printing press appeared as the chief instrument of man's liberation. The coming of the steam engine tallied with the accelerated speed of human thought as it began to shake off its ancient lethargy; and when the expanding human mind could no longer move in a contracted local circle, or remain satisfied with petty selfish differences, the locomotive came forth to meet man's wider range, and to afford him scope for his increased mental activities and enlarged sympathies.

And now another invention has entered the field of actuality; one growing out of, yet more important than, any which have preceded it—that of flying. Man has hitherto employed the solid earth and the less solid water as the medium of material transit, but now he is to make an obedient servant of the tenuous atmosphere, using it to speed, bird-like, directly to his desired destination. And this is an important outward sign of the new stride in evolution which the race is now taking. Rapid and restless changes are marking the present transition period. Old religions and forms of government are passing away. New modes of thought and action are everywhere appearing. Man's consciousness is expanding. The *human* form of consciousness is about to touch, is indeed touching, the point of completion, and from it there will spring, is already springing, the *Divine* form of consciousness which is destined to transform the entire human race. For under that reign of consciousness, nearly everything, as it at present obtains in the world, will be reversed. Man, being then Divine, will act divinely. All those powerful human passions which now dominate the race, and are the chief springs of action will then take a subordinate place, and will be under the control and guidance of man's Divine will and wisdom. He will be master of himself and master of the earth.

Already man has been feeling the growing wings of this new consciousness wherewith he will soar into the highest regions of knowledge and blessedness. For ages, and under the guise of numerous religions, he has aspired to it, and the prophets have foretold it, and now he is to obtain his Divine birthright.

Aviation is the first outward symbol, as it were, of this new mind which is now taking shape. It is also more than a symbol, for it will form the first important material instrument by the aid of which the new consciousness will begin to materialize its glorious ideas and magnificent schemes for the happiness of the race, for the so-called happiness of to-day is misery compared with that blessed state which will obtain on the earth when the Divine condition has become well established.

The beginnings of this new condition, as aided by aviation, will be noticed in the breaking down of certain material limitations between man and man and between nations, and the disappearance of war; along with it will come a free and fraternal industrial intercourse between the nations, and a growing tendency to adopt in practice those fundamental religious principles which are universal, and thus to inaugurate one great world-wide religion. As aviation becomes more perfected, and enters into man's economical schemes, these new conditions—the first seedlings, as it were, of the new consciousness—will begin to appear, for when men are rapidly flitting from country to country, from continent to continent, on "the wings of the wind" they will be brought so close together, both socially and industrially, that the old animosities, which now exist between them, will die out, the old national barriers will quietly break down and disappear, and, without any revolutionary upheaval, the nations will become as one country, sinking all those interests which are not for the mutual good of all nations.

The locomotive is an instance of the above, though in the region of self-consciousness, in that it rendered civil war impossible, making of each nation, formerly divided against itself, a united family working harmoniously together. Aviation, however, will be connected with a higher region of consciousness altogether, namely, the cosmic consciousness, and its results will be much more striking and more far-reaching than those which have hitherto taken place in man's self-conscious condition.

At present we are only in the experimental stage of aviation, but this will be quickly followed by the economic stage, in which flying will be adapted to human travel and mercantile uses, and almost immediately this is reached the new conditions in societies and nations will begin to manifest themselves, and once having commenced, they will gradually absorb the old forms of life, using them as material on which to feed their growing beauty and grandeur. And new and grand men will arise having this higher consciousness, and they will be the leading instruments in establishing this new order of things upon the earth.

THE NEW COURAGE

The virtue of courage is generally referred to in its physical manifestation, and it is significant in this particular—that its symbol is a beast of prey, namely, the lion. The dictionary rendering adheres to this physical aspect of courage, for on turning up the word I find its meanings are given as "bravery, fearlessness, intrepidity"; no other rendering being given. The soldier is the human type of courage, and the current sayings concerning courage are: "As courageous as a lion" and "As brave as a soldier."

The lion and the soldier are alike fearless in attack and defense, and both will forfeit life rather than yield; but it is an entirely animal physical attack and defense. Courage, however, cannot be confined to this phase—indeed, this is its lowest manifestation,—for it has many aspects, many modes of action, and as man rises in the moral and spiritual scale, his courage becomes transmuted, taking a newer and higher form; but before proceeding to the highest form of courage, which is the subject of this article, it is necessary that the lower forms should be first considered.

With the physical form of courage already referred to all are familiar. It is common both to animals and men. It arises in fearlessness. Its two-fold mode of action is *attack and defense.* It will be seen, however, that this kind of courage is inevitably associated with suffering, even with destruction and death, as daily manifested both in the animal and human spheres of life; self-protection being its dominant motive, whether in attack or defense.

But man is not only and merely an animal, a physical being; he is also a moral and intellectual being; and along with his moral evolution he began to develop a higher kind of courage—not the highest or the *New Courage* herein referred to; but yet a great advance on the purely animal courage—namely, *moral courage.* In physical courage the other person's body or property is attacked, while one's own body or property is defended. In moral courage the other person's ideas, opinions, or principles are attacked, one's own ideas, opinions, and principles being defended. There is the same fearlessness, the same attack and defense so far as the spirit of courage is concerned, but as regards its letter, these conditions have undergone a change; their physical aspect has disappeared, and, having undergone a process of transmutation, has reappeared in a new form, for moral courage is concerned, not with persons as persons, but with their principles; it is, indeed, purely mental, and while it is still concerned with destruction and is associated with suffering, the destruction is a bloodless and intellectual one, namely, the destruction of other men's opinions, and its suffering is mental and not physical.

This form of courage is now generally recognized, and is always referred to as *moral courage,* to distinguish it from common or physical courage. It is, without doubt, a comparatively recent development in the evolution of the race, and is entirely absent from animals. A few thousand years ago it was, in all probability, an exceeding rare and new faculty, and it is still in process of development, large numbers of the race not yet having evolved it; for while it is probable that at least seventy-five per cent of the race possess a considerable development of physical courage, it is doubtful whether twenty per cent possess any marked degree of moral courage; so much so that those in full possession of it are marked off from their fellows as men of a higher grade of character, and generally—though not necessarily and always—as leaders of men in their particular sphere of action.

But the New Courage, up to a consideration of which the preceding remarks have been leading, is a still higher form of courage; is, indeed, as much above and beyond moral courage as moral courage is above and beyond physical courage; and is as separate and distinct from it as that is from its precedent form. I have called it the New Courage because it is now new in the race; its manifestation being at present very rare, and, therefore, little understood. Though very different from moral courage, it results from it, just as moral courage though very different from physical courage results from it. Physical courage is of the animal; moral courage is of the human; the New Courage is of the Divine. The New Courage is, therefore, Divine fearlessness as distinguished from animal or human fearlessness.

This Divine fearlessness has a two-fold aspect. It at first consists in fearlessly attacking and overcoming the enemies within one's own mind—instead of the enemies without, as in the other two forms of courage—and is afterwards characterized by an entirely new method of conduct toward others, especially where external enmity and opposition have to be met. It is its latter and perfected stage with which we are here concerned—that is, with its outward manifestation.

We have seen how a man having physical courage acts in defense of his life and property; also how a man having moral courage acts in defense of his opinions; and now, how does one act who has Divine courage?

He who has the New Courage does not attack other men or defend himself; does not attack their opinions or defend his own; he is the defender of all men, and that from which he defends them is their own folly, their own ungoverned passions. While never seeking to protect himself, he so acts as to shield others from their deadliest enemy, namely, the evil within themselves.

Both physical and moral courage make much noise. In the one there is the clash of arms and the roar of artillery, along with the shouts of the victorious and the groans of the dying; in the other, there is the fierce war of opinions and the clamor of conflicting tongues. But in the New Courage there is a profound silence; yet this silence has more influence and enduring power in *one man* than that noise has in entire humanity. The New Courage may, indeed, be described as *the courage to be silent.* Thus, when the man of Divine courage is attacked, abused, or slandered, he remains serenely silent. Yet this is not a proud and selfish silence. It is a silence based upon a right knowledge of life, and having a profound and beneficent purpose; that purpose being the good of the attacking person (and, through him, of all mankind) by protecting him from the evil passion by which he is so injuriously influenced.

To remain silent, calm, and compassionate in the midst of a seething sea of human passions externally pressing upon one—to achieve this requires a lofty courage such as is yet almost unknown to men; so much so that the few men who have it, although misunderstood and persecuted through life, are afterwards worshiped by mankind as Divine and miraculous beings. And here we see how this courage continues to operate even after its possessor is gone from mortal vision. The physically courageous man conquers another in fight; the morally courageous man conquers the opinions of many men, and wins thousands to his cause; but the divinely courageous man conquers the world, and his conquest is one of blessedness and peace, and not of bloodshed or party strife.

In the New Courage, attack and defense, as they obtain in the two lower kinds of courage, have entirely disappeared; nevertheless, they have not been destroyed; they still exist in the spirit, but have become blended into one, have been transmuted into a sublime and universal *kindness;* for when the Divine man refrains from engaging in combat with his adversary, and lets him go feeling that he has all the victory, it is because his thought is all for his mistaken enemy, and not for his own defense. He is prompted by a profound compassion for his enemy, a compassion based on Divine and perfect knowledge; and if his silent act does not always subdue the passions of his adversary at the time being, it subdues the passions of thousands of men through hundreds of future generations, merely by its recital; so great and far-reaching is the power of one deed of truth.

In the New Courage, then, silent kindness (and by this is meant something vastly different from that human impulse commonly called kindness) is both attack and defense. Instead of attempting to conquer passion by fiercer passion—which is the human way—it conquers it, and far more successfully, by its opposite, namely, *gentleness,* which is the Divine way. In the human sense, passion is not opposed at all, but is left alone; yet, in reality, it is opposed by something far more powerful than passion, for in all combats between Divine gentleness and human passion gentleness is the supreme victor. Thus, the man of Divine courage, while viewed from the lower standards of bravery, is not protecting or defending himself, and may for the time being be regarded as a coward, is, in reality, defending himself far more perfectly and successfully than the passionate fighters and partisans; for he who protects his enemy with love, and shields all men with the acts of Divine gentleness, is throwing around himself an eternal shield and protection.

For instances of this New Courage one has to go to the Great Spiritual Leaders of the race, so rare is it. The most striking instance is that of Jesus, who, when mocked, smitten, and crucified, did not retaliate, or offer the least resistance, or speak a word in self-defense; and the fact that the rabble taunted Him with the accusation "He saved others, Himself He cannot save" seems to show that they regarded Him both as an impostor and a coward. Think of the sublime courage required to pass through such an ordeal, and you will have some conception as to how far the New Courage transcends the ordinary human forms of bravery. That transcendent act of courage, too, is to-day universally recognized as Divine, and it still continues to lift men above their warring, selfish passions.

When the Buddha was abused and falsely accused by his enemies He always remained silent, and it not infrequently happened that those who came as accusing enemies went away as worshiping friends and disciples, so powerful was His silent gentleness.

It will be long, as we count time, before such courage becomes general in the race; but everything is making toward it. Other men will come who possess it, and then more and more, until at last the race will stand at this Divine level; then selfishness and sorrow will be ended, and the painful conflict of human passions will no more be heard upon earth.

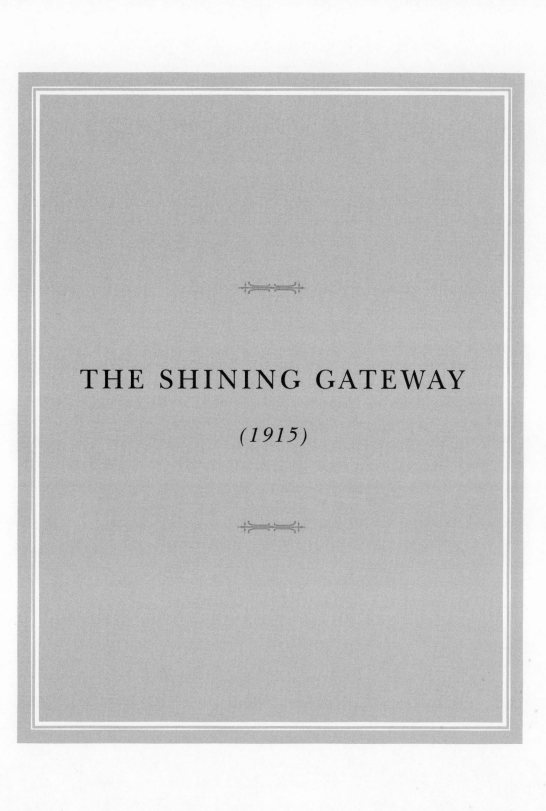

THE SHINING GATEWAY

(1915)

EDITOR'S FOREWORD

Students of the works of James Allen all over the world will welcome with joy another book from his able pen. In this work we find the *Prophet of Meditation* in one of his deepest and yet most lucid expositions. How wonderfully he deals with fundamental principles! Here the reader will find no vague statement of generalities, for the writer enters with tender reverence into every detail of human experience. It is as though he came back to *The Shining Gate,* and, standing there, he reviewed all the way up which his own feet have travelled, passing over no temptation that is common to man; knowing that the obstacles that barred his ascending pathway, or the clouds that at times obscured his vision, are the common experiences of all those who have set their faces towards the heights of Blessed Vision. As we read his words now, he seems to stand and beckon to us, saying, "Come on, my fellow Pilgrims; it is straight ahead to the Shining Gateway; I have blazed the track for you." In sending forth this, another posthumous volume from his pen, we have no doubt but that it will help many and many an aspiring soul up to the heights, until at last they too stand within *The Shining Gateway.*

—LILY L. ALLEN
Bryngoleu,
Ilfracombe, England

CONTENTS

THE SHINING GATEWAY
OF MEDITATION

Be watchful, fearless, faithful, patient, pure:
By earnest meditation sound the depths
Profound of life, and scale the heights sublime
Of Love and Wisdom. He who does not find
The Way of Meditation cannot reach
Emancipation and enlightenment.

The unregenerate man is subject to these three things—*desire, passion, sorrow.* He lives habitually in these conditions, and neither questions nor examines them. He regards them as his life itself, and cannot conceive of any life apart from them. To-day he desires, to-morrow he indulges his passions, and the third day he grieves; by these three things (which are always found together) he is impelled, and does not know why he is so impelled; the inner forces of desire and passion arise, almost automatically, within him, and he gratifies their demands *sans* question; led on blindly by his blind desires, he falls, periodically, into the ditches of remorse and sorrow. His condition is not merely unintelligible to him, it is unperceived; for so immersed is he in the desire (or self) consciousness that he cannot step outside of it, as it were, to examine it.

To such a man the idea of rising above desire and suffering into a new life where such things do not obtain seems ridiculous. He associates all life with *the pleasurable gratification of desire,* and so, by the law of reaction, he also lives in the misery of afflictions, fluctuating ceaselessly between pleasure and pain.

When reflection dawns in the mind, there arises a sense (dim and uncertain at first) of a calmer, wiser, and loftier life; and as the stages of introspection and self-analysis are reached, this sense increases in clearness and intensity, so that by the time the first three stages are fully completed, a conviction of the reality of such a life and of the possibility of attaining it is firmly fixed in the mind. Such conviction, which consists of a steadfast belief in the supremacy of purity and goodness over desire and passion, is called *faith.* Such faith is the stay, support, and comfort of the man who, while yet in the darkness, is searching earnestly for the Light, which breaks upon him for the first time in all its dazzling splendour and ineffable majesty when he enters the Shining Gateway of Meditation. Without such faith he could not stand for a single day against the trials, failures, and difficulties which beset him continually, much less could he courageously fight and overcome them, and his final conquest and salvation would be impossible.

Upon entering the stage of meditation, faith gradually ripens into knowledge, and the new regenerate life begins to be realised in its quiet wisdom, calm beauty, and ordered strength, and day by day its joy and splendour increase.

The final conquest over sin is now assured. Lust, hatred, anger, covetousness, pride and vanity, desire for pleasure, wealth, and fame, worldly honour and power—all these have become dead things shortly to pass away for ever; there is no more life nor happiness in them; they have no part in the life of the regenerate one, who knows that he can never again go back to them, for now the "old man" of self and sin is dead, and the "new man" of Love and Purity is born within him. He has become (or becomes, as the process of meditation ripens and bears fruit) a new being, one in whom Purity, Love, Wisdom, and Peacefulness are the ruling qualities, and wherein strifes, envies, suspicions, hatreds, and jealousies cannot find lodgment. "Old things have passed away, and, behold, all things have become new"; men and things are seen in a different light, and a new universe is unveiled; there is no confusion; as out of the inner chaos of conflicting desires, passions, and sufferings the new being arises, there arises in the outer world of apparently irreconcilable conditions a new Cosmos, ordered, sequential, harmonious, ineffably glorious, faultless in equity.

Meditation is a process both of *purification* and *adjustment.* Aspiration is the purifying element, and the harmonising power resides in the intellectual train of thought involved.

When the stage of meditation is reached and entered upon, two distinct processes of spiritual transmutation are reached and entered upon, two distinct processes of spiritual transmutation begin to take place, namely:

1. Transmutation of passion
2. Transmutation of affliction

The two conditions proceed simultaneously, as they are interdependent, and act and react one upon the other. Passion and affliction, or sin and suffering, are two aspects of one thing, namely, the *self* in man, that self which is the source of all the troubles which afflict mankind. They represent *power,* but power wrongly used. Passion is a lower manifestation of a divine energy which possesses a higher use and application. Affliction is the limitation and negation of that energy, and is therefore a means of restoring harmony. It says, in effect, to the self-bound man, "Thus far shalt thou go and no farther." The man of meditation transfers the passional energy from the realm of evil (self-following) to the realm of good (self-overcoming). To-day he reflects, to-morrow he overcomes his passions, and the third day he rejoices. The mind is drawn from its downward tendency, and is directed upwards. The base metal of error is transmuted into the pure gold of Truth. Lust, hatred, and selfishness disappear; and purity, love, and goodwill take their place. As the stage proceeds, the mind becomes more and more firmly fixed in the higher manifestations, and it becomes increasingly difficult for it to think and act in the lower; and just in the measure that the mind is freed from the lower, violent, and inharmonious activities, just so much is passion transmuted into power, and affliction into bliss.

This means that there is no such thing as affliction to the sinless man. When sin is put away, affliction disappears.

Selfhood is the source of suffering; Truth is the source of bliss.

When the unregenerate man is abused, slandered, misunderstood, or persecuted, it causes him intense suffering; but when these things are brought to bear on the regenerate man, there arises in him the rapture of heavenly bliss. None but he who has put away the great enemy, self, under his feet can fully enter into and understand the saying:

> ye, when men shall revile you, and persecute you, and shall say all manner of evil against you falsely, for my sake. Rejoice, and be exceeding glad.

And why does the righteous (regenerate) man rejoice under those conditions which cause such misery to the unrighteous (unregenerate) man? It is because, having overcome the evil in himself, he ceases to see evil without. To the good man all things are good, and he utilises everything for the good of the world. To him persecution is not an evil; it is a good. Having acquired insight, knowledge, and power, he, by meeting that persecution in a loving spirit, helps and uplifts his persecutors, and accelerates their spiritual progress, though they themselves know it not at the time. Thus he is filled with unspeakable bliss because he has conquered the forces of evil; because, instead of succumbing to those forces, he has learned how to use and direct them for the good and gain of mankind. He is blessed because he is at one with all men, because he is reconciled to the universe, and has brought himself into harmony with the Cosmic Order.

The following symbol will perhaps help the mind of the reader to more readily grasp what has been explained:

LOVE, LIGHT, AND LIFE

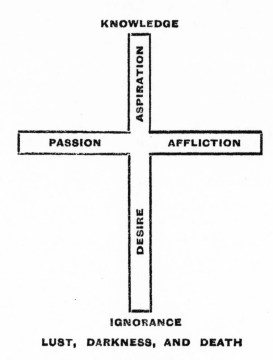

LUST, DARKNESS, AND DEATH

There is at first the underworld of *lust, darkness,* and *death,* which is associated with ignorance; rooted in this is the foot of the cross—*desire*; in the body of the cross, desire branches out into two arms—the right (active or positive) arm, *passion,* being equalised and balanced by the left (passive or negative) arm of affliction; uniting these, and rising out of them at the head of the cross, is aspiration; here, wounded and bleeding, rests the thorn-crowned head of humanity; at the end of this, and right at the summit of the cross, is *knowledge,* which, while being at the apex of the self-life, is the base of the Truth-life; and above rises the heavenly world of *Love, Light,* and *Life.*

In this supremely beautiful world the regenerate man lives, even while living on this earth. He has reached Nirvana, the Kingdom of Heaven. He has taken up his cross, and there is no more sin and suffering; desire and passion and affliction are passed away. Harmony is restored, and all is bliss and peace.

The cross is the symbol of pain. Desire is painful, passion is painful, affliction is painful, and aspiration is painful; this is why these things are symbolised by a cross which has two pairs of conflicting poles. Affliction is the harmonising and purifying element in passion; aspiration is the harmonising and purifying element in desire. Where the one is, the other must be also. Take away the one, and the other disappears. Suffering, or affliction, is necessary to counteract passion; aspiration, or prayer, is necessary to purge away desire; but for the regenerate man all these things are ended; he has risen into a new life and a new order of things—the consciousness of purity; lacking nothing, and being at one with all things, he does not need to pray for anything; redeemed and reconciled, contented and in peace, he finds nothing in the universe to hate or fear, and his is both the duty and the power to work without ceasing for the present good and the ultimate salvation of mankind.

TEMPTATION

I know that sorrow follows passion; know
That grief and emptiness and heartache wait
Upon all earthly joys; so am I sad;
Yet Truth must be, and being, can be found;
And though I am in sorrow, this I know—
I shall be glad when I have found the Truth.

The only external tempters of man are *the objects of sensation.* These, however, are powerless *in themselves* until they are reflected in his mind as desirable objects to possess. His only enemy, therefore, is his *coveting of the objects of sensation.* By ceasing to covet objects of sensation, temptation and the painful fighting against impure desires pass away. This ceasing to covet objects of sensation is called the *relinquishing of* desire; it is *the renunciation of the inner defilement,* by which a man ceases to be the slave of outward things, and becomes their master.

Temptation is a growth, a process more or less slow, the duration of which can be measured by the sage who has gained accurate knowledge of the nature of his thoughts and acts and the laws governing them, by virtue of having subjected himself to a long course of training in mental discipline and self-control. It has its five stages, which can be clearly defined, and their development traced with precision. But the man who is still immersed in temptation has, as yet, little or no knowledge of the nature of his thoughts and acts and the laws governing them. He has lived so long in outward things—in the objects of sensation—and has given so little time to introspection and the cleansing of his heart, that he lives in almost total ignorance of the real nature of his thoughts and acts which he thinks and commits every day. To him, temptation seems to be instantaneous, and his power- lessness to combat the sudden and, apparently, unaccountable onslaught, causes him to regard it as a *mystery*, and mystery being the mother of superstition, he may—and usually does—fall back upon some speculative belief to account for his trouble, such as the belief in an invisible Evil Being, or power, outside himself, who suddenly, and without warning, attacks and torments him. Such a superstition renders him more powerless still, for he has sufficient knowledge to understand that he cannot hope to successfully cope with a being more powerful than himself, and of whose where- abouts and tactics he is altogether unacquainted; and so he introduces other beliefs and supersti- tions which his dilemma seems to necessitate, until at last, in addition to all his sins and sufferings, he becomes burdened with a mass of supernatural beliefs which engross his attention, and take him farther and farther away from the real cause of his difficulty. Meantime he continues to be tempted and to fall, and must do so until by self-subjugation and self-purification he has acquired the abil- ity to trace the relation between cause and effect in his spiritual nature, when, with purified and enlightened vision, he will see that *the moment of temptation is but the fulfilment of those impure desires which he secretly harbours in his own heart.* And, later, with a still purer heart, and when he has gained sufficient control over his wandering thoughts to be able to analyse and understand them, he will see that *the actual moment of temptation itself* has its inception, its growth, and its fruition.

What, then, are the stages in temptation? And how is the process of temptation born in the mind? How does it grow and bear its bitter fruit? The stages are five, and are as follows: 1. *Perception*; 2. *Cogitation*; 3. *Conception*; 4. *Attraction*; and 5. *Desire*.

The first stage is that in which objects of sensation are *perceived as objects.* This is pure percep- tion, and is without sin or defilement. The second stage is that in which objects of sensation are *considered as objects of personal pleasure.* This is a brooding of the mind upon objects, with an unde- fined groping for pleasurable sensation, and is the beginning of defilement and sin. In the third stage objects of sensation are *conceived as objects of pleasure.* In this stage the objects are associated with certain pleasurable sensations, and these sensations are conceived and called up vividly in the mind. In the fourth stage objects of sensation are *perceived as objects of pleasure.* At this stage the pleasure as connected with the object is distinctly defined, yet there is a confusion of *pleasure* and *object*, so that the two appear as one, and a wish to possess the object arises in the mind; there is also a going out of the mind towards the object. The fifth and last stage is an intense desire, a coveting and lusting to possess the object in order to experience the pleasure and gratification which it will afford. With every repetition, in the mind, of the first four stages, this desire is added to, as fuel is added to fire, and it increases in intensity and ardour until at last the whole being is aflame with a burning passion which is blind to everything but its own immediate pleasure and gratification. And when this painful fruition of thought is reached, a man is said to be tempted. There is a still further stage of Action, which is merely the doing of the thing desired, the outworking of the sin already committed in the mind. From desire to action is but a short step.

The following table will better enable the mind of the reader to grasp the process and principle involved:

INACTION—*HOLINESS; REST*

1.	Perception	Objects of Sensation *perceived* as such.
2.	Cogitation	Objects of Sensation *considered* as a source of pleasure.
3.	Conception	Objects of Sensation *conceived* as affording pleasure.
4.	Attraction	Objects of Sensation *perceived* as pleasurable in possession.
5.	Desire	Objects of Sensation *coveted* as such: *i.e.*, desired for personal delight and pleasure.

ACTION—*SIN; UNREST*

Every time a man is tempted, he passes, from *Inaction,* through all the five stages in succession, and his fall is a passing on into *Action.* The process varies greatly in duration according to the nature of the temptation and the character of the tempted; but after much yielding and many falls, the mind becomes so familiar with the transition that it passes through all the stages with such rapidity as to make the temptation appear as an instantaneous, indivisible experience.

The sage, however, never loses sight of the duration of time occupied in the process of temptation, but watches its growth and transition; and just as the scientist can measure the time occupied in the transition of sensation from the brain to the bodily extremities, or from the extremities to the brain, which, ordinarily, appears not to occupy duration, so the sage measures (though by a different method) the passage from pure perception to inflamed desire in a sudden experience of temptation.

This knowledge of the nature of temptation destroys its power, or rather its *apparent* power, for power exists in holiness only. Ignorance is at the root of all sin, and it fades away when knowledge is

admitted into the mind. Just as darkness and the effects of darkness disappear when light is introduced, so sin and its effects are dispersed when knowledge of one's spiritual nature is acquired and
embraced.

How, then, does the sage avoid sin and remain in peace? Knowing the nature of sinful acts—how
they are the result of temptation; knowing also the nature of temptation—how it is the end and
fruition of a particular train of thought, *he cuts off that train of thought at its commencement,* not
allowing his mind to go out into the world of sensation, which is the world of pain and sorrow. He
stands over his mind, eternally vigilant, and does not allow his thoughts to pass beyond the safe
gates of *pure perception.* To him "all things are pure" because his mind is pure. He sees all objects,
whether material or mental, *as they are,* and not as the pleasure-seeker sees them—as objects of personal enjoyment; nor as the tempted one sees them—as sources of evil and pain. His normal sphere,
however, is that of *Inaction,* which is perfect holiness and rest. This is a position of entire indifference to considerations of pleasure and pain, regarding all things from the standpoint of *right,* and
not from that of *enjoyment.* Is, then, the sage, the sinless one, deprived of all enjoyment? Is his life
a dead monotony of inaction—inertia? Truly, he is delivered from all those sensory excitements
which the world calls "pleasure," but which conceal, as a mask, the drawn features of pain; and,
being released from the bondage of cravings and pleasures, he lives without ceasing in the divine,
abiding joy which the pleasure-seeker and the wanderer in sin can neither know nor understand;
but *inaction* in this particular means inaction as regards sin; inaction in the lower animal activities
which, being cut off, their energy is transferred to the higher intellectual and moral activities, releasing their power, and giving them untrammelled scope and freedom.

Thus the sage avoids sin by extracting its root within himself, not allowing it to grow into attraction, to blossom into desire, and to bear the bitter fruits of sinful actions. The unwise man, however,
allows the thought of pleasure to take root in his mind, where its growth evokes sensations which
are pleasant to him, and on these sensations he dwells with enjoyment, thinking in his heart, "So
long as I do not commit the sinful act, I am free from sin." He does not know that his thoughts are
causes the effects of which are actions, and that there is *no escape from sinful acts for him who dwells
in sinful thoughts.* And so the process develops in his mind and blossoms into desire, and in the final
moment of temptation (which is but the moment of opportunity brought into prominence by that
desire), with the coveted object at his unreserved command, the fall of the man into sinful action
is swift and certain.

REGENERATION

Submit to naught but nobleness; rejoice
Like a strong athlete straining for the prize,
When thy full strength is tried; be not the slave
Of lusts and cravings and indulgences,
Of disappointments, miseries, and griefs,
Fears, doubts, and lamentations, but control
Thyself with calmness; master that in thee
Which masters others, and which heretofore
Has mastered thee; let not thy passions rule,
But rule thy passions; subjugate thyself
Till passion is transmuted into peace,
And wisdom crown thee; so shalt thou attain
And, by attaining, know.

Having considered and examined the nature of temptation in its five interdependent stages, let us now turn to the process of regeneration, and also consider its nature, so that the reader who has already received some measure of enlightenment may be still further guided in his strenuous climbing towards the Perfect Life.

The five stages in regeneration (already enumerated) are: 1. Reflection; 2. Introspection; 3. Self-analysis; 4. Meditation; and 5. Pure Perception.

The first stage in a pure and true life is that of *thoughtfulness.* The thoughtless cannot enter the right way in life. Only the reflective mind can acquire wisdom. When a man, ceasing to go after enjoyment, brings himself to a standstill in order to examine his position, and to reflect upon the condition of the world and the meaning of life, then he has entered upon the first stage of regeneration. When a man begins to think seriously, and with a deep and noble purpose in view, he has stepped out of the broad way where the thoughtless and the frivolous clutch at the bubbles of pleasure, and has entered the narrow way where the thoughtful and the wise comprehend eternal verities. Such a man's liberation from sin and suffering is already assured; for though he is, as yet, surrounded by much uncertainty, he is already realising a foretaste of the peace which awaits him; his passions, though still strong, are quieter; his mind is calmer and clearer; his intercourse with others is purer and graver; and in his moments of deepest thought he sees, as in a vision, the strength and calmness and wisdom which he knows will one day be his well-earned possessions.

Thus he passes on to the second stage.

Reflecting day by day, with ever-increasing earnestness, upon life in all its phases, he comes to perceive the passions and desires in which men are involved, and realises the sorrows which are connected with their strangely ephemeral existence. He sees the burning fevers of lusts and ambitions and cravings for pleasure, and the chilling agues of anxieties and fears, and the uncertainty of slowly approaching death, and he aspires to know the meaning of it all; is eager to find the source and cause of what seems so sorrowful and inexplicable. Recognising himself as a unit in humanity, as one involved in like passions and sorrows with all other men, he vaguely understands that somehow the secret of all life is inevitably bound up with his own existence, and so, unsatisfied with the surface theories which are based on observation only, and which still leave him subject to passions and sorrows, and the prey of anxieties and fears, he turns his thoughts inwardly upon his own mind, thinking, perchance, that the wished-for revelation of wisdom and peace awaits him there. Thus he becomes *introspective,* and so he passes on to the third stage.

When the introspective habit is fully ripened and acquired, there is called up in the mind a subtle process of inductive thought by the aid of which the innermost recesses of the man's nature, and, therefore, of all humanity, begin to unveil themselves, and yield up their secrets to the penetrating insight of the patient searcher who, unravelling now the tangled threads of thought, and tracing out the warp and woof of the web of life as it is woven in the mental processes and by the swift-flying shuttle of thought, begins, for the first time, to somewhat clearly comprehend the inner causes of human deeds, and the meaning and purpose of existence. As this process of thought is proceeded with, the desires and passions are purified away from the mind; the calmness necessary to a right perception of Truth is acquired; and gradually the fixed principles of things are presented to the comprehension, and the eternal laws of life axe coherently grasped by the understanding.

And now, quietly, and almost as imperceptibly as the soft light of dawn stealing upon the sleeping world, the neophyte, with mind purified, calmed, and controlled, passes into the fourth stage, and opens his long-sleeping eyes upon the rising light of Truth. He becomes habitually meditative, and in meditation he finds the master-key which unlocks the Door of Knowledge. It is at this advanced stage in the process of regeneration that the sinner becomes the saint, and the pupil is transformed into the master; for here the process of transmutation, hitherto slow and painful, is greatly accelerated, so that the spiritual forces formerly spent in pleasures, gratifications, passions, and afflictions are now conserved, controlled, and turned into channels of productive and reproductive thought, and so wisdom is born in the mind, and bliss, and peace.

As skill and power are acquired in meditation, the fifth and last stage is reached, where the perfect insight of the seer and the sage is evolved, so that the facts of life are grasped, and the laws and principles of things stand revealed. Here the man is altogether regenerated, is purified and per-fected; all human passions are conquered, and human sorrows transcended. Here things are seen *as they are*; all the intricacies of life stand out naked in the light of Truth, and there is no more doubt and perplexity, no more sin and anguish; for he whose pure and enlightened eyes perceive the hid-den causes and effects which operate infallibly in human life—he who knows how the bitter fruits of passion ripen, and where the dark waters of sorrow spring—he it is who no more sins and no more sorrows. Lo! he has come to peace.

The five stages so passed through may be thus presented:

IGNORANCE—*SIN; SUFFERING*

1. Reflection   Deep and earnest thought on the nature and meaning of life.
2. Introspection   Looking inwardly for the causes and effects which operate in life.
3. Self-analysis   Searching the springs of thought and purifying the motives in
                         order to find the truth of life.
4. Meditation   Pure and discriminative thought on the facts and principles of life.
5. Pure Perception   Insight. Direct knowledge of the laws of life.

ENLIGHTENMENT—*PURITY; PEACE*

The whole process of regeneration may be likened to the growth of a plant. At first the small seed of *reflection* is cast into the dark soil of ignorance; then the little rootlets come forth and grope about for light and sustenance (introspection); next the strenuous *self-examination* is as the plant reaching upwards toward the light; and then the development of the bud and opening flower of *meditation,* ending at last in that pure and wise *insight* which is the spiritual glory of the sage, the perfect flower of enlightenment.

Thus beginning in sin and suffering, and passing through thoughtfulness, self-searching, self-purification, meditation, and insight, the seeker after the pure life and the divine wisdom reaches at last the undefiled habitation of a spotless life, and so passes beyond the dark halls of suf-fering, knowing the perfect Law.

ACTIONS AND MOTIVES

Obey the Right,
And wrong shall ne'er again assail thy peace,
Nor error hurt thee more: attune thy heart
To Purity, and thou shalt reach the Place
Where sorrow is not, and all evil ends.

It has been said that "the way to hell is paved with good intentions," and one frequently hears sin excused on the ground that it was done with a "good motive."

There are actions which are bad-in-themselves, and there are actions which are good-in-themselves, and good intentions cannot make the former good—selfish intentions cannot make the latter bad. Foremost among actions which are bad-in-themselves are those which are classified as "criminal" by all civilised communities. Thus murder, theft, adultery, libel, etc., are always bad, and it is not necessary to inquire into the motive which prompts them. Black and white remain black and white to all eternity, and are not altered by specious argumentations. A lie is eternally a lie, and no number of good intentions can turn it into a truth. If a man tell a lie with a good intention, he has none the less uttered a lie; if a man speak the truth with a selfish intention, he has none the less spoken the truth.

Besides those actions above mentioned, there are others which, while not classified by the law of the land as criminal, are yet recognised as wrong by nearly all intelligent people—actions pertaining to social and family life, and to our everyday relations with our fellowmen. Thus when a child wilfully violates its duty to its parents, the father does not stop to inquire into the motives of the child, but metes out the due correction, because the act of disobedience is *wrong-in-itself*.

The reader may here ask, "In being taught, then, to regard the motive, the condition of heart, as all important, and the act as secondary, have we been taught wrongly?" No, you have not. The motive *is* all important, for it determines the nature of the act, and here we must distinguish between *intentions* and *motives*. When people speak of good and bad motives, they nearly always mean good or bad intentions—that is, the action is done with a certain object, good or bad, in view. The motive is the deeply seated *cause* in the mind, the habitual condition of heart; the intention is the *purpose* in view. Thus an act may spring from an impure motive, yet be done with the best intention. It is possible for one to be involved in wrong motives, and yet at the same time to be so charged with good intentions as to be continually intruding himself on other people, and interfering in their business and their lives under the delusion that they "need his help."

Intentions are more or less superficial, and are largely matters of impulse, while motives are more deeply seated, and are concerned with a man's fixed moral condition. A man may do an action to-day with a good intention, and in a few weeks time do the same action with a bad intention; but in both instances the motive underlying the action will be the same.

In reality a wrong act cannot spring from a right motive, although it may be guided by a good intention. A man who can resort, whether habitually or under stress of temptation, to murder, theft, lying, or other actions known as bad, is in a dark, confused condition of mind, and is not capable of acting from right motives. Such acts can only spring from an impure source; and this is why the Great Teachers rarely refer to motives, but always refer to actions. In their precepts they tell us what actions are bad and what are good, without any reference to motive, for the bad and good acts-in-themselves are the fruits of bad and good motives. "By their fruits you shall know them."

In being exhorted to "judge not," we are not taught to persuade ourselves that grapes are figs and figs grapes, but must employ our judgment in clearly distinguishing between the two; so in like manner must we distinguish with unmistakable clearness between bad actions and good actions, so as to avoid the former and embrace the latter; for only in this way can one purify his heart and render himself capable of acting from right motives. A clear perception of what is bad or good, both in ourselves and others, is not false judgment, it is wisdom. It is only when one harbours groundless suspicion about others, and reads into their actions bad and selfish intentions, that he falls into that judging against which we are warned, and which is so pernicious.

There is no need to doubt the good intentions of those about us, while, at the same time, being fully alive to a knowledge of those bad actions which were better left undone, and those good actions which were better done; taking care not to do the former, and to do the latter ourselves, thus teaching by our lives instead of accusing and condemning others. Numberless wrong actions are committed every day with good intentions; and this is why so many good purposes are frustrated and end in disappointment, because the underlying motive is impure, and the good fruit which is sought does not appear; the act is out of harmony with the good intent; the means are not adapted to the end. Bad actions bring forth bitter fruit; good actions bring forth sweet fruit.

The law runs, "Thou shalt not kill; thou shalt not steal; thou shalt not commit adultery"; not "Thou shalt not kill, steal, or commit adultery *with a bad motive*."

Wrong actions are always accompanied with self-delusion, and the chief form which such self-delusion assumes is that of self-justification. If a man flatter himself that he can commit a sinful act, and yet be free from sin because he is prompted by a "pure motive," no limit can be set to the evil which he may commit.

It will be found that bad actions, in the majority of instances, are accompanied with good intentions. The object of the slanderer generally is to protect his fellow-men from one another. Troubled with foolish suspicions, or smarting under the thought of injury, he warns men against each other, speaking only of their bad qualities, and, in his eagerness, distorting the truth. His intention is good, namely, to protect his neighbours; but his motive is bad, namely, hatred of those whom he slanders. Such a man's good intention is frustrated by his bad action, and he at last only succeeds in separating himself from all truth-loving people.

The sore of a bad action is not cured by plastering it over with good intentions, nor is the cause of the defilement removed from the heart.

Men who are involved in bad actions cannot work from pure motives. An issue of foul water always proceeds from an impure source; and an issue of impure actions proceeds from a heart that is defiled.

It greatly simplifies life, and solves all complex problems of conduct, when certain actions are recognised as eternally bad, and others as eternally good, and the bad are for ever abandoned, and final refuge is taken in the good.

The wise and good perform good actions; and motive, act, and intention being harmoniously adjusted, their lives are powerful for good, and free from disappointment, and the good fruit of their efforts appears in due season. They do not need to defend their actions by subtle and specious arguments, not to enter into interminable metaphysical speculations concerning motives; but are content to act, and to leave their actions to bear their own fruit.

Let us not try to persuade ourselves that our good intentions will wipe out the results of our bad actions; but let us resort to the practice of good actions; for only in this way can we acquire goodness; only thus can the life be established on fixed principles, and the mind be rendered capable of comprehending, and working from, pure motives.

MORALITY AND RELIGION

The wise man
By adding thought to thought and deed to deed
In ways of good, buildeth his character.
Little by little he accomplishes
His noble ends; in quiet patience works
Diligently.
    Daily he builds into his heart and mind
Pure thoughts, high aspirations, selfless deeds,
Until at last the edifice of Truth
Is finished, and behold! there rises and appears
The Temple of Perfection.

There is no surer indication of confusion and decadence in spiritual matters than the severance of morality from religion. "He is a highly moral man, but he is not religious"; "He is exceptionally good and virtuous, but is not at all spiritual," are common expressions on the lips of large numbers of people who thus regard religion as something quite distinct from goodness, purity, and right-living.

If religion be regarded merely and only as worship combined with adherence to a particular form of faith, then it would be correct to say, "He is a very good man, but is not religious," in some instances, just as it would be equally correct to say, "He is an immoral man, but is very religious," in other instances, for murderers, thieves, and other evil-doers are sometimes devout worshippers and zealous adherents to a creed.

Such a narrowing down of religion, however, would render much of the Sermon on the Mount superfluous, from a religious point of view, and would lead to the confounding of the *means* of religion with its *end*, the idolising of the *letter* of religion to the exclusion of the *spirit*; and this is what actually occurs when morality is severed from religion, and is regarded as something alien and distinct from it.

Religion, however, has a broader significance than this, and the most obscure creed embodies in its ritual some longing human cry for that goodness, that virtue, that morality, which many, with thoughtless judgment, divorce from religion. And is not a life of moral excellence, of good and noble character, of pure-heartedness, the very end and object of religion? Is it not the substance and spirit, of which worship and adherence to a form of faith are but the shadow and letter?

In religion, as in other things, there are the means and the end, the methods and the attainment. Worship, beliefs about God, adherence to creeds—these are some of the means; goodness, virtue, morality—these are the end. The methods are many and various, and they are embodied in countless forms of faith; but the end is one—it is moral grandeur!

Thus the moral man, far from being irreligous because he may not openly profess some form of worship, possesses the substance of religion, diffuses its spirit, has attained its end; and when the sweet kernel of religion is found and enjoyed, the shell, protective and necessary in its place, has served its purpose, and may be dispensed with.

Let not this, however, be misunderstood. The "moral" man does not refer to one who has only the outward form of morality, appearing moral in the eyes of the world, but keeping his vices secret; nor does it refer to him whose morality extends only to legal limits; nor to those who are proud of their morality—for pride is the reverse of moral—but to those who delight in purity, who are gracious, gentle, unselfish, and thoughtful, who, being good at heart, pour forth the fragrance of pure thoughts and good deeds. By the "moral" is meant the good, the pure, the noble, and the true-hearted.

A man may call himself Christian, Jew, Buddhist, Mohammedan, Hindu—or by any other name—and be immoral; but if one is pure-hearted, if he is true and noble and beautiful in character—in a word, if he is moral—then he is an inhabitant of the "Holy City" in which there is "no temple"; he is, by example and influence, a regenerator of mankind; he is one of the company of the Children of Light.

MEMORY, REPETITION,
AND HABIT

I shall gain,
By purity and strong self-mastery,
The awakened vision that doth set men free
From painful slumber and the night of grief.

When a particular combination of words has been repeated a number of times, it is said to have been committed to memory—that is, it can then be repeated without visual reference to the words themselves, and without pause or effort; indeed, the words have then a tendency to repeat themselves in the mind, and sometimes people are troubled with the ringing of a refrain, or the repetition of a sentence in the mind, which they find it very difficult to get rid of and forget.

There is a sense in which the whole of life is a process of committing to memory. At first there is *act,* from act springs *experience*, from experience arises *recollection*, from recollection *repetition*, and from repetition is formed *habit*; hence proceeds impulse, faculty, character, individualised existence.

Life is a repetition of the same things over again. There is very little difference between the days and years in the life of a man; one is almost entirely a repetition of the other. Every being is an accumulation of experiences gathered, learnt, and woven into the life by a ceaseless series of repetitions extending over an incalculable number of lives which thread their way through eons of time.

The life of a man, from the germ-cell to maturity, is a repetition, in synthesis, of the entire process of evolution. There is a cosmic memory at the root of all growth and progress, which is an informing and sustaining principle in the process of evolution.

The sensuous memory of man is fickle and ephemeral, but the supersensuous memory which is inherent in all matter, building up forms and faculty, is infallible in its reproduction of experiences.

Life is ceaseless reiteration. Nature ever travels over old and familiar ground. Man is daily repeating that which he has learnt, though the schools of experience in which the lessons were acquired may be long forgotten; but the acquired habit is not forgotten; it is carried forward and continues to act. The unconscious and automatic ease which marks the play of faculty is not the ready-made mechanism of an arbitrary creator; it is *skill acquired by practice*; it is the consummation of millions of repetitions of the same thought and act.

Thoughts and deeds long persisted in become at last spontaneous impulses.

It is a profound truth that "there is nothing new under the sun." It is possible and highly probable that, in the round of eternity, even all our modern inventions and mechanical marvels have been produced innumerable times on this or other worlds. In this world, new combinations of matter appear from time to time, but are they new in the universe? Who dare say that, in the mind which overarches eternity, the cosmic memory is not reproducing things long since fashioned out of itself?

Nothing can be added to, or taken from, the universe. Its matter can neither be increased nor decreased. Chemical combinations of matter vary, but matter itself cannot vary. Life likewise does not change. In the forms of life there is continuous flux, but in the principle of life there is no increase or diminution. Forms come forth only to retreat and disappear; but that which disappears is not lost; the memory of it is retained, and it continues to be repeated. Eternal disintegration is balanced by eternal restitution.

The mind of man is not separate from the Eternal Mind; in its daily repetitions is indelibly written the record of all its past. *Character is an accumulation of deeds.* Each man is the last reckoning in the long sum of evolution, and there is no falsification of the account. The mind continues to automatically perform the habit which encloses a million repetitions of the same deed. Compared with this ineffaceable, unconscious memory, the memory of three score years and ten is as a fading vapour to an Egyptian Pyramid. The tendencies, impulses, and habits of which a man is a victim are the repetitions of his accumulated deeds. They enfold the destiny which he has wrought. The grace, goodness, and genius which a man exhibits without conscious effort are the fruits of the accumulated labours of his mind. He repeats with ease that which was learned by painful labour. The wise man sees a reflection of himself in the fate which overtakes him.

Life flows in channels. Every man is in a rut. Men tell their fellows to "get out of their ruts," but they themselves are in ruts of another kind. The flow of law, of nature, cannot be avoided, but it can be utilised. We cannot avoid ruts, but we can avoid bad ones; we can follow along good ones.

In their training and education, the children of to-day are strictly confined to ways which are worn by the feet of a thousand generations. In his fixed habits and characteristics, the man of to-day is reviving the actions of a thousand lives.

It is true that men are bound; but it is equally true that they can unbind. The law by which a man becomes the sorrowful victim of his own wrong deeds is a blessèd, and not a cursèd, law; for by the same law he can become the instrument of all that is good. Habits chain a man, but he himself forged the links. He whose inner eye has opened to perceive the law does not complain. The bondage of evil is a heavy slavery, but the bondage of good is a blessèd service.

The will of man is powerless to alter the law of life, but it is powerful to obey it. The Great Law makes for good; it puts a heavy penalty on evil. Man can break his chains, and shake himself free; and when he enters earnestly upon the work of self-liberation, all the universe will be with him in his labour. Repetition and habit he cannot avoid, but he can set going repetitions that are harmonious; he can form habits that will crystallise into pure and noble characteristics.

In the self-built archives of the mind are stored away the entire records of man's evolution. Man is an epitomised history of the world. In his outbursts of rage we hear again the roar of the lion in the forest; in his selfish schemings to secure his coveted ends we see the tiger stalking its prey; his lusts, revenges, hatreds, and fears are the instinct born of primeval experiences. The universe does not forget; life remembers and restores.

Between the sensuous and the supersensuous worlds is the Lethean stream, the river of forgetfulness. Only he who has passed into the supersensuous world—the world of pure goodness—remembers with the Memory of Life which transcends a million deaths. Only he whose will obeys the Universal Will, whose heart is in harmony with the Cosmic Order, receives the vision which pierces through the vale of time and matter, and sees the before and the beyond.

Man quickly forgets, and it is well that he forgets; the universe remembers and records. The repetition of an evil deed is its own retribution; the repetition of a good deed is its own reward. The deepest punishment of evil is evil; the highest reward of good is good. When a deed is done, it is not ended; it is but begun; it remains with the doer—to curse him, if evil; to bless him, if good. Deeds accumulate by repetition, and they remain as character, and in character is both curse and blessing.

Suffering inheres in the discordant repetition of evil; bliss inheres in the rhythmic repetitions of good. Seeing that we cannot escape the law of repetition, let us choose to do those things which are good; and as one establishes habits of purity, the divine memory will be awakened within him.

WORDS AND WISDOM

I would find
Where Wisdom is, where Peace abides, where Truth,
Majestic, changeless, and eternal, stands
Untouched by the illusions of the world;
For surely there is Knowledge, Truth, and Peace
For him who seeks.

Thoughts, words, acts—these combine to make up the entire life of every individual. Words and acts are thoughts expressed. We think in words. In the process of thinking, words are stored up in the consciousness, where they await expression and use as occasion may call them forth.

Words fit the mind which received them; they are the tally of the intellect which uses them. The meaner the mind, the more meagre is the vocabulary. A limited and a capacious intellect alike expresses itself through a limited and an extensive use of words. A great mind expresses itself by the vehicle of flowing and noble language.

Words stand for conceptions. Conceptions are embodied in words. At the moment that a conception is formed in the mind, its corresponding word arises in the thought. Conceptions and words cannot be hidden away indefinitely. Sooner or later they will come forth into the outer world of expression. The matter of the universe is in ceaseless circulation. Its hidden things are continuously coming forth into open and visible life. Likewise the mental operations of men are ever in active circulation, and their hidden thoughts are daily expressing themselves in words and acts. The words and actions of every man are determined by the thoughts in which he habitually dwells.

Speech is audible thought. A man reveals himself through his speech. Whether he is pure or impure, foolish or wise, he makes his inner condition known through his speech. The foolish man is known by the way in which he talks; the wise man is known by the purity, gravity, and excellence of his speech. "He who would gain a knowledge of men," says Confucius, "must first learn to understand the meaning of words."

All wise men, saints, and great teachers have declared that the first step in wisdom is to control the tongue. The disciple of speech is a mental disciple. When a man controls his tongue, he controls his mind; when he purifies his speech, he purifies his mind. Speech and mind cannot be separated. They are two aspects of character.

A man may read Scripture, study religions, and practise mystical arts; but if he allows his tongue to run loosely, he will be as foolish at the end of all his labours as he was at the beginning.

A man may not read Scripture, nor study religions, nor practise ascetic arts; but if he controls his tongue, and studies how to speak wisely and well, he will become wise.

Wisdom is perceived in the words which are its expression. We speak of certain men—of Shakespeare for instance—as being wise. We never saw Shakespeare, and we know very little of his life; how, then, do we know he was wise? By his words only. Where there are wise words, we know there is a wise mind. A foolish man may, like a parrot, *repeat* wise words, but a wise man *frames* wise sentences; his wisdom is shown in originally expressed language.

Why do men speak of words as being bad or good, degrading or inspiring, low or lofty, weak or strong? Is it not because they unconsciously recognise that words cannot be dissociated from thoughts? Why do pure-minded people avoid a man who habitually uses impure language? Is it not because they know that such words proceed from an unclean mind?

It is impossible for any being to give utterance to words which are not already lodged in his mind in the form of thought. The impure mind cannot speak pure words; the pure mind cannot speak impure words. The ignorant cannot speak learnedly, nor the learned ignorantly. The foolish man cannot speak wisely, nor the wise foolishly.

Altered speech follows an altered mind. When a man turns from evil to good, his conversation becomes cleansed. As a man increases in wisdom, he watches, modifies, and perfects his speech.

If the foolish and the wise are known by their words, what, then, is the speech of folly, and what the language of wisdom?

A man is foolish:

If he talks aimlessly and incoherently.
If he engages in impure conversations
If he utters falsehood.
If he speaks ill of the absent, and carries about evil reports concerning others.
If he frames flattering words.
If he utters violent and abusive words.
If his speech is irreverent, and his words are directed against the great and good.
If he speaks in praise of himself.

A man is wise:

If he talks with purpose and intelligence.
If his conversation is chaste.

If he utters words of sincerity and truth.

If he speaks well of, and in defence of, the absent.

If he speaks words of virtuous reproof.

If his speech is gentle and kindly.

If he talks reverently of the great and good.

If he speaks in praise of others.

We are all, now and always, justified and condemned by our words. The law of Truth is not held in abeyance, and every day is judgment day. For "every idle word" which one speaks he is at once "called to account" in an immediate and certain loss of happiness and influence. By the words which we habitually utter we publish to the universe the degree of our intelligence and the standard of our morality, and receive back through them the judgment of the world. The fool thinks he is harshly judged and badly treated by others, not knowing that his real scourge is his own ungoverned tongue.

To control the tongue, to discipline the speech, to strive for the use of purer and gentler words— this is a very lowly thing, and one that is much despised; but it cannot be neglected by him who eagerly aspires to walk the way of wisdom.

TRUTH MADE MANIFEST

Upon the lofty Summits of the Truth,
Where clouds and darkness are not, and where rests
Eternal Splendour; there, abiding Joy
Awaits thy coming.
Be watchful, fearless, faithful, patient, pure:
By earnest meditation sound the depths
Profound of life, and scale the heights sublime
Of Love and Wisdom.

Truth is rendered visible through the media of deeds. It is something seen and not heard. Words do not contain the Truth; they only symbolise it. Good deeds are the only vessels which contain Truth.

It has been frequently said that *being* must precede *doing*. Being always does precede doing; but being and doing cannot be arbitrarily separated. A man's deeds are the expression of himself. Acts are the language of Reality. If a man's inner being is allied to Truth, his deeds will speak it forth; if with error, his deeds will make manifest that error.

No man can hide what he is. He must necessarily act, and every time he acts he reveals himself.

In the light of Reality no man can deceive humanity or the universe; but he can deceive himself.

Deeds of purity, love, gentleness, patience, humility, compassion, and wisdom are Truth made manifest. These qualities cannot be contained between the covers of a book, but only the words which refer to them; they are Life.

Deeds of impurity, hatred, anger, pride, vanity, and folly are error making itself known. A man's deeds are the publication of himself to the world.

Truth cannot be comprehended through reading, but only by correcting and converting one's self. Precepts are aids to the acquirement of wisdom, but wisdom is acquired only by practice.

If a man would know what measure of Truth he possesses, he should ask himself, "What am I? What are my deeds?"

Men dispute about words, thinking that Truth is heard and read. Truth is neither heard nor read; it is *seen*.

Good deeds are the visible embodiments of Truth; they are messengers of Knowledge; angels of Wisdom; but the eye of error is dark, and cannot see them.

SPIRITUAL HUMILITY

Who would be the companion of the wise,
And know the Cosmic Splendour; he must stoop
Who seeks to stand; must fall who fain would rise;
Must know the low, ascending to the high;
He who would know the Great must not disdain
To diligently wait upon the small:
He wisdom finds who finds humility.

Throughout the Sacred Scriptures of all religions there runs, like a silver thread, the teaching of Humility. Not only all the Scriptures, but the sages of all time have declared that only through the portal of humility is it possible for man to enter into the possession of the Life of Truth; and as that life is entirely of a Spiritual Nature, so the humility that leads to it is purely and absolutely spiritual; and being such, it can never be materialised, can never be embodied in a dogma, or laid down as a formula. It is not an outward thing, nor does it consist of that practice of self-abasement that has usurped its name.

But priests have taught, and many have been led to believe, that self-depreciation is true humility, while in reality it is its extreme antithesis. Self-depreciation is self-degradation; nay, it is even a sort of self-destruction, it is spiritual suicide. The man who believes that all his righteousness is as filthy rags, that there is no good thing in him, and that he can never rise by any effort of his own, is, by that very attitude of his mind, rendering himself impotent; he is strangling the Spirit; he is undermining and disintegrating all that is highest and noblest in his character. Instead of building up his character he is engaged in despoiling it, "As a man thinketh in his heart, so is he"; what our thoughts are, such are our characters. We are in reality beings composed of thoughts; thoughts are the bricks which we are continually laying down in the building of our souls. If we put a large percentage of rotten bricks into the building, we shall build but a miserable hovel, and every self-depreciating thought is a brick that is already crumbling. It will be found to be a rule marvellously accurate in its application that those who continually live in this attitude of self-depreciation are throughout life, or, at any rate, until they strike a nobler attitude, wretched failures. I can bring to my mind many such men that I have known. How can it be otherwise? How can a man who has no faith in himself ever win the confidence of others, or accomplish anything worthy? Moreover, such a man has not, cannot possibly have, any faith in human nature; despising himself, he despises all; and as a result, by the unerring law of cause and effect, all men despise him. Yet it is a strange fact that the men who maintain this faith-destroying attitude of mind invariably profess to have the greatest faith in God; yea, look upon it as an infallible witness to their superior spiritual faith. But I ask this question, Does not true faith, like true charity, begin at home? In the growth of the soul faith in one's self comes first, next faith in human nature, and finally faith in God. That faith which professes to have the latter to the exclusion of the two former is false faith, the outcome of false humility.

Another kind of false humility is that of *personal abasement* to an individual or to established authority. This is humility materialised or subverted. It is the worship of Dagon, the bowing of the knee to Baal, the slavish adoration of the Golden Calf. No man can persist in it without undermining his character, and ultimately dissipating his spiritual and mental energies. Humility to man or to any temporal authority is degrading and slavish; humility to the Most High is grandly beautiful.

Spiritual humility is closely allied to faith, and the more there is of humility the more there is of faith. It is the key-note of all real greatness. In proof of this I have only to refer to the great sages, saints, and reformers of all time. The greatest of them are those who had the greatest share of spiritual humility. True humility, as distinguished from false, has a strengthening power, an upbuilding force. It inspires and invigorates the soul, spurring it to greater and ever greater endeavour.

Of what, then, does this humility consist? Is it the bending of the knee to ask personal favours of Deity? Is it the blind petitioning of God to accomplish for us our petty and narrow designs? Nay, these are its counterfeits. True humility is far above and beyond all this. It is the deepest and holiest aspiration of the human heart, where deep within, hidden from all sacrilegious gaze, it works, a silent mighty power, purifying, transforming, the man of flesh and self; entering its solitary grandeur, the alienated soul returns to the footstool of its God, and bathes, in blissful rapture, in the light of His all-embracing Love. It is a state that can only be entered into by rising above one's *lower self*. It is in fact the submergence of the self in the *non-self*; the submission of passion and intellect to the Supreme; it is the attitude of a human soul adoring its highest conceptions.

Such humility takes its possessor above all that is mean and poor in his nature, into the very presence of God, making him calm, strong, noble, self-reliant, and Godlike. It is the Wine of Life to all aspiring souls. The soul that has not felt its power is dead.

It may sound like a paradox, but it is nevertheless true, that the more a man has of humility the more he has of *independence*. But the seeming paradox will be made clear if we think for a moment of the lives of such teachers of humility as Jesus, Buddha, Confucius, Socrates, Jacob Boehme, George Fox, and indeed of all the great religious reformers. These men walked erect, because, yielding themselves up to the simplicity of humility, they walked with God.

The humility that causes a man to go, metaphorically speaking, on all fours is spurious, and is as debasing and destructive as the real humility is elevating and strengthening. Why should we go amongst our fellows like cringing, fearful beasts, calling ourselves miserable sinners? Shall we ever rise above sin by so doing? Is it possible to rise by ceaselessly contemplating our absolute unworthiness? No, we can only rise by continually contemplating the Highest. There may be much that is unworthy in a man's heart, but there is also a sacredness, a dignity, a divinity about it; let us dwell upon that. Let us continually contemplate the goodness, the purity, and the essential beauty of human nature. Let us ceaselessly search for the Divinity in our own souls, and, finding it through the door of humility, we shall then recognise the invisible God in all men. By so doing, we rise above the binding limitations of our selfish desires, and enter the larger, healthier, holier life of Love.

SPIRITUAL STRENGTH

> All things are holy to the holy mind,
> All uses are legitimate and pure,
> All occupations blest and sanctified,
> And every day a Sabbath.

A clear and firm head must precede and accompany a clean and gentle heart. Without the first the second is impossible, for the qualities of purity and gentleness can only be reached through a clear perception of right and wrong, and by the exercise of an irresistible will. The strength of a powerful animal, or of that animal force in man which enables him to gain the victory over others by attack and resistance, is weakness compared with that quiet, patient, invincible will by which a man overcomes himself, and tames to obedience, and trains to the service of holy purposes, the savage passions of his nature.

Every dog can bark and fight, and every foolish man can rail, abuse, fence with hard words, and give way to fits of bad temper; these things are easy and natural to him, and require no effort and no strength. But the wise man puts away all such follies, and trains himself in self-control—trains himself to act unerringly from fixed principles, and not from the fleeting impulses of an unstable nature.

He who succeeds in so training himself is able to train others, in a small degree by precept, but largely and chiefly by practice or example, for it is pre-eminently the prerogative of the wise to teach by their actions. The mockeries of Herod, the accusations of the people, and the fanatical persecutions of the priests all failed to draw from Jesus the word of complaint, bitterness, or self-defence. Such sublime acts of silence and self-control continue to reach, for ages, both individuals and nations, with far greater power and effect than all the words and books uttered and written by the world's vast army of priests and learned commentators.

To retaliate and fight belongs to the animal in man as it belongs to the beast of the forest; but to refuse to be swayed from the practice of a divine principle by any external pressure—to stand firm and unalterable in goodness and truth alike amid blame and praise—this belongs to the divine in man and in the universe.

To alter one's conduct in order to please others, or to avoid their censure or misunderstanding can never lead to spiritual strength.

That divine kindness which always accompanies spiritual understanding and strength is something very different from merely saying pleasant words—for pleasant words are not always true words—but consists in doing *what is best for the eternal welfare of the other person or persons.*

The weak father, who is unfit to train children, only considers how he can escape trouble with his children, and so he slurs over their acts of disobedience and selfishness, and tries to please them. But the strong father, who considers the future character and welfare of his children, knows how and when to administer a severe reproof, fully understanding that the few minutes' pain caused by his rebuke may save his child from years of suffering as a result of loose living which is fostered by parental neglect. The strong, kind, unselfish father, whose care is for his children's good, and not for his own immediate comfort, knows not only how to be tender in affection, but *tender in discipline,* knows how to stretch out the strong and (to the child at the time) severe arm of restraint to save his little ones when they would ignorantly wander away in wrong paths.

So the man of spiritual strength cannot be merely a weak framer of smooth words, but a doer of right actions, an utterer of words that are vital and true, and, therefore, eternally kind.

The spiritually weak man shrinks from right when it is brought (as by its nature it must be brought) in opposition to his desires, and he embraces sin because it is pleasant. The spiritually strong man shrinks from sin, more especially when it is presented to him in a pleasant garb, and embraces right, even though by so doing he will bring upon himself the odium of those who are ignorant of divine principles and their beneficent application.

The man of spiritual understanding is as unbending as a bar of steel where right is concerned, knowing that right alone is good; he is as unresisting as water where self is concerned, knowing that self alone is evil. Acting from imperishable principles and not from the fleeting desires of self, his actions partake of the imperishable nature of the principles from which they spring, and continue to afford instruction and inspiration through unnumbered generations.

It is always the portion of one who so acts to be misunderstood. The majority live in their desires and impulses, following them blindly as they are brought into operation by external stimuli, and do not understand what is meant by acting dispassionately from right and fixed principles, with entire freedom from self-interest. Such will necessarily misunderstand and misjudge the right-doer, regarding him as cold and cruel in his unbending adherence to right, or as weak and cowardly in his quiet refusal to passionately defend himself. He will, therefore, "be accused of many things"; but this will not cause him any suffering, nor will he be troubled or disturbed thereby, for the truth which he practises is a source of perpetual joy, and he will be at rest in the knowledge that there are those who will understand and follow, that he is working for the ultimate good even of his accusers, and that, by manifesting the truth in his daily actions, he is in the company of those divinely strong ones who are leading the world into ways of quietness and peace.

JAMES ALLEN: A MEMOIR

By Lily L. Allen

from *The Epoch* (February–March 1912)

JAMES ALLEN: A MEMOIR

By Lily L. Allen

> Unto pure devotion
> Devote thyself: with perfect meditation
> Comes perfect act, and the right-hearted rise—
> More certainly because they seek no gain—
> Forth from the bands of body, step by step.
> To highest seats of bliss.

James Allen was born in Leicester, England, on November 28th, 1864. His father, at one time a very prosperous manufacturer, was especially fond of "Jim," and before great financial failures overtook him, he would often look at the delicate, refined boy, poring over his books, and would say, "My boy, I'll make a scholar of you."

The Father was a high type of man intellectually, and a great reader, so could appreciate the evident thirst for education and knowledge which he observed in his quiet studious boy.

As a young child he was very delicate and nervous, often suffering untold agony during his school days through the misunderstanding harshness of some of his school teachers, and others with whom he was forced to associate, though he retained always the tenderest memories of others—one or two of his teachers in particular, who no doubt are still living.

He loved to get alone with his books, and many a time he has drawn a vivid picture for me, of the hours he spent with his precious books in his favourite corner by the home fire; his father, whom he dearly loved, in his arm chair opposite also deeply engrossed in his favourite authors. On such evenings he would question his father on some of the profound thoughts that surged through his soul—thoughts he could scarcely form into words—and the father, unable to answer, would gaze at him long over his spectacles, and at last say: "My boy, my boy, you have lived before"—and when the boy eagerly but reverently would suggest an answer to his own question, the father would grow silent and thoughtful, as though he *sensed* the future man and his mission, as he looked at the boy and listened to his words—and many a time he was heard to remark, "Such knowledge comes not in one short life."

There were times when the boy startled those about him into a deep concern for his health, and they would beg him not to *think so much*, and in after years he often smiled when he recalled how his father would say—"Jim, we will have you in the Churchyard soon, if you think so much."

Not that he was by any means unlike other boys where games were concerned. He could play leap-frog and marbles with the best of them, and those who knew him as a man—those who were privileged to meet him at "Bryngoleu"—will remember how he could enter into a game with all his heart. Badminton he delighted in during the summer evenings, or whenever he felt he could.

About three years after our marriage, when our little Nora was about eighteen months old, and he about thirty-three, I realized a great change coming over him, and knew that he was renouncing everything that most men hold dear that he might find Truth, and lead the weary sin-stricken world to Peace. He at that time commenced the practice of rising early in the morning, at times long before daylight, that he might go out on the hills—like One of old—to commune with God, and meditate on Divine things. I do not claim to have understood him fully in those days. The light in which he lived and moved was far too white for my earth-bound eyes to see, and a *sense of it only* was beginning to dawn upon me. But I knew I dare not stay him or hold him back, though at times my woman's heart cried out to do so, waiting him all my own, and not then understanding his divine mission.

Then came his first book, "From Poverty to Power." This book is considered by many his best book. It has passed into many editions, and tens of thousands have been sold all over the world, both authorized and pirated editions, for perhaps no author's works have been more pirated than those of James Allen.

As a private secretary he worked from 9 a.m. to 6 p.m., and used every moment out of office writing his books. Soon after the publication of "From Poverty to Power" came "All These Things Added," and then "As a Man Thinketh," a book perhaps better known and more widely read than any other from his pen.

About this time, too, the "Light of Reason" was founded and he gave up all his time to the work of editing the Magazine, at the same time carrying on a voluminous correspondence with searchers after Truth all over the world. And ever as the years went by he kept straight on, and never once looked back or swerved from the path of holiness. Oh, it was a blessed thing indeed to be the chosen one to walk by the side of his earthly body, and to watch the glory dawning upon him!

He took a keen interest in many scientific subjects, and always eagerly read the latest discovery in astronomy, and he delighted in geology and botany. Among his favourite books I find Shakespeare, Milton, Emerson, Browning, The Bhagavad-Gita, the Tao-Tea-King of Lao-Tze, the Light of Asia, the Gospel of Buddha, Walt Whitman, Dr. Bucke's Cosmic Consciousness, and the Holy Bible.

He might have written on a wide range of subjects had he chosen to do so, and was often asked for articles on many questions outside his particular work, but he refused to comply, consecrating his whole thought and effort to preach the Gospel of Peace.

When physical suffering overtook him he never once complained, but grandly and patiently bore his pain, hiding it from those around him, and only we who knew and loved him so well, and his kind, tender Doctor, knew how greatly he suffered. And yet he stayed not; still he rose before the dawn to meditate, and commune with God; still he sat at his desk and wrote those words of Light and Life which will ring down through the ages, calling men and women from their sins and sorrows to peace and rest.

Always strong in his complete manhood, though small of stature physically, and as gentle as he was strong, no one ever heard an angry word from those kind lips. Those who served him adored him; those who had business dealings with him trusted and honoured him. Ah! how much my heart prompts me to write of his self-sacrificing life, his tender words, his gentle deeds, his knowledge and his wisdom. But why? Surely there is no need, for do not his books speak in words written by his own hand, and will they not speak to generations yet to come?

About Christmas time I saw the change coming, and understood it not—blind! blind! blind! I could not think it possible that *he* should be taken and *I* left.

But we three—as if we knew—clung closer to each other, and loved one another with a greater love—if that were possible—than ever before. Look at his portrait given with the January "Epoch," and reproduced again in this, and you will see that even then our Beloved, our Teacher and Guide, was letting go his hold on the physical. He was leaving us then, and we didn't know it. Often I had urged him to stop work awhile and rest, but he always gave me the same answer, "My darling, when I stop I must go, don't try to stay my hand."

And so he worked on, until that day, Friday, January 12, 1912, when, about one o'clock he sat down in his chair, and looking at me with a great compassion and yearning in those blessed eyes, he cried out, as he stretched out his arms to me, "*Oh, I have finished, I have finished, I can go no further, I have done.*"

Need I say that everything that human aid and human skill could do was done to keep him still with us. Of those last few days I dare scarcely write. How could my pen describe them? And when we knew the end was near, with his dear hands upon my head in blessing, he gave his work and his beloved people into my hands, charging me to bless and help them, until I received the call to give up my stewardship!

"I will help you," he said, "and if I can I shall come to you and be with you often."

Words, blessed words of love and comfort, *for my heart alone* often came from his lips, and a sweet smile ever came over the pale calm face when our little Nora came to kiss him and speak loving words to him, while always the gentle voice breathed the tender words to her—"*My little darling!*"

So calmly, peacefully, quietly, he passed from us at the dawn on Wednesday, January 24, 1912. "Passed from us," did I say? Nay, only the outer garment has passed from our mortal vision. He lives! and when the great grief that tears our hearts at the separation is calmed and stilled, I think that we shall know that he is still with us. We shall again rejoice in his companionship and presence.

When his voice was growing faint and low, I heard him whispering, and leaning down to catch the words I heard—"At last, at last—at home—my wanderings are over"—and then, I heard no more, for my heart was breaking within me, and I felt, for *him* indeed it was "*Home at last!*" but for me— And then, as though he knew my thoughts, he turned and again holding out his hands to me, he said: "I have only one thing more to say to you, my beloved, and that is I love you, and I will be waiting for you; good-bye."

I write this memoir for those who love him, for those who will read it with tender loving hearts, and tearful eyes; for those who will not look critically at the way in which I have tried to tell out of my lonely heart this short story of his life and passing away—for *his* pupils, and, therefore, *my* friends.

We clothed the mortal remains in *pure white linen,* symbol of his fair, pure life, and so, clasping the photo of the one he loved best upon his bosom—they committed all that remained to the funeral pyre.

ABOUT THE AUTHOR

James Allen was born in Leicester, England, on November 28, 1864. He took his first job at fifteen to support his family, after his father was murdered while looking for work in America in 1879. Allen worked as a factory knitter and later as a private secretary with various manufacturing companies. In 1901, he published his first book, *From Poverty to Power*. The following year, he left secretarial work to devote himself full time to writing and in 1903 completed his third, and best-known, work: *As a Man Thinketh*. Allen soon moved with his wife, Lily, and daughter, Nora, to Ilfracombe, England, where he continued to write books and articles, and, with Lily, to publish his spiritual journal, *The Light of Reason*, later retitled *The Epoch*. He died at age forty-seven on January 24, 1912, most likely of consumption. Allen completed nineteen books during his career, several of which were published posthumously by his wife. All are included in this volume. While not widely known during his lifetime, Allen came to be seen as pioneering voice of contemporary inspirational literature, his work inspiring many of the twentieth century's leading writers of motivational thought, including Norman Vincent Peale, Napoleon Hill, Robert Collier, and Dale Carnegie.

Look for these favorites from

TARCHER SUCCESS CLASSICS

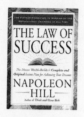

The Law of Success
by Napoleon Hill
978-1-58542-689-8

The Master-Key to Riches
by Napoleon Hill
978-1-58542-689-8

The Magic Ladder to Success
by Napoleon Hill
978-1-58542-710-9

*The Think and Grow
Rich Workbook*
by Napoleon Hill
978-1-58542-711-6

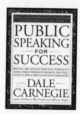

Public Speaking for Success
by Dale Carnegie
978-1-58542-492-4

Riches Within Your Reach!
by Robert Collier
978-1-58542-767-3

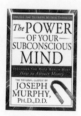

*The Power of Your
Subconscious Mind*
by Joseph Murphy
978-1-58542-768-0

*The Game of Life and
How to Play It*
by Florence Scovel Shinn
978-1-58542-745-1

How to Prosper in Hard Times
by Napoleon Hill, James Allen, et al
978-1-58542-755-0